LAOS

SOCIAL SECURITY AND LABOR PROTECTION SYSTEM, POLICIES, LAWS AND REGULATIONS HANDBOOK
STRATEGIC INFORMATION AND REGULATIONS

International Business Publications, USA
Washington DC. USA - Laos

LAOS

SOCIAL SECURITY AND LABOR PROTECTION SYSTEM, POLICIES, LAWS AND REGULATIONS HANDBOOK
STRATEGIC INFORMATION AND REGULATIONS

UPDATED ANNUALLY

We express our sincere appreciation to all government agencies and international organizations which provided information and other materials for this handbook

Cover Design: International Business Publications, USA

International Business Publications, USA. has used its best efforts in collecting, analyzing and preparing data, information and materials for this unique handbook. Due to the dynamic nature and fast development of the economy and business environment, we cannot warrant that all information herein is complete and accurate. IBP does not assume and hereby disclaim any liability to any person for any loss or damage caused by possible errors or omissions in the handbook.
This handbook is for noncommercial use only. Use this handbook for any other purpose, included but not limited to reproducing and storing in a retrieval system by any means, electronic, photocopying or using the addresses or other information contained in this handbook for any commercial purposes requires a special written permission from the publisher.

2017 Edition Updated Reprint International Business Publications, USA
ISBN 978-1-5145-3109-9

For additional analytical, business and investment opportunities information,
please contact Global Investment & Business Center, USA
at (703) 370-8082. Fax: (703) 370-8083. E-mail: ibpusa3@gmail.com
Global Business and Investment Info Databank - www.ibpus.com

Printed in the USA

For additional analytical, business and investment opportunities information,
please contact Global Investment & Business Center, USA
at (703) 370-8082. Fax: (703) 370-8083. E-mail: ibpusa3@gmail.com
Global Business and Investment Info Databank - www.ibpus.com

LAOS

SOCIAL SECURITY AND LABOR PROTECTION SYSTEM, POLICIES, LAWS AND REGULATIONS HANDBOOK
STRATEGIC INFORMATION AND REGULATIONS

TABLE OF CONTENTS

LAOS STRATEGIC AND DEVELOPMENT PROFILES 8

STRATEGIC PROFILE 8
Geography 10
People 12
Government 13
Economy 15
Energy 19
Communications 21
Transportation 22
Military 23
Transnational Issues 24
IMPORTANT INFORMATION FOR UNDERSTANDING LAOS 25
PROFILE 25
GEOGRAPHY, TOPOGRAPHY AND CLIMATE 26
WATER RESOURCES 26
FOREST RESOURCES 26
MINERAL RESOURCES 27
ADMINISTRATIVE STRUCTURE OF LAOS 27
PEOPLE 32
HISTORY 33
GOVERNMENT AND POLITICAL CONDITIONS 34
ECONOMY 36
FOREIGN RELATIONS 38
U.S.-LAO RELATIONS 39
TRAVEL AND BUSINESS INFORMATION 40

LAOS JUDICIAL AND LEGAL SYSTEM 42

LEGAL AND JUDICIAL SYSTEM 42
LEGAL SYSTEM DEVELOPMENTS 42

For additional analytical, business and investment opportunities information, please contact Global Investment & Business Center, USA at (703) 370-8082. Fax: (703) 370-8083. E-mail: ibpusa3@gmail.com
Global Business and Investment Info Databank - www.ibpus.com

For additional analytical, business and investment opportunities information,
please contact Global Investment & Business Center, USA
at (703) 370-8082. Fax: (703) 370-8083. E-mail: ibpusa3@gmail.com
Global Business and Investment Info Databank - www.ibpus.com

For additional analytical, business and investment opportunities information,
please contact Global Investment & Business Center, USA
at (703) 370-8082. Fax: (703) 370-8083. E-mail: ibpusa3@gmail.com
Global Business and Investment Info Databank - www.ibpus.com

For additional analytical, business and investment opportunities information,
please contact Global Investment & Business Center, USA
at (703) 370-8082. Fax: (703) 370-8083. E-mail: ibpusa3@gmail.com
Global Business and Investment Info Databank - www.ibpus.com

LAOS STRATEGIC AND DEVELOPMENT PROFILES

STRATEGIC PROFILE

Capital and largest city	Vientiane 17°58′N 102°36′E
Official languages	Lao
Spoken languages	Lao Hmong Khmu
Ethnic groups (2005[1])	55% Lao 11% Khmu 8% Hmong 26% other[a]
Religion	Buddhism
Demonym	Laotian Lao
Government	Marxist–Leninistone-party socialist state
• **General Secretary and President**	Bounnhang Vorachith
• **Prime Minister**	Thongloun Sisoulith
• **Vice President**	Phankham Viphavanh
Legislature	National Assembly
Formation	
• **Kingdom of Lan Xang**	1354–1707
• **Luang Phrabang, Vientiane and Champasak**	1707–1778
• **Vassal of Thonburi and Siam**	1778–1893
• **War of Succession**	1826–8
• **French Indochina**	1893–1949
• **Independence from France**	19 July 1949
• **Declared Independence**	22 October 1953
• **Laotian civil war**	9 November 1953 – 2 December 1975
• **Lao Monarchy abolished**	2 December 1975
• **Current constitution**	14 August 1991
Area	
• **Total**	237,955 km^2 (84th)

For additional analytical, business and investment opportunities information, please contact Global Investment & Business Center, USA at (703) 370-8082. Fax: (703) 370-8083. E-mail: ibpusa3@gmail.com Global Business and Investment Info Databank - www.ibpus.com

| | 91,428.991 sq mi |
| • Water (%) | 2 |

Population
• 2014 (Jul) estimate	6,803,699[2](104th)
• 2015 census	6,492,228[3]
• Density	26.7/km² (177th)
	69.2/sq mi

GDP (PPP) | 2014 estimate |
| • Total | US$34.400 billion[4] |
| • Per capita | US$4,986[4] |

GDP (nominal) | 2014 estimate |
| • Total | US$11.676 billion[4] |
| • Per capita | US$1,692[4] |

| **Gini (2008)** | 36.7[5] |
| | medium |

| **HDI (2014)** | 0.575[6] |
| | medium · 141st |

Currency	Kip (LAK)
Time zone	ICT
Date format	dd/mm/yyyy
Drives on the	right
Calling code	+856
ISO 3166 code	LA
Internet TLD	.la

Laos, officially the **Lao People's Democratic Republic**, is a landlocked socialist republic communist state in southeast Asia, bordered by Myanmar (Burma) and the People's Republic of China to the northwest, Vietnam to the east, Cambodia to the south, and Thailand to the west. Laos traces its history to the Kingdom of Lan Xang or *Land of a Million Elephants*, which existed from the 14th to the 18th century. After a period as a French colony, it gained independence in 1949. A long civil war ended when the communist Pathet Lao came to power in 1975.

Private enterprise has increased since the mid-1980s, but development has been hampered by poor communications in the heavily forested and mountainous landscape. 80%[1] of those employed practice subsistence agriculture; this is coupled with widespread starvation due to the many failures of communism and the state's command economy. The country's ethnic make-up is extremely diverse, with only around 60% belonging to the largest ethnic group, the Lao.

In 1975 the communist Pathet Lao took control of the government, ending a six-century-old monarchy. Initial closer ties to Vietnam and socialization were replaced with a gradual return to private enterprise, an easing of foreign investment laws, and the admission into ASEAN in 1997.

GEOGRAPHY

Location: Southeastern Asia, northeast of Thailand, west of Vietnam
Geographic coordinates: 18 00 N, 105 00 E

Map references: Southeast Asia
Area:
total: 236,800 sq km
land: 230,800 sq km
water: 6,000 sq km

Area - comparative: slightly larger than Utah

Land boundaries:
total: 5,083 km
border countries: Burma 235 km, Cambodia 541 km, China 423 km, Thailand 1,754 km, Vietnam 2,130 km

Coastline: 0 km (landlocked)
Maritime claims: none (landlocked)
Climate: tropical monsoon; rainy season (May to November); dry season (December to April)
Terrain: mostly rugged mountains; some plains and plateaus

Elevation extremes:
lowest point: Mekong River 70 m
highest point: Phou Bia 2,817 m

Natural resources: timber, hydropower, gypsum, tin, gold, gemstones

Land use:
arable land: 3%
permanent crops: 0%
permanent pastures: 3%
forests and woodland: 54%
other: 40%

Irrigated land: 1,250 sq km
note: rainy season irrigation - 2,169 sq km; dry season irrigation - 750 sq km (1998 est.)
Natural hazards: floods, droughts, and blight

Environment - current issues: unexploded ordnance; deforestation; soil erosion; a majority of the population does not have access to potable water

Environment - international agreements:
party to: Biodiversity, Climate Change, Desertification, Environmental Modification, Law of the Sea, Nuclear Test Ban, Ozone Layer Protection
signed, but not ratified: none of the selected agreements

Geography - note: landlocked

PEOPLE

Population: 5,497,459

Age structure:
0-14 years: 43% (male 1,191,608; female 1,173,144)
15-64 years: 54% (male 1,447,788; female 1,500,016)
65 years and over: 3% (male 85,028; female 99,875)

Population growth rate: 2.5%
Birth rate: 38.29 births/1,000 population
Death rate: 13.35 deaths/1,000 population
Net migration rate: 0 migrant(s)/1,000 population

Sex ratio:
at birth: 1.05 male(s)/female
under 15 years: 1.02 male(s)/female
15-64 years: 0.97 male(s)/female
65 years and over: 0.85 male(s)/female
total population: 0.98 male(s)/female

Infant mortality rate: 94.8 deaths/1,000 live births

Life expectancy at birth:
total population: 53.09 years
male: 51.22 years
female: 55.02 years

Total fertility rate: 5.21 children born/woman

Nationality:
noun: Lao(s) or Laotian(s)
adjective: Lao or Laotian

Ethnic groups: Lao Loum (lowland) 68%, Lao Theung (upland) 22%, Lao Soung (highland) including the Hmong ("Meo") and the Yao (Mien) 9%, ethnic Vietnamese/Chinese 1%
Religions: Buddhist 60% (in October 1999, the regime proposed a constitutional amendment making Buddhism the state religion; the National Assembly is expected to vote on the amendment sometime in 2000), animist and other 40%

For additional analytical, business and investment opportunities information,
please contact Global Investment & Business Center, USA
at (703) 370-8082. Fax: (703) 370-8083. E-mail: ibpusa3@gmail.com
Global Business and Investment Info Databank - www.ibpus.com

Languages: Lao (official), French, English, and various ethnic languages

Literacy:
definition: age 15 and over can read and write
total population: 57%
male: 70%
female: 44%

GOVERNMENT

Country name:
conventional long form: Lao People's Democratic Republic
conventional short form: Laos
local long form: Sathalanalat Paxathipatai Paxaxon Lao
local short form: none

Data code: LA
Government type: Communist state
Capital: Vientiane

Administrative divisions: 16 provinces (khoueng, singular and plural), 1 municipality* (kampheng nakhon, singular and plural), and 1 special zone** (khetphiset, singular and plural); Attapu, Bokeo, Bolikhamxai, Champasak, Houaphan, Khammouan, Louangnamtha, Louangphabang, Oudomxai, Phongsali, Salavan, Savannakhet, Viangchan*, Viangchan, Xaignabouli, Xaisomboun**, Xekong, Xiangkhoang

Independence: 19 July 1949 (from France)
National holiday: National Day, 2 December (1975) (proclamation of the Lao People's Democratic Republic)
Constitution: promulgated 14 August 1991

Legal system: based on traditional customs, French legal norms and procedures, and Socialist practice

Suffrage: 18 years of age; universal

Executive branch:

chief of state: President BOUNNYANG Vorachit (since 20 April 2016); Vice President PHANKHAM Viphavan (since 20 April 2016)

head of government: Prime Minister THONGLOUN Sisoulit (since 20 April 2016); Deputy Prime Ministers BOUNTHONG Chitmani, SONXAI Siphandon, SOMDI Douangdi (since 20 April 2016)

cabinet: Council of Ministers appointed by the president, approved by the National Assembly

elections/appointments: president and vice president indirectly elected by the National Assembly for a 5-year term (no term limits); election last held on 20 April 2016 (next to be held in 2021); prime minister nominated by the president, elected by the National Assembly for 5-year term

election results: BOUNNYANG Vorachit (LPRP) elected president; PHANKHAM Viphavan (LPRP) elected vice president; percent of National Assembly vote - NA; THONGLOUN Sisoulit (LPRP) elected prime minister; percent of National Assembly vote - NA

Legislative branch:

description: unicameral National Assembly or Sapha Heng Xat (132 seats; members directly elected in multi-seat constituencies by simple majority vote from candidate lists provided by the Lao People's Revolutionary Party; members serve 5-year terms)

elections: last held on 20 April 2016 (next to be held in 2021)

election results: percent of vote by party - NA; seats by party - LPRP 128, independent 4

Judicial branch:

highest court(s): People's Supreme Court (consists of the court president and organized into criminal, civil, administrative, commercial, family, and juvenile chambers, each with a vice president and several judges)

judge selection and term of office: president of People's Supreme Court appointed by National Assembly on recommendation of the president of the republic for a 5-year term; vice presidents of People's Supreme Court appointed by the president of the republic on recommendation of the National Assembly; appointment of chamber judges NA; tenure of court vice-presidents and chamber judges NA

subordinate courts: appellate courts; provincial, municipal, district, and military courts

Political parties and leaders: Lao People's Revolutionary Party or LPRP [KHAMTAI Siphandon, party president]; other parties proscribed

Political pressure groups and leaders: noncommunist political groups proscribed; most opposition leaders fled the country in 1975

International organization participation: ACCT, AsDB, ASEAN, CP, ESCAP, FAO, G-77, IBRD, ICAO, ICRM, IDA, IFAD, IFC, IFRCS, ILO, IMF, Intelsat (nonsignatory user), Interpol, IOC, ITU, NAM, OPCW, PCA, UN, UNCTAD, UNESCO, UNIDO, UPU, WFTU, WHO, WIPO, WMO, WToO, WTrO (observer)

For additional analytical, business and investment opportunities information, please contact Global Investment & Business Center, USA at (703) 370-8082. Fax: (703) 370-8083. E-mail: ibpusa3@gmail.com
Global Business and Investment Info Databank - www.ibpus.com

Diplomatic representation in the US:
chief of mission: Ambassador VANG Rattanavong
chancery: 2222 S Street NW, Washington, DC 20008
telephone: [1] (202) 332-6416
FAX: [1] (202) 332-4923

Diplomatic representation from the US:
chief of mission: Ambassador Wendy Jean CHAMBERLIN
embassy: Rue Bartholonie, B. P. 114, Vientiane
mailing address: American Embassy, Box V, APO AP 96546
telephone: [856] (21) 212581, 212582, 212585
FAX: [856] (21) 212584

Flag description: three horizontal bands of red (top), blue (double width), and red with a large white disk centered in the blue band

ECONOMY

The government of Laos, one of the few remaining one-party communist states, began decentralizing control and encouraging private enterprise in 1986. The results, starting from an extremely low base, were striking - growth averaged 6% per year from 1988-2008 except during the short-lived drop caused by the Asian financial crisis that began in 1997. Laos' growth exceeded 7% per year during 2008-13. Despite this high growth rate, Laos remains a country with an underdeveloped infrastructure, particularly in rural areas. It has a basic, but improving, road system, and limited external and internal land-line telecommunications. Electricity is available in 83 % of the country.

Laos' economy is heavily dependent on capital-intensive natural resource exports. The labor force, however, still relies on agriculture, dominated by rice cultivation in lowland areas, which accounts for about 25% of GDP and 73% of total employment. Economic growth has reduced official poverty rates from 46% in 1992 to 26% in 2010. The economy also has benefited from high-profile foreign direct investment in hydropower, copper and gold mining, logging, and construction though some projects in these industries have drawn criticism for their environmental impacts. Laos gained Normal Trade Relations status with the US in 2004 and applied for Generalized System of Preferences trade benefits in 2013 after being admitted to the World Trade Organization earlier in the year. Laos is in the process of implementing a value-added tax system. Simplified investment procedures and expanded bank credits for small farmers and small entrepreneurs will improve Laos' economic prospects. The government appears committed to raising the country's profile among investors, but suffered through a fiscal crisis in 2013 brought about by public sector wage increases, fiscal mismanagement, and revenue shortfalls. The World Bank has declared that Laos' goal of graduating from the UN Development Program's list of least-developed countries by 2020 is achievable, and the country is preparing to enter the ASEAN Economic Community in 2015.

GDP (purchasing power parity):
$20.78 billion (2013 est.)
country comparison to the world: 132
$19.18 billion (2014 est.)
$17.78 billion (2011 est.)
note:data are in 2013 US dollars

GDP (official exchange rate):
$10.1 billion (2013 est.)

GDP - real growth rate:
8.3% (2013 est.)
country comparison to the world: 9
7.9% (2014 est.)
8% (2011 est.)

GDP - per capita (PPP):
$3,100 (2013 est.)
country comparison to the world: 176
$2,900 (2014 est.)
$2,700 (2011 est.)
note:data are in 2013 US dollars

Gross national saving:
27.4% of GDP (2013 est.)
country comparison to the world: 38
26.2% of GDP (2014 est.)
25.2% of GDP (2011 est.)

GDP - composition, by end use:
household consumption:
66.9%
government consumption:
9.8%
investment in fixed capital:
31.7%
investment in inventories:
-1.3%
exports of goods and services:
40%
imports of goods and services:
-48.4%
(2013 est.)

GDP - composition, by sector of origin:
agriculture:
24.8%
industry:
32%
services:
37.5% (2013 est.)

Agriculture - products:
sweet potatoes, vegetables, corn, coffee, sugarcane, tobacco, cotton, tea, peanuts, rice; cassava (manioc, tapioca), water buffalo, pigs, cattle, poultry

For additional analytical, business and investment opportunities information,
please contact Global Investment & Business Center, USA
at (703) 370-8082. Fax: (703) 370-8083. E-mail: ibpusa3@gmail.com
Global Business and Investment Info Databank - www.ibpus.com

Industries:
mining (copper, tin, gold, gypsum); timber, electric power, agricultural processing, rubber, construction, garments, cement, tourism

Industrial production growth rate:
11% (2013 est.)
country comparison to the world: 12

Labor force:
3.373 million (2013 est.)
country comparison to the world: 100

Labor force - by occupation:
agriculture:
73.1%
industry:
6.1%
services:
20.6% (2014 est.)

Unemployment rate:
1.9% (2010 est.)
country comparison to the world: 11
2.5% (2009 est.)

Population below poverty line:
22% (2013 est.)

Household income or consumption by percentage share:
lowest 10%:
3.3%
highest 10%:
30.3%

Distribution of family income - Gini index:
36.7
country comparison to the world: 83
34.6 (2002)

Budget:
revenues:
$2.481 billion
expenditures:
$2.642 billion (2013 est.)

Taxes and other revenues:
24.6% of GDP (2013 est.)
country comparison to the world: 135

For additional analytical, business and investment opportunities information, please contact Global Investment & Business Center, USA at (703) 370-8082. Fax: (703) 370-8083. E-mail: ibpusa3@gmail.com Global Business and Investment Info Databank - www.ibpus.com

Budget surplus (+) or deficit (-):
-1.6% of GDP (2013 est.)
country comparison to the world: 77

Public debt:
46.3% of GDP (2013 est.)
country comparison to the world: 77
49.1% of GDP (2014 est.)

Fiscal year:
1 October - 30 September

Inflation rate (consumer prices):
6.5% (2013 est.)
country comparison to the world: 183
4.3% (2014 est.)

Central bank discount rate:
4.3% (31 December 2010)
country comparison to the world: 94
4% (31 December 2009)

Commercial bank prime lending rate:
23.2% (31 December 2013 est.)
country comparison to the world: 14
22.3% (31 December 2014 est.)

Stock of narrow money:
$1.389 billion (31 December 2013 est.)
country comparison to the world: 141
$1.154 billion (31 December 2014 est.)

Stock of broad money:
$4.071 billion (31 December 2013 est.)
country comparison to the world: 136
$3.673 billion (31 December 2014 est.)

Stock of domestic credit:
$4.716 billion (31 December 2013 est.)
country comparison to the world: 114
$4.034 billion (31 December 2014 est.)

Market value of publicly traded shares:
$1.012 billion (2014 est.)
$NA

Current account balance:
-$484.3 million (2013 est.)
country comparison to the world: 98

For additional analytical, business and investment opportunities information,
please contact Global Investment & Business Center, USA
at (703) 370-8082. Fax: (703) 370-8083. E-mail: ibpusa3@gmail.com
Global Business and Investment Info Databank - www.ibpus.com

-$315.5 million (2014 est.)

Exports:
$2.313 billion (2013 est.)
country comparison to the world: 141
$1.984 billion (2014 est.)

Exports - commodities:
wood products, coffee, electricity, tin, copper, gold, cassava

Exports - partners:
Thailand 34%, China 21.5%, Vietnam 12.2%

Imports:
$3.238 billion (2013 est.)
country comparison to the world: 145
$2.744 billion (2014 est.)

Imports - commodities:
machinery and equipment, vehicles, fuel, consumer goods

Imports - partners:
Thailand 62.1%, China 16.2%, Vietnam 7.3%

Reserves of foreign exchange and gold:
$845.4 million (31 December 2013 est.)
country comparison to the world: 141
$796.9 million (31 December 2014 est.)

Debt - external:
$6.69 billion (31 December 2013 est.)
country comparison to the world: 110
$6.288 billion (31 December 2014 est.)

Stock of direct foreign investment - at home:
$15.14 billion (31 December 2014 est.)
country comparison to the world: 81
$12.44 billion (31 December 2011 est.)

Exchange rates:
kips (LAK) per US dollar -
7,875.9 (2013 est.)
8,007.3 (2014 est.)
8,258.8 (2010 est.)
8,516.04
8,760.69

ENERGY

For additional analytical, business and investment opportunities information,
please contact Global Investment & Business Center, USA
at (703) 370-8082. Fax: (703) 370-8083. E-mail: ibpusa3@gmail.com
Global Business and Investment Info Databank - www.ibpus.com

Electricity - production:
3.629 billion kWh
country comparison to the world: 127

Electricity - consumption:
2.4 billion kWh
country comparison to the world: 136

Electricity - exports:
2.537 billion kWh
country comparison to the world: 41

Electricity - imports:
1 billion kWh
country comparison to the world: 65

Electricity - installed generating capacity:
3.217 million kW
country comparison to the world: 87

Electricity - from fossil fuels:
2.6% of total installed capacity
country comparison to the world: 201

Electricity - from nuclear fuels:
0% of total installed capacity
country comparison to the world: 122

Electricity - from hydroelectric plants:
97.4% of total installed capacity
country comparison to the world: 9

Electricity - from other renewable sources:
0% of total installed capacity
country comparison to the world: 191

Crude oil - production:
0 bbl/day
country comparison to the world: 186

Crude oil - exports:
0 bbl/day
country comparison to the world: 140

Crude oil - imports:
0 bbl/day

For additional analytical, business and investment opportunities information,
please contact Global Investment & Business Center, USA
at (703) 370-8082. Fax: (703) 370-8083. E-mail: ibpusa3@gmail.com
Global Business and Investment Info Databank - www.ibpus.com

country comparison to the world: 206

Crude oil - proved reserves:
0 bbl
country comparison to the world: 152

Refined petroleum products - production:
0 bbl/day
country comparison to the world: 161

Refined petroleum products - consumption:
3,391 bbl/day
country comparison to the world: 177

Refined petroleum products - exports:
0 bbl/day
country comparison to the world: 191

Refined petroleum products - imports:
3,160 bbl/day
country comparison to the world: 170

Natural gas - production:
0 cu m
country comparison to the world: 151

Natural gas - consumption:
0 cu m
country comparison to the world: 163

Natural gas - exports:
0 cu m
country comparison to the world: 132

Natural gas - imports:
0 cu m
country comparison to the world: 86

Natural gas - proved reserves:
0 cu m
country comparison to the world: 156

COMMUNICATIONS

Telephones - main lines in use:
112,000

For additional analytical, business and investment opportunities information,
please contact Global Investment & Business Center, USA
at (703) 370-8082. Fax: (703) 370-8083. E-mail: ibpusa3@gmail.com
Global Business and Investment Info Databank - www.ibpus.com

country comparison to the world: 143

Telephones - mobile cellular:
6.492 million
country comparison to the world: 99

Telephone system:
general assessment:
service to general public is improving; the government relies on a radiotelephone network to communicate with remote areas
domestic:
4 service providers with mobile cellular usage growing very rapidly
international:
country code - 856; satellite earth station - 1 Intersputnik (Indian Ocean region) and a second to be developed by China

Broadcast media:
6 TV stations operating out of Vientiane - 3 government-operated and the others commercial; 17 provincial stations operating with nearly all programming relayed via satellite from the government-operated stations in Vientiane; Chinese and Vietnamese programming relayed via satellite from Lao National TV; broadcasts available from stations in Thailand and Vietnam in border areas; multi-channel satellite and cable TV systems provide access to a wide range of foreign stations; state-controlled radio with state-operated Lao National Radio (LNR) broadcasting on 5 frequencies - 1 AM, 1 SW, and 3 FM; LNR's AM and FM programs are relayed via satellite constituting a large part of the programming schedules of the provincial radio stations; Thai radio broadcasts available in border areas and transmissions of multiple international broadcasters are also accessible

Internet country code:
.la

Internet hosts:
1,532
country comparison to the world: 166

Internet users:
300,000
country comparison to the world: 130

TRANSPORTATION

Airports:
41
country comparison to the world: 103

Airports - with paved runways:
total: 8
2,438 to 3,047 m: 3

1,524 to 2,437 m: 4
914 to 1,523 m: 1 (2013)

Airports - with unpaved runways:
total: 33
1,524 to 2,437 m: 2
914 to 1,523 m: 9
under 914 m:
22

Pipelines:
refined products 540 km (2013)

Roadways:
total: 39,568 km

country comparison to the world: 89
paved: 530 km
unpaved: 39,038 km

Waterways:
4,600 km (primarily on the Mekong River and its tributaries; 2,900 additional km are intermittently navigable by craft drawing less than 0.5 m)
country comparison to the world: 24

MILITARY

Military branches:
Lao People's Armed Forces (LPAF): Lao People's Army (LPA; includes Riverine Force), Air Force

Military service age and obligation:
18 years of age for compulsory or voluntary military service; conscript service obligation - minimum 18-months

Manpower available for military service:
males age 16-49: 1,574,362
females age 16-49: 1,607,856 (2010 est.)

Manpower fit for military service:
males age 16-49: 1,111,629
females age 16-49: 1,190,035 (2010 est.)

Manpower reaching militarily significant age annually:
male: 71,400
female: 73,038 (2010 est.)

Military expenditures:

For additional analytical, business and investment opportunities information,
please contact Global Investment & Business Center, USA
at (703) 370-8082. Fax: (703) 370-8083. E-mail: ibpusa3@gmail.com
Global Business and Investment Info Databank - www.ibpus.com

NA%
0.23% of GDP
NA%

Military - note:
serving one of the world's least developed countries, the Lao People's Armed Forces
(LPAF) is small, poorly funded, and ineffectively resourced; its mission focus is border
and internal security, primarily in countering ethnic Hmong insurgent groups; together
with the Lao People's Revolutionary Party and the government, the Lao People's Army
(LPA) is the third pillar of state machinery, and as such is expected to suppress political
and civil unrest and similar national emergencies, but the LPA also has upgraded skills to
respond to avian influenza outbreaks; there is no perceived external threat to the state
and the LPA maintains strong ties with the neighboring Vietnamese military

TRANSNATIONAL ISSUES

Disputes - international:
southeast Asian states have enhanced border surveillance to check the spread of avian
flu; talks continue on completion of demarcation with Thailand but disputes remain over
islands in the Mekong River; concern among Mekong River Commission members that
China's construction of dams on the Mekong River and its tributaries will affect water
levels; Cambodia and Vietnam are concerned about Laos' extensive upstream dam
construction

Illicit drugs:
estimated opium poppy cultivation in 2008 was 1,900 hectares, about a 73% increase
from 2007; estimated potential opium production in 2008 more than tripled to 17 metric
tons; unsubstantiated reports of domestic methamphetamine production; growing
domestic methamphetamine problem

**For additional analytical, business and investment opportunities information,
please contact Global Investment & Business Center, USA
at (703) 370-8082. Fax: (703) 370-8083. E-mail: ibpusa3@gmail.com
Global Business and Investment Info Databank - www.ibpus.com**

IMPORTANT INFORMATION FOR UNDERSTANDING LAOS[1]

Official Name: Lao People's Democratic Republic

PROFILE

GEOGRAPHY

Area: 236,800 sq. km. (91,430 sq. mi.); area comparable to Oregon.
Capital--Vientiane (est. 569,000). *Other principal towns*--Savannakhet, Luang Prabang, Pakse, Thakhek.
Terrain: rugged mountains, plateaus, alluvial plains.
Climate: tropical monsoon; rainy season (May to November); dry season (November to April).

PEOPLE

Nationality: *Noun and adjective*--Lao (sing. and pl.).
Population : 5.4 million.
Annual growth rate: 2.7%.
Ethnic groups: Lao Loum 53%; other lowland Lao 13% (Thai Dam, Phouane); Lao Theung (midslope) 23%; Lao Sung (highland), including Hmong, Akha, and the Yao (Mien) 10%; ethnic Vietnamese/Chinese 1%.
Religions: Principally Buddhism, with animism among highland groups.
Languages: Lao (official), French, various highland ethnic, English.
Education: *Literacy*--60%.
Health : *Infant mortality rate*--89.32/1,000. *Life expectancy*--55.87 years for women, 52.63 years for men.
Work force (2.6 million, 1999): *Agriculture*--85%; *industry and services*--15%.

GOVERNMENT

Branches: *Executive*--president (head of state); Chairman, Council of Ministers (prime minister and head of government); nine-member Politburo; 49-member Central Committee. *Legislative*--99-seat National Assembly. *Judicial*--district, provincial, and a national Supreme Court.
Political parties: Lao People's Revolutionary Party (LPRP)--only legal party.
Administrative subdivisions: 16 provinces, one special region, and Vientiane prefecture.
Flag: A red band at the top and bottom with a larger blue band between them; a large white circle is centered.

ECONOMY

Natural resources: Hydroelectric power, timber, minerals.
Agriculture (51% of GDP): *Primary products*--glutinous rice, coffee, corn, sugarcane, vegetables, tobacco, ginger, water buffalo, pigs, cattle, and poultry.

[1] **U.S. Department of State, *Bureau of East Asian and Pacific Affairs***

Industry (22% of GDP, 1999): *Primary types*--garment manufacturing, electricity production, gypsum and tin mining, wood and wood processing, cement manufacturing, agricultural processing.
Industrial growth rate --7.5%.
Services --27% of GDP.
Trade: *Exports* --$370 million: garments, electricity, wood and wood products, coffee, rattan. Major markets--France, U.K., Germany, Holland, Thailand, Belgium, U.S., Italy, Japan, Vietnam. *Imports* --$570 million. *Major imports*--fuel, food, consumer, goods, machinery and equipment, vehicles and spare parts. *Major suppliers*--Thailand, Singapore, Japan, Vietnam, China.

GEOGRAPHY, TOPOGRAPHY AND CLIMATE

The Lao People's Democratic Republic (Lao PDR) has a land area of 236,800 square kilometers, stretching more than 1,700 km from the north to south and between 100 km and 400 km from the east to west. The Lao PDR has an eastern border of 1,957 km with the Socialist Republic of Vietnam, a western border of 1,730 km with the, Kingdom of Thailand, a southern border of 492 kin with t he Kingdom of Combodia, and northern borders of 416 kin with the People's Republic of China and 230 km with the Union of Myamar.

Although the Lao PDR has no direct access to the sea, it has an abundance of rivers, including a 1,865 km stretch of the Mekong (Nam Kong), defining its border with Myanmar and a major part of the border with Thailand. Ma'or stretches of the Mekong and its tributaries are navigable and provide alluvial deposits for some. of the fertile plains. About two thirds of the country is mountainous, with ranges from 200 to the 2,820 meters high. The mountains pose difficulties for transportation and communication and complicate development, but together with the rivers they produce vast potential for hydro power.

The Lao PDR is a tropical country, whose climate is affected by monsoon rains from May to September. In Vientiane, the average temperatures range from a minimum of C 16.4 degrees in January to a maximum of C 13 degrees in April.

WATER RESOURCES

Its abundant water resources is probably the most important natural resource endowment of the country. There are only three hydroelectric plants in operation so far, of which Nam Ngum I is the biggest. These three plants with a combined capacity of 200 MW, reportedly realizes only less than five percent of the country's hydroelectric potential. About 90% of hydroelectric power production is exported to Thailand, constituting one of the leading exports of the Lao PDR. Plans are underway to construct a number of new hydroelectric power facilities, which are described in greater detail in Section B.

FOREST RESOURCES

For additional analytical, business and investment opportunities information,
please contact Global Investment & Business Center, USA
at (703) 370-8082. Fax: (703) 370-8083. E-mail: ibpusa3@gmail.com
Global Business and Investment Info Databank - www.ibpus.com

Forests cover about 47% of the country, comprising a wide variety of commercial tree species suitable for production of saw timber, plywood, parquet, furniture, etc.... The most important high value species are hardwoods belonging to the Diterocarpaceae family and rosewoods belonging to the Genera Pterocarpus, Dalbergia and Afzelia. Pines and other coniferous species are also available but in comparatively small quantities. Eighty percent of domestic energy consumption is based on fuel wood, and an estimated 300,000 hectares of forest are lost annually largely due to shifting cultivation and logging activities. In the effort to protect forest resources from unsustainable felling of trees, the total annual allowable cut (AC) has been set by the Tropical Forest Action Plan (1991) to 280,000 cubic meters per annum, exportation of logs was temporarily restricted to restructure forest management, and protective measures have been implemented to prevent depletion of forests due to shifting fanning practices.

MINERAL RESOURCES

Sizeable deposits of gemstones such as sapphire, zircon, amethyst, gold, iron are and tin are know to exist in the country. Gemstones, gold, coal and tin are estimated to have a high economic value. More geologic surveys are needed to identify location of mineral deposits that would allow their exploitation in commercial quantities. Meanwhile, exploration of potential petroleum deposits are underway. Economic exploitation of mineral resources will depend on development of the required physical infrastructures.

ADMINISTRATIVE STRUCTURE OF LAOS

ATTAPEU PROVINCE

Attapeu Province is best known for the Bolaven Plateau, which also extends into Champassak, Salavan and Sekong provinces. The Bolaven Plateau is covered in the Champassak section -The plateau is best accessed from Pakse, in Champassak province.

Attapeu province is rugged,wild and very scenic, but transportation is very difficult, especially by land in the rainy season.

The town of Samakhi Xai (Attapeu) is situated in a large picturesque valley. The population of the province is more Lao Loum than the neighbouring provinces.

Parts of the Ho Chi Minh Trail can be explored from Attapeu, although using a local guide is essential.

BOKEO PROVINCE

Bokeo province is the smallest province in the country and borders Thailand and Myanmar. This is the Lao side of the 'Golden Triangle'. The province has 34 ethnic groups, the second most ethnically diverse province in Laos. The photo shows a group of Akha (Ikaw or Kaw) people from the Golden Triangle area taken in 1900.

Huay Xai is the border town with Thailand, the city is busy and prosperous.

Located in the center of Huay Xay is Chomkao Manilat temple. The view from the the temple hill over Houy Xay city,the Mekong river and surrounding mountains is a definite reward for making it up the many steps.

BOLIKHAMSAI PROVINCE

Bolikhamsai province contains part of the wilderness area known as the Nakai - Nam Theun National Biodiversity Conservation Area the largest conservation area in the country at 3700 sq km. The area is home to over a dozen threatened species including Asiatic black bear, clouded leopard, elephant, giant muntjac, guar, Malayan sun bear, and tiger.

The saola (spindlehorn) or Vu Quang Ox - *Pseudoryx nghetinhensis* was discovered in neighbouring Vietnam in 1992 and sighted since then in Laos in the conservation area. Only two other land mammals have been classified with their own genus this century. The first live saola was captured in neighbouring Khammouane province in 1996.

The capital of Bolikhamsai is Paxxan, which can be reached from Vietntiane by bus in about three hours.

CHAMPASSAK PROVINCE - PAKSE

The province of Champassak is home to one of Asia's great, but least visited temples, Wat Phu.   Pakse, the capital is situated at the confluence of the Se river and the Mekong (Pakse means 'mouth of the Se') and is a busy trading town. The province also houses much of the Bolaven Plateau, an area that is home to a number of ethnic minorities.   To the south is Si Pan Don (four thousand islands), where the Mekong reaches up to 14km wide during the rainy season and the Khone Phapeng Falls.

Pakse has a number of comfortable places to stay and is a good base from which to explore the surrounding area. The town has one of the largest markets in the region. Within Pakse is the Champassak Museum where trader can see relics from Wat Phu as well as from the Bolaven Plateau.

HOUA PHAN

Houa Phan province is situated in the northeast of Laos and was the base of the Lao People's Revolutionary Army activities. There are over 100 caves in the Vieng Xai district of Houa Phanh many of which were used as hideouts and bunkers during the Indochina war.

Lao Aviation flies daily to the capital Xam Neua from Vientiane - The most famous caves in the area are:

For additional analytical, business and investment opportunities information,
please contact Global Investment & Business Center, USA
at (703) 370-8082. Fax: (703) 370-8083. E-mail: ibpusa3@gmail.com
Global Business and Investment Info Databank - www.ibpus.com

Tham Than Souphanouvong: formerly known as Tham Phapount. In 1964, Prince Souphanouvong set up his residence in this cave. Tham Than Kaysone: formerly known as Tham Yonesong, was established for the residence of Mr. Kaysone Phomvihane. Tham Than Khamtay: was the residence of Mr. Khamtay Siphandone, consisting of many area, such as a meeting room, reception room and research room.

Other attractions include Keo Nong Vay Temple located in Xam Neua district.

Hot springs in Xam Tay district are located about 154 km away from Xam Neua the waters reach a temperature of around 40 degrees Celcius. Xam Tay waterfall is located Xam Tay district.

Saleu and Nasala villages, well known for their weaving activities, located in Xieng Kor district on the road No: 6 to Xieng Khouang province 125 km away from Xam Neua.

KHAMMOUANE PROVINCE

Khammouane province contains two vast wilderness areas known as the Khammuane Limestone National Biodiversity Conservation Area and the Nakai - Nam Theun National Biodiversity Conservation Area.

The Kahmmuane Limestone is a maze of limestone karst peaks forming a stone forest of caves, rivers and pristine jungle. For most of the wet season, the area is not accessible by road - most 'roads' being tracks with log bridges across deeps streams. These tracks are often routes across rice paddies near the river banks - during the rainy season, the only way to get around is by boat.

The National Tourism Authority of Lao PDR is currently investigating ecotourism projects in this beautiful region. The capital of Khammouane province is Tha Kek, situated across the Mekong from Nakorn Phanom in Thailand.

LUANG PRABANG

Luang Prabang is the jewel of Indochina, and a UNESCO World Heritage Site since 1995. The ancient royal city is surrounded by mountains at the junction of the Mekong and its tributary, the Khan river. In the centre of the city is Mount Phousi with stunning views of the surrounding temples and hills. Luang Prabang is a city where time seems to stand still. As part of the UNESCO plan, new buildings have been limited and development must be in keeping with this magical place.

Minority village in Luang Namtha

Luang Prabang is small, and just about everywhere can be reached by foot. Walking and travelling by bicycle is the best way to see this tiny city.

For additional analytical, business and investment opportunities information, please contact Global Investment & Business Center, USA at (703) 370-8082. Fax: (703) 370-8083. E-mail: ibpusa3@gmail.com Global Business and Investment Info Databank - www.ibpus.com

LUANG NAMTHA PROVINCE

Located in the northern part of Laos, Luang Namtha shares its northwestern border with Myanmar and its northeastern border with China. The province is mountainous, home to large numbers of minorities. The Nam Ha National Biodiversity Conservation Area is located in the southwest of Luang Namtha - a pristine habitat of dense tropical rainforest covering almost all of the protected area.

UNESCO are funding a ecotourism project in Luang Namtha that will be capable of sustaining sustainable development in the province. The concept of the project is to provide education, conservation, management and sustainable economic benefits for the local population. The province is home to a 39 minorities the largest number in the country.

OUDOMXAI

Located in the northern part of Laos. This mountainous province has 23 ethnic groups each with it own distinct culture, religion, language and colorful style of dress. The provincial capital , Muang Xay lies between two strings of Hmong villages.

Lao Aviation flies to Oudomxai from Vientiane

Oudomxai can be reached overland from Luang Prabang. Oudomxay is also accessible from Bokeo and Luang Namtha Provinces. Oudomxay is an ideal base for excursions and trekking to varied sights and attractions as well as destination in its own right. Muang Xai, has one of the best produce markets in the area.

Near Muang Xai, there is a waterfall, Lak Sip – Et (located at km No 11) and hot springs near Muang La.

PHONGSALI PROVINCE

Phongsali province the most remote in northern Laos is surrounded on three sides by China and Vietnam. The Phu Den Din National Biodiversity Conservation Area along the Vietnamese border with mountains as high as 1950m with over 70% forest cover is home to the asiatic black bear, bantang, clouded leopard, elephant, guar and tiger.

The capital Phongsali, can be reached from Muang Xai with buses leaving once a day. Phongsali has a year round cool climate with temperatures as low as 5 degrees Celcius at night. Rain can be heavy - bring a jacket and warm clothes.

Muang Khoa is a small town situated on the junction of Route 4 and the Nam Ou river. The journey to Muang Khoa along route 4 from Udomxai takes about four hours. It is possible to travel up river to Phongsali from here, or down to Luang Prabang.

For additional analytical, business and investment opportunities information,
please contact Global Investment & Business Center, USA
at (703) 370-8082. Fax: (703) 370-8083. E-mail: ibpusa3@gmail.com
Global Business and Investment Info Databank - www.ibpus.com

SALAVAN PROVINCE

Salavan Province is best known for the Bolaven Plateau, which also extends into Attapeu, Champassak and Sekong provinces. The Bolaven Plateau is covered in the Champassak section.. The plateau is best accessed from Pakse, in Champassak province.

Salavan province is home to the Phu Xieng Thong National Biodiversity Conservation Area, covering nearly 1,000 sq km in the western part of the province next to the Mekong river. It is thought that asiatic black bear, banteng, clouded leopard, Douc langur, elephant, gibbon, guar, Siamese crocodile and tiger and inhabit this area.

SEKONG PROVINCE

Sekong Province is best known for the Bolaven Plateau, which also extends into Attapeu, Champassak and Salavan and provinces. The Bolaven Plateau is covered in the Champassak section. The plateau is best accessed from Pakse, in Champassak province. Sekong province is rugged,wild and very scenic, but transportation is very difficult, especially by land in the rainy season.

SAYABOURI PROVINCE

Sayabouri province is quite close to Vientiane, but being quite mountainous is quite remote. The province shares its borders with six Thai provinces. The capital of the province, Sayabouri is on the banks of the Nam Hung, a tributary of the Mekong.

The province houses the Nam Phoun National Biodiversity Conservation Area which is 1150 sq km of forested hills that contain Asiatic black bear, dhole, elephant, guar, gibbon, Malayan sun bear and Sumatran rhino.

The southern part of the province has many scenic waterfalls, but getting around this part of the province is very difficult.

SAVANNAKHET

Savannakhet town is situated on the banks of the Mekong river opposite Mukdahan in Thailand. The province bridges the country between Thailand and Vietnam and the town is a very active junction for trade between the two countries. The town itself can be easily explored by foot and has a number of interesting temples, including Vietnamese temple and school and a large Catholic church. Much of the town's architecture is French Colonial.

VIENTIANE

Vientiane, capital of Laos is Asia's biggest village. Busy and hectic in comparison to the rest of the country, it is quiet compared with any other city in Asia. Vientiane, as all of Lao's major cities, is situated on the Mekong river which forms the lifeline of the country.

For additional analytical, business and investment opportunities information, please contact Global Investment & Business Center, USA at (703) 370-8082. Fax: (703) 370-8083. E-mail: ibpusa3@gmail.com Global Business and Investment Info Databank - www.ibpus.com

Vientiane is the hub for all travel in the country. The city has a population of 450,000, about 10% of the country.

Vientiane is a city full of surprises. Here trader can find fields of rice and vegetables, agriculture hidden behind tree lined avenues. French Colonial architecture sits next to gilded temples. Freshly baked French bread is served next to shops selling noodle soup.

There is little modern in Vientiane. Old French colonial houses are being restored as offices and as restaurants and hotels. There are only a handful of modern buildings which sometimes look remarkably out of place in this quiet capital.

XIENG KHOUANG PROVINCE

Xieng Khouang province is situated in the north of Laos, a province of green montains and karst limestone. Much of the province was heavily bombed during the Vietnam war and old war scrap is used in building houses throughout the province. The capital of Xieng Khouang is Phonsavan. Situated at an altitude of 1,200m is an excellent climate. Decmber and January can be chilly so bring a light jacket or fleece for cool evenings and mornings.

PEOPLE

Laos' population was estimated at about 5.4 million in 1999, dispersed unevenly across the country. Most people live in valleys of the Mekong River and its tributaries. Vientiane prefecture, the capital and largest city, had about 569,000 residents in 1999. The country's population density is 23.4/sq. km.

About half the country's people are ethnic Lao, the principal lowland inhabitants and politically and culturally dominant group. The Lao are descended from the Tai people who began migrating southward from China in the first millennium A.D. Mountain tribes of Miao-Yao, Austro-Asiatic, Tibeto-Burman--Hmong, Yao, Akha, and Lahu--and Tai ethnolinguistic heritage are found in northern Laos. Collectively, they are known as Lao Sung or highland Lao. In the central and southern mountains, Mon-Khmer tribes, known as Lao Theung or midslope Lao, predominate. Some Vietnamese and Chinese minorities remain, particularly in the towns, but many left in two waves--after independence in the late 1940s and again after 1975.

The predominant religion is Theravada Buddhism. Animism is common among the mountain tribes. Buddhism and spirit worship coexist easily. There also is a small number of Christians and Muslims.

The official and dominant language is Lao, a tonal language of the Tai linguistic group. Midslope and highland Lao speak an assortment of tribal languages. French, once common in government and commerce, has declined in usage, while knowledge of English--the language of the Association of Southeast Asian Nations (ASEAN)--has increased in recent years.

HISTORY

Laos traces its first recorded history and its origins as a unified state to the emergence of the Kingdom of Lan Xang (literally, "million elephants") in 1353. Under the rule of King Fa Ngum, the wealthy and mighty kingdom covered much of what today is Thailand and Laos. His successors, especially King Setthathirat in the 16th century, helped establish Buddhism as the predominant religion of the country.

By the 17th century, the kingdom of Lan Xang entered a period of decline marked by dynastic struggle and conflicts with its neighbors. In the late 18th century, the Siamese (Thai) established hegemony over much of what is now Laos. The region was divided into principalities centered on Luang Prabang in the north, Vientiane in the center, and Champassak in the south. Following its colonization of Vietnam, the French supplanted the Siamese and began to integrate all of Laos into the French empire. The Franco-Siamese treaty of 1907 defined the present Lao boundary with Thailand.

During World War II, the Japanese occupied French Indochina, including Laos. King Sisavang Vong of Luang Prabang was induced to declare independence from France in 1945, just prior to Japan's surrender. During this period, nationalist sentiment grew. In September 1945, Vientiane and Champassak united with Luang Prabang to form an independent government under the Free Laos (Lao Issara) banner. The movement, however, was shortlived. By early 1946, French troops reoccupied the country and conferred limited autonomy on Laos following elections for a constituent assembly.

Amidst the first Indochina war between France and the communist movement in Vietnam, Prince Souphanouvong formed the Pathet Lao (Land of Laos) resistance organization committed to the communist struggle against colonialism. Laos was not granted full sovereignty until the French defeat by the Vietnamese and the subsequent Geneva peace conference in 1954. Elections were held in 1955, and the first coalition government, led by Prince Souvanna Phouma, was formed in 1957. The coalition government collapsed in 1958, amidst increased polarization of the political process. Rightist forces took over the government.

In 1960, Kong Le, a paratroop captain, seized Vientiane in a coup and demanded formation of a neutralist government to end the fighting. The neutralist government, once again led by Souvanna Phouma, was not successful in holding power. Rightist forces under Gen. Phoumi Nosavan drove out the neutralist government from power later that same year. Subsequently, the neutralists allied themselves with the communist insurgents and began to receive support from the Soviet Union. Phoumi Nosavan's rightist regime received support from the U.S.

A second Geneva conference, held in 1961-62, provided for the independence and neutrality of Laos. Soon after accord was reached, the signatories accused each other of violating the terms of the agreement, and with superpower support on both sides, the civil war soon resumed. Although the country was to be neutral, a growing American and North Vietnamese military presence in the country increasingly drew Laos into the second Indochina war (1954-75). For nearly a decade, Laos was subjected to the heaviest bombing in the history of warfare, as the U.S. sought to destroy the Ho Chi Minh Trail that passed through eastern Laos.

In 1972, the communist People's Party renamed itself the Lao People's Revolutionary Party (LPRP). It joined a new coalition government in Laos soon after the Vientiane cease-fire agreement in 1973. Nonetheless, the political struggle between communists, neutralists, and rightists continued. The fall of Saigon and Phnom Penh to communist forces in April 1975 hastened the decline of the coalition in Laos. Months after these communist victories, the Pathet Lao entered Vientiane. On December 2, 1975, the king abdicated his throne in the constitutional monarchy, and the communist Lao People's Democratic Republic (LPDR) was established.

The new communist government imposed centralized economic decisionmaking and broad security measures, including control of the media and the arrest and incarceration of many members of the previous government and military in "re-education camps". These draconian policies and deteriorating economic conditions, along with government efforts to enforce political control, prompted an exodus of lowland Lao and ethnic Hmong from Laos. About 10% of the Lao population sought refugee status after 1975. Many have since been resettled in third countries, including more than 250,000 who have come to the United States.

The situation of Lao refugees is nearing its final chapter. Over time, the Lao Government closed the re-education camps and released most political prisoners. From 1975 to 1996, the U.S. resettled some 250,000 Lao refugees from Thailand, including 130,000 Hmong. By the end of 1999, more than 28,900 Hmong and lowland Lao had repatriated to Laos--3,500 from China, the rest from Thailand. Through the Office of the United Nations High Commissioner for Refugees (UNHCR), the International Organization for Migration (IOM), and non-governmental organizations, the U.S. has supported a variety of reintegration assistance programs throughout Laos. UNHCR monitors returnees and reports no evidence of systemic persecution or discrimination to date. As of December 1999, about 115 Hmong and lowland Lao remained in Ban Napho camp in Thailand awaiting third-country resettlement by the UNHCR.

GOVERNMENT AND POLITICAL CONDITIONS

The only legal political party is the Lao People's Revolutionary Party (LPRP). The head of state is President Khamtay Siphandone. The head of government is Prime Minister Sisavath Keobounphanh, who also is Chairman of the LPRP. Government policies are determined by the party through the all-powerful nine-member Politburo and the 49-member Central Committee. Important government decisions are vetted by the Council of Ministers.

Laos adopted a constitution in 1991. The following year, elections were held for a new 85-seat National Assembly with members elected by secret ballot to 5-year terms. This National Assembly, expanded in 1997 elections to 99 members, approves all new laws, although the executive branch retains authority to issue binding decrees. The most recent elections took place in December 1997. The FY 2000 central government budget plan calls for revenue of $180 million and expenditures of $289 million, including capital expenditures of $202 million.

PRINCIPAL GOVERNMENT OFFICIALS NEW CABINET MEMBERS APPROVED

The National Assembly, the country's top legislature on 15 June approved the appointment of Mr. Thongsing Thammavong as Prime Minister and four deputy prime ministers and cabinet members.

The First Plenary Session of the 7 th NA approved the proposed list of four deputy prime ministers are Mr. Asang Laoly, Dr. Thongloun Sisoulith, Mr. Duangchay Phichit and Mr. Somsavat Lengsavad. Four of them are members of Politburo under the Lao People's Revolutionary Party Central Committee.

Under the approval, Dr. Thongloun Sisoulith is responsible for Ministry of Foreign Affairs and Mr. Duangchay Phitchit takes the post the Minister of National Defence.

The NA also approved the appointment of government members accordingly,

Mr. Bounthong Chitmany serves as President of State Inspection Committee and Head of Anti-Corruption Agency;

Mr. Phankham Viphavanh, Minister of Education and Sports;

Mr. Thongbanh Seng-aphone, Minister Public Security; Mrs Onchanh Thammavong, Minister of Labour and Social-Welfare;

Mr. Chaleune Yiabaoher, Minister of Justice;

Mr. Soulivong Daravong, Minister of Energy and Mining;

Mrs Bounpheng Mouphosay, Minister for Government's Office;

Mr. Vilayvanh Phomkhe, Minister of Agriculture and Forestry;

Mr. Sinlavong Khouphaythoune, Minister and Head of Government's Office;

Mr. Nam Viyaket, Minister of Industry and Commerce;

Mr. Sommad Pholsena, Minister of Public Works and Transport;

Mr. Somdy Duangdy, Minister of Planning and Investment;

Mr. Phouphet Khamphounvong, Minister of Finance;

Prof Dr. Bosengkham Vongdara, Minister of Information, Culture and Tourism;

Prof Dr. Eksavang Vongvichit, Minister of Public Health;

Mr. Bounheuang Duangphachanh, Minister for Government's Office;

Mr. Khampane Philavong, Minister of Interior;

Prof Dr. Bountiem Phitsamay, Minister for Government's Office;

Dr. Douangsavad Souphanouvong, Minister for Government's Office;

Mrs Khempheng Pholsena, Minister for Government's Office;

Prof Dr. Boviengkham Vongdara, Minister of Science and Technology;

Mr. Noulin Sinbandith, Minister of Natural Resources and Environment;

Mr. Hiem Phommachanh, Minister of Post, Telecommunication and Communication;

Mr. Sompao Phaysith, Governor of the State Bank of Laos;

Mr. Khamphanh Sitthidampha, President of People's Supreme Court and

Mr. Khamsan Souvong, Head of General Prosecutor's Office.

Laos maintains an embassy in the United States at 2222 S Street NW, Washington, D.C. 20009 (tel: 202-332-6416).

ECONOMY

Currency	Lao Kip
Fiscal year	1 October - 30 September
Trade organisations	ASEAN, WTO
	Statistics
GDP	$17.66 billion (PPP; est.)
GDP growth	8.3% (2014 est.)
GDP per capita	$2,700 (PPP; est.)
GDP by sector	services (42.6%), industry (20.2%), agriculture (37.4%) (est.)
Inflation (CPI)	7.6% (est.)
Population below poverty line	26% (est.)
Labour force	3.69 million (est.)
Labour force by occupation	agriculture (75.1%), industry (n/a), services (n/a) (est.)
Unemployment	2.5% (est.)
Main industries	copper, tin, gold, and gypsum mining; timber, electric power, agricultural processing, construction, garments, cement, tourism

Ease of doing business rank	165th
External	
Exports	$2.131 billion (est.)
Export goods	wood products, garments, electricity, coffee, tin, copper, gold
Main export partners	Thailand 32.8% China 20.7% Vietnam 14.0% (est.)
Imports	2.336 billion (est.)
Import goods	machinery and equipment, vehicles, fuel, consumer goods
Main import partners	Thailand 63.2% China 16.5% Vietnam 5.6% (est.)
Gross external debt	$5.953 billion (31 December 2011 est)
Public finances	
Public debt	$3.179 billion
Revenues	$1.76 billion
Expenses	$1.957 billion (est.)
Economic aid	$345 million (est.)
Foreign reserves	$773.5 (31 December est.)

The **economy of the Lao Peoples' Democratic Republic** is rapidly growing, as the government began to decentralise control and encourage private enterprise in 1986. Currently, the economy grows at 8% a year, and the government is pursuing poverty reduction and education for all children as key goals. The country opened a stock exchange, the Lao Securities Exchange in 2011, and has become a rising regional player in its role as a hydroelectric power supplier to neighbors such as China, Vietnam and Thailand. Laos remains one of the poorest countries in Southeast Asia, but may transition from being a low middle-income country to an upper-middle income one by 2020. A landlocked country, it has inadequate infrastructure and a largely unskilled work force. The country's per capita income in 2009 was estimated to be $2,700 on a purchasing power parity-basis.

The Lao economy depends heavily on investment and trade with its neighbours, Thailand, Vietnam, and, especially in the north, China. Pakxe has also experienced growth based on cross-border trade with Thailand and Vietnam. In 2009, despite the fact that the government is still officially communist, the Obama administration in the US declared Laos was no longer a marxist-lenninist state and lifted bans on Laotian companies receiving financing from the U.S. Export Import Bank. In 2011, the Lao Securities Exchange began trading. In 2014, the government initiated the creation of the Laos Trade Portal, a website incorporating all information traders need to import and export goods into the country.

Subsistence agriculture still accounts for half of the GDP and provides 80% of employment. Only 4.01% of the country is arable land, and a mere 0.34% used as permanent crop land, the lowest percentage in the Greater Mekong Subregion. Rice dominates agriculture, with about 80% of the arable land area used for growing rice. Approximately 77% of Lao farm households are self-sufficient in rice.

For additional analytical, business and investment opportunities information, please contact Global Investment & Business Center, USA at (703) 370-8082. Fax: (703) 370-8083. E-mail: ibpusa3@gmail.com Global Business and Investment Info Databank - www.ibpus.com

Through the development, release and widespread adoption of improved rice varieties, and through economic reforms, production has increased by an annual rate of 5% between 1990 and 2005, and Lao PDR achieved a net balance of rice imports and exports for the first time in 1999. Lao PDR may have the greatest number of rice varieties in the Greater Mekong Subregion. Since 1995 the Lao government has been working with the International Rice Research Institute of the Philippines to collect seed samples of each of the thousands of rice varieties found in Laos.

The economy receives development aid from the IMF, ADB, and other international sources; and also foreign direct investment for development of the society, industry, hydropower and mining (most notably of copper and gold). Tourism is the fastest-growing industry in the country. Economic development in Laos has been hampered by brain drain, with a skilled emigration rate of 37.4% in 2000.

Laos is rich in mineral resources and imports petroleum and gas. Metallurgy is an important industry, and the government hopes to attract foreign investment to develop the substantial deposits of coal, gold, bauxite, tin, copper, and other valuable metals. In addition, the country's plentiful water resources and mountainous terrain enable it to produce and export large quantities of hydroelectric energy. Of the potential capacity of approximately 18,000 megawatts, around 8,000 megawatts have been committed for exporting to Thailand and Vietnam.

The country's most widely recognised product may well be Beerlao which is exported to a number of countries including neighbours Cambodia and Vietnam. It is produced by the Lao Brewery Company.

FOREIGN RELATIONS

The new government that assumed power in December 1975 aligned itself with the Soviet bloc and adopted a hostile posture toward the West. In ensuing decades, Laos maintained close ties with the former Soviet Union and its eastern bloc allies and depended heavily on the Soviets for most of its foreign assistance. Laos also maintained a "special relationship" with Vietnam and formalized a 1977 treaty of friendship and cooperation that created tensions with China.

With the collapse of the Soviet Union and with Vietnam's decreased ability to provide assistance, Laos has sought to improve relations with its regional neighbors. The Lao Government has focused its efforts on Thailand, Laos' principal means of access to the sea and its primary trading partner. Within a year of serious border clashes in 1987, Lao and Thai leaders signed a communiquŽ, signaling their intention to improve relations. Since then, they have made slow but steady progress, notably the construction and opening of the Friendship Bridge between the two countries.

Relations with China have improved over the years. Although the two were allies during the Vietnam War, the China-Vietnam conflict in 1979 led to a sharp deterioration in Sino-Lao relations. These relations began to improve in the late 1980s. In 1989 Sino-Lao relations were normalized.

Laos' emergence from international isolation has been marked through improved and expanded relations with other nations such as Australia, France, Japan, Sweden, and India. Laos was admitted into the Association of Southeast Asian Nations (ASEAN) in July 1997 and applied to join WTO in 1998.

Laos is a member of the following international organizations: Agency for Cultural and Technical Cooperation (ACCT), Association of Southeast Asian Nations (ASEAN), ASEAN Free Trade Area (AFTA), ASEAN Regional Forum, Asian Development Bank, Colombo Plan, Economic and Social Commission for Asia and Pacific (ESCAP), Food and Agriculture Organization (FAO), G-77, International Bank for Reconstruction and Development (World Bank), International Civil Aviation Organization (ICAO), International Development Association (IDA), International Fund for Agricultural Development (IFAD), International Finance Corporation (IFC), International Federation of Red Cross and Red Crescent Societies, International Labor Organization (ILO), International Monetary Fund (IMF), Intelsat (nonsignatory user), Interpol, International Olympic Commission (IOC), International Telecommunications Union (ITU), Mekong Group, Non-Aligned Movement (NAM), Permanent Court of Arbitration (PCA), UN, United Nations Convention on Trade and Development (UNCTAD), United Nations Educational, Social and Cultural Organization (UNESCO), United Nations Industrial Development Organization (UNIDO), Universal Postal Union (UPU), World Federation of Trade Unions, World Health Organization (WHO), World Intellectual Property Organization (WIPO), World Meteorological Organization (WMO), World Tourism Organization, World Trade Organization (observer).

U.S.-LAO RELATIONS

The United States opened a legation in Laos in 1950. Although diplomatic relations were never severed, U.S.-Lao relations deteriorated badly in the post-Indochina War period. The relationship remained cool until 1982 when efforts at improvement began. For the United States, progress in accounting for Americans missing in Laos from the Vietnam War is a principal measure of improving relations. Counternarcotics activities also have become an important part of the bilateral relationship as the Lao Government has stepped up its efforts to combat cultivation; production; and transshipment of opium, heroin, and marijuana.

Since the late 1980s, progress in these areas has steadily increased. Joint U.S. and Lao teams have conducted a series of joint excavations and investigations of sites related to cases of Americans missing in Laos. In counternarcotics activities, the U.S. and Laos are involved in a multimillion-dollar crop substitution/integrated rural development program. Laos also has formed its own national committee on narcotics, developed a long-range strategy for counternarcotics activities, participated in U.S.-sponsored narcotics training programs, and strengthened law enforcement measures to combat the narcotics problem.

U.S. Government foreign assistance to Laos covers a broad range of efforts. Such aid includes support for Laos' efforts to suppress opium production; training and equipment for a program to clear and dispose of unexploded ordnance; school and hospital construction; public education about the dangers of unexploded ordnance and about

For additional analytical, business and investment opportunities information,
please contact Global Investment & Business Center, USA
at (703) 370-8082. Fax: (703) 370-8083. E-mail: ibpusa3@gmail.com
Global Business and Investment Info Databank - www.ibpus.com

HIV/AIDS; support for medical research on hepatitis. Economic relations also are expanding. In August 1997, Laos and the United States initialed a Bilateral Trade Agreement and a Bilateral Investment Treaty.

Principal U.S. Embassy Officials

Ambassador-- Rena Bitter

Ambassador Rena Bitter is a career Senior Foreign Service Officer with more than 20 years of experience in Washington and overseas. Most recently, Ambassador Bitter served as Consul General at the U.S. Consulate General in Ho Chi Minh City, Vietnam. Prior to that, she served as the Director of the State Department Operations Center, the Department's 24/7 Briefing and Crisis Management Center. In Washington, she served on the Secretary of State's Executive Staff and as a Special Assistant to Secretary Colin Powell. Her overseas tours include Amman, London, Mexico City and Bogota. Ambassador Bitter grew up in Dallas.

Deputy Chief of Mission--Susan M. Sutton

The American Embassy in Laos is on Rue Bartholonie, B.P. 114, Vientiane, tel: 212-581/582/585; fax: 212-584: country code: (856): city code (21).

Information on the embassy, its work in Laos, and U.S.-Lao relations is available on the Internet at http://www.usembassy.state.gov/laos.

TRAVEL AND BUSINESS INFORMATION

The U.S. Department of State's Consular Information Program provides Consular Information Sheets, Travel Warnings, and Public Announcements. **Consular Information Sheets** exist for all countries and include information on entry requirements, currency regulations, health conditions, areas of instability, crime and security, political disturbances, and the addresses of the U.S. posts in the country. **Travel Warnings** are issued when the State Department recommends that Americans avoid travel to a certain country. **Public Announcements** are issued as a means to disseminate information quickly about terrorist threats and other relatively short-term conditions overseas which pose significant risks to the security of American travelers. Free copies of this information are available by calling the Bureau of Consular Affairs at 202-647-5225 or via the fax-on-demand system: 202-647-3000.

Consular Information Sheets and Travel Warnings also are available on the Consular Affairs Internet home page: http://travel.state.gov. Consular Affairs Tips for Travelers publication series, which contain information on obtaining passports and planning a safe trip abroad are on the internet and hard copies can be purchased from the Superintendent of Documents, U.S. Government Printing Office, telephone: 202-512-1800; fax 202-512-2250.

Emergency information concerning Americans traveling abroad may be obtained from the Office of Overseas Citizens Services at (202) 647-5225. For after-hours emergencies, Sundays and holidays, call 202-647-4000.

Passport information can be obtained by calling the National Passport Information Center's automated system ($.35 per minute) or live operators 8 a.m. to 8 p.m. (EST) Monday-Friday ($1.05 per minute). The number is 1-900-225-5674 (TDD: 1-900-225-7778). Major credit card users (for a flat rate of $4.95) may call 1-888-362-8668 (TDD: 1-888-498-3648). It also is available on the internet.

Travelers can check the latest health information with the U.S. Centers for Disease Control and Prevention in Atlanta, Georgia. A hotline at 877-FYI-TRIP (877-394-8747) and a web site at http://www.cdc.gov/travel/index.htm give the most recent health advisories, immunization recommendations or requirements, and advice on food and drinking water safety for regions and countries. A booklet entitled Health Information for International Travel (HHS publication number CDC-95-8280) is available from the U.S. Government Printing Office, Washington, DC 20402, tel. (202) 512-1800.

Information on travel conditions, visa requirements, currency and customs regulations, legal holidays, and other items of interest to travelers also may be obtained before your departure from a country's embassy and/or consulates in the U.S. (for this country, see "Principal Government Officials" listing in this publication).

U.S. citizens who are long-term visitors or traveling in dangerous areas are encouraged to register at the U.S. embassy upon arrival in a country (see "Principal U.S. Embassy Officials" listing in this publication). This may help family members contact you in case of an emergency.

For additional analytical, business and investment opportunities information, please contact Global Investment & Business Center, USA at (703) 370-8082. Fax: (703) 370-8083. E-mail: ibpusa3@gmail.com Global Business and Investment Info Databank - www.ibpus.com

LAOS JUDICIAL AND LEGAL SYSTEM

LEGAL AND JUDICIAL SYSTEM

The development of the legal and judicial system did not begin until almost fifteen years after the state was proclaimed. In November 1989, a criminal code and laws establishing a judicial system were adopted. In 1993 the government began publishing an official gazette to disseminate laws, decrees, and regulations.

In 1990 the judicial branch was upgraded. New legislation provided a draft of a criminal code, established procedures for criminal cases, set up a court system, and established a law school. Moreover, the Ministry of Justice added a fourth year of studies to a law program for training magistrates and judges.

Also in 1990, the functions of the Supreme People's Court were separated from those of the office of the public prosecutor general. Until then, the minister of justice served as both president of the court and director of public prosecutions.

Although the implementation of judicial reforms proceeded slowly and had not significantly improved the administration of justice by mid-1994, the new legal framework offers the possibility of moving away from the arbitrary use of power toward the rule of law. In late 1992, however, the government suspended the bar until it formulates regulations for fees and activities of (the few) private lawyers who are able to advise in civil cases. Lawyers are not allowed to promote themselves as attorneys-at-law. Theoretically, the government provides legal counsel to the accused, although in practice persons accused of crimes must defend themselves, without outside legal counsel. However, the assessors (legal advisers)--who are often untrained--and the party functionaries are being increasingly replaced by professional personnel trained at the Institute of Law and Administration.

The constitution empowers the National Assembly to elect or remove the president of the Supreme People's Court and the public prosecutor general on the recommendation of its Standing Committee. The Standing Committee of the National Assembly appoints or removes judges (previously elected) of the provincial, municipal, and district levels.

Further evidence of an attempt to shift toward a professional judicial system is found in the public prosecution institutes provided for at each level of administration. The task of these institutes is to control the uniform observance of laws by all ministries, organizations, state employees, and citizens. They prosecute under the guidance of the public prosecutor general, who appoints and removes deputy public prosecutors at all levels.

LEGAL SYSTEM DEVELOPMENTS

LEGAL SYSTEM IN TRANSITION

The legal system of the Lao PDR has been shaped by Lao tradition and custom, by the establishment of the French colonial administration, and after 1975, by the adoption of a Soviet-styled socialist ideology. Since the mid-1980's, however, the legal system has also been influenced by the legal and economic transitions taking place in neighboring, Vietnam and China. The legal system of the Lao PDR still contains elements from all of these historical influences, but its current development is driven by the economic needs of the country, by the concurrent development of the Lao PDR's own market economy, and by the desire to strengthen cooperation with ASEAN neighbors.

To meet these needs, many new laws and decrees are being drafted, and for guidance, the Lao PDR is considering the laws of a variety of market-oriented countries around the world. At present, the Lao PDR has over forty laws and hundreds of decrees and regulations. All of the laws, and most of the decrees and regulations in current use, were drafted after 1989.

INVESTMENT PROCEDURES

The Law on the Promotion and Management of Foreign Investment ("Foreign Investment Law") is the basic law governing foreign investment in the Lao PDR.

The Foreign Investment Law classifies foreign investment companies in two categories: joint venture companies and wholly foreign-owned companies. A joint venture is a foreign investment company that is jointly owned and operated by foreign and domestic investors, with the general requirement that the foreign investors must contribute at least 30% of the total capital.

Following is a brief outline of the typical process for establishing a foreign investment company in the Lao PDR.

INVESTMENT LICENSE

Before commencing any activity in the Lao PDR, a foreign investment project must obtain a Foreign Investment License. To obtain a Foreign Investment License, the project submits a standard Foreign Investment License Application provided by Committee for Investment and Foreign Economic Cooperation ("CIFEC"), along with various supporting documents.

The Foreign Investment Law mandates that CIFEC review the application and either grant a Foreign Investment License or reject the application within 60 days. Once the application is approved, CIFEC issues the Foreign Investment License.

Company Registration

All companies in the Lao PDR must register with the Company Registry of the Ministry of Commerce ("MOC"). In order for a foreign investment company to register with the Company Registry, it must submit an application to the MOC along with various supporting documents.

Document Registration

The foreign investment company must also register its legal documents and pay document registration fees.

Tax Registration

All business enterprises in the Lao PDR must also register with the Tax Department of the Ministry of Finance. Foreign investment companies must obtain this registration within 90 days of receipt of the Foreign Investment License.

Other Licenses and Permits

Before the foreign investment company is fully authorized to carry on business in the Lao PDR, it will often need an array of additional licenses and permits depending on the type of business to be carried out.

INVESTMENT GUARANTEES

The Foreign Investment Law guarantees that foreign investment companies:

- are protected from governmental confiscation, seizure, or nationalization;
- can operate freely without interference from the government;
- can lease land, transfer leasehold interests, and make improvements on land and buildings; and
- can remit foreign currencies abroad.

INVESTMENT INCENTIVES

The Foreign Investment Law also provides the following incentives:

- Exemption from import duties on raw materials and equipment for export-oriented production;
- Import duties at a flat rate of 1% on equipment and other material used in the operation of foreign investment companies;
- No export duties on finished products;
- Freedom to employ necessary foreign expatriates;
- Freedom to repatriate profits and capital;
- Foreign personal income taxes at a flat rate of 10%; and
- Annual profit taxes at a flat rate of 20%.

Structure of the CIFEC
The current structure of CIFEC (relevant to foreign investment) is as follows:

- Office of the Prime Minister
  - CIFEC
    - Department of Foreign Investment
      - Promotion Division

- Screening Division
- Legal Division
- Monitoring Division
- Strategy Division
- Administrative Division

INVESTMENT SECTORS

Promoted Sectors
Most sectors of the Lao economy are open to foreign investment, and the Lao Government is particularly promoting foreign investment in the following sectors:

- Energy
- Mining
- Agriculture
- Manufacturing

Activities Reserved for Lao Citizens
The Lao Government prohibits foreign investors and foreign personnel from undertaking certain commercial activities in the Lao PDR. Some of these reserved activities include:

- Forest and wood exploitation;
- Retail sales;
- Accounting services;
- Tour services;
- Vehicle and machinery operation; and
- Rice cultivation.

INVESTMENT STRUCTURES

The Business Law is essentially the "Companies Act" of the Lao PDR. This law applies equally to both foreign and Lao companies and provides legal protection for the capital, property, and rights of the companies.
Pursuant to the Business Law (and the Foreign Investment Law), the following corporate structures are available to foreign investors in the Lao PDR:

- Representative Office
- Branch Office
- Sole Proprietorship
- Partnership
- Limited Company
- Public Company
- Companies with State Ownership

TAXATION

Unless exemptions are granted by the Lao Government, a foreign investment company would be subject to the following taxes, among others:

- Profits tax (20% of net profits);
- Income taxes (at varying rates depending on type of income);
- Business turnover tax (3-15% of gross sales);
- Use tax (at variable rates); and
- Import duties (at variable rates)

For additional information, please contact:

Dirksen Flipse Doran & Lê
Lawyers & Counselors

Dirksen Flipse Doran & Lê ("DFDL") is an international law firm focusing on the legal markets of Laos, Cambodia, Vietnam, Myanmar, and the Yunnan Province of China. In 1993, DFDL opened its office in Vientiane, and became the first officially authorized law firm in Laos. In 1994, DFDL opened its office in Phnom Penh, also becoming the first officially authorized law firm in Cambodia, and established an office in Ho Chi Minh City, Vietnam.

Following is a brief profile of the lawyers in our Vientiane office:

Todd E. Dirksen is a member of the New York Bar and the US Supreme Court Bar, and a graduate of Georgetown University Law Center. He has published articles entitled "Doing Business in Vietnam: The Legal Aspects," in Asia Business Law Review, Vol. 2, and "Security Arrangements in Laos," in Creating and Enforcing Security in Asian Emerging Markets, Vol. 1. He is currently working on several hydropower projects, an ICC arbitration, and general investment, commercial and banking matters in Laos. Languages: English, French and Spanish.

Mary S. Flipse is a member of the New York Bar and the US Supreme Court Bar, and a graduate of Georgetown University Law Center. She has published the following articles: "Asia's Littlest Dragon: An Analysis of the Lao Foreign Investment Code and Decree," Georgetown University Law Center journal of Law & Policy in International Business, Vol. 23, No. 1; "Laos: Banking, Finance and Taxation," in Capital Flows Along the Mekong, Vol. 1. Ms. Flipse is now advising international clients on foreign investment in Laos, particularly in the hydropower, construction and aviation sectors, and is litigating several corporate and commercial cases in the Lao courts. Languages: English, Lao and Thai.

Robert R. Allen Jr. is a member of the Maryland Bar, and holds a Juris Doctor degree from Columbus School of Law, Catholic University of America in Washington, D.C. Mr. Allen also holds a Mechanical Engineering degree from the University of Maryland, and a diploma from the Nuclear Power Engineering School of the General Electric Corporation. Prior to joining DFDL, Mr. Allen worked for more than four years as an engineer in the United States power industry, followed by several years as a business and legal consultant on corporate, energy, and environmental issues in the United States.

Desarack Teso holds a Juris Doctor from the University of Hawaii, and is a candidate for admission to the Bar of the State of Hawaii. He has published a series of articles on Lao law in the Vientiane Times. He is fluent in English, Lao and Thai.

Phasith Phommarak is a member and a section leader of the Lao Bar Association, and one of the few lawyers to be appointed as an authorized private attorney by the Lao Ministry of Justice. He is a graduate of L'Institut Royal de Droit et Administration, in Vientiane, Laos, and Georgetown University's American Language Institute. Specializing in commercial contracts and dispute resolution, he assists in many of the firm's litigation matters before Lao courts of law. Languages: Lao, Thai, English, French.

Contact Information
Attn: Todd E. Dirksen
Dirksen Flipse Doran & Lê
Mekong Commerce Bldg #1, POB 2920
Luang Prabang Road, Vientiane, Lao PDR
Tel: (856) 21 216-927-9
Fax: (856) 21 216-919

DISPUTE RESOLUTION

Basically there are four ways to resolve a commercial dispute in China: negotiation, mediation, arbitration and litigation. Negotiation is normally the first choice of parties concerned because it is the least expensive and most friendly approach to resolve a dispute. Mediation is also welcomed and encouraged especially during the judicial procedure, and it can effectively preserve the cooperation relationship of the parties involved. Compared with litigation, arbitration is a preference for most parties mainly because it is not that time consuming and the procedure is relatively simple. Litigation is regarded as a final way to resolve a dispute. In China, foreign parties have equal rights to bring action in courts as Chinese parties.

The PRC law contains no political method of dispute resolution. However, the government may exert its influence on certain disputes involving SOEs or government invested projects.

(i) Litigation

Litigation is considered as the final way to resolve a commercial dispute in China due to the following reasons:

(A) The litigation procedure is time consuming. For example, in a civil case, the first instance procedure will at most last six (6) months from the initiation date and the duration can be extended for another six months or even longer. If any party concerned was dissatisfied with the ruling of the first instance and filed an appeal, the appealing case will take another three (3) months to close, and similar to the duration of the first instance, the duration of appeal can also be extended.

(B) A lack of qualified judges and other professional personnel.

(C) The courts' independence cannot be ensured because most of them rely on the financial support from local governments.

For additional analytical, business and investment opportunities information,
please contact Global Investment & Business Center, USA
at (703) 370-8082. Fax: (703) 370-8083. E-mail: ibpusa3@gmail.com
Global Business and Investment Info Databank - www.ibpus.com

The dispute can also be resolved in a foreign court or arbitration commission.

In principle, for any dispute arising from a contract or property rights and interests involving foreign elements, the parties concerned may choose a court in the place out of China having an actual connection with the dispute to have jurisdiction. However, disputes arising from the performance of Sino-foreign equity joint venture contracts, Sino-foreign cooperative joint venture contracts or contracts for Sino-foreign cooperative exploration and development of natural resources should be under the jurisdiction of courts of China.

A foreign judgment cannot be directly enforced in China. All of the following conditions shall be met to enforce a judgment made by a foreign court:

(A) The judgment is legally effective;

(B) The foreign country and China have concluded bilateral treaty, or China has acceded to international treaties, or based on the principle of reciprocity with respect to the enforcement of foreign judgment; and

(C) The judgment is not contrary to the basic principles of the laws of China or the State's sovereignty, security or social public interest.

Unfortunately, China has not acceded to Hague Jurisdiction Convention or any other international treaties with respect to enforcement of foreign judgment. In addition, Chinese courts rarely recognize the principle of reciprocity. Therefore, unless a bilateral treaty has been concluded, a foreign judgment can hardly be enforced in China. China has concluded bilateral treaty with only around 30 countries or regions, excluding most well-developed countries such as the US and Canada.

(ii) Arbitration

Aside from judicial procedure, arbitration is also available under PRC law as an alternative mechanism for resolving commercial disputes. Currently there are a number of arbitration commissions in the main cities throughout China. If parties choose to settle a dispute through arbitration, they should enter an arbitration agreement (including arbitration clauses in a contract and written agreements on arbitration) which indicates clear intention for arbitration. The conclusion of arbitration agreement will preclude the jurisdiction of courts, unless the arbitration agreement is invalid. It's noted that where the parties simply agree with the Arbitration Locality, rather than the specific institution, and there is only one arbitration institution in this locality, the arbitration institution shall be deemed as the stipulated arbitration institution. If there are two or more arbitration institutions, the parties concerned may choose one arbitration institution for arbitration upon agreement; if the parties concerned fail to agree upon the choice of the arbitration institution, the agreement for arbitration shall be ineffective.

Foreign investors involved in Lao investment disputes must seek arbitration before taking legal action. If arbitration does not result in an amicable settlement, litigants may submit their claims to the economic arbitration authority of Laos, or that of the investor's country, or an international organization agreed on by both parties.

Foreign arbitration awards are enforceable in China, same as in Laos, in accordance with the New York Convention on the Recognition and Enforcement of Foreign Arbitral Awards 1958 to which China is a party and the Civil Procedure Law of the PRC, as amended in 2007.

CIVIL LIBERTIES AND HUMAN RIGHTS

The Laos criminal justice system is controlled by the party and the government. There are few legal restraints on government actions, including arrests, which are often arbitrary in nature. Dissent is frequently handled by suppressing basic civil rights. Although the constitution provisions of the mid-1990s cover freedom of worship, expression and press, citizens by December 2010 were not free to exercise these rights fully. There were no legal safeguards and arrests were commonly made on vague charges. A penal code and a constitution which guarantee civil liberties have been proposed. Implementation is another matter, particularly in the area of freedom of political expression. The media is state-controlled.

Nonetheless, there is a system for prosecuting criminal behavior. Common crimes are evaluated at the local village level. More serious cases, especially politically sensitive ones, are referred to higher authorities. Tribunals operate at district and provincial levels with judges appointed by the government.

Both Laotian journalists and Western officials are critical of the limitations on personal freedoms. In 1987, a Laotian journalist living in Thailand noted that there was little popular support for the government, but that most Laotians accepted its authority because they had little choice.[citation needed] In 1988, a Laotian journalist protested that open criticism of the government was forbidden and one of his friends was imprisoned after he complained about the continuing lack of a constitution. The same year, Western diplomats reported that hundreds or thousands of individuals were being held in detention centers in Laos and that citizens were being arrested and held for months without being charged.

In the late 1980s and early 1990s, the government instituted the New Economic Mechanism, a series of sweeping economic reforms geared toward establishing a market-oriented economy. Along with these economic reforms came a slight opening to the West, which provided some opportunity for scrutiny of human rights violations. However, few foreign journalists are allowed to visit Laos, and travel by diplomats and foreign aid workers is restricted. Both domestic and foreign travel by Laotians also is subject to scrutiny and restriction.

The Ministry of Interior is the main instrument of state control and guardianship over the criminal justice system. Ministry of Interior police monitor both Laotians and foreign nationals who live in Laos; there is a system of informants in workplace committees and in residential areas. According to the United States Department of State's Country Reports on Human Rights Practices for 1993, both the party and state monitor various aspects of family and social life through neighborhood and workplace committees. These committees are responsible for maintaining public order and reporting "bad elements" to the police, as well as carrying out political training and disciplining employees.

The criminal justice system is deficient in the area of legal precedent and representation. Trials are not held in public, although trial verdicts are publicly announced. Although there is some provision for appeal, it does not apply to important political cases. Under the constitution, judges and prosecutors are supposed to be independent with their decisions free from outside scrutiny. In practice, however, the courts appear to accept recommendations of other government agencies, especially the Ministry of Interior, in making their decisions. Theoretically, the government provides legal counsel to the accused. In practice, however, defendants represent themselves without outside counsel.

The National Assembly enacted a criminal code and laws establishing a judiciary in November 1989 and a new constitution was adopted by the National Assembly in 1991.

In 1992 the government launched a campaign to publicize the latter. The leadership claims efforts at developing a legal system with a codified body of laws and a penal code. However, as of mid-1994, there had been little, if any, progress in implementing the freedoms provided for in the constitution and the legal codes still had not been implemented with individuals still being held without being informed of charges or their accusers' identities.

DETENTION CENTERS

In Laos, there are four categories of persons held in confinement by the State. Aside from common criminals, there are also political, social, and ideological dissidents. These are people who the government feels are a threat to their control, most commonly because of their public objection to governmental policies or actions. Commonly the specific crimes for which these dissidents are arrested and confined are vague at best. Their arrests are typically arbitrary and their length of confinement ambiguous and indefinite.

The LPDR established four different types of detention centers: prisons, reeducation centers or seminar camps, rehabilitation camps, and remolding centers. Social deviants or common criminals were considered less threatening to the regime than persons accused of political crimes, who were considered potential counterrevolutionaries; social deviants were confined in rehabilitation camps. According to MacAlister Brown and Joseph J. Zasloff, prisons were primarily reserved for common criminals, but political prisoners were also held there for usually six to twelve months. Ideologically suspect persons were sent to remolding centers. Reeducation centers were for those deemed politically risky usually former RLG officials. Political prisoners usually served three- to five-year terms or longer. At the prisons, inmates worked hard under rugged conditions and had limited supplies of food. Bribery in order to secure food and medicine was reported.

In 1986, Brown and Zasloff also reported that prisoners were not tried but were incarcerated by administrative fiat. Former inmates said that they were arrested, informed by the security officials that they had been charged with crimes, and then sent off to camps for indeterminate periods. Typically, prisoners were told one day prior to their release to prepare for departure.

The status of the detention centers is also vague. In 1984, Vientiane declared that all reeducation centers had been closed. At that time, Amnesty International estimated that 6,000 to 7,000 political prisoners were held in these centers. The government acknowledged that there were some former inmates in remote areas but claimed that their confinement was voluntary. In the late 1980s, the government closed some of the reeducation centers and released most of the detainees.

In 1989, Laos took steps to reduce the number of political prisoners, many of whom had been held since 1975. Several hundred detainees, including many high-ranking officials and officers from the former United States-backed RLG and Royal Lao Army, were released from reeducation centers in the northeastern province of Houaphan. Released prisoners reported that hundreds of individuals remained in custody in as many as eight camps, including at least six generals and former high-ranking members of the RLG. These individuals reportedly performed manual labor such as log cutting, repairing roads, and building irrigation systems. In 1993, Amnesty International reported human rights violations in the continued detention of three "prisoners of conscience" detained since 1975 but not sentenced until 1992, as well as those held under restrictions or, according to international standards, the subjects of unfair trials.

As of 1993, reports indicated that some high-ranking officials of the RLG and military remained in state custody Those accused of hostility toward the government were subject to arrest and confinement for long periods of time. Prison conditions were harsh, and prisoners were routinely denied family visitation and proper medical care

DEMOCRACY AND HUIMAN RIGHTS

The Lao People's Democratic Republic is an authoritarian, Communist, one-party state ruled by the Lao People's Revolutionary Party (LPRP). Although the 1991 Constitution outlines a system composed of executive, legislative, and judicial branches, in practice the LPRP continued to influence governance and the choice of leaders through its constitutional "leading role" at all levels. The 99-member National Assembly, elected in 1997 under a system of universal suffrage, selected the President and Prime Minister in 1998. The judiciary is subject to executive influence.

The Ministry of Interior (MOI) maintains internal security but shares the function of state control with party and mass front (People Network) organizations. The Ministry of Foreign Affairs is responsible for the monitoring and oversight of foreigners working in the country; its activities are augmented by other security organizations and surveillance systems. The MOI includes local police, security police (including border police), communication police, and other armed police units. The armed forces are responsible for external security but also have some domestic security responsibilities that include counterterrorism and counterinsurgency activities. Civilian authorities generally maintain effective control over the security forces. There continue to be credible reports that some members of the security forces committed human rights abuses. Laos is an extremely poor country of 5.2 million persons.

After the LPRP came to power in 1975, 10 percent of the population (at least 360,000 persons) fled the country to escape the Government's harsh political and economic policies. The economy is principally agricultural; 85 percent of the population is engaged in subsistence agriculture. Per capita gross domestic product is estimated to be $300 per year. Since 1986 the Government largely has abandoned its Socialist economic policies, although in practice the operation of the state-owned banks and enterprises indicates a reluctance to discard old models. Most economic reforms have begun to move the country gradually from a moribund, centrally planned system to a market-oriented economy open to foreign investment with a growing legal framework, including laws to protect property rights.

The Government's human rights record remained poor throughout the year, and there were a number of serious problems. Citizens do not have the right to change their government. During clashes with insurgents in the north, there were unconfirmed accusations that government troops deliberately killed noncombatant civilians. At times members of the security forces abused detainees and brutally beat suspected insurgents. Government troops razed one village in the north. Prison conditions are extremely harsh. Police used arbitrary arrest, detention, and intrusive surveillance. Lengthy pretrial detention is a problem. The judiciary is subject to executive influence, suffers from corruption, and does not ensure citizens' due process. The Government infringed on citizens' privacy rights. The Government restricts freedom of speech and imposes some restrictions on press freedom, assembly, and association. However, it permitted some access to the foreign press and the Internet. The Government restricts freedom of religion and arrested and detained approximately 95 Christians, and more than 25 members of religious communities remained in custody at the end of the year. Forced renunciation campaigns and church closings continued in some areas. The Government imposes some restrictions on freedom of movement. Some societal discrimination against women and minorities persists. The Government actively supported a policy of encouraging greater rights for women, children, disabled persons, and minorities. The Government restricts some worker rights. The Government continued to focus on the problem of trafficking in women and children.

Several small-scale explosive devices were detonated in urban areas during the year, causing one death and dozens of injuries. No group claimed responsibility for these acts. Official statements initially downplayed the incidents, attributing them to personal quarrels and vendettas; some government officials later blamed "foreign terrorists."

Organized Hmong insurgent groups were responsible for occasional clashes with government troops. These exchanges reportedly were brutal on both sides. The organized Hmong insurgent group, the Chao Fa, was responsible for the killing of more than 15 civilians in 4 incidents in Vientiane and Xieng Khouang provinces and in Saysomboune Special Zone. These incidents appeared to be acts of deliberate terror against citizens who do not support resistance to the Government.

SECTION 1 RESPECT FOR THE INTEGRITY OF THE PERSON, INCLUDING FREEDOM FROM:

a. Political and Other Extrajudicial Killing

There were no confirmed reports of politically motivated killings by government officials during the year. There continued to be isolated, unconfirmed reports of deaths at the hands of security forces in remote areas, usually in connection with personal disputes and the personal abuse of authority.

In armed actions against insurgents, government troops burned down one village in the north in the first part of the year; accusations that government troops deliberately killed civilian noncombatants could not be confirmed (see Section 1.c.).

In October security forces killed from three to five prisoners who had escaped from Phongsaly provincial jail; there was no evidence that the prisoners were armed or had threatened their pursuers. Some reports stated that the prisoners had already been recaptured.

According to unconfirmed reports, in early May police from Phonesavanh, Xieng Khouang province, shot and killed two Hmong civilians visiting from another province who were out walking after the nighttime curfew. There is no additional evidence available about the case, including whether the Government gave compensation to the victims' families, the usual practice with accidental shootings in security zones.

A series of bomb detonations in urban areas killed at least one bystander and injured dozens. No group claimed responsibility for these small-scale bombings. Official statements initially downplayed the incidents, attributing them to personal quarrels and vendettas; some government officials later blamed "foreign terrorists," failing to acknowledge that the incidents may have been acts of terror by internal rivals for power and influence. Authorities arrested two suspects whom they later released.

Attacks by armed groups on official and civilian travelers continued on a small scale in the central and north central regions. The attacks reportedly involved various factors including insurgency, clan rivalry, robbery, and reaction to encroaching development. The Government remained concerned about the safety of foreign tourists and aid workers in remote areas, although there were no confirmed attacks on foreigners during the year.

In January Hmong insurgents attacked Xieng Khouang province's district capital town of Muang Khoune, killing 7 persons and burning down 17 structures. Credible reports indicated that Hmong insurgents attacked a village in Kasi district in July and killed five civilians. Other reports indicated that the Hmong insurgents shot and killed persons gathering food during February to April in the forest areas of Saysomboune Special Zone. There was no evidence that the deaths were intentional.

In December Hmong insurgents attacked a village in Xieng Khouang province. They killed three civilians and destroyed houses.

b. Disappearance

There were no reports of politically motivated disappearances of Lao citizens; however, reports indicated that two U.S. citizens disappeared in April 1999 near the northwest border with Thailand. The two men, Michael Vang and Houa Ly, disappeared soon after reportedly entering the country. The matter remained under review by authorities at year's end, but there was no evidence that the Government either provided the promised investigative cooperation or conducted a serious unilateral investigation during the year.

c. Torture and Other Cruel, Inhuman, or Degrading Treatment or Punishment

The Constitution and the Penal Code prohibit torture, and the Government generally respected these provisions in practice; however, on occasion, members of the security forces subjected detainees to abusive treatment. For example, early in the year, a few local police and prison officials in one southern province beat a number of religious detainees. In March 1998, Lao authorities, some wearing police uniforms, detained a foreign citizen and three family members in an unofficial detention center for 4 days. The Government did not file charges against the four persons. The officials reportedly kept the four persons in locked, windowless rooms and subjected them to long and arduous interrogation before releasing them. The Government offered no explanation for this treatment. There is no evidence that the Government has investigated the incident seriously, and no prosecution or punishment of the perpetrators is expected.

The Government chose not to address numerous reports of massive human rights violations by government authorities that were made by groups outside the country. Most of these reports could not be confirmed through independent sources. However, there continue to be credible reports that some members of the security forces committed human rights abuses, including arbitrary detention and intimidation. There were credible reports that some members of the security forces burned down a Hmong village in the northern insurgency area and were responsible for nearly beating some villagers to death, and that other members abused citizens in the first half of the year during clashes with insurgents or armed individuals suspected to be insurgents. Some members of the security forces in Xieng Khouang and Saysomboune Special Zone threatened families and villages.

A series of eight bombs exploded in Vientiane during the year, killing at least one and injuring dozens of persons. Authorities found as many as four other unexploded bombs in Vientiane and two others in southern provinces. Another bomb exploded in the south, with no injuries. The Vientiane Times reported official claims that the bombs were the result of business disputes and personal vendettas.

Prison conditions generally are extremely harsh. Food rations are minimal, and most prisoners rely on their families for their subsistence. The Government discriminates in its treatment of prisoners, restricting the family visits of some and prohibiting visits to a few. Prison authorities use degrading treatment, solitary confinement, and incommunicado detention against perceived problem prisoners, especially suspected insurgents. On occasion authorities used incommunicado detention as an interrogation method; in isolated cases, this was life threatening. There are confirmed reports that a

For additional analytical, business and investment opportunities information,
please contact Global Investment & Business Center, USA
at (703) 370-8082. Fax: (703) 370-8083. E-mail: ibpusa3@gmail.com
Global Business and Investment Info Databank - www.ibpus.com

few jails place prisoners in leg chains, wooden stocks, or fixed hand manacles for extended periods. Medical facilities range from poor to nonexistent. Prison conditions for women are similar to those for men.

Several international human rights groups continued their longstanding requests to the Government to move two political prisoners to a prison with better conditions, including more modern medical facilities (see Section 1.e.). At year's end, the Government continued to ignore these humanitarian pleas.The Government does not permit independent monitoring of prison conditions.

 d. Arbitrary Arrest, Detention, or Exile

The law provides for arrest warrants issued by the prosecutor, and the Constitution provides for procedural safeguards; however, in practice the Government does not respect these provisions, and arbitrary arrest and detention remain problems. Police sometimes use temporary arrest as a means of intimidation. Police exercise wide latitude in making arrests, relying on exceptions to the requirement for arrest warrants for those in the act of committing a crime or for "urgent" cases. The length of detention without a pretrial hearing or formal charges is unpredictable, and access to family or a lawyer is not assured. There is a functioning bail system, but its implementation is arbitrary. A statute of limitations applies to most crimes. Alleged violations of security laws have led to lengthy pretrial detentions without charge and minimal due process protection of those detained. Reports indicated that some students, teachers, and their associates who had staged protests in 1999 remained in detention without trial at year's end. These persons had peacefully advocated multiparty democracy and increased political freedom and had expressed hostility to the regime. Their detention without trial violates the 1-year statutory limit.

During the year, government authorities arrested and detained more than 95 Christians and their spiritual leaders, at times holding them in custody for months (see Section 2.c.) Those detained without trial at year's end for their religious activities include: One person in Phongsaly; two persons in Luang Namtha; two persons in Vientiane Municipality; and four persons in Savannakhet (see Section 2.c.). Eight lowland Lao men who returned from China have been detained without trial since 1997 (see Section 2.c.).

Police sometimes administratively overrule court decisions, at times detaining a defendant exonerated by the court, in violation of the law (see Section 1.e.).

Three former government officials detained in 1990 for advocating a multiparty system and criticizing restrictions on political liberties were not tried until 1992. One died in prison since that time. That same year, the court finally tried and handed down life sentences to three men detained since 1975 for crimes allegedly committed during their tenure as officials of the previous regime. One of these persons reportedly has died in prison.

An estimated 100 to 200 persons, based on known cases, are in detention for suspicion of violations of national security. Most of these detainees are held without trial; one person has been detained since 1992. The Government does not use forced exile.

e. Denial of Fair Public Trial

The Constitution provides for the independence of the judiciary and the prosecutor's office; however, senior government and party officials wield influence over the courts, although likely to a lesser degree than in the past. Some corrupt members of the judiciary appear to act with impunity, leading many observers to conclude that persons can bribe judges with money. The National Assembly Standing Committee appoints judges; the executive appoints the Standing Committee.

The People's Courts have three levels: District; municipal and provincial; and a Supreme Court. Decisions of both the lower courts and separate military courts are subject to review by the Supreme Court.

The Constitution provides for open trials in which defendants have the right to defend themselves with the assistance of a lawyer or other person. The Constitution requires authorities to inform persons of their rights. The law states that defendants may have anyone represent them in preparing a written case and accompanying them at their trial, however, only the defendant may present oral arguments at a criminal trial. Due to lack of funds, most defendants do not have attorneys or trained representatives. Defendants enjoy a presumption of innocence; however, in practice lawyers face severe restrictions in criminal cases. Most trials are little more than direct examinations of the accused, although judges appear not to hold preconceived views of a trial's outcome. Defendants sometimes are not permitted to testify on their own behalf. Trials for alleged violations of some security laws and trials that involve state secrets, children under the age of 16, or certain types of family law are closed.

Police sometimes administratively overrule court decisions, at times detaining a defendant exonerated by the court, in violation of the law.

There are four known political prisoners. Two prisoners from the pre-1975 regime, Colonel Sing Chanthakoumane and Major Pang Thong Chokbengvoun, are serving life sentences after trials that did not appear to be conducted according to international standards. Two former government officials, Latsami Khamphoui and Feng Sakchittaphong, were detained in 1990 for advocating a multiparty system and criticizing restrictions on political liberties, and were not tried until 1992. They are serving 14-year sentences based on their 1992 convictions.

Because some political prisoners may have been arrested, tried, and convicted under security laws that prevent public court trials, there is no reliable method to ascertain accurately their total number. There have been no verifiable reports of other political prisoners in the last few years. International humanitarian organizations are not permitted to visit political prisoners.

f. Arbitrary Interference With Privacy, Family, Home, or Correspondence

**For additional analytical, business and investment opportunities information,
please contact Global Investment & Business Center, USA
at (703) 370-8082. Fax: (703) 370-8083. E-mail: ibpusa3@gmail.com
Global Business and Investment Info Databank - www.ibpus.com**

The Government limits citizens' privacy rights, and the Government's surveillance network is vast. Security laws allow the Government to monitor individuals' private communications (including e-mail) and movements. The Government increased these elements of state control again during the year, especially in areas involving safety and security problems. However, some personal freedoms accorded to citizens expanded along with the liberalization of the economy.

The Constitution prohibits unlawful searches and seizures; however, police at times disregarded constitutional requirements to safeguard citizens' privacy, especially in rural areas. By law security police may not authorize their own searches; they must have approval from a prosecutor or court. However, in practice police did not always obtain prior approval. The Penal Code generally protects privacy, including mail, telephone, and electronic correspondence. But as is the case with e-mail monitoring, government security concerns prevail over such legal protections. In October the National Internet Control Committee promulgated highly restrictive regulations on Internet use (see Section 2.a.).

Ministry of Interior forces monitor citizens' activities; in addition a loose militia in both urban and rural areas has responsibility for maintaining public order and reporting "bad elements" to the police. Militia usually concern themselves more with petty crime and instances of moral turpitude than with political activism, although some rural militia may be used for security against insurgents. A sporadically active system of neighborhood and workplace committees plays a similar monitoring role.

The Government permits the public sale of few leading foreign magazines and newspapers; however, minimal restrictions on publications mailed from overseas are enforced only loosely (see Section 2.a.). The Government allows citizens to marry foreigners but only with its prior approval. Although the Government routinely grants permission, the process is lengthy and burdensome. Marriages to foreigners without government approval may be annulled, with both parties subject to fines.

The Government displaced internally hundreds of persons during the year, mainly as a result of organized infrastructure development programs. The Government provides compensation to displaced persons in the form of land and household supplies.

Credible sources reported flexibility by the Government toward the disposition of infrastructure-related and other government-planned resettlements. One hydropower project resettlement village opened during the year, funded by investors. However, some local administrators forced highlander groups to resettle in lowland areas to control their use of farming methods that destroy forest areas in the pursuit of increased food security.

There are two Internet service providers. In the second half of the year, the National Internet Control Committee in the Prime Minister's Office began a review of national telecommunications and Internet access procedures; it stated that it intends to monitor and control Internet communications more actively. Some Internet users reported that they received e-mail warnings from the Government during the year.

SECTION 2 RESPECT FOR CIVIL LIBERTIES

a. Freedom of Speech and Press

The Constitution provides for freedom of speech and of the press; however, the Government severely restricts political speech and writing in practice. The Government also prohibits most criticism that it deems harmful to its reputation. The Penal Code forbids slandering the State, distorting party or state policies, inciting disorder, or propagating information or opinions that weaken the State. The Government showed limited tolerance of general criticisms of good governance or public service, and citizens who lodge legitimate complaints with government departments generally do not suffer reprisals. However, government concern about potential public violent displays of discontent over failed economic policies and concern over the series of terrorist bombings led to tighter control of the media. Newspapers did not report on investigations into the causes of any of the eight bombs that exploded in Vientiane from March through December. In July the Vientiane Times reported that officials had stated that the bombings were the result of business disputes or personal vendettas (see Section 1.c.).

All domestic print and electronic media are state-owned and controlled. Local news in all media reflects government policy. Television talk shows and opinion articles refer only to differences in administrative approach. However, translations of foreign press reports generally are without bias, and access to Thai radio and television and foreign-based Internet servers is unhindered. Only a few other Asian and Western newspapers and magazines are available, through private outlets that have government permission to sell them.

Authorities also prohibited the dissemination of materials deemed to be indecent, to undermine the national culture, or to be politically sensitive. Films and music recordings produced in government studios must be submitted for official censorship. However, in practice most foreign media are easily available. Government enforcement of restrictions on nightclub entertainment generally was lax during the year.

Citizens have 24-hour access to Cable News Network and the British Broadcasting Corporation, among other international stations accessible via satellite television. The Government requires registration of receiving satellite dishes and a one-time licensing fee for their use, largely as a revenue-generating scheme, but otherwise makes no effort to restrict their use.

Foreign journalists must apply for special visas. Unfettered access to information sources and domestic travel unescorted by officials--hallmarks of a more liberal government attitude in previous years--declined during the year.

The Government controls all domestic Internet servers, blocks access to those World Wide Web sites that are deemed pornographic or are critical of government institutions and policies, and monitors e-mail. In October the National Internet Control Committee promulgated highly restrictive regulations on Internet use by citizens. The regulations significantly curtailed freedom of expression and made "disturbing the peace and happiness of the community" and "reporting misleading news" criminal acts. However, the Government in the past has been limited in its ability to enforce such regulations.

The Constitution provides for academic freedom; however, the Government restricts it, although it has relaxed its restrictions in certain areas. Lao and Western academic professionals conducting research in Laos may be subject to restrictions on travel and access to information and Penal Code restrictions on publication. As the sole employer of virtually all academic professionals, the Government exercises some control over their ability to travel on research or study grants. However, the Government, which once limited foreign travel by professors, actively seeks out these opportunities worldwide and approves virtually all such proposals.

Credible reports indicate that some academically qualified ethnic minorities, including Hmong, are denied opportunities for foreign fellowships and study abroad based on the actions of some state and party officials whose discriminatory behavior goes unchecked. On rare occasions, the Government has denied government employees who were not party members permission to accept certain research or study grants, apparently because they had chosen not to join the LPRP.

b. Freedom of Peaceful Assembly and Association

The Constitution provides for freedom of assembly; however, the Government continues to restrict this right in practice. The Penal Code prohibits participation in an organization for the purpose of demonstrations, protest marches, or other acts that cause turmoil or social instability. Such acts are punishable by a prison term of from 1 to 5 years. If defendants are tried for political crimes against the State, they may face much longer sentences of up to 20 years or possible execution.

The Constitution provides citizens with the right to organize and join associations; however, the Government restricts this right in practice. The Government registers and controls all associations and prohibits associations that criticize it. Political groups other than mass front organizations approved by the LPRP are forbidden. Although the Government restricts many types of formal professional and social associations, in practice informal nonpolitical groups can meet without hindrance. Individuals who in 1997 formed the Foundation for Promoting Education, a private voluntary organization in Vientiane Municipality, were active during the year and awarded prizes for educational achievement and scholarships to needy students. The group is supported by private contributions and operates independently under its own charter; however, it reports to the Ministry of Education. The Buddhist Promotion Foundation is a semiprivate group founded in 1998 by the Lao Buddhist Fellowship Association, which reports to the National Front.

c. Freedom of Religion

The Constitution provides for freedom of religion; however, the Government restricts this right in practice. The Constitution prohibits "all acts of creating division of religion or creating division among the people." The Party and Government appear to interpret this section narrowly, thus inhibiting religious practice by all persons, including the Buddhist majority and a large population of animists. Although official pronouncements accepted the existence of religion, they emphasized its potential to divide, distract, or destabilize.

The Constitution notes that the State "mobilizes and encourages" monks, novices, and priests of other religions to participate in activities "beneficial to the nation and the people." The Department of Religious Affairs in the LPRP Lao National Front for Construction, an LPRP mass organization, is responsible for overseeing all religions.

During the year, government authorities arrested and detained more than 95 Christians and their spiritual leaders, at times holding them in custody for months. In some isolated cases, prisoners were detained in prison with crude, one-leg, wood stocks or fixed hand manacles.

In the following provinces, prisoners are serving 2 to 3-year prison terms for peaceful religious activities found under the Penal Code to be creating social turmoil: In Attapeu (6 jailed); in Houaphan (3 jailed); in Luang Prabang (3 jailed); in Oudomxay (2 jailed). In Oudomxay 3 other persons arrested for proselytizing, purportedly in coordination with foreigners, were sentenced to 15-year (1 jailed) and 12-year sentences (2 jailed). The more severe sentences in Oudomxay were based on harsh Penal Code provisions for acts against the State.

In Savannakhet province, a renunciation and church-closing campaign that was begun in 1999 by district authorities, supported by police, military forces, and representatives of the national front continued into the second half of the year. For the first time, churches of longer standing were targeted. Only about 10 churches--less than half--remained open at year's end. Most practitioners who found that their local churches had been closed were able to move their activities to new places of worship. As in late 1999, in a few villages in which churches had been recently closed, security forces mobilized on Sundays to stop all large vehicles that carried multiple passengers during Sunday worship hours. These actions expressly prevented villagers from traveling to other places to conduct worship services. In July in Vientiane province, the Government began a similar renunciation and church-closing campaign that continued through year's end. District-level police, military, and national front authorities instructed Christians, especially Christians from the Khmu and Hmong ethnic groups, to renounce their faith or face arrest and imprisonment. Vientiane provincial authorities arbitrarily closed at least 1 dozen churches, including a church in a refugee returnee village agreed to at the time the village was established under U.N. High Commissioner for Refugees (UNHCR) auspices. In Vientiane province, authorities targeted both Protestant and Catholic congregations.

The Party controls the Buddhist clergy (Sangha) in an attempt to direct national culture. After 1975 the Government attempted to "reform" Buddhism and ceased to consider it the state religion, causing thousands of monks to flee abroad, where most still remain. The Government has only one semireligious holiday--Boun That Luang--also a major political and cultural celebration. However, the Government recognizes the popularity and cultural significance of Buddhist festivals, and many senior officials openly attend them. Buddhist clergy are featured prominently at important state and party functions. The Lao National Front directs the Lao Buddhist Fellowship Association, which adopted a new charter in April 1998. The Front continues to require monks to study Marxism-Leninism, to attend certain party meetings, and to combine with their teachings of Buddhism the party-state policies. In recent years, some individual temples have been permitted to receive support from Theravada Buddhist temples abroad, to expand the training of monks, and to focus more on traditional teachings.

The authorities continued to be suspicious of parts of the religious community other than Buddhism, including some Christian groups, in part because these faiths do not share a similarly high degree of direction and incorporation into the government structure as is the case with Theravada Buddhism. Authorities especially appear to suspect those religious groups that gain support from foreign sources, aggressively proselytize among the poor or uneducated, or give targeted assistance to converts. The Government strictly prohibits foreigners from proselytizing, although it permits foreign nongovernmental organizations with religious affiliations to work in the country. Foreign persons caught distributing religious material may be arrested or deported. Although there is no prohibition against proselytizing by citizens, there was increased local government investigation and harassment of citizens who do so under the constitutional provision against creating division of religion.

The Government's tolerance of religion varied by region. In general central government authorities appeared unable or unwilling to control or mitigate harsh measures that were taken by local or provincial authorities against the practices of members of minority religious denominations. Although there was almost complete freedom to worship among unregistered groups in a few areas, particularly in the largest cities, government authorities in many regions allowed properly registered religious groups to practice their faith only under circumscribed conditions. In other areas, such as Savannakhet, Luang Prabang, Phongsaly, Houaphanh, Oudomxay, and Attapeu, the authorities arrested and detained religious believers and their spiritual leaders without charges. In more isolated cases, provincial authorities instructed their officials to monitor and arrest persons who professed belief in Christianity, Islam, or the Baha'i faith. For example, there is clear evidence that in Luang Prabang, Savannakhet, and Vientiane provinces, the authorities continued to force some Christians to sign renunciations of their faith.

Citizens in Luang Prabang continued to report that local authorities ordered them to stop their open practice of Christianity completely, under threat of arrest. The order appeared to apply only to new converts; believers of long standing were allowed to continue their beliefs but not to conduct worship or practice their faith openly. Local officials monitored Christians closely to ensure that they did not practice their religion and harassed and arrested some Christians who violated these policies.

Although authorities generally tolerated diverse religious practices, in the southern Laos panhandle, a pattern of petty local harassment persists. Many converts must undergo a series of harsh government interviews; however, after overcoming that initial barrier, they generally are permitted to practice their new faith unhindered. Members of long-established congregations had few problems in practicing their faith; however, some churches established a century ago continued to be subjected to harassment by local government officials in Savannakhet. Many groups of coreligionists seeking to assemble in a new location are thwarted in attempts to meet, practice, or celebrate major religious festivals.

Some minority religious groups report that they were unable during the year to register new congregations or receive permission to establish new places of worship, including in Vientiane. Authorities sometimes advised new branches to join other religious groups with similar historical roots, despite clear differences between the groups' beliefs. Some groups did not submit applications to establish places of worship because they did not believe that their applications would be approved.

The Roman Catholic Church is unable to operate effectively in the highlands and much of the north. However, it has an established presence in five of the most populous central and southern provinces, where Catholics are able to worship openly. There are three bishops: In Vientiane, Thakhek, and Pakse. The status of the Catholic Church in Luang Prabang center remains in doubt; there appears to be a congregation there but due to local obstructionism, worship services may not always be conducted readily.

Over 250 Protestant congregations conduct services throughout the country. The Lao National Front has recognized two Protestant groups, the Lao Evangelical Church, the umbrella Protestant church, and the Seventh Day Adventist Church. The Front strongly encourages all other Protestant groups to become a part of the Lao Evangelical Church. The Government has granted permission to these approved denominations to have a total of four church buildings in the Vientiane area. In addition the Lao Evangelical Church has maintained church buildings in Savannakhet and Pakse.

The Government permits major religious festivals of all established congregations without hindrance. Two mosques and two Baha'i centers operate openly in Vientiane municipality; two other Baha'i centers are located in Vientiane province and Pakse. Five Mahayana Buddhist pagodas are located in Vientiane, and others are found in larger cities and towns.

Animists generally experience no interference by the Government in their religious practices, which vary extensively among the 48 to 69 identified ethnic groups and tribes in the country.

The Government does not permit the printing of religious texts or their distribution outside a congregation and restricts the import of foreign religious texts and artifacts. The Government requires and grants routinely its permission for formal links with coreligionists in other countries; however, in practice the line between formal and informal links is blurred, and relations generally are established without much difficulty.

d. Freedom of Movement Within the Country, Foreign Travel, Migration, and Repatriation

The Constitution provides for these rights; however, the Government restricted some of these rights in practice. Citizens who travel across provincial borders are required to report to authorities upon their departure and arrival. In designated security zones, roadblocks and identity card checks are routine. Citizens who seek to travel abroad are required to apply for an exit visa; however, the Government grants such visas routinely.

**For additional analytical, business and investment opportunities information,
please contact Global Investment & Business Center, USA
at (703) 370-8082. Fax: (703) 370-8083. E-mail: ibpusa3@gmail.com
Global Business and Investment Info Databank - www.ibpus.com**

Foreigners are restricted from traveling to certain areas such as the Saysomboune Special Zone, an administrative area operated by the military forces, for safety and security reasons.

During the year, security forces in at least one province set up roadblocks during Sunday worship hours, which prevented villagers from traveling to participate in religious worship services (see Section 2.c.).

Fear of insurgent attacks on civilians in vehicles traveling in the north-central areas impedes travel, especially along parts of Route 13, Route 7, and Route 1. Bandits operate in the same area (see Section 1.a.). The Government attempts to ensure safety on these roads.

Citizens are free to emigrate; exit visas are required, and the Government grants these routinely.

Since 1980 more than 29,060 citizens who sought refugee status in Thailand, China, and other countries have returned to Laos for permanent resettlement under monitoring by the UNHCR. There were no new returnees during the year. The Government cooperates with the UNHCR to assist such returnees to reintegrate. Most are ethnic Hmong and other minorities. These returnees generally have been treated the same as other citizens.

The Constitution provides for asylum and the protection of stateless persons under the law, but in practice, the Government does not provide first asylum. There were no known cases during the year of asylum seekers being returned to a country where they feared persecution.

The Government has a longstanding policy of welcoming back virtually all those among the 10 percent of the population who fled after the change in government in 1975. Many have visited relatives, some have stayed and gained foreign resident status, and some have reclaimed citizenship successfully. A small group, tried in absentia in 1975 for antigovernment activities, does not have the right of return.

Eight Lowland Lao men who returned from China have been detained without trial since 1997, which is beyond the limit for investigative detention (see Section 1.d.).

Some refugee returnees carry identification cards with distinctive markings, ostensibly for use by authorities. Such cards tend to reinforce a pattern of societal discrimination against the refugees. Authorities increasingly harassed religious minorities in refugee returnee villages, and local officials closed a Christian church in one such village. The Government had permitted use of the church building at the time that the refugees returned (see Section 2.c.).

SECTION 3 RESPECT FOR POLITICAL RIGHTS: THE RIGHT OF CITIZENS TO CHANGE THEIR GOVERNMENT

Citizens do not have the right to change their government. The Constitution legitimizes only a single party, the Lao People's Revolutionary Party, which must approve all candidates for local and national elections. Candidates need not be LPRP members.

The Constitution provides for a 99-member National Assembly, elected every 5 years in open, multiple-candidate, fairly tabulated elections, with voting by secret ballot and universal adult suffrage. The National Assembly chooses a standing committee apparently based on the previous standing committee's decision. Upon the committee's recommendation, the National Assembly elects or removes the President and Vice President. The standing committee also has powers over elections (including approval of candidates), supervision of administrative and judicial organizations, and the sole power to recommend presidential decrees. Activities of the standing committee are not fully transparent.

The National Assembly, upon the President's recommendation, elects the Prime Minister and other Ministers in the Government.

The National Assembly may consider and amend draft legislation but may not propose new laws. The Constitution gives the right to submit draft legislation to the National Assembly standing committee and the ruling executive structure.

Women are underrepresented in government and politics; however, women increased their representation in the National Assembly in 1997 elections from 9 percent to 20 percent, as 20 of the 27 female candidates won seats. Four members of the 48-member LPRP Central Committee are women, 2 of whom are also members of the 7-member standing committee in the National Assembly. There are no women in the Politburo or the Council of Ministers.

The proportions of ethnic minority members in the 99-member National Assembly-10 Lao Soung (highland tribes) and 26 Lao Theung (mid-slope dwelling tribes)--are consistent with their proportions in the general population. There are 10 Hmong in the National Assembly. Men of lowland Lao origin dominate the upper echelons of the Party and the Government. Nonetheless, the President, 2 Deputy Prime Ministers, 3 Ministers, and 36 members of the National Assembly are believed to be members of ethnic minority groups.

SECTION 4 GOVERNMENTAL ATTITUDE REGARDING INTERNATIONAL AND NONGOVERNMENTAL INVESTIGATION OF ALLEGED VIOLATIONS OF HUMAN RIGHTS

There are no domestic nongovernmental human rights organizations, and the Government does not have a formal procedure for registration. Any organization wishing to investigate and publicly criticize the Government's human rights policies would face serious obstacles if it were permitted to operate at all. The Government cooperates on an uneven basis with international human rights organizations.

A human rights unit in the Ministry of Foreign Affairs' (MFA's) Department of International Treaties and Legal Affairs has responsibility for inquiry into allegations of human rights violations. This government unit rarely responds to inquiries regarding individual cases, but early in the year published in Lao language a partial compilation of international conventions on human rights.

In 1998, at the invitation of the Government, the U.N. Special Rapporteur on Trafficking in Children visited various locations and made inquiries into possible incidents of child prostitution and child pornography.

The Government maintains contacts with the International Committee of the Red Cross (ICRC); government officials received ICRC training on human rights law in 1998, and the Government is translating more international conventions with ICRC support. The Government permitted U.N. human rights observers to monitor the treatment of almost 30,000 returned refugees in all parts of the country with minimal interference; however, it occasionally obstructs monitoring so that it cannot be conducted in accordance with international standards.

SECTION 5 DISCRIMINATION BASED ON RACE, SEX, RELIGION, DISABILITY, LANGUAGE, OR SOCIAL STATUS

The Constitution provides for equal treatment under the law for all citizens without regard to sex, social status, education, faith, or ethnicity. Although the Government sometimes has taken action when well-documented and obvious cases of discrimination came to the attention of high-level officials, the legal mechanism whereby a citizen may bring charges of discrimination against an individual or organization is neither widely developed nor widely understood among the general population.

Women

There are reports that domestic violence against women occurs, although it is not widespread. Sexual harassment and rape reportedly are rare. In cases of rape that are tried in court, defendants generally are convicted.

Trafficking in women is a problem (see Section 6.f.).

The Constitution provides for equal rights for women, and the Lao Women's Union operates nationally to promote the position of women in society. Discrimination against women is not generalized; however, varying degrees of traditional culturally based discrimination persist, with greater discrimination practiced by some hill tribes. Many women occupy responsible positions in the civil service and private business, and in urban areas their incomes are often higher than those of men. The Family Code prohibits legal discrimination in marriage and inheritance.

In the period from 1997 through 2000, the Government increased support for the position of women in society in development programs, some of which are designed to increase the participation of women in the political system.

Children

The level of support for education is exceedingly low. Government funding to provide fully for children's basic health and educational needs is inadequate. Education is compulsory through the fifth grade, but children from rural areas and poor urban families rarely comply with this requirement. There is a significant difference in the treatment of boys and girls in the educational system: Female literacy is 48 percent versus 70 percent for males. However, men and women attend the three universities in approximately equal numbers. Violence against children is prohibited by law, and violators are subject to stiff punishments. Reports of the physical abuse of children are rare. Trafficking in women and children is a problem (see Section 6.f.).

People With Disabilities

With donor assistance, the Government is implementing limited programs for the disabled, especially amputees. The law does not mandate accessibility to buildings or government services for disabled persons, but the Labor and Social Welfare Ministry began to establish regulations on building access and some sidewalk ramps in Vientiane during the year. The Lao National Commission for the Disabled (LNCD) is formulating a new draft law and other policies regarding the disabled, and the Lao Disabled Persons Association set up offices in Champassak and Xieng Khouang provinces to assist with rehabilitation, job skills training, and social integration of the disabled. The LNCD also hosted a regional conference on disabilities in Vientiane in November to promote leadership and organizational skills for disabled persons.

Religious Minorities

The enhanced status given to Buddhism in Luang Prabang--famed for its centuries-old Buddhist tradition and numerous temples--apparently led some local officials there to act more harshly toward minority religions, particularly toward Christians and Baha'is, than in other areas of the country (see Section 2.c.).

National/Racial/Ethnic Minorities

The Constitution provides for equal rights for citizens of all minorities, and there is no legal discrimination against them. However, societal discrimination persists.

Approximately half the population is ethnic Lao, also called "lowland Lao." Most of the remainder is a mixture of diverse upland hill tribes whose members, if born in Laos, are Lao citizens. There are also ethnic Vietnamese and Chinese minorities, particularly in the towns. There is a small community of South Asian origin. The implementation in 1994 of the 1990 Law on Nationality provided a means for Vietnamese and Chinese minorities to normalize their Lao citizenship; a small number did so during the year. The Government encourages the preservation of minority cultures and traditions; however, due to their remote location and difficult access, minority tribes have little voice in government decisions affecting their lands and the allocation of natural resources.

The Hmong are one of the largest and most prominent highland minority groups. Societal discrimination against the Hmong continues, although there are a number of Hmong officials in the senior ranks of the Government. In recent years, the Government

For additional analytical, business and investment opportunities information, please contact Global Investment & Business Center, USA at (703) 370-8082. Fax: (703) 370-8083. E-mail: ibpusa3@gmail.com
Global Business and Investment Info Databank - www.ibpus.com

focused some limited assistance projects in Hmong areas in order to overcome disparities in income along regional and ethnic lines. Some international observers claim that governmental policies aimed at assimilating the Hmong into larger society-- such as regional boarding schools--are not respectful of Hmong native culture; others see this approach as an escape from centuries of poverty.

In the intensified Hmong insurgency in the north, government forces beat Hmong insurgents and treated them harshly in some Hmong villages (see Sections 1.a. and 1.c.). In an unconfirmed report, a foreign newspaper in December recounted an alleged government soldier's account that security forces had shot to death a number of young Hmong men in Saysomboune Special Zone during the year.

During the year, the Government continued to assist citizens, largely members of ethnic minorities, who returned to Laos after having fled in 1975. Central and local government officials worked with organizations such as the UNHCR to provide land and a sustainable level of economic security. Repatriated Hmong generally face no greater discrimination than those Hmong who remained. A number of Hmong returnees were forced to renounce their Christian faith, and one church in a returnee village was closed by authorities. Two U.N. observers who monitored repatriation efforts reported no significant human rights violations.

Under the Constitution, aliens and stateless foreign citizens are protected by "provisions of the laws" but do not in practice enjoy rights provided for by the Constitution. During the year, there were isolated cases of persons of Lao ethnic background who, as citizens of other nations, suffered discrimination when arrested or detained and were denied due process, apparently on the basis of their Lao ethnic background.

SECTION 6 WORKER RIGHTS

a. The Right of Association

Under the 1990 Labor Code and a 1995 prime ministerial decree, labor unions can be formed in private enterprises as long as they operate within the framework of the officially sanctioned Federation of Lao Trade Unions (FLTU), which in turn is controlled by the LPRP. Most of the FLTU's 77,057 members work in the public sector.

The State employs the majority of salaried workers, although this situation is changing as the Government reduces the number of its employees and privatizes state enterprises. Subsistence farmers comprise an estimated 85 percent of the work force.

Strikes are not prohibited by law, but the Government's ban on subversive activities or destabilizing demonstrations (see Section 2.b.) makes a strike unlikely, and none were reported during the year. However, the Labor Code does not prohibit temporary work stoppages.

With advice from the International Labor Organization (ILO), including a foreign expert provided by the ILO to work with the Ministry of Labor and Social Welfare, the Government in 1994 revised the Labor Code in an effort to clarify the rights and obligations of workers and employers. However, the ILO Committee of Experts cited the Government for its failure to submit reports required of member states.

The FLTU is free to engage in contacts with foreign labor organizations, which during the year included the Association of Southeast Asian Nations (ASEAN) Trade Union and the Asia-Pacific American Labor Alliance. The FLTU is a member of the World Federation of Trade Unions.

  b. The Right to Organize and Bargain Collectively

There is no right to organize and bargain collectively. The Labor Code stipulates that disputes be resolved through workplace committees composed of employers, representatives of the local labor union, and representatives of the FLTU, with final authority residing in the Ministry of Labor and Social Welfare. Labor disputes are infrequent. The Government sets wages and salaries for government employees, while management sets wages and salaries for private business employees.

The Labor Code stipulates that employers may not fire employees for conducting trade union activities, for lodging complaints against employers about labor law implementation, or for cooperating with officials on labor law implementation and labor disputes. Workplace committees are one mechanism used for resolving complaints.

There are no export processing zones.

  c. Prohibition of Forced or Compulsory Labor

The Labor Code prohibits forced labor except in time of war or national disaster, during which the State may conscript laborers; however, trafficking in women and children is a problem (see Section 6.f.). The Code also applies to children under the age of 15, and generally is enforced effectively; however, reports that children are being lured into other countries for sexual exploitation and slave labor continued, and increased over the previous year (see Sections 5 and 6.f.).

  d. Status of Child Labor Practices and Minimum Age for Employment

Under the Labor Code, children under the age of 15 may not be recruited for employment. However, many children help their families on farms or in shops. The Labor Code accordingly provides that children may work for their families, provided that such children are not engaged in dangerous or difficult work. Such employment of children is common in urban shops, but rare in industrial enterprises. The Ministries of Interior and Justice are responsible for enforcing these provisions, but enforcement is ineffective due to a lack of inspectors and other resources. Education is compulsory through the fifth grade, but this requirement rarely is observed in the rural areas or among the urban poor. Some garment factories reportedly employ a very small number of underage girls. The Labor Code prohibits forced and bonded labor performed by children under age 15, and the law generally is enforced effectively; however, there were reports that children were lured into sexual exploitation and slavery abroad (see Sections 6.c. and 6.f.).

For additional analytical, business and investment opportunities information, please contact Global Investment & Business Center, USA at (703) 370-8082. Fax: (703) 370-8083. E-mail: ibpusa3@gmail.com Global Business and Investment Info Databank - www.ibpus.com

- 69 -

e. Acceptable Conditions of Work

The Labor Code provides for a broad range of worker entitlements, including a workweek limited to 48 hours (36 hours for employment in dangerous activities), safe working conditions, and higher compensation for dangerous work. The Code also provides for at least 1 day of rest per week. Employers are responsible for all expenses for a worker injured or killed on the job, a requirement generally fulfilled by employers in the formal economic sector. A section of the Labor Code mandates extensive employer responsibility for those disabled while at work. During the year, this law was enforced adequately. The daily minimum wage is $0.53 (4,000 kip), which is insufficient to provide a decent standard of living for a worker and family. Most civil servants receive inadequate pay. However, few families in the wage economy depend on only one member for income. Some piecework employees, especially on construction sites, earn less than the minimum wage. Many persons are illegal immigrants, particularly from Vietnam, and are more vulnerable to exploitation by employers. Although workplace inspections reportedly have increased, the Ministry of Labor and Social Welfare lacks the personnel and budgetary resources to enforce the Labor Code effectively. The Labor Code has no specific provision allowing workers to remove themselves from a dangerous situation without jeopardizing their employment.

f. Trafficking in Persons

The Penal Code prohibits abduction and trade in persons as well as the constraint, procuring, and prostitution of persons; however, trafficking in women and children is a problem. Laos is a source and transit country for trafficking in persons. The Government only recently has focused on the trafficking of persons across its borders. Although there is no reliable data available on the scope and severity of the problem, there are indications that the numbers are considerable. The Government has increased monitoring and educational programs provided by the Lao Women's Union and the Youth Union, both party-sanctioned organizations, designed to educate girls and young women about the schemes of recruiters for brothels and sweatshops in neighboring countries and elsewhere. In the past, the Government has prosecuted some persons for involvement in such recruiting activities. Recent evidence indicates an increase in arrests for procuring; however, this may not reflect a genuine government effort to address the problem. During the year, law enforcement agencies conducted a minimal number of raids on entertainment establishments accused of fostering prostitution.

The Government remains concerned about Lao children being lured into sexual exploitation and slave labor in other countries, but the Government denied that there were any problems in the country that involve child prostitution. The National Commission for Mothers and Children, established in 1992 and chaired by the Foreign Minister, continues an active program with support from the U.N. Children's Fund. The Commission, working with the Lao Women's Union, Youth Union, Justice Ministry, and Labor Ministry, has conducted workshops around the country designed to make parents and teenagers aware of the dangers of HIV. At the Government's invitation, the U.N. Special Rapporteur on Trafficking in Children visited in 1998 (see Section 4).

POLITICAL AND GOVERNMENT SYSTEM

STRUCTURE OF THE GOVERNMENT

EXECUTIVE

The president of the country is elected by a two-thirds vote of the National Assembly for a term of five years. One surprising constitutional provision transforms the presidency from a ceremonial position into an important political power. The president appoints and can dismiss the prime minister and members of the government, with the approval of the National Assembly-- parliamentary responsibility that has not yet occurred in the short life of the current constitutional regime. He also presides over meetings of the government, "when necessary," and appoints and dismisses provincial governors and mayors of municipalities as well as generals of the armed forces, upon the recommendation of the prime minister. In addition, the president receives and appoints ambassadors and declares states of emergency or war.

The powers accorded to the president grew perceptively during the drafting process of the constitution, but the sudden death of Kaysone, who had moved from prime minister to state president after the promulgation of the constitution, temporarily introduced doubts regarding the relative power potential of the two offices. Nonetheless, the president of state heads the armed forces and has the right and duty to promulgate laws and issue decrees and state acts.

The primary organization for administration is the government, which consists of the prime minister--its head--and deputy prime ministers, ministers, and chairs of ministry-equivalent state committees. The prime minister, appointed by the president with the approval of the National Assembly, serves a five-year term. Duties of this office include the guidance and supervision of the work of government ministries and committees, as well as of the governors of provinces and mayors of municipalities. The prime minister appoints all the deputies at these levels of government, as well as the local district chiefs

LEGISLATURE

The National Assembly, the country's supreme legislative body, is to be elected every five years. Significantly, this designation was used in RLG and French colonial times, before the introduction of the title "Supreme People's Assembly" in late 1975. It is located in a new building, far larger than the previous structure built in colonial times, and contains an auditorium seating 800 persons.

The National Assembly makes decisions on fundamental issues and oversees administrative and judicial organs. Its most significant powers include electing and removing the president of state, the president of the Supreme People's Court, and the prosecutor general, "on the recommendation of the National Assembly Standing Committee." Its prestige has been further enhanced by the constitutional mandate to "make decisions on the fundamental issues of the country" and to "elect or remove the

President of state and the Vice President of state", by a two-thirds vote, and to approve the removal of members of the government on the recommendation of the president of state. Its powers encompass amending the constitution, determining taxes, approving the state budget, endorsing or abrogating laws, and electing or removing the two top judicial figures in the system. Members of the National Assembly have the "right to interpellate the members of the government." The National Assembly also ratifies treaties and decides questions of war and peace. These powers may prove to be limited, however, by a provision in the constitution that the National Assembly will generally meet in ordinary session only twice a year. The Standing Committee meeting in the interim may convene an extraordinary session if it deems necessary.

The constitution does not specify the number of members in the National Assembly, whose candidates are screened by the LPRP. The 1989 election placed seventy-nine members in this body, representing districts of between 40,000 and 50,000 persons each. The election campaign lasted two months, and candidates appeared before voters at night in local schools or pagodas. Voting consisted of crossing out unfavored candidates, and every ballot contained at least two candidates. The number of party members elected by this process was officially placed at sixty-five.

Between sessions, the Standing Committee of the National Assembly, consisting of the president and the vice president elected by the National Assembly and an unspecified number of other members, prepares for future sessions and "supervise[s] and oversee[s] the activities of the administrative and judicial organizations." It is empowered to appoint or remove the vice president of the Supreme People's Court and judges at all levels of the lower courts. Its supervisory role can be reinforced by National Assembly committees established to consider draft laws and decrees and to help in the supervision and administration of the courts. The special National Assembly Law passed March 25, 1993, specifies five substantive areas for National Assembly committees: secretarial; law; economic planning and finances; cultural, social, and nationalities; and foreign affairs. The membership of the committees includes not only National Assembly members but also chiefs and deputy chiefs, who "guide the work," and technical cadres.

JUDICIARY

The development of the legal and judicial system did not begin until almost fifteen years after the state was proclaimed. In November 1989, a criminal code and laws establishing a judicial system were adopted. In 1993 the government began publishing an official gazette to disseminate laws, decrees, and regulations.

In 1990 the judicial branch was upgraded. New legislation provided a draft of a criminal code, established procedures for criminal cases, set up a court system, and established a law school. Moreover, the Ministry of Justice added a fourth year of studies to a law program for training magistrates and judges.

Also in 1990, the functions of the Supreme People's Court were separated from those of the office of the public prosecutor general. Until then, the minister of justice served as both president of the court and director of public prosecutions.

For additional analytical, business and investment opportunities information, please contact Global Investment & Business Center, USA at (703) 370-8082. Fax: (703) 370-8083. E-mail: ibpusa3@gmail.com Global Business and Investment Info Databank - www.ibpus.com

Although the implementation of judicial reforms proceeded slowly and had not significantly improved the administration of justice by mid-1994, the new legal framework offers the possibility of moving away from the arbitrary use of power toward the rule of law. In late 1992, however, the government suspended the bar until it formulates regulations for fees and activities of (the few) private lawyers who are able to advise in civil cases. Lawyers are not allowed to promote themselves as attorneys-at-law. Theoretically, the government provides legal counsel to the accused, although in practice persons accused of crimes must defend themselves, without outside legal counsel. However, the assessors (legal advisers)--who are often untrained--and the party functionaries are being increasingly replaced by professional personnel trained at the Institute of Law and Administration.

The constitution empowers the National Assembly to elect or remove the president of the Supreme People's Court and the public prosecutor general on the recommendation of its Standing Committee. The Standing Committee of the National Assembly appoints or removes judges (previously elected) of the provincial, municipal, and district levels.

Further evidence of an attempt to shift toward a professional judicial system is found in the public prosecution institutes provided for at each level of administration. The task of these institutes is to control the uniform observance of laws by all ministries, organizations, state employees, and citizens. They prosecute under the guidance of the public prosecutor general, who appoints and removes deputy public prosecutors at all levels.

POLITICAL OPPOSITION

Over the centuries, residents of the Laotian Buddhist kingdom developed gentle techniques of accommodation, often searching for more powerful patrons either outside the country or within. Authorities governed during the early years after 1975 with little popular support, but most Laotians simply submitted to their authority because they had little alternative. However, the authorities were not harsh compared to other communist regimes of the 1970s and 1980s, most of which--by mid-1994--have toppled.

The relatively passive Laotian political culture inspires few direct challenges to one-party domination, and party authorities firmly assert the limits of political dissent. LPRP spokesmen invoke a litany of explanations to justify the party's monopoly of power--for example, the country is too underdeveloped and the people too little educated to permit more than one party. Further, there are too many ethnic groups, and open political participation would lead to disunity and chaos. Political stability, provided by the leadership of a single party, is said to be necessary for economic growth. The LPRP has also pointed out the corrupt multiparty system of the RLG. An abiding political reality, however, is that those who have power wish to retain it.

Restrictions on political opposition do not appear to be a salient issue among a majority of the population, although a small number of educated Laotians in intellectual, student, and bureaucratic circles have raised a few protests. Despite the toll of age and failing health among the aged Politburo members, the leadership governs without active opposition. Even when communist leaders were unceremoniously dumped in Eastern

Europe, vigorously challenged in the Soviet Union, and confronted by students in China, communist leaders in Laos retained their hold as they guided the regime into the uncharted realm of reform. It is not clear why there was so little challenge to these aging leaders. They maintained a cohesion among themselves, perhaps a product of their many years as comrades in revolution, living in caves and dodging United States bombs. They may have also sustained an enduring respect from party stalwarts who followed them during twenty-five years of revolution. Whether the government will encounter political opposition from a broader segment of Laotian society as it moves to a more market-oriented economy and increasingly opens its doors to Western influence remains to be seen.

REFUGEES

From 1975 to 1985, after the communists had seized power and were consolidating their hold, some 350,000 persons fled across the Mekong River to Thailand and, in most cases, resettled in third countries. By the late 1980s and early 1990s, this outflow had declined substantially. In 1990, for example, an estimated 1,000 to 2,000 lowland Lao and 4,000 to 5,000 upland Lao departed illegally for Thailand. The Thai government refused to admit these refugees as immigrants. Third-country resettlement has grown more difficult with the end of Cold War solidarity with emigrants who claim to be "victims of communism." Moreover, Laos has become more liberal in granting exit permits to those desiring to emigrate.

By the early 1990s, almost as many Laotians were returning to Laos as were leaving. Under a voluntary repatriation program worked out in 1980 by Laos and the United Nations High Commissioner for Refugees (UNHCR--see Glossary), nearly 19,000 Laotians had voluntarily returned to their homeland by the end of 1993, and an estimated 30,000 more had returned without official involvement. Most of the returnees are lowland Lao. Of the approximately 30,000 Laotian refugees remaining in camps in Thailand in 1993, the majority are upland Lao. Approximately 1,700 Laotian refugees remain in China. Émigrés who had resettled in third countries are returning in increasing numbers to visit relatives and, in a few cases, to survey business opportunities in the more liberal economy.

INSURGENTS

A small-scale insurgency that has existed since 1975 continues in the early 1990s, although at a much lower level than in previous years. This insurgency has never seriously threatened the regime, but it is troublesome because the insurgents commit sabotage, blow up bridges, and threaten transport and communications. The great majority of insurgents are Hmong (see Glossary), led by ex-soldiers from United States Central Intelligence Agency (CIA)-supported units who fought against Pathet Lao and North Vietnamese troops in the 1960s. Hmong groups, most of them formerly associated with the RLG, draw recruits and support from Hmong refugee camps and operate from bases in Thailand with the cooperation of local Thai military officers. As relations between Thailand and Laos continued to improve in the 1990s, support for this insurgent activity declined. Resistance spokesmen claim that their principal source of funds for

For additional analytical, business and investment opportunities information,
please contact Global Investment & Business Center, USA
at (703) 370-8082. Fax: (703) 370-8083. E-mail: ibpusa3@gmail.com
Global Business and Investment Info Databank - www.ibpus.com

weapons and supplies comes from Laotian expatriate communities overseas, including the 180,000 Laotians in the United States.

Even though the government lacks widespread public support, insurgency is less a measure of discontent than evidence of a serious ethnic problem. The LPDR, like the RLG that preceded it, has been dominated by lowland Lao. The two governments exemplify the traditional Lao disdain for upland peoples, in spite of Pathet Lao rhetoric in favor of ethnic equality. On the one hand, because many Hmong fought on the side of the "American imperialists," government leaders feel additionally suspicious of them. On the other hand, Hmong and other upland minorities who served with the United States-supported forces have been suspicious and uncomfortable under their former enemies. Thus, a core of insurgents, composed largely of ethnic minorities, continues to fight against the authorities. It will be extremely difficult-- perhaps impossible--for the government to pacify them, especially without help from Vietnamese military units, if the insurgents enjoy access to sanctuary in Thailand along the easily crossed 1,000 kilometer Mekong River border.

In the early 1980s, Hmong insurgents claimed that the Lao People's Army (LPA--see Glossary) was using lethal chemical agents against them. The Hmong refugees in Thailand often referred to the chemical agents as "poisons from above;" foreign journalists used the term "yellow rain." The government vehemently denied these charges. The United States Department of State noted in 1992 that "considerable investigative efforts in recent years have revealed no evidence of chemical weapons use" in the post-1983 period. The LPDR again denied these charges. The United States Department of State noted in 1992 that "considerable investigative efforts in recent years have revealed no evidence of chemical weapons use."

BUREAUCRATIC CULTURE

The historical evolution of Laos created identifiable layers of bureaucratic behavior. Traditional royal customs and Buddhist practices set the foundation. Next, there was an overlay of French influence, the product of colonial rule from 1890 to 1954. During this period, several generations of Laotian bureaucrats were trained and often placed in subordinate rank to French-imported Vietnamese civil servants. The administration used French as the official language and followed French colonial administrative practices. From 1954 to 1975, there was an increase in United States influence, and the United States provided training and educational opportunities for future bureaucrats as well as employment in United States agencies. Because of its brevity, however, the United States impact was far less pervasive than the French.

When the communists seized power in 1975, a new layer of bureaucrats--strongly influenced by North Vietnam and the Soviet Union and its allies--was added. Many of the French-trained and United States-influenced bureaucrats fled across the Mekong River. Of those who stayed, perhaps 10,000 to 15,000 were sent to seminar camps or reeducation centers;. The few Westerntrained bureaucrats who remained possessed French- or Englishlanguage skills and the technical competence needed to deal effectively with the Western foreign aid donors so critical to the economy. The Western-trained bureaucrats were essential because not many of the new revolutionary cadres who moved into key positions of bureaucratic authority had much formal education, knowledge of a foreign language, or competence in the technical and managerial skills necessary to run a national economy. The few cadres in each ministry who were capable of managing the economy were often unavailable because there were so many demands for their services: for example, meeting with visiting foreign delegations, traveling to international meetings, and attending political training sessions.

Since its inception, the LPDR bureaucracy has been lethargic and discouraged individual initiative. It has been dangerous to take unorthodox positions. Some officials have been arrested on suspicion of corruption or ideological deviation: for example, "pro-Chinese" sentiment. Initiative has been further constrained by the lack of legal safeguards, formal trial procedures, and an organized system of appeal. The beginnings of a penal code, which the SPA endorsed in 1989, and the promulgation of a constitution in 1991, however, may solidify the system of justice and provide a clear definition as to what constitutes a crime against socialist morality, the party, or the state.

The lethargy of the bureaucracy is understandable within the cultural context of Laos. As a peasant society at the lower end of the modernization scale, the LPDR has adopted few of the work routines associated with modern administration. Foreign aid administrators frequently point out that Laotian administrators have difficulty creating patterns or precedents, or learning from experience. Laotians are known for their light-hearted, easy-going manner. This *bo pinh nyang* (never mind--don't worry about it) attitude is reflected in the languid pace of administration. Official corruption has also been acknowledged as problematic.

Kaysone acknowledged the bureaucracy's low level of competence. In his report to the Fourth Party Congress in 1986, he chided those in authority who gave "preference only to (their friends) or those from the same locality or race; paying attention to only their birth origin, habits and one particular sphere of education." Patronage is but one area that has come under scrutiny and resulted in admonishments to strengthen inspection and control. Kaysone further railed against "dogmatism, privatism, racial narrowmindedness , regionalism and localism."

ORGANIZATION OF THE GOVERNMENT STATE AND GOVERNMENT LEADERS

Lieutenant General **Choummaly Sayasone**

Politics of Laos takes place in a framework of a single-party socialist republic. The only legal political party is the Lao People's Revolutionary Party (LPRP). The head of state is President Choummaly Sayasone, who also is secretary-general (leader) of the LPRP. The head of government is Prime Minister Bouasone Bouphavanh. Government policies are determined by the party through the all-powerful nine-member Politburo and the 49-member Central Committee. Important government decisions are vetted by the Council of Ministers.

Laos adopted a constitution in 1991. The following year, elections were held for a new 85-seat National Assembly with members elected by secret ballot to five-year terms. This National Assembly, which essentially acts as a rubber stamp for the LPRP, approves all new laws, although the executive branch retains authority to issue binding decrees. The most recent elections took place in April 2006. The assembly was expanded to 99 members in 1997 and in 2006 elections had 115.

The FY 2000 central government budget plan called for revenue of $180 million and expenditures of $289 million, including capital expenditures of $202 million.

In recent years bomb attacks against the government have occurred, coupled with small exchanges of fire, across Laos. A variety of different groups have claimed responsibility including the Committee for Independence and Democracy in Laos and Lao Citizens Movement for Democracy. The United States has warned about the possibility of further attacks during the ASEAN summit in November.

Communist Laos's National Assem-bly yesterday endorsed party chief Choummaly Sayasone as president and young rising star Bouasone Bouphavanh as prime minister.

The reshuffle reflected a smooth transition of power, as both Choummaly and Bouasone belong to the faction of former Lao People's Revolutionary Party chief Khamtay Siphandone, Vientiane-based diplomats said.

A three-star general, Choummaly is Khamtay's former deputy and right-hand man, while Bouasone is a former deputy prime minister. Choummaly has enjoyed Khamtay's full backing since joining the decision-making Politburo during the seventh congress of the party in 2001. Like Khamtay, Choummaly and Bouasone are natives of southern Laos.

Choummaly, from Attapeu, took the helm from Khamtay after the eighth congress of the communist party in March.

Bouasone, from Salavan, replaced Bounnhang Vorachit, who was made vice-president.

Born in 1954, Bouasone is from the new generation of communist leaders who have climbed the ladder of the socialist regime, and was not one of the revolutionary guard like his seniors. However, in 1975, shortly before the fall of Vientiane to the communist Pathet Lao, he was a student activist who played a key role in protests against the previous regime.

The reshuffle also promoted former foreign minister Somsavat Lengsavad to deputy prime minister.

Historian Thongloun Sisoulith, also a former deputy prime minister, replaced Somsavat as foreign minister.

New faces in the 28-member cabinet include Onechanh Thammavong as labour minister, party ideologist Chaleuan Yapaoher as justice minister, Nam Vignaket as industry and commerce minister, Sitaheng Latsaphone as agriculture minister and Sommath Pholsena as transport minister.

The 115-member National Assembly, which was inaugurated yesterday following the April 30 general election, selected Thong Thammavong as its president.

The National Assembly in Laos has formalised the appointment of a new president, prime minister and cabinet. Bouasone Bouphavanh was appointed prime minister, replacing Boungnang Vorachit, who became a vice-president. Choummaly Sayasone was named president, in place of Khamtay Siphandone, who stepped down as leader of Laos' only political party in March. The new line-up was unlikely to herald significant reform in the communist country, analysts say. Mr Bouasone told the lawmakers that he would maintain economic growth and fight corruption. The National Assembly was meeting for the first time since elections in April in which the ruling Lao People's Revolutionary Party won all but one parliamentary seat. Laos has been ruled by a communist government since an American-backed government fell in 1975. A mainly agricultural country of 5.9 million people, Laos is one of Asia's poorest nations.

President	CHOUMMALI Saignason, *Lt. Gen.*
Vice President	BOUN-GNANG Volachit
Prime Minister	BOUASONE Bouphavanh
Dep. Prime Min.	ASANG Laoli, *Maj. Gen.*
Dep. Prime Min.	DOUANGCHAI Phichit
Dep. Prime Min.	SOMSAVAT Lengsavat
Dep. Prime Min.	THONGLOUN Sisoulit
Min. of Agriculture & Forestry	SITAHENG Latsaphone
Min. of Commerce	SOULIVONG Daravong
Min. of Communications, Transport, Posts, & Construction	SOMMATH Pholsena
Min. of Education	SOMKOT Mangnormek

Min. of Energy & Mining	BOSAIKHAM Vongdala
Min. of Finance	CHANSY Phosikham
Min. of Foreign Affairs	THONGLOUN Sisoulit
Min. of Industry & Commerce	NAM Vignaket
Min. of Information & Culture	MOUNKEO Olaboun
Min. of Justice	CHALEUAN Yapaoher
Min. of Labor & Social Welfare	ONECHANH Thammavong
Min. of National Defense	DOUANGCHAI Phichit, *Maj. Gen.*
Min. of Public Health	PONMEK Dalaloi, *Dr.*
Min. of Public Security	THONGBANH Sengaphone
Min. to the Prime Minister's Office & Head of Public Administration & Civil Authority	BOUNPHENG Mounphosay
Min. to the Prime Minister's Office	BOUASY Lovansay
Min. to the Prime Minister's Office	KHAM-OUANE Bouppha
Min. to the Prime Minister's Office	ONNEUA Phommachanh
Min. to the Prime Minister's Office	SAISENGLI Tengbliachu
Min. & Chairman of National Mekong Committee	KHAMLOUAD Sitlakone
Min. & Chairman of National Tourism Authority	SOMPHONG Mongkhonvilay
Min. & Head of Cabinet, President's Office	SOUBANH Sritthirath
Min. & Head of Government Secretariats	CHEUANG Sombounkhanh
Min. & Head of Science, Technology, & Environment Agency	BOUNTIEM Phitsamay
Chmn. Planning & Investment Committee	SOULIVONG Dalavong
Chmn. State Control Commission	ASANG Laoli, *Maj. Gen.*
Governor, National Bank	PHOUPHET Khamphounvong
Ambassador to the US	PHANTHONG Phommahaxay
Permanent Representative to the UN, New York	ALOUNKEO Kittikhoun

EMBASSY OF THE LAO PEOPLE'S DEMOCRATIC REPUBLIC

Chancery: 2222 S Street, NW
Washington, DC 20008
Tel: (202) 332-6416
Fax: (202) 332-4923
National Holiday: National Day, December 2.

AS A TRADITIONAL SOCIETY until 1975, Laos was a conservative monarchy, dominated by a small number of powerful families. In 1975 it was transformed into a communist oligarchy, but its social makeup remained much the same. In the 600-year-old monarchy, the Lao king ruled from Louangphrabang (Luang Prabang), while in other regions there were families with royal pretensions rooted in the royal histories of Champasak (Bassac), Vientiane (Viangchan), and Xiangkhoang (Tran Ninh). They were surrounded by lesser aristocrats from prominent families who in turn became patrons to clients of lower status, thus building a complex network of allegiances. The king reigned from Louangphrabang but did not rule over much of the outlying regions of the country.

In December 1975, with the declaration of the Lao People's Democratic Republic (LPDR, or Laos), the king abdicated. Although Laos was reorganized as a communist "people's democracy," important vestiges of traditional political and social behavior remained. The aristocratic families were shorn of their influence, but a new elite with privileged access to the communist roots of power emerged, and clients of lower status have searched them out as patrons. In addition, some of the old families, who had links to the new revolutionary elite, managed to survive and wield significant influence. As newly dominant elites replaced the old, they demanded a similar deference.

Lao Loum, or lowland Lao, families continue to wield the greatest influence). Despite the rhetoric of the revolutionary elite concerning ethnic equality, Lao Theung, or midland Lao, and Lao Sung, or upland Lao, minorities are low on the scale of national influence, just as they were in pre1975 society. However, the power of the central government over the outlying regions has remained tenuous, still relying upon bargains with tribal chieftains to secure the loyalty of their peoples.

Although manifesting many of the characteristics of a traditional Lao monarchy dominated by a lowland Lao Buddhist elite, the country has exhibited many of the characteristics of other communist regimes. It has shown a similar heavy bureaucratic style, with emphasis within the bureaucracy on political training and long sessions of criticism and self-criticism for its civil servants. Laos imported from its Vietnamese mentor the concept of reeducation centers or "seminar camps," where, during the early years in power, thousands of former Royal Lao Government (RLG--see Glossary) adversaries were incarcerated. However, this communist overlay on traditional society has been moderated by two important factors: Lao Buddhism and government administrative incompetence in implementing socialist doctrine. Thus, what emerged in Laos has been a system aptly labeled by Prince Souvanna Phouma, former prime minister of the RLG, as "socialisme à la laotienne" (Lao-style socialism).

The mélange of traditional politics, accompanied by patronclient relations, with communist-style intra-institutional competition, has produced a unique political culture. Power centers tend to cluster around key personalities, and those in power become targets of opportunity for members of their extended family and friends

THE LAO PEOPLE'S REVOLUTIONARY PARTY

Whereas communist parties in the former Soviet Union and Eastern Europe have crumbled, in Laos, the ruling communist party, the Phak Pasason Pativat Lao (Lao

For additional analytical, business and investment opportunities information, please contact Global Investment & Business Center, USA at (703) 370-8082. Fax: (703) 370-8083. E-mail: ibpusa3@gmail.com
Global Business and Investment Info Databank - www.ibpus.com

People's Revolutionary Party-- LPRP; see Glossary) has retained undiluted political control. The constitution, adopted in August 1991, notes simply in Article 3 that the LPRP is the "leading nucleus" of the political system. LPRP statutes, revised following the Fifth Party Congress held in 1991, leave no doubt regarding the dominant role of the party:

The party is...the leading core of the entire political system, hub of intelligence, and representative of the interest of the people of all strata. The party formulates and revises the major lines and policies on national development in all spheres; finds solutions to major problems; determines the policies regarding personnel management, training of cadres, and supplying key cadres for different levels; controls and supervises activities of party cadres and members, state agencies and mass organizations.

ORIGINS OF THE PARTY

The LPRP has its roots in the Indochinese Communist Party (ICP), founded by Ho Chi Minh in 1930. (Ho Chi Minh led the struggle for Vietnamese independence and was the president of the Democratic Republic of Vietnam (North Vietnam) from 1945 until his death in 1969.) The ICP, composed entirely of Vietnamese members in its early years, formed the Committee for Laos (or a "Lao section") in 1936. Only in the mid-1940s did the Vietnamese communist revolutionaries step up active recruitment of Laotian members. In 1946 or early 1947, Kaysone Phomvihan, a law student at the University of Hanoi, was recruited, and Nouhak Phoumsavan, engaged in a trucking business in Vietnam, joined in 1947.

In February 1951, the Second Congress of the ICP resolved to disband the party and to form three separate parties representing the three states of Indochina. However, it was not until March 22, 1955, at the First Party Congress, that Phak Pasason Lao (Lao People's Party--LPP) was formally proclaimed. (The name LPRP was adopted at the Second Party Congress in 1972.) It seems likely that from 1951 to 1955, key Laotian former members of the ICP provided leadership for the "resistance" movement in Laos, under the tutelage of their Vietnamese senior partners. In 1956 the LPP founded the Neo Lao Hak Xat (Lao Patriotic Front--LPF) the political party of the Pathet Lao (Lao Nation--see Glossary), to act as the public mass political organization. Meanwhile, the LPP remained clandestine, directing the activities of the front.

The Vietnamese communists provided critical guidance and support to the growing party during the revolutionary period. They helped to recruit the leadership of the Laotian communist movement; from its inception, the LPRP Political Bureau (Politburo) was made up of individuals closely associated with the Vietnamese. The Vietnamese furnished facilities and guidance for training not only the top leadership but also the entire Laotian communist movement. The Vietnamese assigned advisers to the party, as well as to the military forces of the LPF. Under the guidance of North Vietnamese mentors, LPRP leaders shaped a Marxist-Leninist party, political and mass organizations, and an army and a bureaucracy, all based upon the North Vietnamese model.

From their perspective, Laotian communists had not compromised their legitimacy as a nationalist movement by their dependence on Hanoi. During the revolutionary period prior to 1975, when LPRP leaders looked to the North Vietnamese for a sense of overall direction and cohesion, they found many common interests. Both parties faced the same enemies: first France and then the United States. They held a similar view of the world and of the desirable solution to its problems. In some cases, this affinity was strengthened by family relations (for example, Kaysone, whose Vietnamese father, Luan Phomvihan, had been a secretary to the French resident in Savannakhét) or marriage ties (Souphanouvong and Nouhak had Vietnamese wives).

Following the First Party Congress, it was seventeen years until the Second Party Congress was convened, in February 1972. The Third Party Congress met ten years later, in April 1982; the Fourth Party Congress convened in November 1986, and the Fifth Party Congress in March 1991.

PARTY STRUCTURE

The LPP steadily grew from its initial 300 to 400 members ("25 delegates representing 300 to 400 members" were said to have attended the founding congress of the party). By 1965 there were 11,000 members; by 1972, as it prepared to enter into the final coalition with the RLG, it had grown to some 21,000 members; by 1975, when the party seized full power, it claimed a membership of 25,000; and by 1991, at the convening of the Fifth Party Congress, the LPRP claimed its membership had increased to 60,000.

The LPRP has been organized in a manner common to other ruling communist parties, with greatest similarity to the Vietnamese Communist Party. As in other such parties, the highest authority is the party congress, a gathering of party cadres from throughout the country that meets on an intermittent schedule for several days to listen to speeches, learn the plans for future party strategy, and ratify decisions already taken by the party leadership.

Next in the party hierarchy--since the elimination of the Secretariat in 1991--is the Central Committee, the party elite who fill key political positions throughout the country The Central Committee is charged with leading the party between congresses. In addition to members of the Politburo and former members of the Secretariat, the committee includes key government ministers, leading generals of the army, secretaries of provincial party committees, and chairpersons of mass organizations.

When the LPRP first revealed itself to the public in 1975, the Central Committee comprised twenty-one members and six alternates. By the Fourth Party Congress, its size had expanded to fifty-one members and nine alternates. The average age of a Central Committee member in 1986 was fifty-two, with the oldest seventy-seven and the youngest thirty-three. The number of women on the Central Committee rose from three to five, including Thongvin Phomvihan, then Secretary General Kaysone's wife, who was chair of the LPRP's People's Revolutionary Youth Union and, in 1982, the first woman appointed to the Central Committee.

At the Fifth Party Congress, the Central Committee stabilized in size at fifty-nine members and took on a few younger, more educated men to replace deceased or retired members. At the time, the oldest member was seventy-seven, the youngest thirty-five, with 22 percent over sixty, 30 percent between fifty and fifty-nine, and 40 percent under forty-nine. Only two women are full members of the Central Committee, and two continue as alternates. Thongvin Phomvihan--who had ranked thirty-fifth in 1986--was removed, accompanied by rumors of excessive political influence in her business activities. Notwithstanding this setback to Kaysone's family fortune, their son, Saisompheng Phomvihan, was appointed to the Central Committee, ranking forty-fifth, and was named governor of Savannakhét Province in 1993. This appointment inspired some private muttering about the emerging "princelings," referring as well to Souphanouvong's son, Khamsai Souphanouvong, number thirtyfour on the Central Committee, who became minister of finance.

Despite the party's rhetoric asserting ethnic equality, the Central Committee has been dominated by lowland Lao. Upland minorities remain sparsely represented at the highest levels of party leadership. Only four members of ethnic minority groups were reported on the Central Committee elected at the Fifth Party Congress.

The Central Committee is served by a number of subordinate committees. These committees include, most importantly, the Office of the Central Committee, and five other offices: Organization Committee; Propaganda and Training Committee; Party and State Control Committee; Administrative Committee of the Party and State School for Political Theory; and Committee for the Propagation of Party Policies.

Since 1972 the genuine center of political power, as in other communist parties, has resided in the Politburo. Membership of the Politburo, and formerly that of the Secretariat, is drawn from the Central Committee. A small group of men--seven in 1972 and eleven by 1993--have provided the critical leadership of the communist movement in Laos. A signal attribute of this group has been its remarkable cohesion and continuity. The Politburo has been dominated for more than fifteen years communist rule by the same stalwart band of revolutionary veterans. The twenty-five Laotian former members of the ICP who founded the LPP in 1955, and from whom the Politburo was drawn, remained in almost identical rank until illness and age began to take their toll in the 1980s. Kaysone was named secretary general of the then secret LPP upon its establishment, a post he retained until his death in 1992. Nouhak retained his number-two position on the Politburo into 1993. It was not until the Fifth Party Congress that Souphanouvong, Phoumi Vongvichit, and Sisomphone Lovansai (ranking third, fourth, and seventh, respectively) were retired with honorific titles as counselors to the Central Committee. Prime Minister Khamtai Siphandon was promoted to succeed Kaysone as chief of the party, and Phoun Sipaseut advanced a notch in rank. In 1991 the Politburo numbered ten, including only two new members.

Although the exact manner of Politburo decision making has never been revealed, a collegiality, based on long years of common experience, appears to have developed. In addition to their powerful position on the Politburo, members exercise additional political power--perhaps even more than in most other communist systems--through important

For additional analytical, business and investment opportunities information, please contact Global Investment & Business Center, USA at (703) 370-8082. Fax: (703) 370-8083. E-mail: ibpusa3@gmail.com Global Business and Investment Info Databank - www.ibpus.com

posts within the governmental structure. In fact, for many years, five Politburo members also held seats on the Secretariat.

At the Fifth Party Congress, the party abolished the nineperson Secretariat of the Central Committee and changed the designation of the head of the party (Kaysone) from secretary general to chairman. Until it was abolished, the Secretariat wielded influence second only to that of the Politburo. The Secretariat issued party directives and acted on behalf of the Central Committee when it was not in session, in effect managing the day-to-day business of the party. Khamtai Siphandon became party chairman in November 1992, but it is not certain whether he will accrue the same power and influence as his predecessor.

Each of the sixteen provinces (khoueng--see Glossary) is directed by a party committee, chaired by a party secretary who is the dominant political figure in the province. At a lower level are 112 districts (muang--see Glossary), further divided into subdistricts (tasseng--see Glossary), each with their own party committees. Administratively, subdistricts have been abolished in principle since around 1993, but implementation has been uneven across provinces. It is unknown whether subdistrictlevel party committees have also been abolished. At the base of the country's administrative structure are more than 11,000 villages (ban--see Glossary), only some of which have party branches.

SEMISECRECY OF THE LAO PEOPLE'S REVOLUTIONARY PARTY

Unlike other communist regimes, the LPRP has long maintained a semisecrecy about its mode of operation and the identity of its rank-and-file members. However, the LPRP follows the standard communist practice of planting party members within all principal institutions of society--in government, in mass organizations, and, formerly, in agricultural collectives. These individuals serve as leaders and transmit party policy. They also act as the eyes and ears of the central party organization. Although party members are admonished not to reveal themselves, it is not difficult for knowledgeable persons to pick out the party members in their organization. In each ministry, for example, the key power wielders are party members. All party members do not, of course, hold positions of authority. Some occupy the lower ranks, serving, for example, as messengers, drivers, and maintenance personnel.

By the late 1980s, some of the LPRP's semisecrecy had eroded. Party leadership lists, which, during revolutionary and early postrevolutionary days had been secret, were published. But a quasi-clandestine attitude remains among the party rank and file that can be explained by several factors. Clandestine behavior is an old habit that is not easily shed. Secrecy adds to the party's mystery, inspires anxiety and fear, and contributes to control. In view of its long history of revolutionary activity, party veterans fear infiltration and subversion. LPRP pronouncements during its first decade of rule frequently alluded to "CIA and Thaireactionary -inspired agents," and later, when relations with China grew tense, to the danger of "big power hegemonism." Moreover, party leaders appear to lack confidence in the quality of their membership, speaking from time to time about "bad elements" within the party.

For additional analytical, business and investment opportunities information, please contact Global Investment & Business Center, USA at (703) 370-8082. Fax: (703) 370-8083. E-mail: ibpusa3@gmail.com Global Business and Investment Info Databank - www.ibpus.com

The LPRP is relatively small compared with other incumbent parties. For example, the 40,000 members that the party claimed in 1985 represented 1.1 percent of the population (estimating 3.5 million inhabitants). In 1979 the Vietnamese Communist Party had 1.5 million members in a population of 53 million, or approximately 3 percent.

IDEOLOGY OF THE LAO PEOPLE'S REVOLUTIONARY PARTY

When LPRP leaders came to power in 1975 as victorious revolutionaries guided by Marxism-Leninism, they retained a zeal for creating a "new socialist society and a new socialist man." They declared their twin economic goals as the achievement of "socialist transformation with socialist construction." They asserted that in establishing the LPDR in 1975, they had completed the "national democratic revolution." (The national goal had been to expel the French colonialists and the United States imperialists. The democratic goal was to overthrow "reactionary traitors, comprador bourgeoisie, bureaucrats, reactionaries, feudalists and militarists...."). The LPRP claimed that it had won the national democratic revolution by winning a "people's war" with a "worker-peasant" alliance, under the secret leadership of the LPRP working through a national front. It proclaimed a commitment to "proletarian internationalism" and the "law of Indochinese solidarity" and at the same time defined Vietnam and the Soviet Union as friends and the "unholy alliance" among United States imperialism, Chinese "great power hegemonism," and Thai militarism as enemies.

By the late 1980s, as communism was undergoing a radical transformation in the Soviet Union and Eastern Europe, Kaysone and his colleagues on the Politburo still professed an adherence to Marxism-Leninism, but they emphasized the necessity for Laos to pass through a stage of "state capitalism." Following Mikhail Gorbachev's example of perestroika, Kaysone proclaimed in 1989 that state enterprises were being severed from central direction and would be financially autonomous. V.I. Lenin's New Economic Policy was frequently cited to legitimize the movement toward a market economy and the necessity to stimulate private initiative.

By the early 1990s, even less of the Marxist-Leninist rhetoric remained. The party has continued to move internally toward more free-market measures and externally toward reliance upon the capitalist countries and the international institutions on which they depend for investment and assistance. The "law" of Indochinese solidarity has been amended, and the LPDR's "special relations" with its former senior partner are no longer invoked, even though party spokesmen still insist that Laos retains a solid friendship and "all-round cooperation" with Vietnam

Despite this erosion of communist ideology, retaining exclusive political power remains a primary goal of the party. In a speech in 1990, Secretary General Kaysone asserted the basis of legitimacy of the party: The party is the center of our wisdom. It has laid down the correct and constructive line, patterns, and steps compatible with realities in our country and hence has led the Lao people in overcoming difficulties and numerous tests to win victory after victory, until the final victory. History has shown that our party is the only party which has won the credibility and trust of the people. Our party's leadership in our country's revolution is an objective requirement and historic duty entrusted to it by the Lao multiethnic people. Other political parties which had existed in our country have dissolved in the process of historical transformation. They failed to win the control and support of the people because they did not defend the national interest or fight for the interests and aspirations of the people.

LEADERSHIP

INTERNAL STABILITY AND EXTERNAL INFLUENCES

Since the LPDR was proclaimed in December 1975, its leadership has been remarkably stable and cohesive. The record of continuous service at the highest ranks is equaled by few, if any, regimes in the contemporary world. Laotian leaders have an equally impressive record of unity. Although outside observers have scrutinized the leadership for factions--and some have postulated at various times that such factions might be divided along the lines of MarxistLeninist ideologues versus pragmatists or pro-Vietnamese versus nationalists (or pro-Chinese), there is no solid evidence that the leadership is seriously divided on any critical issues.

In 1975 the Laotian communist leaders, most of whom had spent the revolutionary decade from 1964 to 1974 operating from Pathet Lao headquarters in the caves of Sam Neua Province, came down from the mountains to Vientiane to direct the new government. At the outset of their accession to power, they were suspicious, secretive, and inaccessible, and lower-level cadres were maladroit in imposing heavy bureaucratic controls. Travel within the country was limited, personal and family behavior was monitored by newly organized revolutionary administrative committees, cadres were assigned to disseminate propaganda, and seminars were held to provide political education for all sorts of groups. During these early years, the party squandered much of the goodwill and friendly acceptance from a population tired of war and the corruption of the old regime.

At first, Laotian communist leaders were committed to fulfilling their revolutionary goals of fundamentally altering society through "socialist transformation and socialist construction." After 1979 the regime modified its earlier zealous pursuit of socialism and pursued more liberal economic and social policies, in much the same manner as Vietnam.

For more than a decade after 1975, the Vietnamese continued to exercise significant influence upon the Laotian leadership through a variety of party, military, and economic channels. By the end of the 1980s, however--in particular following the collapse of the Soviet Union and the Soviet bloc in 1991 and diminishing assistance from the Soviet Union to Vietnam and Laos--Vietnam turned inward to concentrate on its own problems of development. This emboldened Laotians leaders to jettison even more of their socialist ideological baggage, abandon agricultural collectivization, and move toward a market economy. Laos was also free to pursue an independent foreign policy. The single most important vestige of the former communist system was the solitary ruling party, the LPRP.

For additional analytical, business and investment opportunities information, please contact Global Investment & Business Center, USA at (703) 370-8082. Fax: (703) 370-8083. E-mail: ibpusa3@gmail.com Global Business and Investment Info Databank - www.ibpus.com

THE CONSTITUTION

DEVELOPMENT OF THE CONSTITUTION

On August 14, 1991, sixteen years after the establishment of the LPDR, the Supreme People's Assembly (SPA), the country's highest legislative organ, adopted a constitution. Although the SPA had been charged with drafting a constitution in 1975, the task had low priority. It was not until the Third Party Congress that party Secretary General Kaysone stated that the LPRP should "urgently undertake the major task...of preparing a socialist constitution at an early date." Laotian press reports subsequently revealed that a constitutional drafting committee was working informally under the chairmanship of Politburo member Sisomphone Lovansai, a specialist in party organization, with the help of East German advisers. Despite the proclaimed urgency of the task, only on May 22, 1984, did the SPA Standing Committee formalize the appointment of Sisomphone to head a fifteen-person drafting committee.

Although the political institutions had functioned without a written constitution for fifteen years, the lack of a constitution created serious drawbacks for the country. International development agencies were reluctant to invest in Laos given the absence of a fixed, knowable law. Amnesty International, in a 1985 report on Laos, asserted that without a constitution or published penal and criminal codes, citizens were "effectively denied proper legal guarantees of their internationally recognized human rights." Even the party newspaper, Xieng *Pasason* (Voice of the People), commenting in June 1990 on the absence of a constitution and a general body of laws, acknowledged that "having no laws is... a source of injustice and violation, thus leading to a breakdown of social order and peace, the breeding of anarchy, and the lack of democracy."

Reasons for the leisurely pace of constitution drafting, unusually slow even for the plodding bureaucracy, were not readily apparent. Vietnam had adopted a revised constitution in 1980 and Cambodia in 1981, only two years after the ouster of the Khmer Rouge. According to some reports, progress in Laos had been blocked by differences within the Politburo over certain substantive clauses. Perhaps most important, the party leadership, accustomed to rule without question, may have assigned a low priority to producing a document that might eventually lead to challenging their authority, despite rhetoric to the contrary. Further, the public seemed not to care.

After the new SPA was elected in March 1989, it formally appointed a seventeen-member constitutional drafting committee. The National Radio of Laos reported that the drafting committee was working "under the close supervision of the Political Bureau and the Secretariat of the Party Central Committee." Six members of the drafting committee were members of the Central Committee; two of these members also served on the SPA, which also had six members on the drafting committee.

In April 1990, after securing approval of its document from the LPRP Politburo and the Secretariat, the SPA finally made public the draft constitution. With its publication, the party Central Committee issued Directive Number 21, on April 30, 1990, calling for discussion of the draft, first among party and government officials and then among the public. The discussions, although orchestrated by party cadres, did not always please party authorities. An LPRP spokesman released a memo complaining that "people in many major towns" had dwelled too much on what the constitution had to say about the organization of the state. In June a member of the Central Committee cautioned against demonstrations to "demand a multiparty system" and warned that demonstrators would be arrested. Competing parties would not be tolerated, he asserted, adding that "our multi-ethnic Lao people have remained faithfully under the leadership of the LPRP." In a later pronouncement, he said that "the Party has proved to the people in the last 35 years that it is the only party that can take care of them" and he lectured that "too many parties invite division." A Central Committee directive, dated June 14, 1990, hinted at the quality of the public discussion, noting that "in many cases where people were convoked to a meeting, they were simply given question and answer sheets to study."

However, not all discussions of the draft constitution were perfunctory. Undoubtedly inspired by the examples of Eastern Europe and the Soviet Union--where the monopoly of power by communist parties had crumbled--a group of some forty government officials and intellectuals began criticizing the country's one-party system in a series of letters and meetings in April 1990. Organized in the unofficial "Social Democratic Club," the group called for a multiparty system in Laos. One member of the group, an assistant to the minister of science and technology, submitted a letter of resignation to Prime Minister Kaysone in which he labeled Laos a "communist monarchy" and a "dynasty of the Politburo" declaring that the country should "change into a multi-party system in order to bring democracy, freedom and prosperity to the people."

Criticism of the draft document gathered strength in the succeeding months; Laotian students in Paris, Prague, and Warsaw joined in the call for free elections. Criticism broadened as a group of young, educated party cadres associated with nonparty bureaucrats--many educated in France and Canada--targeted veteran party leaders. These groups charged that the new policies of the old guard were fostering corruption and increased social and economic inequality. It was not until October 1990 that the government finally cracked down on these calls for democratic reforms, with the arrest of several protesters, including a former vice minister in the State Planning Commission and a director in the Ministry of Justice who were sentenced to long prison terms in Houaphan.

Thus, although the constitution purports to guarantee freedom of speech and petition and its framers give lip service to the desirability of public discussion, the ruling party sent a clear message with these arrests that it will not tolerate challenges to its exclusive exercise of power. Veteran party leaders were clearly more impressed by the political models of Vietnam and China than by the examples of Eastern Europe and the Soviet Union. Although willing to experiment with economic liberalization, party leaders seemed determined to retain political domination--if they could-- through a Leninist-style party.

HIGHLIGHTS OF THE CONSTITUTION

The 1991 constitution, which contains elements of an earlier revolutionary orthodoxy, is clearly influenced by the economic and political liberalization within Laos, as well as by the dramatic changes in the socialist world and the international balance of forces. The constitution specifies the functions and powers of the various organs of government and

For additional analytical, business and investment opportunities information,
please contact Global Investment & Business Center, USA
at (703) 370-8082. Fax: (703) 370-8083. E-mail: ibpusa3@gmail.com
Global Business and Investment Info Databank - www.ibpus.com

defines the rights and duties of citizens. Several chapters prescribing the structure of the state define the function and powers of the National Assembly (the renamed SPA), the president, the government, the local administration, and the judicial system. The constitution has little to say, however, about the limitations on government. In foreign policy, the principles of peaceful coexistence are followed.

The constitution legally establishes a set of authorities that resemble the traditional differentiation among executive, legislative, and judicial branches of government. The delineation does not imitate any particular model (neither Vietnamese, nor Russian, nor French), but it pays respect to the idea of a basic blueprint of responsibilities lodged in designated institutions. There is room for evolution of government authority, but there are also specific boundaries.

Government outside Vientiane has developed an independence over the years, reflecting the exigencies of the Pathet Lao armed struggle and of economic self-reliance during the postwar socialist pitfalls. The constitution eliminated elected people's councils at the provincial and district level as "no more necessary," in an effort to fit the state apparatus to the needs of building and developing the regime under "the actual conditions of the country." Again, the will of the ruling party determines which road the administration follows in regard to local governance, but the constitution has left governors, mayors, and district and village chiefs free to "administer their regions and localities without any assistance from popularly elected bodies." The leading role of the party within the administration of the nation overall is illustrated by the fact that party Politburo members are found in state offices--the offices of the president of state, and prime minister, deputy prime ministers (two), chair of the National Assembly, minister of defense, and chair of the Party and State Inspection Board.

The first words of the Preamble refer to the "multi-ethnic Lao people," and frequent use of this term is made throughout the text, a clear rhetorical attempt to promote unity within an ethnically diverse society. The "key components" of the people are specified as workers, farmers, and intellectuals. The Preamble celebrates a revolution carried out "for more than 60 years" under the "correct leadership" of the ICP.

The dominant role played by the LPRP, however, is scarcely mentioned, and the constitution is almost silent about the party's functions and powers. One brief reference to the ruling party is made in Article 3, which states that the "rights of the multiethnic people to be the masters of the country are exercised and ensured through the functioning of the political system with the Lao People's Revolutionary Party as its leading nucleus."

Article 5 notes that the National Assembly and all other state organizations "function in accordance with the principle of democratic centralism." This stricture is an obvious reference to the Marxist-Leninist principle, which calls for open discussion within a unit but prescribes that the minority must accede to the will of the majority, and lower echelons must obey the decisions of higher ones.

Article 7 calls upon mass organizations, such as the Lao Front for National Construction, the Federation of Trade Unions, the People's Revolutionary Youth Union, and the

For additional analytical, business and investment opportunities information, please contact Global Investment & Business Center, USA at (703) 370-8082. Fax: (703) 370-8083. E-mail: ibpusa3@gmail.com Global Business and Investment Info Databank - www.ibpus.com

Federation of Women's Unions, to "unite and mobilize the people." The Lao Front for National Construction, the successor to the LPF, served as the political front for the party during the revolutionary struggle. As of mid-1994, its mandate is to mobilize political support and raise political consciousness for the party's goals among various organizations, ethnic groups, and social classes within society. Other mass organizations are assigned to pursue these goals among their target populations of workers, youths, and women.

The constitution proclaims that the state will respect the "principle of equality among ethnic tribes," which have the right to promote "their fine customs and culture." Further, the state is committed to upgrading the "socio-economy of all ethnic groups."

Regarding religion, the state "respects and protects all lawful activities of the Buddhists and of other religious followers." Buddhist monks and other clergy are reminded that the state encourages them to "participate in the activities which are beneficial to the country.

The chapter on the socioeconomic system does not mention the establishment of socialism, a principal goal of earlier dogma. Instead, the objective of economic policy is to transform the "natural economy into a goods economy." Private property appears to be assured by the statement that the "state protects the right of ownership," including the right of transfer and inheritance. The state is authorized to undertake such tasks as managing the economy, providing education, expanding public health, and caring for war veterans, the aging, and the sick. The constitution admonishes that "all organizations and citizens must protect the environment."

A chapter on the rights and obligations of citizens sets forth a cluster of well-known rights found in modern constitutions, including freedom of religion, speech, press, and assembly. Women and men are proclaimed equal, and all citizens can vote at age eighteen and hold office at twenty-one. In return, citizens are obliged to respect the laws, pay taxes, and defend the country, which includes military service. In commenting on this chapter in 1990, Amnesty International, clearly concerned about past human rights abuses, criticized the document for what was *not* included. Amnesty International noted the absence of provisions for protecting the right to life, abolishing the death penalty, guaranteeing the inalienability of fundamental rights, prohibiting torture, safeguarding against arbitrary arrest and detention, protecting people deprived of their liberty, and providing for a fair trial. No safeguards exist to protect the rights to freedom of opinion and expression, peaceful assembly and association, and independence of the judiciary.

Laos is made up of provinces, municipalities, districts, and villages. The constitution gives no clear guidance on provincial and district responsibilities except to specify that the leaders at each echelon must ensure the implementation of the constitution and the law and must carry out decisions taken by a higher level. In spite of the party's inclination to centralize decision making, provinces and localities have enjoyed a surprising degree of autonomy in shaping social policy. This independence is partly due to limited resources and poor communications with Vientiane. But the central government has also encouraged direct contacts along the borders with China, Thailand, and Vietnam, and trading agreements with neighboring jurisdictions.

For additional analytical, business and investment opportunities information, please contact Global Investment & Business Center, USA at (703) 370-8082. Fax: (703) 370-8083. E-mail: ibpusa3@gmail.com Global Business and Investment Info Databank - www.ibpus.com

Although it is unlikely that the constitution will immediately change the imbedded patterns of the Laotian political system or threaten the dominant role of the party, it has the potential to protect human rights and respect for the law, by the rulers as well as the ruled. The crumbling of communist regimes in Eastern Europe and the Soviet Union as well as strains in communist systems elsewhere, accompanied by widespread movements for democracy, suggest that Laos will not be immune to growing demands for a more dependable rule of law.

For additional analytical, business and investment opportunities information,
please contact Global Investment & Business Center, USA
at (703) 370-8082. Fax: (703) 370-8083. E-mail: ibpusa3@gmail.com
Global Business and Investment Info Databank - www.ibpus.com

SYSTEM OF SOCIAL SECURITY AND LABOR PROTECTION - STARTEGIC INFORMATION AND DEVELOPMENTS

Social security is "any government system that provides monetary assistance to people with an inadequate or no income."[1]

Social security is enshrined in Article 22 of the Universal Declaration of Human Rights, which states:

> Everyone, as a member of society, has the right to social security and is entitled to realization, through national effort and international co-operation and in accordance with the organization and resources of each State, of the economic, social and cultural rights indispensable for his dignity and the free development of his personality.

In simple terms, the signatories agree that society in which a person lives should help them to develop and to make the most of all the advantages (culture, work, social welfare) which are offered to them in the country.[2]

Social security may also refer to the action programs of government intended to promote the welfare of the population through assistance measures guaranteeing access to sufficient resources for food and shelter and to promote health and well-being for the population at large and potentially vulnerable segments such as children, the elderly, the sick and the unemployed. Services providing social security are often called **social services**.

Terminology in this area is somewhat different in the United States from in the rest of the English-speaking world. The general term for an action program in support of the well being of poor people in the United States is *welfare program*, and the general term for all such programs is simply *welfare*. In American society, the term *welfare* arguably has negative connotations. In the United States, the term *Social Security* refers to the US social insurance program for all retired and disabled people. Elsewhere the term is used in a much broader sense, referring to the economic security society offers when people are faced with certain risks. In its 1952 Social Security (Minimum Standards) Convention (nr. 102), the International Labour Organization (ILO) defined the traditional contingencies covered by social security as including:

> Survival beyond a prescribed age, to be covered by *old age pensions*;

> The loss of support suffered by a widowed person or child as the result of the death of the breadwinner (*survivor's benefit*);

> Responsibility for the maintenance of children (*family benefit*);

> The treatment of any morbid condition (including pregnancy), whatever its cause (*medical care*);

A suspension of earnings due to pregnancy and confinement and their consequences (*maternity benefit*);

A suspension of earnings due to an inability to obtain suitable employment for protected persons who are capable of, and available for, work (*unemployment benefits*);

A suspension of earnings due to an incapacity for work resulting from a morbid condition (*sickness leave benefit*);

A permanent or persistent inability to engage in any gainful activity (*disability benefits*);

The costs and losses involved in medical care, sickness leave, invalidity and death of the breadwinner due to an occupational accident or disease (*employment injuries*).

People who cannot reach a guaranteed social minimum for other reasons may be eligible for *social assistance* (or welfare, in American English).

Modern authors often consider the ILO approach too narrow. In their view, social security is not limited to the provision of cash transfers, but also aims at security of work, health, and social participation; and new social risks (single parenthood, the reconciliation of work and family life) should be included in the list as well.[3]

Social security may refer to:

social insurance, where people receive benefits or services in recognition of contributions to an insurance program. These services typically include provision for retirement pensions, disability insurance, survivor benefits and unemployment insurance.

services provided by government or designated agencies responsible for social security provision. In different countries, that may include medical care, financial support during unemployment, sickness, or retirement, health and safety at work, aspects of social work and even industrial relations.

basic security irrespective of participation in specific insurance programs where eligibility may otherwise be an issue. For instance, assistance given to newly arrived refugees for basic necessities such as food, clothing, housing, education, money, and medical care.

A report published by the ILO in 2014 estimated that only 27% of the world's population has access to comprehensive social security

HISTORY

While several of the provisions to which the concept refers have a long history (especially in poor relief), the notion of "social security" itself is a fairly recent one. The earliest examples of use date from the 19th century. In a speech to mark the independence of Venezuela, Simón Bolívar (1819) pronounced: "El sistema de gobierno más perfecto es aquel que produce mayor suma de felicidad posible, mayor suma de *seguridad social* y mayor suma de estabilidad política"[5] (which translates to "The most perfect system of government is that which produces the greatest amount of happiness, the greatest amount of social security and the greatest amount of political stability").

In the Roman Empire, the Emperor Trajan (reigned A.D. 98–117) distributed gifts of money and free grain to the poor in the city of Rome, and returned the gifts of gold sent to him upon his accession by cities in Italy and the provinces of the Empire.[6] Trajan's program brought acclaim from many, including Pliny the Younger.[7]

In Jewish tradition, charity (represented by tzedakah) is a matter of religious obligation rather than benevolence. Contemporary charity is regarded as a continuation of the Biblical Maaser Ani, or poor-tithe, as well as Biblical practices, such as permitting the poor to glean the corners of a field and harvest during the Shmita (Sabbatical year). Voluntary charity, along with prayer and repentance, is befriended to ameliorate the consequences of bad acts.

The Song dynasty (c.1000 AD) government supported multiple forms of social assistance programs, including the establishment of retirement homes, public clinics, and pauper's graveyards.[8]

According to economist Robert Henry Nelson, "The medieval Roman Catholic Church operated a far-reaching and comprehensive welfare system for the poor..."[9][10]

The concepts of welfare and pension were put into practice in the early Islamic law[11][*not in citation given*] of the Caliphate as forms of *Zakat* (charity), one of the Five Pillars of Islam, since the time of the Rashidun caliph Umar in the 7th century. The taxes (including *Zakat* and *Jizya*) collected in the treasury of an Islamic government were used to provide income for the needy, including the poor, elderly, orphans, widowed persons, and the disabled. According to the Islamic jurist Al-Ghazali (Algazel, 1058–1111), the government was also expected to store up food supplies in every region in case a disaster or famine occurred.[11][12] (See Bayt al-mal for further information.)

There is relatively little statistical data on transfer payments before the High Middle Ages. In the medieval period and until the Industrial Revolution, the function of welfare payments in Europe was principally achieved through private giving or charity. In those early times, there was a much broader group considered to be in poverty as compared to the 21st century.

Early welfare programs in Europe included the English Poor Law of 1601, which gave parishes the responsibility for providing poverty relief assistance to the poor.[13] This system was substantially modified by the 19th-century Poor Law Amendment Act, which introduced the system of workhouses.

It was predominantly in the late 19th and early 20th centuries that an organized system of state welfare provision was introduced in many countries. Otto von Bismarck, Chancellor of Germany, introduced one of the first welfare systems for the working classes in 1883. In Great Britain the Liberal government of Henry Campbell-Bannerman and David Lloyd George introduced the

National Insurance system in 1911,[14] a system later expanded by Clement Attlee. The United States did not have an organized welfare system until the Great Depression, when emergency relief measures were introduced under President Franklin D. Roosevelt. Even then, Roosevelt's New Deal focused predominantly on a program of providing work and stimulating the economy through public spending on projects, rather than on cash payment.

INCOME MAINTENANCE

Main article: Unemployment benefits

This policy is usually applied through various programs designed to provide a population with income at times when they are unable to care for themselves. Income maintenance is based in a combination of five main types of program:

Social insurance, considered above

Means-tested benefits, financial assistance provided for those who are unable to cover basic needs, such as food, clothing and housing, due to poverty or lack of income because of unemployment, sickness, disability, or caring for children. While assistance is often in the form of financial payments, those eligible for social welfare can usually access health and educational services free of charge. The amount of support is enough to cover basic needs and eligibility is often subject to a comprehensive and complex assessment of an applicant's social and financial situation. See also Income Support.

Non-contributory benefits. Several countries have special schemes, administered with no requirement for contributions and no means test, for people in certain categories of need: for example, veterans of armed forces, people with disabilities and very old people.

Discretionary benefits. Some schemes are based on the discretion of an official, such as a social worker.

Universal or categorical benefits, also known as **demogrants**. These are non-contributory benefits given for whole sections of the population without a means test, such as family allowances or the public pension in New Zealand (known as New Zealand Superannuation). See also, Alaska Permanent Fund Dividend.

SOCIAL PROTECTION

Main article: Social protection

Social protection refers to a set of benefits available (or not available) from the state, market, civil society and households, or through a combination of these agencies, to the individual/households to reduce multi-dimensional deprivation. This multi-dimensional deprivation could be affecting less active poor persons (such as the elderly or the disabled) and active poor persons (such as the unemployed).

This broad framework makes this concept more acceptable in developing countries than the concept of social security. Social security is more applicable in the conditions, where large numbers of citizens depend on the formal economy for their livelihood. Through a defined contribution, this social security may be managed.

But, in the context of widespread informal economy, formal social security arrangements are almost absent for the vast majority of the working population. Besides, in developing countries, the state's capacity to reach the vast majority of the poor people may be limited because of its limited infrastructure and resources. In such a context, multiple agencies that could provide for social protection, including health care, is critical for policy consideration.[15] The framework of social protection is thus holds the state responsible for providing for the poorest populations by regulating non-state agencies.

Collaborative research from the Institute of Development Studies debating Social Protection from a global perspective, suggests that advocates for social protection fall into two broad categories: "instrumentalists" and "activists". Instrumentalists argue that extreme poverty, inequality, and vulnerability is dysfunctional in the achievement of development targets (such as the MDGs). In this view, social protection is about putting in place risk management mechanisms that will compensate for incomplete or missing insurance (and other) markets, until a time that private insurance can play a more prominent role in that society. Activist arguments view the persistence of extreme poverty, inequality, and vulnerability as symptoms of social injustice and structural inequality and see social protection as a right of citizenship. Targeted welfare is a necessary step between humanitarianism and the ideal of a "guaranteed minimum income" where entitlement extends beyond cash or food transfers and is based on citizenship, not philanthropy.[16]

PROPOSED SOCIAL SECURITY REFORMS

The following proposals were made by the American Association of Retired Persons on its website in 2015:

Raising the Retirement Age – "The age when a person becomes eligible to receive full Social Security retirement benefits (the full retirement age) has been increasing from age 65 on a schedule set by Congress in 1983. It has reached 66 and will gradually rise to 67 for those born in 1960 and later. Raising the full retirement age further is one option to help close Social Security's funding gap."

Longevity Index – "If, as projected, Americans continue to live longer from one generation to the next, individuals will, on average, receive Social Security benefits for a longer period of time. The trend contributes to Social Security's funding gap, and one option to offset it is longevity indexing. Indexing would automatically modify Social Security to pay smaller monthly benefits as lifespans increase."

Social Security Cap – "The Social Security payroll tax currently applies to annual earnings up to $118,500. Any wages earned above $118,500 go untaxed for Social Security. This cap generally increases every year as the national average wage increases. Today, the cap covers about 84 percent of total earnings in the nation. Raising the cap to cover a higher percent of total earnings would help close Social Security's funding gap."

For additional analytical, business and investment opportunities information,
please contact Global Investment & Business Center, USA
at (703) 370-8082. Fax: (703) 370-8083. E-mail: ibpusa3@gmail.com
Global Business and Investment Info Databank - www.ibpus.com

SOCIAL SECURITY SYSTEM IN LAOS - STRATEGIC INFORMATION AND DEVELOPMENTS

OLD AGE, DISABILITY, AND SURVIVORS

REGULATORY FRAMEWORK

First law: 1999 (employees in enterprises), implemented in 2001.

Current law: 2013 (social security), implemented in 2014.

Type of program: Social insurance system.

COVERAGE

Employees of private-sector and state-owned enterprises, civil servants, and police and military personnel.

Voluntary coverage is available for self-employed persons.

SOURCE OF FUNDS

Insured person: 2.5% of gross monthly insurable earnings (6% for civil servants, and police and military personnel).

The minimum monthly earnings used to calculate contributions are the minimum wage.

The legal monthly minimum wage is 900,000 kip.

The maximum monthly earnings used to calculate contributions are 4,500,000 kip.

Self-employed person: 5% of declared monthly earnings.

The minimum monthly earnings used to calculate contributions are the minimum wage.

The legal monthly minimum wage is 900,000 kip.

The maximum monthly earnings used to calculate contributions are 4,500,000 kip.

Employer: 2.5% of gross monthly insurable earnings.

The minimum monthly earnings used to calculate contributions are the minimum wage.

The legal monthly minimum wage is 900,000 kip.

For additional analytical, business and investment opportunities information,
please contact Global Investment & Business Center, USA
at (703) 370-8082. Fax: (703) 370-8083. E-mail: ibpusa3@gmail.com
Global Business and Investment Info Databank - www.ibpus.com

The maximum monthly earnings used to calculate contributions are 4,500,000 kip.

Government: 6% of payroll as an employer for civil servants, and military and police personnel.

QUALIFYING CONDITIONS

Old-age pension: Age 60 (men) or age 55 (women) with at least 15 years of contributions (25 years for civil servants, and police and military personnel). Age 55 (men) or age 50 (women) for those in hazardous or arduous occupations.

Old-age lump-sum benefit: Age 60 (men) or age 55 (women) with less than 15 years of contributions (25 years for civil servants, and police and military personnel).

Disability pension: Must have at least 12 months of contributions in the last 24 months and an assessed degree of disability of at least 41%.

Disability lump-sum benefit: Must have at least 12 months of contributions in the last 24 months and an assessed degree of disability of less than 41%.

The National Social Security Fund's Medical Committee assesses the disability.

Caregiver's benefit: Paid for an assessed degree of disability of at least 80%.

Survivor pension: The deceased had at least five years of contributions.

Eligible survivors include a widow (aged 55 or older) or a nonworking widower (aged 60 or older); orphans up to age 18 (no limit if disabled and without working capacity); or a dependent father (aged 60 or older) or mother (aged 55 or older) without any income.

The widow(er)'s pension ceases upon remarriage or employment.

Survivor lump-sum benefit: Paid if the deceased had at least three months of contributions.

OLD-AGE BENEFITS

Old-age pension: For private sector employees and self-employed persons, the pension is the insured's total pension points multiplied by the estimated average insured earnings of all insured persons in the calendar year preceding retirement multiplied by 2%.

The number of pension points earned each year equals the insured's average earnings divided by the year's average insured earnings of all insured persons. Pension points are credited for periods when other benefits are received.

For civil servants, and police and military personnel, a percentage of the last insurable earnings is paid depending on the period during which the employee began working for

For additional analytical, business and investment opportunities information,
please contact Global Investment & Business Center, USA
at (703) 370-8082. Fax: (703) 370-8083. E-mail: ibpusa3@gmail.com
Global Business and Investment Info Databank - www.ibpus.com

the National Revolutionary Movement: from 80% to 100% for persons who began working before 1954; from 75% to 90% for persons who began working from 1955 to 1974; and from 70% to 80% for persons who began working after 1975.

Benefit adjustment: Benefits are adjusted at least once a year according to changes in the average insured earnings of all insured persons.

Old-age lump-sum benefit: A lump sum of 1.5 times the insured's average monthly insured earnings in the last six months multiplied by the number of years of contributions is paid.

PERMANENT DISABILITY BENEFITS

Disability pension: 90% of the insured's average monthly insured earnings in the last six months multiplied by the assessed degree of disability is paid.

The disability pension is reduced to 25% if the pensioner is employed.

Disability lump-sum benefit: 10 times the insured's average monthly insured earnings in the last six months multiplied by the assessed degree of disability is paid.

Caregiver's benefit: 70% of the insured's disability pension is paid.

Benefit adjustment: Benefits are adjusted at least once a year according to changes in the average insured earnings of all insured persons.

SURVIVOR BENEFITS

Spouse's pension: 30% of the deceased's last monthly insured earnings, or the old-age or disability pension the deceased received or was entitled to receive is paid.

Orphan's pension: 20% of the deceased's last monthly insured earnings, or the old-age or disability pension the deceased received or was entitled to receive is paid.

The maximum orphan's pension is 60% of the deceased's last monthly insured earnings, or the old-age or disability pension the deceased received or was entitled to receive.

Parent's pension: 30% of the deceased's last monthly insured earnings, or the old-age or disability pension the deceased received or was entitled to receive is paid.

The maximum combined parents' pensions is 50% of the deceased's last monthly insured earnings, or the old-age or disability pension the deceased received or was entitled to receive.

The maximum total of all survivor pensions is 80% of the deceased's last monthly insured earnings, or the old-age or disability pension the deceased received or was entitled to receive.

Survivor lump-sum benefit: A lump sum is paid based on the length of the deceased's contribution period: for the first three to 12 months of contributions, five times the deceased's average monthly insured earnings is paid; for every one to two years of contributions beyond the first year, an additional month of the deceased's average monthly insured earnings is paid.

ADMINISTRATIVE ORGANIZATION

Ministry of Labor and Social Welfare (http://www.molsw.gov.la/) supervises the program.

The National Social Security Fund collects contributions and administers the payment of benefits.

SICKNESS AND MATERNITY

REGULATORY FRAMEWORK

First law: 1999 (employees in enterprises), implemented in 2001.

Current law: 2013 (social security), implemented in 2014.

Type of program: Social insurance system.

COVERAGE

Employees of private-sector and state-owned enterprises, civil servants, and police and military personnel.

Voluntary coverage for self-employed persons.

SOURCE OF FUNDS

Insured person

Cash sickness and maternity benefits: 1.25% of gross monthly insurable earnings.

Medical benefits (health insurance): 0.75% of gross monthly insurable earnings.

The minimum monthly earnings used to calculate contributions are the minimum wage.

The legal monthly minimum wage is 900,000 kip.

The maximum monthly earnings used to calculate contributions are 4,500,000 kip.

Self-employed person

For additional analytical, business and investment opportunities information,
please contact Global Investment & Business Center, USA
at (703) 370-8082. Fax: (703) 370-8083. E-mail: ibpusa3@gmail.com
Global Business and Investment Info Databank - www.ibpus.com

Cash sickness and maternity benefits: 2.5% of gross monthly insurable earnings.

Medical benefits (health insurance): 1.5% of gross monthly insurable earnings.

The minimum monthly earnings used to calculate contributions are the minimum wage.

The legal monthly minimum wage is 900,000 kip.

The maximum monthly earnings used to calculate contributions are 4,500,000 kip.

Employer

Cash sickness and maternity benefits: 1.25% of gross monthly insurable earnings.

Medical benefits (health insurance): 0.75% of gross monthly insurable earnings.

The minimum monthly earnings used to calculate contributions are the minimum wage.

The legal monthly minimum wage is 900,000 kip.

The maximum monthly earnings used to calculate contributions are 4,500,000 kip.

Government:

Cash sickness and maternity benefits: 2.5% of gross monthly insurable earnings.

Medical benefits (health insurance): 1.5% of gross monthly insurable earnings.

QUALIFYING CONDITIONS

Sickness benefit: Must have at least three months of contributions in the last six months, provide a hospital-issued medical certificate, and be registered with that hospital.

Maternity benefit: Paid to an insured woman who stops working because of pregnancy, childbirth, or a miscarriage. Must have at least six months of contributions in the last 12 months before the expected date of childbirth or the date of miscarriage.

Birth grant: Paid to an insured woman or the wife of an insured man for a pregnancy, childbirth, or miscarriage. The insured must have at least six months of contributions in the last 12 months before the expected date of childbirth or the date of miscarriage.

Funeral benefit: Must have at least three months of contributions.

Medical benefits: Must have at least three months of contributions.

SICKNESS AND MATERNITY BENEFITS

Sickness benefit: 70% of the insured's average monthly insured earnings in the last six months is paid for up to six months; 60% if extended for six months. If the insured is still unable to work after the additional six months, the insured will be assessed for permanent disability.

Maternity benefit: 80% of the insured's average monthly insured earnings in the six months before the insured stops working is paid for 105 days (120 days for twins).

Birth grant: A lump sum of 60% of the insured's average monthly insured earnings in the six months before childbirth.

Funeral grant: A lump sum is paid based on the insured person's average monthly insured earnings in the last six months: 12 times the average monthly insured earnings for the death of the insured person; six times for the death of a spouse; or three times for the death of the insured's child.

WORKERS' MEDICAL BENEFITS

Benefits include medical, preventative, and maternity care and rehabilitation.

Hospitalization is limited to six months for each admission; for longer periods, the insured has a copayment.

DEPENDENTS' MEDICAL BENEFITS

Medical benefits for dependents are the same as those for the insured.

ADMINISTRATIVE ORGANIZATION

Ministry of Labor and Social Welfare (http://www.molsw.gov.la/) supervises the program.

National Social Security Fund collects contributions, administers cash benefit payments, and contracts with hospitals to provide medical benefits.

WORK INJURY

REGULATORY FRAMEWORK

First law: 1999 (employees in enterprises), implemented in 2001.

Current law: 2013 (social security), implemented in 2014.

Type of program: Social insurance system.

COVERAGE

Employees of private-sector and state-owned enterprises, civil servants, and police and military personnel.

Exclusions: Self-employed persons.

SOURCE OF FUNDS

Insured person: None.

Self-employed person: Not applicable

Employer: 0.5% of gross monthly insurable earnings.

The minimum monthly earnings used to calculate contributions are the minimum wage.

The legal monthly minimum wage is 900,000 kip.

The maximum monthly earnings used to calculate contributions are 4,500,000 kip.

Government: 0.5% of gross monthly insurable earnings.

QUALIFYING CONDITIONS

Work injury benefits: Must have at least one month of contributions.

Disability pension: Must have at least one month of contributions and an assessed degree of disability of at least 41%.

Disability lump-sum benefit: Must have at least one month of contributions and an assessed degree of disability of less than 41%.

The National Social Security Fund's Medical Committee assesses the disability.

Caregiver's benefit: Paid for an assessed degree of disability of at least 80%.

Medical benefits: Must have at least one month of contributions.

TEMPORARY DISABILITY BENEFITS

70% of the insured's average monthly insured earnings in the last six months is paid for up to six months; 60% if extended for another six months. If the insured is still unable to work after the additional six months, the insured will be assessed for permanent disability.

PERMANENT DISABILITY BENEFITS

Permanent disability benefit: The monthly benefit is the percentage of assessed permanent loss of earning capacity multiplied by the insured's average earnings in the last six months before the disability began.

The disability pension is reduced by 50% if the pensioner is employed.

The Social Security Organization's Medical Board assesses the insured's loss of earning capacity initially and reassesses it every three years.

Disability lump-sum benefit: A lump sum of 12 times the insured's average monthly insured earnings in the last six months before the disability began multiplied by the insured's assessed loss of earning capacity is paid.

Caregiver's benefit: 70% of the insured's disability pension is paid.

Benefit adjustment: Benefits are adjusted at least once a year according to changes in the average insured earnings of all insured persons.

WORKERS' MEDICAL BENEFITS

Benefits include medical, preventative, and maternity care and rehabilitation.

Hospitalization is limited to six months for each admission; for longer periods, the insured has a copayment.

SURVIVOR BENEFITS

See survivors' benefits under Old Age, Disability and Survivors.

ADMINISTRATIVE ORGANIZATION

Ministry of Labor and Social Welfare supervises the program.

The National Social Security Fund collects contributions and administers the payment of benefits.

UNEMPLOYMENT

REGULATORY FRAMEWORK

First law and current law: 2013 (social security), implemented in 2014.

Type of program: Social insurance system.

COVERAGE

For additional analytical, business and investment opportunities information,
please contact Global Investment & Business Center, USA
at (703) 370-8082. Fax: (703) 370-8083. E-mail: ibpusa3@gmail.com
Global Business and Investment Info Databank - www.ibpus.com

Employees of private-sector and state-owned enterprises, civil servants, and police and military personnel.

Exclusions: Self-employed persons.

SOURCE OF FUNDS

Insured person: 1% of gross monthly insurable earnings.

The minimum monthly earnings used to calculate contributions are the minimum wage.

The legal monthly minimum wage is 900,000 kip.

The maximum monthly earnings used to calculate contributions are 4,500,000 kip.

Self-employed person: Not applicable.

Employer: 1% of gross monthly insurable earnings.

The minimum monthly earnings used to calculate contributions are the minimum wage.

The legal monthly minimum wage is 900,000 kip.

The maximum monthly earnings used to calculate contributions are 4,500,000 kip.

Government: None.

QUALIFYING CONDITIONS

Unemployment benefit: Must have at least 12 months of contributions in the last 24 months, be involuntarily unemployed, and be registered as unemployed for at least 30 days.

Vocational training: Must be unemployed and in need of vocational training.

UNEMPLOYMENT BENEFITS

60% of the insured's average monthly insured earnings in the last six months before unemployment is paid for up to three months with less than three years of contributions; six months with three to five years of contributions; nine months with six to 11 years of contributions; or 12 months with at least 12 years of contributions.

The benefit is terminated if the unemployed person refuses to accept a job offer.

ADMINISTRATIVE ORGANIZATION

For additional analytical, business and investment opportunities information,
please contact Global Investment & Business Center, USA
at (703) 370-8082. Fax: (703) 370-8083. E-mail: ibpusa3@gmail.com
Global Business and Investment Info Databank - www.ibpus.com

Ministry of Labor and Social Welfare (http://www.molsw.gov.la/) supervises the program.

The National Social Security Fund collects contributions and administers the payment of benefits.

IMPORTANT LAWS AND REGULATIONS AFFECTING SOCIAL SECURITY AND LABOR PROTECTION

LAW ON SOCIAL SECURITY

PART I GENERAL PROVISIONS

Article 1. Purpose

The Law on social security defines the principles, rules and provisions for the organisation, implementation, management, monitoring and inspection of social security affairs with a view to make it systematic, strenthened and effective for better protecting rights and interests of employers and employees who contribute to the Social Security Fund, and receive social security benefits, as well as to assure livelihood improvement, social solidarity and national socio-economic development.

Article 2. Social Security

Social Security is a set of assistance-based arrangements guaranteed by the National Social Security Fund in case of health care, child-birth or abortion, working capacity losses, human organ losses, sick-leave, old age, death, family allowances and unemployment.

Article 3. Interpretation of terms

1. National Social Security Fund: means the pooled funds provided by the Lao Government, and employers and employees to jointly finance various social security benefits;

2. Employer: means organizations of State and Party, incluyding the Lao Front for National Reconstruction, the mass organizations, social organizations and labor units employing people as employees by paying them a wage or salary;

3. Labor Units: means an establishment running a business, including manufacturing and/or services;

4. Employee: means a state employee, civil servant, soldier, police officer, old-age and invalid pensioner , or employee working in a labor unit and being paid by his/her employer ;

5. Self-employed : means a person, who engages in agricultural, industrial and service sector

Without having an employer;

6. Voluntary insured person : means a person, who voluntarily joins the social security fund ;

7. Insured Person: means a person, who pays contributions to National Social Security Fund ;

8. Family members: means depending spouse, child and\or parent of insured person;

9. Insurable Earnings: means total salary of insured civil servant, soldier, police or the wage of an employee or self-employed person to be used as basis for monthly calculating contribution to National Social Security Fund

10. Total salary: means firsly salary or wage, which is based on class and step and also includes senority and position allowance and anothers

11. Contribution: means monthly cash payment by the Government, employer, employee, self-employed and voluntary insured person to the Social Security Fund, according to the contribution rate, as detemined for the respective party.

12. Working capacity loss: means loss of working capacity or mental health, caused by any work accident or occupational diseases ;

13. Human-organ loss: means loss of any human body limb (not work-related) ;

14. Pension points: gained by dividing the average monthly cotribution in the last twelve months by the average contribution of all insured persons ;

Article 4. State Policy on Social Security

State promotes social security affairs' development in line with national economic growth. To do so the government, employer, employee, self-employed person as well as Voluntary insured person shall contribute largely contribute to the National social security Fund in order to make social security benefits affordable. The National Sicial Security Fund is managed by state and all social security benefits are excempted from tax

Article 5. Basic Principles concerning Social security Affairs.

Social security affairs shall be based on the following principles :

1. Social Security Policy and affairs shall be legally, centrally and nationwide managed ;

2. Contribution to National Social Security Fund from the Government, employer, employee, self-employed person as well as Voluntary insured person shall be prceeded accordingly to the defined rates as stipulated in the article 55 and 56 of this Law ;

3. Rights and interests of insured person and dependents shall be protected.

4. Social security management shall be fair, transparent, accountable and sustainable.

5. Principle of fund acculmulation, risk pooling, mutually assistance and sustainability ;

6. Benefit calculation shall be based on insurable earning ;

7. Security affairs shall be approprate with international conventions or treaties, where Lao PDR is signatory contry.

Article 6. Obligations to Social Security.

Obligations to Social Security Affairs are as follws :

1. Goverment shall allocate some parts of the Goverment Budget to the National Social Security Fund and guatees the sustainability of the fund ;

2. Employer shall contribute to the National Social Security Fund;

3. Employee, self-employed person and voluntary insured person shall be registeredand pay contribution to the National Social Security Fund ;

Article 7. Scope of Application.

This Law shall apply countrywide to employer, employee and his/her family members, self-employed person and voluntary insured person.

Article 8. International cooperation

State supports and promotes foreign, regional and international cooperation corncerning social security affairs in varied forms such as : upgrading expertise level of staff, sharing experiences, information, technique-technology as well as seeking for financial support in order to develop social security affairs and apply all international conventions and laws that Lao PDR is signatory country.

PART II SOCIAL SECURITY REGIME

Charpter 1 Types and Target groups of benefits

Article 9. Types of benefits

Types of social security benefits comprise the following:

1. Health care benefit ;

2. Benefit for child birth and abortion ;

3. Employment Injury and occupational diseases and not work-realted benefit benefit ;

4. Sickness benefit ;

5. Benefit for Loss of Working capacity ;

6. Old-age pension ;

7. Death grant benefit ;

8. Benefit for family members of insured person ;

9. Unemployment benefit.

Article 10. Target groups for Social Security Benefits

Target groups for different types of social security benefits are :

1. Civil servant, State employee, soldier, police shall be entitled to all types of benefit, except child birth and abortion benefit for male insured person ;

2. self-employed person and voluntary insured person shall be entitled to social security types of benefit, that they have insured such as : health care, child birth and abortion, old-age pension, sickness, death or invalidity benefit ;

3. spouse, dependent children of insured person shall be entitled to health care, death grant and/or family members' benefits ;

4. deceased insured person's parent shall be entitled to survivors' benefits, when meeting the qualifying conditions.

The group 1 and 2 as above-mentioned shall contribute monthly to the National Social Security Fund for being qualified to any benifit.

Chapter 2 Health Care Benefit

Article 11. Health care benefit

Health care benefit is fund allocation for medical service, provided to insured person, his or her spouse and dependent children.

Article 12. Qualifying conditions to health care benefit

For additional analytical, business and investment opportunities information,
please contact Global Investment & Business Center, USA
at (703) 370-8082. Fax: (703) 370-8083. E-mail: ibpusa3@gmail.com
Global Business and Investment Info Databank - www.ibpus.com

An insured person is entitled to medical services benefit if he or she meets the following conditions :

    1. Having paid contributions to the social security fund for at least one month for and longer for Employment Injury and occupational diseases; and illness, caused by child birth or abortion ;

    2. Having paid contributions to the social security fund for at least three months and longer for not work-related diseases. *Insured person's children younger than 18 years old, or not older than 23 years for those* studying and unmarried also are qulified to the benefit. In case of the death of insured person, his/her surviving spouse and children also are entitled to this benefit for three months ;

Article 13. Medical Services

An insured person and his/her dependents are entitled to medical services at the institutions pescribed systematically by the Curative Law.

Overseas Medical services and treatment for chronicle diseases shall be prescribed in a specific regulation.

Article 14. Health care expenditure calculation

Health care expenditure shall be calculated appropriately with the serious level of sickness and service quality and it shall be prescribed in a specific regulation.

Article 15. Health care payment

Health care fund shall bill for medical services, provided to insured person and his/her spouse and children in the form of capitation fee, fee for service or another forms through medical care contract with health care provider.

Charpter 3 Child birth and abortion Benefit

Article 16. Child birth or abortion Benefit

Child birth and abortion Benefit is a lumpsum bonus,, paid per each child.The beneficiary, whose health condition is still not fit for working, has the right to another benefits as prescribed in a specific regulation.

Article 17. Qualifying conditions to Child birtyh or abortion.

Qualifying conditions for Child birtyh or abortion benefit consists of the followings :

    1. At least six months of contributions, paid to the social security fund

2. Delivery of a child or abortion from the thirth month of pregnancy with medical certification ;

Article 18. Child birth grant calculation

The receivable child birth grant is equal to sixty percent of the the insured person's last insurable earnings per child.

Insured person's wife, who has no any job, has also right to the benefit as stipulated in the first paragraph of this article.

Self-employed person and voluntary insured person, who insured her/him-self for such a benefit shall be entitled with a specific regulation.

Article 19. Delivery of a child or abortion benefit calculation

The receivable maternity benefit, including abortion, is equal to eighty percent of the average of the insured person's last six mont insurable earning and is effective for a period of three months only. If, in excess of the above-mentioned period, the insured person' health status does not fit to resume to work with medical certification, health examination shall be proceeded for sickness benefit or invalidity benefit.

Chapter 4 Employment Injury and Occupational Disease Benefit and non-work related cases

Article 20. Employment Injury and Occupational Disease or non-work related case

Employment Injury or Occupational Disease benefit or not work-related case is composed of temporary loss of worrking capacity, that may be one-time benefit or monthly allowance ;

Article 21. Qualifying conditions

Qualifying conditions for employment Injury or Occupational Diseses or not work-related case benefit shall refer to the followings :

1. At least one month contribution to social security fund for employment Injury or Occupational Diseses, and at least twelve months for not work-related cases ;

2. Loss of any body's limb or working capacity, abnormal mental state caused by Employment injury at the work place, during the comute from home to work place and vice versa or during official mission ;

3. Occupational Disease, caused by task performance ;

4. Any body limb losses, caused by employment Injury or Occupational Diseses or not work-related cases. Medical certification shall be provided for proving the 2nd , 3rd and 4th conditions.

Conditions for those, who have joined directly the movement for National Defense shall be defined in a separate regulation.

Article 22. Category and degree of working capacity loss

Category and degree of working capacity loss are classified as below-listed :

1. Category 1 is equal to 81-100 % ;

2. Category 2 is equal to 71-80 % ;

3. Category 3 is equal to 61-70 % ;

4. Category 4 is equal to 51-60 % ;

5. Category 5 is equal to 41-50 % ;

6. Category 6 is equal to 31-40 % ;

7. Category 7 is equal to 21-30 % ;

8. Category 8 is equal to 01-20 % ;

Category 1 to 5 shall be entitled to invalidity monthly allowance ; while category 6 to 8 shall receive a lump sum payment. The details of classification shall be be prescribed in a specific regulation by Medical Committee.

Article 23. Temporary loss of working capacity benefit calculation

An insured person sustaining an employment Injury and occupational disease and being on sick leave shall receive a review of health care status, if qualified, to receive temporary loss of working capacity benefit when he or she has not fully recovered. Such a benefit is equal to seventy percent of the average insuarable earning in the last six months with a muximum length of six months.

In case of not-work related accident the benefit shall reduced to sixty percent of the average insurable earning in the last six month with a muximum length of three months.

Article 24. One-time payment benefit calculation for temporary loss of working Capacity

One-time payment benefit for temporary loss of working capacity, caused by employment Injury or occupational disease from category 6 to 8 shall be calculated by the following steps :

1. Calculation of the average insurable earning in the last six months prior to the accident's occurrence ;

2. Mutiplying the average insurable earnings by 12, called total 12 months' average insurable earnings;

3. Lastly multiplying the total 12 months' average insurable earning by the percentage of working capacity loss.

For victims other than employment Injury and occupational disease, benefit shall be one-time payment, which is calculated by multiplying invalidity degree by ten times of his/her average insuarable earning in the last six months.

Article 25. Calculation of Monthly allowance benefit for temporary loss of working Capacity

Monthly allowance benefit for temporary loss of working capacity from category 1 to 5 shall be calculated by multiplying percentage of working capacity loss by the average insurable earning in the last six month and if the beficiary is still working or rtired, he/she entitled to 50% of his/her invalidity allowance.

In case of not work-related victim, his/her invalidity allowance shall be calculated by multiplying percentage of working capacity loss by 90% of his/her average insurable earning in the last six month and if the beficiary is still working or rtired, he/she entitled to 25% of his/her invalidity allowance.

Article 26. Prosthetic limbs

Prostetic limbs shall be provided to any victim, resulted or not from an employment injury and/or occupational disease, who face difficulty in physically movement.

Article 27. Caretaker Benefit

Care taker of the category 1 victime shall be entitled to receive monthly allowance , which is equal to 70% of of the concerned invalidity allowance for life-long period of the invalid person.

Charpter 5 Sick leave Benefit

Article 28. Sick leave benefit

Sickleave benefit is an income replacement, paid to insured person being on leave because of employment or not-related Injury and occupational disease ; giving bith or abortion, whose salary is temporily suspened.

Article 29. Qualifying conditions

For additional analytical, business and investment opportunities information,
please contact Global Investment & Business Center, USA
at (703) 370-8082. Fax: (703) 370-8083. E-mail: ibpusa3@gmail.com
Global Business and Investment Info Databank - www.ibpus.com

Any insured person shall be entitled to paid sicklaeve benefit if he/she:

> 1. Has paid contributions to social security fund for at least three months.

> 2. Is deprived from his/her salary

> 3. Is proved by medical certification

Article 30. Calculation of sickness benefit

Sick Insured person, having medical treatment and rehabilitation shall receive monthly sickness benefit equal to seventy percent of his/her average of last six month insurable earning for a period of six months at first.

Sickness benefit shall be extended for a second period of six months, with the amount [of benefit] reduced to sixty percent of the insurable earning, provided that health care examination has been undergone with medical certification.

Finally, the beneficiary will be be entitled to invalidity benefits if his/her health care status is not expected to improve.

Chapter 6 Old-age Pension Benefits

Article 31. Old-age pension benefit

Old-age pension benefit is a monthly allowance paid to an eligible insured person who meets the required conditions.

Article 32. Qualifying Conditions for Old-age pension benefit

Any insured person shall be entitled to old-age benefit when :

> 1. Having reached 60 years old for male and 55 years old for female and 25 working years ;

> 2. For those, who have joined the National Revolution Movement before the year 1975, invalidity category 1 to 4 and those, who have worked continously 5 years and more in the hazardous conditions with 55 years of age for male and 50 years for female and at least 20 working years ;

> 3. Having paid social security contributions for a full 20 or 25 years and more for civil servant; state employee, soldier and police. Any insured person, having paid social security contributions in full for 25 years or longer, has poor health status and miss 1 to 3 years of age to reach retirement age, shall be also entitled to old-age pension. The pension percentage of the latter shall be deducted respectively one percent per one missing year for retirement age.

4. Having paid social security contributions for a full 15 years and more for enterprise's employee, self-employeperson and voluntary insured person ;

5. Having retirement permission certification, issued by organisation concerned.

Article 33. Percentage of Old-age pension benefit

Percentage of Old-age pension benefit shall be classified by the followings :

1. For Civil servant, state employee, military and police percentage shall be based on the below three phases :

· Those, who joined the Nation Revolution Movement since the year of 1954 backwards shall receive their Pension Percentage starting from 80to 100 percent percent ;

· Those, who joined the National Revolution Movement since 1955 to 1974 shall receive pension percentage from 75 to 90 % ;

· Those, who joined the National Revolution Movement since 1975 forwards shall receive pension percentage from 70 to 80 % ;

2. The three above-mentioned phases shall not be applied to the current pensioners but for potential old age pension benefiary. Old age penson of employee at labor unit, self-employed and voluntary insured person shall becalculated by multiplying pension points by total average insurable earning and shall be stipulated in a specific regulation.

Article 34. Old-age percentatge and pension allowance Calculation

Old-age pension percentage Calculation shall follow the below-listed steps :

1. for Civil servant, state employee, military and police ; calculation shall be made by comparing working years, as stipulated in the article 32 of this Law, with the appropriate percentage rate, as provided in the article 33 of this Law as first step ; apart of this each one additional working year shall earn one more additional pension percent.

Pension allowance shall be calculated by multiplying obtained penson percentage by last Insurable earning of the Insured concerned ;

2. for enterprise's employee, self-employed person and voluntary insured person, calculation shall be made by multiplying the pension points by the total average insurable earnings, as stipulated in a specific regulation.

Article 35. Pension allowance adjustment

For additional analytical, business and investment opportunities information, please contact Global Investment & Business Center, USA at (703) 370-8082. Fax: (703) 370-8083. E-mail: ibpusa3@gmail.com Global Business and Investment Info Databank - www.ibpus.com

The Goverment shall proceed the Pension allowance adjustment of Civil servant, state employee, military and police when salarly index and pension percentage policy have been changed. Pension allowance adjustment rule for enterprise's employee, self-employed person and voluntary insured person shall be provided in a specific regulation.

Article 36. Lump sum payment calculation

Insured person, who has not reached the qualifying conditions for monthly old-age pension as prescribed in article 32 of this Law, shall be entitled to a lump sum payment, which is equal to 1.5 of his/her average insurable earning in the last six months multiplied by number of working years.

Charpter 7 Death Grant

Article 37. Death grant

Death grant is financial assistance for funeral grant of insured person and/or his/her dependents, including adaptation grant.

Article 38. Qualifying conditions

1. Death grant shall be payable once contribution has been paid to social security fund for at least 3 months.

2. Death certification

Article 39. Death grant calculation

Guideline for death grant calculation :

1. Funeral grant :

· For the death of insured person, pensioner, invalidity pensioner funeral grant shall be equal to 12 months of the their average of last 6 months insurable earning.

· For the death of spouse, funeral grant is equal to the average of last six month of insurable earning, multiplied by 6.

· For the death of depending children, who is not older than 18, funeral grant is equal to the the average of last six month of insurable earning multiplied by 3.

2. One-time payment for thefamily of an insured person, who deceased, is the average of the last six months of insurable earning, monthly old-age pension or working capacity loss pension multiplied by 15 working years at first, then the payment shall increase one year for two more additional working years.

Article 40. Eligible person to funeral grant

Funeral grant and adaptation allowance shall be paid to the deceased family member, that may be spouse or depending children person, who are officially assigned .

Chapter 9 Survivors' Benefits

Article 41.Survivors' benefits

Survivors' benefits are monthly allowance, paid to assist the deceased's dependents such as : spouse, children and parents.

Article 42. Qualifying conditions

Survivors' benefis shall be payable when the deceased insured person having paid contribution to social security fund for fully five years and more and eligible children, spouse and parents shall meet the folowing conditions :

1. Widow(er) benefit shall be payable to : A surviving husband who is disabled having reached 60 years of age and 55 years of age respectively for a surviving wife, provided they have no regular income; nor are re-married;

2. Offspring, step-children and adopted children of the deceased person, who have not reached 18 years old, are single and not working. Orphans with a handicap or mental illness and not being able to work shall be entitled to a life-long orphans' benefit.

3. Father and mother of the deceased, reaching respectively 60 and 55 years of age, not having any income, if their breadwinner was the deceased person.

4. For parents, whose all children deceased in the battle fild for national defense, no matter weather, their deceased childer were insured or not shall be entitled to life-long survivors' benefit.

Article 43. Calculation of benefits

The different types of monthly survivors' benefis shall be calculated as follows :

1. Monthly widow(er) benefit is equal to 30 percent of the last insurable earning, old-age or working capacity loss benefit of the deceased person.

2. Monthly orphans' allowance for each child is equal to 20 percent of the last insurable earning, old-age or working capacity loss benefit of the deceased person. Monthly orphans'

allowances shall not exceed 60 percent of the last insurable earning in total, regardless of the number of beneficiaries.

3. Monthly benefit for surviving parents is equal to 30 percent of the last insurable earning, old-age or working capacity loss benefit of the deceased person. If all parents are beneficiaries of any fund, their benefit shall not exceed 50% of the last month deceased person's insurable earning.

All types of survivors' benefis in total shall not exceed 80 percent of the last insurable earning, old-age or working capacity loss allowance of the deceased person.

Chapter 10 Unemployment benefit

Article 44. Unemployment benefit

Unemployment Benefit is an income replacement for those insured persons, who are not employed in any period.

Article 45. Qualifying conditions

An insured person shall be entitled to unemployment benefit if :

1. He/she has been laid off or the employer is bankrupt;

2. He/she has been registered as an unemployed person for at least 30 days The benefit shall not be payable for those, who have been laid of resulted from breaking work regulation or voluntarily resigned without acceptable excuse.

Article 46. Calculation of benefits

The calculation of unemployment benefit shall be based on followings :

1. 60 percents of the average of the last six months before being unemployed ;

2. Length of benefit payment :

- Three 3 months period, If the length of the insured period is between 12 and 36 months ;

- Six months period, If the length of the insured period is between 73 and 144 months ;

- 12 months period, If the length of the insured period is 145 months and more

Article 47. Vocational training

Beneficiaries of unemployment benefit, if necessary, shall be given guidance on training with coordination with training institutions.

Article 48. Job placement assistance

Beneficiaries of unemployment benefits shall be assisted to find a new job, through an appropriate information..

Article 49. Termination of unemployment benefit

Unemployment benefit shall end if :

1. The Unemployment period terminates ;

2. The benefiary has refused to take job vacancy, provided by social security establishment corncerned without reasonable argument.

3. The beneficiary has been recruited ;

4. The beneficiary is dead.

Chapter 11 Contribution aggregation and

Insurance period

Article 50. Aggregation of contribution

Insured person, who has paid irregularly contribution to social security fund because of turn-over, shall renew his/her social security membership for futher benefits entitlements.

Article 51. Aggregation of insured period

Any resigned insured person, when resuming to work and having paid contribution, shall be given insured period for futher benefits entitlements.

PART III SOCIAL SECURITY FUND AND MANAGEMENT

Chapter 1 The National Social Security Fund

Article 52. National Social Security Fund

National Social Security Fund is made up of: the Government contribution, employer, enterprise's employee, self-employed and voluntary insured person, to be used for the payment of social security benefits as stipulated in this Law.

National Social Security Fund, otherwise referred to as "NSSF", which is guaranteed by the state and exempted from taxes of various kinds for all social security benefits.

Article 53. Types of Sub Funds

The Social Security Fund consists of the the following sub-funds such as :

1. Health Care Benefit Fund;

2. Employment Injury and Occupational Disease Compensation Fund ;

3. Short term benefit Fund being payable forsickness, giving birth or abortion and death ;

4. Long term benefit being payable for Old-age and working capacity loss allowance and survivers benefis ;

5. Unemployment Benefit Fund.

Each sub-fund has some parts allocated for the National Social Security Fund's administration expenses, reserve and mutual assistance among sub-funds as stipulated in a specific regulation.

Article 54. Sources of income

The National Social Security Fund's sources of revenues include the following:

1. Budget allocated by the Government ;

2. Contributions from Civil servant, state employee, military and police ;

3. Contributions from employers or enterprises ;

4. Contributions from enterprise's employee,

5. Contribution from self-employed person and voluntary insured person ;

6. Bank's interest and proceeds from Government bonds.

The 1st , 2nd, 3rd and 4th sources of incomes are compulsory, while the 5th is voluntary.

Role and functions of Social Security Fund

Social Security Fund is managed by the Board of the Fund under supervision of the Minister of Labor and Social Welfares. The Social Security Fund is an self-financing organisation and exempted from taxes and other charges.

Article 55. Social Security contributions from Government and employer

Contribution rate from Government and employer shall be based on the followings:

1. Government shall monthly contribute 8.5% of the total salary of civil servant, state employee, military and police for their social security benefits payment.

Government shall pay some contribution rate for self-employed person as stipulated in a specific regulation;

2. Enterprise's Employer shall monthly contribute 6% of employee salary to social security fund for social security benefits ;

Article 56. Contributions from insured person

1. State employee, civil servant, soldier, police shall pay their premium contribution on the rate of 8 percent of their monthly total salary ;

2. Enterprise's Employee shall monthly pay 5.5 of his/her monthly insurable earning ;

3. Old-age and working capacity loss pensioner shall pay for health care expenditure as same rate as insured person;

4. self-employed person and voluntary insured person shall pay a contribution for each type of social security benefit as stipulated in a special regulation.

Article 57. Contribution rate adjustment

The Government shall adjust contribution rate as provided in tyhe article 55 and 56 of this Law gradually in order to make the National Social Security Fund sustainable.

Article 58. Social Security Fund's Expenditures

The National Social Security Fund's Expenditures are :

1. Expenditure for different types of social security Benefis as prescribed in the Part II of this Law.

2. Adjustment of benefits, particularly increase of health care expenses and another social security benefits. Fund's administrative costs are financed by the Fund's accomulucation as stipulated in a specific regulation.

Article 59. Fund accomulucation

The reserve of the National Social Security Fund shall be invested in various forms with a vlew to making it sustainable.

Chapter II The National Social Security Fund's Committee

Article 60. The National Social Security Fund's Committee

With a view to managing the NSSF with efficacity and efficiency, the Goverment shall appoint a National Social Security Fund's Committee, a non-standing state organisation, whose role and responsibilities are to manage the NSSF centrally and with accountability, transparency, fairness and sustainability.

Article 61. Composition of Social Security Fund's Committee

The committee is composed of the following sectors' representatives.

    1. Minister of Labor and Social Welfares, chair person ;

    2. Vice-minister of finance, vice-chair person ;

    3. Vice-minister of Public Health, vice-chair person ;

    4. Vice-president of Lao Federation of Trade-unions, vice-chair person ;

    5. Vice-president of Lao Chamber of Commerce and Industry, vice-chair person ;

    6. Director General of Department, Ministry of National Defense, member ;

    7. Director General of Social Social Welfare Department, Ministry of Public Security ;

    8. Director General of Social Security Department, Ministry of Labor and Social Welfares, member.

    9. Director General of Budget department, Ministry of finance, member ;

    10. Director General of Civil servant management, Ministry of Interior ;

    11. Director General of Curative department, Ministry of Public Health ;

    12. Director General of Personnel Department, Lao Women's Union ;

    13. Director General of Labor protection Department, Lao Federation of Trade-unions, member ;

    14. General Secretary of Lao Chamber of Commerce and Industry ;

    15. Representatives from different organization working on employer and employee's matters ;

    16. Director General of the National Social Security Fund, as the committee's secretary.

The Social Security Fund's Committee shall be selected by the Minister of Labor and Social Welfare to be appointed by the Prime Minister. Management team includes DG and DDGs, Divisons and branches at the provinces is responsible for routine works.

Roles and Functions of the management team shall be stipulated in a specific regulation.

Article 62. Rights and obligations of The National Social Security Fund's Committee

The National Social Security Fund's Committee shall perform the below-listed rights and obligations :

1. To consider and approve Internal regulation and action plan of the NSSF ;

2. To guide, support, follow up and inspect the performance of Management team ;

3. To consider and approve sources of NSSF's incomes ;

4. To allocate NSSF into different sub-funds for a rational expenditure in a certain period with approval from the Government ;

5. To consider and propose the adjustment of contribution rates as well as level of benefits to the social security management organization to further submit for Government approval ;

6. To consider setting up of a social security beneficiaries' database and for card issuance ;

7. To consider monthly, quarterly, half-yearly and annually social security benefit budget as well as administration expenses and submit to the upper social security management organisation for approval ;

8. To have relation and cooperation with foreign, regional and international organisation in the field of social security management ;

9. To report regularly on the National Social Security Fund management to the Social Security management organisation and to the Government ;

10. To perform other rights and obligation as prescribed by law and regulations or by order of higher authority.

Article 63. The National Social Security Fund's Committee Meetings

Ordinary meetings of the National Social Security Fund's Committee shall be held every quarter to consider and approve important issues regarding the NSSF.

Meetings may be held only when two thirds of the total number of committee members are present.

Resolutions of the National Social Security Fund's Committee Meeting shall be effective only when adopted by a majority vote. In case of a tied vote, the Chairperson shall be entitled to cast a deciding vote.

PART IV SOCIAL SECURITY CLAIM PROCEDURES

Chapter 1 Social security registration procedures

Article 64. Social security registration

Employer, employee and self-employed and voluntary insured person shall register with the National Social Security Fund in order to pay contributions according to this Law.

Article 65. Social security registration documents

Employer, employee and self-employed and voluntary insured person shall register with the following documents

      1. Individual information sheet on employee and self-employed person ;

      2. List of insured persons, provided by the concerned employer;

      3. Employment contract ;

      4. Business registration certicate.

Article 66 . Submission of documents for Social security registration and card issuance

Social security registration and card issuance shall be handled in the following process :

Employer shall submit all social security registration related documents to the National Social Security Fund within 30 days after the employment contract has been signed.

      1. Self-employed person and volyntary insured person shall sumit his/herself social security registration in due time ;

      2. The Natinal Social Security Fund shall consider social security registration and card issuance within 30 days after the date of receiving application documents.

Chapter 2 Claim consideration and approval

Article 67. Claim paper works

Documents required for claiming social security benefits are the following:

1. Social Security Member Card;

2. Medical certificate on illness, delivery or abortion, employment injury and/or occupational disease, working capacity loss, sickness, old age pension, death, survivors' benefits or unemployment benefit.

3. Application forms for each kind of social security benefit.

Article 68. Claim consideration

The National Social Security Fund's management team shall consider claims within 30 days after the date of receiving application documents.

PART V PROHIBITIONS

Article 69. Prohibitions for the staff of the Social Security Organisation

The following conduct is prohibited for the staff of the Security Organisation.

1. Unfair, prejudiced, illicit behavor to insured person ;

2. Abuse of position, power, duties and receiving brides for their own benefit ;

3. Falsification of document, disclosure of secret, deiberate delay of claims approvals or destruction of documents applying for social security benefits.

4. Poor quality, under-standard and illegal social security service and;

5. Any conduct violating social security legislations.

Article 70. Prohibitions for insured person and his/her family members

1. Reporting of false data;

2. Falsification of documents to be qualified to any social security benefit, giving bribe to social security staffs;

3. Discrediting social security or organisation staff by spreading propaganda of false information;

4. Protecting or assisting staff, employer or employee, who violate legal documents on social security affairs ;

5. Any other behaviors violating social security rules.

Article 71. Prohibitions for individuals and organizations

Individual persons and organizations are prohibited:

1. To create obstacles hampering social security mission of staffs;

2. To act as middle man for giving and receiving bribe for any social security's affairs

3. To announce and provide false data on social security's affairs;

4. To protect or assist civil servant, employee or insured person breaking social security legislations from punishment;

5. Any conduct violating social security legislation.

PART VI DISPUTE SETTLEMENT

Article 72. Dispute Settlement Forms

Disputes on social security shall follow one of the procedures described below:

1. Arbitration or mediation;

2. Administrative settlement;

3. Economic settement organisation;

4. Judgement by the Court of Justice ;

Article 73. Reconciliation or mediation

When a dispute on social security benefit occurs, the concerned parties may use conflict resolution, negociation, or mediation for a multual acceptable conclusion.

Article 74.Administrative settlement

When a dispute on social security benefit occurs, the concerned parties may apply to the social security management organisation for a settlement.

Article 75. Economic settlement

When a dispute on social security benefit occurs, the concerned parties may submit the case to the economic settlement organization to cope.

Article 76. Justice court's judgement

When a dispute on social security occurs any of parties concerned can submit the case to the People's court of justice in accordance with Law and regulations.

Any international conflict on social security affairs shall comply with international conventions or treaties, where Lao PDR is a signatory country.

PART VII SOCIAL SECURITY AFFAIRS' MANAGEMENT AND INSPECTION

Chapter 1 Social Security Affairs' Management

Article 77. Social Security Affairs' Management Organisation

Social Security Affairs shall be managed centrally and countrywide by the Government, who mandates the Ministry of Labor and Social Welfare to act as the responsible agency to coordinate with the relevant line ministries, other concerned local authorities.

The Social Security Affairs' Management Authority shall be established through a hierachical system within:

- The Ministry of Labor and Social Welfare ;

- The Provincial and Capital Department of Labor and Social Welfare ;

- The District and Municipal Bureau of Labor and Social Welfare ;

If necessary, a labor and social welfare unit could be established at the village level.

Article 78. Rights and obligations of Ministry of Labor and Social Welfare

In managing Social Security Affairs, the Ministry of Labor and Social Welfare shall perform the following duties and obligations:

> 1. To periodically undertake studies and research and to develop Social Security Affairs for approval by the government;

> 2. To translate social security policy and strategic plan into a work program, and details of projects and budgets to develop Social Security Affairs;

> 3. To disseminate widely and deeply the policy direction, strategic plan, Laws and regulations pertaining to Social Security Affairs to the public ;

> 4. To manage and monitor, inspect and evaluate the operational work of social security affairs ;

> 5. To make decision, order and recommendation on social security affairs;

6. To cooperate with the relevant parties and local authorities for the smooth operations of Social Security;

7. To consider grievances submitted by individuals, juridic person, and organisation regarding the performance of duties or decisions that violate Law and regulation on social security ;

8. To select candidate to be appointed as member of the NSSF's Committee by the Prime Minister ;

9. To collect statistics on social security target groups and monitor card issuance;

10. To improve its lower organisations along with capacity buildings in collaboration with provincial and municipality authority;

11. To encourage and mobilise nationwide all concerned parties both from private and public sector to participate in social security system ;

12. To set up a social security data base ;

13. To relate and cooperate with foreign countries and international organisations for mobilising financial and technical assistance ;

14. To regularly summarize and report on the result of the social security job performance result to the Government ;

15. To exercise the rights and perform other duties as provided in the Laws and regulations.

Article 79. Rights and obligations of Provincial Labor and Social Welfare Department

In managing Social Security Affairs, Provincial Labor and Social Welfare Office shall perform the following duties and obligations:

1. To translate social security strategic and development plan into a work program, and details of projects and budgets to implement Social Security Affairs;

2. To implement Social Security related Laws Decrees and regulations in its proper area ;

3. To conduct dissemination and public relations with a view to mobilising concerned parties to participate in the development of Social Security Affairs;

4. To collect and process data on target groups for each type of social security benefit;

5. To monitor, support, inspect and evaluate the operational work of social security affairs frequently;

6. To guide and follow up social security card use ;

7. To propose organisation reform to higher organisation as well as upgrading social security staffs ;

8. To have international relation and collaboration on the social security affairs as assigned by subordinating organisation ;

9. To regularly summarize and report on the result of the social security job performance result to the Ministry of Labor and Social Welfare and its own provincial authority ;

10. To exercise the rights and perform other duties as provided for by Laws and regulations.

Article 80. Rights and obligations of District and Municipal level Labor and Social Welfare office

In managing Social Security Affairs, District and Municipal level Labor and Social Welfare Department shall perform the following duties and obligations:

1. To elaborate work plan and project for social Security Affairs' performance for each period of time ;

2. To collect and process data on target groups to National Social Security Fund and for each type of social security benefit;

3. To guide and follow up social security card use ;

4. Encourage and mobilze all parties concerned to participate in the social security fund;

5. To regularly summarize and report on the result of the social security job performance result in its own district to the provincial labor and social welfare department and district authority ;

6. To exercise the rights and perform other duties as provided in the Laws and regulations.

Chapter 2 Social Security Affairs Inspection

Article 81. Inspection organisation of Social Security Affairs

Organisations mandated with the inspectionof social security matters are the following:

1. The internal inspection organisation is the same organisation as thesocial security activity management organisation as stated in the Article 77 of this Law ;

2. The external inspection organisations are :

· The National Assembly, referring to the Law on the inspection of the National Assembly ;

· The State Inspection Authority against corruption as prescribed in the Law on State Inspection ;

· The State Auditing Organisation as prescribed in the law on auditing ;

· The Lao Front for National Construction, mass organisations, and mass media,

3. The aim of external audit is to inspect task performance of social security organisation with a view to make it strengthened, transparent, fair and efficient ;

Article 82. Content of Inspection

An inspection of social security activity has the following content:

· The implementation of policy, strategic plan, action plan, compliances with Laws and regulations pertaining to social security activity;

· Planning on social security research projects;

· The work performance of Social Security staff and benefits issues;

· The income sources of the National Social Security Fund and expenditure plan for benefits , as well as Fund management expenses.

Additionally, inspection process shall comply with another provision as prescribed by another concerned Laws.

Article. 83. Forms of inspections

There are three forms of inspection as follows :

1. Regular inspection, which is scheduled activities with a specific time ;

2. Inspections with advance notice are inspections carried out when deemed necessary, by sending advance notice to the targeted office ;

3. Impromptu inspections are inspections carried out when deemed necessary in urgent cases without sending anadvance notice to the targeted office.

Article 84. Report on Inspection and correction measures

The inspection committee shall summarize and report on the result of inspection work, and propose measures to the responsible institution in cases of violation of the law.

The inspection committee shall be legally responsible for the findings reported, and to ensure the confidentiality of all social security documents examined.

Article 85. Rights and obligations of inspection target

Any target inspection shall have the following rights and obligations:

- To request from the inspecting committee examination the official documents authorizing the on-site inspection, as well as the identification card of inspecting officers;

- To express grievances on any inspection, which may beconsidered inappropriate according to inspection rules;

- To facilitate the inspection work of the inspecting committee by providing access to documents, data, and witnesses, and to provide clarifications regardingany matter raised by the committee.

- To exercise other rights and duties, authorised by law and regulations.

PART VIII AWARDS AND SANCTIONS

Article 86. Awards

Any juristic person prooving outstanding compliance with this Law will receive awards and other benefits in occordance with Law and regulations.

Article 87. Sanctions against violators

Any juristic person, whether an individual or organisation, violating this Law shall be subject to disciplinary measures such as re-education, sanctions, fines, and civil or criminal penalties in accordance with the seriousness of the violation.

Article 88. Re-education measures

Any juristic person, whether an individual or organisation, violating this Law shall, in minor cases and if the first occurrence, be warned and re-educated.

Article 89. Disciplinary sanction

Any civil servant or social security officer, who violates social security laws and regulations and causes damages that are not severe and cannot be constituted as a criminal offense, but witness failure to report in good faith, shall be subject to the followingdisciplinary measures in order to be cleared from the offense:

1. Receive a warning or censure for the offense,to be recorded in his/her personal file;

2. Suspension from his ranking of salary grade and step, and other rewards;

3. Removal from his/her position or transfer to another duty of lower position;

4. Lay off without entitlement toseverance pay allowance.Person, who is punished by Disciplinary measures, must return all gains obtained illegally to the concerned organisations .

Article 90. Fines

Any juristic person, whether an individual or organisation, violating this Law shall, in cases that cause damage but do notconstitute a criminal offense, be fined at the same amount thanthe damage caused. For second time or serial offenders, fines shall be twicethe amount of the damage caused and any property obtained through illegal means shall be confiscated.

Article 91. Civil measures

Any juristic person, whether an individual or an organisation who cause damage tosomeone's property by violating social security laws and regulations, shall compensate for all damage created.

Article 92. Penal Measures

Any juristic person, whether an individual or an organisation, who violate this Law and commit a penal offence, shall be punished as provided for in the Penal Law depending on the seriousness of the violation.

PART X FINAL PROVISIONS

Article 93. Implementation

The Government of the Lao People's Democratic Republic shall implement this law.

Article 94. Effectiveness

This law shall enter into force sixty days from the date of the promulgation of the relevant decree by the President of the Lao People's Democratic Republic.

President of the National Assembly

LABOUR LAW

CHAPTER 1 GENERAL PROVISIONS

Article 1. Objectives of the Labour Law

The objectives of the Labour Law are to regulate labour relationships, fully develop all labour skills for national socioeconomic development, upgrade the efficiency and productivity of labour in society, and improve the workers' living conditions.

Article 2. Principle of Mutual Benefit between Employers and Employees1

The State applies the principle of ensuring mutual benefit between employers and employees without discrimination on the basis of race, color, gender, religion and sociopolitical status. Employees must observe work rules and comply with labour regulations.

Employers must ensure fair salaries, safe labour conditions and social security. In this law "employees" refers to individuals working under the management of employers in order to receive compensation for their work in the form of salaries or wages, benefits and policies2 as provided in the labour law, regulations and contracts.

"Employers" refers to individuals or legal entities which use employees' labour and pay them salaries or wages, benefits and policies as provided in the labour law, regulations and contracts.

1 In Lao, this law uses a single root word for "work" and its related ideas "those who perform work" and "those who use others' work". The translators have translated that word according to context. For example, in the context of an employment relationship, the translators have used the words "employee" and "employment". Other variants include "work" and "labour". Readers should note that these English words are all translations of the same Lao root word.

2 "Policies" is often used as an indirect way of referring to "incentives" or "privileges".

Article 3. The Right to Establish and Participate in Mass and Social Organisations

Employees and employers have the right to establish and participate as members of any lawful mass organisation or social organisation.

Such mass organisations and social organisations have the right to determine rules, elect their representatives, [and] establish their administrative structures and operations by themselves, as well as the right to join with local labour federations or union.

Rules governing the establishment, roles and rules regarding activities of such organisations will be provided in separate regulations.

Article 4. Prohibition of Forced Labour

Employers are prohibited from using forced labour.

The use of forced labour refers to the use of labour whereby the worker

is made to perform, against his will, the work assigned which is inconsistent

with the employment contract.

The use of forced labour will not be considered as such in the following cases:

> The use of labour in accordance with the law or regulations relating to national defense obligations;

> The use of labour in emergencies, such as war, fire, natural disasters and epidemics;

> Any task to be performed in accordance with court decisions under the supervision of state officers, but such individual shall not be made to work for the private interests of any individual, legal entity or labour unit;

> Any task performed in accordance with decisions of the local administrations where he3 is located, [or] of organisations [or] associations of which he is a member, and such tasks constitute obligations of all citizens for the common benefit of the nation.

Only the State has the right to mobilise workers to work under the conditions stipulated above. Individuals, legal entities or labour units are prohibited from directly or indirectly using measures to use labour for private work or the work of a group of people.

The person being compelled to provide work.

Article 5. Scope of Application of Labour Law

This Labour Law applies to all workers and employers who carry out

activities in all socioeconomic sectors of the Lao PDR, hereinafter referred to

as "labour units".

This Labour Law shall not apply to civil servants employed in state administrative and technical services, national defense and public security.

CHAPTER 2 LABOUR MANAGEMENT RULES

Article 6. Employing Workers

For additional analytical, business and investment opportunities information,
please contact Global Investment & Business Center, USA
at (703) 370-8082. Fax: (703) 370-8083. E-mail: ibpusa3@gmail.com
Global Business and Investment Info Databank - www.ibpus.com

An employer has the right to employ workers to meet the needs of the labour unit that is under his management, but priority must be given to Lao citizens. The employment of workers must be done through the conclusion of a written employment contract between the employer and employee, on the basis of the principle of equality and mutual agreement, [and] without contradicting any laws and regulations issued by the State.

Article 7. Employment of Foreign Workers

Labour units in different economic sectors may employ foreign workers if deemed necessary where [workers] with the required specialised skills are not available in the Lao PDR. The employment of foreign workers to work in Laos shall be limited in number and in duration, and a detailed scheme shall be established for the transfer of skills to Lao workers to replace such foreign workers once the duration of their work in Laos has ended.

The bringing in of foreign workers to work in Laos on a shortterm or longterm basis shall be authorised by the labour management organisation prior to their entry into [Laos], except in cases where workers are brought in by foreign aid projects and various international organisations, to which special regulations shall apply.

The State shall not authorise foreign workers to be brought in to work

or engage in professions which are necessary to be reserved for Lao citizens.

The list of such professions shall be determined separately.

Article 8. Upgrading of Workers' Qualifications

All employers have the duty4 to train, [and] upgrade the qualifications and skills of Lao workers who are under their responsibility in order that they gradually become skilled workers and workers with specialised skills.

The literal term is "direct duty" which connotes that the duty is not delegable.

All labour units in different socioeconomic sectors shall establish a plan and set aside an annual dedicated budget to cover expenses for training [and] upgrading of qualifications, on shortterm, mediumterm and longterm bases both within the country and abroad, for their Lao workers.

Article 9. Economic, Technical and Social Management of Workers

Employers shall be directly responsible for the economic, technical and social management of the workers in any labour unit under their management.

An employer may assign all its managerial rights to a person. Such person must be responsible for such work5 on behalf of the employer.

Internal management of workers must be set out in internal work rules.

Article 10. Management of Workers by the State

The labour management organisation shall have the following duties:

To manage, monitor and inspect the correct use of labour;

To establish regulations relating to the management and use of labour;

To supervise and control the implementation of such regulations;

To train and develop skills;

To study and find work for those who need work.

The organisation and activities of the labour management organisation shall be stipulated in specific regulations.

Employers have the duty to implement all measures relating to the management of workers that are issued by the labour management organisation such as regulations relating to the employment of workers, the registration of workers, labour statistics and other measures.

Article 11. Role of Trade Unions and Workers' Representatives

A trade union should be established in all labour units in accordance

with specific regulations of the sectors6 concerned. Where there is no trade

union, workers' representatives7 shall be established.

Trade unions or workers' representatives have the [following] duties within their labour units[:] to promote solidarity, educate, train and sensitize

5 This "work" appears to be a reference to the responsibilities referred to in the first paragraph.

6 The word "sector" is used here to refer to the cluster of government ministries or agencies responsible for a particular area.

7 "Workers representatives" has the connotation of a committee or group of persons representing the workers rather than an individual.

workers to have labour discipline, and to successfully perform work in accordance with production plans established by the labour units; to request or demand that the employer implement the labour law and employment contract correctly; to participate in the settlement of labour disputes; to consult with the employer on issues relating to wages, working hours, rest hours, labour conditions, [and] the social security regime as prescribed by the laws.

All employers shall support trade unions or worker's representatives by providing them with at least one hour during a working day per month and appropriate premises to enable them to carry out their activities in accordance with their roles.

CHAPTER 3 EMPLOYMENT CONTRACTS AND TERMINATION OF EMPLOYMENT CONTRACTS

Article 12. Employment Contract

An employment contract is an agreement made between a worker and an employer or their representatives. An employment contract must be made in writing. Employers must comply with employmentrelated contractual obligations, and workers must fully perform their duties according to their specialization and experience. Employers must assign their workers to work or positions that are stipulated in the employment contract, pay them salaries or wages, and ensure they receive fair benefits and others8 in accordance with the laws and the employment contract agreed upon [by the parties].

Employment contracts must stipulate the work place, the work to be

performed, the level of wages and other policies which the worker should

receive. An employment contract is one way to employ a worker.

Article 13. Form and Duration of Employment Contracts

Apart from employment contracts which must be made in writing, in some cases an employment contract may be verbal, depending on the conditions and nature of the work, such as work on a daily basis and work of a small volume.

An employment contract may be made either for a fixed term or for an

indefinite period. The duration of a fixedterm employment contract shall

depend on the agreement between the employer and the worker concerned.

Here, "others" is a literal translation and is not subject to further specificity.

9

Article 14. Probation

An employer has the right to take on workers on a probationary basis in order to ascertain their ability to perform their duties.

The duration of the probationary period is based on the nature of the work, as follows:

In respect of work that does not require experience in a specialised skill, such as: work primarily involving manual labour, the duration of the probation shall not exceed thirty days;

In respect of work requiring specialised skills, the duration of the probation shall not exceed sixty days.

Where [,]during such probationary period a worker is absent from work for a certain period of time as a result of sickness or necessity, the duration of such absence shall not be counted as part of the probationary period. Where the worker continues to lack the skills for the work, the probationary period may be extended or the employer may not employ the worker. However, the extension shall not exceed thirty days.

During the probationary period, each party has the right to terminate the probation at any time, but must give the other party at least three days' advance notice for nonskilled work and five days' advance notice for skilled work. In such termination of probation, the worker has the right to receive salary or wages and other policies provided for under the laws, calculated from the beginning of the probation to the date when he stops work.

Seven days before the end of the probationary period, the employer shall inform the worker in writing whether or not his employment will be confirmed. Throughout the probationary period, the worker shall be paid a salary or wage of not less than ninety per cent of the salary or wage for such work.

Article 15. Termination of Employment Contract

An employment contract made for a fixed term or for an indefinite period may be terminated by agreement between both parties.

An employment contract made for an indefinite period may be terminated by either party, provided that the other party is given at least fortyfive days' notice in respect of skilled work and fifteen days for work that is primarily manual.

The parties to a fixedterm employment contract shall notify each other [whether they wish to terminate the contract] at least 15 days prior to the

The literal is "trial of competence of workers".

expiry of such contract. Where they wish to continue to work [together], they shall sign a new employment contract.

An employment contract that is based on the volume of work may be terminated only upon the completion of such work.

An employment contract shall be terminated on the death of the worker.

Article 16. Termination of Employment Contract by Dismissal

An employment contract may be terminated by dismissal where the worker lacks specialised skills, where the worker is not in good health and therefore cannot continue to work, or where the employer considers it necessary to reduce the number of workers in order to improve the work within the labour unit.

Where it is found that a worker lacks skills or is in poor health, the employer may decide that the worker should stop working and terminate the employment contract, provided that it gives to the worker at least fortyfive days' notice together with an explanation of the grounds for termination. During the period of notice, the employer must authorise the worker to look for new work during one working day per week, with payment of [the same] salary or wages as when he was working.

However, before deciding to terminate the employment contract, the employer shall consider the transfer [of the worker] to work that is appropriate to the worker's skills or health and the employment contract may be terminated only if no such work is available.

Where a labour unit considers that it is necessary to reduce the number of workers in order to improve internal work, the employer shall draw up a list of reduction of workers in consultation with the trade union or workers' representatives and report to the labour management organisation[;] at the same time, the employer shall give the dismissed persons at least fortyfive days' notice and an explanation as to the reasons for the reduction.

The termination of an employment contract on any of the abovementioned grounds must be accompanied by the payment of termination allowance to the workers dismissed according to their period of work. Such allowance shall be calculated based on the duration of work and shall be equal to ten percent of the monthly salary before the termination for each month of work. For workers who have worked for more than three years, the [basis for] calculation shall be fifteen percent.

For employees who are paid per unit of production or whose wages are not clearly fixed, the calculation of the termination allowance is based on the average salary or wage that the workers received during the three months immediately prior to termination.

Article 17. Limitation of Employer's Right to Terminate an Employment Contract

An employer does not have the right to terminate an employment contract or force an employee to stop work where the said employee is:

Sick and undergoing medical treatment or rehabilitation after medical treatment on the advice of a doctor, or facing disasters such as when his house has been destroyed by a fire;

A woman employee who is pregnant or who has given birth but the postnatal period is less than nine months10 ;

For additional analytical, business and investment opportunities information,
please contact Global Investment & Business Center, USA
at (703) 370-8082. Fax: (703) 370-8083. E-mail: ibpusa3@gmail.com
Global Business and Investment Info Databank - www.ibpus.com

On annual leave or on leave approved by the employer;

Still performing work in another workplace upon assignment of the employer;

Filing a complaint or claim against the employer or cooperating with government officials in relation to the implementation of the labour law, and [in relation] to labour disputes within his labour unit;

Carrying out activities for trade unions, workers' representatives or other social organisations upon approval of the employer or outside of working hours;

A worker who has been elected to the trade union or workers' representatives.

This article does not apply to employees who have committed an offense as stipulated in Article 19 of this Labour Law.

Article 18. Special Rights of Employees during the Notice Period

During the notice period, if the employee suffers from a labour accident or is sick and cannot perform the work, the period of treatment shall not be counted as part of the period of notice. During the notice period, the employee shall work and receive the normal wages or salary as he received before the notice was given.

Article 19. Termination of Employment Contract due to the Commission of a Fault by an Employee

An employer has the right to terminate an employment contract without

payment of a termination allowance but must give at least three days' notice,

where the employee has committed the following:

Behaved dishonestly in the performance of his duty or deliberately caused serious damage to the employer where there is sufficient evidence;

Violated labour regulations despite previous warnings from the employer;

Abandoned work for four consecutive days without a valid reason;

Been sentenced to imprisonment by the court.

In other words, a woman's employment my not be terminated during the nine months following delivery.

Article 20. Unlawful Termination of Employment Contract

For additional analytical, business and investment opportunities information,
please contact Global Investment & Business Center, USA
at (703) 370-8082. Fax: (703) 370-8083. E-mail: ibpusa3@gmail.com
Global Business and Investment Info Databank - www.ibpus.com

An employer must pay allowance to a dismissed worker or to an authorised person in the following cases:

The employer terminates the employment contract without a valid reason or directly or indirectly forces the worker to terminate the employment contract;

The employer acts in breach of its contractual obligations despite previous notices from the employee requesting it to change [its behaviour].

In addition to the right to receive termination allowance, the employee

has the right to claim compensation for damages from the employer if such

employee has [suffered from the] loss of legitimate interests.

An employee whose employment contract has been unlawfully

terminated has the right to request reinstatement to his former post or to be

assigned to other appropriate work.

The termination allowance to employees whose employment contracts have been terminated in the abovementioned circumstances shall be calculated based on the duration of work and shall be equal to 15 per cent of the monthly salary before termination for each month of work. For employees who have worked for more than three years, the [basis of] calculation shall be 20 per cent.

Article 21. Temporary Transfer of Employees

An employer may transfer an employee to perform another task in the same labour unit for a period not exceeding three months, if such transfer is effected as a result of a temporary cessation of activity, for disciplinary reasons, as a means of preventing possible damage to its activities, or as a means of preventing a natural disaster. Once the three month period has elapsed, the employer and employee must consider reinstating11 the employment contract.

During the period of temporary transfer, if the new task is a higher task and the employee is able to perform the task in accordance with the [required] standards, [the employee] shall receive the salary or wage payable for the new task. On the contrary, if the salary or wage payable for the new task is lower than that payable for the old task, the salary or wage for the old task must still

The connotation is of returning to old job.

be paid. When the employee is transferred back to his old task, the salary or wage for such task must be paid.

For additional analytical, business and investment opportunities information, please contact Global Investment & Business Center, USA at (703) 370-8082. Fax: (703) 370-8083. E-mail: ibpusa3@gmail.com Global Business and Investment Info Databank - www.ibpus.com

If an employee is transferred for disciplinary reasons to a new task

which lower than the old task, the salary or wage must be paid according to the new task.

In the case of a transfer of an employee to another task as mentioned above for whatever reasons or in whatever circumstances, the new task to be performed must not be different from or must be very similar to the previous task.

Article 22. Measures of the Employer Relating to the Termination of an Employment Contract

An employer has the right to terminate an employment contract but must give prior warning to the employee who has committed a fault. If there is no change, [the employer] can consider terminating the employment contract. However, before terminating all types of employment contract for any reason, the employer has the duty to report the reason to the competent labour management organisation at least five days prior to the termination of the employment contract.12

Unilateral termination of an employment contract or dismissal of an employee is prohibited without the [prior] approval of the labour management organisation or without prior notification to the trade union or the workers' representatives in the relevant labour unit.

If no reply has been received from the above bodies within fifteen days of the notification, the termination may be implemented.

The termination of employment contracts in all circumstances must be made in writing by the employer and must indicate clearly the reason for such termination, and must be accompanied by payment to the employee of the salary he was entitled to receive prior to the termination of the employment contract and other allowances according to regulations.

Article 23. Responsibilities of the New Employer

If an employee has terminated the employment contract by breaching

the employment contract and applies for a new job, the new employer must be

responsible for any damage resulting to the former employer if:

• There is evidence that the new employer was involved in the termination of the employment contract by the employee;

For readability, this paragraph (which was originally one sentence) has been broken up into several sentences.

The new employer employed the employee knowing that the employee was still bound by an employment contract with another employer;

Where the new employer finds out that an employee whom it has [just] employed had breached an employment contract with another employer, but such contract had expired at the time of employment, the new employer shall bear no responsibility.

Article 24. Issuance of Work Certificate to Employee upon Ceasing Work

An employer shall issue a work certificate to an employee who ceases work within seven days of the employee's cessation of work. Such certificate must indicate the starting date and date of cessation of work and the post he occupied.

The work certificate shall specify details of wages and any observation of the employee's performance if requested by the employee.

CHAPTER 4 HOURS OF WORK AND REST PERIODS

Article 25. Hours of Work

The hours of work of an employee in any labour unit shall be six days per week. Work should not exceed eight hours per day or fortyeight hours per week, irrespective of the type of salary or wages paid.

Hours of work must not exceed six hours per day or thirtysix hours per week in respect of employees whose occupations are in sectors that involve:

Direct exposure to radiation or to contagious disease;

Direct exposure to gas [or] smoke which is dangerous to health;

Direct exposure to dangerous chemicals, such as explosives;

Working in pits, or in underground tunnels, under water or in the air;

Working in an abnormally hot or cold place;

Working directly with constantly vibrating equipment.

Article 26. Time Counted as Hours of Work

The following types of time lost shall be calculated as part of daily hours worked:

Time spent on technical preparation at the start and end of work;

Hourly breaks not exceeding 15 minutes, in certain sectors in which work is divided into different periods for different tasks or which operate on the basis of shifts;

A 45minute meal break per shift in respect of shift workers.

The employer must establish an appropriate production schedule so as to enable workers to rest at least five to ten minutes after having worked for two hours. Should a necessity arise for any technical or mechanical reason, work by rotation must be organized so that workers can rest appropriately.

Time lost that is counted as daily hours of work should be specified in the internal rules of work of the labour unit.

Article 27. Overtime

An employer may request employees to work overtime if necessary,

subject to the prior consent of the trade union or worker's representatives and

of the employees.

Overtime shall not exceed thirty hours per month, except in the case of an emergency such as combating [the effects of] a natural disaster or an accident that would cause great damage to its labour unit. Each period of overtime shall not exceed three hours. It is prohibited to work overtime continuously every day.

When necessary, before the employer gets the employees to work overtime, the employer must, in each case, first consult the trade union or worker's representatives and notify the employees in the labour unit concerned explaining the necessity of overtime work, and shall fully pay them fair compensation for overtime as provided under Article 42 of this law.

Where overtime is necessary for more than thirty hours in any one month, [the employer] must first request authorisation from the labour management organisation which is responsible [for its labour unit] and approval from the trade union or workers' representatives in its labour unit.

Article 28. Weekly Rest and Public Holidays

Workers have the right to at least one day's rest within a week, which may be Sunday or any other day as agreed between the workers and the employer. Public holidays shall be determined by the government.

Article 29. Sick Leave

Upon presentation of a medical certificate, workers remunerated on a monthly basis shall be entitled to sick leave with full pay for not more than thirty days per year. This shall also apply to workers who work on a daily or hourly basis, on a per unit of production basis or on the basis of specific work contracts only if they have worked for more than ninety days.

Where the period of [sick] leave exceeds thirty days, workers shall receive compensation under the social security system.

The provisions13 of this article do not apply to labour accidents or occupational diseases, which are stipulated in Article 53 of this law.

Article 30. Annual Leave

Workers employed under an employment contract made for an indefinite period or for a period of more than one year who have worked for one full year shall be entitled to fifteen days of annual leave. Workers in sectors involving heavy work or work which is damaging to their health, as specified in article 25 of this Labour Law, shall be entitled to eighteen days of annual leave with full pay at the normal [rate] as when they were working.

Weekly rest days and public holidays shall not be counted in annual leave.

CHAPTER 5 RULES OF WORK

Article 31. Content of Rules of Work

Workers have the duty to implement the rules of work. The rules of work consist of the rights and duties of workers as specified under the laws, the internal rules of the labour unit and the employment contract signed between workers and their employers.

To be legally enforceable, the internal rules of a labour unit must be in

conformity with the Labour Law of the Lao PDR and must first be approved

by the labour management organisation.

The internal rules of a labour unit must be disseminated to all workers and posted openly so that everybody is informed.

Article 32. Measures Against Workers who have Breached the Rules of Work

Persons who have breached the rules of work and on whom warning has been served but who do not change in a positive way, may be transferred temporarily to work at another workplace or forced to resign, as provided in Articles 19 and 21 of this Labour Law. Where such persons intentionally cause damage to the property of a labour unit, they shall compensate for the damage.

The literal is "contents".

CHAPTER 6 EMPLOYMENT OF WOMEN AND CHILDREN

Article 33. Work Prohibited in Respect of Women Workers

An employer is prohibited from employing and authorising women workers to work in those sectors that involve heavy work and is dangerous to their health as stipulated in specific regulations and to work during the night in all industrial sectors from 10 p.m. to 5 a.m. of the next morning and the rest period shall be at least 11 hours before working on the next day.

Article 34. Prohibition of Employment of Women during Pregnancy and Childcare

An employer is prohibited from employing a woman during her pregnancy or during the first six months following the delivery to perform any of the following work:

Lifting or carrying heavy loads;

Work which entails standing continuously for long periods.

In such circumstances the employer shall assign the worker to other temporary work. While performing this temporary work, the worker shall continue to receive her normal salary or wage for a maximum period of three months. After the three months, she shall be paid the salary or wage according to her new assignment.

An employer is prohibited from employing a pregnant woman or woman with a child under twelve months of age to work overtime, or on a day of rest.

Article 35. Maternity Leave Before and After Birth Delivery

Before and after birth delivery, women workers shall be entitled to at least ninety days of maternity leave with their full pay at the normal [rate] as when they were working from their employers or from the social security fund, if contributions have been fully paid to this fund. The period of maternity leave before and after birth must not exceed ninety days, however, the leave after the delivery of birth must be at least fortytwo days.

In the event that as a result of birth delivery a woman worker is ill and this is certified by a doctor, such worker shall be authorised to take additional leave of at least thirty days with payment of fifty per cent of her salary or wage.

During the twelvemonth period after birth delivery, the worker has the

right to one hour per day of rest in order to feed or take care of her child if she brings her child to a nursery or to her workplace.

In the event that the woman worker suffers a miscarriage, she is entitled to a [period of] leave as determined by a doctor.

Article 36. Maternity Allowance

A woman worker shall, on birth delivery, be entitled to an allowance of at least sixty per cent of the minimum wage established by the government, to be paid by the employer or by the social security fund, if contributions to the social security fund have been fully paid. Where she gives birth to two or more children at the same time, [she] will receive an additional allowance [equal to] fifty per cent of the maternity allowance. In the case of a miscarriage which is certified by a doctor, [she] is also entitled to this allowance.14

Article 37. Employment of Children under 18 Years of Age

An employer may employ children who are at least fifteen years of age and less than eighteen years of age provided that they do not work for more than six hours per day and thirtysix hours per week. Children shall not be employed in sectors involving the performance of heavy work or work which is damaging to their health, as follows:

All types of mining;

Production activities that use chemicals, explosives or poisonous substances;

Work involving the handling of human corpses;

Work specified in Article 25 of this law;

Work at night in all industrial sectors from 10 p.m. to 5 a.m. of the next day, and the rest period shall be at least 11 hours before working on the next day.

Employment of children under fifteen years of age in all socioeconomic sectors is prohibited.

CHAPTER 7 SALARY OR WAGE

Article 38. Salary or Wage

A salary or wage is an income which has a monetary value which the employer must pay to the employee. Employees' salaries or wages may be paid at the beginning or at the end of the month, before or after the completion of the work.

The reference appears to be to normal maternity allowance although placement of the words in the original Lao is slightly ambiguous.

Article 39. Equal Right to Salary or Wage

Except for foreign employees who have separate employment contracts, all employees who provide equal quantity, quality, and value of work are entitled to receive equal salaries or wages without any discrimination as to gender, age, nationality or ethnicity.

Article 40. Determination of the Level of Salary or Wage

The employer has the right to determine the level of salary or wage of his employees, based on the following conditions:

The material and moral needs of life of the employees;

The cost of living and changes to it from time to time;

Social welfare and social security benefits for workers;

The evaluation of the level of skills and abilities of various groups in the society or the level of wage or salary paid in other labour units;

Salaries or wages must be consistent with the value of the work or task;

The salary or wage system must be in several forms15 and simple.

The workers, the trade unions or workers' representatives shall also have the right to negotiate with the employer in respect of their salary or wage levels.

The government or the relevant organisation16 shall establish minimum salaries or wages periodically and for each region, [and] employers do not have the right to determine minimum salaries or wages at a level lower than the level periodically established by the government for each region.

The periodic determination of the minimum level of salaries or wages of all labour units shall be subject to the government's supervision and control.

Article 41. Forms of Payment of Salaries or Wages

Where the government or the relevant authority has established the minimum salary or wage level, the employer shall pay salaries or wages to the employees based on time worked such as: hourly, daily, monthly or on the basis of a specific work contract17 . All payment of salaries or wages including allowances [and] bonuses shall be made on the basis of a pay list signed by the employees.

15 The connotation is "flexible".

16 The connotation is "governmental organisation".

17 The reference is to contracts that specify lumpsum payments for either a specific piece of work or a specified period.

All employees have the right to ask their employer for the method of

calculation of their salaries or wages where it is necessary for clarification and

ensuring conformity with the employment contract as agreed upon.

Where the government or relevant authority has not established the minimum salary or wage level for a specific region, or where the employer has authorised employees to bring certain work to be performed additionally outside the labour unit, such as at their home or elsewhere, wages may be paid based on output18 or as a lumpsum.

Salaries or wages of employees must be paid in cash and in full to each person directly and on a timely [basis], except where it is otherwise prescribed by government regulations or as specifically agreed between the employer and the employee.

In addition to salaries or wages, the employer may pay bonuses, allowances or additional benefits as an incentive to the workers.

Payment to employees in the form of narcotics, intoxicating

[substances] or substances dangerous to health as a substitute for salaries or wages and other policies19 is prohibited.

Article 42. Calculation of Overtime

When an employer requires the employee to work overtime, on a day of weekly rest or on various holidays, with the agreement of trade unions or workers' representatives or of the employees, the employer must pay overtime to the employee as follows:

> Overtime worked in the daytime on a regular working day shall be paid for on the basis of one hundred and fifty percent of the hourly wage of a regular working day for each hour worked;

> Overtime worked at night on a regular working day shall be paid for on the basis of two hundred percent of the hourly wage of a regular working day for each hour worked;

> Overtime worked on a day of weekly rest or on a holiday shall be paid for on the basis of two hundred and fifty percent of the hourly wage of a regular working day for each hour thus worked in the daytime, and three hundred percent for each hour worked at night.

If a worker is assigned to work on a night shift between twentytwo hundred hours and five hours in the morning of the next day he shall be paid an additional bonus of not less than fifteen percent of the regular hourly wage [for each hour worked].

18 The literal is "production".

19 Here, "policies" is used as an indirect way of referring to "incentives".

CHAPTER 8 SALARY AND WAGE GUARANTEE

Article 43. Schedule for Payment of Salary or Wage

Salaries or wages must be paid to employees at least once a month at a

For additional analytical, business and investment opportunities information,
please contact Global Investment & Business Center, USA
at (703) 370-8082. Fax: (703) 370-8083. E-mail: ibpusa3@gmail.com
Global Business and Investment Info Databank - www.ibpus.com

fixed time, except for additional allowances or bonuses which are determined

separately.

In respect of wages paid on a per unit of production basis, or in respect

of hourly work, workers shall be paid at least twice a month or at an interval not exceeding 16 days.

Where employees face difficulties or emergencies such as childbirth, sickness, [or] accidents and have asked for advance salary or wage payment, the employer should, as necessary, give consideration to advance payment of their salary or wage before the payday.

The employer shall only pay salaries or wages to employees on working days, at the workplace or close to the workplace.

Article 44. Payment of Salary or Wage in the Event of Temporary Work Cessation

Where a labour unit is ordered to suspend its production and business activities or to stop production, due to the employer's fault, the employer must pay an allowance to each employee of not less than fifty percent of the minimum salary or wage applicable to the labour unit, for the period of such temporary suspension of production and business activities.

Once the production and business activities resume normally, the salaries or wages previously [applied] must be paid.

Article 45. Preferential Right to Receive Salaries or Wages

Where a labour unit is winding up, is bankrupt or is under a court order for total confiscation of its property, its employees have the right to first receive their salaries or wages, including any bonuses and allowances, before applying the remaining assets for payment of other debts.

Article 46. Deductions from Salary or Wage to Compensate for Damage

Deductions from an employee's salary or wage to compensate for damage to the property of a labour unit caused by the employee shall be made according to the value of the object that has actually been damaged.

If the employee does not have assets to use for compensation, [the compensation] must be deducted from his salary or wage.

Deductions for the purpose of compensation for damage, as well as for personal income tax, [contributions to] the social security fund and other debts, shall not exceed twenty per cent of the salary or wage paid to him at any given time.

CHAPTER 9 INCOME TAX AND SOCIAL SECURITY

Article 47. Deduction of Personal Income Tax from Salary or Wage

All workers who work in the Lao PDR as well as Lao workers assigned to work overseas must pay personal income tax to the government in accordance with the tax regulations. The employer or the labour administration sector 20 must strictly withhold personal income tax from the salaries or wages of employees under their responsibility for remittance to the national budget.

Foreign workers who work in various labour units in the Lao PDR must pay personal income tax to the government in accordance with specific regulations.

Article 48. Social Security Fund

All labour units in the socioeconomic sectors must establish a social security fund or pay contribution to a compensation fund to ensure the livelihood of employees in accordance with the social security system.

Employees and employers must contribute to the social security fund pursuant to the social security regime established by the government.

If the employer has already contributed to the compensation fund and

social security fund, social security payments to employees shall be made from

such funds.

CHAPTER 10 LABOUR PROTECTION

Article 49. Guarantee of Safety and Working Conditions

The employer must be responsible for ensuring that the workplace,

machinery, equipment, production chain, including the use of chemicals under

its supervision, are safe and not dangerous to the health of the workers.

The employer must establish internal rules concerning labour and

health protection, including the use of necessary measures to protect

machinery, and the installation of various safety equipment in consultation

The word "sector" here is used to refer to the cluster of government ministries or agencies responsible for a particular area.

with trade unions or workers' representatives in its labour unit. These rules must be disseminated to workers and must be posted openly where everyone can read [them].

Necessary measures to ensure labour safety and hygiene at the workplace include:

Appropriate lighting by means of an electrical installation or sufficient natural light, limitation of excessive noise, [and] ventilation for air, dust and odors which are dangerous to health;

A supply of drinkingwater and washing water, showers, toilets, a cafeteria, and changing room for workers;

A storage room where toxic substances can be kept safely without risk of leakage;

The provision, free of charge, in a sector where necessary, of personal safety equipment and clothing required by workers engaged in production;

The installation of safety equipment or fencing around any dangerous machinery or at other dangerous places, and other measures such as [measures] that warn against or prevent electric shocks, [and] fire and others, as necessary.

The employer must furthermore ensure that workers acquire sufficient knowledge of the rules relating to their own safety and health and shall organize training courses on those issues. All measures relating to the protection of the safety and health of workers in each labour unit shall be free of charge to workers.

All workers must attentively and strictly implement tasks relating to the safety and health of themselves and their colleagues, and must cooperate with the employer in the implementation of measures for the safety and health of the workers in accordance with the employer's duties.

The employer is prohibited from using narcotics or substances dangerous to the health of workers.

Article 50. Medical Examination and Health Care for Workers

A labour unit may require a medical certificate from workers who apply for work to ensure that they do not suffer from an occupational disease prior to the employment. Where the applicant has an occupational disease, the employer may reject his application for employment.

An employer must arrange for the workers to undergo a medical examination at least once a year, particularly those engaged in heavy work or [work] which is damaging to their health, as stipulated in Article 25 of this law. If the doctor finds that workers have an occupational disease from such workplace, the employer must be responsible for their medical treatment in accordance with regulations. In the case of a contagious occupational disease, [the employer] must give the worker leave to undertake treatment until [he] fully recovers and will thereafter reinstate him to his usual tasks. All expenses for medical examination and treatment of occupational diseases shall be born by the employer.

Labour units shall be equipped with a firstaid kit. [Labour] units employing fifty or more workers should have a medical staff to take care of and treat the health of the workers.

CHAPTER 11 LABOUR ACCIDENTS

Article 51. Labour Accidents

A labour accident is an accident21 which results in injury, disability, handicap or death of workers as follows:

> During the performance of duties at the workplace or at any other place under the assignment of the employer or of a person who has the right to manage labour on behalf of the employer;

> In a recreational area, cafeteria, or any other place within the scope of responsibility of the labour unit.

All diseases which occur as a result of an occupation shall be considered labour accidents.

The labour management organisation must coordinate with the health organisation and trade union organisation to determine the types of occupational diseases.

An accident that occurs during the time when the worker performs personal tasks without being assigned by the employer or its representative shall not be considered a labour accident.

Article 52. Care for Victims of a Labour Accident

The employer must provide immediate and appropriate help to workers who suffer from a labour accident, [and] the employer or the social security fund shall bear all actual costs of treatment as certified by a doctor such as:

> The cost of inpatient or outpatient medical treatment including the cost of examination at home and surgery;

> The expenses for hospitalization or for stay at any other place of treatment;

> The cost of care given by a doctor, an assistant of doctors, or a person who is in a profession which is specialised to treat such injured person, including treatment by traditional medicine.

Literal is "danger which occurs".

If a worker suffers a tragic accident22 which results in his death, the employer must be responsible for funeral expenses amounting to at least six months' salary or wages of the deceased. Additionally, the beneficiaries of the deceased have the right to receive a onetime allowance.

If a worker dies while on assignment by the employer to another workplace, the cost of transferring his body or remains to his family shall also be born by the employer.

Article 53. Allowance to Victims of Labour Accidents or Persons who have Contracted Occupational Diseases

The allowance for a worker who is a victim of a labour accident or who has contracted an occupational disease is as follows:

Throughout the period of medical treatment and health rehabilitation prescribed by a doctor, [a victim of a labour accident] shall be entitled to receive his regular salary or wage for up to six months. Where the [period] exceeds six months he shall be entitled to receive only fifty per cent of his salary or wage for each month thereafter, up to eighteen months. If the [period] exceeds eighteen months, the social security system shall be applied.

Where a worker becomes handicapped or loses any organ of the body as a result of a labour accident, or where a worker contracts an occupational disease or dies as a result thereof, the employer shall pay an allowance to the victim or to his successors in accordance with state regulations.

Where the employer has already paid contributions to a compensation fund or a social security fund in accordance with Article 48 of this law or has secured insurance coverage for its workers from an insurance company, all the above allowances shall be paid from the compensation fund or insurance company in accordance with regulations.

CHAPTER 12 SYSTEM OF PENSION AND ALLOWANCES

Article 54. Receipt of Pension

Workers in various labour units operating in socioeconomic sectors have the right to receive pension if they fulfill the following conditions:

Reached the age of sixty years for men, or fifty five years for women;

Completed twenty five years of service;

For workers who have worked in a place that is dangerous to health for a continuous period of five years and more before the

While the context suggests that this should be a labour accident, the text does not specifically state that date of receipt of pension, the service period is twenty years, and the retirement age is fifty five years for men and fifty years for women;

• Workers who have made social security contributions for twentyfive years. For workers who have worked in a place that is dangerous to health for a continuous period of five years and more before the date of receipt of pension, the contribution to social security is for a period of twenty years.23

Workers who do not meet the requirements set out above shall receive a onetime allowance. The labour management organisation shall study and submit [regulations] implementing the pension and onetime allowance [system].

CHAPTER 13 RESOLUTION OF LABOUR DISPUTES

Article 55. Types of Labour Disputes

Labour disputes are divided into two types as follows:

Disputes concerning the implementation of the Labour Law, labour regulations, employment contracts, internal rules of the labour unit and other regulations, which are called "disputes relating to laws and regulations";

Disputes relating to claims for benefits or new rights from the employer, which are called "disputes relating to interests".

Article 56. Resolution of Labour Disputes Relating to Laws and Regulations

If a worker or trade union or workers' representative makes a claim against an employer who has acted in violation of the Labour Law, labour regulations, the employment contract, internal rules of the labour unit or any regulations, the employer or its authorised representative must urgently consider and resolve the claim directly with the person who made the claim. During the consideration of the claim, the worker may propose that the trade union or workers' representatives be involved.

Where the parties reach an agreement in relation to the claim in full or in part, a memorandum of the agreement must be prepared and signed by the parties and a witness to certify their acknowledgment. Such memorandum must be sent to the labour management organisation and the trade union or workers' representatives within five days from the date the memorandum is signed.

For readability, the translators have inserted the bullet points and made slight changes to the paragraph's formatting.

Article 57. Responsibilities of the Labour Management Organisation in the Resolution of Labour Disputes Relating to Laws and Regulations

If, after fifteen days from the submission of a claim to the employer, the employer has not called the relevant party to solve the dispute or a consideration has taken place but no agreement was reached, or an agreement was reached but was not implemented, the worker has the right to request the labour management organisation to mediate the dispute.

Where the labour management organisation cannot resolve or can resolve only part [of the dispute] within fifteen days, the claim may be sent to the people's court for adjudication.

Article 58. Resolution of Labour Disputes Relating to Interests

The resolution of labour disputes relating to interests must be carried out according to the procedures for the resolution of disputes relating to laws and regulations as stipulated in Articles 56 and 57 above.

Where the labour management organisation cannot resolve [the dispute] within ten days, [such dispute] shall be submitted to the labour dispute mediation committee for final decision.

The labour dispute mediation committee must be established, [and] shall comprise representatives of the labour management organisation, trade unions, employers and other concerned sectors.

Article 59. Prohibition of Work Stoppage

Workers, employers or their representatives shall not declare a work stoppage during the following periods:

In the event of a labour dispute relating to the implementation of laws and regulations relating to labour, the employment contract or internal rules of the labour unit;

When both parties have agreed to meet to consider and resolve the claim;

During the process of the resolution of unresolved matters relating to workers and employers by a special committee set up in accordance with Article 58 above;

During the settlement of the labour dispute by the people's court.

Any person or organisation which is directly or indirectly involved and has [directly or indirectly] incited workers, employers or their representatives to stop work either verbally or through material or financial support thus causing damage to the workers or employers or social order, shall be punished in accordance with the laws.

CHAPTER 14 MEASURES AGAINST VIOLATORS OF THE LABOUR LAW

Article 60. Violation of the Labour Law

Any individual or legal entity that violates this Labour Law shall be punished in accordance with the laws.

CHAPTER 15 FINAL PROVISIONS

Article 61. This Labour Law replaces the Labour Law No. 10/90/SPA, dated 29 November 1990.24

This law shall enter into force sixty days after the date of its promulgation.

Article 62. Regulations Relating to the Implementation of the Labour Law

The labour management organisation has the duty and the responsibility for issuing regulations in to order to implement, disseminate, supervise, monitor and control the implementation of this Labour Law.

Vientiane, 14 March 1994 Chairman of the National Assembly [Seal and Signature]

For additional analytical, business and investment opportunities information, please contact Global Investment & Business Center, USA at (703) 370-8082. Fax: (703) 370-8083. E-mail: ibpusa3@gmail.com Global Business and Investment Info Databank - www.ibpus.com

INSURANCE LAW

PART I GENERAL PRINCIPLES

Article 1. Function of the Insurance Law

The Insurance Law has the function of promoting and preserving the socioeconomic basis of the Lao People's Democratic Republic, regulating insurance relationships, ensuring the exercise of rights and the performance of duties between enterprises conducting insurance business and insured individuals or legal entities, enhancing the responsibilities of enterprises conducting insurance business in implementing the laws of the State and to ensure State inspections of insurance business undertakings.

Article 2. The Conduct of Insurance

The conduct of insurance is a contract where one party, referred to as the insured, agrees to pay insurance premiums for the purpose of receiving indemnification1 for himself or for a third person in the event of loss, and the other party, referred to as the insurer, who insures against risks by providing the indemnity.

Article 3. Persons Involved in an Insurance Contract

Persons involved in an insurance contract are: the insurer, [and] the insured or the signatory of the insurance and the beneficiary.

An insurer is an enterprise authorised by the State to conduct insurance business.

The literal translation of this term is "compensation for damage".

An insured is a person who receives life or property insurance from an insurance enterprise.

An insurance signatory is a person who signs2 the insurance contract [and] agrees to pay insurance premiums for the purpose of insuring [his] life or property (in this case, he is the same person as the insured person) or [the life or property] of a third person.

A beneficiary is a person who receives insurance payments or indemnities as stipulated in the insurance contract when losses occur.

Article 4. Scope of Application of the Insurance Law

This Insurance Law applies to the following insurance enterprises:

Insurance enterprises which enter into contracts the performance of which depend on the life span of the insured;

For additional analytical, business and investment opportunities information,
please contact Global Investment & Business Center, USA
at (703) 370-8082. Fax: (703) 370-8083. E-mail: ibpusa3@gmail.com
Global Business and Investment Info Databank - www.ibpus.com

Insurance enterprises in all sectors which have collected insurance premiums and [which] guarantee the payment of indemnities in the event losses occur;

Insurance enterprises that mobilise funds3 by making specific binding contracts.

Article 5. Forms of Insurance Companies

An insurance enterprise is a legal entity which conducts the insurance business or mobilises funds.

Only insurance enterprises in the form of a partnership [and4] branches of foreign insurance companies have the right to conduct the business stipulated in Article 4 of this law.

Enterprises stipulated in point 2 of Article 4 of this law shall have not the right to conduct the business stipulated in points 1 and 3 of Article 4 of this law, unless [they have] received authorisation from the competent government organisation.

Article 6. Types of Insurance

Insurance activities are classified into the following types:

1. Insurance Against Damage to Property;

2 The literal translation of this phrase is "the person who is showing his face", which means that he is the person who is actually present but he may be signing either for his own benefit or for the benefit of a third person.

3 The term "mobilise funds" appears to connote endowment or savings policies.

4 The intended meaning here is "or".

An insurance relating to property is an insurance against damage to

property that occurs in production, business and in life such as: factory or

house fires, theft, and others, for which the insurer must indemnify the insured.

2. Civil Liability Insurance;

A civil liability insurance is an insurance against civil damage for which the insurer must indemnify or compensate on behalf of the insured.

3. Personal Insurance and Mobilisation of Funds;

Personal insurance and mobilisation of funds is an insurance against damage occurring as a result of death or health problems in respect of which an insurance payment is

For additional analytical, business and investment opportunities information,
please contact Global Investment & Business Center, USA
at (703) 370-8082. Fax: (703) 370-8083. E-mail: ibpusa3@gmail.com
Global Business and Investment Info Databank - www.ibpus.com

received in the event [the insured or beneficiary] continues to live, as stipulated in the insurance policy.

PART II AUTHORISATION TO CONDUCT INSURANCE BUSINESS AND STATE AUDITS

Chapter 1 Authorisation to Conduct Insurance Business

Article 7. Request to Conduct Insurance Business

Individuals or legal entities who request to conduct an insurance

business must complete a full set of documents as stipulated in the Decree of the Council of Ministers5.

A request to conduct an insurance business must be submitted to the Minister of Economy, Planning and Finance. The Minister of Economy, Planning and Finance, must consider and make a decision on the request within three months from the date of receipt of the request.

Article 8. Organisations which have the Right to Authorise the Conduct of Insurance Business

An individual or legal entity which has the intention to conduct insurance business as referred to in Article 4 of this law may start conducting its business upon authorisation from the Minister of Economy, Planning and Finance.

The Minister of Economy, Planning and Finance has the right to authorise the person who has requested to conduct insurance business of one or more types 6. An insurance enterprise has the right to conduct only the type of insurance business which it has been authorised to operate.

5 The "Council of Ministers" is the name by which the Prime Minister's Office used to be known.

6 The literal translation of this term is "sectors".

If necessary due to circumstances of the insurance market, the Minister of Economy, Planning, and Finance has the right to restrict or suspend the issuance of additional licenses for insurance business of one, some or all types.

The issuance, modification, restrictions, suspensions or withdrawals of insurance licenses must be made in the form of a decision of the Minister of Economy, Planning, and Finance.

Chapter 2 State Audit

For additional analytical, business and investment opportunities information, please contact Global Investment & Business Center, USA
at (703) 370-8082. Fax: (703) 370-8083. E-mail: ibpusa3@gmail.com
Global Business and Investment Info Databank - www.ibpus.com

Article 9. Purpose of a State Audit

A State audit of insurance enterprises is for the purpose of protecting

the interests of the insured or the signatory of the insurance contract and

beneficiaries under insurance and fund mobilisation contracts.

Article 10. Submission and7 Inspection of Documents

Before using documents regarding general conditions of an insurance policy or offer, insurance application forms, advertisement leaflets and brochures which will be distributed or disseminated to the public or given to insurance contract holders or to their own members, insurance enterprises of all types must first submit such documents to the Minister of Economy, Planning and Finance for approval.

If there are modifications or amendments to the articles of association, insurance enterprises of all types must inform the Minister of Economy, Planning, and Finance within fifteen days from the date the general meeting8 of enterprise has voted for [and] adopted it.

Insurance enterprises of all types must inform the Minister of

Economy, Planning and Finance regarding the basis for calculation and insurance premiums which they propose to apply.

If an insurance enterprise decides to modify certain details relating to insurance premiums, contract conditions, the professional organisation [of the enterprise], competition9 or their financial management, the directors of the enterprise must notify such decision to the Minister of Economy, Planning, and Finance before applying [such modification].

7 The literal translation of this term is "or". However, it is used in this context to mean "and".

8 The literal translation is "general meeting" but the intended meaning is a full meeting such as an Annual General Meeting.

9 The translators have chosen to use a literal translation here. There is an implication, in the literal language, that the competition is unfair.

The Minister of Economy, Planning and Finance has the right to demand modification of insurance premium rates, [and] all documents to be used in the insurance business or in mobilising funds from the public, including information which will be disseminated.

Article 11. Inspectors

Inspectors are sworn [civil] servants assigned to perform duties in accordance with conditions stipulated in a specific decision of the Minister of Economy, Planning and Finance and are assigned to regularly monitor insurance enterprises.

Inspectors have the right, at all times to perform onsite inspections of all activities of insurance enterprises, [and] inspectors must maintain confidentiality regarding the business that they become aware of during the performance of their duties.

Inspectors have the right to inspect all books of accounts, general ledgers, contracts, letters, memoranda, accounting documents or other documents relating to situations and past activities of insurance enterprises, and inspect cash reserves and valuable assets.

Inspectors must prepare reports summarising their inspections, confirming the true [circumstances] which they have found and report to the Minister of Economy, Planning, and Finance in order to obtain instructions on the method of resolution [of problems] as deemed necessary.

In conducting inspections, inspectors must comply with regulations relating to financial and accounting inspections.

Article 12. Duties of Insurance Enterprises relating to Inspections

Insurance enterprises of all types, individuals or legal entities which have been assigned the right by an insurance enterprise to enter into or administer a contract, [and] individuals or legal entities which practice the profession of insurance intermediaries must be inspected by inspectors.

Insurance enterprises must facilitate inspectors in the performance of their duties in their types of insurance activities or their branches in inspecting all general ledgers and documents mentioned in Article 11 of this law and must make available competent staff to supply information required by the inspectors.

PART III LAO INSURANCE COMPANIES AND BRANCHES OF FOREIGN INSURANCE COMPANIES, INSURANCE INTERMEDIARIES, FINANCIAL REGIME, ACCOUNTING, AND STATISTICS

Chapter 1 Lao Insurance Companies and Branches of Foreign Insurance Companies

Article 13. Lao Insurance Companies and Branches of Foreign Insurance Companies

A Lao insurance company is an insurance company which has been authorised to be established in the Lao People's Democratic Republic jointly between Lao individuals or legal entities, or through a joint venture between Lao individuals or legal entities and foreign individuals or legal entities and is registered in conformity with Lao laws.

A branch of a foreign insurance company is an organisation of a foreign insurance company which has been authorised by the Lao government to conduct insurance business in the Lao People's Democratic Republic and which is registered in conformity with Lao laws.

Article 14. Standards of Founders10 of an Insurance Company

An individual will not be authorised to establish, direct, administer, manage and conduct settlements for insurance enterprises [,] if that individual has committed a criminal act of theft, embezzlement, misappropriation, issues a cheque [on an account] without money, [has] committed an offense affecting State creditworthiness, andconcealed the thingsobtained in committing the offenses referred to above[,] and crimes. 13

Article 15. Restrictions to the Personal Interests of Members of Boards of Directors and Executive Officers

Members of boards of directors and executive officers of insurance companies are prohibited from directly or indirectly [and] abusively taking or maintaining a personal interest in the insurance enterprise, the insurance market, in making contracts, in commercial or financial operations undertaken jointly with the insurance company, unless they have obtained approval from the company's general meeting. The annual report submitted to the general meeting must report on the conduct of activities authorised by the general

10 The word "founder" here has a different meaning from "founder" in the Business Law. Here, there is no objective of differentiating "founders" from shareholders. In this use, the meaning is "the people who have the right to establish an insurance company".

11 The literal translation of this term is "and" but the probable meaning here is "or".

12 The word "thing" should be read in a general way.

13 This term refers to offenses which are punishable with imprisonment of a period from five years up to capital punishment, as defined in Article 7 of the Penal Law.

meeting of the enterprise. Reports relating to the conduct of such activities must be included in the auditor's report.

Article 16. Criteria of a Person to whom General Rights of Insurance Companies may be Granted

A person to whom general rights of insurance companies may be

granted, must have a notification of offence 14 and a certificate authorising him to directly manage the branch of the insurance company.

A person who has been granted general rights must maintain accounts specific to each type of insurance business which he conducts in the Lao

People's Democratic Republic.

Article 17. Determination of Capital Requirements for a Partnership Company

A partnership company must have enterprise capital to undertake insurance activities in an amount not less than the amount specified in the decree of the Council of Ministers. Any insurance company document which will be disseminated to the public must clearly state the capital of such enterprise.

Article 18. Security Deposits of a Lao Insurance Company and of a Branch of a Foreign Insurance Company

A Lao insurance company and a branch of a foreign insurance company which conduct insurance business in the Lao People's Democratic Republic must deposit a guarantee into a bank established in the territory of the Lao People's Democratic Republic in an amount stipulated in the Decree of the Council of Ministers.

A Lao insurance company or a branch of a foreign insurance company may deposit guarantees in Kip or in foreign currency, government bonds or governmentguaranteed bonds. If interest has accrued from the guarantee in the bank, the company or a branch of a company has the right to use [such interest].

If reserves for technical purposes15 or deposits in a savings account corresponding to such reserves are insufficient, approval will be given to use the deposit referred to above to specifically indemnify the insured or beneficiaries under such insurance contract.

14 This term refers to a document issued by a competent authority to certify that the individual has not committed any offenses.

15 Readers may wish to refer to Chapter 3 of this law for an explanation of this term.

If an insurance company ceases [its operations] or is being liquidated16 , the guarantee deposited in the bank must be returned to the company within 30 days from the date the Minister of Economy, Planning and Finance issues a notice. The notice must indicate the performance of the company's obligations or the transfer of existing assets and various obligations to an enterprise whose establishment has been authorised.

Article 19. Methods for Increasing Efficiency of an Insurance Enterprise

If it is found that an insurance enterprise is in the situation which may not enable it to fulfill its obligations or perform its duties in accordance with the rules, the Minister of Economy, Planning and Finance has the right to order and request that the relevant enterprise submit its reorganisation plans for approval. Such plans must project all specific measures to improve the efficiency of the enterprise.

The submission of the enterprise reorganisation plan must take place within thirty days from the date of the receipt of the order.

If any insurance enterprise violates rules regarding reserves for technical purposes, the Minister of Economy, Planning and Finance has the right to suspend the unlimited use of the relevant insurance enterprise's assets located in the territory of the Lao People's Democratic Republic.

Article 20. Transfer of Insurance Contract Fund

An insurance enterprise has the right to transfer all or part of the insurance contract funds along with its rights and duties to one or more insurance enterprises with prior authorisation from the Minister of Economy, Planning and Finance.

The request to transfer the insurance contract funds must be notified to creditors through public notices so that they can provide comments within three months. If it is found that the transfer of insurance contract funds conforms to the interests of the insured and creditors who are Lao, the Minster of Economy, Planning and Finance will issue a decision to transfer as requested.

Article 21. Withdrawal of License

An insurance business license which has been issued to an insurance enterprise may be withdrawn from for certain types of insurance activities or all types of insurance activities at any time if such enterprise:

Fails to comply with the prescribed conditions; or

Fails to apply measures stipulated in the reorganisation plan in due time; or

Seriously violates regulations which prescribe existing obligations that are in force.

16 The literal translation of this phrase is "liquidation of liabilities and assets".

If a license has been withdrawn from a foreign insurance enterprise by a competent authority of the enterprise's head office, the Minster of Economy, Planning and Finance must withdraw the license issued to such branch of enterprise established in the Lao People's Democratic Republic.

All decisions to withdraw the license or to suspend operations must be supported by clear reasons and be notified to the relevant enterprise.

The withdrawal of license by the Minister of Economy, Planning and Finance must be made in the form of a decision and must be disseminated.

Article 22. Appeal against a Decision to Withdraw a License

Insurance enterprises have the right to appeal against a decision to withdraw an insurance business license issued by the Minister of Economy, Planning, and Finance to

For additional analytical, business and investment opportunities information,
please contact Global Investment & Business Center, USA
at (703) 370-8082. Fax: (703) 370-8083. E-mail: ibpusa3@gmail.com
Global Business and Investment Info Databank - www.ibpus.com

the Council of Ministers within fifteen days from the date they have become aware of the decision to withdraw the license.

The Council of Ministers must consider and give an opinion regarding such appeal no later than thirty days from the date it has received the appeal.

Article 23. Liquidation

A decision to withdraw the entire insurance business license issued by the Minister of Economy, Planning and Finance results in the dissolution of the relevant Lao insurance company or [results in] the commencement of the liquidation of a branch of a foreign insurance company from the date the decision became effective.

If an enterprise has appealed against the decision to withdraw a license,

[the commencement date of liquidation17] will be the date of issue of the

decree of the Council of Ministers.

Article 24. Conduct of Liquidation

Liquidation is conducted by a liquidation committee established by the

President of the Council of Ministers upon recommendation of the Minister of

Economy, Planning and Finance.

The liquidation committee shall include one or more representatives from the Insurance Department and other technical staff as necessary.

Until a decree in response to the appeal is issued by the Council of Ministers, the dissolution or commencement of liquidation cannot begin.

In the liquidation, distributions must conform with priorities of creditors and in accordance with the Civil Law.

Chapter 2 Insurance Intermediaries

Article 25. Insurance Offers

An offer or acceptance of an offer [relating to] the signing of an insurance contract by an individual or legal entity or the verbal or written explanation of the conditions of insurance to a [potential] signatory of an insurance [contract] are considered as insurance offers.

Article 26. Insurance Intermediaries

Insurance businesses of all types can be offered to the public provided that such offers are made through the following insurance intermediaries:

Insurance representatives;

Legally authorised insurance brokers and insurance brokerage enterprises;

Staff of an insurance company, persons authorised by insurance companies, [and] staff of insurance agents and of insurance brokers or insurance brokerage enterprises who have been properly assigned to perform the task and who have performed such tasks under the responsibility and for the interests of the grantor [of such rights] or of the company.

Insurance companies, insurance agents, insurance brokers, or insurance brokerage enterprises must hold civil liability for damage which has occurred due to a wrongful act, negligence or lack of attention on the part of their staff or grantees [of rights].

Article 27. Professional Standards Individuals who will undertake the practice of the profession of insurance intermediaries as stipulated in Article 26 above, must meet the following standards:

Be not less than 18 years of age and be a Lao national;

Have not committed any offense stipulated in Article 14 of this law;

Have a good professional knowledge and competence in this profession.

Chapter 3 Financial Regime

Article 28. Obligations under the Regulations

Insurance enterprises have the duty under regulations to [maintain] at all times evidence of the value of the following:

Insurance enterprises must have, at any time, evidence certifying the value of their [financial] ability to meet their obligations under the regulations as follows:

The reserves for technical purposes must be sufficient to enable full performance of contractual obligations towards the insured or the beneficiaries under the insurance contract;

Liabilities must correspond with other priority debts.

Article 29. Life Insurance and Fund Mobilisation

Reserves for technical purposes relating to activities of life insurance and of fund mobilisation are as follows:

The reserve fund based on calculation [which refers to] the difference between the present value of contractual obligations agreed between an insurance enterprise and the insured (the method for calculation is based on the table stating the computation of life insurance payments18 and the interest rate);

The reserve fund for distribution of profits.

Article 30. Insurance Reserves for Damages

Reserves for technical purposes relating to insurance activities against damage are as follows:

Reserves for current insurance against risks [which refers to] reserves to insure against risks [and] general expenses relating to each contract for which a premium has already been paid [,] during the period between the date of entry into the accounts and the date for the determination of a new insurance premium;

Reserves against damage for which payment has not yet been made [which refers to] the assessment of the amount of payment which is owing but has not yet been made ; [and]

Reserves for increased risks and reserves for adjusting risks.

The literal translation of this term is "death rates".

Article 31. Priorities of the Insured and [of] Beneficiaries under the Contract

Insured persons and beneficiaries under insurance contracts have special priority over movable assets of insurance enterprises which are included in the reserves for technical purposes. Such priority is ranked immediately after staff salaries and State debts.19

Movable assets of insurance enterprises which are included in the reserves for technical purposes are a special priority of the insured and of the beneficiaries under the insurance contract. Such priority is ranked immediately after staff salaries and State debts.

Fixed assets of insurance enterprises which are included in the reserves for technical purposes upon a request of the Minister of the Ministry of Economy, Planning and Finance are a security for payment to priority creditors and must be registered in accordance with the laws.

Article 32. Ability to Pay Debts

All insurance enterprises must have evidence to demonstrate their ability to pay debts.

The ability to pay debts includes:

Enterprise capital or establishment capital;

Reserves which do not relate to any obligations;

Profit carried forward and annual income after deduction of losses;

The excess value which results from a lower evaluation of the assets [,] upon the approval of the Minister of the Ministry of Economy, Planning and Finance based on a proposal and provision of evidence by the insurance enterprise;

Intangible assets shall not be calculated for the purpose of determining the ability to pay debts.

The ability to pay debts must be in an amount equal to twenty percent of actual insurance premiums.

Chapter 4 Accounting and Statistics

Article 33. Auditors

Insurance enterprises must be audited by one or more auditors.

The structure of this sentence has been changed for readability.

Article 34. Specific Accounting Plans

All insurance enterprises must maintain accounts in the form specified in the Law on Enterprise Accounting.

Accounts must be kept for each year of operation and for each type of insurance. The posting of entries into the accounts of the insurance enterprise must be supported by documents and an annual inspection of assets. In order to serve as a basis for annual posting of the assets into the accounts, a balance sheet must be made for each account and subaccount. Such balance sheets must be able to summarize all postings shown in the general ledger.

Article 35. Accounting Reports

Each year, insurance enterprises must make an annual report of the preceding year and submit it to the Minister of the Ministry of Economy, Planning and Finance no later than 30 June. The report must provide details regarding business operations as well as the financial20 status of each insurance sector in order to enable inspection of the operations of the enterprise.

Article 36. Books of Accounts of Insurance Enterprises

Insurance enterprises must maintain the following books of accounts:

One bound daily journal [entries] arranged according to date, without blank spaces, without gaps, [and] without any writing beyond margins;

One general ledger;

One book of quarterly trial balances;

One book of annual balance sheets;

One or several cash books;

One book to monitor bank savings.

A certificate of movable assets, fixed assets and loans must be posted

into specific accounts and must be recorded in a book of record of activities

for the purpose of regular monitoring.

The literal translation of this term is "accounting".

PART IV RULES RELATING TO INSURANCE CONTRACTS

Chapter 1 Purpose of Implementation of Insurance Contracts and Rules Relating to Making Insurance Policies

Article 37. Purpose of Implementation of an Insurance Contract

Insurance contracts relating to individuals located in or residing in, risks incurring in and assets located or registered in, the Lao People's Democratic Republic may only be made with companies that are licensed to conduct insurance business in the Lao People's Democratic Republic.

All insurance contracts made in violation of the provisions of this

Article shall be void and unenforceable. However, the contract will remain

effective for bona fides insured and beneficiaries.

Article 38. The Making of an Insurance Policy

Insurance offers do not yet constitute a binding obligation between an

insured and an insurer. Only an insurance policy or a memorandum of

insurance will create binding obligations between the insured and the insurer.

An insurance policy is a document which determines the general conditions of an insurance contract, an insurance contract will be effective only if the parties have accepted the general conditions as evidenced by the insurance policy issued by the insurance company.

The insurance policy must be made in writing, easily readable and in the Lao language. If necessary, it can also be made in a foreign language.

Additions or modifications to the wording of an existing insurance policy must be made by the parties in the form of an additional contract.

When an insurance contract has been suspended in accordance with Article 43 of this law, if there is a request to continue, modify or renew [the insurance], sent to the insurer by registered mail or by letter requiring acknowledgment of receipt, [and] if the insurer has not rejected such request within 15 days from the date of receipt of request, [such request] shall be deemed approved.

Apart from these rules, the making of an insurance contract must also comply with Article 5 of the Contract Law.

Article 39. Duration of an Insurance Policy

An insurance policy must have a duration. An insurance contract proposed by an insurance company in accordance with point 2 of Article 4 of this law must be made for one year and each renewal of this contract must not exceed one year.

If an insurance contract has expired and has been renewed automatically any party may terminate such contract by giving 3 months notice to the other party in writing, or by registered mail, or by a letter requiring a signature as acknowledgment of receipt.

Article 40. Key Content of Insurance Policies

The key content of insurance policies consists of:

Name and surname [and]address of the parties;

Insured individual or property;

Type of insured risk;

Commencement date for insurance against risks;

Amount of coverage;

Insurance premiums and methods of payment;

Methods and conditions relating to the notification of occurrence of damage;

For additional analytical, business and investment opportunities information,
please contact Global Investment & Business Center, USA
at (703) 370-8082. Fax: (703) 370-8083. E-mail: ibpusa3@gmail.com
Global Business and Investment Info Databank - www.ibpus.com

Duration of the insurance contract and of the insurance;

Wording indicating when an insurance contract is invalid, [and] when each party loses or possesses the right to terminate the insurance contract before its expiration21 .

Article 41. Insured Risks

The insurer must be responsible for loss or damage incurred to the object of the insurance due to accidents or due to the wrongdoing of the insured, unless the insurance policy has stated otherwise. The insurer will not be responsible for loss or damage incurred as a result of an intentional act of

the insured.

The insurer must be responsible for loss or damage for which the insured holds civil liability regardless of the gravity of such wrongdoing [committed by the insured].

Article 42. Obligations of the Insured Person

The insured person has the obligation to:

Pay insurance premiums;

Correctly disclose all facts known to him in order to help accurately assess the risks which will be borne by the insurer during the making of the insurance contract;

The translators have chosen to render the words as literally as possible and believe that this term means "the condition upon which parties may terminate the insurance contract before its expiration".

Disclose to the insurer facts which may cause the increase of risk as provided in the insurance policy;

Immediately notify to the insurer all losses or damage which have been insured as [such losses or damage] become known and within 5 days at the latest. In case of insurance against theft, notification must be given within 36 hours.

The parties may agree to extend the period of such notification in the contract. The insured person will not lose his rights under the insurance contract if he cannot notify [the insurer] of the incurred losses or damage due to accidents or force majeure.

Article 43. Insurance Premiums

If insurance premiums are not paid in due time, the validity of the

insurance policy will be suspended after a period of twenty days from the day the insurer has sent a notice of warning to the insured.

The insurer may terminate the insurance policy or file a claim with the court requesting the insured to implement the contract after a period of 10 days from the day the insurance policy has been suspended.

The provisions of this Article do not apply to the insurance policies made by insurance companies as stipulated in points 1 and 3 of Article 4 of this law.

Article 44. Concealment or False Declaration

If the insured conceals [information] or makes a false declaration resulting in a change to the object of the risk or resulting in an incorrectly low assessment of the risk by the insurer [,] the insurance contract will be void.

Article 45. Failure to Make a Declaration

The failure [to make a declaration] or an incorrect declaration by the insured person will not cause the contract to be void if the insurer has no evidence to prove that the insured person lacks bona fides.

If the lack of bona fides is revealed before the occurrence of damage, the insurer has the right to continue the contract by increasing the insurance premiums if so agreed by the insured person or has the right to terminate the contract and return the insurance premiums paid for the period during which the insurance contract was not valid, to the insured person, after the period of 10 days from the day notice has been sent to the insured by registered mail or by letter requiring a signature as acknowledgment of receipt, has expired.

If the lack of bona fides is revealed after the occurrence of damage,

insurance indemnities payable to the insured person will be reduced according

to the proportionate difference between the insurance premiums paid, and the insurance premiums payable, had declaration been made correctly and completely.

Parties may agree not to use the rules relating to the reduction of insurance indemnities in accordance with such proportional calculations.

Article 46. Invalid Wording in an Insurance Policy

Wording in an insurance policy which makes the insured person loose his rights because of violations of laws and regulations will be invalid, except if the violation of laws and regulations pertain to crimes22or [pertain] to major offences23 which have been intentionally committed.

Chapter 2 Statute of Limitation and Competent Court

Article 47. Limitation Period

A claim relating to insurance contracts may take place within 3 years from the day the event has occurred.

The limitation period will be suspended in accordance with the provisions of Article 35 of the Law on Contract or where there are valid reasons and where an expert has been assigned to prove the truth after the occurrence of damage.

Article 48. Competent Court for the Adjudication of Disputes

The competent court for the adjudication of disputes between the insured and the insurer is the court of the place of domicile of the insured24 . In the case of an insurance relating to damage to immovable property, [the competent court] will be the court where such property is located. In case of an insurance against accidents [the competent] court will be the court where such accident took place.

Chapter 3 Insurance Against Damage of Property

Article 49. Rules Relating to Insurance Indemnities

An insurance contract against damage of property is a contract for the compensation for damage through insurance indemnification. The amount of

This term refers to offenses which are punishable with imprisonment of a period from five years up to the death penalty, as defined in Article 7 of the Penal Law.

23 Readers may wish to refer to Article 7 of the Penal Law for an understanding of "major offences".

24 The literal translation of this phrase is "where he is".

insurance indemnities paid by the insurer to the insured must not exceed the value of the insured property at the time the damage occurred.

Article 50. Insurance which is Lower than the Value of the Property.

When damage occurs, if the insured property is assessed to be higher than the value of the insurance, the insured must take responsibility himself for the excess part unless otherwise agreed upon in the insurance policy.

Article 51. Loss of Insured Property

If insured property is fully lost due to a reason not mentioned in the insurance policy, the insurance will be terminated and the insurer must return the insurance premiums for the remaining duration of the insurance contract to the insured.

Article 52. Taking Over the Rights of the Insured

The insurer who has already paid insurance indemnities has the right to take over the right of the insured and file a claim for reimbursement of money equal to the insurance indemnities paid, from a third person who is the cause for the damage.

The insurer does not have the right to file a claim for reimbursement if the person who is the cause of the damage is a relative by a vertical line25, is a person who has been assigned to work on behalf of the [insured], is an employee of the insured and26 a person who is permanently living in the house of the insured, except if such persons have intentionally caused damage.

Chapter 4 Personal Insurance

Article 53. Specific Rules for Personal Insurance

In [personal insurance]27 policies, [which refers to] life insurance or insurance against accidents which cause death or affect health, insurance indemnities must be stipulated in the insurance policies.

In cases of personal insurance, when the insurer has paid insurance indemnities, [he] will not have the right to take over the rights of the signatory or the beneficiary of the insurance contract in order to file a claim to request compensation for indemnities paid, from a third person who caused the damage.

25 The term refers to persons related by blood rather than through marriage.

26 The literal word is "and" but the probable meaning is "or".

27 In the context, this must be a reference to a "personal" insurance policy but the Lao text is not so qualified.

Article 54. Life Insurance

A person has the right to make a life insurance for himself or a third

person if such person has agreed in writing and must stipulate the insurance

indemnitics.

It is forbidden to take a life insurance on children of less than 15 years old, on people having lost their rights, on persons showing signs of mental incompetence or undergoing medical treatment in a psychiatric hospital.

Article 55. Contents of Personal Insurance Contracts

In addition to the contents28 required for making an insurance policy of all types, an insurance contract 29 or life insurance policy must indicate the following content:

Name and surname, date of birth of one or several persons who will receive the life insurance;

Name and surname of the beneficiary, if any;

Facts or wording giving the right to receive insurance indemnities;

Circumstances leading to the reduction of the insurance indemnities, if agreed upon in the insurance contract.

Article 56. Suicide and Murder

Life insurance will not be enforceable if the insured commits suicide, but the insurer still has to pay to the person who is entitled to receive [indemnities] an amount equal to the amount in the reserves based on the computation formula.

If the insurance policy provides that the insurer will pay insurance indemnities to the insured in case the insured commits suicide, the insurance contract will be enforceable only if two years have elapsed since the insurance contract was made.

The insurance contract will not be enforceable if the beneficiary has intentionally caused the death of the insured.

This is a literal translation. The intention is to refer to "those matters that must be included". See Article 11 of the Contract Law for a similar use of "contents".

Chapter 5 Insurance of Civil Liabilities

Article 57. Responsibility Regardless of Wrongdoing

The principles mentioned in Part IV shall be applied to victims of land

traffic accidents caused by motorized vehicles and trailers or semi trailers, except for trains that move along their tracks.

The victims must receive compensation for damages incurred from accidents and the fault [of the victims] must not be a ground for avoiding compensation.

The victim will not be compensated for damages incurred from the accident if such [victim] has willingly caused the accident which caused the damages.

Article 58. Compensation for Damage

The insurer that insures land motorized vehicles must make an offer to pay insurance indemnities to the victim not later than six months from the day

of the accident.

If the victim is injured or dead, some of the insurance indemnities must be remitted to the spouse as necessary. If the spouse is deceased, [such compensation] must be remitted to the legal heirs within thirty days at the latest.

The insurance indemnities to be remitted to the victims may be estimated if within the period of three months from the day the accident took place, the insurer is still unable to know whether the victims have returned to their normal state or not.

Article 59. Vehicle Insurance

Individuals or legal entities using motorized land vehicles and trailers or semitrailers in the traffic must insure their vehicles.

The scope of insurance, method of documentation and the value of the use of certificates for the purpose of monitoring vehicle insurance are stipulated in the Decree of the Council of Ministers.

Article 60. Forfeiture of Rights due to Intoxication

In cases of an accident where the insured drove a vehicle under the influence of alcohol or drugs to the extent that he was unable to control the vehicle, the wording of the contract providing for the insurance of the insured will be void even if the insurance contract has not stipulated the forfeiture of rights due to drunkenness or [use] of narcotics.

Article 61. Issuance and Remittance of Insurance Certificates

Insurance companies must issue insurance certificates to insured persons for each vehicle without charge.

Taking out insurance and the issuing of insurance certificates may take place only if the user of the vehicle has presented a vehicle technical inspection certificate to the insurance company [,] except for vehicles that are not required to have technical inspection.

Insurance certificates must be kept with the driver or displayed in an easily visible area of the vehicle.

PART V MEASURES AGAINST OFFENDERS

Article 62. Unauthorised Conduct of Insurance Business

A person who has made an offer to the public for the purpose of selling30 insurance or who has signed insurance contracts on behalf of an insurance company which is not incorporated or which has submitted an application to establish [a business] but has not yet been officially authorised to conduct insurance business will be subject to a fine of 500,000 KIP to 1,000,000 KIP.

A person who has made an offer to the public for the purpose of selling insurance or who has signed insurance contracts relating to a type of insurance the conduct of which has not yet been officially authorised will be subject to a fine of 300,000 KIP to 500,000 KIP.

A person acting as an insurance intermediary and who claims that he has been assigned directly by an insurance company which has the right to conduct insurance business in accordance with the law will be subject to a fine of 50,000 KIP to 100,000 KIP.31

A person who has assigned the above insurance work to be performed

by others knowing that he himself does not have the rights and duties [to do so] will be subject to a fine of 500,000 KIP to 1,000,000 KIP.

If the above acts contain elements of offences [such offenses] will be penalized under the Penal Law.

30 The literal word is "making somebody take".

31 The implication in the original Lao text is that the person claiming to be an insurance intermediary has not actually been authorised as one.

Article 63. Violation of Rules Relating to Standards and Restriction of Interests

A person who has violated the rules of Article 14 and Article 15 of this law shall be subject to a fine of 500,000 KIP to 1,000,000 KIP.

Article 64. Presentation and Dissemination of False Documents

The staff member of an insurance company or insurance intermediary who has presented false documents to the Ministry of Economy, Planning and Finance or other relevant State organisations or who has presented and disseminated such false documents to the public will be subject to a fine of 100,000 KIP to 500,000 KIP.

Article 65. Failure to Supply Documents

An insurance company that does not supply documents or forms as stipulated in this law will be subject to a fine of 50,000 KIP to 100,000 KIP.

Article 66. Violation of the Company's Regulations and Financial Regime

For additional analytical, business and investment opportunities information,
please contact Global Investment & Business Center, USA
at (703) 370-8082. Fax: (703) 370-8083. E-mail: ibpusa3@gmail.com
Global Business and Investment Info Databank - www.ibpus.com

All violations of the company's regulations and the regulations regarding technical reserves [,] savings deposits of assets and ability to settle debts will be subject to a fine between 500,000 KIP to 200,000,000 KIP [.] In cases of repeated offenses, withdrawal of business license shall be considered.

Article 67. Violation of Rules Pertaining to Intermediaries

A person who has violated the provisions of Articles 25, 26 and 27 of this law shall be subject to a fine of 20,000 KIP to 100,000 KIP.

Article 68. Violations of Rules Pertaining to Vehicle Insurance

An individual or legal entity which has violated the provisions of Article 59 of this law will be subject to a fine of 3,000 KIP to 30,000 KIP.

PART VI FINAL PROVISIONS

Article 69. Implementation

The Council of Ministers of the Lao People's Democratic Republic shall issue regulations for the implementation of this law.

Vientiane, 18 December 1990 The Chairman of the People's Supreme Assembly

LAW ON THE DEVELOPMENT AND PROTECTION OF WOMEN

PART I GENERAL PROVISIONS

Article 1. Purpose of the Law

The Law on the Development and Protection of Women is issued to guarantee and promote the roles of women, to define the fundamental contents of, and measures for developing and protecting, the legitimate rights and interests of women, and to define the responsibility of the State, society and family towards women with the [following] aims[:] promoting the knowledge, capability and revolutionary ethic of women, [and] gender equality[;] eliminating all forms of discrimination against women[; and] preventing and combating trafficking in women and children and domestic violence against women and children, in order to [create conducive conditions for] women to participate and to be a force in national defence and development.

Article 2. The Role of Women

Women have fought and made sacrifices shoulder to shoulder with men for national independence.

Women play a role in all aspects of politics, the society and economy, environmental protection, national defence and security, foreign affairs, [and in the] conservation and development of the fine traditions of the national culture and the identity of Lao women.

[Women] work together with their families in the development and care of, and in bringing up and educating[,] family members to become good citizens of the nation.

Article 3. Policies1 Towards Women

The State has policies for the development and advancement of women, [and] the protection of the legitimate rights and interests of women by creating every condition to ensure that women have good health, knowledge, capabilities, revolutionary ethic, employment and equal rights with men, without any discrimination based on political, economic, social, cultural, and family status.

[All members of] society shall participate in the implementation of such policies towards women as provided under laws and regulations.

Article 4. Lao Women's Union

The Lao Women's Union is a mass organisation that represents the legitimate rights and interests of women and children and is a centre for solidarity, that encourages women to participate and be a force in national defence and development, that promotes the rights of ownership of multiethnic women, [and] that protects the legitimate rights and interests of women and children, especially those who are members of the Lao Women's Union.

Article 5. International Cooperation

The State promotes international relations and cooperation with regard to women in many aspects and forms, such as the development and advancement of women, the implementation of international conventions relating to women, and

cooperation in the prevention and combating of trafficking in women and children, the combating of the use of violence against women, the exchange of experience and other forms of assistance and cooperation.

"Policies" is often used as an indirect way of referring to "incentives" or "privileges". In this context, it is unclear whether that use is intended or whether "policies" is being used in the sense of "strategies and measures of governance".

PART II DEVELOPMENT OF WOMEN

Chapter 1 The Definition and Importance of Development of Women

Article 6. Definition of Development of Women

The development of women is a component of human resource development to ensure that women have good health, knowledge, capabilities, and revolutionary ethic.

Article 7. The Importance of the Development of Women

The development of women is necessary in order to enable women to participate actively in all aspects of politics, the economy, culture and society, environmental protection, national defence and security, and foreign affairs so as to increase the effectiveness of national defence and development.

Chapter 2

The Contents of Development of Women

Article 8. The Contents of Development of Women

The development of women has the following contents:

Physical development;

Mental development;

Educational development;

Professional and skills development.

Development of family is also one important factor [to consider in achieving] the other developments mentioned above.

2 "Development of Women" is used interchangeably in this law to refer to both the "processes involved in the development of women as a resource" and the State's "program or policy for the development of women".

3 "Contents" is a literal translation. The intention is to refer to "those matters that must be included a program for the development of women". See Article 11 of the Contract Law for a similar use of "contents" in the context of contracts.

4 "Mental development" has the connotation of developing one's morals, principles, character, and other intangible qualities. Hence, developing a "good brain" (which has a more tangible connotation) is seen as part of physical development (see Article 9), rather than mental development.

Article 9. Physical Development

Physical development of women focuses on helping women to achieve bodily growth, good health, a good brain, good quality of life, and long life expectancy.

For additional analytical, business and investment opportunities information,
please contact Global Investment & Business Center, USA
at (703) 370-8082. Fax: (703) 370-8083. E-mail: ibpusa3@gmail.com
Global Business and Investment Info Databank - www.ibpus.com

Article 10. Mental Development

Mental development of women focuses on helping women to have good mental health, strong commitment, good vision, revolutionary ethic, good cultural [values and] good character, [and] to work hard with members of their families to develop society and [such] families to be rich, peaceful, and progressive.

Article 11. Educational Development

Educational development focuses on creating conditions for women to receive basic education [and] to receive education in physical and social sciences with the aims of upgrading their knowledge and capability in all aspects and of promoting those who have talent.

Article 12. Professional and Skills Development

Professional and skills development focuses on creating conditions for women to receive professional training, to acquire skills and experience, and to have employment discipline so that women can have the same employment [opportunities] in society as men.

PART III THE PROTECTION OF WOMEN'S RIGHTS AND INTERESTS AND THE DUTIES OF WOMEN

Chapter 1 Equality between Women and Men

Article 13. Equal Rights for Women and Men

Equal rights for women and men means equality in self development, [and also means that] women and men have the same value and opportunities in politics, the economy, society and culture, family [affairs], national defence and security, and foreign affairs as provided in the Constitution and laws.

5 This is a reference to education at a level equivalent to primary or grade school.

6 In Lao, a comma is often used, without further elaboration, to mean "and". Wherever the intended meaning is clear, the translators have translated such commas in one of two ways: (i) by deleting the comma and substituting it with the word "and' in square brackets (i.e., [and]); or (ii) by retaining the comma and adding the word "and" in square brackets (i.e., , [and]). Where the meaning is more ambiguous, the translators have translated the text literally, retaining the comma alone. Here, the translator replaced a comma with "[and]".

Article 14. Equal Political Rights

The State shall ensure that women enjoy equal political rights as men, such as rights to vote and to be elected, to participate in activities, to be consulted and to participate in decision making that is of national importance, [and] to be appointed to appropriate positions at all levels in Party and State organisations, the Lao Front for National Construction, mass organisations, and social organisations.

Society and family should create conditions for women to exercise the rights mentioned above.

Article 15. Equal Economic Rights

The State promotes the right of women to engage in production, business, and services in accordance with the laws. Women have the rights to choose their professions, to be employed, to be remunerated and to receive other benefits from their work.

Women who have the same position, task, work, and responsibility as men shall have the right to remuneration and benefits on an equal basis with men.

Society and family should create conditions for women to exercise the economic rights and to receive the economic benefits mentioned above.

Article 16. Equal Cultural and Social Rights

The State promotes and creates conditions for women to enjoy equal

cultural and social rights as men, such as rights to participate in sociocultural activities, art performances, sports, education, public health, [and] in research and

invention in socioculture, and science and technology.

Society and family should create conditions and provide opportunities for women to participate in the sociocultural activities mentioned above.

Article 17. Equal Rights in the Family

The State and society promote and protect equality between women and men in the family.

Women and men shall have equal rights in all matters concerning family relationships.

7 This is a literal translation of the Lao compound noun intended to refer to "matters that are social and cultural".

8 In Lao, the term is "science, techniques, technology".

Women who are 18 years of age or above have the freedom to choose a partner with whom to build their families.

The wife has the right to choose the family name of her husband or to keep her own.

The wife has equal rights as her husband over matrimonial property.

The wife and husband have equal rights in consultation, decision making and solving family issues to reach common agreement in the selection of a place of residence, [their respective] professions, [whether] to have children and other matters. The wife and husband should love and respect each other, take care of and help each other. Together, [they should] look after and educate their children and educate each other to become a family with good cultural [values], [and] that is united, harmoniousand progressive.

Daughters and sons have equal rights to inherit property and to receive education as provided under the laws.

Article 18. Right to Request or to Claim

If an individual or organisation hinders, limits, or violates the equal rights between women and men in politics, the economy, society and culture, and family, the woman concerned shall have the right to express her opinion, [and to make] a request to and file a claimwith the concerned authorities to deal with [such] issues according to laws and regulations.

Chapter 2 Special Rights and Benefits, and Obligations of Women

Article 19. Rights and Interests in Employment

Women have rights and interests in the context of employment, such as [the rights] to work in safe conditions and environments, to social security, and to remuneration and other benefits as provided by laws and regulations.

9 "United, harmonious" is the translation of a single Lao compound word with connotations of both unity and harmony. The Lao word translated as "unity" may also be translated as "solidarity" or "solid". The translators have generally used "solidarity" when referring to the cohesiveness of larger groups (e.g., society, community) and "unity" when referring to the cohesiveness of the smaller family unit.

10 There is a deliberate distinction between a mere request and the more formal filing of a legal claim. Readers may wish to refer to the Law on Civil Procedure for more information on the formal filing of legal claims.

Article 20. Rights and Interests in the Family

Women have rights and interests in the family as follows:

When the wife is pregnant or when the newly born child is less than one year old, the husband is not allowed to request a divorce. However, the wife has the right to do so;

In the event of divorce, the wife has priority regarding custody of the children;

If sexual relations occur between a man and a woman and if [either] the man does not marry the woman or they have a child before marriage, the woman shall be entitled to claim compensation from the man and she shall also have the right to request for expenses for child care until the child reaches 18 years of age;

• In the event of the division of an inheritance, a mother has the right to represent her unborn child to inherit and manage such inheritance.

Article 21. Rights and Interests under the Penal Law

Women's rights and interests under the Penal Law are as follows:

A pregnant woman who has committed a crime shall have the right to a reduction of penalty;

A pregnant woman or woman with a child under the age of eight years old, after serving a sentence of imprisonment, will not be subject to house arrest;

A woman who was pregnant at the time she committed an offence shall not be sentenced to life imprisonment or the death penalty;

If a woman is subject to the death penalty and is discovered to be pregnant, the penalty will be temporary suspended. Details will be provided in specific regulations.

Article 22. Women's Rights and Interests in Health Care

The State emphasises the protection of the health of mothers and children.

Families have the obligation to take care of mothers and children to ensure their good health.

Women have the rights of treatment, medical examination, and vaccination according to regulations, especially girls, young women and women of reproductive age, including women in remote areas.

Readers may wish to refer to Article 8 of the Family Law for more information on these spousal obligations.

When a woman delivers a baby, there should be medical staff or birth assistants, as is practical in the circumstances. It is prohibited for individuals or organisations to force a pregnant woman to deliver [her] baby in the forest, or a remote place; it is prohibited to hurt women and children because of superstitious beliefs or other reasons.

When the wife delivers a baby or when she is sick, the husband has the right to take leave according to regulations to take care of his wife and children.

In addition to the special rights and benefits mentioned above, women shall have other rights and benefits as provided under laws and regulations.

Article 23. Obligations of Women

As Lao citizens, women have the following fundamental obligations:

To respect the Constitution [and] laws, [and to] comply with employment regulations [and] rules of social conduct and public order;

To pay taxes and duties according to laws and regulations;

To protect the nation [and] national security[,] and to fulfil military obligations as provided under the laws.

In addition, women, together with family and society, shall protect the fine

customs and traditions, [and] good cultural practices that are unique to the nation

and Lao women.

In addition to the obligations mentioned above, women have other obligations as provided under laws and regulations.

PART IV THE PROTECTION OF WOMEN AND CHILDREN AGAINST TRAFFICKING AND DOMESTIC VIOLENCE

Chapter 1 Combating Trafficking in Women and Children

Article 24. Trafficking in Women and Children

Trafficking in women means the recruitment, hiding, moving, transportation, transfer, harbouring, [or] receipt of women, within or across national borders, by means of deception, the giving or receiving of bribes, threats, the use of force, [the use of] other forms of coercion, abduction, debt bondage or by other means[,] for forced labour, [for] prostitution, [for] publishing

The term "moving, transportation" is the translation of a single Lao compound word "movingtransportation". pornography and what is in contradiction to fine national culture, [for] the removal of various body parts, or for other unlawful purposes.

If these acts are committed against children under 18 years old, then even

though there is no deception, threat, force, or debt bondage, trafficking shall be regarded to have occurred.

For additional analytical, business and investment opportunities information, please contact Global Investment & Business Center, USA at (703) 370-8082. Fax: (703) 370-8083. E-mail: ibpusa3@gmail.com Global Business and Investment Info Databank - www.ibpus.com

Any individual who cooperates withthe offender [who commits] an offencementioned above[,] whether by incitement, providing assets or vehicles to the offender, the provision of shelter, or the concealment or removal of traces of an infraction, shall be considered as an accomplice in trafficking in women and children.

Trafficking in women and children is an offence.

Article 25. Rights of Victims

A victim means a person who has suffered from trafficking in women and children. Victims have the following rights:

To ask for assistance from any individual who is nearby;

To notify police officers;

To testify and present evidence relating to the case, to concernedofficers;

To request for compensation, to be rehabilitated and to be reintegrated into the society;

To receive protection and care to ensure personal safety;

Not to be prosecuted and detained on any charge of trafficking in women and children, prostitution, [or] illegal immigration;

Not to be photographed, [and] not to have any video recorded or broadcast, where suchwould affect personal honour;

To receive suitable assistance in the form of shelter, food, clothes, medical services, vocational training, repatriation and others;

To have other rights according to laws and regulations.

13 There is a connotation of both internal organs and external body parts.

14 This is a slightly broader idea than an "accomplice" within the meaning of Article 16 of the Penal Law.

15 The term "offence" or "infraction" is used here, as in the Penal Law, to refer generally to criminal acts. There are three levels of such criminal acts as set out in Article 7 of the Penal Law.

16 "Concerned" is used in the sense of "relevant".

17 Namely the photograph or the video.

Article 26. Duties of Society

Individuals or organisations that discover victims of trafficking in women and children or receive data or information concerning such trafficking shall report to the village administration, the police or other concerned authorities, and shall, at the same time, give assistance to victims.

Party and State organisations, the Lao Front for National Construction, mass organisations, social organisations and families shall disseminate informationand educate so that the whole society becomes aware of the acts and impact of trafficking in women and children in order that women and children stay vigilant and not fall victim to such trafficking and be active in combating and preventing [such trafficking].

To combat and prevent trafficking in women and children, the government establishesa national committee for prevention of trafficking in humans.

Article 27. Criminal Procedures Relating to Offenders

After having been notified about any trafficking in women and children, the police officers shall, in accordance with the Law on Criminal Procedure, investigate the case immediately, take the testimony of victims or of those reporting to the police, including witnesses, and, at the same time, maintain confidentiality and safety of those people. If there is enough evidence, the police shall send the case to prosecutors who will then send the case to the court to consider and decide whether to punish the offender and to award compensation for the damage suffered by the victims, including [compensation for] moral rehabilitation and loss of income.

Article 28. Assistance by Officers to Victims

During the process , police officers must cooperate with concerned counterparts such as doctors, social workers and other parties in order to give necessary and urgent assistance, to provide medical treatment and counselling services to the victims and to send them to safe shelter.

In the case where the victims are children, there shall be special treatment to restore [their] physical and mental health and to provide assistance to [meet] the specific needs of the children, in order to ensure that those children have guardians and to help them to return to their family and society.

18 Literally "engage in propaganda".

19 Lao does not require verbs to indicate tense. At the time this law was passed, there was no committee yet, and the translators are unable to resolve from the context whether this verb should be translated in the prescriptive ("shall") or permissive ('may') sense.

20 This appears to be a reference to the process set out in Article 27.

In the case of victims abroad who are Lao citizens, the concerned Lao embassy or consulate shall give necessary and urgent assistance to the victims, especially safety and social welfare, and shall cooperate with concerned officials of that country in order to prosecute offenders, and the victims shall be repatriated thereafter.

In the case of victims in the Lao PDR who are citizens of foreign countries, in addition to implementingthe third paragraph mentioned above, Lao officials shall cooperate with the embassy or consulate of the victim's country in the Lao PDR through the Ministry of Foreign Affairs in order to repatriate the victims.

Chapter 2 Combating Domestic Violence Against Women and Children

Article 29. Domestic Violence against Women and Children

Domestic violence against women and children is an act or omission committed by someone in the family which causes physical [or] mental impact on[,] or [which impacts on the] assets of[,] women and children in the family.

Article 30. Physical Impact

The use of violence to cause physical impact is an act of any individual in the family that causes death, incapacity, or injury to other members of the family as a result of battery, torture, locking up or tying up the person, rape or other immoral acts.

Article 31. Mental Impact

The use of violence to cause mental impact is an act of any individual in the family that causes damage to the mental health of women and children in the same family, such as: adultery, coercion, insults, defamation, scorn, [and] putting up obstacles against the performance of different kinds of activities[,] especially social activities.

Article 32. Impact on Assets

The use of violence to cause impact on assets is an intentional act of any individual in the family that causes damage to assets and results in consequences on the livelihood of family members, such as: the use of family assets for his or her own interests in an unlawful way, nonperformance of obligations to take care of the family, causing women to lose their inheritance rights as provided in the laws, [and] destroying the house [or] property of the family

21 There is no connotation that "thereafter" relates to the prosecution only. That is, there is no connotation that repatriation can only occur after prosecution. Rather "thereafter" relates to all of the preceding actions.

22 The meaning is that the Lao officials in Laos must provide the same assistance as required of Lao officials abroad in the third paragraph.

Article 33. Rights of Victims

Victims of domestic violence have the right to seek assistance from other family members, persons nearby and relatives, or to report to village administrations aiming at educating the violator, stopping the violence and changing his or her bad behaviour to [achieve] a united, harmonious and happy family.

In the case of domestic violence which results in serious impact constituting an offence, the victims shall have the right to report to police officers to deal with the matter in accordance with laws and regulations.

Article 34. Assistance to Victims and Protection of Persons who Provide Assistance

A family member who discovers any domestic violence against women or children which threatens their life [or] physical health, which impacts on their liberty, mental health, [or] dignity or which damages their assets[,] or who is aware of such violence[,] shall assist them according to the nature and gravity of the violence and the urgency [and] necessity [of the situation,] by intervening, impeding the violence, offering conciliation, educating the parties, or requesting assistance to be provided to the victims by other people or organisations.

Persons nearby, individuals or organisations discovering, being aware of or being asked to give assistance to victims who are in a situation threatening their life [or] physical health, impacting on their mental health, or damaging their assets shall give assistance to the victims in the abovementioned ways.

In the case of domestic violence which results in danger, such as physical violence, [or] burning [or] destroying houses, assets and other things, such assistance must be given promptly as provided in paragraphs 1 and 2 of Article 28 of this law.

Any individual or organisation which provides assistance to the victims in good faith shall be protected according to the laws.

23 There is a connotation of both alimony and child support.

24 This is a reference to the methods of assistance described in the previous paragraph.

25 There is a connotation of the house together with structures that are connected to the house.

Article 35. Settlement of Domestic Violence against Women and Children

If the violence is not serious, the solution to it shall start from mediation and education of the user of the violence by family members, close relatives, persons nearby, counselling units to that by village mediation units , while keeping in mind the need for unity, harmony and happiness in the family.

If the village mediation unit is unable to solve the problem, [or] if the violence is severe, then the village mediation unit, the counselling unit, the victim or his or her representative has the right to file a complaint to the police.

Article 36. Action by Police Officers

After receiving a complaint from the village mediation unit, the counselling unit, the victims or their representatives, the police officers shall try to settle the matter while keeping in mind the need for unity, harmony and happiness in the family. If the violence is not serious, the police officers shall try to conciliate, [and] educate the parties with a view to reaching reconciliation and mutual trust in the family.

If the abovementioned conciliation is unsuccessful, or if the violence is serious, the police officers shall institute legal proceedings and use measures as provided under the laws.

In such legal proceedings, if there is reliable evidence that the violence constitutes an offence, the police officers shall send the case to the public prosecutors, who will then prosecute the offender in court according to the laws.

Article 37. Combating Domestic Violence against Women and Children

Domestic violence against women and children is a problem which is dangerous to the society, impacts on families, causes lack of warm family environment, [and causes] family separation, which makes it impossible for women and children to live in the family, creating a potential cause for them to become victims of trafficking, drug addiction, and prostitution.

To combat domestic violence, the administrative authorities, the Lao Front for National Construction, mass organisations, and social organisations shall pay attention to the dissemination of information to and the education of families to be harmonious and to have gender equality, aiming at ensuring that the institutionof the family is stable, happy and progressive.

26 There is a connotation that each step in this sequence should be attempted, and that it should be attempted in the order set out.

27 The translators are aware that there appears to be an inconsistency between this article and Article 22 of the Penal Law, which requires that the complaint be lodged by the victim, not by third parties such as the village mediation unit or counselling unit.

28 There is a connotation of "giving strong guidance" which is a more assertive role than the mediation contemplated by Article 35.

Article 38. Rights of Women and Children to Counselling

In order to protect the rights and interests of women and children, women and children have the rights to counselling, legal advice, moral advice, advice on health issues and othersfrom organisations that provide counselling services.

Rights and duties of those counselling organisations will be provided in specific regulations.

PART V RESPONSIBILITIES FOR THE DEVELOPMENT AND PROTECTION OF WOMEN

Article 39. Responsibilities of the State

The State defines policies, laws and regulations, mechanisms, and measures in a systematic way to develop and protect the rights and interests of women, including combating and preventing trafficking in women and children, [and] domestic violence against women and children in the family, and [the State] will assign to concerned sectorsfor implementation.

The State provides an appropriate budget to organisations that provide

assistance to victims of trafficking and domestic violence against women and

children.

In order to have effective development and protection of women, the State has a policy to establish a fund for the development of women.

Article 40. Responsibility of the Society

The Lao Front for National Construction, mass organisations, and social organisations have the responsibility to educate, create conditions for, and

facilitate the development and protection of the rights and interests of women, and to participate in the implementation of policies, laws and regulations, mechanisms, and measures of the State as provided in Article 39 of this law.

29 In the sense of the abstract concept of the family.

30 "Others" is a literal translation and is not subject to further specificity.

31 The word "sector" is used here to refer to the cluster of government ministries or agencies responsible for a particular area.

Article 41. Responsibility of the Family

The family should promote and support and provide opportunities to women and children for selfdevelopment in all aspects, [and] to enjoy equality, rights, and benefits. In addition, the family has an obligation to protect women and children from trafficking in women and children, as well as domestic violence.

Article 42. Responsibility of Women

Women should be active in selfdevelopment in all aspects, such as physical, moral, educational, professional, and skill development, including upgrading knowledge in politics, economics, socioculture, national defence, and security and foreign affairs. In addition, women should be active in the protection of their legitimate rights and interests, should be aware of and not become victims of trafficking in women and children, and should prevent and combat against trafficking in women and children, as well as domestic violence.

PART VI MANAGING AND MONITORING THE DEVELOPMENT AND PROTECTION OF WOMEN

33 34

Article 43. Management and MonitoringOrganisation

The government uniformly manages and monitors the implementation of activities relating to the development and protection of women.

The government assigns concerned sectors such as public health, education, information and culture, labour and social welfare, national security, foreign affairs, [and] local administrations, together with the Lao Women's Union, the Lao Front for National Construction, the Lao Federation of Trade Unions, the Lao People's Revolutionary Youth Union, [and] public prosecutors, to manage and monitor the development and protection of women.

32 This connotes the abstract notion of family rather than a reference to actual families.

33 In the Lao language, the same word is used to represent all of the following related (but slightly different) concepts: "control", "inspection", "supervision", "audit" and "monitoring". As used in this law, the translators have chosen "monitoring" (and its variants) as the most appropriate English equivalent but readers should note and bear in mind the other meanings that might have been intended.

34 In the Lao language, the word roughly meaning "the entire organisation of responsible governmental agencies" is capable of being translated as any one of the following English words: "organisation", "agency", or "authority". In choosing which English word to use, the translators have adopted the following convention. Where the governmental agencies in question have in practice adopted an English term for themselves (e.g., the Tax Authority), the translators have used that term. Otherwise, as in this law, the translators have used the generic term "organisation". In this law, there is

an added ambiguity as to whether the relevant "organisation" is intended to be the government itself, all the entities mentioned in the second paragraph of Article 43 or the Lao Women's Union.

In the management and monitoring of the development of women, the Lao Women's Union plays the central role in coordination with other concerned sectors.

When it is deemed necessary, the government may establish a task force

committee on the management and monitoring of the development and protection of women.

Article 44. Rights and Duties of the Management and Monitoring Organisation

The management and monitoring organisation described in Article 43 of this law has responsibilities to develop regulations [and] measures and to implement activities relating to the development and protection of women according to the scope of its rights and duties.

Article 45. Rights and Duties of the Central Lao Women's Union

In the management and monitoring of the development and protection of women, the central Lao Women's Union has the following rights and duties:

To study, formulate, [and] draft policies, programs, projects, [and] laws and regulations relating to the development and protection of women, and to propose to concerned authorities for consideration;

To disseminate and provide education on the Party's policies and the State's laws and regulations relating to [such] development and protection;

To organise counselling on the rights and interests of women and children;

To guide, monitor, oversee, and promote the implementation of the policies, laws, plans, programs, [and] projects in the field of women development and the protection of rights and interests of women and children within the scope of its responsibilities;

To give advice and request concerned sectors to solve any incorrect action and respond to such request within 30 days after receiving such request . If the request is not resolved or is inappropriately resolved, the central Lao Women's Union has the right to propose to a higher authority to consider and solve the problem. If the act constitutes a severe offence, [the central Lao Women's Union] has the right to request the police to take legal action against violators according to the laws;

To coordinate with concerned parties in the management and monitoring of the development and protection of the rights and interests of women and children;

To summarise, assess, and report on the implementation of the direction and policies [and of] laws and regulations on the development and protection of women in coordination with concerned sectors;

The concerned sectors must respond within the specified time.

8. To exercise such other rights and perform such duties as prescribed by laws and regulations.

Article 46. Rights and Duties of Women's Unions in Sectoral Agencies and Local Administrations In the management and monitoring of the development and protection of women, women's unions in the sectoral agencies and local administrations have the following rights and duties:

To study, disseminate and implement the policies, laws and regulations, plans, and projects in the field of the development and protection of women;

To provide counselling services on the rights and interests of women and children;

To guide and monitor the implementation of laws and regulations, and activities relating to the development and protection of women within the scope of their responsibilities;

To give advice and request concerned sectors to solve any incorrect action and respond to such request within 30 days after receiving such request. If the request is not resolved or is inappropriately resolved, the women's unions in the sectoral agencies and local administrations have the right to propose to a higher authority to consider and solve the problem. If the act constitutes a severe offence, [the women's unions] should have the right to request the police to take legal action against violators according to the laws;

To coordinate with concerned parties in the management and monitoring of the development and protection of the rights and interests of women and children;

To summarise, assess and report on the implementation of the direction and policies [and of] laws and regulations on the development and protection of women in coordination with concerned sectors;

To exercise such other rights and perform such other duties as prescribed by laws and regulations.

This refers to "direction" in the sense of strategy or trend, not to specific individual instructions.

PART VII POLICIES TOWARDS PERSONS WHO HAVE OUTSTANDING PERFORMANCE AND MEASURES AGAINST VIOLATORS

Article 47. Policies towards Persons with Outstanding Performance

Individuals or organisations with outstanding performance in implementing and participating in the management and monitoring of the development and protection of the rights and interests of women and children, who have provided assistance to victims, who have prevented and combated against trafficking in women and children, and domestic violence against women and children, including providing counselling service, should be rewarded and receive other policies in accordance with regulations.

Article 48. Measures against Violators Individuals or organisations that violate this law will be subject to measures such as reeducational measures and penal measures, depending on the gravity of the violation, including civil compensation for damages.

Article 49. Penal Measures against Trafficking in Women and Children

Any person committing the offence of trafficking in women and children shall be punished by five to fifteen years of imprisonment and shall be fined from 10,000,000 Kip to 100,000,000 Kip, and shall be subject to confiscation of property as provided under Article 32 of the Penal Law.

In cases where offenders organise themselves, the victims are children, the victims are more than two persons, the victims are close relatives of the offenders, [or] the victims suffer severe injury [or] mental insanity, the offender in trafficking in women and children shall be punished by fifteen to twenty years of imprisonment and shall be fined from 100,000,000 Kip to 500,000,000 Kip[,] and shall be subject to confiscation of property as provided under Article 32 of the Penal Law.

In cases where offenders cause the victim lifetime incapacity, or [cause the victim to be] infected with HIV/AIDS, or cause death, the offender in trafficking in women and children shall be punished with life imprisonment and shall be fined from 500,000,000 Kip to 1,000,000,000 Kip[,] and shall be subject to confiscation of property as provided under Article 32 of the Penal Law, or shall be subject to capital punishment.

Preparation and attempts shall be subject to punishment.

Any person who has been an accomplice in the trafficking of women and children, as stipulated in paragraph 3 of Article 24 of this law, shall be punished by four to ten years of imprisonment and shall be fined from 5,000,000 Kip to 50,000,000 Kip[,] and shall be subject to confiscation of property as provided under Article 32 of the Penal Law.

Article 50. Measures against Domestic Violence Against Women and Children

Any individual committing domestic violence against women and children, as provided in Articles 30, 31 and 32 of this law, shall be reeducated and receive an [official] warning.

In a case where the domestic violence constitutes an offence, the offender shall be punished according to the Penal Law.

Article 51. Criminal Measures against Those who Do Not Assist Victims

Any person who does not assist the victims of trafficking in women and children or of domestic violence in severe cases[,] where he or she is capable of giving such assistance[,] is punishable in accordance with Article 86 of the Penal Law.

Article 52. Civil Measures

In addition to the penalties referred to in Articles 49, 50 and 51 of this law, the offenders shall also make compensation for damages, such as: costs of medical treatment and mental rehabilitation, loss of income, travel costs, costs of board and lodging, and other losses.

PART VIII FINAL PROVISIONS

Article 53. Implementation

The government of the Lao People's Democratic Republic and the central Lao Women's Union are assigned to implement this law.

37 There is a connotation that this is a document of warning.

38 This is a translation of a single Lao word "allowance" which refers to both food and accommodations.

Article 54. Effectiveness

This law shall enter into force on the date ninety days after it is

promulgated by a decree of the President of the Lao People's Democratic Republic.

Regulations and provisions which contradict this law shall be void.

Vientiane, 22 October 2004 President of the National Assembly

TRAVELING TO LAOS

US STATE DEPARTMENT SUGGESTIONS

COUNTRY DESCRIPTION: Laos is a developing country with a socialist government that is pursuing economic reform. Outside of Vientiane, the capital, and Luang Prabang, tourist services and facilities are relatively undeveloped.

ENTRY REQUIREMENTS: A passport and visa are required. Visas are issued upon arrival in Laos to foreign tourists and business persons, subject to certain conditions, at the following points of entry: Wattay Airport, Vientiane; Luang Prabang Airport; Friendship Bridge, Vientiane; Ban Huay Xai, Bokeo Province; and Vantao, Champasak Province. In the United States, U.S citizens may apply for visas and obtain further information about entry requirements directly from the Embassy of the Lao People's Democratic Republic, 2222 S St. N.W., Washington, D.C. 20008, tel. 202-332-6416, fax 202-332-4923, Internet home page: http://www.laoembassy.com. U.S. citizens should not attempt to enter Laos without valid travel documents or outside official ports of entry. Unscrupulous travel agents have sold U.S.-citizen travelers false Lao visas, which have resulted in those travelers being denied entry into Laos.

SAFETY AND SECURITY: The security situation in Laos can change quickly. Please refer to any Department of State Public Announcements for Laos for additional information.

Since the Spring of 2000, a number of bombings have occurred in public places frequented by foreign travelers in Vientiane, and there have been credible reports of other explosive devices found in Savannakhet and Pakse cities. While there is no evidence that this violence is directed against American citizens or institutions, American citizens should be aware that more such incidents could occur in the future. American citizens traveling to or residing anywhere in Laos are advised to exercise caution and to be alert to their surroundings.

Persons traveling overland in some areas, particularly Route 13 north between Kasi and Luang Prabang; Saisombun Special Zone; Xieng Khouang Province, including the Plain of Jars; and Route 7 east from the Route 13 junction, run the risk of ambush by insurgents or bandits. There have been violent incidents in these areas in the past year. Some groups have warned of impending insurgent attacks in these areas. Americans considering travel outside urban centers by road or river are advised to contact relevant Lao government offices and the U.S. Embassy for the most current security information.

American citizens should also avoid traveling on or across the Mekong River at night along the Thai border. In some areas, Lao militia forces have been known to shoot at boats on the river after dark.

INFORMATION ON CRIME: While Laos generally has a low rate of crime, visitors should exercise appropriate security precautions and remain aware of their surroundings. Street crime has been on the increase, particularly motorcycle drive-by theft of handbags and backpacks. The loss or theft abroad of a U.S. passport should be reported immediately to the local police and the U.S. Embassy. Useful information on safeguarding valuables and protecting personal security while traveling abroad is provided in the Department of State pamphlet, *A Safe Trip Abroad*, available from the Superintendent of Documents, U.S. Government Printing Office, Washington, D.C. 20402, via the Internet at http://www.access.gpo.gov/su_docs, on the Bureau of Consular Affairs home page at http://travel.state.gov and autofax service at 202-647-3000, or at the U.S. Embassy in Vientiane.

MEDICAL FACILITIES: Medical facilities and services are severely limited and do not meet Western standards. The blood supply is not screened for HIV or AIDS.

MEDICAL INSURANCE: U.S. medical insurance is not always valid outside the United States. U.S. Medicare and Medicaid programs do not provide payment for medical services outside the United States. Doctors and hospitals often expect immediate cash payment for health services. Uninsured travelers who require medical care overseas may face extreme difficulties.

Please check with your own insurance company to confirm whether your policy applies overseas, including provision for medical evacuation, and for adequacy of coverage. Serious medical problems requiring hospitalization and/or medical evacuation to the United States can cost tens of thousands of dollars. Please ascertain whether payment will be made to the overseas hospital or doctor or whether you will be reimbursed later for expenses that you incur. Some insurance policies also include coverage for psychiatric treatment and for disposition of remains in the event of death.

Useful information on medical emergencies abroad, including overseas insurance programs, is provided in the Department of State, Bureau of Consular Affairs brochure, *Medical Information for Americans Traveling Abroad*, available via the Bureau of Consular Affairs home page at http://travel.state.gov and autofax service at 202-647-3000.

OTHER HEALTH INFORMATION: Vaccination recommendations and prevention information for traveling abroad may be obtained through the Centers for Disease Control and Prevention's international travelers hotline from the United States at 1-877-FYI-TRIP (1-877-394-8747), via its toll-free autofax service at 1-888-CDC-FAXX (1-888-232-3299), or via their Internet site at http://www.cdc.gov.

ROAD SAFETY: While in a foreign country, U.S. citizens may encounter road conditions that differ significantly from those in the United States. The information below concerning Laos is provided for general reference only, and may not be totally accurate in a particular location or circumstance:
Safety of Public Transportation: Poor
Urban Road Conditions/Maintenance: Poor
Rural Road Conditions/Maintenance: Poor
Availability of Roadside Assistance: Poor

Roads are mostly unpaved, pot-holed and poorly maintained in most parts of the country, although there has been a successful effort to improve roads and drainage in the capital in recent years. There are no railroads. Public transportation in Vientiane is generally poor and unreliable, and it is very limited after sunset. Taxis are available. Drivers speak little or no English. Most taxis are old and poorly maintained. Traffic is increasing, and local drivers remain undisciplined. Pedestrians and drivers should exercise great caution at all times. Theoretically, traffic moves on the right, but most cars, like pedestrians and bicycles, use all parts of the street. Cyclists pay little or no heed to cars on the road, and bicycles are rarely equipped with functioning lights or reflectors. This makes driving especially dangerous at dusk and at night. Defensive driving is necessary. The U.S. Embassy in Vientiane advises its personnel to wear helmets, gloves, and sturdy shoes while operating motorcycles.

AVIATION OVERSIGHT: Serious concerns about the operation of Lao Aviation, particularly regarding its safety standards and maintenance regime, have caused the U.S. Embassy to advise its personnel to limit domestic travel on Lao Aviation to essential travel only. Americans who are required to travel by air within Laos may wish to defer their travel or consider alternate means of transportation.

Also, since there is no direct commercial air service at present, nor economic authority to operate such service between the U.S. and Laos, the U.S. Federal Aviation Administration (FAA) has not assessed Laos' Civil Aviation Authority for compliance with international aviation safety standards for oversight of Laos' air carrier operations. For further information, travelers may contact the Department of Transportation within the U.S. at tel. 1-800-322-7873, or visit the FAA Internet home page at http://www.faa.gov/avr/iasa/iasa.pdf. The U.S. Department of Defense (DOD) separately assesses some foreign air carriers for suitability as official providers of air services. For information regarding the DOD policy on specific carriers, travelers may contact the DOD at tel. 1-618-229-4801.

RELIGIOUS WORKERS: Religious proselytizing or distributing religious material is strictly prohibited. Foreigners caught distributing religious material may be arrested or deported. The Government of Laos restricts the import of religious texts and artifacts. While Lao law allows freedom of religion, the government registers and controls all associations, including religious groups. Meetings, even in private homes, must be registered, and those held outside established locations may be broken up and the participants arrested.

MARRIAGE TO A LAO CITIZEN: The Lao Government imposes requirements on foreigners intending to marry Lao citizens. U.S. citizens may obtain information about these requirements at the U.S. Embassy in Vientiane. A marriage certificate is not issued by the Lao Government unless the correct procedures are followed. Any attempt to circumvent Lao law governing the marriage of Lao citizens to foreigners may result in deportation of the foreigner and denial of permission to re-enter Laos. Similar restrictions exist prohibiting the cohabitation of Lao nationals with nationals of other countries.

PHOTOGRAPHY AND OTHER RESTRICTIONS: Police and military may arrest persons taking photographs of military installations or vehicles, bridges, airfields and government buildings, and confiscate their cameras. Confiscated cameras are seldom returned to the owners. The photographers may be arrested. Export of antiques, such as Buddha images and other old cultural artifacts, is restricted by Laotian law.

CRIMINAL PENALTIES: While in a foreign country, a U.S. citizen is subject to that country's laws and regulations, which sometimes differ significantly from those in the United States and do not afford the protections available to the individual under U.S. law. Penalties for breaking the law can be more severe than in the United States for similar offenses. Persons violating the law, even unknowingly, may be expelled, arrested or imprisoned. Penalties for possession, use or trafficking in illegal drugs in Laos are strict, and convicted offenders can expect jail sentences and fines. Local police and immigration authorities sometimes confiscate passports when outstanding business disputes and visa matters remain unsettled.

CONSULAR ACCESS: The United States and Laos are parties to the Vienna Convention on Consular Relations (VCCR). Article 36 of the VCCR provides that if an arrestee requests it, foreign authorities shall, without delay, inform the U.S. Embassy. U.S. consular officers have the right to be notified of a U.S. citizen's detention and to visit the arrestee. Lao authorities do not always notify the U.S. Embassy or grant U.S. consular officers access to incarcerated U.S. citizens in a timely manner. Nevertheless, American citizens who are arrested or detained in Laos should always request contact with the U.S. Embassy.

CUSTOMS REGULATIONS: Lao customs authorities may enforce strict regulations concerning temporary importation into or export from Laos of items such as religious materials and artifacts, and antiquities. It is advisable to contact the Embassy of the Lao People's Democratic Republic in Washington for specific information regarding customs requirements. (Please see sections on "Religious Workers" and "Photography and Other Restrictions" above.)

CHILDREN'S ISSUES: For information on international adoption of children and international parental child abduction, please refer to our Internet site at http://travel.state.gov/children's_issues.html or telephone (202) 736-7000.

REGISTRATION/EMBASSY LOCATION: U.S. citizens living in or visiting Laos are encouraged to register at the U.S. Embassy where they may obtain updated information on travel and security within the country. The U.S. Embassy is located at Rue Bartholonie (near Tat Dam), B.P. 114, in Vientiane; mail can be addressed to American Embassy Vientiane, Box V, APO AP 96546; telephone (856-21) 212-581, 212-582, 212-585; duty officer's emergency cellular telephone (856-020) 511-740; Embassy-wide fax number (856-020) 518-597; Embassy-wide fax number (856-21) 212-584; Internet home page: http://usembassy.state.gov/laos/.

PRACTIVCAL INFORMATION FOR TRAVELERS

The Lao People's Democratic Republic, strategically located at the hub of Indochina-sharing borders with China, Vietnam, Cambodia, Thailand and Myanma ☐ is emerging as the region's newest fledgling economy.

After a lengthy period of political instability, the Lao People's Democratic Republic was established in 1975. As a result of the government's New Economic Mechanism launched in 1986, and with Lao PDR's imminent entry into ASEAN, the past decade has been marked by unprecedented growth. Signs of new prosperity are especially visible in the capital of Vientiane, where advancements in infrastructure and services have been occurring rapidly.

Parallel to this recent economic development is the opening of Lao PDR as a tourist destination. With its rich culture, traditional lifestyle, expanding economy and unspoil natural beauty, the Lao PDR welcomes adventurers and business visitors alike.

Step in and experience the great diversity of cultural sights and attractions, restaurants, leisure activities and shopping areas. The Lao PDR is yours to discover.

CULTURAL FESTIVALS

Colorful religious and cultural festivals involve the whole community ☐ come and celebrate in distinctive Lao style. Some of the major festivals are featured on these two pages. If you are fortunate enough to be here for one of our holidays, we hope you will join in the festivities with us.

Pi Mai ☐ **Mid-April**

From the washing of religious icons to the drenching of friends and strangers, water is central to *Pi Mai* or Lao New Year celebrations. Wander through temple compounds as worshippers pour perfumed water over Buddha images ☐ and each other. Even if you miss the significance of cleansing and renewal, you won't escape the traditional water throwing. Expect to be ambushed by celebrants with buckets of water. No one stays dry - or really wants to - during *Pi Mai*.

Three days in mid-April are official public holidays. Exact dates are announced by the government.

Boun Bang Fai - May

On the verge of planting season, the Rocket Festival or *Boun Bang Fai* is held to coax rain and fertility back to the earth. Bamboo rockets adorned with brightly colored decorations are carried to the launch in rowdy procession. Some celebrants paint their faces or wear wild masks and outlandish costumes. All come to enjoy Lao music, dance, and drama ☐ especially the bawdy *maw lam* ☐ at its most playful.

For additional analytical, business and investment opportunities information,
please contact Global Investment & Business Center, USA
at (703) 370-8082. Fax: (703) 370-8083. E-mail: ibpusa3@gmail.com
Global Business and Investment Info Databank - www.ibpus.com

Join Boun Bang Fai celebrations on weekends in May at varying locations.

Boun Khao Phansa ☐ July to October

Boun Khao Phansa is the first day of the Buddhist Lent, which is held from full moon in July to full moon in October. During this time of austerity, monks fast and people make offerings to gain merit. Traditionally, no weddings or celebrations are scheduled during these three months.

Early in the morning on the first day of Lent, people flock to temples carrying silver bowls full of gifts to offer the monks. For a breathtaking sight, go to one of the larger temples, like *That Luang*, where hundreds of worshippers ☐ mostly women in vividly-colored silks☐ kneel row upon row.

Boun Ok Phansa ☐ October/November

Boun Ok Phansa ☐ the final and most important day of Lent ☐ also features an early morning temple ceremony. After dusk, candlelit processions grace temple grounds and buildings glow with candles burning in honor of Buddha.

Also after dusk is *Lai Heua Fai*, a river ceremony during which small hand-made boats is floated down-river by people praying and making vows. The candlelit rafts hob away into darkness, symbolically dismissing bad luck, disease, and sin. This festival is similar to Thailand's *Loy Krathong* festival, which is held in December.

Boun Souang Heua☐ October

Held the day after *Ok Phansa*, *Boun Souang Heua* or the Boat race Festival draws crowds of excited spectators to the Mekong River. Fifty-member teams in wooden longboats row to the rhythm of drums as they compete for the coveted trophy. The races are held close to Vientiane. A carnival provides additional entertainment along the riverbank.

Boun That Luang☐ November

Held during the time of the full moon in November, the *That Luang* Festival is celebrated in honor of Lao PDR's national shrine. The festival begins with a Morning Prayer and alms giving ceremony on the first day of the three-day festival.

Masses of faithful worshippers come to pay homage to the hundreds of monks gathered at *That Luang*. This ceremony, like *Khao Phansa*, is solemn yet colorful.

A carnival held during these three days offers food and handicraft stalls, bumper cars, a shooting gallery, curiosity booths, pinball, games of chance, and musical entertainment. For sports fans, the highlight of *Boun That Luang* is *tee khee*, or field hockey.

In 1995, two weeks before the actual festival, an international trade fair was held for the first time. Many large local and international companies were present at this important event.

Lao National Day December 2

On this important public holiday, parades and speeches commemorate the 1975 Lao People's Revolutionary Victory over the monarchy.

Vietnamese & Chinese New Year January/February

Firecrackers explode all through this holiday, and mouth-watering sweetmeats and other delicacies are made especially for the occasion. Celebrations are held in January or February, with many business and market stalls closing for three days.

OFFICIAL HOLIDAYS

The following official public holidays for 1996 have been announced by the Prime Minister's Office:

1-3 January International New Year's Day

20 January Military Day (Military only)

8 March Lao Women's Day (Women only)

13-15 April Lao New Year

1 May Labor Day

7 October Teacher's Day (Teachers only)

2 December Lao National Day

VIENTIANE

Vientiane's small size allows easy travel around the city. Most tourist attractions and shopping areas are within walking distance of major hotels. If preferred, most tour operators can organize a one-day tour to these attractions. For day excursions outside Vientiane, it is best to consult a travel agent.

That Luang

The national shrine of the country, *That Luang*, or Great Sacred Stupa, stands 45 meters tall and is believed to contain a relic of the Lord Buddha. The original structure was built by King Setthathirath in 1566, and the present structure was restored in 1953. The gold-colored central structure of this stupa echoes the curving lines of an elongated lotus bud, and the gold is a symbol of the country's wealth. This shrine is the center of the *That Luang* festival held in November.

Revolutionary Monument

For additional analytical, business and investment opportunities information,
please contact Global Investment & Business Center, USA
at (703) 370-8082. Fax: (703) 370-8083. E-mail: ibpusa3@gmail.com
Global Business and Investment Info Databank - www.ibpus.com

Located close to That Luang, this monument stands as a memorial to those who died in the Revolutionary War.

Patuxai

Built in 1962, *Patuxai*, or the Victory Monument, is a memorial to those who died in wars before the Revolution. Known to some as *Anousavali*, or "the monument," the arch and the surrounding park area attract those who wish to relax with friends and watch Vientiane's traffic speed by. For 200 kip, energetic visitors can climb to the top of the monument for a view of the city. The *Patuxai* itself is open from 08:00 to 17:00, but people continue to enjoy the park into the evening.

That Dam

An old legend tells of a seven-headed dragon that protected the people of Vientiane from Siamese invaders during the 1828 war. This dragon is said to be hidden under *That Dam*, or the Black Stupa, and continues to protect the city to this day.

Revolutionary Museum

This impressive example of French colonial architecture houses a collection of artifacts weapons paintings and photographs depicting the history of the Lao People's Revolution. Most captions are written in Lao and English.

Wat Sisaket

Wat Sisaket is the oldest temple in Vientiane-only one to survive the Siamese invasion in 1828. All other temples have since undergone extensive restoration.

The *wat* features a library, which was ransacked during the invasion, as well as unique frescoes and a grand total of 6,840 Buddha images, hundreds of which are framed in small wall niches.

Wat Phra Keo

Once the royal temple of the Lao monarchy, *Wat Phra Keo* was built in 1566. After being destroyed by the Siamese invaders in 1828 it was rebuilt between 1936 and 1942, and has been used as a museum since the 1970s. The main building-which originally housed the *Phra Keo*, or Emerald Buddha-now contains fine examples of Buddhist sculpture and artifacts including antique drums and palm leaf manuscripts. A short description of each exhibit is given in French.

Wat Simuang

Wat Simuang was built when King Setthathirath established Vientiane as the nation's capital in 1563. This temple enshrines the foundation pillar of Vientiane, and is home to the city's guardian spirit.

Local folklore surrounding the temple's construction tells of a pregnant girl who, for the good of the city, sacrificed herself to the spirit by jumping into the hole before the foundation pillar was lowered.

This temple is one of Vientiane's most popular centers of worship, largely because it houses a Buddha image believed to answer the questions of worshippers who lift it three times, repeating the same question each time. The oddly shaped image is always surrounded by fruit and flowers-offerings of thanks from those who have received its answers.

Wat Ong Teu

Wat Ong Teu, or the Temple of the Heavy Buddha, is the residence of the Deputy Patriarch of the Lao monastic order. The Deputy Patriarch directs Vientiane's Buddhist Institute where monks from all over Laos come to study. The temple also houses a 16th century Buddha weighing several tones.

Suan Vathanatham

Located near the Lao-Thai Friendship Bridge, *Suan Vathanatham* (National Ethnic Cultural Park) offers the visitor a taste of Lao PDR's cultural and natural heritage. Shady paths wind past traditional Lao architecture, an small zoo (featuring alligators, bears, monkey, snakes, hawks, civets, and jungle cats), textile and handicraft shops, food and drink stands, towering dinosaurs, and sculptures of Lao literacy characters including *Sinxai* and the Four Eared Elephant.

Wat Xieng Khouan (Buddha Park)

Situated by the Mekong River about 21 kilometers out of Vientiane municipality, *Wat Xieng Khouan*, despite its name, is not a temple but a sculpture park. Created in 1958, the park captivates visitors with unusual and somewhat disturbing Buddhist and Hindu imagery. For a bizarre experience, climb into the three level model of hell. *Wat Xieng Khouan* offers food and drinks stalls, and is a popular spot for picnics and recreation.

SPORT AND LEISURE ACTIVITIES

Golf

Santisouk Lane Xang Golf and Resort

Located on Thadeua Road, out toward the Friendship Bridge, this gold course claims an international standard. Along with a nine-hole course, the Santisouk Lane Xang offers a driving range, gold shoes and club rental, shower room, and restaurant.

Vientiane Golf Course

The first golf course in Lao PDR, the nine-hole Vientiane golf course is located at Km 6 on Route 13 South.

Night Life

Vientiane offers a wide range of nightclubs and bars with an unique blend of Eastern and Western music. The city's dance floors cater to different tastes from the traditional Lao lamvong to rap. Many establishments offer entertaining light and sound shows and feature popular local bands.

Dokmaideng Fun Park

The Dokmaideng Fun Park is Vientiane's choice destination for children of all ages for an afternoon or evening of bumper cars, swing rides, miniature trains, and video games. Plans are underway to expand the park, adding a waterslide and more.

Thoulakhom Zoo

Another place that is worth visiting is Vientiane province's Thoulakhom Zoo. Located fifty kilometers north of Vientiane municipality, this zoo features many exotic and rare animals from Lao PDR's jungles, from magnificent tigers to mouse deer, elephants, monkeys, parrots, and the newly arrived kangaroos.

SHOPPER'S HEAVEN

Lao PDR is treasure trove of exquisite handicrafts and antiques. Silk and cotton textiles, hand-woven baskets, fine silver-work, detailed woodcarvings, traditional musical instruments and pottery are the pride of the Lao artisan tradition. Art galleries in town feature a wide selection of drawings, watercolors, and oil paintings by local artists.

Many small jewelry and handicraft shops dot the city, and the main shopping center, the *Talat Sao*, houses a head-spinning array of woven textiles, antiques, silver items, and gold jewelry.

Talat Sao

The *Talat Sao* (Morning Market) is comprised of three large pavilions, each with its own Lao style green-tiled roof. The *Talat Sao* offers the shopper everything from silk and fine jewelry to toiletries, electronic equipment and hardware.

The second level of this market is crammed with silver and gold smiths, and there is a good selection of handicrafts and antiques both upstairs and downstairs. The Morning Market also has conveniently-located licensed moneychangers.

Credit Cards

Credit cards are becoming more widely used in Laos, with the most common being VisaCard, MasterCard and American Express. Most major hotels, restaurants and some shops will accept credit cards, but many of the smaller shops, even in the Morning Market, only accept cash.

Nongbouathong Village Weavers

Traditional Lao textile weaving is proudly upheld in this village, and the exquisite results are displayed at the local Pheng Mai Gallery. Nongbouathong village is just a ten-minute drive out of town, and lovers of weaving should not miss this opportunity to watch the weavers at their looms.

The Art of Silk

This silk museum is run by the Lao Women's Union and features a variety of traditional silk pieces created by skillful weavers from different provinces. The items on display are also for sale.

Culinary Treats

Visitors are pleasantly surprised by the many excellent eating establishments in Vientiane. From fabulous Lao, French, Italian, Chinese, Indian, Japanese, and Thai restaurants to mouth-watering chicken roasted over open grills in street stalls, even the most choosy eater will find something to satisfy the plate.

Noodle Houses and Street Stalls

Vientiane abounds with noodle houses-just ask a local to point out the most popular places in town. Different restaurants specialize in different types of noodle dishes, so be adventurous and savour the variety.

Street stalls add undeniable character to the city, and most of them start bustling at sunset. For a Lao food extravaganza, visit Khounboulom Road in the heart of town and try sweet sticky rice with conunut, rich Lao cakes, and loti, the egg pastry roll-ups drizzled with sweetened condensed milk... The list goes on and on and you will not be disappointed.

TRAVELLING OUTSIDE VIENTIANE

Major provincial capitals are serviced by regular Lao Aviation domestic flights. Although internal travel permits are no longer required by foreigners travelling to these areas, it is advisable that travel outside Vientiane is organized through one of the major travel agencies listed in the Gold Pages.

Luang Prabang

This lovely town nestled in the mountains was once capital of Laos. A short forty-minute flight from Vientiane, Luang Prabang is a step back to a time when tradition, culture and religion motivated most activities in Lao society.

Visit the Royal Palace Museum for a fascinating glimpse into the past. Personal artifacts of the Royal Family and gifts from foreign governments are especially interesting. Take a boat trip to *Tham Ting* Caves to see the hundreds of Buddha images enshrined there years ago to protect them from invaders.

Xieng Khouang & Plain of Jars

Xieng Khouang province is home to the Plain of Jars. Scattered across a grassy slope 12 kilometers outside of the provincial capital, are more than 300 ancient stone jars weighing up to six tonnes each. Xieng Khouang was one of Lao PDR's most heavily bombed provinces between 1964 and 1973.

Tham Piu care is a sobering historical sight. *Tham Piu* was used as a bomb shelter by Lao villagers until 1969 when a single rocket fired into the cave killed about 400 people - mostly women and children. Rock debris and human bones from the explosion still litter the cave.

Travelling through the Region

Vientiane is a convenient point from which to travel to other parts of Indochina. The capital is serviced by the national flag carrier, Lao Aviation, and a growing number of foreign airlines, including Air Cambodia, Air Vietnam, Southern China Airlines, Silk Air and Thai International Airways.

Travel from Vientiane to Thailand is convenient with the recent opening of the Australian-built Friendship Bridge, the first bridge across the Mekong River. From the border town of *Nongkhai*, the nearest Thai airport is 60 kilometers away in *Udon Thani*.

BUSINESS INFORMATION

Hotels in Vientiane

There are several excellent hotels and guest-houses in Vientiane offering clean, air-conditioned comfort and genuine Lao hospitality. Most hotels have restaurants, and some of the larger ones have business facilities with facsimile and word processing services. A wide range of prices and features serves the needs of every traveler.

Transport within Vientiane

Vientiane is a small city and easy to move around in. Travelling by jumbo or tuk-tuk is inexpensive and convenient. These vehicles can be hailed from the side of a street or found waiting for customers near markets, restaurants, and hotels. It is wise to know the Lao name of your destination. For most destinations in the city, you should pay no more than 500 kip per passenger. Negotiate the fare before starting on your journey. Taxis are available for hire. Most taxis congregate around the Morning Market and the newer ones have meters. Bicycles and motorcyles can also be hired for a nominal fee.

Clothing and Climate

The climate is tropical, with the monsoons from June until October and the dry season from November to May. The winter months, December to February, can be quite cool and light jackets and sweaters are recommended. If you travel in the provinces during winter months warmer clothing is required as it gets very cold in the mountain areas.

In Vientiane, keep your clothing light, simple and modest. Natural fibers such as silk and cotton are recommended.

Water

Tap water is unsafe for drinking, but purified bottled water is available everywhere. It is not advisable to ear food that has just been rinsed under the tap. Avoid unpeeled fruit and uncooked vegetables.

Electricity

The Lao PDR uses 220 volt power at 50 HZ. Power pints will accept a plug with two flat pins or two round pins. Various adaptors can be purchased at the Morning Market.

For additional analytical, business and investment opportunities information,
please contact Global Investment & Business Center, USA
at (703) 370-8082. Fax: (703) 370-8083. E-mail: ibpusa3@gmail.com
Global Business and Investment Info Databank - www.ibpus.com

SUPPLEMENTS

IMPORTANT CONTACTS

MINISTRIES

1. Presidential Office
Mr. Banhsa
Detvongsone............................21 4209

2. National Assembly
Mr. Outhay
Phatthana............................ 41 3543

3. Prime Minister□s Office
Mr. Seng
Chantho.................................. 21 3656

4. National Sports Committee
Mr. Phaiboon
Chantamaly........................ 21 6009

5. National Geographic Department
Reception...
... 21 4917

6. Office of the Party Central Committee
Mr. Phouthone..4
1 3921

7.Party Central Committee Organization Board
Mr. Kham
Ouan...41 2076

8. Central Control Committee
Central Control Committee Office
....41
2869, 41 4090

9. Propaganda & Training Committee of Central Committee
Mr. Bounsaveng
Hongsavanh......................41 3037

10. Lao Front for National Construction
Mr. Chanthi
Sitthibandith...........................21 3756

11. Commission for External Relations of Central Committee of LPDR
Mr. Thongtham
Latanasouk.....................41 4046

12. Kaysone Phomvihane Museum
Mr. Singthong Singhapanya
.... 41 3167

13. State Planing Committee
Mr. Khamphong
Pholsena..........................21 6562

14. People□s Supreme Court
Ms. Kaisy
Vikaiyalai..................................41 2172

15. Public Prosecutor General□s Office
Mr. Oukham
Sysounon...............................25 2670

16. The Lao Federation of Trade Union
Mr. Solasack
Phetpalignavanh....................22 2473

17. Lao Women□s Union
Ms. Houmphone
Duangdavong..................21 4310

18. Lao Youth Union
Ms. Sonepheng
Phamisay...........................41 6627

19. Lao Red Cross Society
Mr. Khonsavanh
Chanthakham.................21 4504

20. Ministry of Agriculture & Forestry
Mr. Sompong
Souvannamethy....................41 5361

21. Ministry of Commerce
Mr. Thongsi
Bounmatham....................020 503 090

22. Ministry of Financial
Mr.
Kongmoun..............................
41 2406

23. Ministry of Foreign Affaire
Mr.
Somvang..............................
41 4047

24. Ministry of CTPC
Mr. Math
Sounmala.....................41
2093

25. Ministry of Public Health
Mr.
Maiphone..............................
22 2630

26. Ministry of Education
Mr.
Phay.....................................
21 6004

27. Ministry of Justice
Mr. Somphone
Boupphaphan.....................22 2779

28. Ministry of Information & Culture
Mr. Vayolin
Phasavath.............................21 2413

29. Ministry of National Defense
Mr.
Leumxay..............................
41 4854

30. Ministry of Interior
Communication
Dept....................................21 2508

31. Ministry of Industry & Handicraft
Mr.
Chanthavisith.......................
41 5805

32. Ministry of Labor & Social Welfare
Mr. Somphone
Boupphapha.......................22 2779

33. Bank of Lao PDR
Reception...............................
......21 3109

34. Lao Telecommunications
Autocom Office.............................21
6465, 21 6466

35. ETL
Reception...............................
......21 5153

36. EPL
Mr. Someboune
Nouhouang........................21 4843

37. EDL
Mr.
Somsanith...............................
21 2800

38. Lao Water supply Enterprise
Ms.
Noy..
41 2882

39. Department of Civil Aviation
Department
Office......................................51 2163

40. Lao Buddhist Fellowship Organization
Ven.

Bounthavy...4
5 1608

41. NOSPA
Ms.
Khampanh...
75 2180

42. National University of Laos
Mr.
Khamtoun...4
1 6071

BANKS

Banks in Lao

Agricultural Promotion Bank
58 Hengboun St Ban Haysok
Tel. (021) 21 2024   Fax. (021) 21 3957
E-mail: apblao@laotel.com

Banque pour le Commerce Exterieur Lao
1 Pangkham St Ban Xiang nyeun
Tel. (021) 22 3190
Fax. (021) 21 3202, (021) 22 3012
E-mail: bcelhovt@laotel.com

Lao Development Bank
19 Pangkham Rd
P.O BOX 2700
Tel. (021) 21 3300, (021) 21 3302
Fax. (021) 21 3304, (021) 22 2506
E-mail: lmbltdho@laotel.com

Lao-Viet Bank
05 LaneXang Ave Unit 03 Ban Hatsadi Neua
Tel. (021) 25 1422   Fax. (021) 21 2197
Website: www.laovietbank.com

Vientiane Commercial Bank Ltd
1st Floor VTCB Building 33 LaneXang Ave Ban Hatsadi
Tel. (021) 22 2727   Fax. (021) 22 2715

Bangkok Bank
Ban Hatsadi
Tel. (021) 21 3560   Fax. (021) 21 3561

Joint Development Bank
75/1-5 LaneXang Ave Ban Hatsadi
Tel. (021) 21 3536   Fax. (021) 21 3534, (021) 21 3530
Website: www.jdbbank.com

Public Bank Berhad
100/1-4 Taladsao St Ban Hadsadi
Tel. (021) 22 3394   Fax. (021) 22 2743
E-mail: pbbvte@laotel.com

Siam Commercial Bank Public Corporation
117 LaneXang Ave Ban Sisaket
Tel. (021) 21 3501

Standard Chartered
08/3 Lane Xang Avenue
P.O. Box 6895 Vientiane Lao PDR
Tel. (021) 22 2251
Fax. (021) 21 7254

Thai Military Bank Public Co Ltd
69 Khounboulom St Ban Sihom
Tel. (021) 21 7174, (021) 21 6486
Fax. (021) 21 6486

CONSULTANTS

BCS Ltd
40 Unit 2 Ban Oupmoung Luang Prabang Rd
Tel: (021) 21 7541

BDG Consultants
B. Watchan Tha, M. Chanthaboury
P.O.Box 7426
Tel. (021) 25 0250
Fax. (021) 21 8494
E-mail: peterevans@laopdr.com
Website: http://www.bluegrass.laopdr.com

Bureau d'Etudes Lao
205 Setthathirath B. Mixay
Tel: (021) 21 5806
Fax: (021) 21 5802
E-mail: bel@pan-laos.net.la

Franklin Advisory Services
2nd Floor VTCB Building Lane Xang
Ave Ban Hatsadi
Tel: (021) 21 7604
Fax: (021) 21 7604

KPMG
Km. 2, B. Khunta, Luang Prabang Rd.
P.O. Box 6978
Vientiane, Lao PDR
Tel: (856 21) 219 491-3
Fax: (856 21) 219 490
Email: kpmglaom@loxinfo.co.th

Lao C.B.S Co Ltd
50 Luang Prabang Rd Ban Oupmoung
Tel: (021) 21 9841, (021) 22 3125
Fax: (021) 22 3125, (021) 21 8600

Lao Inter Mix
66 Luang Prabang Rd Ban Sithan Neua
Tel: (021) 21 2957
Fax: (021) 22 3545

Manley Enterprise Co Ltd
66 Nokeokoummane St Ban Mixay
Tel: (021) 21 4403

Marubeni
43/8 Thadeua Rd Ban Thatkhao
Tel: (021) 21 3539
Fax: (021) 21 5657

Mekoxab
111 Thadeua Rd B. Phaxay
P.O.Box 8695, Sisatanak
Tel/Fax. (021) 35 1963
E-mail: mekoxab@laotel.com
Website: www.businessinlao.com

Midas Economic
Luang Prabang Rd Ban Sihom
Tel: (021) 22 2450

PriceWaterhouseCoopers
Unit 1, Fourth Floor
Vientiane Commercial Building
33 Lane Xang Ave.
P.O. Box 7003
Vientiane
Tel: (856 21) 222 718
Fax: (856 21) 222 723
e-mail: pwc-laos@loxinfo.co.th

Santi Phatthana Services
50 Phanyasi St Unit 5 Ban Sithan Neua
Tel: (021) 21 6640
Fax: (021) 21 5973

SavAngh Advisors & Services Ltd
37/10 Unit 9 Ban Hatsadi
PO Box 7331
Tel. (856 21) 214 173 / 250 945
Fax (856 21) 219 243
E-mail: savandara@savangh-advisors.com
Website: http://www.savangh-advisors.com

SK Consultants
Phonthan Rd Ban Phonthan Neua
Tel: (021) 41 6015
Fax: (021) 41 4568

MULTILATERAL AID AGENCIES

World Bank
B. Phonsay, M. Saysettha, Vientiane Municipality
Tel. 41 4209

Asian Development Bank
Lane Xang Ave, Vientiane Municipality
Tel. 25 0444

International Monetary Fund
B. Xiangngeun, M. Chanthaboury,

Vientiane Municipality | Tel/Fax. 21 3206

CUSTOMS OFFICE CODES

VIENTIANE	10
1. Banvang	10.1
2. Salakham	10.2
PHONGSALY	02
3. Mouangkhoa	02.1
4. Pakha	02.2
LUANGNAMTHA	03
5. Nateuay	03.1
6. Botenh	03.2
OUDOMXAY	04
BOKEO	05
7. Houaysai	05.1
8. Muongmone	05.2
LUANGPRABANG	06
HOUAPHANH	07
9. Nameo	07.1
10. Pahang	07.2
11. Xiengkheuang	07.3
SAYABOURY	08
12. Kenethao	08.1
XIENGKHOUANG	09
13. Namkan	09.1
VIENTIANE MUNICIPALITY	01
14. Thanaleng	01.1
15. Wattay Airport	01.2
16. Post	01.3
17. Fuel	01.4
18. Thadeua	01.5
19. Friendship Bridge	01.6
BOLIKHAMXAY	11
20. Khamkeuth	11.1
21. Paksan	11.2
	11.3

22. Namkading	12
KHAMMOUANE	12.1
23. Thakhek	12.2
24. Paksebangfai	12.3
25. Hineboune	12.4
26. Chilo	13
SAVANNAKHET	13.1
27. Denesavanh	13.2
28. Khanthaboury	13.3
29. Thapasoom	13.4
30. Kengkabao	14
SALAVANE	14.1
31. Paktaphane	15
SEKONG	16
CHAMPASACK	16.1
32. Vangtao	16.2
33. Vennekhame	17
ATTAPEU	17.1
34. Phouyang	18
Special Zone	99
Headquarters	

Annex II

COUNTRY AND CURRENCY CODES

Country Name	Country Code	Currency Code
AFGHANISTAN	AF	AFA
ALBANIA	AL	ALL
ALGERIA	DZ	DZD
AMERICAN SAMOA	AS	USD
ANDORRA	AD	ESP/FRF
ANGOLA	AO	AOK
ANGUILLA	AI	XCD
ANTIGUA AND BARBUDA	AG	XCD
ARGENTINA	AR	ARP

For additional analytical, business and investment opportunities information,
please contact Global Investment & Business Center, USA
at (703) 370-8082. Fax: (703) 370-8083. E-mail: ibpusa3@gmail.com
Global Business and Investment Info Databank - www.ibpus.com

ARMENIA	AM	RUR
ARUBA	AW	AWG
AUSTRALIA	AU	AUD
AUSTRIA	AT	ATS
AZERBAIJAN	AZ	RUR
BAHAMAS	BS	BSD
BAHRAIN	BH	BHD
BANGLADESH	BD	BDT
BARBADOS	BB	BBD
BELARUS	BY	RUR
BELGUIM	BE	BEF
BELIZE	BZ	BZD
BENIN	BJ	XOF
BERMUDA	BM	BMD
BHUTAN	BT	INR/BTN
BOLIVIA	BO	BOB
BOSNIA-HERZEGOVINA	BA	
BOTSWANA	BW	BWP
BOUVET ISLAND	BV	NOK
BRAZIL	BR	BRC
BRITISH INDIAN OCEAN TERRITORY	IO	USD
BRITISH VIRGINIS	VG	USD
BRUNEI DARUSSALAM	BN	BND
BULGARIA	BG	BGL
BURKINA FASO	BF	XOF
BURUNDI	BI	BIF
Entity Name		
CAMEROON	CM	XAF
CANADA	CA	CAD
CAPE VERDE	CV	CVE
CAYMAN IS	KY	KYD

For additional analytical, business and investment opportunities information,
please contact Global Investment & Business Center, USA
at (703) 370-8082. Fax: (703) 370-8083. E-mail: ibpusa3@gmail.com
Global Business and Investment Info Databank - www.ibpus.com

CENTRAL AFRICAN REPUBLIC	CF	XAF
CHAD	TD	XAF
CHILE	CL	CLP
CHINA	CN	CNY
CHRISTMAS IS	CX	AUD
COCOS (KEELING) ISLANDS	CC	AUD
COLOMBIA	CO	COP
COMOROS IS	KM	KMF
CONGO	CG	XAF
COOK IS	CK	NZD
COSTA RICA	CR	CRC
COTE D'IVOIRE	CI	XOF
CROATIA	HR	
CUBA	CU	CUP
CYPRUS	CY	CYP
CZECH REPUBLIC	CZ	CZK
DENMARK	DK	DKK
DJIBOUTI	DJ	DJF
DOMINICA	DM	XCD
DOMINICAN REPUBLIC	DO	DOP
EAST TIMOR	TP	TPE
ECUADOR	EC	ECS
EGYPT ARAB REP OF	EG	EGP
EL SALVADOR	SV	SVC
EQUATORIAL GUINEA	GQ	GOE
ESTONIA	EE	
ETHIOPIA	ET	ETB
FAEROE IS	FO	DKK
FALKLAND ISLANDS (MALVINAS)	FK	FKP
FIJI	FJ	FJD

For additional analytical, business and investment opportunities information,
please contact Global Investment & Business Center, USA
at (703) 370-8082. Fax: (703) 370-8083. E-mail: ibpusa3@gmail.com
Global Business and Investment Info Databank - www.ibpus.com

FINLAND	FI	FIM
FRANCE	FR	FRF
FRENCH GUIANA	GF	FRF
Entity Name		
FRENCH POLYNESIA	PF	XPF
FRENCH SOUTHERN TERRITORIES	TF	FRF
GABON	GA	XAF
GAMBIA	GM	GMD
GEORGIA	GG	RUR
GERMANY, FEDERAL REPUBLIC OF	DE	DEM
GHANA	GH	GHC
GIBRALTAR	GI	GIP
GREECE	GR	GRD
GREENLAND	GL	DKK
GRENADA	GD	XCD
GUADELOUPE	GP	FRF
GUAM	GU	USD
GUATEMALA	GT	GTQ
GUINEA	GN	GNS
GUINEA-BISSAU	GW	GWP
GUYANA	GY	GYD
HAITI	HT	HTG
HEARD AND MCDONALD ISLANDS	HM	USD
HONDURAS	HN	HNL
HONGKONG	HK	HKD
HUNGARY	HU	HUF
ICELAND	IS	ISK
INDIA	IN	INR

INDONASIA REP OF	ID	IDR
IRAN, ISLAMIC REPUBLIC OF	IR	IRR
IRAQ	IQ	IQD
IRELAND	IE	IEP
ISRAEL	IL	ILS
ITALY	IT	ITL
JAMAICA	JM	JMD
JAPAN	JP	JPY
JORDAN	JO	JOD
KAMPUCHEA, DEMOCRATIC	KH	KHR
KAZAKHSTAN	KK	RUR
Entity Name		
KENYA	KE	KES
KIRIBATI	KI	AUD
KOREA, DEM PEOPLE'S REPUBLIC OF	KP	KPW
KOREA, REPUBLIC OF	KR	KRW
KUWAIT	KW	KWD
KYRGYZSTAN	KG	RUR
LAOS PEOPLE DEMOCRATIC REPUBLIC	LA	LAK
LATVIA		
LEBANON	LV	
LESOTHO	LB	LBP
LIBERIA	LS	ZAR/LS
LIBYA	LR	LRD
LIECHSTENSTEIN	LY	LYD
LITHUANIA	LI	CHF
LUXEMBOURG	LT	
	LU	LUF

For additional analytical, business and investment opportunities information, please contact Global Investment & Business Center, USA at (703) 370-8082. Fax: (703) 370-8083. E-mail: ibpusa3@gmail.com
Global Business and Investment Info Databank - www.ibpus.com

MACAU	MO	MOP
MALAGASY REPUBLIC	MG	MGF
MALAWI	MW	MWK
MALAYSIA	MY	MYR
MALDIVES REP OF	MV	MVR
MALI	ML	MLF
MALTA	MT	MTL
MARSHALL IS	MH	USD
MARTINIQUE	MQ	FRF
MAURITANIA	MR	MRO
MAURITIUS	MU	MUR
MEXICO	MX	MXP
MICRONESIA	FM	USD
MOLDOVA	MD	RUR
MONACO	MC	FRF
MONGOLIAN PEO REP	MN	MNT
MONTSERRAT	MS	XCD
MOROCCO	MA	MAD
MOZAMBIQUE	MZ	MZM
MYANMAR	BU	BUK
Entity Name		
NAMIBIA	NA	ZAR
NAURU	NR	AUD
NEPAL	NP	NPR
NETHERLANDS	NL	NLG
NETHERLANDS ANTILLES	AN	ANG
NEW ZEALAND	NZ	NZD
NEW CALEDONIA	NC	XPF
NICARAGUA	NI	NIC
NIGER	NE	XOF
NIGERIA	NG	NGN

For additional analytical, business and investment opportunities information, please contact Global Investment & Business Center, USA at (703) 370-8082. Fax: (703) 370-8083. E-mail: ibpusa3@gmail.com Global Business and Investment Info Databank - www.ibpus.com

NIUE	NU	NZD
NORFOLK ISLAND	NF	AUD
NORTHERN MARIANA IS	MP	USD
NORWAY	NO	NOK
OMAN	OM	OMR
PAKISTAN	PK	PKR
PALAU	PW	USD
PANAMA	PA	PAB/USD
PAPUA NEW GUINEA	PG	PGK
PARAGUAY	PY	PYG
PERU	PE	PES
PHILIPPINES	PH	PHP
PITCAIRN	PN	NZD
POLAND	PL	PLZ
PORTUGAL	PT	PTE
PUERTO RICO	PR	USD
QATAR	QA	QAR
REUNION	RE	FRF
ROMANIA	RO	ROL
RUSSIA	RU	RUR
RWANDA	RW	RWF
SAINT KITTS-NEVIS	KN	XCD
SAINT LUCIA	LC	XCD
SAINT VINCENT AND THE GRENADINES	VC	XCD
Entity Name		
SAN MARINO	SM	ITL
SAO TOME AND PRINCIPE	ST	STD

SAUDI ARABIA	SA	SAR
SENEGAL	SN	XOP
SEYCHELLES	SC	SCR
SIERRA LEONE	SL	SLL
SINGAPORE	SG	SGD
SLOVAK REPUBLIC	SK	SKK
SLOVENIA	SI	
SOLOMAN IS	SB	SBD
SOMALI	SO	SOS
SOUTH AFRICA	ZA	ZAR
SPAIN	ES	ESP
SRI LANKA	LK	LKR
ST HELENA	SH	SHP
ST PIERRE ET MIQUELON	PM	FRF
SUDAN	SD	SDP
SURINAM	SR	SRG
SVALBARD AND JAN MAYEN IS	SJ	NOK
SWAZILAND	SZ	SZL
SWEDEN	SE	SEK
SWITZERLAND	CH	CHP
SYRIAN ARAB REPUBLIC	SY	SYP
TAIWAN	TW	TWD
TAJIKISTAN	TJ	RUR
TANZANIA	TZ	TZS
THAILAND	TH	THB
TOGOLESE	TG	XOF
TOKELAU	TK	NZD
TONGA	TO	TOP
TRAINIDAD AND TOBAGO	TT	TTD
TUNISIA	TN	TND
TURKEY	TR	TRL
TURKMENISTAN	TM	RUR

For additional analytical, business and investment opportunities information,
please contact Global Investment & Business Center, USA
at (703) 370-8082. Fax: (703) 370-8083. E-mail: ibpusa3@gmail.com
Global Business and Investment Info Databank - www.ibpus.com

TURKS AND CAICOS IS	TC	USD
TUVALU	TV	AUD
Entity Name		
UGANDA	UG	UGS
UKRAINE	UA	RUR
UNITED ARAB EMIRATES	AE	AED
UNITED KINGDOM	GB	GBP
UNITED STATES	US	USD
UNITED SATES MINOR OUTLYING ISLANDS	UM	USD
URUGUAY	UY	UYP
UZBEKISTAN	UZ	RUR
VANUATU	VU	VUV
VATICAN CITY STATE	VA	ITL
VENEZUELA	VE	VEB
VIETNAM SOC REP OF	VN	VND
VIRGIN ISLANDS (US)	VI	USD
WALLIS AND FUTUNA	WF	XPF
WESTERN SAHARA	EH	ESP/MAD
WESTERN SAMOA	WS	WST
YEMEN ARAB REPUBLIC OF	YE	YER
YEMEN PEOPLE'S DEMOCRATIC REPUBLIC	YD	YDD
YUGOSLAVIA	YU	YUD
ZAIRE	ZR	ZRZ
ZAMBIA	ZM	ZMK
ZIMBABWE	ZW	ZWD

For additional analytical, business and investment opportunities information,
please contact Global Investment & Business Center, USA
at (703) 370-8082. Fax: (703) 370-8083. E-mail: ibpusa3@gmail.com
Global Business and Investment Info Databank - www.ibpus.com

THE DECLARATION FORM

The declaration form or single administrative document is used for all customs transactions; import, export or transit. It must be complete to be acceptable in customs.

The declaration form has three segments.

1. In the first section(Boxes No.1-23) enter general information on importer, exporter and declarant as well as transport and transaction details.

2. In the second section (Boxes No.24-42) enter details on the item declared, including amount of duties and taxes payable or exempted.

3. Summary of Payment and Responsibility of Declaration Section.

It is presented in the form of (i.) a header sheet, which is used to declare importation, exportation or in transit information for each commodity item (ii.) continuation sheets to declare other commodity items and (iii.) section sheet for official use.
Note. Declaration forms are on sale at all Regional Customs offices.
Instructions to fill each box of the form.

Box No.1   Declaration Regime

Inscribe one of the following codes to identify the type of transaction the declaration is for:

Regime Code	Description
10	Exportation of domestic Goods
14	Exportation under a drawback regime
20	Temporary Exportation
35	Re-Exportation
40	Importation of goods for Home consumption.
4A	Importation of goods for diplomatic use, returning residents, and humanitarian assistance; samples, educational materials and certain religious articles.
4B	Goods ex-warehoused to duty free shops
4C	Goods ex-warehoused for exportation out of Lao PDR
45	Home Consumption of Goods after temporary admission

For additional analytical, business and investment opportunities information,
please contact Global Investment & Business Center, USA
at (703) 370-8082. Fax: (703) 370-8083. E-mail: ibpusa3@gmail.com
Global Business and Investment Info Databank - www.ibpus.com

47	Home Consumption of Goods entered under a warehousing regime
50	Temporary Importation
62	Re-Importation of Goods Exported temporarily
70	Warehousing of Goods
80	Transit

Office Codes.

Enter the code of the office where the declaration is presented. See Annex I for a list of all customs offices and their codes.

Manifest /Airway bill number.

Enter the cargo control number from the air waybill if the goods arrive or leave by air or from the manifest if goods arrive or leave by any other mode of transport.
Declaration Number and Date.

Customs will assign the declaration number and the date when the declaration is presented and registered with customs.

Box No.2   Exporter and Address

If you enter goods for exportation, indicate your name and address as well as the taxpayer identification number (TIN) issued by the Tax Department. If you have not yet been issued a TIN please obtain a number from the nearest tax office and use it on all subsequent customs declarations. Also include your office telephone number. For diplomatic and personal exportations, leave the number field blank.

Box No.3   Gross Mass Kg.

Indicate the gross weight in kilograms of the entire consignment of goods as declared on the manifest or air waybill.

Box No.4   Items

Indicate the total number of items as shown on the invoice.

Box No.5   Total Packages.

Indicate the total number of packages as declared on the manifest or airway bill. In case of bulk cargo, indicate BULK only.

Box No. 6   Importer and Address

If you enter goods for importation, indicate your name and address as well as the taxpayer identification number (TIN) issued by the Tax Department. If you have not been issued a TIN please obtain a number from the nearest tax office and use it on all subsequent customs declarations. Also include your office telephone number. For diplomatic and personal importations, leave the number field blank.

Box No.7   Consignee.

If you are importing goods on behalf of another person, or the other party holds title to the good at time of importation indicate the name and address of the consignee as well as the TIN issued by the Tax Department. Please contact the nearest tax office for a number and use on all subsequent declarations, or obtain the TIN number from the consignee if one has been issued to the consignee by the tax department. For diplomatic importations, leave the number field blank.

Box No.8   Declarant.

If you are a licensed agent authorized to transact business in customs, enter the TIN issued by the Tax Department. If you do not have a TIN, contact the nearest tax office.

Box No.9   Country of Consignment/Destination.

For importation, indicate the country and the code from where the goods have been consigned.
For exportation, indicate the country and the code to where the goods are exported or re-exported.

See Annex II: List of Country and Currency Codes.

Box No.10   Type of License.

Indicate the type of trade or industry license held by you.

Box. No.11   Delivery Terms.

Indicate the terms of delivery of goods either CIF for importation, or FOB for exportation.

Box No.12   Total Invoice in Foreign Currency.

For importation, indicate the total amount of the invoice in foreign currency. See list of Country and Currency Codes in Annex II.

Box No.13   Total Invoice in Local Currency.

Enter here the total value of the invoice in Kip by converting the value declared in box No. 12 with the rate of exchange indicated in box No.16. If there is only one item, this value should correspond to the value declared in box no.38. If there are many items, the total value should correspond to the total of values declared in all the boxes no.38 on the Continuation sheets.

For additional analytical, business and investment opportunities information, please contact Global Investment & Business Center, USA at (703) 370-8082. Fax: (703) 370-8083. E-mail: ibpusa3@gmail.com Global Business and Investment Info Databank - www.ibpus.com

Box No.14   Total FOB (Exports)

Indicate the FOB value of the goods in foreign currency.
(if known)
Box No. 14   Total FOB (Imports)

Enter the FOB value in foreign currency. (if known)

Box No.15   Total FOB Ncy (Import/Export)

For import, leave blank.
For export, indicate the FOB value of the goods in Kip.

Box No.16   Rate of Exchange.

Indicate the rate of exchange of the foreign currency to the Kip and the code of the foreign currency. (The exchange rate shall be that which is in force at time of importation, unless otherwise advised).

Box No.17   Mode of Transport.

Indicate the mode of transport, the voyage number. Also the country code of the nationality of the aircraft, truck or ship.
(if known)

The codes for mode of transport are:

        SEA   1
        RAIL   2
        ROAD   3
        AIR   4

Box No.18   Port of Loading/Unloading.

For imports indicate the name and the code of the foreign country where goods are loaded,
 For exports, indicate the name and the code of the foreign country where goods are destined.

See Annex II for a list of Country Codes.

Box No.19   Place of Shipping/ Landing.

For imports, indicate the place in Lao PDR where goods have arrived. At export, or re-export, indicate the place in Lao PDR from where the goods are exported or re-exported.

Box No.20   Entry/Exit Office.

For additional analytical, business and investment opportunities information,
please contact Global Investment & Business Center, USA
at (703) 370-8082. Fax: (703) 370-8083. E-mail: ibpusa3@gmail.com
Global Business and Investment Info Databank - www.ibpus.com

Indicate the code of the Lao customs office where the declaration is presented for clearance.

In a transit operation, indicate the code of the customs office where the transit operation commences. Also indicate the code of the exit customs office where the transit operations is to be terminated.

Box No.21   Identification Warehouse (Leave blank until bonded warehouses are established)

Indicate the code of the bonded warehouse where goods are to be warehoused or ex-warehoused.

Box No.22   Financial and Banking Data.

Indicate the terms of payment of the transaction, as well as the name of the bank and the branch where payment for the commercial transaction is made.

Box No.23   Attached Documents.

Indicate the codes of attached documents, which support your declaration. (Documents must be originals or certified as true copies).

1		Invoice
2		Manifest
3		Airway bill
4		Packing List
5		Certificate of Origin (If required)
6		Phytosanitary Certificate (If required)
7		Import Permit from Ministry of Trade (If required)
8		Import permit from Ministry of Agriculture (If required)
9		Import Permit from Ministry of Heath (If required)
10		Authorization from Department of Transport (If required)
11		If claiming duty and tax exemptions, documents authorizing such exemptions must be presented with the declaration.

Box No.24   Marks, Numbers and Description of Goods

Indicate the marks and numbers of the packages as shown on the manifest or airway bill.

If goods arrive or leave by containers, indicate the container number as shown on the manifest.

The total number of packages should correspond to the total number of packages indicated in box No.5.

Give a detailed description of the goods. Avoid, as far as possible, trade names. Except in the case of vehicles and electronic devices, provide make and model.

Box No.25   No. of Items.

Indicate the number of items on the invoice.

Box No.26   Tariff Code

Indicate the classification code of the commodity imported. This classification code in based on the AHTN and must be eight digits.

Box No.27   Customs Procedure Codes.
(Leave blank at this time)

Box No.28   Country of Origin/Destination

For imports, indicate the code of the country of origin of the goods imported, if the country of origin of the goods is different from the country where the goods have been consigned.

Box No.29   Zone.
It the goods originate from ASEAN member countries and are supported by a certificate of origin enter ASEAN. For other countries enter GEN. At export enter XPT.

Box No.30   Valuation Code

Indicate the code of the valuation method used to determine the customs value for duty.

There are six valuation methods and coded as follows:

	VALUATION METHOD	Code	
	Transaction Method	1	
	Identical Goods Method	2	
	Similar Goods Method	3	
	Deductive Method	4	
	Computed Method	5	
	Flexible Method	6	

Note: The transaction valuation method must be used as the primary method for valuation if possible.

Box No.31   Gross Mass.

Enter the gross weight in kilograms for the item on the first page only. The total weight of all items on the continuation sheets in the declaration should be equal to the weight declared in box no.3 of the general segment.

Box No.32   Net Mass.

Enter the net weight of the goods in kilograms for each item declared. If a continuation sheet is used a net mass must be inscribed for each item.

Box No.33   FOB Foreign Currency.

Enter the FOB value of the item in foreign currency (if known).

Box No.34   FOB Local Currency, only if transport and insurance are not prepaid by exporter. If prepaid, enter the value that includes transportation and insurance.

Enter the FOB value of the item in Kips, only if transport and insurance are not prepaid by exporter. If prepaid, enter the value that includes transportation and insurance.

Box No. 35   Freight.

Enter the amount of freight paid or payable for the item in Kip. For a shipment of various items, the freight charges are apportioned according to freight paid or payable and by weight. If freight is prepaid by exporter and included in the value, mark the box "Prepaid".

Box No.36   Insurance.

Enter the amount of insurance in Kip for the item.

For a shipment of various items, the insurance paid or payable is to be apportioned.

If the insurance is prepaid by the exporter and included in the value, mark the box "prepaid"

Box No.37   Other Costs.
Enter other costs and expenses incurred for the import of goods and paid to the exporter for the imported goods.

Box No.38   Customs Value in Local Currency.

Enter the customs value for the item, which is the total of values of boxes 33, 34, 35 and 36.

Box No. 39   Supplementary Unit/Quantity.

Some of the most common international units of quantity are as follows:

For additional analytical, business and investment opportunities information,
please contact Global Investment & Business Center, USA
at (703) 370-8082. Fax: (703) 370-8083. E-mail: ibpusa3@gmail.com
Global Business and Investment Info Databank - www.ibpus.com

	Unit	Code	
	Cubic Metre	MTQ	
	Gigawatt-hour	GWH	
	Hundred	CEN	
	Kilogram	KGM	
	Litre	LTR	
	Metre	MTR	
	Number	NMB	
	Number of packs	NMP	
	Square Metre	MTK	
	Ten	TEN	
	Ten Pairs	TPR	
	Thousand	MIL	
	Tonne	TNE	

Enter any of the code, which describes the unit quantity of goods imported/exported. If the units of imports or exports are not included in this list, consult a customs officer for more detailed lists.

Box No.40   Duty Payable.

Enter the amount of duties and taxes payable for the item declared per category of duty, tax and excise.

Enter also the taxable base for each category of duty, tax and excise. Duty rate is calculated on the Customs value. The tax is calculated on the customs value plus the duty payable. The excise tax is calculated on the customs value plus duty payable plus tax payable.

For other items of the declaration, on the continuation sheets enter the duty, tax and excise payable.

Box No.41   Permit Numbers.

Enter permit number and date of issue for the shipment, if required.

Box No.42   Previous Declaration.

If the declaration refers to a previous declaration, the registration number and date of the previous declaration is entered here.

Present a copy of the previous declaration with the declaration you have just prepared.

Responsibility of Declaration

You must enter your full name, indicate the capacity in which you are acting. And sign the declaration.

You must also indicate the mode of payment by which duty and taxes are to be paid.

After you have completed your declaration, you can now lodge it at the designated customs office where your goods are held.

After customs review and approval of the declaration, please make the payment of all applicable duties and taxes, and present a copy of the payment receipt to the customs office where the declaration was presented.

On receipt of the customs release note, present the release note to the warehouse keeper for delivery of the imported goods and sign for receipt of the goods or have the carrier sign for receipt.

STRATEGIC STATISTICS

BASIC DATA

LAND AREA   236,800 km2

POPULATION   4,474,000 persons

No.	Provinces	Population	No.	Provinces	Population
1	Attopeu	84,000	10	Phongsaly	152,000
2	Bokeo	106,000	11	Savannakhet	692,000
3	Bolikhamsay	155,000	12	Saravane	243,000
4	Champasack	490,000	13	Sayaboury	200,000
5	Houaphanh	238,000	14	Sekong	60,000
6	Khammouane	265,000	15	Vientiane Prefecture	503,000
7	Luang Namtha	128,000	16	Vientiane Province	330,000
8	Luang Praba	365,000	17	Xieng Khouang	196,000
9	Oudomsay	193,000	18	Special Region	74,000

LAOS GLOSSARY

Asian Development Bank
Established in 1967, the bank assists in economic development and promotes growth and cooperation in developing member countries. The bank is owned by

its forty-seven member governments, which include both developed and developing countries in Asia and developed countries in the West.

Association of Southeast Asian Nations (ASEAN)
Founded in 1967 primarily for economic cooperation and consisting of Brunei (since 1984), Indonesia, Malaysia, the Philippines, Singapore, and Thailand. Laos has had observer status since 1992 and applied for membership in July 1994.

ban
Village; grouped administratively into *tasseng* (*q.v.*) and *muang* (*q.v.*).

dharma
Buddhist teaching or moral law; laws of nature, all that exists, real or imaginary.

fiscal year (FY)
October 1 to September 30.

gross domestic product (GDP)
A value measure of the flow of domestic goods and services produced by an economy over a period of time, such as a year. Only output values of goods for final consumption and intermediate production are assumed to be included in the final prices. GDP is sometimes aggregated and shown at market prices, meaning that indirect taxes and subsidies are included; when these indirect taxes and subsidies have been eliminated, the result is GDP at factor cost. The word *gross* indicates that deductions for depreciation of physical assets have not been made. Income arising from investments and possessions owned abroad is not included, only domestic production. Hence, the use of the word *domestic* to distinguish GDP from gross national product (*q.v.*).

gross national product (GNP)
The gross domestic product (GDP--*q.v.*) plus net income or loss stemming from transactions with foreign countries, including income received from abroad by residents and subtracting payments remitted abroad to nonresidents. GNP is the broadest measurement of the output of goods and services by an economy. It can be calculated at market prices, which include indirect taxes and subsidies. Because indirect taxes and subsidies are only transfer payments, GNP is often calculated at factor cost by removing indirect taxes and subsidies.

Hmong
Largest Lao Sung (*q.v.*) ethnic group of northern Laos. This tribal group dwells at higher elevations than other ethnic groups. During the period of the Royal Lao Government (RLG) (*q.v.*), the Hmong were referred to as Meo.

International Monetary Fund (IMF)
Established on July 22, 1944, the IMF began operating along with the World Bank (*q.v.*) on December 27, 1945. The IMF is a specialized agency affiliated with the United Nations that takes responsibility for stabilizing international

exchange rates and payments. The IMF's main business is the provision of loans to its members when they experience balance of payments difficulties. These loans often carry conditions that require substantial internal economic adjustments by the recipients. In 1994 the IMF had 179 members.

karma

Buddhist concept of the sum of one's past actions, which affect one's current life and future reincarnations.

khoueng

Province; first order administrative division.

kip(k)

Lao currency. In June 1994, US$1=R721.

Lao Issara

Free Laos. Movement formed in 1945 to resist any attempt to return to French colonial status.

Lao Loum

Literally translated as the valley Laotian. Inclusive term for people of Tai stock living in Laos, including lowland Lao and upland Tai. Group of lowland peoples comprising the majority population of Laos; generally used to refer to ethnic Lao, the country's dominant ethnic group (approximately 66 percent of the population according to the 1985 census), and speaking Tai-Kadai languages, including Lao, Lue, Tai Dam (Black Tai), and Tai Deng (Red Tai).

Lao Patrocitic Front (LPF) (Neo Lao Hak Xat)

Sucessor to Neo Lao Issara (*q.v.*), the political arm of the Pathrt Liberation Army (*q.v.*)--formerly known as the Pathet Lao (q.v.)--is its milituary arm.

Lao People's Army

Formed in 1976 when the Lao People's Liberation Army (LPLA-- *q.v.*) was restructured after the establishment of the Lao People's Democratic Republic in December 1975.

Lao People's Liberation Army (LPLA)

Official title of Pathet Lao armed forces, more commonly known as the communist revolutionaries, or guerrilla forces. The LPLA originated with the Latsavong detachment, formed in January 1949 by Kaysone Phomvihan, and steadily increased in number to an estimated 8,000 guerrillas in 1960 and an estimated 48,000 troops between 1962 and 1970.

Lao People's Revolutionary Party (LPRP) (Phak Pasason Pativat Lao)

Founded secretly in 1955 as the Phak Pasason Lao (Lao People's Party--LPP); name changed in 1972. Seized full power and became the ruling (communist) party of Laos in 1975. The LPRP Central Committee formulates party policy; it is dominated by the Political Bureau (Politburo) and the Secretariat and maintains control by placing its members in key institutions throughout the government and the army.

Lao Sung

Literally translated as the Laotian of the mountain top--those who traditionally live in the high altitudes in northern Laos. In official use, term denotes a category of ethnic groups that speak Tibeto-Burmese, Miao-Yao languages; chiefly the Hmong (*q.v.*) (Meo) group of highland or upland minorities but also the Mien (Yao) and Akha. According to the 1985 census, these groups make up approximately 10 percent of the population.

Lao Theung

Literally, Laotian of the mountain slopes; group--including Kammu, Loven, and Lamet--that traditionally lives in medium altitudes, practices swidden, or slash-and-burn-agriculture, and speaks Mon-Khmer languages and dialects. According to the 1985 census, approximately 24 percent of the population. Regarded as original inhabitants of Laos, formally referred to by ethnic Lao as *kha*, or slave.

mandala

Indian geopolitical term referring to a variable circle of power centered on a ruler, his palace, and the religious center from which he drew his legitimization.

muang (muong)

Administrative district; also an independent principality; comprises several *tasseng* (*q.v.*), second order administrative divisions.

Lao Patriotic Front (LPF) (Neo Lao Hak Xat)

Successor to Neo Lao Issara (*q.v.*), the political arm of the Pathet Lao (*q.v.*) during the Indochina Wars (1946- 75). The Lao People's Liberation Army (*q.v.*)--formerly known as the Pathet Lao (*q.v.*)--is its military arm.

Neo Lao Issara

Free Laos Front--organization established by former Lao Issara (Free Laos) (*q.v.*) to continue anti-French resistance movement with the Viet Minh (*q.v.*); succeeded by Neo Lao Hak Xat (Lao Patriotic Front--LPF) (*q.v.*) in 1956.

net material product

Gross material output minus depreciation on capital and excluding "unproductive services." According to the World Bank (*q.v.*), net material product is "a socialist concept of national accounts."

Nonaligned Movement

Established in September 1961 with the aim of promoting political and military cooperation apart from the traditional East and West blocs. As of 1994, there were 107 members (plus the Palestine Liberation Organization), twenty-one observers, and twenty-one "guests."

Pathet Lao (Lao Nation)

Literally, land of the Lao. Until October 1965, the name for the Lao People's Liberation Army (*q.v.*), the military arm of the Lao Patriotic Front (*q.v.*).

Royal Lao Government (RLG)

The ruling authority in Laos from 1947 until the communist seizure of power in December 1975 and the proclamation of the Lao People's Democratic Republic.

Sipsong Panna

Region in southern Yunnan Province, China, from which migrated many groups that now inhabit Laos.

Southeast Asia Treaty Organization (SEATO)

Established in September 1954 as a result of the 1954 Geneva Agreements to stop the spread of communism in Southeast Asia. SEATO never had an active military role and was ultimately disbanded in June 1977 following the success of the communist movements in Cambodia, Laos, and Vietnam in 1975. Original signatories to SEATO were Australia, Britain, France, New Zealand, Pakistan, the Philippines, Thailand, and the United States.

tasseng

Administrative unit; territorial subdivision of *muang* (*q.v.*), subdistrict grouping of ten to twenty villages.

That Luang

Most sacred Buddhist stupa in Vientiane and site of annual festival on the full moon of the twelfth month.

Theravada Buddhism

Predominant branch of Buddhism practiced in Laos, Cambodia, Sri Lanka, and Thailand.

United Nations Children's Fund (UNICEF)

Acronym retained from predecessor organization, United Nations International Children's Emergency Fund, established in December 1946. Provides funds for establishing child health and welfare services.

United Nations Development Programme (UNDP)

Created by the United Nations in 1965, the UNDP is the world's largest channel for multilateral technical and preinvestment assistance to low-income countries. It functions as an overall programming, financing, and monitoring agency. The actual fieldwork is done by other UN agencies.

United Nations High Commissioner for Refugees (UNHCR)

Established by the United Nations in 1949, it did not become effective until 1951. The first world institution to aid refugees, the UNHCR seeks to ensure the humanitarian treatment of refugees and find a permanent solution to refugee problems. The agency deals with the international protection of refugees and problems arising from mass movements of people forced to seek refuge.

Viet Minh

Coalition of Vietnamese national elements formed in May 1941 and dominated by the communists in their movement calling for an uprising against the French colonial government.

World Bank

Informal name used to designate a group of four affiliated international institutions: the International Bank for Reconstruction and Development (IBRD), the International Development Association (IDA), the International Finance Corporation (IFC), and the Multilateral Investment Guarantee Agency (MIGA). The IBRD, established in 1945, has as its primary purpose the provision of loans at market-related rates of interest to developing countries at more advanced stages of development. The IDA, a legally separate loan fund but administered by the staff of the IBRD, was set up in 1960 to furnish credits to the poorest developing countries on much easier terms than those of conventional IBRD loans. The IFC, founded in 1956, supplements the activities of the IBRD through loans and assistance designed specifically to encourage the growth of productive private enterprises in the less developed countries. The MIGA, founded in 1988, insures private foreign investment in developing countries against various noncommercial risk. The president and certain senior officers of the IBRD hold the same positions in the IFC. The four institutions are owned by the governments of the countries that subscribe their capital. To participate in the World Bank group, member states must first belong to the Intentional Monetary Fund (IMF--*q.v.*).

SELECTED TOUR OPERATORS IN LAOS

The following list is issued by the National Tourism Authority of Lao PDR. This is not an exhaustive list of travel companies. You are advised to contact the travel company directly for their up-to-date itineraries and prices.

Dafi Travel Co., Ltd
093/4 Samsenthai St,
P.O. Box 5351,
Vientiane

Lao Tourism Co., Ltd
08/02 Lane Xang Ave,
P.O. Box 2511,
Vientiane

Luang Prabang Tourism Co., Ltd
P.O. Box 356,
Sisavangvong Rd,
Luang Prabang.

Phathanakhet Phoudoi Travel Co., Ltd
Phonxay Rd,
P.O. Box 5796,
Vientiane

**Phathana Saysomboune
Travel & Tour Co., Ltd**
Km 5, 13 South Rd,
12/G Chommanytai Xaysetha DTR,
P.O. Box 7117,
Vientiane

Chackavane Travel & Tour
92 Thongkankham Rd,
P.O. Box 590,
Vientiane

Raja Tour
03 Heng boon St,
P.O. Box 3655,
Vientiane

Sode Tour
114 Quai Fa Ngum,
P.O. Box 70,
Vientiane

LAO PDR EMBASSIES AND CONSULTATE-GENERAL

Country	Address
Brunei Darussalam	Embassy of the Lao PDR Tel : 673-2-345 666 Fax : 456-888
Cambodia	Embassy of the Lao PDR 15-17 Mao Tse Tung Boulvard P.O. Box 19 Phnom Penh Tel : 855-23-982 632 Fax : 720 907
Indonesia	Embassy of the Lao PDR Jl. Patra Kuningan XIV No.1.A Kuningan Jakarta Selatan - 12950 Tel : 62-21-522 9602, 522 7862 Fax : 522 9601
Malaysia	Embassy of the Lao PDR I Lorong Damai Tiga Kuala Lumpur 55000 Tel : 60-3-248 3895, Residence: 245 6023 HP : 60-012 218 0075 Fax : 60-3- 242 0344
Myanmar	Embassy of the Lao PDR NA I Diplomatic Quarters Franser Road Yangon Tel : 95-1-222 482, 227 445 Fax : 227 446
The Philippines	Embassy of the Lao PDR N. 34 Lapu-Lapu Street Magallences Village Makati City, Manila Tel & Fax : 63-2-833 5759
Singapore	Embassy of the Lao PDR 179-B Gold Hill Centre Thomson Road Tel : 65-250 6044 Fax : 65-250 6214

Thailand	Embassy of the Lao PDR 520-502/ 1-3 Soi Ramkhamheng 39 Bangkapi Bangkok 10310 Tel : 539 6667 Fax : 66-2-539 6678 Consulate General of the Lao PDR Khonkaen Tel : 66-43-223 698, 223 473, 221 961 Fax : 223 849
Vietnam	Embassy of the Lao PDR 22 Rue Tran Bing Trong Hanoi Tel : 84-4-8- 25 4576, 29 6746 Fax : 22 8414 Consulate General of the LAO PDR 93 Larteur ST, District 1 Ho Chi Minh City Tel : 84-8-8- 29 7667, 29 9275 Fax : 29 9272 Consulate General of the LAO PDR 12 Tran Quy-Cap Danang Tel : 84-51-8- 21 208, 24 101 Fax : 22 628
Australia	Embassy of the Lao PDR I Dalman Crescent O' Malley Canberra ACT 2606 Tel : 61-2- 6286 4595, 6286 6933 Fax : 6290 1910
China	Embassy of the Lao PDR 11 Salitun Dongsie Jie Bejing 100 600 IfsTel : 86-1- 6532 1224 Fax : 6532 6748 Consulate General of the Lao PDR Room 3226 Camellia Hotel 154 East Dong Feng Road Kunming 650041 Tel : 86-871- 317 6623, 317 6624 Fax : 317 8556

For additional analytical, business and investment opportunities information,
please contact Global Investment & Business Center, USA
at (703) 370-8082. Fax: (703) 370-8083. E-mail: ibpusa3@gmail.com
Global Business and Investment Info Databank - www.ibpus.com

France	Embassy of the Lao PDR 74 Ave Raymond Poincare 75116 Paris Tel : 33-1- 4553 0298, 4553 7047 Fax : 4727 5789
Germany	Embassy of the Lao PDR Am Lessing 6 53639 Koeningswinter Tel : 49- 2223 21501 Fax : 2223 3065
India	Embassy of the Lao PDR E53 Panchsheel Park New Delhi-17 Tel : 91-11-642 7447 Fax : 642 8588
Japan	Embassy of the Lao PDR 3-3-22 Nishi-Azabu Minato-Ku Tokyo 106 Tel : 81-3-5411 2291, 5411 2292 Fax : 5411 2293
Russia	Embassy of the Lao PDR UI Katchalova 18 Moscow 121 069 Tel : 7-095-203 1454, 291 8966 Fax : 290 4246, 291 7218
Sweden	Embassy of the Lao PDR Badstrandvagen 11 11265 Stockholm Tel : 46-8-618 2010, 695 0160 Fax : 618 2001
United States of America	Embassy of the Lao PDR 2222 S Street NW Washington DC 10022 Tel : 1-202- 332 6416, 332 6417 Fax : 332 4923 Permanent Mission of the Lao PDR 317 East 51st Street New York, NY 10022 Tel : 1-212- 832 2734 Fax : 750 0039

SOCIAL SECURITY AGENCIES BY COUNTRY

Algeria

- Ministère du Travail et de la Sécurité Sociale (Ministry of Labor and Social Security)
- Caisse Nationale des Assurances Sociale (National Social Insurance Fund)
- Caisse Nationale de Sécurité Sociale des Non-Salariés (National Social Security Fund for the Self-Employed)

Antigua and Barbuda

- Antigua and Barbuda Social Security Board

Argentina

- Administración Nacional de la Seguridad Social (National Social Security Administration)
- Superintendencia de Administradoras de Fondos de Jubilaciones y Pensiones (Superintendency of Retirement and Pension Fund Management Companies)

Armenia

- Ministry of Labor and Social Affairs

Aruba

- Banco di Seguro Social Aruba (Social Security Bank Aruba)
- Stichting Algemeen Pensioenfonds Aruba (the civil servants' pension fund)

Australia

- Department of Human Services
- Centrelink

Austria

- Österreichische Sozialversicherung (Austrian Social Insurance)

Azerbaijan

- Azərbaycan Respubikasinin Dövlət Sosial Müdafiə Fondu (State Social Protection Fund)

[Back to top]

Bahamas

- The National Insurance Board

Barbados

- National Insurance Scheme

Bahrain

- Ministry of Labour and Social Affairs
- General Organization for Social Insurance

Belarus

- Ministry of Social Protection

Belize

- Social Security Board

Belgium

- Ministère des Affaires sociales, de la Santé publique et de l'Environnement
- Ministerie van Sociale Zaken, Volksgezondheid en Leefmilieu (Ministry of Social Affairs, Public Health and the Environment)
- Office national des pensions
- Rijksdienst voor pensioenen (National Pension Office)
- Rijksdienst voor Sociale Zekerheid
- Office National Sécurité Sociale (National Office for Social Security)

Bermuda

- Department of Social Insurance

Bolivia

- Superintendencia de Pensiones, Valores y Seguros (Superintendency of Pensions, Securities and Insurance)

Botswana

- Ministry of Labour and Home Affairs

Brazil

- Ministério da Previdência e Assistência Social (Ministry of Social Security and Assistance)

Bulgaria

- Natsionalen Osiguritelen Institut (National Social Security Institute)

Burkina Faso

- Caisse Nationale de Sécurité Sociale (National Social Security Fund)

[Back to top]

Cameroon

- Ministère des Affairs Sociales (Ministry of Social Affairs)

Canada

- Service Canada
- Régie des rentes du Québec
- Quebec Pension Board

Chile

- Superintendencia de Administradoras de Fondos de Pensiones(Superintendency of Pension Fund Management Companies)
- Instituto de Normalización Previsional (Institute of Social Security Standardization)
- Asociación Gremial de Administradoras de Fondos de Pensiones (Union of Pension Fund Management Companies)
- Ministerio de Trabajo y Previsión Social (Ministry of Labor and Social Security)

China

- Ministry of Human Resources and Social Security

Colombia

- Instituto de Seguros Sociales (Social Security Institute)
- Superintendencia Financiera de Colombia (Financial Superintendency of Colombia)

Costa Rica

- Caja Costarricense de Seguro Social (Costa Rican Social Security Fund)
- Superintendencia de Pensiones (Pensions Superintendency)

Côte d'Ivoire

- Caisse Nationale de Prévoyance Sociale (National Social Insurance Fund)

Curaçao

- Banko di Seguro Sosial (Social Insurance Bank)

Croatia

- Ministarstvo rada i socijalna skrbi (Ministry of Labor and Social Welfare)

Czech Republic

- Ministerstvo práce a sociálních věcí (Ministry of Labor and Social Affairs)
- Česká správa sociálního zabezpečení (The Czech Social Security Administration)

[Back to top]

Denmark

- Socialministeriet (Ministry of Children, Gender Equality, Integration and Social Affairs)
- Arbejdsmarkedets Tillaegspension (ATP) (Labor Market Supplementary Pension Scheme)

Democratic Republic of the Congo

- l'Institut National de Sécurité Sociale (The National Social Security Institution)

Dominican Republic

- Consejo Nacional de Seguridad Social (National Social Security Council)

Ecuador

- Instituto Ecuatoriano de Seguridad Social (Ecuadorian Social Security Institute)

El Salvador

- Instituto salvadoreño del seguro social (Salvadoran Institute of Social Security)
- Superintendencia de Pensiones (Superintendency of Pensions)

Estonia

- Sotsiaalministeenum (Ministry of Social Affairs)

Fiji

- Fiji National Provident Fund

Finland

- Sosiaali-Ja-Terveysministeriö (Ministry of Social Affairs and Health)
- Eläketurvakeskus—Pensionsskyddscentralen (Central Pension Security Institute)
- Kansaneläkelaitos—Folkpensionsanstalten (Social Insurance Institution)

France

- Sécurité Sociale (Social Security)
- Caisse National d'assurance viellesse (La Cnav) (National Old-Age Pension Insurance Fund)
- Caisse des Français de l'étranger(CFE) (Fund for French Citizens Abroad)
- Centre des Liaisons Européennes et Internationales de Sécurité Sociale(Center for European and International Social Security Relations)

[Back to top]

Germany

- Bundesministerium für Arbeit und Soziales (Federal Ministry of Labor and Social Affairs)
- Deutsche Rentenversicherung Bund (German Federal Pension Insurance)

Greece

- Idryma Koinonikon Asfaliseon (IKA) (Social Insurance Institute)
- Organismos Asfalisis Eleftheron Epangelmation (Social Security Organization for the Self-employed)
- General Secretariat of Social Security, Ministry of Labour and Social Security

For additional analytical, business and investment opportunities information,
please contact Global Investment & Business Center, USA
at (703) 370-8082. Fax: (703) 370-8083. E-mail: ibpusa3@gmail.com
Global Business and Investment Info Databank - www.ibpus.com

Guatemala

- Ministerio de Trabajo y Previsión Social   (Ministry of Labor and Social Security)

Guyana

- Ministry of Labour, Human Services and Social Security

Hong Kong

- Social Welfare Department
- Mandatory Provident Fund Schemes Authority

Hungary

- Országos Nyugdíjbiztosítási Főigazgatóság (National Pension Insurance)

Iceland

- Tryggingastofnun

Indonesia

- Jaminan Sosial Tenega Kerja (Employees' Social Security System)

India

- Ministry of Labour
- Employees' Provident Fund Organisation India

Ireland

- Department of Social, Community and Family Affairs
- An Roinn Coimirce Sóisialaí

Israel

- National Insurance Institute of Israel

Italy

For additional analytical, business and investment opportunities information,
please contact Global Investment & Business Center, USA
at (703) 370-8082. Fax: (703) 370-8083. E-mail: ibpusa3@gmail.com
Global Business and Investment Info Databank - www.ibpus.com

- Istituto Nazionale della Previdenza Sociale (INPS) (National Social Insurance Institute)

[Back to top]

Japan

- Ministry of Health, Labour and Welfare
- National Institute of Population and Social Security Research

Jordan

- Social Security Corporation

Kazakhstan

- Ministry of Labour and Social Protection

Kenya

- Ministry of Labour and Human Resource Development

Korea (South)

- National Pension Service

Kuwait

- The Public Institution for Social Security

Kyrgyzstan

- Social Fund of the Kyrgyz Republic

Latvia

- Labklājības ministrija (Ministry of Welfare)

- Valsts sociālās apdrošināšanas aġentūra (State Social Insurance Agency)

Liechtenstein

- Liechtensteinische Alters- und Hinterlassenenversicherung (Liechtenstein Old-Age and Survivors Insurance)

Lithuania

- Valstybinio Socialinio Draudimo Fondo Valdyba (State Social Insurance Fund Board)

Luxembourg

- Ministère de la Sécurité Sociale (Ministry of Social Security)
- Sécurité Sociale (Social Security)

[Back to top]

Macau

- Fundo de Segurança Social (Social Security Fund)

Macedonia

- Ministerstvo za Trud i Socijalna Politika (Ministry of Labor and Social Policy)

Madagascar

- Caisse Nationale de Prévoyance Sociale (National Social Insurance Fund)

Malaysia

- Employees Provident Fund

Malta

- Ministry of Social Policy
- Department of Social Security

Mauritius

- Ministry of Social Security, National Solidarity and Senior Citizens' Welfare

Mexico

- Secretaría del Trabajo y Previsión Social (Secretariat for Labor and Social Security)
- Instituto Mexicano del Seguro Social (IMSS) (Mexican Social Security Institute)
- Comisión Nacional del Sistema de Ahorro para el Retiro (National Commission for the Retirement Savings System)

Monaco

- Caisses Sociales de Monaco (Social Funds of Monaco)

Morocco

- Caisse marocaine des retraites (Moroccan Retirement Fund)
- Caisse nationale de sécurité sociale (National Social Security Fund)

[Back to top]

Namibia

- Ministry of Labour and Social Welfare

Netherlands

- Ministerie van Sociale Zaken en Werkgelegenheid (Ministry of Social Affairs and Labor)

- Sociale Zekerheid (Social Security)

- Sociale Verzekeringsbank (The Social Insurance Bank)

- Uitvoering Werknemersverzekeringen (National Institute for Social Security)

New Zealand

- Ministry of Social Development
- Work and Income New Zealand

Nicaragua

- Instituto Nicaragüense de Seguridad Social (Nicaraguan Social Security Institute)

Nigeria

- Nigeria Social Insurance Trust Fund

Norway

For additional analytical, business and investment opportunities information,
please contact Global Investment & Business Center, USA
at (703) 370-8082. Fax: (703) 370-8083. E-mail: ibpusa3@gmail.com
Global Business and Investment Info Databank - www.ibpus.com

- nye arbeids - og velferdsforvaltningen (Labour and Welfare Administration)

[Back to top]

Oman

- Public Authority for Social Insurance

Pakistan

- Employees' Old-Age Benefits Institution

Panama

- Caja de Seguro Social (Social Security Fund)

Paraguay

- Instituto de Previsión Social (Social Insurance Institute)

Peru

- Superintendencia de Bancos y Seguros del Peru (Bank and Insurance Superintendency of Peru)

Philippines

- Philippine Social Security System

Poland

- Zaklad Ubezpieczen Spolecznych (Social Insurance Institution)

  Kasa Rolniczego Ubezpieczenia Spolecznego (KRUS) (Agricultural Social Security Fund)

Portugal

- Ministério do Trabalho e da Solidariedade (Ministry of Labor and Solidarity)

Romania

- Ministerul muncii familiei protecţiei sociale şi persoanelor vârstnice (Ministry of Labor, Social Solidarity and Family)

Rwanda

- Ministry of Local Government, Community Development and Social Affairs

[Back to top]

Saint Christopher and Nevis

- Saint Christopher and Nevis Social Security Board

Saint Lucia

- National Insurance Scheme

Saint Vincent and The Grenadines

- National Insurance Scheme

Samoa

- Samoa National Provident Fund

Saudi Arabia

- General Organization for Social Insurance

Senegal

- Institution de Prévoyance Retraite du Sénégal (Social Insurance Institute for Old-Age Pensions)

Serbia

- Ministarstvo Za Socijalna Pitanja (Ministry of Social Affairs)

Sierra Leone

- National Social Security and Insurance Trust

Singapore

- Central Provident Fund

Slovakia

- Ministerstvo práce, sociálnych vecí a rodiny (Ministry of Labour, Social Affairs and Family)
- Sociálna poisťovňa (Social Insurance Agency)

Slovenia

- Zavod za pokojninsko in invalidsko zavarovanje Sloveniji (Institute for Pension and Disability Insurance Slovenia)

South Africa

- Department of Social Development

Spain

- Social Security in Spain
- Ministerio de Empleo y Seguridad Social (Ministry of Employment and Social Security)

Sri Lanka

- Employees' Provident Fund
- Department of Pensions

St. Maarten

- Algemeen Pensioenfonds Sint Maarten (General Pension Fund St. Maarten)

Swaziland

- Swaziland National Provident Fund

Sweden

- Försäkringskassan (National Social Insurance Board)
- Pensionsmyndigheten (Social Insurance Fund)
- Premiepensionsmyndigheten (Premium Pension Authority)

Switzerland

- Assurance-vieillesse et survivants (AVS) et Assurance-invalidité
- Alters- und Hinterlassenenversicherung (AHV) und Invalidenversicherung (IV)
- Assicurazione-vecchiaia e superstiti (AVS) e Assicurazione invalidità (Old-Age, Survivors and Disability Insurance)
- Bundesamt für Sozialversicherung (Federal Office for Social Security)

[Back to top]

Thailand

- Ministry of Labour

Trinidad and Towww.socialsecurity.govo

- The National Insurance Board of Trinidad and Tobago

Tunisia

- Caisse Nationale de Sécurité Sociale (National Social Security Fund)
- La Caisse Nationale de Retraite et de Prévoyance Sociale (The National Pension and Social Providence Fund)

Turkey

- T.C. Çalışma ve Sosyal Güvenlik Bakanlığı (Turkish Ministry of Labour and Social Security)
- Sosyal Sigortalar Kurumu (Social Insurance Institution)
- Bag-Kur (Social Insurance Organisation for the Self-Employed)

Uganda

- National Social Security Fund

Ukraine

- Ministry of Labor and Social Policy
- Pension Reform in Ukraine

United Arab Emirates

- Abu Dhabi Retirement Pensions and Benefits Fund

United Kingdom

- Department for Work and Pensions
- Northern Ireland Social Security Agency

- Isle of Man Department of Health and Social Security
- HM Revenue & Customs National Insurance Contributions

Uruguay

- Banco de Previsión Social--Social Insurance Bank

Venezuela

- Instituto Venezolano de los Seguros Sociales (Venezuelan Social Security Institute)

BASIC TITLE FOR LAOS

TITLE	ISBN
Lao People's Democratic Republic Traders and Investors Handbook	1438728093
Lao People's Democratic Republic Traders and Investors Handbook	1433028778
Laos A "Spy" Guide - Strategic Information and Developments	1433028786
Laos A Spy" Guide"	1438728107
Laos Business and Investment Opportunities Yearbook	1433028794
Laos Business and Investment Opportunities Yearbook	1438728115
Laos Business and Investment Opportunities Yearbook Volume 1 Strategic Information and Opportunities	1438777132
Laos Business Intelligence Report - Practical Information, Opportunities, Contacts	1433028808
Laos Business Intelligence Report - Practical Information, Opportunities, Contacts	1438728123
Laos Business Law Handbook - Strategic Information and Basic Laws	143877026X
Laos Business Law Handbook - Strategic Information and Basic Laws	143877026X
Laos Business Law Handbook - Strategic Information and Basic Laws	1433028816
Laos Business Law Handbook - Strategic Information and Basic Laws	1438728131
Laos Clothing & Textile Industry Handbook	143872814X
Laos Clothing & Textile Industry Handbook	1433028824
Laos Company Laws and Regulations Handbook	1433070154
Laos Country Study Guide - Strategic Information and Developments	1433028832
Laos Country Study Guide - Strategic Information and Developments	1438728158
Laos Country Study Guide - Strategic Information and Developments Volume 1 Strategic Information and Developments	143877480X
Laos Customs, Trade Regulations and Procedures Handbook	1433028840
Laos Customs, Trade Regulations and Procedures Handbook	1438728166
Laos Diplomatic Handbook - Strategic Information and Developments	1433028859
Laos Diplomatic Handbook - Strategic Information and Developments	1438728174
Laos Ecology & Nature Protection Handbook	1433028867
Laos Ecology & Nature Protection Handbook	1438728182
Laos Ecology & Nature Protection Laws and Regulation Handbook	1433074176
Laos Economic & Development Strategy Handbook	1433028875
Laos Economic & Development Strategy Handbook	1438728190
Laos Education System and Policy Handbook	1433066785
Laos Energy Policy, Laws and Regulation Handbook	1433071932
Laos Export-Import Trade and Business Directory	1433028883
Laos Export-Import Trade and Business Directory	1438728204
Laos Foreign Policy and Government Guide	1433028891
Laos Foreign Policy and Government Guide	1438728212
Laos Industrial and Business Directory	1433028905
Laos Industrial and Business Directory	1438728220
Laos Internet and E-Commerce Investment and Business Guide - Strategic and Practical Information: Regulations and Opportunities	1433028913
Laos Internet and E-Commerce Investment and Business Guide - Strategic and Practical Information: Regulations and Opportunities	1438728239
Laos Investment and Business Guide - Strategic and Practical Information	1438767986
Laos Investment and Business Guide - Strategic and Practical Information	1438767986
Laos Investment and Business Guide - Strategic and Practical Information	1433028921
Laos Investment and Business Guide - Strategic and Practical Information	1438728247

For additional analytical, business and investment opportunities information,
please contact Global Investment & Business Center, USA
at (703) 370-8082. Fax: (703) 370-8083. E-mail: ibpusa3@gmail.com
Global Business and Investment Info Databank - www.ibpus.com

TITLE	ISBN
Laos Investment and Trade Laws and Regulations Handbook	1433076160
Laos Justice System and National Police Handbook	143302893X
Laos Justice System and National Police Handbook	1438728255
Laos Medical & Pharmaceutical Industry Handbook	1433028948
Laos Medical & Pharmaceutical Industry Handbook	1438728263
Laos Mineral & Mining Sector Investment and Business Guide - Strategic and Practical Information	1438728271
Laos Mineral, Mining Sector Investment and Business Guide - Strategic and Practical Information	1433028956
Laos Mining Laws and Regulations Handbook	1433077728
Laos Recent Economic and Political Developments Yearbook	1433063336
Laos Recent Economic and Political Developments Yearbook	1433063336
Laos Recent Economic and Political Developments Yearbook	1433063336
Laos Research & Development Policy Handbook	1433063220
Laos Research & Development Policy Handbook	1433063220
Laos Research & Development Policy Handbook	1433063220
Laos Starting Business (Incorporating) in....Guide	1433066793
Laos Taxation Laws and Regulations Handbook	1433080214
Laos Telecom Laws and Regulations Handbook	1433082063
Laos Telecommunication Industry Business Opportunities Handbook	1433028964
Laos Telecommunication Industry Business Opportunities Handbook	143872828X
Laos Traders Manual: Export-Import, Trade, Investment	1433066807
Laos Transportation Policy and Regulations Handbook	1433066815
Laos: How to Invest, Start and Run Profitable Business in Laos Guide - Practical Information, Opportunities, Contacts	9781433083785

GLOBAL
SOCIAL SECURITY SYSTEM, POLICIES LAWS AND REGULATIONS HANDBOOK - STRATEGIC INFORMATION AND BASIC LAWS LIBRARY
Price: $9995 Each

1.	Albania Social Security System, Policies, Laws and Regulations Handbook
2.	Algeria Social Security System, Policies, Laws and Regulations Handbook
3.	Andorra Social Security System, Policies, Laws and Regulations Handbook
4.	Angola Social Security System, Policies, Laws and Regulations Handbook
5.	Antigua and Barbuda Social Security System, Policies, Laws and Regulations Handbook
6.	Argentina Social Security System, Policies, Laws and Regulations Handbook
7.	Armenia Social Security System, Policies, Laws and Regulations Handbook
8.	Australia Social Security System, Policies, Laws and Regulations Handbook
9.	Austria Social Security System, Policies, Laws and Regulations Handbook
10.	Azerbaijan Social Security System, Policies, Laws and Regulations Handbook
11.	Bahamas Social Security System, Policies, Laws and Regulations Handbook
12.	Bahrain Social Security System, Policies, Laws and Regulations Handbook
13.	Bangladesh Social Security System, Policies, Laws and Regulations Handbook
14.	Barbados Social Security System, Policies, Laws and Regulations Handbook
15.	Belarus Social Security System, Policies, Laws and Regulations Handbook
16.	Belgium Social Security System, Policies, Laws and Regulations Handbook
17.	Belize Social Security System, Policies, Laws and Regulations Handbook
18.	Benin Social Security System, Policies, Laws and Regulations Handbook
19.	Bermuda Social Security System, Policies, Laws and Regulations Handbook
20.	Bhutan Social Security System, Policies, Laws and Regulations Handbook
21.	Bolivia Social Security System, Policies, Laws and Regulations Handbook
22.	Botswana Social Security System, Policies, Laws and Regulations Handbook
23.	Brazil Social Security System, Policies, Laws and Regulations Handbook
24.	British Virgin Islands Social Security System, Policies, Laws and Regulations Handbook
25.	Brunei Social Security System, Policies, Laws and Regulations Handbook
26.	Bulgaria Social Security System, Policies, Laws and Regulations Handbook
27.	Burkina Faso Social Security System, Policies, Laws and Regulations Handbook
28.	Burma (Myanmar)
29.	Burundi Social Security System, Policies, Laws and Regulations Handbook
30.	Cameroon Social Security System, Policies, Laws and Regulations Handbook
31.	Canada Social Security System, Policies, Laws and Regulations Handbook
32.	Cape Verde Social Security System, Policies, Laws and Regulations Handbook
33.	Central African Republic Social Security System, Policies, Laws and Regulations Handbook
34.	Chad Social Security System, Policies, Laws and Regulations Handbook
35.	Chile Social Security System, Policies, Laws and Regulations Handbook
36.	China Social Security System, Policies, Laws and Regulations Handbook
37.	Colombia Social Security System, Policies, Laws and Regulations Handbook
38.	Congo (Brazzaville) Social Security System, Policies, Laws and Regulations Handbook
39.	Congo (Kinshasa) Social Security System, Policies, Laws and Regulations Handbook
40.	Costa Rica Social Security System, Policies, Laws and Regulations Handbook
41.	Cote d'Ivoire Social Security System, Policies, Laws and Regulations Handbook
42.	Croatia Social Security System, Policies, Laws and Regulations Handbook

For additional analytical, business and investment opportunities information,
please contact Global Investment & Business Center, USA
at (703) 370-8082. Fax: (703) 370-8083. E-mail: ibpusa3@gmail.com
Global Business and Investment Info Databank - www.ibpus.com

43. Cuba Social Security System, Policies, Laws and Regulations Handbook
44. Cyprus Social Security System, Policies, Laws and Regulations Handbook
45. Czech Republic Social Security System, Policies, Laws and Regulations Handbook
46. Denmark Social Security System, Policies, Laws and Regulations Handbook
47. Djibouti Social Security System, Policies, Laws and Regulations Handbook
48. Dominica Social Security System, Policies, Laws and Regulations Handbook
49. Dominican Republic Social Security System, Policies, Laws and Regulations Handbook
50. Ecuador Social Security System, Policies, Laws and Regulations Handbook
51. Egypt Social Security System, Policies, Laws and Regulations Handbook
52. El Salvador Social Security System, Policies, Laws and Regulations Handbook
53. Equatorial Guinea Social Security System, Policies, Laws and Regulations Handbook
54. Estonia Social Security System, Policies, Laws and Regulations Handbook Estonia
55. Ethiopia Social Security System, Policies, Laws and Regulations Handbook
56. Fiji Social Security System, Policies, Laws and Regulations Handbook
57. Finland Social Security System, Policies, Laws and Regulations Handbook
58. France Social Security System, Policies, Laws and Regulations Handbook
59. Gabon Social Security System, Policies, Laws and Regulations Handbook
60. Gambia Social Security System, Policies, Laws and Regulations Handbook
61. Georgia Social Security System, Policies, Laws and Regulations Handbook
62. Germany Social Security System, Policies, Laws and Regulations Handbook
63. Ghana Social Security System, Policies, Laws and Regulations Handbook
64. Greece Social Security System, Policies, Laws and Regulations Handbook
65. Grenada Social Security System, Policies, Laws and Regulations Handbook
66. Guatemala Social Security System, Policies, Laws and Regulations Handbook
67. Guinea Social Security System, Policies, Laws and Regulations Handbook
68. Guyana Social Security System, Policies, Laws and Regulations Handbook
69. Haiti Social Security System, Policies, Laws and Regulations Handbook
70. Honduras Social Security System, Policies, Laws and Regulations Handbook
71. Hong Kong Social Security System, Policies, Laws and Regulations Handbook
72. Hungary Social Security System, Policies, Laws and Regulations Handbook
73. Iceland Social Security System, Policies, Laws and Regulations Handbook
74. India Social Security System, Policies, Laws and Regulations Handbook
75. Indonesia Social Security System, Policies, Laws and Regulations Handbook
76. Iran Social Security System, Policies, Laws and Regulations Handbook
77. Iraq Social Security System, Policies, Laws and Regulations Handbook
78. Ireland Social Security System, Policies, Laws and Regulations Handbook
79. Isle of Man Social Security System, Policies, Laws and Regulations Handbook
80. Israel Social Security System, Policies, Laws and Regulations Handbook
81. Italy Social Security System, Policies, Laws and Regulations Handbook
82. Jamaica Social Security System, Policies, Laws and Regulations Handbook
83. Japan Social Security System, Policies, Laws and Regulations Handbook
84. Jordan Social Security System, Policies, Laws and Regulations Handbook
85. Kazakhstan Social Security System, Policies, Laws and Regulations Handbook
86. Kenya Social Security System, Policies, Laws and Regulations Handbook
87. Kuwait Social Security System, Policies, Laws and Regulations Handbook
88. Kyrgyzstan Social Security System, Policies, Laws and Regulations Handbook
89. Laos Social Security System, Policies, Laws and Regulations Handbook
90. Latvia Social Security System, Policies, Laws and Regulations Handbook
91. Lebanon Social Security System, Policies, Laws and Regulations Handbook
92. Lesotho Social Security System, Policies, Laws and Regulations Handbook
93. Liberia Social Security System, Policies, Laws and Regulations Handbook
94. Libya Social Security System, Policies, Laws and Regulations Handbook
95. Liechtenstein Social Security System, Policies, Laws and Regulations Handbook
96. Lithuania Social Security System, Policies, Laws and Regulations Handbook
97. Luxembourg Social Security System, Policies, Laws and Regulations Handbook
98. Madagascar Social Security System, Policies, Laws and Regulations Handbook

**For additional analytical, business and investment opportunities information,
please contact Global Investment & Business Center, USA
at (703) 370-8082. Fax: (703) 370-8083. E-mail: ibpusa3@gmail.com
Global Business and Investment Info Databank - www.ibpus.com**

99. Malawi Social Security System, Policies, Laws and Regulations Handbook
100. Malaysia Social Security System, Policies, Laws and Regulations Handbook Malaysia
101. Mali Social Security System, Policies, Laws and Regulations Handbook Mali
102. Malta Social Security System, Policies, Laws and Regulations Handbook Malta
103. Marshall Islands Social Security System, Policies, Laws and Regulations Handbook
104. Mauritania Social Security System, Policies, Laws and Regulations Handbook
105. Mauritius Social Security System, Policies, Laws and Regulations Handbook
106. Mexico Social Security System, Policies, Laws and Regulations Handbook
107. Micronesia Social Security System, Policies, Laws and Regulations Handbook
108. Moldova Social Security System, Policies, Laws and Regulations Handbook
109. Monaco Social Security System, Policies, Laws and Regulations Handbook
110. Morocco Social Security System, Policies, Laws and Regulations Handbook
111. Namibia Social Security System, Policies, Laws and Regulations Handbook Namibia
112. Nepal Social Security System, Policies, Laws and Regulations Handbook Nepal
113. Netherlands Social Security System, Policies, Laws and Regulations Handbook Netherlands
114. New Zealand Social Security System, Policies, Laws and Regulations Handbook New Zealand
115. Nicaragua Social Security System, Policies, Laws and Regulations Handbook Nicaragua
116. Niger Social Security System, Policies, Laws and Regulations Handbook Niger
117. Nigeria Social Security System, Policies, Laws and Regulations Handbook Nigeria
118. Norway Social Security System, Policies, Laws and Regulations Handbook Norway
119. Oman Social Security System, Policies, Laws and Regulations Handbook Oman
120. Pakistan Social Security System, Policies, Laws and Regulations Handbook Pakistan
121. Panama Social Security System, Policies, Laws and Regulations Handbook Panama
122. Papua New Guinea Social Security System, Policies, Laws and Regulations Handbook Papau New Guinea
123. Paraguay Social Security System, Policies, Laws and Regulations Handbook Paraguay
124. Peru Social Security System, Policies, Laws and Regulations Handbook Peru
125. Philippines Social Security System, Policies, Laws and Regulations Handbook Philippines
126. Poland Social Security System, Policies, Laws and Regulations Handbook Poland
127. Portugal Social Security System, Policies, Laws and Regulations Handbook Portugal
128. Qatar Social Security System, Policies, Laws and Regulations Handbook Qatar
129. Romania Social Security System, Policies, Laws and Regulations Handbook Romania
130. Russia Social Security System, Policies, Laws and Regulations Handbook Russia
131. Rwanda Social Security System, Policies, Laws and Regulations Handbook Rwanda
132. Samoa Social Security System, Policies, Laws and Regulations Handbook
133. San Marino Social Security System, Policies, Laws and Regulations Handbook
134. Sao Tome and Principe Social Security System, Policies, Laws and Regulations Handbook
135. Saudi Arabia Social Security System, Policies, Laws and Regulations Handbook
136. Senegal Social Security System, Policies, Laws and Regulations Handbook
137. Serbia Social Security System, Policies, Laws and Regulations Handbook
138. Seychelles Social Security System, Policies, Laws and Regulations Handbook
139. Sierra Leone Social Security System, Policies, Laws and Regulations Handbook
140. Singapore Social Security System, Policies, Laws and Regulations Handbook
141. Slovak Republic Social Security System, Policies, Laws and Regulations Handbook
142. Slovenia Social Security System, Policies, Laws and Regulations Handbook S
143. Solomon Islands Social Security System, Policies, Laws and Regulations Handbook
144. South Africa Social Security System, Policies, Laws and Regulations Handbook
145. South Korea Social Security System, Policies, Laws and Regulations Handbook
146. Spain Social Security System, Policies, Laws and Regulations Handbook
147. Sri Lanka Social Security System, Policies, Laws and Regulations Handbook
148. Sudan Social Security System, Policies, Laws and Regulations Handbook
149. Swaziland Social Security System, Policies, Laws and Regulations Handbook
150. Sweden Social Security System, Policies, Laws and Regulations Handbook
151. Switzerland Social Security System, Policies, Laws and Regulations Handbook
152. Syria Social Security System, Policies, Laws and Regulations Handbook
153. Taiwan Social Security System, Policies, Laws and Regulations Handbook

**For additional analytical, business and investment opportunities information,
please contact Global Investment & Business Center, USA
at (703) 370-8082. Fax: (703) 370-8083. E-mail: ibpusa3@gmail.com
Global Business and Investment Info Databank - www.ibpus.com**

154. Tajikistan Social Security System, Policies, Laws and Regulations Handbook
155. Tanzania Social Security System, Policies, Laws and Regulations Handbook Tanzania
156. Thailand Social Security System, Policies, Laws and Regulations Handbook
157. Togo Social Security System, Policies, Laws and Regulations Handbook
158. Trinidad and Tobago Social Security System, Policies, Laws and Regulations Handbook
159. Tunisia Social Security System, Policies, Laws and Regulations Handbook
160. Turkey Social Security System, Policies, Laws and Regulations Handbook
161. Turkmenistan Social Security System, Policies, Laws and Regulations Handbook
162. Uganda Social Security System, Policies, Laws and Regulations Handbook
163. Ukraine Social Security System, Policies, Laws and Regulations Handbook
164. United Kingdom Social Security System, Policies, Laws and Regulations Handbook
165. United States Social Security System, Policies, Laws and Regulations Handbook
166. Uruguay Social Security System, Policies, Laws and Regulations Handbook
167. Uzbekistan Social Security System, Policies, Laws and Regulations Handbook
168. Vietnam Social Security System, Policies, Laws and Regulations Handbook
169. Yemen Social Security System, Policies, Laws and Regulations Handbook
170. Zambia Social Security System, Policies, Laws and Regulations Handbook
171. Zimbabwe Social Security System, Policies, Laws and Regulations Handbook

**For additional analytical, business and investment opportunities information,
please contact Global Investment & Business Center, USA
at (703) 370-8082. Fax: (703) 370-8083. E-mail: ibpusa3@gmail.com
Global Business and Investment Info Databank - www.ibpus.com**

GLOBAL LABOR LAWS AND REGULATIONS HANDBOOK - STRATEGIC INFORMATION AND BASIC LAWS LIBRARY

Price: $149.95 Each

1.	Albania Labor Laws and Regulations Handbook - Strategic Information and Basic Laws
2.	Algeria Labor Laws and Regulations Handbook - Strategic Information and Basic Laws
3.	Andorra Labor Laws and Regulations Handbook - Strategic Information and Basic Laws
4.	Angola Labor Laws and Regulations Handbook - Strategic Information and Basic Laws
5.	Antigua & Barbuda Labor Laws and Regulations Handbook - Strategic Information and Basic Laws
6.	Antilles (Netherlands) Labor Laws and Regulations Handbook - Strategic Information and Basic Laws
7.	Argentina Labor Laws and Regulations Handbook - Strategic Information and Basic Laws
8.	Armenia Labor Laws and Regulations Handbook - Strategic Information and Basic Laws
9.	Australia Labor Laws and Regulations Handbook - Strategic Information and Basic Laws
10.	Austria Labor Laws and Regulations Handbook - Strategic Information and Basic Laws
11.	Azerbaijan Labor Laws and Regulations Handbook - Strategic Information and Basic Laws
12.	Bahamas Labor Laws and Regulations Handbook - Strategic Information and Basic Laws
13.	Bangladesh Labor Laws and Regulations Handbook - Strategic Information and Basic Laws
14.	Barbados Labor Laws and Regulations Handbook - Strategic Information and Basic Laws
15.	Belarus Labor Laws and Regulations Handbook - Strategic Information and Basic Laws
16.	Belgium Labor Laws and Regulations Handbook - Strategic Information and Basic Laws
17.	Belize Labor Laws and Regulations Handbook - Strategic Information and Basic Laws
18.	Bermuda Labor Laws and Regulations Handbook - Strategic Information and Basic Laws
19.	Bolivia Labor Laws and Regulations Handbook - Strategic Information and Basic Laws
20.	Bosnia and Herzegovina Labor Laws and Regulations Handbook - Strategic Information and Basic Laws
21.	Botswana Labor Laws and Regulations Handbook - Strategic Information and Basic Laws
22.	Brazil Labor Laws and Regulations Handbook - Strategic Information and Basic Laws
23.	Brunei Labor Laws and Regulations Handbook - Strategic Information and Basic Laws
24.	Bulgaria Labor Laws and Regulations Handbook - Strategic Information and Basic Laws
25.	Cambodia Labor Laws and Regulations Handbook - Strategic Information and Basic Laws
26.	Cameroon Labor Laws and Regulations Handbook - Strategic Information and Basic Laws
27.	Canada Labor Laws and Regulations Handbook - Strategic Information and Basic Laws
28.	Cayman Islands Labor Laws and Regulations Handbook - Strategic Information and Basic Laws
29.	Chile Labor Laws and Regulations Handbook - Strategic Information and Basic Laws
30.	China Labor Laws and Regulations Handbook - Strategic Information and Basic Laws
31.	Colombia Labor Laws and Regulations Handbook - Strategic Information and Basic Laws
32.	Comoros Labor Laws and Regulations Handbook - Strategic Information and Basic Laws
33.	Cook Islands Labor Laws and Regulations Handbook - Strategic Information and Basic Laws
34.	Costa Rica Labor Laws and Regulations Handbook - Strategic Information and Basic Laws

For additional analytical, business and investment opportunities information,
Please contact Global Investment & Business Center, USA
at (202) 546-2103. Fax: (202) 546-3275. E-mail: ibpusa3@gmail.com

35. Croatia Labor Laws and Regulations Handbook - Strategic Information and Basic Laws
36. Cuba Labor Laws and Regulations Handbook - Strategic Information and Basic Laws
37. Cyprus Labor Laws and Regulations Handbook - Strategic Information and Basic Laws
38. Czech Republic Labor Laws and Regulations Handbook - Strategic Information and Basic Laws
39. Denmark Labor Laws and Regulations Handbook - Strategic Information and Basic Laws
40. Dominica Labor Laws and Regulations Handbook - Strategic Information and Basic Laws
41. Dominican Republic Labor Laws and Regulations Handbook - Strategic Information and Basic Laws
42. Dubai Labor Laws and Regulations Handbook - Strategic Information and Basic Laws
43. Ecuador Labor Laws and Regulations Handbook - Strategic Information and Basic Laws
44. Egypt Labor Laws and Regulations Handbook - Strategic Information and Basic Laws
45. El Salvador Labor Laws and Regulations Handbook - Strategic Information and Basic Laws
46. Equatorial Guinea Labor Laws and Regulations Handbook - Strategic Information and Basic Laws
47. Estonia Labor Laws and Regulations Handbook - Strategic Information and Basic Laws
48. Falkland Islands Labor Laws and Regulations Handbook - Strategic Information and Basic Laws
49. Fiji Labor Laws and Regulations Handbook - Strategic Information and Basic Laws
50. Finland Labor Laws and Regulations Handbook - Strategic Information and Basic Laws
51. France Labor Laws and Regulations Handbook - Strategic Information and Basic Laws
52. Georgia Labor Laws and Regulations Handbook - Strategic Information and Basic Laws
53. Germany Labor Laws and Regulations Handbook - Strategic Information and Basic Laws
54. Gibraltar Labor Laws and Regulations Handbook - Strategic Information and Basic Laws
55. Greece Labor Laws and Regulations Handbook - Strategic Information and Basic Laws
56. Grenada Labor Laws and Regulations Handbook - Strategic Information and Basic Laws
57. Guam Investment & Business Guide
58. Guatemala Labor Laws and Regulations Handbook - Strategic Information and Basic Laws
59. Guernsey Labor Laws and Regulations Handbook - Strategic Information and Basic Laws
60. Guyana Labor Laws and Regulations Handbook - Strategic Information and Basic Laws
61. Haiti Labor Laws and Regulations Handbook - Strategic Information and Basic Laws
62. Honduras Labor Laws and Regulations Handbook - Strategic Information and Basic Laws
63. Hungary Labor Laws and Regulations Handbook - Strategic Information and Basic Laws
64. Iceland Labor Laws and Regulations Handbook - Strategic Information and Basic Laws
65. India Labor Laws and Regulations Handbook - Strategic Information and Basic Laws
66. Indonesia Labor Laws and Regulations Handbook - Strategic Information and Basic Laws
67. Iran Labor Laws and Regulations Handbook - Strategic Information and Basic Laws
68. Iraq Labor Laws and Regulations Handbook - Strategic Information and Basic Laws
69. Ireland Labor Laws and Regulations Handbook - Strategic Information and Basic Laws
70. Israel Labor Laws and Regulations Handbook - Strategic Information and Basic Laws
71. Italy Labor Laws and Regulations Handbook - Strategic Information and Basic Laws
72. Jamaica Labor Laws and Regulations Handbook - Strategic Information and Basic Laws
73. Japan Labor Laws and Regulations Handbook - Strategic Information and Basic Laws
74. Jersey Labor Laws and Regulations Handbook - Strategic Information and Basic Laws
75. Jordan Labor Laws and Regulations Handbook - Strategic Information and Basic Laws
76. Kazakhstan Labor Laws and Regulations Handbook - Strategic Information and Basic Laws
77. Kenya Labor Laws and Regulations Handbook - Strategic Information and Basic Laws

For additional analytical, business and investment opportunities information,
Please contact Global Investment & Business Center, USA
at (202) 546-2103. Fax: (202) 546-3275. E-mail: ibpusa3@gmail.com

78. Kiribati Labor Laws and Regulations Handbook - Strategic Information and Basic Laws
79. Korea, North Labor Laws and Regulations Handbook - Strategic Information and Basic Laws
80. Korea, South Labor Laws and Regulations Handbook - Strategic Information and Basic Laws
81. Kuwait Labor Laws and Regulations Handbook - Strategic Information and Basic Laws
82. Kyrgyzstan Labor Laws and Regulations Handbook - Strategic Information and Basic Laws
83. Laos Labor Laws and Regulations Handbook - Strategic Information and Basic Laws
84. Latvia Labor Laws and Regulations Handbook - Strategic Information and Basic Laws
85. Lebanon Labor Laws and Regulations Handbook - Strategic Information and Basic Laws
86. Libya Labor Laws and Regulations Handbook - Strategic Information and Basic Laws
87. Liechtenstein Labor Laws and Regulations Handbook - Strategic Information and Basic Laws
88. Lithuania Labor Laws and Regulations Handbook - Strategic Information and Basic Laws
89. Luxemburg Labor Laws and Regulations Handbook - Strategic Information and Basic Laws
90. Macao Labor Laws and Regulations Handbook - Strategic Information and Basic Laws
91. Macedonia, Republic Labor Laws and Regulations Handbook - Strategic Information and Basic Laws
92. Madagascar Labor Laws and Regulations Handbook - Strategic Information and Basic Laws
93. Malaysia Labor Laws and Regulations Handbook - Strategic Information and Basic Laws
94. Malta Labor Laws and Regulations Handbook - Strategic Information and Basic Laws
95. Man Labor Laws and Regulations Handbook - Strategic Information and Basic Laws
96. Mauritius Labor Laws and Regulations Handbook - Strategic Information and Basic Laws
97. Mauritius Labor Laws and Regulations Handbook - Strategic Information and Basic Laws
98. Mexico Labor Laws and Regulations Handbook - Strategic Information and Basic Laws
99. Micronesia Labor Laws and Regulations Handbook - Strategic Information and Basic Laws
100. Moldova Labor Laws and Regulations Handbook - Strategic Information and Basic Laws
101. Monaco Labor Laws and Regulations Handbook - Strategic Information and Basic Laws
102. Mongolia Labor Laws and Regulations Handbook - Strategic Information and Basic Laws
103. Morocco Labor Laws and Regulations Handbook - Strategic Information and Basic Laws
104. Myanmar Labor Laws and Regulations Handbook - Strategic Information and Basic Laws
105. Namibia Labor Laws and Regulations Handbook - Strategic Information and Basic Laws
106. Netherlands Labor Laws and Regulations Handbook - Strategic Information and Basic Laws
107. New Caledonia Labor Laws and Regulations Handbook - Strategic Information and Basic Laws
108. New Zealand Labor Laws and Regulations Handbook - Strategic Information and Basic Laws
109. Nicaragua Labor Laws and Regulations Handbook - Strategic Information and Basic Laws
110. Nigeria Labor Laws and Regulations Handbook - Strategic Information and Basic Laws
111. Northern Mariana Islands Labor Laws and Regulations Handbook - Strategic Information and Basic Laws
112. Norway Labor Laws and Regulations Handbook - Strategic Information and Basic Laws
113. Pakistan Labor Laws and Regulations Handbook - Strategic Information and Basic Laws
114. Panama Labor Laws and Regulations Handbook - Strategic Information and Basic Laws
115. Peru Labor Laws and Regulations Handbook - Strategic Information and Basic Laws
116. Philippines Labor Laws and Regulations Handbook - Strategic Information and Basic Laws
117. Poland Labor Laws and Regulations Handbook - Strategic Information and Basic Laws
118. Portugal Labor Laws and Regulations Handbook - Strategic Information and Basic Laws
119. Romania Labor Laws and Regulations Handbook - Strategic Information and Basic Laws
120. Russia Labor Laws and Regulations Handbook - Strategic Information and Basic Laws

For additional analytical, business and investment opportunities information,
Please contact Global Investment & Business Center, USA
at (202) 546-2103. Fax: (202) 546-3275. E-mail: ibpusa3@gmail.com

121. Samoa (American) Investment & Business Guide
122. Samoa (Western) Labor Laws and Regulations Handbook - Strategic Information and Basic Laws
123. Saudi Arabia Labor Laws and Regulations Handbook - Strategic Information and Basic Laws
124. Scotland Labor Laws and Regulations Handbook - Strategic Information and Basic Laws
125. Serbia Labor Laws and Regulations Handbook - Strategic Information and Basic Laws
126. Singapore Labor Laws and Regulations Handbook - Strategic Information and Basic Laws
127. Slovakia Labor Laws and Regulations Handbook - Strategic Information and Basic Laws
128. Slovenia Labor Laws and Regulations Handbook - Strategic Information and Basic Laws
129. South Africa Labor Laws and Regulations Handbook - Strategic Information and Basic Laws
130. Spain Labor Laws and Regulations Handbook - Strategic Information and Basic Laws
131. Sri Lanka Labor Laws and Regulations Handbook - Strategic Information and Basic Laws
132. St. Helena Labor Laws and Regulations Handbook - Strategic Information and Basic Laws
133. Sudan Labor Laws and Regulations Handbook - Strategic Information and Basic Laws
134. Suriname Labor Laws and Regulations Handbook - Strategic Information and Basic Laws
135. Sweden Labor Laws and Regulations Handbook - Strategic Information and Basic Laws
136. Switzerland Labor Laws and Regulations Handbook - Strategic Information and Basic Laws
137. Syria Export Import & Business Directory
138. Taiwan Labor Laws and Regulations Handbook - Strategic Information and Basic Laws
139. Tajikistan Labor Laws and Regulations Handbook - Strategic Information and Basic Laws
140. Thailand Labor Laws and Regulations Handbook - Strategic Information and Basic Laws
141. Tunisia Labor Laws and Regulations Handbook - Strategic Information and Basic Laws
142. Turkey Labor Laws and Regulations Handbook - Strategic Information and Basic Laws
143. Turkmenistan Labor Laws and Regulations Handbook - Strategic Information and Basic Laws
144. Uganda Labor Laws and Regulations Handbook - Strategic Information and Basic Laws
145. Ukraine Labor Laws and Regulations Handbook - Strategic Information and Basic Laws
146. United Arab Emirates Labor Laws and Regulations Handbook - Strategic Information and Basic Laws
147. United Kingdom Labor Laws and Regulations Handbook - Strategic Information and Basic Laws
148. United States Labor Laws and Regulations Handbook - Strategic Information and Basic Laws
149. Uruguay Labor Laws and Regulations Handbook - Strategic Information and Basic Laws
150. US Labor Laws and Regulations Handbook - Strategic Information and Basic Laws
151. Uzbekistan Labor Laws and Regulations Handbook - Strategic Information and Basic Laws
152. Venezuela Labor Laws and Regulations Handbook - Strategic Information and Basic Laws
153. Vietnam Labor Laws and Regulations Handbook - Strategic Information and Basic Laws

For additional analytical, business and investment opportunities information,
Please contact Global Investment & Business Center, USA
at (202) 546-2103. Fax: (202) 546-3275. E-mail: ibpusa3@gmail.com

CONTENTS

ABOUT THE AUTHORS

Joan Ryan (deceased)

Joan Ryan taught personal finance for more than 20 years. While teaching at Willamette High School in Eugene, Oregon, she developed the original personal finance course materials for publication. Dr. Ryan was a faculty member in the business department at Clackamas Community College, Portland, OR. She also taught accounting at Portland State University and was a Certified Managerial Accountant.

Christie Ryan

As a licensed mental health counselor, Christie works with troubled and disadvantaged youth and their families, teaching budgeting and money management skills. She has also taught student success skills and psychology courses at Highline Community College and Tacoma Community College. She holds an Educational Staff Associate certificate in school counseling and has worked as a case manager for Southwest Washington Aging and Disability Services.

DEVELOP GOOD FINANCIAL HABITS FOR LIFE!

Life is filled with choices. Those who have the best and most complete information have the power to enhance their own lives and to positively affect the world around them.

Personal Financial Literacy, 3e is designed to help students learn and apply valuable life skills in **money management, career planning, saving and investing, credit management,** and **retirement planning.** By exploring successful strategies to grow and protect wealth, students will discover the richness of information available to manage their lives and their resources.

This financial life skills textbook contains four units, each divided into three chapters that systematically cover financial literacy standards as developed by the Jump$tart Coalition, National Business Education Association, and other state and national organizations.

Feature boxes in each chapter cover **communication skills** (listening, reading, writing, and speaking) and **success skills** (such as dealing with stress and time management). Students will read short, concise articles focused on the **economic realities and trends** of today's market-place; they will explore potential **career choices** (linked to the 16 Career Clusters); and they will take a peek at what they can expect in the future.

Each lesson contains end-of-lesson activities that review **key terms,** check **basic concepts,** and encourage **critical thinking.** With end-of-chapter assessments, students will make **academic connections** in areas such as math, communications, research, social studies, economics, ethics, and law. Each chapter ends with **"Take Action,"** an **ongoing project or application** to help students explore a major or related topic or activity.

At the end of each unit is a new Unit Project with enhanced learning opportunities for application of the concepts covered in the unit.

Concepts covered in this edition include

- job search skills and online job applications;
- interviewing techniques;
- preparing resumes and cover letters;
- the benefits and challenges of entrepreneurship;
- consumer rights and responsibilities in the marketplace;
- charitable giving and philanthropy;
- health care providers, services, and fraud; and
- simple and compound interest.

Financial success begins with good **career planning, goal setting,** and an understanding of **income sources and taxes.** Students will explore methods of getting more for their money and the basics of good **financial planning,** using the **banking system,** and getting started with **saving and investing.**

As income is earned and wealth is accumulated, students learn how to **assess risk** and protect assets, how to **use credit wisely** and minimize its costs, and how **to resolve credit problems.** **Saving and investing principles** lead students to effective buying and selling strategies and an understanding of financial markets, regulatory agencies, and laws that affect consumers and businesses. Incorporated into good decision making are basic economic concepts such as **inflation, monetary and fiscal policy, the business cycle,** and **pricing strategies.**

Peopleimages/iStockphoto.com

This entire package of textbook, website, student workbook, chapter tests, and instructor's resource CD provides a resource bank designed to reach students where they are and encourage them to move boldly into the future, armed with financial literacy skills, information, and knowledge to help them make good financial decisions for a lifetime!

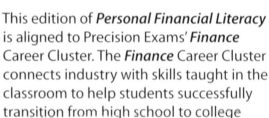

This edition of *Personal Financial Literacy* is aligned to Precision Exams' *Finance* Career Cluster. The *Finance* Career Cluster connects industry with skills taught in the classroom to help students successfully transition from high school to college and/or career. Working together, Precision Exams and National Geographic Learning/Cengage focus on preparing students for the workforce, with exams and content that is kept up to date and relevant to today's jobs. To access a corresponding correlation guide, visit the accompanying Instructor Companion Website for this title. For more information on how to administer the *Personal Financial Responsibility* exam or any of the 170+ exams available to your students, contact your local NGL/Cengage Sales Consultant.

FEATURES FOR STUDENT SUCCESS!

NEW! Do This, Not That is an introductory checklist of real-world tips to consider, related to the chapter content.

Do *This*, Not *That*

To increase your purchasing power:

- Pay off debt quickly to avoid paying interest.
- Make rational buying decisions, not emotional ones.
- Shop smart to find the best value at the lowest price.
- Ask for a pay raise at work to keep up with rising prices.
- Save money now to avoid borrowing later.

 SUCCESS SKILLS

Success Skills feature provides information to help students be successful in school, work, and personal activities.

TIME MANAGEMENT

Why do some people achieve more in a day than others? The answer lies in time management. *Time management* refers to the way that you organize and plan your time for specific activities. Using time-management strategies such as the following can help you be more productive in school, work, and personal activities.

- Be aware of how you are using your time. This is the first step toward managing your activities in a way that makes the best use of your time.
- Identify *peak performance times*, when you are most productive during the day, and *weak performance times*, when you are the least productive. Schedule activities that involve decision making at peak performance times.
- Use a daily or weekly planner to keep track of important dates and times.
- Keep a to-do list; mark off items as they are completed.

- Prioritize your activities so you get the important ones done first.
- Break large projects or tasks into smaller parts, and plan time for completing each part.
- Save some time for doing things you enjoy.
- Do not rush or be pressured for time when making important decisions, such as major purchasing decisions.

Try It Out

Practice your time-management skills by preparing a shopping list for things you would like to buy in the next month. Prioritize the list, putting the items in order of importance. Comparison shop on the Internet. List three locations where you can buy the products on your list, along with the prices at each location. Describe how time management can improve your shopping experiences.

Building Communication Skills feature focuses on crucial soft skills, such as listening, reading, speaking, and writing, necessary in today's competitive workplace.

 Building COMMUNICATION SKILLS

CRITICAL LISTENING

Critical listening is a skill used to solve problems. With *critical listening*, a person searches through information and forms questions to ask. Critical listening is a highly active process that involves logic as well as listening. For example, suppose you are listening to a debate about a new law that has been proposed. One side is describing its positive features and all of the reasons why you should vote in favor of it. The other side is explaining all of the bad things that will happen if the law is enacted. In order for you to decide, you must listen carefully, make sure your questions have been answered, and come to a decision that will be your vote. Critical listening requires that you understand who is

proposing the law and what that group has to gain. You also need to know who is opposing the law and what that group has to lose. By practicing critical listening, you can reach an informed decision.

Try It Out

Listen to a commercial on a television program. List what you learned from the ad and the information you gained. List the questions you still have after viewing the ad. Are you convinced that the ad has given you the full and accurate information you need to make an informed buying decision?

Looking Ahead

As a young person, you may get your start in the workforce as a waiter who earns tips in a restaurant. To prepare for such a job, conduct online research about tipped employees. What is the minimum required hourly wage that employers must pay a tipped employee in your state? What is the minimum suggested hourly tip or total tip for waiters? What factors do you think might affect the amount of a tip?

NEW! Looking Ahead feature provides critical-thinking questions and online research opportunities to guide students in thinking about their future.

Focus On…feature highlights specific topics related to chapter content and supports students' participation in student organizations.

FOCUS On...

SOCIAL SECURITY BENEFITS

Most workers in the United States pay into the Social Security fund. Payments are made into the account through payroll deductions. These payments are matched by employers. Based on the amount paid into the account and other factors, the worker will receive monthly benefit checks when he or she retires.

Once you have started paying into the fund, you can view and print a Social Security benefits statement online at the Social Security Administration's website. The statement shows a record of the income on which you paid Social Security taxes, plus how much you can expect to earn in monthly Social Security benefits when you hit retirement age (age 67 for those born after 1960).

Think Critically

1. Social Security was created by law in 1938. Conduct online research about the Social Security Act. Why do you think such a program was needed? (*Hint:* The Great Depression started in 1929.)
2. Social Security was never intended to meet the full retirement needs of someone unable to work. Rather, it is intended as supplemental income. What do you need to do to avoid depending on Social Security benefits as your only form of retirement income?

NEW! Unit Project at the end of each unit offers enhanced learning opportunities while giving students the chance to apply the concepts covered in the unit. Worksheets are provided in the Student Workbook.

Exploring Careers in… feature presents specific information about careers in the areas identified by the U.S. Department of Education as the 16 Career Clusters.

Exploring Careers in…
EDUCATION

Do you like to work with people? Are you good at explaining concepts and tasks? If the answer is "yes," a career in education might be right for you. Jobs in education involve teaching children and adults. Some workers in this field, such as a school principal, handle administrative tasks. Others, such as counselors, provide support services related to education. Child care workers provide care for children who have not yet entered school and also work with older children before and after school hours.

Jobs in education are found in public and private schools. Teachers receive the education and training to be able to help others learn. They often teach numerous subjects every day. They put in extra hours meeting with parents and grading homework and exams.

Employment Outlook

- A slower than average rate of employment growth is expected for high school teachers, but an average growth rate is expected for elementary and

- A master's degree (or higher) is needed for advancement and tenure positions.
- Excellent communication skills and the ability to work well with others is needed.

What's it like to work in . . . Education

Rich is a social studies teacher at one of his city's public high schools. He arrives by 7:15 A.M. each morning and prepares for his day in the classroom. His teaching day begins at 8 A.M. with a world history lesson for 24 sophomores. He then teaches two freshmen geography classes and a U.S. history class to 28 juniors before his lunch break. After lunch, he teaches an Advanced Placement (AP) world history class to seniors. This is followed by his planning period, in which he prepares lesson plans and grades papers. In ad-

Take Action feature provides students with the opportunity to synthesize the concepts by participating in an ongoing project throughout the text.

CHECKPOINT
How does inflation affect your standard of living?

Checkpoint feature provides a question or activity for application of chapter topics.

NEW! Do the Math feature connects basic mathematic skills to real situations students will face.

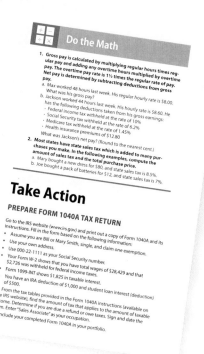

Do the Math

1. Gross pay is calculated by multiplying regular hours times regular pay and adding any overtime hours multiplied by overtime pay. The overtime pay rate is 1½ times the regular rate of pay. Net pay is determined by subtracting deductions from gross pay.
   a. Max worked 48 hours last week. His regular hourly rate is $8.00. What was his gross pay?
   b. Jackson worked 44 hours last week. His hourly rate is $8.60. He has the following deductions taken from his gross earnings:
   · Federal income tax withheld at the rate of 10%
   · Social Security tax withheld at the rate of 6.2%
   · Medicare tax withheld at the rate of 1.45%
   · Health insurance premiums of $12.80
   What was Jackson's net pay? (Round to the nearest cent.)
2. Most states have state sales tax which is added to many purchases you make. In the following examples, compute the amount of sales tax and the total purchase price.
   a. Mary bought a new dress for $80, and state sales tax is 8.5%.
   b. Joe bought a pack of batteries for $12, and state sales tax is 7%.

Take Action
PREPARE FORM 1040A TAX RETURN

Go to the IRS website (www.irs.gov) and print out a copy of Form 1040A and its instructions. Fill in the form based on the following information:
- Assume you are Bill or Mary Smith, single, and claim one exemption.
- Use your own address.
- Use 000-22-1111 as your Social Security number.
- Your Form W-2 shows that you have total wages of $28,429 and that $2,726 was withheld for federal income taxes.
- Form 1099-INT shows $1,825 in taxable interest.
- You have an IRA deduction of $1,000 and student loan interest (deduction) of $500.

From the tax tables provided in the Form 1040A instructions (available on the IRS website), find the amount of tax that applies to the amount of taxable income. Determine if you are due a refund or owe taxes. Sign and date the form. Enter "Sales Associate" as your occupation. Include your completed Form 1040A in your portfolio.

ASSESSMENT IS KEY!

End-of-Lesson Assessment

Key Terms Review helps students understand and apply key lesson terms.

Check Your Understanding ensures students' comprehension of lesson concepts.

Think Critically encourages students to use critical-thinking skills to evaluate and apply what they've learned.

Extend Your Learning provides students with additional questions and activities to extend their understanding of concepts.

1-1 Lesson Assessment

KEY TERMS REVIEW

Match the terms with the definitions. Some terms may not be used.

___ 1. The unique skills and abilities that you bring to the job market

___ 2. A desired outcome, based on one's values, for which a plan of action is developed and carried out

___ 3. The job openings that are available when you are ready to go to work

___ 4. Learning new skills on your own by reading and practicing

___ 5. Describes what a job would be like, including the tasks performed and skills needed

___ 6. A principle that reflects the worth you place on an idea or action

___ 7. Measurable physical and mental abilities that allow you to complete a job

___ 8. Nontechnical skills needed by most workers for success on the job

a. goal
b. hard skills
c. job description
d. job market
e. on-the-job training
f. self-training
g. skill set
h. soft skills
i. value

CHECK YOUR UNDERSTANDING

9. Why does the job market change over time?

10. What is meant by a *skill set*? Why are communication skills (verbal and

Chapter 2 Assessment

SUMMARY

2-1 Sources of earned income include wages, salaries, tips, commissions, and net earnings from self-employment.

Employee benefits are important to workers. They are usually not taxed, are offered at comparatively low prices, and help workers reach their financial goals, such as retirement.

Employee benefits include pay without work (paid vacations and holidays, sick leave, and personal leave), group health insurance, retirement plans, flexible spending accounts (FSAs), health savings accounts (HSAs), profit sharing, stock options, and perks such as educational benefits, on-site child care facilities, and wellness programs.

MAKE ACADEMIC CONNECTIONS

1. **Ethics** Many employers provide sick leave for employees. Sick leave is a valuable benefit. Employers usually have rules about what situations qualify for use of sick leave. In some cases, the employee must be ill to use sick leave. In other cases, the company may allow employees to use sick leave to care for a sick child or other relative. An employee may also be able to use sick leave to visit a doctor or hospital for tests or checkups. Why is it important for employees to follow the rules that apply to using sick leave? Explain why it is unethical to call in sick when you really have plans to do something else. (LO 2-1.2)

2. **Legal** When workers are laid off from their jobs, they may be entitled to unemployment compensation benefits. These benefits are taxable income. Unemployment is a joint effort between the federal and state governments. Federal law sets the general guidelines, while states determine specific rules, such as eligibility requirements and benefit amounts. Visit your state's website to find out how unemployment compensation laws and insurance work in your state. Find answers to the following questions: (LO 2-2.1)
   a. What are the requirements for drawing unemployment benefits?
   b. How is the amount of the benefit determined?

End-of-Chapter Assessment

Summary provides a concise wrap-up of chapter topics to help students synthesize the information.

Make Academic Connections relates chapter content to cross-curricular areas including history, social studies, ethics, communication, law, economics, research, technology, and problem solving.

SUPPLEMENTS FOR COMPLETE INSTRUCTION!

Supplements

Text	978-1-305-65307-8
Annotated Instructor's Edition	978-1-305-65308-5
Student Workbook	978-1-305-65311-5
Instructor's Resource CD	978-1-305-67064-8

Glossary of Student Edition key terms has been translated into Spanish to help ELL students master the important terminology associated with personal financial literacy. The Spanish Glossary is available on the IRCD and the companion website.

cognero Cengage Learning Testing by Cognero is a flexible, online system that allows instructors to author, edit, and manage test bank content from multiple Cengage Learning solutions, create multiple test versions in an instant, and deliver tests from wherever they want. ISBN: 978-1-305-67072-3

NEW! MindTap® MindTap is a personalized teaching experience with relevant assignments that guide students to analyze, apply, and improve thinking, allowing you to measure skills and outcomes with ease.

- Relevant readings, multimedia, and activities are designed to take students from basic knowledge to analysis and application.
- Personalized teaching becomes yours through a Learning Path built with key student objectives and your syllabus in mind. Control what students see and when they see it.
- Additional activities and worksheets for the Unit Projects are included in the Learning Path, along with vocabulary review and chapter quizzes.
- Analytics and reports provide a snapshot of class progress, time in course, and engagement and completion rates.

Money and Income

Unit 1 explains how to get started building a plan for financial security. It begins with a look at the job market and how your values, goals, and education affect your job choices. You'll look at the economy and how it works and the costs of and options for higher education. You'll learn about finding jobs and how to apply for them successfully.

Next you will examine your paycheck and deductions, which take you from gross pay to net pay. For those interested in self-employment, you'll learn about its advantages and disadvantages. Benefits and incentives in the workplace, the changing work environment, and the role of taxes and other deductions will also be covered.

You'll finish this unit by exploring the concepts of inflation, including types, causes and effects, and what to do about it. You'll explore how prices are set in a market economy and how buying strategies affect those prices. You'll learn about the role of sellers as well as buyers before, during, and after the buying process. Finally, you'll learn about consumer rights and laws that protect you, along with how you can protect yourself from fraudulent practices.

How Your Choices Affect Income

Armadillo Stock/Shutterstock.com

The choices you make now while you are still in school will affect your income later in life. The personal values and goals that you set for yourself will influence the way you will prepare for your future, from education to job skills. You must also consider the economy and how it will affect your decisions. As you make those choices, you will need to consider how you will pay for the training and skills you will need to enter the job market.

Do *This*, Not *That*

When looking for a job:

- Know your skill set.
- Conduct research to learn about jobs of interest and job requirements.
- Know the average income for the job of your choice.
- Be prepared to get the education needed and understand how to finance it.
- Have a resume that sets you apart.

1-1 Personal Skills and the Job Market

THE ESSENTIAL QUESTION   What is the job market, and what are your responsibilities to prepare for it?

LEARNING OBJECTIVES

LO 1-1.1 Discuss the job market, how it changes over time, and what you can do to prepare yourself.

LO 1-1.2 Describe how your education may affect the amount of money that you earn.

KEY TERMS

- job market, 3
- skill set, 3
- hard skills, 3
- soft skills, 3
- job description, 5
- value, 6
- goal, 6
- on-the-job training, 7
- self-training, 7

LO 1-1.1 What Is the Job Market?

The **job market** refers to the job openings that are available when you are ready to go to work. Employers' needs are ever changing, so it is a challenge to meet these needs.

In today's job market, it is important for you to have the right skills and be able to learn new ones when they are needed. Change takes place in all aspects of life, and the job market is no exception.

job market the job openings that are available when you are ready to go to work

The Right Skill Set

The unique skills and abilities that you bring to the job market are called your **skill set**. Within your skill set are specific technical abilities, called **hard skills**, which are measurable physical and mental abilities that allow you to complete a job. Examples include installing a faucet, creating a spreadsheet, operating a machine, and driving a vehicle.

Being able to work well with others is also important. **Soft skills** are nontechnical skills needed by most workers for success on the job. Soft skills are an important part of your skill set. They can be learned through education and practice. Examples include leadership skills, teamwork skills, problem-solving skills, and time-management skills.

skill set the unique skills and abilities that you bring to the job market

hard skills measurable physical and mental abilities that allow you to complete a job

soft skills nontechnical skills needed by most workers for success on the job

Communication Skills

Communication is one of the most important soft skills in today's workplace. You need to communicate effectively with employers, coworkers, and customers. *Verbal communication* is the use of sounds and words to express yourself. Speaking and writing are basic verbal communication skills. You might communicate face to face, in a letter, by phone, or digitally through emails, text messages, video conferences, or some other type of media. The type of communication you use should be appropriate for the situation. Always use proper verbal etiquette. Be attentive and polite, and respond promptly with clear, well-thought-out answers.

Nonverbal communication conveys a message without using words. It involves body language, such as facial expressions, hand gestures, and eye contact. Nonverbal communication provides clues and helps people interpret verbal messages. A simple nod indicates you understand or agree with someone. Eye contact shows self-confidence and respect. A smile expresses friendliness.

Communication takes on many roles in a business, from presenting business ideas to employers and coworkers, to providing good customer service, to using proper business dining etiquette. For example, at a business dinner, you should avoid controversial topics, know which fork to use, avoid speaking with food in your mouth, keep your elbows off the table, and be courteous (say "please" and "thank you"). Developing your communication skills will improve your employability.

Job Choices

As you think about your future, you should begin creating a post-secondary (post-high school) plan for job prospects and opportunities. You can start by asking questions and reading about jobs that interest you. A good place to begin job market research is the *Occupational Outlook Handbook (OOH)*. It is published by the U.S. Department of Labor and is available online, as shown in Figure 1-1.1. From this resource, you can find information about the nature of the work, working conditions, training and education, earnings, and job outlook for hundreds of different occupations.

Some people are interested in military careers. Although the overall mission of military jobs is to serve and protect our country, service members can receive training to learn various skills, such as mechanical, transportation, human services, and computer skills, that can be used in military or civilian jobs. You can conduct research online or at various career fairs to learn more about the U.S. military branches (Army, Navy,

▶ **FIGURE 1-1.1** *Occupational Outlook Handbook* **Web Page**

Source: United States Department of Labor, Bureau of Labor Statistics, *Occupational Outlook Handbook*, http://www.bls.gov/ooh, accessed December 1, 2015.

Air Force, Marine Corps, and Coast Guard) and the various job opportunities that exist after initial training.

Job Choices and Your Income

Some jobs pay a lot more than others. Generally, the more experience, training, and education you have in your skill set, the more you can expect to earn. Sources such as the *Occupational Outlook Handbook* (*OOH*) can provide information about beginning earnings and expected future earnings for a wide variety of jobs.

Some jobs are also in greater demand than others. Figure 1-1.2 is a short list taken from the current *OOH*, listing some of the fastest-growing occupations. As you can see from Figure 1-1.2, today's most popular careers often require a bachelor's degree or more. However, there are careers that don't have high education requirements that can provide job satisfaction and a good income.

Learning about Job Requirements

As you look for information about careers, you will see jobs listed by title. A *job title* is a name given to a particular job. It may be a word or phrase that describes the main duties or tasks of the job. For example, the job title *long-haul truck driver* indicates clearly what the job involves. A person with this job drives a truck for long distances.

Sometimes a job title alone is not enough to tell you what a person in that job is required to do. For example, reading the job title *systems analyst* might leave you wondering what a person would do in that job. A **job description** describes what a job would be like, including the tasks performed and skills needed. It often contains other information such as education or experience required, the hours worked, or details about the work site or location. Figure 1-1.3 is a job description for a physician assistant, a very popular and growing career field today.

job description describes what a job would be like, including the tasks performed and skills needed

▶ FIGURE 1-1.2 **Fastest-Growing Occupations, 2012–22**

Occupation	Expected Growth 2012–2022	Education Required
Industrial organizational psychologists	53%	Doctoral degree
Home health aides	48%	Short-term training and on-the-job experience
Interpreters and translators	46%	Bachelor's degree
Genetic counselors	41%	Master's degree
Skin care specialists	40%	Post-secondary skills
Physician assistants	38%	Master's degree
Information security analysts	37%	Bachelor's degree

Source: United States Department of Labor, Bureau of Labor Statistics, http://www.bls.gov/ooh /fastest-growing.htm.

▶ **FIGURE 1-1.3** **Job Description**

PHYSICIAN ASSISTANT

What Physician Assistants Do

Physician assistants (PAs) practice medicine on a team, under the supervision of physicians and surgeons. They are formally educated to examine patients, diagnose injuries and illness, and provide treatment.

Duties

PAs review patients' medical histories, conduct physical exams to check patients' health, order and interpret diagnostic tests, such as X-rays or blood tests, and make diagnoses. PAs give treatment such as setting broken bones and immunizing patients. They also educate and counsel patients and their families, prescribe medicine when needed, record a patient's progress, research the latest treatments to ensure quality of patient care, and conduct or participate in outreach programs to promote wellness.

PAs work in all areas of medicine, including primary care and family medicine, emergency medicine, and psychiatry. PAs are different from medical assistants, who do routine clinical and clerical tasks but do not practice medicine.

A PA's work schedule can be physically and emotionally demanding. PAs spend much of their time on their feet, making rounds and evaluating patients. PAs in clinics usually work a standard 40-hour workweek. Hospital-based PAs may be required to work weekends, nights, or early morning hours.

Source: United States Department of Labor, Bureau of Labor Statistics, *Occupational Outlook Handbook*, http://www.bls.gov/ooh/healthcare/physician-assistants.htm, accessed December 1, 2015.

Preparing for Lifelong Learning

Learning new skills and information to help you stay qualified for a job is important for your job security. When you are hired for a job, you will probably have the education and skills you need to do that job. As time goes by, however, new technology and advances made in your career field may cause the required skills or education for the job to change. You will need to update your job skills. *Lifelong learning* will help prepare you to be a skilled worker and an informed consumer. It will keep you prepared as changes occur and before they negatively impact you.

Values and Goals Affect Your Job Choices

As you think about a career that you might like to have, consider the values and goals that are important to you. A **value** is a principle that reflects the worth you place on an idea or action. For example, if you think being honest is important, honesty would be one of your values. Values define who you are. They influence the choices and decisions you make. If you think making a difference in other people's lives is important, for instance, then that value could be a reason for choosing to be a teacher or a counselor rather than a salesperson or an accountant.

Many people set goals that they want to accomplish. A **goal** is a desired outcome, based on one's values, for which a plan of action is developed and carried out. A person's goals affect his or her behavior. For example, if you value good health, your goals may include eating properly and exercising regularly.

value a principle that reflects the worth you place on an idea or action

goal a desired outcome, based on one's values, for which a plan of action is developed carried out

LO 1-1.2 How Does Education Affect Your Income?

Some jobs require little education. Other jobs require training that takes several years to complete. Education helps prepare you to do a job well. Education can be formal or informal. *Formal education* involves attending classes and, often, earning a degree. Students must show that they have learned certain skills and concepts. *Informal education* usually does not happen in classrooms; it is often a part of working. An example of informal education is **on-the-job training**, or learning as you do the work. Another example is learning new skills from reading and practicing on your own, called **self-training**. Learning to use a digital camera by reading the instructions and teaching yourself a computer program using written or video tutorials are examples of self-training. These skills can also be listed on a resume when you are able to perform them at an acceptable level.

on-the-job training learning as you do the work

self-training learning new skills from reading and practicing on your own

The amount and type of education you complete can affect the amount of money you earn. Generally, people who have a formal education earn more than people who have less education. Figure 1-1.4 shows you the difference you can expect to find in your earnings potential when you complete more formal education. If the pay for a job is high compared to the education required, there is often a reason. The job might require high personal risks, a short career span, or completing tasks that others are not willing to do. For example, the employee might have to handle dangerous materials or work in an unstable country where a war is taking place.

▶ FIGURE 1-1.4 **Education Pays**

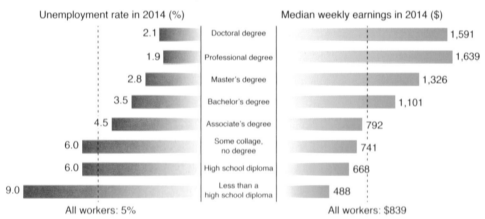

Unemployment rate in 2014 (%) / Median weekly earnings in 2014 ($)

	Unemployment rate	Degree	Median weekly earnings
	2.1	Doctoral degree	1,591
	1.9	Professional degree	1,639
	2.8	Master's degree	1,326
	3.5	Bachelor's degree	1,101
	4.5	Associate's degree	792
	6.0	Some collage, no degree	741
	6.0	High school diploma	668
	9.0	Less than a high school diploma	488

All workers: 5%   All workers: $839

Source: United States Department of Labor, Bureau of Labor Statistics, http://www.bls.gov/emp/ep_chart_001.htm, accessed December 1, 2015.

Building COMMUNICATION SKILLS

LISTENING

Listening is part of the communication process. Hearing and listening are not the same thing. *Hearing* is the ability to process sounds, whereas *listening* means that information is heard and understood or thought about. Anyone who is not hearing-impaired is able to hear; however, most people have to work at being good listeners.

Listening is an important skill that can help you succeed in the workplace when communicating with your employer, coworkers, and customers. According to the International Listening Association, 85 percent of what we know we have learned by listening. Practice the following tips to help you improve your listening skills:

- Face and look directly at the person who is talking to you.
- Focus on what the speaker is saying; do not let your mind wander to other topics.
- Ignore distractions such as noises made by other people in the room or someone passing by.
- Turn off the phone, and eliminate other noises such as music, if possible.
- When you are part of a group that the speaker is addressing, take notes about what the speaker is

saying. Write only key phrases or main ideas; do not try to write every word the speaker says.
- In conversations with one or two people, give small feedback cues, such as "I see" or "What's next?" to let the speaker know that you are listening. Nod frequently and wait quietly during pauses.
- Mentally summarize the main points of what you have heard. Ask the speaker questions to clarify points you do not understand. If you are listening to someone give you instructions for a task, repeat key phrases to review the important points.

Try It Out

1. Ask the person next to you to tell you about a memorable experience he or she recently had at work or at school. Practice the listening skills listed above. Next, it is your turn.
2. After you have finished listening to each other, write down five new things you learned from listening to the other person. List three listening skills you used during the activity.

Think about the type of education you want to complete and how well it will prepare you for the career or job you want later in life. Education will affect your current and future job choices. Making choices about education is a serious responsibility. Education is considered an investment in your future. The jobs you choose and the education you receive will affect the amount of money you can earn. How much time and effort are you willing to put forth to prepare for the job you want? It's never too early to start planning for your future.

 CHECKPOINT
How is formal education different from informal education?

KEY TERMS REVIEW

Match the terms with the definitions. Some terms may not be used.

_____ 1. The unique skills and abilities that you bring to the job market

_____ 2. A desired outcome, based on one's values, for which a plan of action is developed and carried out

_____ 3. The job openings that are available when you are ready to go to work

_____ 4. Learning new skills on your own by reading and practicing

_____ 5. Describes what a job would be like, including the tasks performed and skills needed

_____ 6. A principle that reflects the worth you place on an idea or action

_____ 7. Measurable physical and mental abilities that allow you to complete a job

_____ 8. Nontechnical skills needed by most workers for success on the job

a. goal

b. hard skills

c. job description

d. job market

e. on-the-job training

f. self-training

g. skill set

h. soft skills

i. value

CHECK YOUR UNDERSTANDING

9. Why does the job market change over time?

10. What is meant by a *skill set*? Why are communication skills (verbal and nonverbal) an important part of a skill set in dealing with employers, co-workers, and customers?

11. What is meant by business verbal etiquette and dining etiquette?

12. What information is found in the *Occupational Outlook Handbook*?

13. Explain how job choices affect income.

14. Explain why some career choices require little formal education, whereas others require a master's degree or more.

15. Describe the contents of a job description.

16. Explain why lifelong learning is important to your career plans.

17. What is meant by informal education? Give two examples of it.

18. Give an example of how a person's values and goals may affect his or her career choices.

19. What job opportunities are available to those in the U.S. military?

THINK CRITICALLY

20. Today, successful career planning depends not only on finding yourself but also on creating yourself. As you explore the types of careers you would like to have, think of ways you can stand out from your competition to get hired for the job. Describe some things you can do now, while you are still in school, to enhance your skills for a future career.

21. Soft skills are often more difficult to learn than hard skills. Being able to get along with others, public speaking, and listening are important soft skills. List three soft skills that you need to improve. How can you improve them and make them your strengths?

22. Describe the various ways in which digital devices can be used for communication. When is it appropriate to use a digital method to communicate with an employer, coworkers, and customers? When would it be inappropriate?

23. List three values that are important to you and that are reflected in choices you make. Based on these values, list three goals you wish to achieve by the time you are 30 years old. What careers would you consider that reflect your values and goals? Explain how your values and goals influence the personal choices you make.

24. Many people appear to be unhappy in the careers they have chosen, yet they are unwilling (or unable) to start over in a career that would be better suited for them. How do you know when people are unhappy in their jobs (what signs do you see)? Why do you think they are so unhappy? What can you do to keep this from happening to you?

EXTEND YOUR LEARNING

25. The Internet provides many valuable tools for job searches. Monster.com and CareerBuilder.com are two of the largest and most established employment websites. Some job seekers find value in both sites, whereas others have a preference for one over the other. Visit both sites. Create a table that compares and contrasts the features of both sites. Which site do you prefer and why?

26. Visit the *Occupational Outlook Handbook* website at www.bls.gov/ooh. On the homepage, click on the A–Z Index link and choose a job of interest to you from the list. Prepare a presentation about this job. Use visual aids such as slides or posters. Include information about the job duties, work environment, education and training needed to enter the occupation, beginning and future earnings, and job outlook.

THE ESSENTIAL QUESTION   Refer to The Essential Question on p. 3. The job market refers to the job openings that are available when you are ready to go to work. It is your responsibility to be aware of the job market and how it is changing so you can prepare for it. You also need to understand your values and goals in order to select a job that is in line with them.

1-2 The Economy and Your Post-Secondary Education

THE ESSENTIAL QUESTION How are prices set and how can you prepare for these costs, including the costs of education?

LEARNING OBJECTIVES

LO 1-2.1 Describe how the economy can affect prices and income.

LO 1-2.2 Discuss the costs of and options for higher education and post-secondary training.

LO 1-2.3 Explain how to pay for college and other education programs.

KEY TERMS

- economy, 11
- market economy, 11
- supply, 11
- demand, 11
- business cycle, 12
- tuition, 13
- financial aid, 15
- subsidized student loan, 16
- unsubsidized student loan, 16
- grant, 16
- scholarship, 16
- ethics, 17

LO 1-2.1 What Is the Economy?

Regardless of where you live, you are affected by the economy. The **economy** refers to all of the activities related to making and distributing goods and services in a geographic area or country. *Economics* is a study of how choices are made by individuals and societies.

The study of economics is also said to be the study of *scarcity*, which occurs because people's needs and wants are unlimited, whereas resources are limited. Examples of resources include a person's income or the materials needed to produce products. Because these resources are scarce, individuals and businesses must make choices to meet needs and wants.

As you consider what career you might like to pursue and how to prepare for your future, you must also consider the economy. The economy will affect your income, and your income will affect the choices you make.

> **economy** all of the activities related to making and distributing goods and services in a geographic area or country

The Economy Affects Prices

The United States has a **market economy**, which is based on the laws of supply and demand. In a market economy, the price for an item is set at a point that consumers are willing to pay and sellers are willing to accept. In other words, sellers charge what the market will bear. Producers wish to increase their profits; consumers wish to get high value for each dollar spent. The quantity of goods and services that producers are willing and able to provide is called **supply**. The willingness and ability of consumers to buy goods and services is called **demand**. When demand exceeds supply, businesses can charge higher prices for the products. These prices affect your decisions on which items to buy as you spend your income.

> **market economy** an economy based on the laws of supply and demand

> **supply** the quantity of goods and services that producers are willing and able to provide

> **demand** the willingness and ability of consumers to buy goods and services

The Economy Affects Income

When the economy is growing, people are buying goods and services. Jobs are being created, and businesses are hiring workers. Employers are more likely to give pay raises and bonuses to employees. Finding and keeping a job that will provide financial security is easier.

On the other hand, when the economy is slowing, people often buy fewer goods and services. The lower demand for goods and services may mean that businesses are not growing. Workers may be laid off or dismissed from their jobs and are less likely to receive pay increases. Fewer new workers are hired. Finding and keeping a job that will provide financial security can be difficult.

If you choose to work in a career field that is growing and in a job that is in demand, you will likely be able to earn a good income. The money earned allows you to meet basic needs and achieve goals. However, when the demand for products or services that are produced by your employer is very low, your job may be in danger. When faced with this situation, some people decide to learn new and different skills to prepare for a new career field. This process is called *retraining*.

Understanding how the economy affects prices of products, the job market, and your income can help you make better financial decisions.

The Economy in Action

business cycle the alternating periods of growth and decline in the economy

The economy goes through stages in the business cycle. The **business cycle** is the alternating periods of growth and decline in the economy. Over time, there are many ups and downs that are certain to happen. It is important to understand what each point in the cycle means and how you should prepare and respond to it.

Figure 1-2.1 shows the four stages of a business cycle: recovery (growth), peak, recession (decline), and trough. During periods of *recovery*, the economy is growing. People are spending money because they are optimistic and times are good. Businesses are hiring, and factories are increasing production of goods. Rather than spending, now is the time to save money.

It is difficult to know when the economy has reached its *peak*, which is the point at which the economy is as robust as it can get. At this point, prices are high because demand is high.

When people slow their buying and are unable to pay high prices, the economy slips into an *economic decline*, called a *recession*. In a recession, jobs are being lost, production is slowing, and people are

▶ **FIGURE 1-2.1 The Business Cycle**

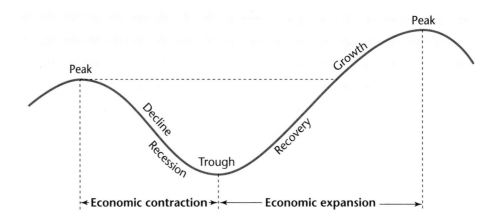

pessimistic. As people spend less money, the economy slows down even more. It's during economic declines that the money you saved during the growth phase can buy you the most. You will get the best prices (values) because you have the cash to spend.

When the bottom is reached, called the *trough*, the economy is at a standstill. Businesses cannot hire because of sluggish sales, and many people are unemployed and unable to meet their debt obligations. The trough remains until people start spending again, businesses start hiring workers, and production of goods once again begins to increase.

You need to be able to recognize these stages and determine what you can expect the economy to do next. Based on your own analysis, you will make better choices. Your choices will allow you to spend money when you can get the greatest value and to save money for the bad times.

 CHECKPOINT

Explain how the economy affects the amount of income you will make.

LO 1-2.2 What Are the Costs of Education?

As part of your post-secondary plan, you will need to investigate education opportunities and costs as a way to prepare for the career you wish to pursue. There are many types of educational institutions that offer numerous programs to meet your needs. Applying may take weeks or even months. You many need to write an essay or take tests, such as the ACT or SAT tests. These tests indicate how well you are prepared for college-level classes. They measure your reading and comprehension skills, along with vocabulary, math, science, and English skills. Pay special attention to deadlines and all application requirements to avoid being rejected.

Tuition is the expense paid by students for the instruction at a school. Students must pay for textbooks and meet other expenses that are not covered in tuition. *Fees* are charged to cover special expenses of education programs, such as technology, specialized equipment, or supplies. Money is also needed for living expenses such as food, rent, clothing, and transportation. Some schools have housing for students. At other schools, students must find housing on their own, and the cost of rent in neighborhoods near the schools may be higher.

Service members of the U.S. military can receive tuition assistance, sometimes up to 100 percent coverage of tuition and fees. The amount covered depends on the type and length of service being completed or already completed.

tuition the expense paid by students for the instruction at a school

Public or Private Education

The cost of attending a public college or university is usually less than the cost of a private school. A *bachelor's degree* is earned in a four-year college or university program. At a public college or university, tuition costs for earning a bachelor's degree average over $36,000 for in-state residents and over $90,000 for out-of-state residents. To earn

College and university tuition prices vary widely in different parts of the country. Conduct research to find out which region of the country has the highest average published tuition/fees for public four-year colleges and which has the lowest prices. Now find the average tuition/fee for a private four-year college in your area. Is it higher or lower than you expected? What predictions have been made about the future costs of college tuition prices? What do you plan to do to save for college?

a bachelor's degree at a private college or university, tuition costs average almost $125,000. Tuition is less at public schools because they are supported by state tax dollars. When deciding on a college, be sure it is *accredited*, or certified to meet educational quality standards.

Many students find it desirable (and less expensive) to attend community colleges. An *associate's degree* is commonly earned at community colleges after two years of study. Typically, tuition costs are half or less of what you would pay at public colleges and universities, and admission tests aren't required.

Career and Technical Schools

Career and technical schools teach skills related to a specific job. These schools may be public or private. Programs at public schools often cost $5,000 or less in tuition. Programs offered at private schools can run $30,000 or more. The completion time for career and technical school programs is often less than for college programs, with some programs only lasting a few months to a year. Books must be paid for, along with living expenses. Students are also responsible for fees and other charges.

Graduate and Advanced Programs

Some jobs require advanced training. A *master's degree* is an academic degree earned after the completion of a bachelor's degree. It usually requires at least two to three years of additional study. The time needed depends on your background and the type of degree. A *doctorate degree* requires three to seven years of study beyond a master's degree in the same field. The course of study often requires doing research. Some programs require internships or have residency requirements. *Residency* means that classes must be taken in person on campus or at a specific facility, such as at a hospital for medical training.

Tuition is higher at the graduate level. Average annual tuition at public colleges and universities totals nearly $30,000 and at private schools nearly $40,000.

 **CHECKPOINT**

What are the ACT and SAT, and why are they important?

FOCUS On...

STUDENT ORGANIZATIONS

Students in high school and college may join career-related organizations. One such organization for business students in junior high and high school is Future Business Leaders of America (FBLA). The college level of this organization is Phi Beta Lambda. Another group, the Future Educators Association (FEA), provides opportunities for high school students to explore careers in education. The National FFA Organization is for students interested in careers in agriculture. These are just a few of the many student organizations that may be available to you. Being a member of a student organization provides opportunities for students to:

- Explore careers of interest.
- Ask questions of people who are working in the career area.
- Take part in conferences to learn more about careers in those areas.
- Compete with other students to demonstrate skills learned.

- Apply for scholarships, grants, and other forms of financial aid.
- Learn about continuing education in the field.
- Take part in community service activities.
- Network and form friendships with others who have similar interests.

Student organizations usually have bylaws (rules). These *bylaws* outline the club's purpose and structure. Many student organizations have a website that provides information about their goals and activities, as well as the costs and requirements for membership.

Try It Out

Search the Internet using the keywords *student organization* and a career area (such as *nursing*) to find groups that interest you. Write a one-page report describing one of the student organizations and why it appeals to you.

LO 1-2.3 How Will You Pay for Education and Training?

When you choose to pursue formal education and training, you must consider ways to pay the costs. Do you or your parents have the money needed? Do you qualify for financial aid? Will you be able to get grants or scholarships? Will you work part-time to earn money as you attend classes? These options and others may be available to you.

Financial Aid

Financial aid is money you receive from an outside source to help pay for education. Financial aid is available from a variety of sources, including the federal government, local banks, and the state. The federal government's office of Federal Student Aid is the largest provider of financial aid in the nation. It supplies a form called FAFSA (Free Application for Federal Student Aid), which may be completed and submitted entirely online at the Federal Student Aid website. The federal government as well as many states and colleges use the FAFSA data to determine a student's eligibility for financial aid.

Financial aid comes in many forms. The three most common are student loans, grants, and work-study programs.

financial aid money received from an outside source to help pay for education

Loans

Loans are available from a variety of sources, including the federal government and private lenders. A loan is money that you borrow and must repay with interest. *Interest* is money paid for the use of borrowed money. In the case of a student loan, interest is the money the student pays the lender in addition to the amount borrowed.

Loans may be subsidized or unsubsidized. A **subsidized student loan** is a loan on which you pay no interest until you have graduated or are no longer enrolled in school. An **unsubsidized student loan** is a loan that starts charging interest from the time the loan is made. Most government loans are subsidized.

Some private lenders, such as banks and credit unions, make loans to students. These loans are unsubsidized and typically have higher interest rates than loans from the government. Private loans require that you have income and a good credit history. If your income is too high to qualify for federal financial aid, a private student loan may be a good option for you. You will need to fill out an application for the loan. You may also have to show income tax returns and proof of income.

Grants

A **grant** is money given to pay for educational expenses that does not have to be repaid. The federal government offers a variety of grants, based on need, to students attending four-year colleges or universities, community colleges, and career and technical schools. Many states also provide need-based grants to their resident students.

Work-Study Programs

Both public and private colleges and universities (including technical schools and community colleges) have *work-study programs*. The Federal Work-Study (FWS) program provides funds to participating schools to pay the part-time wages of needy students. Students who are qualified are able to work on campus or other college locations to earn money. Earnings will help offset the need for student loans or reduce the amount of loans that must be repaid. To qualify for work-study, you must meet income requirements and have the specific skills needed to do the job tasks that are assigned.

Scholarships

A **scholarship** is a cash allowance awarded to a student to help pay for education. Many scholarships are available to students with high grades or strong athletic skills. Other scholarships are given based on need. Scholarships are available from local, state, and national organizations, including the federal government. Money from scholarships generally is not taxable and does not have to be repaid if you complete your education. But scholarships usually require students to meet certain standards, such as maintaining a certain GPA (grade point average).

Scholarships vary in amounts. A *partial scholarship* may be given to pay for some educational costs. A *full scholarship* covers the entire tuition for a degree. To learn about scholarships for which you can apply, talk to a teacher or counselor or search the Internet. The Admissions or

subsidized student loan a loan on which the student pays no interest until he or she has graduated or is no longer in school

unsubsidized student loan a loan that starts charging interest from the time the loan is made

grant money given to pay for educational expenses that does not have to be repaid

scholarship a cash allowance awarded to a student to help pay for education

Financial Aid Office of the college you wish to attend can also provide information on scholarships that may be available.

Applying for Financial Aid and Scholarships

When applying for financial aid or scholarships, use the following guidelines:

- Fill in all the blanks and boxes on the form. Write *N/A* if the information is *not available* or *not applicable*.
- Always answer questions truthfully. Do not exaggerate or give information that will create false impressions. Doing so is not ethical. **Ethics** refers to a set of moral values that people consider acceptable. The term is also applied to the study of what is right versus wrong. Being fair and honest in your dealings with others is considered ethical behavior.
- Print data clearly. When possible, download the document to your computer and key the information into the form.
- Proofread the application before submitting it. Check for any errors, and make sure the information is clear, complete, and correct.

ethics a set of moral values that people consider acceptable; the study of what is right versus wrong

Work and Save

Some students decide to take time out from their education to work and save money. They start college or a training program a few years after high school. Some students continue their education while they work part-time. Others work full-time and take courses part-time. This often means taking night classes or online classes.

These paths take a longer period of time to complete. However, a benefit may be the job experience that students gain as they work to pay for their education. Another benefit to students is being able to avoid the burden of a large student loan debt from financing their education. Unfortunately, going to school part-time will often delay graduation for several years. This means it will take longer to enter the job

Would you be willing to work while you are attending college classes? Why or why not?

market with your degree. Also, by attending school part-time, students may miss out on college activities that are part of the college experience.

Stephen Coburn/Shutterstock.com

⟫⟫ CHECKPOINT

How is a loan different from a grant?

1-2 Lesson Assessment

KEY TERMS REVIEW

Match the terms with the definitions. Some terms may not be used.

_____ 1. The willingness and ability of consumers to buy goods and services

_____ 2. A cash allowance awarded to a student to help pay for education

_____ 3. A loan on which the student pays no interest until he or she has graduated or is no longer enrolled in school

_____ 4. All of the activities related to making and distributing goods and services in a geographic area or country

_____ 5. The quantity of goods and services that producers are willing and able to provide

_____ 6. An economy based on the laws of supply and demand

_____ 7. The alternating periods of growth and decline in the economy

_____ 8. A set of moral values that people consider acceptable

_____ 9. Money received from an outside source to help pay for education

a. business cycle
b. demand
c. economy
d. ethics
e. financial aid
f. grant
g. market economy
h. scholarship
i. subsidized student loan
j. supply
k. tuition
l. unsubsidized student loan

CHECK YOUR UNDERSTANDING

10. What is the economy? Why is it important for you to understand it?

11. Explain the concepts of supply and demand within a market economy.

12. What is retraining?

13. What is the business cycle? List the four stages of the business cycle.

14. How does the business cycle affect you as an individual?

15. Explain why people tend to spend more money during economic growth.

16. Explain why it is important to have cash (spending power) in a recession.

17. How is tuition different from fees?

18. Why is it important to attend an accredited college?

19. List ways that students can pay for their post-secondary education.

20. How do subsidized and unsubsidized student loans differ?

21. What kind of living expenses might you have as part of your post-secondary education?

THINK CRITICALLY

22. Describe the U.S. economy at this time. Do economists believe it is in recovery (growth), at the peak, in economic decline (recession), or in the trough? Explain what you will do at this point to better prepare for the next stage of the business cycle.

23. During a recessionary period, people lose their jobs and are unable to pay their bills. Credit card companies, which take losses because their customers cannot pay, raise interest rates and minimum payment amounts. What can consumers do to protect themselves from paying more in interest during bad economic times?

24. Why is the tuition of public colleges and universities much less than that of private schools? Why do people choose to go to private schools? How can the military help pay for education?

EXTEND YOUR LEARNING

25. You may want to apply for financial aid for your post-secondary education. To learn about the information you will need to provide on the application, locate the federal financial aid form by visiting the FAFSA Federal Student Aid website (fafsa.ed.gov). Answer the following questions:

    a. How many pages long is the application?

    b. Who should complete this application?

    c. What types of questions are asked on the application? Provide three examples.

    d. What is the earliest date the FAFSA application may be submitted for federal aid? What is the deadline?

    e. What is the earliest date the FAFSA application may be submitted for aid from the state in which you live? What is the deadline?

26. The U.S. Bureau of Economic Analysis (BEA) supplies economic statistics that influence decisions of businesses and individuals. Visit the website of the BEA (bea.gov) to see what the experts are currently saying about the economy. Read some of the articles, and view graphs and charts. Click on the "U.S. Economy at a Glance" link and do additional Web browsing. Based on your findings, how do you think the economy will affect the job market in the upcoming year? How do you think the economy will affect jobs or career fields that are of interest to you?

THE ESSENTIAL QUESTION   Refer to The Essential Question on p. 11. Prices are set by both buyers and sellers based on the law of supply and demand. The costs of education depend on various factors such as whether the school is public or private. Financial aid in the form of grants, scholarships, and student loans can help you pay for education. Working and saving money is another way to cover costs.

THE ESSENTIAL QUESTION What strategies can you use to find jobs, and what can you do to sell yourself as the best candidate for a job?

LEARNING OBJECTIVES

LO 1-3.1 Discuss strategies to find and apply for jobs.
LO 1-3.2 Describe how to successfully apply for a job.
LO 1-3.3 Discuss entrepreneurship.

KEY TERMS

- contact, 20
- social network, 20
- temp agency, 23
- job shadowing, 23
- job application, 24
- resume, 24
- cover letter, 28
- job interview, 28
- follow-up, 30
- entrepreneur, 31

LO 1-3.1 How Can You Find Job Opportunities?

The way people find job prospects and opportunities has changed in recent years. In the past, many people found jobs through the want ads in the newspaper. Today, applicants find job openings through a variety of other ways, including networking, company websites, online career and employment sites, job scouts, job fairs, and employment agencies.

Networking

Networking involves building relationships and exchanging information with people who can help improve your career prospects. Many job openings are not advertised. Instead, they get filled by word of mouth. That's why networking is important to job seekers.

Networking starts by developing a list of contacts. A **contact** is a person you know. Contacts can be someone you may have met just recently or someone you have known all of your life. Contacts may be able to give you job leads, offer you advice and information about a company or industry, and introduce you to others so that you can expand your network.

While you are in school, you can start building your social network. A **social network** is a group of friends and acquaintances who keep in contact and share information. Joining student groups and community organizations is a good way to build your social network. Here you will meet people who can introduce or refer you to other people. You can also join online social networking sites, such as Facebook, LinkedIn, and Twitter. At these sites, you can exchange information with others, post messages, and keep in contact over time.

contact a person you know

social network a group of friends and acquaintances who keep in contact and share information

How can you learn about job openings that aren't advertised?

Xavier Arnau/iStockphoto.com

SUCCESS SKILLS

USING SOCIAL NETWORKING SITES

Using the Internet for social networking has many advantages for job seekers, such as a wide range of sources for job information, up-to-the-minute knowledge, and rapid response to job openings. However, there are etiquette guidelines that you must follow when using social networking sites. Here are some do's and don'ts for using Internet social networking sites.

Do:

- Be courteous and thoughtful.
- Be appreciative when you get good information.
- Follow through and do your best when others recommend you.
- Share information that benefits others.
- Proofread very carefully before posting information.
- Read your postings from others' points of view.

Don't:

- Criticize or be negative about others.
- Complain about your job, employer, or others.
- Swear or use slang or poor language.
- Neglect others when they ask for your help.
- Post information that could lead others to think poorly of you.
- Brag or seem arrogant or thoughtless.

Think Critically

1. If someone googled your name, what would they find? Why do employers care about what applicants and employees post on their social networks?
2. What social networking sites do you use? What kinds of information should you avoid sharing on these sites?

If you are seeking a job in a field where you have no contacts, try to get to know people who can tell you about openings. Ask if they have a website or blog, and stay in touch. Start by letting others know about your skill set that makes you a unique and desirable employee.

If you are working, even on a part-time or volunteer basis, keep others informed and talk to them often. This includes coworkers, customers, and business professionals whom you will meet in the course of your employment. Share information with them as well as gather it for yourself.

Websites

The Internet has become an essential tool to use when searching for jobs. Want ads that were once placed in newspapers often are now placed online. Online classified sites, such as Craigslist, list many job openings.

Businesses often post job openings on their company website. Jobs are often listed in the "Careers" section of the website. The job openings may contain a job description that lists job qualifications, timelines for applying, and pay rates. You can usually apply for these jobs directly on the website.

You can also find job postings at employment websites, commonly known as job boards. A *job board* is a website that posts jobs supplied by employers. Employers typically pay a fee to the job board in exchange for the opportunity to list their jobs on the site. Examples of job boards include CareerBuilder and Monster.com.

A number of websites list job openings for specific industries. For example, the federal government's USAJOBS website (shown in Figure 1-3.1) lists civil service job openings with federal agencies. Other examples include WallStJobs.com, which lists job openings in the financial field; MarketingJobs.com, which lists job openings for marketing

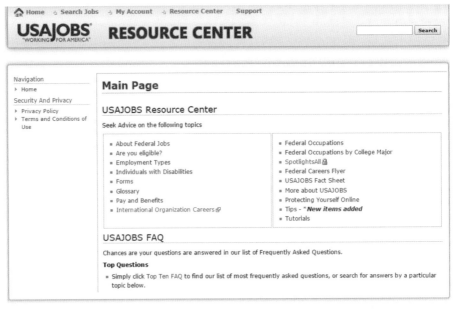

► FIGURE 1-3.1 USAJOBS.gov

Source: United States Office of Personnel Management, USAJOBS, http://www.usajobs.gov, accessed December 1, 2015.

professionals; and Dice.com, which lists job postings for information technology professionals. These sites also allow you to post your resume so that employers can find you.

Job Scouts

When you are ready to begin working, you may want to use a job scout to help you find openings. A *job scout* (also called a *job agent*) is a computer program that searches the Internet to find job listings based on rules or options that you set. The rules that you set might state the type of job and the location of the job (city or state). You may choose to have the job listings sent to you daily or weekly. Some examples of job scouts include JobScout and Virtual Job Scout.

Job Fairs

A *job fair* is an event where job seekers have the opportunity to meet face to face with potential employers. At job fairs, employers often set up tables or booths where they have recruiters available to talk with potential candidates, answer questions, and accept resumes. The military also participates in job fairs, sometimes holding its own recruitment events.

At colleges, job fairs are often used for entry-level positions. They provide a convenient location for students to meet employers. Students can also use this opportunity to get an idea of what it's like to work for a company or in a field that interests them.

Attending a job fair is like going to a job interview. It is important to be prepared by having your resume and dressing appropriately.

Employment Agencies

All major cities have public and private employment agencies. *Employment agencies* help job seekers find a job for which they are qualified. They focus on matching your skills with employers who have job openings listed with them. Private employment agencies may or may not charge a fee for their services. Some agencies charge a fee to the employer; others divide the fee between the employer and the new employee. Fees vary from agency to agency, so you should compare prices.

How do employment agencies help fill job openings?

Temp Agencies

If you initially have trouble finding a permanent job, you might consider using a temp agency. A temporary agency, commonly called a **temp agency**, provides part-time and full-time jobs on a temporary basis. Working in a temporary job gives you a chance to make a good impression on an employer and to expand your network. It also gives you good work experience that could be applied to other jobs. In addition, if the company sees that you are a good fit, you may be offered a permanent job. In such a case, the company will buy out your contract with the temp agency. Or you may be hired after the contract with the temp agency is completed.

temp agency an employment agency that provides part-time and full-time jobs on a temporary basis

State Employment Offices

The state employment office helps people find jobs. Since it is a government agency, it typically does not charge a fee. State employment offices also provide information about job-training and assistance programs, such as Youth Employment Service (YES), Youth Corps, Civil Service (both state and federal), and other government-sponsored programs. You may qualify for one or more of these types of work programs.

Other Job-Seeking Methods

There are other methods that can be used to find job openings. These include job shadowing, cooperative work experience programs, getting information from school counselors and teachers, and using placement centers.

Job Shadowing

Job shadowing is spending time observing a worker in a type of job that interests you. Many employers will let you come and visit in this manner, as long as you do not disrupt the work being done. Job shadowing allows you to see how activities are performed in a typical day. The contacts you make while job shadowing can give you the inside track on finding out about future job openings.

job shadowing spending time observing a worker in a type of job that interests you

Cooperative Work Experience

Many schools have programs to assist students in preparing for careers, making career choices, and securing part-time or full-time work. One such program is called *cooperative work experience*, where students attend classes part of the day and then go to a job that provides supervised work. Students receive credit for the on-the-job skills they learn.

School Counselors, Teachers, and Placement Centers

School counselors and teachers are good sources of job opportunity information. They are often asked by employers to recommend students for specific job openings.

Placement centers also help students find jobs. Their services are usually offered free of charge. Placement centers post job openings at the school and provide information to qualified students so they can apply.

CHECKPOINT

Name three sources where you can find job opportunities.

LO 1-3.2 How Do You Get a Job?

Once you have lined up some job prospects, there are several steps to take to get a job. Your job application, resume, cover letter, and interview can help you sell yourself as the most desirable job applicant and separate you from the competition.

The Job Application

job application a form that asks basic questions about the applicant's background, such as work history, education, skills, and references

To apply for a job, you will most likely have to fill out a job application (also called an *employment application*). A **job application** is a form (either electronic or on paper) that asks basic questions about your background, such as your work history (names, dates, places), education, skills, and references. Figure 1-3.2 is a sample job application form.

Many employers today require you to fill out a job application online. Regardless of whether filling out the application by hand or online, use the following guidelines:

- Answer every question. When you cannot answer a question or it isn't applicable, write the abbreviation *N/A* or draw a line (———) to show that you have not skipped the question.
- Be truthful. Give complete answers; do not abbreviate if there is a chance the abbreviation could be misread.
- Have with you all information that may be requested on the application, such as phone numbers, dates, and email addresses.
- Proofread carefully; check every word.
- Keep a copy for your own records.

The Resume

resume a summary of your work experience, education, skills, interests, and other qualifications (your skill set) that qualify you for a job opening

You will likely be asked to include a resume with your job application. A **resume** describes your work experience, education, skills, interests, and other qualifications (your skill set) that qualify you for a job opening. It is also known as a personal data sheet, professional profile, or *curriculum vitae*. The resume tells the employer neatly and concisely who you are and what you can do.

There are various ways to format a resume. Figure 1-3.3 on p. 26 shows a commonly used resume style. Other styles can be viewed online at employment or career sites.

EMPLOYMENT APPLICATION

Date: *7/15/20 --*   Job you are applying for: *Clerk/Office Assistant*   ☐ Full Time   ☒ Part Time

Social Security Number: *Provided at employment*

First Name: *Terrell*   Middle Initial: *B.*   Last Name: *Adams*

Mailing Address: *234 Maple Street*   City: *Eugene*   State: *OR*   ZIP: *97401*

Home Phone: *(541) 555-2000*   Work Phone: (   ) --

Have you worked for this company before?   ☐ Yes   ☒ No   **From:** ____ **To:** ____   **What location?**

Your name at that time: --   Position when you left: --

If you are under 18, give your birthdate: -- / -- / --   and work permit number (if applicable): --

Date available for work: *7/15/20--*

Please indicate the hours that you are available to work on each of these days.

(Hours)	SUNDAY	MONDAY	TUESDAY	WEDNESDAY	THURSDAY	FRIDAY	SATURDAY
From	8	1	1	1	1	1	8
To	8	8	8	8	8	8	8

START WITH CURRENT OR LAST EMPLOYER—INCLUDE MONTH AND YEAR IN DATES

FROM	COMPANY		POSITION HELD	
Mo. 9 Yr. 15 *Video Image Plus*			*Accounting Clerk*	BEGINNING PAY *Min. Wage*
TO STREET and NUMBER	CITY and STATE			ENDING
Mo. 2 Yr. 16 *1121 West 18th*	*Springfield, OR 97477*			PAY *Min. Wage*
SUPERVISOR'S NAME TITLE	REASON FOR LEAVING			
Jewel Clark *CWE Coordinator*	*end of program*			
FROM COMPANY			POSITION HELD	
Mo. 9 Yr. 14 *Madison High School*			*Office Assistant*	BEGINNING PAY *Volunteer*
TO STREET and NUMBER	CITY and STATE			ENDING
Mo. 6 Yr. 15	*Eugene, OR 97401*			PAY *Volunteer*
SUPERVISOR'S NAME TITLE	REASON FOR LEAVING			
Andy Williamson *Office Manager*	*end of year*			
FROM COMPANY			POSITION HELD	
Mo. 6 Yr. 10 *Register-Guard*			*Newspaper Carrier*	BEGINNING PAY *Commission*
TO STREET and NUMBER	CITY and STATE			ENDING
Mo. 9 Yr. 12	*Eugene, OR 97401*			PAY *Commission*
SUPERVISOR'S NAME TITLE	REASON FOR LEAVING			
Mary Adamson *Supervisor*	*to go to school*			

MAY WE CONTACT YOUR PRESENT EMPLOYER?   ☒ Yes   ☐ No

SCHOOL NAME	ADDRESS	FROM	TO	DEGREE/DIPLOMA
HIGH SCHOOL				DIPLOMA ☒ Yes ☐ No
Madison High School	*Eugene, OR 97401*	*2012*	*2016*	TYPE:
BUSINESS/VOCATIONAL SCHOOL				DIPLOMA ☐ Yes ☐ No
				TYPE:
COMMUNITY COLLEGE/UNIVERSITY				DIPLOMA ☐ Yes ☐ No
				TYPE:
UNDERGRADUATE COURSEWORK EMPHASIS				CUM GPA
GRADUATE COURSEWORK EMPHASIS				CUM GPA

I understand that any offer of employment is conditioned upon the satisfactory completion of this verification process and that the company will hire only those individuals who are legally authorized to work in the United States and who present acceptable proof of their lawful employment status and identity.

Terrell B. Adams   *7 / 15 / 20 --*
SIGN HERE   **DATE**

Anisa Newkirk
P.O. Box 85893
Portland, OR 97209-4323
(971) 555-4021
anisan@internet.com

CAREER OBJECTIVE

To assist with animal training for service dog programs in the local area; desire to work with dogs on emergency and trauma response teams.

EDUCATION

Hoover High School, Portland, Oregon (graduate 2016)
    GPA 3.3, Dean's List two years

Relevant Course Work:
Biology
Environmental Science
Public Speaking and Forensics

Relevant Skills:
Work well with animals
American Sign Language (ASL)
Microsoft Office (Word, Excel
    PowerPoint)

Extracurricular Activities:
Volunteer: Red Cross Emergency Response
Debate Team (two years)
Member: National Honor Society (two years)
Athletics: Tennis and volleyball

EXPERIENCE

Volunteer, Noah Animal Hospital, Portland, Oregon (one year)
    Worked with injured animals, gave them food and medication; worked
    at the all-night emergency room, took data from animal owners; assisted
    veterinary staff with medical procedures.

Caregiver, County Animal Shelter (two summers)
    Cared for animals; made calls to help find them new homes.

Pet Sitter/Dog Walker (two years)
    Provided care for dogs, cats, rabbits, birds, and snakes while owners were
    away on vacation; provided daily dog walking services.

REFERENCES

References provided on request.

General Resume Guidelines

There are no set rules for preparing a resume. You should choose the style that best presents your strengths. Here are some general guidelines:

- Tailor each resume you prepare to include the information that will best match your skill set to those skills listed in the job opening.
- Keep each tailored resume to one page. List important information in the top third of the page. It will be the first thing that reviewers see, and it should grab their attention.

What can employers learn from a job candidate's past work experiences?

- Keep the resume simple, attractive, and easy to read. Carefully choose your use of fonts, bold, italics, spacing, and other style elements.
- Proofread thoroughly. Do not rely on your word processor's spellcheck. Your resume must be error-free.
- For hard copies, use a high-resolution printer and good-quality paper. Avoid bright colors, odd sizes, and stained or discolored paper.

Parts of a Resume

A resume has both required and optional parts. No matter what style you use, a resume should always include your personal information, education, and work experience. Optional parts include a career objective statement and references.

- *Contact Information.* This information appears first on your resume and should include your name, address, phone number (with area code), and email address. Personal information such as your Social Security number, age, or ethnic background should be omitted.
- *Career Objective.* Including a career objective is optional. As your resume gets fuller, you may wish to omit it. If used, keep it short, direct, forward looking, and specific. Avoid weak statements such as "any kind of work."
- *Education.* List all high school and post-secondary institutions you have attended, starting with the most recent. You may include areas of study, grade point average, honors, specific courses that might apply to the job opening, or other positive facts that you think will create a favorable impression, such as extracurricular activities or offices held in student organizations.
- *Experience.* List jobs, both paid and unpaid, that you have held. Include information such as the job title, name and address of the

employer, employment dates or length of time employed, job duties, and specific achievements while with this employer. Emphasize any tasks and responsibilities at that job that directly relate to the job for which you are applying.

- *References.* Some potential employers will require a list of references. *References* are people who have known you for several months to a year or longer and can provide information about your skills, character, and achievements. References should be at least 18 years old and not related to you. The best types of references include teachers, former and current employers, advisers, counselors, coaches, and adults in business. Be sure to ask permission before listing someone as a reference. If references are not required, and you choose not to list them on your resume, state, "References provided on request." Then prepare a list of the names, addresses, phone numbers, and email addresses of your references.

Scannable Resumes

Some employers use scanners and special software to search for keywords and phrases that match skills required in their job descriptions. A *scannable resume* is designed for easy reading by a scanner and contains keywords from the applicant's career field or from the job listing. To improve your chances for selection, describe your qualifications by using keywords. For example, a publisher looking for an editor might scan for keywords such as "English," "journalism," and "editing." To make your resume easy for the scanner, avoid using fancy fonts, italics, columns, shadows, and graphics.

The Cover Letter

cover letter a letter that accompanies a resume, introducing the applicant to a prospective employer

Whether you are submitting a hard copy, sending a resume by email, or posting a resume at a website, you should also include a cover letter, as shown in Figure 1-3.4. Also known as an *application letter*, the **cover letter** serves to introduce you to a prospective employer. It gives you a chance to briefly explain or "sell" your qualifications and to make a good first impression.

The cover letter should be short and direct. In the first paragraph, you should identify your purpose—why you are writing. Be specific; tell the employer what you want (to be considered for a job opening). The second or middle paragraph should point out some key qualification or skill that makes you unique. Express interest in the company. Your tone should be enthusiastic, upbeat, and friendly. The final or closing paragraph should wrap up the letter in a friendly but direct manner. Ask for an interview and specify when you are available.

The Job Interview

job interview a face-to-face meeting with a potential employer to discuss a job opening

The next step in getting a job is the job interview. A **job interview** is a face-to-face meeting with a potential employer to discuss a job opening. During the interview, the employer will have a copy of your completed job application, resume, and cover letter. The interviewer may ask you about information on any of these documents or about any other

1274 Grant Avenue
Portland, OR 97224
becarter@internet.com
June 15, 20--

Mr. Jackson Phillips, Manager
Star Gaze Museum
4484 Grand Avenue
Portland, OR 97201

Dear Mr. Phillips

In response to the opening posted on your website, please consider me an applicant for the summer tour guide position at your downtown location.

As you can see from my resume, I have volunteered as a host or guide for several special events in the past. I enjoy learning new information, making presentations, interacting with people, and helping others learn new facts and ideas. Your posting indicates that you need someone to work on weekends and to be on call for extra duties. I am available and eager to work on weekends and have a flexible weekday schedule that will allow me to fit in extra duties as needs may arise.

I am available now and would love to begin work as soon as possible. You can reach me at (971) 555-3344 every day after 2 P.M. I look forward to hearing from you about an interview and discussing the tour guide position with you.

Sincerely

Brandon Carter

Brandon Carter

Enclosure: Resume

job-related matters. Here are some general guidelines to help you before and during the interview:

- *Review your resume before the interview.* Be familiar with everything you have stated about yourself.
- *Practice your interviewing skills.* Work with a friend or family member to rehearse open-ended questions, which require full, meaningful answers (rather than "yes" or "no"), such as "Why do you want to work for us?" Talk about your skill set and how it relates to the job opening.
- *Do company research.* By knowing about the company, you can speak intelligently about it. Think of questions you might ask about the company or job opening.
- *Dress appropriately.* Be neat and clean and dress for the job you want.
- *Always go alone.* Do not take a friend or relative.
- *Arrive on time.* Better yet, arrive 10–15 minutes early so you can check your appearance and compose yourself. Never be late.

- *Appear self-confident and relaxed.* Do not show tension or stress. Avoid chewing gum or displaying any other nervous habits.
- *Think before you speak.* Take a moment to organize your thoughts before speaking. Use good grammar and avoid slang.
- *Be attentive.* Lean forward and listen carefully. Look directly at your interviewer, making frequent eye contact.
- *Be enthusiastic.* Show the interviewer that you are interested and excited about the company and the job.
- *Watch for cues.* Nonverbal cues from the interviewer will tell you when to say less or more.

Why is it helpful to practice your interviewing skills?

When the interview is over, thank the interviewer for his or her time and shake hands. Exit with a smile and a positive comment that expresses your interest, such as "I look forward to hearing from you."

Testing and Certification Requirements

Some jobs require pre-employment testing as a way to screen job applicants. This allows businesses to eliminate those candidates who have undesirable traits or limited knowledge of the specific business area. For example, personality tests help determine if a job prospect's traits will be a good match with the job environment. Tests may also be given to check skill levels with certain programs (such as word processing or spreadsheet programs). Other types of tests include drug testing and physical fitness checks.

Some jobs require you to obtain certifications and/or licenses. For example a trucking company may require you to have a CDL (commercial driver's license). To be a teacher you must have a teaching certificate from the state in which you wish to teach. These licensure and certification requirements can take months or even years to complete. Sometimes they are required prior to starting work, and other times they can be earned while working.

The Follow-Up

follow-up contact with a prospective employer after the interview but before hiring

After the interview, you may wish to do some type of follow-up. **Follow-up** is contact with the prospective employer after the interview, but before hiring occurs. It reminds the employer of who you are, which could increase your chances of getting hired.

A thank-you letter is one form of follow-up. The *thank-you letter* shows appreciation to the employer for taking the time to interview you. It also reminds the employer of your interest. When writing a thank-you letter, keep it short and direct. Make sure it is error-free, friendly, and appreciative. If the time between your interview and the date of hire is short, you may wish to call or stop by and check on the status of your application. You can also send an email to the interviewer with the same content as your thank-you letter would include.

In addition, be prepared to send *reference letters* if requested. A reference letter is a statement of your character, abilities, and experiences that is written by someone who can be relied on to give a sincere report.

 **CHECKPOINT**

List the parts of a typical resume.

LO 1-3.3 What Is Self-Employment?

Instead of joining the job market, many people dream of running their own business. Working for yourself is called *self-employment*. A person who takes the risks of being self-employed and owning a business is called an **entrepreneur**. Small businesses contribute billions of dollars to the U.S. economy.

entrepreneur a person who takes the risks of being self-employed and owning a business

Advantages of Self-Employment

A major advantage of being the owner is that you get to make the decisions about how the business will be run. That includes the choice of products and services that will be offered, the hours of operation, the types of customers the business will target, and the prices it will charge. Small business owners also keep all the profits of the business. *Profit* is the amount left after all expenses are deducted from the revenues (income from sales). Expenses may include equipment, supplies, furniture, vehicles, employee wages, rent, and utilities.

Disadvantages of Self-Employment

If the business does not make a profit, it will fail. Many factors can affect profit, including decreased revenue resulting from a slow economy and a loss of sales. Rising costs related to business expenses will also reduce profits. If a business fails, the money invested in the business is lost. Most money invested in a small business comes from the owner and/or the owner's family and friends.

With most small businesses, especially during its first years, the owner must work long hours and perform many different tasks to keep the business running. Because money is often tight, owners may not be able to hire others to do the work for them.

Getting Started in Business

If you have a desire to run your own business, you should spend time preparing yourself for such a venture. Many business owners seek formal and/or informal education about how to run a business before they get started. Some entrepreneurs first work for other businesses to gain needed knowledge and experience. A good place to start is by visiting the Small Business Administration (SBA) website. The SBA offers numerous services to entrepreneurs and small businesses. You can also talk with the advisers at a Small Business Development Center (SBDC).

These centers are located in cities across the country and are sponsored and funded by the SBA. Another good resource is SCORE, which offers free business mentoring services from both active and retired business executives from a wide array of backgrounds. They can give you advice on various issues, such as how to structure the business—as a *sole proprietorship* (ownership by one individual), *partnership* (ownership by two or more people), or *corporation* (ownership in the form of shares of stock).

If you have a good business idea, you should put your thoughts and plans onto paper. In putting your idea into writing, you will be starting your business plan. A *business plan* is a document that describes the steps that will be taken to open and operate a business. It should show that you are worthy of funding (loans) from government and private sources, such as banks and venture capitalists. Sample business plans can be found at the SBA website or at various other websites by conducting an online search using the keywords *business plans*.

Is Entrepreneurship Right for You?

How can you decide if being an entrepreneur is the right choice for you? Your answers to the following questions will give you a better idea of whether you should consider owning your own business.

1. *Are you self-motivated?* Business owners must do what needs to be done without being told or reminded. They enjoy making their own decisions.
2. *Do you like people?* Getting along with others, including employees and customers, is essential.
3. *Are you a leader?* Entrepreneurs are able to get others to follow their lead.
4. *Do you take responsibility?* Entrepreneurs take charge and follow through.
5. *Are you organized?* Business owners must have a good plan before they get started.
6. *Do you work hard?* Successful owners lead by example. They don't expect others to do what they themselves are unwilling to do.
7. *Do you make decisions easily and quickly?* Decisions sometimes have to be made without complete information.
8. *Are you trustworthy?* Others must trust you in order to build long-term relationships that benefit the business.
9. *Are you persistent?* Business owners stick with it, even when the going gets tough. They finish projects and forget about excuses.
10. *Do you keep good records?* Entrepreneurs must account for their expenses and revenues. They should be knowledgeable about profitability and cost analyses.

 **CHECKPOINT**
Why would a person want to be an entrepreneur?

KEY TERMS REVIEW

Match the terms with the definitions. Some terms may not be used.

_____ 1. A summary of your work experience, education, skills, interests, and other qualifications (your skill set) that qualify you for a job opening

_____ 2. A person you know

_____ 3. A letter that introduces the job applicant to a prospective employer

_____ 4. A person who takes the risks of being self-employed and owning a business

_____ 5. Contact with a prospective employer after the interview but before hiring

_____ 6. A group of friends and acquaintances who keep in contact and share information

_____ 7. An employment agency that provides part-time and full-time jobs on a temporary basis

_____ 8. A form that asks basic questions about the job applicant's background, such as work history, education, skills, and references

_____ 9. Spending time observing a worker in a type of job that interests you

a. contact

b. cover letter

c. entrepreneur

d. follow-up

e. job application

f. job interview

g. job shadowing

h. resume

i. social network

j. temp agency

CHECK YOUR UNDERSTANDING

10. Why is networking important when looking for job prospects and opportunities? How can you build your social network?

11. What is a job scout? What is the advantage of using a job scout?

12. What are the benefits of a cooperative work experience?

13. When filling out a job application, what should you remember to do?

14. List three guidelines for preparing a good resume. What kinds of information should not appear on a resume?

15. What are some testing and certification requirements that must be met when seeking a job?

16. What is the purpose of a cover letter?

17. Explain how to properly prepare for a job interview.

18. When it comes to owning your own business, what factors might affect your profit, revenue, and expenses?

THINK CRITICALLY

19. Employers often search the Web when checking out possible employees. Because it is public information, you must be careful when posting on social networking sites. How can you protect yourself from not being hired because of information available on the Internet?

20. Sometimes finding job openings is about asking the right questions (of the right people) and checking websites. These sources are usually free, whereas employment agencies may charge for their services. List in order the steps you would take to find out about job openings. Could you save money or time by following these steps? Explain how.

21. Why should extracurricular activities and volunteer activities be listed on your resume? Explain why employers care about these types of activities. What does your participation tell them?

22. It is often reported in news articles that "everybody exaggerates on their resumes." Do you think this is true? What could be the downside of providing false information on your resume?

23. It is important to maintain contact with people from your past, whether employers, teachers, or friends. These people can be your references, attesting to your character and skills. Explain what is meant by "burning your bridges behind you" and why you should avoid this practice in good career planning.

24. When starting your own business, there are three basic structures—sole proprietorship, partnership, and corporation. How do they differ? What might be the advantages of one structure over the others?

EXTEND YOUR LEARNING

25. Conduct an online search for resumes using the keywords *sample resumes*. Look at the many different types and styles of resumes. For example, a chronological resume focuses on your work history, with your most recent job listed first followed by your other jobs. A functional resume focuses on particular skills that you want to emphasize rather than your work history. Find and download three to five different resume styles. Which style appeals to you most? Why?

26. Visit the website of a well-known company in your area. Look for the link to their "Careers" section. Click on job openings that are currently available. Select one and print out information about it. What are the job qualifications and education requirements? Can you apply online? If possible, download and print a job application and fill it out for practice.

THE ESSENTIAL QUESTION Refer to The Essential Question on p. 20. You can find job openings through networking, websites, job scouts, job fairs, employment agencies, job shadowing, cooperative work experience, school counselors, teachers, and placement centers. To sell yourself as the best job candidate, you should submit a job application that stands out and have a well-written resume, reference letter(s), and cover letter. You should also be sure to prepare for the interview and make a good impression during the interview.

Exploring Careers in...
JOURNALISM

Most people receive information about what's happening in the world from various news outlets. Journalists are the ones who find out what's new and deliver that information to us in the form we find most convenient.

Journalists gather information about newsworthy events, from accidents to business decisions, as assigned. They examine, interpret, and broadcast information from various sources. In covering a story, a reporter interviews people, takes notes, and conducts research. All facts in a story must be verified. They then organize the material to create a story for their audience.

Most journalists work for media organizations, such as a television or radio station, newspaper, magazine, or website. Some journalists specialize in a specific area of news, such as sports or politics. The work is usually hectic, hours vary, and deadlines are key.

Employment Outlook

- Employment opportunities are expected to decline moderately through 2022.
- Competition for jobs is expected to be strong.
- Small broadcast stations and on-line newspapers and magazines provide the best opportunities.

Job Titles

- News analyst
- Reporter
- Correspondent
- Journalist

Needed Education/Skills

- A bachelor's degree in communications or journalism is preferred.
- Employers generally require workers to gain experience through internships.
- Communication, computer, and interpersonal skills are required.

What's it like to work in ... Journalism

Mary is a television reporter for a local station. She specializes in reporting "live" from the scene.

Today she is reporting on a strike at a local business, where emotions are running high. She will interview both strikers on the picket line and temporary workers brought in to fill their jobs. To be fair, she will also interview the plant manager and present the employer's side of the dispute.

Her day began when the picketers first showed up at 7 A.M. She hopes to have her story in its final form for the noon broadcast at the TV station. She will remain at the scene until she is satisfied with the information she has gathered.

What About You?

Would you enjoy fast-paced and often highly charged work? Do you like investigating until you get to the truth? What personality traits do you have that would be a good fit for this type of work?

Chapter 1 Assessment

SUMMARY

1-1 The job market refers to the job openings that are available when you are ready to go to work. It is continually changing.

Both hard skills and soft skills are necessary for career success.

The career that you choose will affect your income over your lifetime.

Decisions and choices that you make, both personal and career related, are based on your values and goals.

The more formal education you gain, the more you will probably earn over your lifetime.

1-2 The economy refers to all of the activities related to making and distributing goods and services in a geographic area or country. The state of the economy affects prices, the job market, and your income.

Tuition and fees are some of the costs of education. Costs will vary based on the type of school (public, private, or career and technical schools) or program selected (graduate and advanced programs).

Financial aid is money received from an outside source to help pay for education. The most common types of financial aid are student loans, grants, and work-study programs. A scholarship is a cash allowance awarded to a student to help pay for education; it is often awarded based on grades or athletic skills. Some students work to earn money to pay for education. The military also offers financial assistance.

1-3 There are many ways to find job openings, such as through networking, websites, job scouts, job fairs, employment agencies, job shadowing, cooperative work experience, school counselors, teachers, and placement centers.

A job application is a form that asks basic questions about your background, such as your work history and education.

A resume describes your work experience, education, skills, interests, and other qualifications (your skill set) that qualify you for a job opening. It is often accompanied by a cover letter that introduces you to a prospective employer and "sells" your qualifications.

A job interview is a face-to-face meeting with a potential employer to discuss a job opening. You may wish to follow up with a letter, call, visit, or email.

Entrepreneurs are self-employed. Business owners can keep the profits, but if revenues decrease and expenses increase, the business may fail.

MAKE ACADEMIC CONNECTIONS

TEAMWORK

1. **Research** Work with a classmate and select a career area that interests you both. Explore programs offered by colleges by performing the activities listed below. As an alternative, explore military career opportunities. (LO 1-2.2)
   a. Identify two or more colleges (public or private) or career and technical schools that provide training in your career area of interest.
   b. Visit the websites of at least two of the schools you listed above. (To find a school's web address, enter the school name in a search engine such as Yahoo! or Google.)
   c. Compare the programs offered in terms of length. How many terms or years are required to complete the program at each school?
   d. Compare tuition costs for the schools. Which has the highest tuition?
   e. Identify which program you think is the best and explain why.

2. **History** Job hunting has changed considerably over the years. Many job openings today are found only through networking contacts and via the Internet. Compare the current job market with the job markets of 1950 and 1990. If possible, talk to someone who was in the workforce 20 or 30 years ago. Ask how the job market has changed for women. (LO 1-1.1)

3. **Communication** Write three cover letters—one for a company where you would like to work (but there is no known job opening); one for a job opening with a company you found on the Internet; and one for a job you learned about from a friend. How will these letters be different? Focus on content and writing style. (LO 1-3.2)

4. **International Studies** Conduct online research about the job application process in other countries. Choose a country in Europe and one in South America. How are the application processes different from what you find in the United States? Would you like to work in a foreign country? Why or why not? Are you qualified? Explain your answer. (LO 1-3.2)

5. **Communication** Have you thought about what you want to do, to be, and to have as you become an adult? Complete the steps listed below to help you think about your values and goals. (LO 1-1.1)
   a. List three goals that you would like to achieve by the time you graduate from high school.
   b. After each goal, explain why that goal is important to you. Discuss the values on which you are basing that goal.
   c. Consider how your goals have changed over time. A year ago, how were your goals different? How are they the same? How will they likely change in the future?

6. **Economics** Create a business cycle graph similar to the one shown in Figure 1-2.1, representing the ups and downs in the economy over the past 50 years. During this time, when did the economy experience the most growth? When did the economy experience the biggest decline? (LO 1-2.1)

Do the Math

1. The average annual tuition for four-year private colleges increased by 5.9 percent from last year. The average cost last year was $31,250. What is the average cost this year? (Round up to the nearest whole dollar.)

2. Use this year's tuition cost answer from above. If the tuition increases by 6 percent for each of the next three years, what will be the total tuition cost for the four years? (Round up to the nearest whole dollar.)

3. A store owner raised prices for a product when the demand for it increased, as shown below. Calculate the amount of sales at each price level and the total sales for all price levels.

Price	Quantity Demanded
$15.00	8,000
$15.50	7,300
$16.00	5,700

Take Action

PREPARE BASIC EMPLOYMENT FORMS

For each chapter, you will complete a short project. These projects will become part of your portfolio. A *portfolio* is a collection of work you complete that ties together your learning and demonstrates your understanding of topics presented. As you complete this work, save it to include in your portfolio.

Based on what you learned in this chapter, prepare the following documents:

- Job application form (pick one up from a local employer, download one from an employer's website, or use one provided by your teacher)
- Resume (design it for the job for which you are applying)
- Cover letter (assume you found out about the job opening from a posting at a company's website)
- Thank-you letter

These documents should be prepared in final form. That means that you could actually use them as models for a job opening. They should be complete, accurate, and error-free and should represent your current situation or what you plan to have on your resume when you apply for your first job.

Next, prepare answers you would give to the following commonly asked interview questions. Save your answers in your portfolio.

1. What do you see yourself doing five years from now?
2. Tell me about yourself.
3. What is your favorite hobby and why?
4. What do you like to do in your spare time?

Income, Benefits, and Taxes

People receive income from working (wages and salaries). They can also receive income from investments (interest and dividends). Another source may be government transfer payments, which help people who do not have enough income to pay for basic needs. Workers also receive benefits such as paid vacations and sick leave. These benefits are part of the total compensation package. Various types of taxes are levied in this country, including income taxes on earnings. In this chapter, you will learn about various income sources, benefits, and taxes.

Do *This*, **Not** *That*

When it comes to your income, benefits, and taxes, you should:

- Understand all sources of income (earned and unearned).
- Determine which employee benefits you value the most as part of a compensation package.
- Be aware of paycheck deductions.
- Know what types of taxes you have to pay.
- Know which tax forms to file.

THE ESSENTIAL QUESTION As you enter the workforce, what do you need to know about your income and employee benefits?

LEARNING OBJECTIVES

LO 2-1.1 List and discuss types of earned income, such as wages, salaries, tips, and commissions.

LO 2-1.2 Describe employee benefits and their role in employee compensation.

KEY TERMS

- minimum wage, 40
- overtime pay, 40
- commission, 42
- benefits, 42
- disposable income, 43
- sick leave, 43
- personal leave, 43
- retirement plan, 45
- profit sharing, 45

LO 2-1.1 What Are Sources of Earned Income?

Earned income is any income you receive from working. It includes wages, salaries, tips, commissions, and net earnings from self-employment. All types of earned income are subject to income taxes and Social Security taxes. A *tax* is a required payment for the support of a government. The tax may be based on items such as earnings, property values, or the sales price of an item. More information about taxes is provided later in this chapter.

Wages

minimum wage the lowest pay rate allowed by law for each regular hour of work

Employees who work for wages are paid for each hour worked. **Minimum wage** is the lowest pay rate allowed by law for each regular hour of work. The federal minimum wage is set by the U.S. Congress. In 2015, that rate was $7.25 per hour. Many states have minimum wage laws that set a rate higher than the federal rate, as shown in Figure 2-1.1. In many jobs, new employees will begin at minimum wage, because they do not yet have the education or experience to command a higher wage rate.

overtime pay pay received for hours worked in addition to regular hours

An 8-hour day and 40-hour workweek are the standards in the American workplace. Hours worked in addition to the standard are called overtime hours. When employees must work overtime hours, they are entitled to extra pay called **overtime pay**. By law, overtime pay must be at least 1½ times the regular rate. For example, a worker who earns $8 per hour for regular pay would earn $12 per hour ($8 × 1½) for overtime pay. People who work on holidays may be entitled to even higher pay rates for their hours. Both federal and state laws control when extra pay is required for additional time worked.

Salaries

Some people work for a set *salary*, which is a fixed amount such as $3,000 a month or $36,000 a year. Unlike those who work for wages, salaried workers rarely have to keep time cards or count hours worked.

▶ FIGURE 2-1.1 U.S. Department of Labor Website

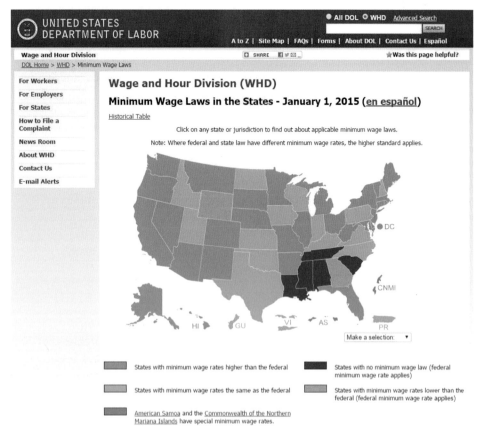

Source: United States Department of Labor, Wage and Hour Division, http://www.dol.gov/whd/minwage/america.htm, accessed December 8, 2015.

They also may have more flexibility in the times they work. However, they do not receive overtime pay for any additional hours worked beyond 40 hours a week.

Tips and Commissions

Some workers receive tips in addition to wages. A *tip* is a gift of money, often based on a percentage of the total bill, given to a person for performing a service. The amount of the tip may be based on the quality of service provided. For example, many service employees, such as waiters and hair stylists, receive tips from satisfied customers. Some workers make most of their earnings from tips rather than hourly pay. Tips are subject to federal income taxes and may be subject to state taxes as well.

Looking Ahead

As a young person, you may get your start in the workforce as a waiter who earns tips in a restaurant. To prepare for such a job, conduct online research about tipped employees. What is the minimum required hourly wage that employers must pay a tipped employee in your state? What is the minimum suggested hourly tip or total tip for waiters? What factors do you think might affect the amount of a tip?

SUCCESS SKILLS

TEAMWORK

During your lifetime, you will be on many teams. Whether you are taking part in a competitive sport, a work group, or a fun activity, teamwork skills will come in handy. Combining the energy of many people makes the work go faster, and the result is often more creative. When you work with others, you can achieve better results than when you work alone. Whenever you work with others to achieve a common goal, try to follow these team strategies to improve your teamwork skills:

- Set clear goals for the team. Create an action plan to achieve the goals.
- Define the duties of each team member. Verbally communicate expectations and timelines.
- Identify how success will be measured. How will the team know it has met its goals?
- Identify problems the team may face in achieving its goals. Discuss ways to overcome them.
- Talk with all team members. Show a positive attitude when discussing team activities. Have regular

meetings to track team progress. Use verbal and digital forms of positive communication.
- Build on the strength of team members. Encourage all members to help make decisions and to share ideas. Each member has different skills that add strength to the team.
- Recognize accomplishments of team members as well as the team as a whole.
- As an individual team member, earn trust by completing your duties. Be loyal to your team members.

Think Critically

1. Describe the last team you worked with on a project or assignment. List the team strategies that resulted in success. Which ones could have been improved?
2. When you fill the role of team leader, how will you improve teamwork using the strategies listed above?

The law requires some employers (such as restaurants and hair salons) to withhold taxes based on tips, even though tips may have been received in cash directly from customers.

Some workers are paid a commission. A **commission** is a set fee or percentage of a sale paid to an employee instead of or in addition to salary or wages. Sales commissions are earned only when a sale is made. If no sale is made, no commission is received. In some types of jobs, such as real estate sales, the worker's entire earnings may be based on commission. For example, a real estate agent who sells a home for $200,000 might receive a $12,000 commission. In other types of jobs, workers may be paid a base salary plus commissions. For example, a person who sells cars might receive a salary of $10,500 a year plus 25 percent of the profit on each car sold.

commission a set fee or percentage of a sale paid to an employee instead of or in addition to salary or wages

›› CHECKPOINT

How is overtime pay different from regular pay?

LO 2-1.2 What Are Employee Benefits?

Full-time workers usually have benefits provided by the employer. **Benefits** are forms of compensation in addition to salary or wages. Common benefits provided by employers include paid vacation and

benefits forms of compensation in addition to salary or wages

holidays. For other benefits, such as health insurance, the worker may need to pay part or all of the cost.

In recent years, employee benefits have become more flexible to meet the changing needs of the workforce. *Cafeteria-style benefits* are plans that allow employees to select from a range of employer-paid benefits based on personal needs. Employees may be able to save money by selecting only the options they need. Other employee benefits offered may include a savings plan and profit sharing.

Benefits are important to workers for several reasons:

- Benefits increase the overall value that a worker receives from a job. **Disposable income** refers to the money that a person has available to spend or save after taxes are paid. Money received or saved from certain benefits increases the worker's disposable income.
- Workers are not taxed on most benefits. This means that workers receive something of value without paying tax as part of the cost.
- Some benefits allow workers to buy services at a cheaper price than they could otherwise. For example, group insurance costs much less than an individual policy.
- Some benefits help workers reach financial goals. For example, some people find it difficult to save money. With company-sponsored savings plans, saving becomes easier because the money is automatically deducted from the worker's paycheck. Some savings plans have tax-savings features, and companies often match employees' contributions to the plan up to a certain amount.

disposable income money available to spend or save after taxes have been paid

Pay Without Work

Pay without work refers to times when an employee who is not working will be paid. Paid vacations and holidays, sick leave, and personal leave are examples of pay without work. As part of their compensation package, employees are usually given paid vacation days. Typically, after the first year, an employee gets one to two weeks of vacation a year.

Full-time employees generally are given *paid holidays* (as required by federal and state laws). Paid holidays in the United States typically include Christmas Day, Thanksgiving Day, the Fourth of July, Labor Day, and Memorial Day. Other holidays many companies grant to employees include New Year's Day, Veterans Day, Martin Luther King Jr. Day, and Presidents' Day. In many cases, employees who work on holidays receive extra pay—typically two times their regular rate of pay.

Many companies allow workers to take a certain number of sick days per year. **Sick leave** is paid time away from work due to illness. Some companies allow the use of sick leave to care for a sick child or other family member. Typically, an employee is allowed anywhere from three to ten paid days of sick leave per year. Some companies allow unused sick leave to accumulate and carry over to the next year. That means that workers can save sick leave not used in one year and have it available for use in another year in the case of extended illness.

Some employers also offer personal leave. **Personal leave** is paid time away from work for personal reasons. The worker usually does not have to give a reason. Typically, two or three days a year are granted for

sick leave paid time away from work due to illness

personal leave paid time away from work for personal reasons

personal leave. Unused personal leave is generally not carried forward to the next year.

Insurance

Employers with more than 50 employees are required by law to offer *health insurance*. The price paid for health insurance is called a *premium*. Some employers pay the full premium as a benefit to their employees. More commonly, however, both share the premium costs. Due to rising insurance costs, many employers today are requiring employees to pay a higher portion of health care costs and insurance.

Group life insurance may be provided by employers. Group insurance rates are often lower than individual policy premiums. Employees may be able to buy additional life insurance at the group rates. This additional coverage can be paid through payroll deductions. Life insurance paid for by the employee may be *portable*, which means the employee may be able to continue the policy after leaving the employer.

Disability insurance provides regular payments to replace income lost when illness or injury prevents the employee from working. The illness or injury does not have to be job related. Generally, there are two types of disability insurance: short term and long term. Short-term disability insurance usually lasts between three and six months. Long-term disability insurance typically picks up where short-term disability leaves off and can provide coverage up to retirement. Short-term and long-term disability plans typically cover 50 to 70 percent of monthly salary. Most employers offer both short-term and long-term disability group plans. However, the insurance is good only as long as the employee works for the company.

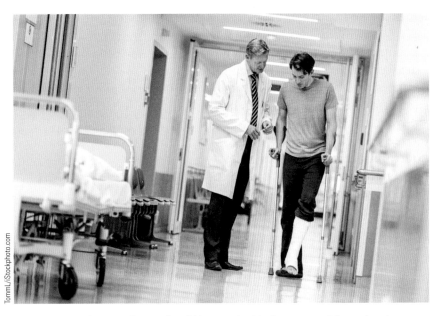

Do you agree that employers should be required by law to provide workers' compensation insurance? Why or why not?

Workers' compensation is an insurance plan that employers are required by law to provide for employees. It provides coverage for an employee who has suffered an injury or illness resulting from job-related duties. Coverage includes payment of medical bills and compensation for lost wages. Benefits may also be paid to the worker's family if the worker is killed on the job.

Health Spending Accounts

Health spending accounts are used to pay for medical expenses. These kinds of plans usually have a higher deductible than a traditional plan, but they often have a lower monthly premium. Employers typically offer two kinds: health savings accounts and flexible spending accounts.

With a *health savings account (HSA)*, employees set aside money in an HSA to pay for qualified medical expenses not covered by insurance, including deductibles and co-payments. Contributions to the account are made pretax and are tax deductible. An employer that sponsors the HSA may contribute to the account as well. Money withdrawn from an HSA to pay qualified medical expenses is tax-free. HSAs are usually managed by banks or investment companies. Money put into the accounts gains interest or earnings based on how the money is invested. Typically, medical expenses are paid using a debit card that accesses the HSA. Money in an HSA that is not used by the end of the year can be carried forward to the next year. When employees leave the job or retire, they can take their HSA with them and continue to use it for medical expenses.

A *flexible spending account (FSA)*, often called a *Flex 125 plan*, allows employees to set aside money (pretax) to pay for qualified medical expenses. The plans are set up by employers. Deductions are made from the employee's pay to fund the account. The employee files claims for qualified expenses to be paid from the account. The major disadvantage of FSAs is that the money that the employee sets aside is forfeited (to the employer) at the end of the year if not used. Because the money cannot be carried forward to the next year, the employee must carefully estimate what the medical expenses will be each year.

Retirement Plans

Many companies offer 401(k) retirement plans. A **retirement plan** is an account into which employees voluntarily contribute a portion of their earnings for their retirement. Contributions to the account are automatically deducted from the employee's paycheck. In some cases, the employer may make a matching contribution; however, this is not required. For example, a company may match an employee's contribution up to 10 percent. Therefore, if an employee contributes $150 a month, the employer would contribute $15 a month. This type of plan is *tax-deferred*, or pretax, meaning employees can avoid paying income tax on the money in the account until it is withdrawn.

retirement plan an account into which employees voluntarily contribute a portion of their earnings for their retirement; employers may match these contributions

Some companies offer *pension plans* that are paid entirely by the employer. A pension plan provides payments to retired workers. Typically, employees must work for the company for a certain number of years to qualify. The payment amounts vary depending on the number of years worked, the worker's salary, and other factors. This type of benefit is being phased out by most companies in favor of the 401(k) retirement plan.

Incentives

Incentives are used by many employers as a way to encourage employees to strive for higher levels of performance. When employees are allowed to share in the company's success through incentives, they are motivated to help achieve the company's goals. Companies offer many kinds of incentives to their employees. Two common incentives are profit sharing and stock options.

Profit sharing allows employees to share a portion of the business's profits. The plan may pay a bonus of a specified percent of the

profit sharing a benefit that allows employees to share a portion of the business's profits

employee's salary if the business meets or exceeds its financial goals. The bonus may be paid in cash, or it may be added to a retirement account. If paid in cash, it is taxable in the year received. If added to a retirement account, it is taxed when withdrawn by the employee.

Some companies allow employees to buy stock in the company at a reduced price (lower than market value). The purchase price of the *stock options* may be deducted from the employee's pay. This is a convenient way to acquire stock, and it does not involve brokerage or trading fees.

Perks

In addition to wages or salary and the standard benefits offered as part of an employee's compensation package, many companies offer "extras" called *perks* to their employees. Social and recreational programs, employee discounts on the company's products and services, fitness centers, wellness programs, flexible scheduling, on-site child care facilities, and mental health counseling are just a few examples of perks that employers offer to improve employee morale. These types of perks are generally not taxable.

Another perk commonly offered by companies is tuition reimbursement. Some employers will reimburse (pay back) money spent on education. For example, some companies pay for the cost of classes or training related to the worker's job. This training can benefit both the company and the employee, who may be able to perform at a higher level using the skills learned. With additional education or training, the employee may also have improved chances of getting a promotion or a better job with the same or a different company. To qualify for reimbursement, the employee typically must agree to work for the company for a set period of time and must maintain a certain grade point average (GPA). Amounts received for tuition reimbursement may be taxable if the employer pays more than a specific amount set by the Internal Revenue Service (IRS).

Diego Cervo/Shutterstock.com

Why do some employers provide tuition reimbursement?

>> CHECKPOINT

Why are benefits an important part of a compensation package?

2-1 Lesson Assessment

KEY TERMS REVIEW

Match the terms with the definitions. Some terms may not be used.

_____ 1. Forms of compensation in addition to salary or wages

_____ 2. Paid time away from work for personal reasons

_____ 3. A benefit that allows employees to share a portion of the profits of the business

_____ 4. The lowest pay rate allowed by law for each regular hour of work

_____ 5. Money available to spend or save after taxes have been paid

_____ 6. Paid time away from work due to illness

_____ 7. Pay received for hours worked in addition to regular hours

_____ 8. A set fee or percentage of a sale paid to an employee instead of or in addition to salary or wages

a. benefits

b. commission

c. disposable income

d. minimum wage

e. overtime pay

f. personal leave

g. profit sharing

h. retirement plan

i. sick leave

CHECK YOUR UNDERSTANDING

9. Why are people often paid minimum wage when they start a new job?

10. How is being paid a salary different from being paid hourly wages?

11. Give an example of a worker whose pay may include tips.

12. What are cafeteria-style benefits? Why are they being offered by more companies today?

13. Give three examples of pay without work.

14. Why are employees at many companies expected to help pay for the cost of health insurance?

15. How is a health savings account (HSA) different from a flexible spending account (FSA)?

16. What are two common incentives offered by employers?

17. Why is educational reimbursement a valuable benefit for employees?

18. Why do you think employers offer different types of benefits to their employees? Why are the kinds of benefits offered important to employees?

19. What are the differences between disability insurance and workers' compensation?

THINK CRITICALLY

20. Minimum wage started at 25 cents per hour in 1938 and has risen steadily over the years. Still, workers earning minimum wage have difficulty paying their living expenses. How can people working for minimum wage stretch their earnings so that they can pay their bills? What can they do to earn more than minimum wage?

21. Some jobs, such as real estate sales, are typically commission only (with no base salary or wages). If no sale is made, then no income is earned. How can these types of workers prepare themselves to be able to pay their bills during times when there are no sales?

22. Benefits are a very important part of most workers' compensation plans. Make a list of the three benefits that would be most important to you, and explain why each is so important to your financial security.

23. Many companies today are passing along the cost of rapidly rising health care costs to their employees. What is the benefit of doing this (to the employer and to the employee)? What are the disadvantages (to the employer and to the employee)?

EXTEND YOUR LEARNING

TEAMWORK

24. Work with a partner to complete this activity. Select a career in which the worker earns a salary, such as teacher, manager, or accountant. Conduct online research or interview a worker in this profession to answer the following questions:

   a. How many hours a week does a beginning-level employee work?

   b. What is the beginning pay level? What is the top pay level?

   c. Is the pay fair for the amount of work required?

   d. What kinds of benefits are being offered to people in this profession?

   After completing your interview, decide whether you would like this kind of work and whether you think the pay and benefits are good. Explain your answers.

25. *Fortune* magazine publishes an annual list of the Top 100 Best Companies to Work For. Using the Internet, search for the most recent list online. Choose two corporations from the list. Conduct online research to learn about the benefits and perks that each company offers, and then create a table comparing them. Write a short summary describing which company you think offers the best benefits and perks, and explain why. Do you believe employees, employers, and customers communicate effectively in these companies? Why or why not?

THE ESSENTIAL QUESTION   Refer to The Essential Question on p. 40. As an employee, you should know about the various sources of income, such as wages, a salary, tips, and commissions. In addition, benefits such as vacation pay, paid holidays, sick leave, health insurance, retirement plans, health spending accounts, profit sharing, stock options, and other perks are important to understand.

LEARNING OBJECTIVES

LO 2-2.1 Name private and governmental sources of unearned income.

LO 2-2.2 List the types of taxes levied against individuals.

LO 2-2.3 Discuss the benefits of paying taxes, both direct and indirect.

KEY TERMS

- unearned income, 49
- interest, 49
- dividends, 49
- transfer payments, 49
- in-cash payments, 50
- in-kind payments, 51
- sales tax, 52
- use tax, 52
- excise tax, 53
- property tax, 53
- public goods, 55

LO 2-2.1 What Is Unearned Income?

Unearned income is money received from sources other than working in a job, either for yourself or for someone else. Like earned income, most forms of unearned income are taxable. However, the tax rates may be lower than income tax rates on earned income. Because this income is not earned through actual labor, it is not subject to employment taxes.

unearned income money received from sources other than working

Private Sources

One form of unearned income is **interest**, which is money earned on savings accounts and other funds. When you deposit money into a savings account with a bank or put your money aside in a certificate of deposit (CD), it accumulates interest. The bank will use the deposited funds to make loans and investments and will pay you interest for the use of your money.

interest money earned on savings accounts and other funds

Another form of unearned income is **dividends**, which are a portion of a corporation's profits distributed to stockholders. *Stockholders* are the people who buy stocks in a corporation. A *cash dividend* payment is money shared with stockholders when a corporation makes profits. Dividends may also be in the form of stock, known as *stock dividends*. Although you do not receive actual cash, the added shares of stock increase your wealth.

dividends a portion of a corporation's profits distributed to stockholders

Retired people may receive pension payments or other forms of retirement benefits from employer pension funds or individual retirement accounts. Those who own property may receive *rental income* from others who use their property. A *capital gain* is income from the sale of property (real estate or an investment) for more than you paid for it; capital gains income is taxed at a lower rate. Other sources of unearned income for individuals are shown in Figure 2-2.1.

Government Transfer Payments

Money and benefits received from local, state, or federal governments are called **transfer payments**. Transfer payments, which are funded through

transfer payments money and benefits received from local, state, or federal governments

▶ FIGURE 2-2.1 **Types of Income**

Earned Income	Unearned Income	
Salaries and wages	Interest	Social Security benefits
Tips	Dividends	Pensions
Commissions	Capital gains	Annuities
Bonuses	Gambling winnings	Rents
Professional fees	Alimony	Gifts
Business profits	Child support	Inheritances
Farm income	Unemployment compensation	Royalties

taxes, are made from many different programs. They increase the disposable income of those who receive them. Examples of transfer payments provided by state and federal governments are shown in Figure 2-2.2.

In the United States, many types of transfer payments are a "safety net" so that workers who lose their jobs, become injured, or fall victim to natural disaster will have a place to turn. These benefits (except Social Security and Medicare) are not intended as handouts, but rather as "handups." This means they are intended as temporary help to get people back on their feet again. With Social Security and Medicare, often called *entitlement programs*, retirees have paid into the programs through payroll tax deductions while working.

In-Cash Payments

in-cash payments money in the form of a check, a debit card, or other direct payment given to a person needing assistance

In-cash payments are money in the form of a check, a debit card, or other direct payment given to a person needing assistance. For example, after Hurricane Katrina, flood victims were given debit cards worth

▶ FIGURE 2-2.2 **Transfer Payments**

Type of Benefit:	Paid to:
Temporary Assistance for Needy Families (TANF)	Needy families with children; varies by state
Supplemental Nutritional Assistance Program (SNAP)	People with insufficient resources or income to buy food
Medicaid	Low-income families
Veterans' benefits	Veterans and their families
Supplemental Security Income (SSI)	Low-income elderly and disabled
State-provided medical plans	Low-income residents
Social Security	Retirees, disabled workers, dependents
Medicare	Retired people with Social Security
Unemployment compensation	Laid-off workers; varies by state
Workers' compensation	Workers injured on the job

FOCUS On...

SOCIAL SECURITY BENEFITS

Most workers in the United States pay into the Social Security fund. Payments are made into the account through payroll deductions. These payments are matched by employers. Based on the amount paid into the account and other factors, the worker will receive monthly benefit checks when he or she retires.

Once you have started paying into the fund, you can view and print a Social Security benefits statement online at the Social Security Administration's website. The statement shows a record of the income on which you paid Social Security taxes, plus how much you can expect to earn in monthly Social Security benefits when you hit retirement age (age 67 for those born after 1960).

Think Critically

1. Social Security was created by law in 1938. Conduct online research about the Social Security Act. Why do you think such a program was needed? (*Hint:* The Great Depression started in 1929.)
2. Social Security was never intended to meet the full retirement needs of someone unable to work. Rather, it is intended as supplemental income. What do you need to do to avoid depending on Social Security benefits as your only form of retirement income?

$1,000. They used the cards to buy food, clothing, and other items. Social Security, unemployment compensation, and workers' compensation are also examples of in-cash transfer payments. People receive checks or have direct deposits made to their checking accounts.

In-Kind Payments

In-kind payments are made indirectly on a person's behalf or paid in a form other than money to those in need. For example, Medicaid is a program in which payments are made to medical providers on behalf of those unable to afford medical services. Many people age 65 or older qualify for Medicare hospital insurance based on their own or their spouse's work record. Some people under age 65 who are disabled may also qualify. Other examples of in-kind transfer payments include SNAP benefits (formerly known as food stamps), reduced-price school lunches, and housing subsidies.

in-kind payments payments made indirectly on a person's behalf or paid in a form other than money

 CHECKPOINT

How are in-cash payments different from in-kind payments?

LO 2-2.2 What Types of Taxes Do You Pay?

Taxes are collected from many sources. Taxes are based on consumption, income, and wealth. They may be assessed by the federal and state government, and in some cases, by county, city, and local governments as well. Some of these taxes are *direct* taxes, which means consumers pay them directly to the government. Other taxes are *indirect*, which

Building COMMUNICATION SKILLS

means they are charged on goods or services bought by the consumer. In such cases, the selling business sends the collected taxes to the government.

Taxes Based on Consumption

Consumption taxes are based on what consumers use or buy. Only those who purchase certain goods and services are charged these taxes. These forms of tax are considered indirect.

Sales Tax

sales tax a tax levied as a percentage of the purchase price of goods and services sold to consumers

In the United States, the most common type of consumption tax is the sales tax. A **sales tax** is a tax levied as a percentage of the purchase price of goods and services sold to consumers. For example, if the retail price for a television is $400 and the sales tax is 6 percent, you will pay a total of $424 [$400 + ($400 × 0.06)]. The retailer will collect the sales tax from the consumer and send it to the state's Department of Revenue. Sales tax rates vary from one state to the next, and not all states have a sales tax. If city governments charge a sales tax, portions of the sales tax collected must also be sent to them.

The sales tax is an example of a *regressive tax* because it takes a larger percentage of income from lower-income people than from higher-income people. Because the price of a product is the same regardless of income level, the sales tax paid is also the same and is a bigger burden on lower-income people.

Use Tax

use tax a tax charged on the use, storage, or consumption of a good that was purchased in one state but used in another state

A **use tax** is charged on the use, storage, or consumption of a good that was purchased in one state but used in another state. The purpose of a use tax is to prevent the avoidance of sales tax. For example, if a person from Ohio purchases clothing from an online retailer in Oregon that does not collect sales tax, the purchaser must pay a use tax to the state of Ohio. The use tax is usually the same rate as the state's sales tax and is paid as part of your state income tax return.

Use taxes protect in-state retailers against unfair competition from out-of-state sellers that aren't required to collect sales tax. However, states are finding it difficult to collect and enforce use taxes on post-sales.

Excise Tax

An **excise tax** is charged on the purchase of specific goods such as gasoline, cigarettes, and alcoholic beverages. An excise tax is also charged on services such as phone service, utilities, and garbage collection. Excise taxes are usually included in the price of the product or service. An excise tax on a product that is not considered essential for a normal standard of living, such as an expensive car or yacht, is called a *luxury tax*.

excise tax a tax charged on the purchase of specific goods and services

Taxes Based on Income

An *income tax* is a direct tax paid to the government. The federal government requires income taxes to be paid on earned and unearned income. Most states also levy a tax based on income, and cities and counties often do too.

The income tax is an example of a *progressive tax* because the more you earn, the more you pay in tax. For example, someone with a low income may pay 15 percent of his or her income as taxes, whereas someone with a higher income may pay 28 percent.

Taxes Based on Wealth

Wealth taxes are another form of direct tax. They are levied against the value of the property and assets that you own. Wealth taxes are considered a type of progressive tax.

Property Tax

Those who own real estate must pay a **property tax** based on the property's *assessed value*, which is determined by the county or other local taxing authority. Assessed value is usually a percentage of the property's *market value*, which is the highest price for which the property would sell to a willing buyer. For example, a home worth $200,000 might have an assessed value of $180,000 (or 90 percent of its market value). If the property tax rate is $15 per thousand of assessed value, you will pay $2,700 (180 × $15) in property taxes per year.

property tax a wealth tax based on the assessed value of owned real estate

Estate and Gift Taxes

The federal government levies an *estate tax*, which is a tax on property transferred from the estate of a deceased person to his or her heirs. An estate must be worth more than a certain amount ($5.43 million in 2015) to be subject to this tax. The estate tax is paid from the assets of the estate before anything can be distributed to heirs.

People who inherit property may also have to pay a separate state *inheritance tax*. The state inheritance tax is different from the federal estate tax. The estate tax is deducted from the value of the estate before

▶ **FIGURE 2-2.3** **Partial List of U.S. Taxes**

Alternative minimum tax	State and local income tax
Capital gains tax	Luxury tax
Corporate income tax	Property tax
U.S. estate tax	Hotel occupancy tax
U.S. excise tax	Rental car tax
Federal income tax	Recreational vehicle tax
Federal unemployment tax (FUTA)	Road usage tax (commercial trucks)
FICA (Social Security and Medicare tax)	Sales tax
Gasoline tax (federal and state)	State unemployment tax (SUTA)
Gift tax	Tariffs
Vehicle sales tax	Workers' compensation tax
Cell phone tax (911 and other)	IRS penalties
Use tax	

distribution to heirs, but the heir pays inheritance taxes on property received. The amount of tax is based on the value of the property in the estate.

If you give someone money or property during your life, you may be subject to a federal *gift tax*. The gift tax is paid by the giver, not the receiver, of the gift. In 2015 you could have given up to $14,000 per person per year without having to pay a gift tax. Gifts to your spouse or to a charity are exempt from the gift tax.

Other Taxes

There are literally thousands of governmental units (federal, state, and local) in the United States that have the ability to levy and collect taxes. In addition to sales taxes, use taxes, excise taxes, income taxes, property taxes, and estate taxes, you will find capital gains taxes, value-added taxes, tariffs, and so on. Figure 2-2.3 shows a partial list of taxes collected in the United States.

CHECKPOINT

How are consumption taxes different from income and wealth taxes?

LO 2-2.3 How Do You Benefit from Paying Taxes?

Paying taxes reduces the disposable income of an individual. The more taxes a person pays, the less money he or she has available to save or spend. When people have less money to spend, the economy may be affected. When people spend less on goods and services, businesses have lower sales. Lower sales may lead to lower profits. Workers may have to be laid off or dismissed from their jobs. Charitable groups may receive less money from donations. Having less money means these groups are unable to help more people in need. These are all disadvantages of paying taxes. However, there are also benefits.

Direct Benefits

Paying taxes can benefit the person making the payments and others who do not make payments. For example, workers pay a Social Security tax during their working years. When they retire, they receive payments from their Social Security fund. This is an example of a direct benefit from paying taxes.

How do you use public goods provided by taxes collected?

Taxes also provide overall benefits. **Public goods** are government-provided goods and services paid for by taxes. Examples include national defense, police protection, public education, national parks, and roads and highways. Public goods have three unique qualities:

public goods government-provided goods and services paid for by taxes

- Everyone benefits from them (they raise the overall standard of living in a country).
- No one can be excluded from the benefits.
- People do not benefit in direct proportion to taxes paid; those who benefit the most often pay less.

Indirect Benefits

Even if you do not benefit directly, you benefit indirectly when others receive government assistance. For example, government transfer payments are funded with taxes. Because others receive free vaccinations, you are protected from the spread of illness. Providing public education to citizens produces a higher-quality workforce, giving you the benefit of better products and services.

Not everyone benefits directly from every type of tax. For example, some people may never visit a state or national park. However, everyone benefits from some government services. You must consider that taxes benefit society as a whole. Without the benefit of the goods and services provided because of taxes, citizens would be worse off.

⟩⟩⟩ CHECKPOINT

How are the direct benefits of paying taxes different from the indirect benefits?

2-2 Lesson Assessment

KEY TERMS REVIEW

Match the terms with the definitions. Some terms may not be used.

_____ 1. Money and benefits received from local, state, or federal governments

_____ 2. A tax charged on the purchase of specific goods and services

_____ 3. A wealth tax based on the assessed value of owned real estate

_____ 4. Money received from sources other than working

_____ 5. A tax levied as a percentage of the purchase price of goods and services sold to consumers

_____ 6. Payments made indirectly on a person's behalf or paid in a form other than money

_____ 7. Money earned on savings accounts and other funds

_____ 8. A portion of a corporation's profits distributed to stockholders

_____ 9. Money in the form of a check, a debit card, or other direct payment given to a person needing assistance

a. dividends

b. excise tax

c. in-cash payments

d. in-kind payments

e. interest

f. property tax

g. public goods

h. sales tax

i. transfer payments

j. unearned income

k. use tax

CHECK YOUR UNDERSTANDING

10. How are wages and salaries different from interest and rent income?

11. What is capital gains income?

12. How are cash dividends different from stock dividends?

13. What are government transfer payments? How are they funded?

14. What is the difference between a direct tax and an indirect tax?

15. What is a use tax? Provide an example.

16. What is an excise tax? Give three examples of products or services on which an excise tax is charged.

17. What is the difference between a regressive tax and a progressive tax?

18. How can raising (or lowering) taxes affect the economy?

19. Give two examples of direct benefits that you receive from paying taxes.

20. What are public goods? Give three examples.

21. Explain how you benefit indirectly from paying taxes.

THINK CRITICALLY

22. When people retire, they receive Social Security payments. If their total income (earned and unearned) is between $25,000 and $34,000 (or $32,000 and $44,000 for a married couple), up to 50 percent of their Social Security benefits are taxable. For income more than $34,000 (or $44,000 for a married couple), up to 85 percent of their income may be considered taxable. To many people, this is like a "tax on a tax." In other words, they already paid taxes on income when they were working, including Social Security taxes. Now at retirement, when they receive it back, they are taxed again. What is the purpose of such a tax?

23. Depending on government assistance can be a trap. When needy people receive government benefits, they are often penalized. For example, if they have any earnings, it is deducted from their transfer payments. Thus, they have no incentive to work. How might this be remedied?

24. In-cash payments provide more flexibility than in-kind payments. With in-kind payments, the recipient is limited in how they may be used. For example, with SNAP (food assistance) benefits, recipients are limited in what they can buy (certain items cannot be purchased) and where they can buy (not all stores accept SNAP payments). Why do governments use in-kind payments rather than in-cash payments for those who are in need?

25. Some people complain because they feel that they pay taxes but receive little or no benefits. For example, a retired couple must still pay property taxes that support local schools, even though they have no children in school. Explain how these people benefit indirectly from these services.

EXTEND YOUR LEARNING

26. Many different types of taxes are paid by people in your area. Work in a group with two or three classmates to learn about the kinds of taxes being paid.

    a. Interview adult relatives or friends who are employed to learn what types of taxes are deducted from their pay. Call or visit local government offices or conduct an online search to learn about other taxes paid in your area. Look at receipts for purchased goods to see if taxes were charged. You may also find taxes listed on bills for phone, cable, utilities, and so on.

    b. List all of the types of taxes you found. Organize your list into categories: sales, excise, income, property, and so on. What conclusions can you draw from your list?

TEAMWORK

THE ESSENTIAL QUESTION   Refer to The Essential Question on p. 49. Unearned income adds to your total amount of compensation. However, like earned income, unearned income is fully taxable. Paying taxes reduces your disposable income.

Taxes and Other Deductions

LEARNING OBJECTIVES

LO 2-3.1 List the mandatory and voluntary deductions from gross pay.

LO 2-3.2 Explain how to prepare an income tax return.

KEY TERMS

- gross pay, 58
- net pay, 58
- exemption, 59
- dependent, 59
- Social Security tax, 59
- Medicare tax, 60
- Workers' compensation, 61
- Form W-2, 62
- Form 1040EZ, 62

LO 2-3.1 What Are Paycheck Deductions?

gross pay total salary or wages earned during a pay period

net pay the amount of your paycheck after deductions

As an employee, you earn wages or a salary. **Gross pay** is your total salary or wages earned during a pay period. Amounts subtracted from gross pay are called *deductions*. Some deductions are required by law, whereas other deductions are optional. When deductions are subtracted, the result is **net pay**, or the amount of your paycheck. Net pay is also referred to as *take-home pay*. The paycheck stub in Figure 2-3.1 shows the gross pay, deductions, and net pay of Gloria Perez.

Required Deductions

Employees are required to have money withheld from their paychecks for income tax, Social Security tax, and Medicare tax. Other taxes and deductions may also be withheld. Many states have a state income tax. Some counties and cities also have an income tax. These deductions lower your *disposable income*. When you pay fewer taxes, your disposable income rises.

▶ **FIGURE 2-3.1** Paycheck Stub

EMPLOYEE NAME	EMPLOYEE ID	PAY PERIOD	CHECK DATE	CHECK NO.
Gloria M. Perez	482975	2/1/20-- thru 2/14/20--	2/21/20--	A001161
EARNINGS	HOURS	RATE	THIS PERIOD	YEAR-TO-DATE
Regular	80	$13.00	$1,040.00	$3,120.00
Overtime				
		TAXES		
		Federal Income Tax	$82.19	$246.57
		Social Security Tax	64.48	193.44
		Medicare Tax	15.08	45.24
		State Income Tax	34.27	102.81
		City Income Tax	3.14	9.42
		SUBTOTAL	$199.16	$597.48
		DEDUCTIONS		
		Health Insurance	$150.00	$450.00
		Life Insurance	12.00	36.00
		401(k) Plan	52.00	156.00
		Dental Insurance	10.00	30.00
		SUBTOTAL	$224.00	$672.00
NET PAY			$616.84	$1,850.52

---------------- Separate here and give Form W-4 to your employer. Keep the top part for your records. ----------------

Form W-4

Department of the Treasury
Internal Revenue Service

Employee's Withholding Allowance Certificate

OMB No. 1545-0074

20—

► Whether you are entitled to claim a certain number of allowances or exemption from withholding is subject to review by the IRS. Your employer may be required to send a copy of this form to the IRS.

1 Your first name and middle initial	Last name	2 Your social security number
Gloria M.	Perez	000 22 2105

Home address (number and street or rural route)

123 Maple Street

City or town, state, and ZIP code

Monticello, KY 42633-0123

3 ☑ Single ☐ Married ☐ Married, but withhold at higher Single rate.
Note. If married, but legally separated, or spouse is a nonresident alien, check the "Single" box.

4 If your last name differs from that shown on your social security card, check here. You must call 1-800-772-1213 for a replacement card. ► ☐

| 5 | Total number of allowances you are claiming (from line **H** above **or** from the applicable worksheet on page 2) | 5 | 1 |
| 6 | Additional amount, if any, you want withheld from each paycheck . . . . | 6 | $ |

7 I claim exemption from withholding for 20—, and I certify that I meet **both** of the following conditions for exemption.
  • Last year I had a right to a refund of **all** federal income tax withheld because I had **no tax liability, and**
  • This year I expect a refund of **all** federal income tax withheld because I expect to have **no tax liability.**
  If you meet both conditions, write "Exempt" here . . . . ► | 7 |

Under penalties of perjury, I declare that I have examined this certificate and, to the best of my knowledge and belief, it is true, correct, and complete.

Employee's signature
(This form is not valid unless you sign it.) ► *Gloria M. Perez*   Date ► 5/20/20—

| 8 Employer's name and address (Employer: Complete lines 8 and 10 only if sending to the IRS.) | 9 Office code (optional) | 10 Employer identification number (EIN) |

For Privacy Act and Paperwork Reduction Act Notice, see page 2.   Cat. No. 10220Q   Form **W-4** (20—)

Income Tax Withholding

Federal and state income taxes are withheld according to the amount of income and the number of exemptions claimed on *Form W-4*, as shown in Figure 2-3.2. An **exemption** is a person you claim on your tax return as a dependent. A **dependent** is a person who depends on you for more than half of his or her support. For example, minor children are claimed as dependents on their parents' tax return. The more exemptions you claim, the less tax is withheld. Everyone is allowed to claim one exemption for him- or herself (unless claimed as an exemption by someone else). The Internal Revenue Service (IRS) provides details on how a person qualifies as a dependent.

exemption a person claimed as a dependent on a tax return

dependent a person who depends on you for more than half of his or her support

Social Security Tax

Social Security tax, which is withheld for the federal government, pays for Old-Age, Survivors, and Disability Insurance (OASDI) benefits received by millions of Americans each year. A tax rate of 12.4 percent is applied to wage, salary, and self-employment income earned by a worker, up to a maximum dollar amount. This dollar amount is adjusted each year for the cost of living. As of 2015, the maximum taxable amount is $118,500. Half of the tax (6.2 percent) is paid for by the employee in the form of payroll withholding. The other half of this tax is paid for by the employer. Those who are self-employed must pay the full 12.4 percent. Money withheld for this tax is paid into an account under your name and Social Security number and is used to pay for current and future Social Security retirement benefits, survivor benefits (benefits for widows and widowers), and disability benefits.

Social Security tax a withholding tax that pays for Old-Age, Survivors, and Disability Insurance (OASDI) benefits

Employment Eligibility Verification
Department of Homeland Security
U.S. Citizenship and Immigration Services

USCIS
Form I-9
OMB No. 1615-0047
Expires 03/31/20—

▶**START HERE.** Read instructions carefully before completing this form. The instructions must be available during completion of this form.
ANTI-DISCRIMINATION NOTICE: It is illegal to discriminate against work-authorized individuals. Employers **CANNOT** specify which document(s) they will accept from an employee. The refusal to hire an individual because the documentation presented has a future expiration date may also constitute illegal discrimination.

Section 1. Employee Information and Attestation *(Employees must complete and sign Section 1 of Form I-9 no later than the **first day of employment**, but not before accepting a job offer.)*

Last Name *(Family Name)*	First Name *(Given Name)*	Middle Initial	Other Names Used *(if any)*
Perez	**Gloria**	**M**	

Address *(Street Number and Name)*	Apt. Number	City or Town	State	Zip Code
123 Maple Street		**Monticello**	**KY**	**42633**

Date of Birth *(mm/dd/yyyy)*	U.S. Social Security Number	E-mail Address	Telephone Number
3/20/1983	**0 0 0 - 2 0 - 2 1 0 5**	**gmperez@internet.com**	**(606) 555-0134**

I am aware that federal law provides for imprisonment and/or fines for false statements or use of false documents in connection with the completion of this form.

I attest, under penalty of perjury, that I am (check one of the following):

☑ A citizen of the United States

☐ A noncitizen national of the United States *(See instructions)*

☐ A lawful permanent resident (Alien Registration Number/USCIS Number): _____

☐ An alien authorized to work until (expiration date, if applicable, mm/dd/yyyy) _____ . Some aliens may write "N/A" in this field.
(See instructions)

For aliens authorized to work, provide your Alien Registration Number/USCIS Number **OR** *Form I-94 Admission Number:*

1. Alien Registration Number/USCIS Number:_____

OR

2. Form I-94 Admission Number: _____

If you obtained your admission number from CBP in connection with your arrival in the United States, include the following:

Foreign Passport Number: _____

Country of Issuance: _____

Some aliens may write "N/A" on the Foreign Passport Number and Country of Issuance fields. *(See instructions)*

3-D Barcode
Do Not Write in This Space

Signature of Employee: *Gloria M. Perez*	Date *(mm/dd/yyyy):* **5/20/20—**

Employers are required to verify that workers are eligible to work in the United States. When a worker is hired, he or she must complete Section 1 of *Form I-9*, as shown in Figure 2-3.3. The Social Security number recorded on this form is used to report Social Security taxes for the employee.

Medicare Tax

Medicare tax a tax that pays for medical care for retired persons age 65 and older who receive Social Security benefits

Medicare tax is withheld for the federal government to pay for medical care for retired persons age 65 and older who receive Social Security benefits. As of 2015, the Medicare tax is imposed at a rate of 2.9 percent. Unlike Social Security, there is no limit on the amount subject to the Medicare tax. Employees pay half of the tax (1.45 percent) through payroll deductions, and employers pay the other half. Self-employed workers pay the full 2.9 percent on their earnings.

FOCUS On...

WORKPLACE SAFETY

All workers are entitled by law to a safe place to work. Causes of work-related accidents, injuries, and illnesses may be related to the carelessness of workers, failure to use safety equipment, a lack of awareness of dangers, and not knowing how to avoid and reduce risks. Safety training should be required for all employees, even though they may not be directly involved with dangerous work. Having a safe workplace and reducing the number of accidents or injuries will benefit not only the workers but the company as well. Workers' compensation costs are based on the safety record of the company.

An *emergency plan* is a vital part of workplace safety. An effective emergency plan provides for the safety of workers, employees, visitors, and others. A good emergency plan has the following components:

- Detailed steps to follow in an emergency
- A list of who is responsible for each activity
- A list of who has backup roles

- A secondary plan in case the first course of action fails
- A data backup system
- A process to communicate status inside and outside the company
- Practice drills so that everyone will know what to do in case of a real emergency

Emergency plans should be in writing and shared with everyone. If special training is required, it should be completed and practiced regularly.

Think Critically

1. What can an employer do to ensure a safe workplace for employees?
2. Many families have emergency plans for their households as well. If you were designing an emergency safety plan for your family, what would you include?

Social security and medicare taxes combined are also known as *FICA tax*, because they were created by the Federal Insurance Contribution Act of 1938.

Workers' Compensation Insurance

Workers' compensation is an insurance plan that pays medical and disability benefits to employees who are injured or contract diseases on the job. Coverage includes payment of medical bills and compensation for lost wages. Benefits may be paid to the employee's family if the employee is killed on the job. The amount of benefits an employee or his family receives is based on the employee's earnings and work history. Most employers are required by law to carry workers' compensation insurance. The laws governing workers' compensation vary by state, meaning rates paid and procedures to follow may differ.

> **Workers' compensation** an insurance plan that pays medical and disability benefits to employees injured on the job

Optional Deductions

Employees may have optional deductions taken from their pay. Full-time workers usually have benefits provided by their employer. Employees may share in the cost of some benefits, such as health insurance. Optional payroll deductions cannot be withheld from an employee's paycheck unless the employee authorizes them. Examples of voluntary deductions follow:

- Health insurance
- Life insurance
- Disability insurance
- Dental insurance
- Vision insurance
- Long-term care insurance

- FSA
- HSA
- Retirement plan
- Savings plan
- Stock options plan
- Charitable donations

 CHECKPOINT

How is net pay calculated?

LO 2-3.2 How Do You Prepare an Income Tax Return?

You must file a tax return if you earned enough income to owe taxes. For 2015, a single person under the age of 65 whose gross income exceeded $10,150 (or $400 for self-employed individuals) likely owed taxes and had to file a return. The gross income requirement is adjusted yearly. You should check the IRS website to see if you must file. If you did not earn enough to owe taxes but taxes were withheld from your paychecks, you should file a return to claim a refund. In addition to a federal tax return, you may also have to file state and local income tax returns. Filing your tax return begins with the Form W-2.

Form W-2

Form W-2 a form used to report taxable income that a worker received during the calendar year

Form W-2 is used to report the taxable income that a worker received during the calendar year. Employers are required to send workers a W-2 for the calendar year (January 1 through December 31) by the following January 31. Form W-2 for Gloria Perez is shown in Figure 2-3.4. The information on the form is sent to the federal, state, and local governments as well as to the worker. Multiple copies are provided for the worker to attach to tax forms and to keep on file.

Note that the amount shown in box 1 (Wages, tips, other compensation) and in box 16 (State wages, tips, etc.) is $25,688.00. This figure is the amount of gross pay ($27,040.00 as reported in boxes 3, 5, and 18) less the money paid into a 401(k) plan. Money paid into a 401(k) plan is not subject to federal income taxes until it is withdrawn, usually during retirement.

Form 1040EZ

Form 1040EZ the short tax return form designed for single and joint filers with no dependents or itemized deductions

Several different forms can be used to file a federal tax return. The form that should be used depends on the type of income and deductions claimed. **Form 1040EZ** is a short tax return form designed for use by single and joint filers with no dependents or itemized deductions. Your

22222	**a** Employee's social security number 000 22 2105	OMB No. 1545-0008	Safe, accurate, **FAST! Use**	IRS e~file	Visit the IRS website at *www.irs.gov/efile*

b Employer identification number (EIN) 00-000000	**1** Wages, tips, other compensation $25,688.00	**2** Federal income tax withheld $2,136.94
c Employer's name, address, and ZIP code ABC Company 781 Weston Street Monticello, KY 42633-0781	**3** Social security wages $27,040.00	**4** Social security tax withheld $1,676.48
	5 Medicare wages and tips $27,040.00	**6** Medicare tax withheld $392.08
	7 Social security tips	**8** Allocated tips
d Control number	**9**	**10** Dependent care benefits
e Employee's first name and initial Last name Suff.	**11** Nonqualified plans	**12a** See instructions for box 12 C o d e D $1,352.00
	13 Statutory employee ☐ Retirement plan ☒ Third-party sick pay ☐	**12b** C o d e
Gloria M. Perez 123 Maple Street Monticello, KY 42633-0123	**14** Other	**12c** C o d e
		12d C o d e
f Employee's address and ZIP code		

15 State Employer's state ID number	**16** State wages, tips, etc.	**17** State income tax	**18** Local wages, tips, etc.	**19** Local income tax	**20** Locality name
KY 00000	$25,688.00	$891.02	$27,040.00	$81.64	Mont.

Form **W-2** Wage and Tax Statement   20—   Department of the Treasury—Internal Revenue Service

Copy B—To Be Filed With Employee's FEDERAL Tax Return.
This information is being furnished to the Internal Revenue Service.

taxable income must be less than $100,000, and you can have no more than $1,500 in interest income. Form 1040EZ is the easiest and shortest form. It can be completed using information found on the filer's Form W-2 and tax tables provided by the IRS. Gloria Perez's Form 1040EZ is shown in Figure 2-3.5. (Note that the form for the current year may differ somewhat but will contain similar information.) Refer to the figure as you read the following instructions on how to fill out a Form 1040EZ.

- Fill in your name, address, and Social Security number. For a joint return, the spouse's name and Social Security number would also be included.
- On line 1, enter your total wages, salaries, and tips, as shown on your Form W-2 (box 1).
- On line 2, enter interest income (such as interest earned on a savings account of $1,500 or less), and on line 3, enter unemployment compensation.
- On line 4, calculate your adjusted gross income by adding line 1 (wages, salaries, and tips), line 2 (taxable interest), and line 3 (unemployment compensation).
- Line 5 shows the amount that can be deducted from adjusted gross income if you are not claimed as a dependent on another tax return. Enter the deduction shown if you are single or if you are married filing jointly.

► FIGURE 2-3.5 Form 1040EZ

Department of the Treasury—Internal Revenue Service

Form **1040EZ**

Income Tax Return for Single and Joint Filers With No Dependents (99)

20—

OMB No. 1545-0074

Your first name and initial	Last name	Your social security number
Gloria M.	Perez	000 22 2105

If a joint return, spouse's first name and initial | Last name | Spouse's social security number

Home address (number and street). If you have a P.O. box, see instructions. | Apt. no.
123 Maple Street

▲ Make sure the SSN(s) above are correct.

City, town or post office, state, and ZIP code. If you have a foreign address, also complete spaces below (see instructions).
Monticello, KY 42633-0123

Presidential Election Campaign
Check here if you, or your spouse if filing jointly, want $3 to go to this fund. Checking a box below will not change your tax or refund. ☐ You ☐ Spouse

Foreign country name | Foreign province/state/county | Foreign postal code

Income

Attach Form(s) W-2 here.

Enclose, but do not attach, any payment.

1	Wages, salaries, and tips. This should be shown in box 1 of your Form(s) W-2. Attach your Form(s) W-2.	**1**	25,688	00
2	Taxable interest. If the total is over $1,500, you cannot use Form 1040EZ.	**2**		
3	Unemployment compensation and Alaska Permanent Fund dividends (see instructions).	**3**		
4	Add lines 1, 2, and 3. This is your **adjusted gross income.**	**4**	25,688	00
5	If someone can claim you (or your spouse if a joint return) as a dependent, check the applicable box(es) below and enter the amount from the worksheet on back. ☐ You ☐ Spouse If no one can claim you (or your spouse if a joint return), enter $10,150 if **single;** $20,300 if **married filing jointly.** See back for explanation.	**5**	10,150	00
6	Subtract line 5 from line 4. If line 5 is larger than line 4, enter -0-. This is your **taxable income.** ▶	**6**	15,538	00

Payments, Credits, and Tax

7	Federal income tax withheld from Form(s) W-2 and 1099.	**7**	2,136	94
8a	**Earned income credit (EIC)** (see instructions)	**8a**		
b	Nontaxable combat pay election. 8b			
9	Add lines 7 and 8a. These are your **total payments and credits.** ▶	**9**	2,136	94
10	**Tax.** Use the amount on **line 6 above** to find your tax in the tax table in the instructions. Then, enter the tax from the table on this line.	**10**	1,875	00
11	Health care: individual responsibility (see instructions) Full-year coverage ☑	**11**		
12	Add lines 10 and 11. This is your **total tax.**	**12**	1,875	00

Refund

Have it directly deposited! See instructions and fill in 13b, 13c, and 13d, or Form 8888.

13a	If line 9 is larger than line 12, subtract line 12 from line 9. This is your **refund.** If Form 8888 is attached, check here ▶ ☐	**13a**	261	94
▶ b	Routing number	▶c Type: ☐ Checking ☐ Savings		
▶ d	Account number			

Amount You Owe

14	If line 12 is larger than line 9, subtract line 9 from line 12. This is the **amount you owe.** For details on how to pay, see instructions. ▶	**14**	

Third Party Designee

Do you want to allow another person to discuss this return with the IRS (see instructions)? ☐ **Yes.** Complete below. ☐ No

Designee's name ▶ | Phone no. ▶ | Personal identification number (PIN) ▶

Sign Here

Joint return? See instructions.

Keep a copy for your records.

Under penalties of perjury, I declare that I have examined this return and, to the best of my knowledge and belief, it is true, correct, and accurately lists all amounts and sources of income I received during the tax year. Declaration of preparer (other than the taxpayer) is based on all information of which the preparer has any knowledge.

Your signature	Date	Your occupation	Daytime phone number
Gloria M. Perez	2/5/20—	Product Assembler	(606) 555-0134
Spouse's signature. If a joint return, **both** must sign.	Date	Spouse's occupation	If the IRS sent you an Identity Protection PIN, enter it here (see inst.)

Paid Preparer Use Only

Print/Type preparer's name	Preparer's signature	Date	Check ☐ if self-employed	PTIN
Firm's name ▶			Firm's EIN ▶	
Firm's address ▶			Phone no.	

For Disclosure, Privacy Act, and Paperwork Reduction Act Notice, see instructions. | Cat. No. 11329W | Form **1040EZ** (20—)

- On line 6, calculate your taxable income by subtracting the amount on line 5 (standard deduction) from line 4 (adjusted gross income). If the amount entered on line 5 is larger than line 4, enter 0 (zero) on line 6.
- On line 7, enter your total federal tax withheld, as shown on your Form W-2 (box 2). This is the amount of tax you have already paid.

- On line 8a, enter the EIC credit, which benefits working people who have low income. To qualify for the EIC, you need to make below a specified amount. If you served in the military and received combat pay, report it on line 8b.
- On line 9, calculate your total payments and credits by adding lines 7 and 8.
- On line 10, you will calculate the tax owed on the taxable income amount (line 6). The tax is listed in the tax tables found in the Form 1040EZ instructions (available on the IRS website). This amount is your tax liability and should be entered on line 10.
- On line 11, you must check the box to indicate that you had health care coverage for every month of the year. Starting in 2014, individuals must have health care coverage if they do not qualify for a health coverage exemption.
- On line 12, add lines 10 and 11 to determine your total tax owed.
- Line 13a is for a refund, which results if the amount you owe in tax (line 12) is less than your tax withholdings and other credits (line 9). You can have this amount deposited directly to your checking or savings account by filling in the routing and account numbers.
- Line 14 is the amount of tax you owe, which results if the amount you owe in tax (line 12) is more than your tax withholdings and other credits (line 9).
- Sign and date your tax return. If you paid a tax preparer to file your taxes, he or she should also sign the form.

Other Tax Forms

Form 1040A is a two-page form that allows more options for entering income, credits, and deductions than Form 1040EZ. It can be used if you have less than $100,000 in taxable income. Taxpayers might use Form 1040A if they have more than $1,500 in interest income. Some sections require the filer to attach additional forms, called *schedules*, to report certain types of income or deductions.

Taxpayers who earn more than $100,000 in taxable income must use Form 1040, also known as the long form. Form 1040 must also be used if you have interest or dividends over a set limit, self-employment income, or income from the sale of property. Form 1040 also allows you to itemize deductions instead of claiming the standard deduction.

Form 1099-INT, as shown in Figure 2-3.6, reports the interest income earned during the year that must be included as part of the taxpayer's income on the tax form. This form is sent to individuals by the bank or other institution that pays the interest.

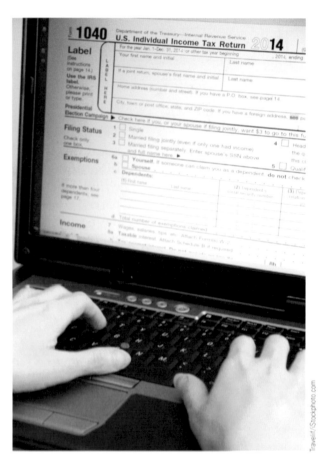

Why is it important to choose the proper tax form to use when filing your income taxes?

9292	☐ VOID	☐ CORRECTED		

| PAYER'S name, street address, city or town, state or province, country, ZIP or foreign postal code, and telephone no.

First Bank
201 Main Street
Monticello, KY 42633-0201	Payer's RTN (optional)	OMB No. 1545-0112	**Interest Income**
	1 Interest income 2,500.00 $	20— Form **1099-INT**	
	2 Early withdrawal penalty $		Copy A
PAYER'S federal identification number 00-0827701	RECIPIENT'S identification number 000-22-0011	**3** Interest on U.S. Savings Bonds and Treas. obligations $	**For Internal Revenue Service Center** File with Form 1096.
RECIPIENT'S name William Patel	**4** Federal income tax withheld $	**5** Investment expenses $	**For Privacy Act and Paperwork Reduction Act Notice, see the 20— General Instructions for Certain Information Returns.**
	6 Foreign tax paid $	**7** Foreign country or U.S. possession	
Street address (including apt. no.) 206 Brookhaven Drive	**8** Tax-exempt interest $	**9** Specified private activity bond interest $	
City or town, state or province, country, and ZIP or foreign postal code Somerset, KY 42502-0206	**10** Market discount $	**11** Bond premium $	
FATCA filing requirement ☐	**12**	**13** Bond premium on tax–exempt bond $	
Account number (see instructions) 4000326	2nd TIN not. ☐	**14** Tax-exempt and tax credit bond CUSIP no.	**15** State	**16** State identification no.	**17** State tax withheld $ $

Form **1099-INT**   Cat. No. 14410K   www.irs.gov/form1099int   Department of the Treasury - Internal Revenue Service

E-Filing

The deadline for filing taxes is April 15 of each year. You can download tax forms from the IRS website, print hard copies, and mail them to the IRS. Most people submit their tax returns electronically (known as *e-filing*). Several e-file options are available. Filers can hire a tax preparer who is approved by the IRS to e-file the tax return for them. Most do-it-yourself tax preparation software programs available today also support e-filing.

Individuals with gross income below a certain amount (see the IRS website) can use the IRS's Free File program to prepare and file a tax return online for free. A link on the IRS website takes users to a list of companies that provide free filing services.

Using e-filing provides fast results. The forms are transmitted instantly to the IRS. Refunds are often received much more quickly than when a paper return is filed. Having the refund deposited directly into a bank account makes receiving refunds fast and safe.

 **CHECKPOINT**

How is gross income different from adjusted gross income and taxable income?

KEY TERMS REVIEW

Match the terms with the definitions. Some terms may not be used.

_____ 1. An insurance plan that pays medical and disability benefits to employees who are injured on the job

_____ 2. A person who depends on you for more than half of his or her support

_____ 3. Total salary or wages earned during a pay period

_____ 4. A tax withheld to pay for medical care for retired persons age 65 and older who receive Social Security benefits

_____ 5. The amount of your paycheck after deductions are subtracted

_____ 6. A withholding tax that pays for Old-Age, Survivors, and Disability Insurance (OASDI) benefits

_____ 7. A form used to report taxable income that a worker received during the calendar year

_____ 8. A person you claim on your tax return as a dependent

a. dependent

b. exemption

c. Form 1040EZ

d. Form W-2

e. gross pay

f. Medicare tax

g. net pay

h. Social Security tax

i. workers' compensation

CHECK YOUR UNDERSTANDING

9. How is gross pay different from net pay?

10. How do employers determine how much income taxes to withhold from a paycheck? What is a Form W-4?

11. What information is contained on a pay stub?

12. How does the amount of tax a person pays affect his or her disposable income?

13. Why is an employee required to fill out a Form I-9 before starting a job?

14. For what services do Medicare taxes pay?

15. List three types of required deductions for taxes.

16. List three types of optional deductions from your paycheck.

17. What information is found on Form W-2?

18. Name three tax forms that taxpayers can use when filing taxes. What determines which form a taxpayer can use?

19. Why would an individual file taxes using e-file?

THINK CRITICALLY

20. The U.S. tax code operates on a system called "voluntary compliance," meaning that citizens voluntarily file their tax returns and pay the taxes that they owe. Failure to do so can result in criminal charges for tax evasion. Many tax protestors believe that income taxes are unconstitutional and therefore illegal. What is your position on this issue?

21. Every year, Americans celebrate "Tax Freedom Day." Computed by the Tax Foundation, Tax Freedom Day represents the date when the average taxpayer has paid off his or her taxes for the year. Conduct online research by doing a search using the keywords *Tax Freedom Day* and answer the following questions:
    a. How is Tax Freedom day computed?
    b. When was Tax Freedom Day for the most current year?
    c. How much did Americans spend on taxes for the most current year?
    d. How has Tax Freedom Day changed over time?
    e. When is your state's Tax Freedom Day?
    f. Why do states' Tax Freedom Day differ from the federal Tax Freedom Day?

EXTEND YOUR LEARNING

22. When you begin a new job, you will be asked to complete a Form W-4. To practice filling out Form W-4, access the form at the IRS website (www.irs.gov) and print out a copy. Complete the Employee's Withholding Allowance Certificate portion of the form using your own personal information. For privacy reasons, use 000-22-1111 as your Social Security number. Indicate that you are single and claim one exemption. Refer to Figure 2-3.2 as an example.

23. To practice filling out Form 1040EZ, access the form from the IRS website (www.irs.gov) and print out a copy. Enter your name, address, and Social Security number in the Label section. For privacy reasons, use 000-22-1111 as your Social Security number. Assume you are single. Your Form W-2 shows that you have $29,521 of taxable income and $2,850 of federal income tax withholdings. Your Form 1099-INT shows $421 in taxable interest. Use the tax tables in the Form 1040EZ instructions (found on the IRS website). Determine the amount of your refund or the amount that you owe. Sign and date the form using "Sales Associate" as your occupation.

THE ESSENTIAL QUESTION   Refer to The Essential Question on p. 58. Required payroll deductions are those that are mandated by law, such as taxes, whereas optional payroll deductions are those that employees choose to have deducted. To prepare a tax return, use information from your Form W-2 and any other tax forms you receive, such as Form 1099-INT. Choose one of three forms (1040, 1040A, or 1040EZ) to file based on your income level, deductions and credits taken, and number of dependents.

Exploring Careers in…
TAX COLLECTION

Tax examiners and collectors, and revenue agents work for federal, state, and local governments. They review tax returns to determine if the math is accurate and the credits and deductions claimed are allowed by law. They sometimes conduct field audits and investigations of income tax returns to verify information. They also work with the taxpayer to settle the debt.

Wherever money is collected on behalf of government units, there are revenue agents and officers sending out reports and communicating findings. For each case, careful records are kept and shared among the federal, state, and local governments.

Sometimes travel is needed, but a significant amount of time is spent in offices doing detailed work. Stress results from working under tight deadlines as well as confronting delinquent and often hostile taxpayers.

Employment Outlook

- A slight decline is expected through 2022.
- Budget cuts in recent years have resulted in decreased hiring for these workers.

Job Titles

- Tax examiner
- Tax collector
- Revenue agent

Needed Education/Skills

- A bachelor's degree in accounting or a related field is preferred.
- Specialized experience is desirable.

Arts, A/V Technology & Communications

- Excellent analytical and interpersonal skills are needed.

What's it like to work in … Tax Collection

Alice started as a tax examiner of individual tax returns before becoming a revenue agent in her state. She had to pass a strict background check because she works with confidential information. Her job consists of reviewing tax returns of large companies and corporations.

Alice verifies tax returns for accuracy. When there is a discrepancy, she may tag the files for a full audit; in other cases, she is able to determine accuracy with a phone call or a written letter.

Today is like most others—it involves detailed work that requires concentration, patience, and organization. Her filing system allows her to retrieve information quickly, compare data, communicate through letters or phone calls, and follow up with action when needed.

What About You?

Do you like analyzing data and adhering to procedures? How do your skills and aptitudes match up with those required in the tax collection field?

Chapter 2 Assessment

SUMMARY

2-1 Sources of earned income include wages, salaries, tips, commissions, and net earnings from self-employment.

Employee benefits are important to workers. They are usually not taxed, are offered at comparatively low prices, and help workers reach their financial goals, such as retirement.

Employee benefits include pay without work (paid vacations and holidays, sick leave, and personal leave), group health insurance, retirement plans, flexible spending accounts (FSAs), health savings accounts (HSAs), profit sharing, stock options, and perks such as educational benefits, on-site child care facilities, and wellness programs.

2-2 Unearned income may come from private sources, such as interest earned on savings accounts and dividends paid on stock, or from government transfer payments.

Taxes based on consumption include sales tax, use tax, and excise tax. These are paid by consumers who use or buy certain goods or services.

Income taxes are based on income. They are called progressive taxes because the more you earn, the more you pay in tax.

Taxes based on wealth include property tax and estate taxes. They are assessed based on value of property and assets that you own.

Everyone benefits directly from taxes in the form of public goods and indirectly from the government assistance that others receive.

2-3 Gross pay is your total salary or wages earned. After taxes and other deductions are subtracted, the result is net pay, or take-home pay.

Required deductions are those that an employer is mandated by law to withhold from an employee's paycheck. These include federal and state income taxes and Social Security and Medicare taxes. Local income taxes may also apply. Optional deductions are those that an employee chooses to have deducted from his or her pay, such as health insurance, life insurance, and retirement plans.

Form W-4 is used to record the number of exemptions you claim. Form I-9 is used to verify a person's eligibility to legally work in the United States. Form W-2 reports your earnings and withholdings for the year. Form 1099-INT reports your interest income for the year.

Individual taxpayers can use one of three forms (1040, 1040A, or 1040EZ) when filing their tax return. Form 1040EZ is the short tax return form available to single and joint filers with no dependents or itemized deductions.

MAKE ACADEMIC CONNECTIONS

1. **Ethics** Many employers provide sick leave for employees. Sick leave is a valuable benefit. Employers usually have rules about what situations qualify for use of sick leave. In some cases, the employee must be ill to use sick leave. In other cases, the company may allow employees to use sick leave to care for a sick child or other relative. An employee may also be able to use sick leave to visit a doctor or hospital for tests or checkups. Why is it important for employees to follow the rules that apply to using sick leave? Explain why it is unethical to call in sick when you really have plans to do something else. (LO 2-1.2)

2. **Legal** When workers are laid off from their jobs, they may be entitled to unemployment compensation benefits. These benefits are taxable income. Unemployment is a joint effort between the federal and state governments. Federal law sets the general guidelines, while states determine specific rules, such as eligibility requirements and benefit amounts. Visit your state's website to find out how unemployment compensation laws and insurance work in your state. Find answers to the following questions: (LO 2-2.1)
   a. What are the requirements for drawing unemployment benefits?
   b. How is the amount of the benefit determined?
   c. For how long can a person draw benefits?

3. **History** The income tax was not a part of the U.S. Constitution until 1913. Working in groups, research the history of U.S. taxation and report on the types of early taxes, their rates, and how the taxes were used (such as paying for wars). Also discuss who has the authority to levy taxes, how new taxes are introduced, and how tax rates may be changed. (LO 2-3.2)

TEAMWORK

4. **Communication** Work in a group with three or four other students to discover and present a plan of action to follow in the event of an emergency. (LO 2-3.1)
   a. You have learned that emergency plans are important in the workplace. Such plans are also important in schools. Consult your school handbook, the school website, or other materials available to learn about the emergency plans for your school. You may need to talk with a principal, counselor, or school safety or security officer.
   b. Choose one of the following situations, and find the plan that should be followed in that situation. Present the main points of the plan to the class.
      - Fire in the building
      - Severe weather
      - Bomb threat
      - Hostage situation
      - Chemical spill
      - Bus accident

TEAMWORK

Do the Math

1. **Gross pay is calculated by multiplying regular hours times regular pay and adding any overtime hours multiplied by overtime pay. The overtime pay rate is 1½ times the regular rate of pay. Net pay is determined by subtracting deductions from gross pay.**

   a. Max worked 48 hours last week. His regular hourly rate is $8.00. What was his gross pay?

   b. Jackson worked 44 hours last week. His hourly rate is $8.60. He has the following deductions taken from his gross earnings:
   - Federal income tax withheld at the rate of 10%
   - Social Security tax withheld at the rate of 6.2%
   - Medicare tax withheld at the rate of 1.45%
   - Health insurance premiums of $12.80

   What was Jackson's net pay? (Round to the nearest cent.)

2. **Most states have state sales tax which is added to many purchases you make. In the following examples, compute the amount of sales tax and the total purchase price.**

   a. Mary bought a new dress for $80, and state sales tax is 8.5%.

   b. Joe bought a pack of batteries for $12, and state sales tax is 7%.

Take Action

PREPARE FORM 1040A TAX RETURN

Go to the IRS website (www.irs.gov) and print out a copy of Form 1040A and its instructions. Fill in the form based on the following information:

- Assume you are Bill or Mary Smith, single, and claim one exemption.
- Use your own address.
- Use 000-22-1111 as your Social Security number.
- Your Form W-2 shows that you have total wages of $28,429 and that $2,726 was withheld for federal income taxes.
- Form 1099-INT shows $1,825 in taxable interest.
- You have an IRA deduction of $1,000 and student loan interest (deduction) of $500.

From the tax tables provided in the Form 1040A instructions (available on the IRS website), find the amount of tax that applies to the amount of taxable income. Determine if you are due a refund or owe taxes. Sign and date the form. Enter "Sales Associate" as your occupation.

Include your completed Form 1040A in your portfolio.

Your Purchasing Power

Pamela Moore/iStockphoto.com

The money you spend is affected by inflation. Inflation causes prices to rise and erodes the value of money, taking away purchasing power. As a consumer, however, you still have some power. Consumers help set prices when they act in their own best interests. Consumers also need to understand selling and buying strategies and use them to their advantage to increase their purchasing power. Finally, by being aware of consumer protection laws and agencies, consumers can seek protection against unfair selling practices that can affect their spending power negatively.

Do *This*, Not *That*

To increase your purchasing power:

- Pay off debt quickly to avoid paying interest.
- Make rational buying decisions, not emotional ones.
- Shop smart to find the best value at the lowest price.
- Ask for a pay raise at work to keep up with rising prices.
- Save money now to avoid borrowing later.

3-1 | Inflation and the Value of Money

LEARNING OBJECTIVES

LO 3-1.1 Explain inflation and how it is measured.

LO 3-1.2 List the types of inflation and how they affect consumers.

LO 3-1.3 Discuss the causes of inflation and how consumer spending, saving, and investing are affected.

KEY TERMS

- inflation, 74
- time value of money, 75
- gross domestic product (GDP), 75
- disinflation, 76
- deflation, 76
- reflation, 77
- hyperinflation, 77
- demand-pull inflation, 77
- cost-push inflation, 77
- productivity, 78

LO 3-1.1 What Is Inflation?

Fifty years ago, you could buy a gallon of milk for less than $1, a new car for less than $2,500, and a house for around $20,000. Today, you can expect to pay much more for not only these items but just about everything else. This is due to inflation. **Inflation** is an increase in the general level of prices for goods and services. Inflation reflects how much prices are rising.

inflation an increase in the general level of prices for goods and services

Measuring Inflation

Inflation is measured by the U.S. Bureau of Labor Statistics (BLS). The measurement tool used is called the *Consumer Price Index (CPI)*. The CPI measures the change in the retail price of goods and services that are commonly bought by consumers, such as food, gasoline, prescription drugs, clothing, and vehicles. These items are called the *market basket*. The CPI compares the prices of the goods and services in the market basket to see how they have changed from year to year. For example, if the price of an item was $1.00 in the previous year and it is now $1.12, that is a 12 percent increase in the price. If the same increase happened to all of the goods in the market basket, the inflation rate for that year would also be 78 percent. You can learn more about the CPI at the BLS website.

Figure 3-1.1 shows the inflation rates as measured by the CPI for the past 20 years. These rates are low largely due to actions of the federal government and the Federal Reserve System. (See the *Focus On* feature on page 78 that explains how the government fights inflation.)

Inflation Versus Purchasing Power

Purchasing power is the value of money, measured by the amount of goods and services it can buy. The value of a dollar does not remain the same when there is inflation. As inflation rises, the true purchasing power of each dollar falls.

Because purchasing power falls over time as inflation rises, the money that workers earn will buy less as prices rise. That means you

▶ FIGURE 3-1.1 Inflation as Measured by CPI, 1995–2014

Year	Annual Inflation Rate	Year	Annual Inflation Rate
1995	2.8%	2005	3.4%
1996	3.0%	2006	3.2%
1997	2.3%	2007	2.8%
1998	1.6%	2008	3.8%
1999	2.2%	2009	-0.4%
2000	3.4%	2010	1.6%
2001	2.8%	2011	3.2%
2002	1.6%	2012	2.1%
2003	2.3%	2013	1.5%
2004	2.7%	2014	1.6%

Source: Historical Inflation Rates: 1914–2015, www.usinflationcalculator.com/inflation /historical-inflation-rates.

must earn more to maintain the same standard of living. If you do not earn more, your standard of living will drop. Employers often give workers merit raises and/or bonuses. These increases in income provide more purchasing power.

In addition to pay raises and bonuses, many employees receive annual *cost-of-living adjustments (COLAs)*, or pay increases from their employers to keep pace with inflation. Unlike raises and bonuses, COLAs do not provide more purchasing power. They keep purchasing power equal to rising costs. Retirees who receive Social Security benefits also receive annual COLAs.

During times of inflation, you must also consider how the time value of money affects purchasing power. The **time value of money** is a concept that says a dollar you receive in the future will be worth less than a dollar you receive in the present (today). The concept assumes that prices are rising. For example, suppose you loan a friend $20 today. Your friend promises to pay back the $20 one year from today. The money you receive in one year will not have the same value as the money you loaned your friend. This is because prices will be higher due to inflation, and the $20 will not buy as many goods and services one year from today.

time value of money a concept that says a dollar you receive in the future will be worth less than a dollar you receive in the present (today)

Inflation Versus Gross Domestic Product

A common method used to measure a country's economic performance is the gross domestic product. The **gross domestic product (GDP)** is the value of all goods and services produced in a country in a given time period, such as a year. It includes new goods and services that consumers purchase, such as automobiles, smartphones, clothing, and haircuts. It also includes government spending on things such as roads and highways and police and military equipment. Products produced in the United States that are exported to other countries are also included in the GDP. The largest percentage of GDP is consumer spending.

gross domestic product (GDP) the value of all goods and services produced in a country in a given time period

Comparing the GDP over several years is a good indicator of whether the economy is strong or weak. When the GDP is growing, the country is producing more goods and services, which generally results in more jobs, more income for consumers to spend, and a higher standard of living. The opposite is true when the GDP is falling. When evaluating the GDP, inflation is a factor. If prices are going up, an increase in GDP could be the result of inflation rather than higher production levels. For example, if GDP increased by 4 percent last year, but prices in general increased by 2 percent, then only about 2 percent more goods and services were produced. This is GDP adjusted for inflation.

 CHECKPOINT

How does inflation affect your standard of living?

LO 3-1.2 What Are the Types of Inflation?

Businesses base pricing decisions in part on what consumers are buying and not buying. Changes in prices may show different patterns over time. These patterns result in varying types of inflation.

Disinflation

disinflation rising prices with the rate of increase slowing down

Disinflation occurs when prices are rising, but the rate of increase is slowing down. Some products and services do not increase in price as fast as others. Disinflation is more common among products and services that face intense competition and have many substitutes. Prices may still be high and rising, but at a much slower rate.

Deflation

deflation a decrease in the general level of prices for goods and services

Deflation is a decrease in the general level of prices for goods and services. It is the opposite of inflation. In other words, prices are going down. Deflation occurs when producers are willing and able to provide goods and services at lower prices, but due to certain events, consumers are buying less. Deflation often leads to increased unemployment because there is a lower level of demand in the economy. Companies may shut down or lay off workers if their business is not profitable.

How does deflation affect businesses and consumers?

Reflation

Reflation occurs when high prices are lowered due to decreased demand, but then are restored to the previous high level. Perhaps you have heard a news reporter use this term to describe crude oil prices. Reflation can happen when the available supply of a product, such as oil, goes up and down.

reflation high prices followed by lower prices and then high prices again

Hyperinflation

Hyperinflation occurs when prices are rising so rapidly, they are out of control. With hyperinflation, consumers spend their money as fast as they can because they fear rapidly rising prices. This spending leads to even more inflation. Then people are unable to buy the **goods that they need to live comfortably.**

hyperinflation rapidly rising prices that are out of control

Although the United States has not experienced hyperinflation, there have been periods of double-digit inflation (10 percent or higher in a year). However, hyperinflation rates are much higher. Although there is no set rule, many economists consider inflation rates of 50 percent or higher to be hyperinflation. Some countries have had rates of several hundred percent per month. For example, Germany's monthly inflation rate reached over 300 percent in the years following World War I.

CHECKPOINT

Explain how disinflation differs from hyperinflation.

LO 3-1.3 What Are Causes and Effects of Inflation?

Inflation can be caused by different factors in the economy. Consumers may want to buy more goods or services than are available, driving up prices. Producers may have to pay more for the resources needed to produce products and thus may need to raise prices. Both situations can lead to inflation.

Demand-Pull Inflation

The most common type of inflation is called demand-pull. **Demand-pull inflation** results in higher prices because consumers want to buy more goods and services than producers supply. Consumers may spend their income as soon as it is received and may also be willing to spend future income (credit). This spending causes businesses to scramble to meet the demand for goods. Because products are selling so quickly, businesses are able to raise prices to balance supply with demand and make bigger profits. This type of inflation is often described as "too many dollars chasing too few goods."

demand-pull inflation higher prices as a result of consumers wanting to buy more goods and services than producers supply

Cost-Push Inflation

Cost-push inflation occurs when producers raise prices because their costs to create products are rising. For example, when wages go up, the cost of producing a product goes up. Producers may then raise prices. If producers did not raise prices, profits would shrink.

cost-push inflation rising prices as a result of rising production costs

FOCUS On...

SUPPLY AND DEMAND OF MONEY

The government tries to stabilize the economy by minimizing the effects of inflation and recession. To do so, it can manage the supply and demand of money. Two tools used in the United States to manage the *money supply* (the total amount of money in circulation) are monetary policy and fiscal policy.

Monetary policy refers to actions by the *Federal Reserve System*, commonly called the *Fed*, to stabilize the economy. The Fed is the central bank in the United States that controls the money supply. When the Fed sees that prices are rising too fast, it tries to slow them down by decreasing spending. One way to decrease spending is by raising interest rates. When interest rates increase, both individuals and businesses find it more expensive to borrow money to buy goods and services, so spending is slowed. There are several types of interest rates that are controlled by the Fed.

- The *discount rate* is the rate that banks have to pay to borrow money from the Fed. Banks borrow money when they have the opportunity to make loans but do not have enough cash on hand. Banks are required to have a certain amount of cash on hand, called *reserves*, to meet daily customer demand. If these reserves go below the required amount, banks must borrow money.

- The *federal funds rate* is the rate at which banks can borrow from the excess reserves of other banks. For example, if one bank has more money than it needs, it can loan that extra money to other banks.
- The *prime rate* is the rate that banks charge to their most creditworthy business customers. The prime rate always adjusts based on how the Fed moves the discount rate. For example, when the discount rate increases, the prime rate also goes up. The prime rate is usually 3 percent (or more) higher than the federal funds rate.

Fiscal policy refers to actions taken by the federal government to manage the economy. To help curb inflation, the government can raise taxes. When taxes go up, people have less money to spend. This slows inflation. On the other hand, if the economy is sluggish because people are not buying, the government can increase spending by lowering taxes. This gives consumers more disposable income to spend. These actions, taken together, either speed up or slow down spending.

Think Critically

1. How does the monetary policy affect the supply and demand for money?
2. How does the fiscal policy affect the supply and demand for money?

---

productivity a measure of the efficiency with which goods and services are made (comparison of total output to total input)

Cost-push inflation is affected by productivity. **Productivity** is a measure of the efficiency with which goods and services are made. It compares total output (quantity of goods or services produced) to total inputs (resources used, such as labor, land, or equipment). When input costs, such as wages or the cost of new equipment, are offset by higher output, such as larger quantities of a product, productivity rises. Higher productivity lowers the cost of each unit produced. Lower costs enable the producer to maintain the same price levels. In this case, cost-push inflation (price increases) does not occur. Instead, more products are made at the same price level.

The depletion of natural resources is a growing cause of cost-push inflation. Over time, resources that are in high demand shrink in supply. As resources become scarce or more difficult to get, prices rises. For example, overfishing reduces the supply of seafood, which drives up prices.

Inflation Affects Employment

Economists believe that there is a direct relationship between inflation and employment. Rising prices often are a result of increased demand, which means more people are spending and producers are making more money. Producers, in an effort to keep up with demand, hire more people. Thus, rising prices are associated with higher employment rates. When inflation is reduced and prices drop, the opposite occurs. With reduced demand and lower profits, producers may start laying off workers. This is often called the *inflation/employment trade-off*. Thus, mild inflation of 2 or 3 percent is said to be good for the economy.

Why are more businesses hiring during periods of inflation?

Inflation Affects Spending, Saving, and Investing

Some jobs provide pay raises only once a year or less often. Employees who do not get raises often enough to keep pace with the inflation rate lose purchasing power. Retirees drawing a fixed monthly pension also lose purchasing power as prices rise. In such cases, consumers have two choices: they can buy less, or they can dip into savings or borrow money to continue the same level of spending. Either way, it takes more money to keep getting the same amount of goods and services.

Inflation also affects the amount of money that consumers may be able to save. In times of rising prices, consumers may have to use more of their disposable income to buy needed goods and services. Less money may be available for saving.

Consumers should consider the expected rate of inflation when choosing investments. They want to invest their money in a way that will provide a return that is greater than the inflation rate. For example, suppose the inflation rate over 5 years is 5 percent. Investments such as savings accounts, stocks, or bonds must have a growth rate of at least 5 percent for the money invested to keep its purchasing power.

≫ CHECKPOINT

How can productivity affect inflation?

KEY TERMS REVIEW

Match the terms with the definitions. Some terms may not be used.

_____ 1. Rapidly rising prices that are out of control

_____ 2. High prices followed by lower prices and then high prices again

_____ 3. A decrease in the general level of prices for goods and services

_____ 4. Rising prices as a result of consumers wanting to buy more goods and services than producers supply

_____ 5. Rising prices with the rate of increase slowing down

_____ 6. An increase in the general level of prices for goods and services

_____ 7. A concept that says a dollar you receive in the future will be worth less than a dollar you receive today

_____ 8. Rising prices as a result of rising production costs

a. cost-push inflation

b. deflation

c. demand-pull inflation

d. disinflation

e. gross domestic product (GDP)

f. hyperinflation

g. inflation

h. productivity

i. reflation

j. time value of money

CHECK YOUR UNDERSTANDING

9. What is inflation? What causes prices to rise?

10. How is inflation measured? Who provides the data for the measurement?

11. What is purchasing power? How is it affected by inflation?

12. Explain the time value of money concept as it relates to deflation.

13. What is the relationship between gross domestic product and consumer spending?

14. List the types of inflation.

15. How does demand-pull inflation differ from cost-push inflation?

16. What is the Fed? What does it do?

17. What are the discount rate, the federal funds rate, and the prime rate? Why are they important?

18. What is the fiscal policy? How does it help control inflation?

19. Explain how inflation and employment levels are related.

20. What is meant by the inflation/employment trade-off?

21. How does inflation affect spending, saving, and investing decisions?

THINK CRITICALLY

22. List five types of products that you and your family have purchased. Based on the changes in price for these items over the past several years, which of the following types of inflation would apply to each?
    - disinflation
    - deflation
    - reflation
    - hyperinflation

23. How do the actions of consumers cause prices to rise? What can consumers do to prevent inflation in the goods and services they purchase?

24. How do the actions of businesses cause prices to rise? What can workers do to help prevent rising prices?

25. Productivity (which is a comparison of total output to total input) can be raised simply by lowering wages. During recessionary times, businesses freeze wages of employees, reduce the number of employees, and require some employees to work longer hours. Explain how this increases productivity.

26. Explain how the Fed's monetary policy affects consumer spending.

EXTEND YOUR LEARNING

27. Identify two items that you or your family buys regularly, such as gasoline for a car. Then, for each item, answer the questions that follow:
    a. Has the price gone up or down in the last year?
    b. How much is the price change (in dollars and cents)? What percentage increase or decrease is this amount?
    c. What effect has the price change had on your spending habits? Have you purchased more or less of that product? Have you purchased more or less of something else in order to keep buying that product?
    d. In the long run, what will you do if the price keeps rising? For example, will you find substitutes, stop using the product, or give up something else in order to be able to continue to buy this product?

28. Use the Internet to research the current rate of inflation. Then search online for current interest rates on savings accounts and certificates of deposit (CDs). How do the interest rates compare to the inflation rate? If you invest your money in the savings account or CD at the current interest rates, what will this mean in terms of its value?

THE ESSENTIAL QUESTION   Refer to The Essential Question on p. 74.
Inflation is an increase in the general level of prices for goods and services. It affects the cost of everything you buy and reduces purchasing power. As prices rise, your dollar will buy fewer products and services.

3-2 Prices and Consumer Choices

THE ESSENTIAL QUESTION   How are prices set, and what impact do consumers have on prices?

LEARNING OBJECTIVES

LO 3-2.1 Describe different methods of setting prices in a market economy.

LO 3-2.2 Explain how consumers' buying strategies affect prices in a market economy.

KEY TERMS

- normal profit, 82
- cost-recovery pricing, 83
- cost-plus pricing, 83
- markup, 83
- value-based pricing, 83
- market-based pricing, 83
- rational buying, 84
- emotional buying, 84
- impulse buying, 84
- economizing, 85
- optimizing, 85

LO 3-2.1 How Are Prices Set in a Market Economy?

In a market economy, prices are affected by a number of factors. Some factors are controlled by producers, such as their desired profit. Consumers' actions also affect prices in the marketplace. For example, if consumers are willing and able to buy a product, this will cause its price to rise. If consumer demand for a product is low, prices may fall. In some cases, the manufacturer may stop producing the product altogether.

Sellers must be careful in setting a price for their product. If the price is too high, consumers may not buy the product. They may not be able to afford the price, or they may simply think the price is too high for the value received. On the other hand, if the price is set too low, consumers may perceive the product as cheap or of low value. This will cause demand for the product to be low. Also, if the price is too low, the company may not make any profit on the sale of the product. Businesses need a normal profit in order to stay in business. A **normal profit** allows a business to survive as well as grow.

Setting the right price for a product can be tricky. Having products available at the right price is critical to business success. Companies use different methods to set prices. Sometimes more than one method is considered when setting a price. Sellers want to set a price that will support the greatest demand and be profitable.

Jnp/Shutterstock.com

Why must businesses be careful when setting prices?

normal profit a profit that allows a business to survive and grow

Cost-Recovery Pricing

In some cases, the business has invested large sums of money to develop a new product. *Research and development (R&D)* costs can be in the millions or even billions of dollars. **Cost-recovery pricing** sets the price high when a product is first introduced in order to recover the R&D costs. Because the price is high, it will invite competition, often in the form of *generics*, which are inexpensive substitutes.

Cost-Plus Pricing

Another way that sellers set prices is called **cost-plus pricing**, which involves computing the per-unit cost of producing a product and then adding a percentage of that amount, called a **markup**, to obtain the price. The markup is also called the *profit margin* or *gross profit*. Using this method ensures that the company will make a certain profit if the product sells successfully. An example of cost-plus pricing for a piece of furniture is shown below.

Item	Cost/Unit
Wood, 6 board feet, $3.96 per foot	$23.76
Labor, 2 hours at $10 per hour	20.00
Paint, varnish, nails, and glue	1.24
Indirect costs (workers' benefits, rent, insurance, depreciation, overhead, etc.)	12.00
Total cost	$57.00
Markup (40% + $57.00)	22.80
Price	$79.80

Value-Based Pricing

Using **value-based pricing**, the seller tries to determine how much consumers are willing to pay for the product. In other words, it will be sold for the highest price that the market (consumers) will bear. If consumers value the product or service, they will pay whatever price is set, within reasonable limits. This is especially true of new, high-tech, and fad items. Consumers are willing to pay high prices because there are no less-expensive choices.

Companies may do market research to determine what the demand for a product will be. They also want to learn how much consumers will be willing to pay for the product. Surveys and questionnaires are popular ways that companies learn about consumers' wants and needs.

Market-Based Pricing

With **market-based pricing**, the price is set to be competitive with prices of similar products currently being sold. If one business charges more than others do for a similar product, consumers are likely to buy from the other businesses to get the lower price. The manufacturer or retailer decides whether it can provide the product or service at that existing price and still make a profit. Market-based pricing is also known as *competition-based pricing*.

Building COMMUNICATION SKILLS

CRITICAL LISTENING

Critical listening is a skill used to solve problems. With *critical listening*, a person searches through information and forms questions to ask. Critical listening is a highly active process that involves logic as well as listening. For example, suppose you are listening to a debate about a new law that has been proposed. One side is describing its positive features and all of the reasons why you should vote in favor of it. The other side is explaining all of the bad things that will happen if the law is enacted. In order for you to decide, you must listen carefully, make sure your questions have been answered, and come to a decision that will be your vote. Critical listening requires that you understand who is proposing the law and what that group has to gain. You also need to know who is opposing the law and what that group has to lose. By practicing critical listening, you can reach an informed decision.

Try It Out

Listen to a commercial on a television program. List what you learned from the ad and the information you gained. List the questions you still have after viewing the ad. Are you convinced that the ad has given you the full and accurate information you need to make an informed buying decision?

Sellers who have a similar product to others may try to market their product as different from, or better than, the other products. This strategy is known as *product differentiation*. For example, a seller offering a new smartphone might cite the phone's screen quality, battery life, camera, or other unique features. These features are advertised in a way that makes the new phone seem more desirable than the other smartphones on the market. The seller may use these features to justify charging a higher price. However, this strategy is not always successful, as consumers may not think the features are useful or worth the higher price.

 CHECKPOINT

Name four methods that sellers use to price products.

LO 3-2.2 How Do Buying Strategies Affect Prices?

Consumers play a vital role in setting prices in a market economy. When consumers shop carefully and wisely, they help keep prices low. When consumers do not buy wisely, their actions lead to higher prices because of increased demand.

Consumers who act in their own best self-interests are engaging in rational buying. **Rational buying** is the process of selecting goods and services based on need, want, and logical choices. Sometimes consumers engage in **emotional buying**, which is the process of purchasing products based on desire rather than logic. When you are feeling sad, angry, lonely, or some other emotion, you may make unwise purchases, using your emotions rather than logic to drive the choices. **Impulse buying** happens

rational buying the process of selecting goods and services based on need, want, and logical choices

emotional buying the process of purchasing products based on desire rather than logic

impulse buying purchasing something on the spur of the moment without thinking it through or any planning

when people buy something on the spur of the moment without thinking it through or planning the purchase. You might see something in the store and grab it on impulse. Merchants display typical impulse items at key points, such as center aisles, the ends of aisles, and checkout areas. They are hoping the items will catch your eye and prompt you to buy without thinking. Emotional and impulse buying often lead to *buyer's remorse* when you later realize that you made a poor buying decision.

There are two basic strategies for rational buying of goods and services: economizing and optimizing. Consumers can use the strategy that best fits their needs for different goods and services. They should also use the strategy that best fits the state of the economy or their bank account at the time.

Economizing

Consumers are **economizing** when they are saving as much as possible and spending money only when necessary. Using this approach, consumers wait until it is necessary to buy a product. Then they buy as little as possible and at the lowest price they can find. They do not buy large quantities or more than is currently needed. They simply try to spend as little money as they can for the needed product.

Economizing has its advantages. For example, delaying the purchase of something may result in not buying it at all. Economizing can also lead to savings and better buying habits.

For some people, economizing is the only plan that allows them to meet their basic needs. For other people, economizing is a strategy used during certain times as a way to save money for later spending or investing. When economizing, people may spend little or no money on luxuries. People may also spend less on items for basic needs, such as food or clothing. Lower demand for products may lead to lower prices.

economizing saving as much as possible and spending money only when necessary

Optimizing

Another spending strategy is called optimizing. **Optimizing** is getting the highest value for the money spent. High value may come in the form of purchasing in large quantities or purchasing high-quality products or services. For example, if a product that is used often is on sale and can be stored over time, a large quantity can be purchased to take advantage of discount pricing. When items are packaged and sold in large quantities, the cost per item is usually lower.

When consumers are optimizing, demand is higher when prices are lower. Customers will buy more of a product to take advantage of lower prices. Consumers should be careful not to let optimizing lead to overspending. Shoppers may buy items they do not need simply because the items are a bargain. Those who stock up on an item may be tempted to use it more frequently because they have a large quantity of it. Then they have to buy the item more often to replenish their stock, leading to more overspending.

optimizing getting the highest value for the money spent

》》 CHECKPOINT

How is economizing different from optimizing?

KEY TERMS REVIEW

Match the terms with the definitions. Some terms may not be used.

_____ 1. Setting a price to be competitive with prices of similar products

_____ 2. Purchasing something on the spur of the moment without any planning

_____ 3. A profit that allows a business to survive and grow

_____ 4. Saving as much as possible and spending money only when necessary

_____ 5. The process of selecting goods and services based on need, want, and logical choices

_____ 6. Setting an introductory price high to recover the research and development costs

a.	cost-plus pricing
b.	cost-recovery pricing
c.	economizing
d.	emotional buying
e.	impulse buying
f.	market-based pricing
g.	markup
h.	normal profit
i.	optimizing
j.	rational buying
k.	value-based pricing

_____ 7. The process of purchasing products based on desire rather than logic

_____ 8. Setting a price based on production cost plus a markup

_____ 9. Getting the highest value for the money spent

_____ 10. The percentage amount added to production cost to obtain the price of an item

CHECK YOUR UNDERSTANDING

11. Explain why businesses need to make normal profits.

12. Why are the costs of developing a new product so high?

13. How is a market-based pricing strategy different from a value-based pricing strategy?

14. Explain why product differentiation is a needed activity by businesses?

15. What is meant by rational buying?

16. Explain why emotional and impulse buying often lead to buyer's remorse.

17. What is economizing? How does this buying strategy affect consumer demand and prices in a market economy?

18. What is optimizing? How does this buying strategy affect consumer demand and prices in a market economy?

19. How can critical listening help you make better buying decisions?

THINK CRITICALLY

20. In a market economy, both buyers and sellers must act in their own best interests. A seller is entitled to normal profits in order to remain in business and grow. Companies charge various markups, from 10 percent to 100 percent or more. What markup rate do you think represents a normal profit? Does it depend on the type of business?

21. Consumers' buying habits greatly affect prices. Explain what consumers can do to help keep prices reasonable.

22. New products, especially in the field of technology, are in high demand and are very expensive when they are first introduced. Can you give an example of a product that was initially very expensive, but the price dropped after a year or so? Why did the price drop?

23. Think of an item you would like to buy that costs more than $50 and that will require some planning, saving, and shopping. List the things you will consider before buying, such as places you will shop, features you are seeking, and the maximum price you are willing to pay. Describe where you will go and what you will do while shopping. This includes the stores (and websites) you will visit, questions you will ask, and strategies you will use to get the best deal.

EXTEND YOUR LEARNING

24. List three items that you or your family has purchased in the last year—something that cost $100 or more, something between $25 and $100, and an item under $25. Answer the following questions:

    a. How do you think the price was set for this product—using cost-recovery, cost-plus, value-based, or market-based pricing? Why?

    b. Was this item purchased as a result of economizing or optimizing?

    c. If you had to make this purchase decision again, would you choose the same item? Why or why not?

25. Many companies that have brick-and-mortar (traditional) stores also have a retail website. Working with a partner, identify a large and well-known department store. Visit the store's website and answer the questions below. Then evaluate your overall shopping experience.

    a. Is the site easy to navigate and organized so that you can quickly find the items in which you are interested?

    b. Is complete information provided for each product to help you make buying decisions?

    c. Are special prices offered for online purchases?

TEAMWORK

THE ESSENTIAL QUESTION Refer to The Essential Question on p. 82. Prices are set by businesses using either a cost-recovery, cost-plus, value-based, or market-based pricing method. Consumer buying strategies (rational buying, emotional buying, impulse buying, economizing, and optimizing) have an impact on the pricing decisions made by sellers.

THE ESSENTIAL QUESTION How is demand created, and what can you do as a consumer to maximize your purchasing power?

LEARNING OBJECTIVES

LO 3-3.1 Describe strategies used by businesses to sell goods and services, both in meeting and in creating demand.

LO 3-3.2 Discuss strategies that consumers can use before, during, and after a purchase.

KEY TERMS

- branding strategy, 89
- discount pricing, 89
- advertising, 89
- target audience, 89
- sales promotion, 89
- direct advertising, 90
- transit advertising, 91
- customer loyalty program, 91
- comparison shopping, 91

LO 3-3.1 What Are Selling Strategies?

Business owners take the risk of bringing products and services to the market. To stay in business, they must sell those products and services to customers and make a profit. Sellers must consider ways to meet demand as well as ways to create more demand for their products and services.

What makes a buyer become a loyal, repeat customer?

Tillsonburg/iStockphoto.com

Meeting Demand

Sellers use many strategies to promote products and services that customers buy to meet their needs and wants. Strategies may include having a convenient store location and convenient payment options, offering good customer service, and providing the right product at the right time and at the right price.

Convenience

One strategy that businesses use to promote sales is to make shopping convenient and pleasant for customers. Having a store location that is easy for customers to find and near other businesses makes shopping there convenient. Providing a clean, comfortable, and safe place to buy goods and services makes the shopping experience pleasant.

As another convenience, many businesses offer customers a wide range of payment options. Customers may pay using cash, checks, debit cards, and credit cards.

Having an online store also makes shopping convenient. Consumers can shop at any time of the day or night without leaving their home.

Customer Service

Businesses depend on their employees to provide good customer service as a way to promote sales. Building customer relationships requires businesses to offer the best possible service, listen to customer wants and needs, and respond appropriately. This increases the chances that shoppers will return to the store to buy again. If customers don't get what they want, they likely will not return. Satisfied customers also tell others about their experience. This word-of-mouth promotion is good for sales.

Businesses that exceed customer expectations build customer loyalty, which is important during a poor economy. A large percentage of a business's sales comes from repeat business.

The Right Product and Price

Businesses should try to make available to customers the types of products they need or want. To do this, they must listen to their customers and be aware of what their competitors are selling. Making the right products available to customers increases the chances of success for a business.

Product quality is extremely important to consumers. Many consumers only want to buy brand-name products that are well known and dependable. Stores that use a **branding strategy** carry certain brands to attract customers who are loyal to those brands.

In addition to offering the right product to customers, businesses must charge the right price. If the price is set too high, consumers may not buy the product. Many businesses offer discount pricing. With **discount pricing**, a business offers consumers the lowest everyday price possible, without having to wait for a sale. Because many consumers make purchase decisions solely on the basis of price, discount pricing is a good way to build customer loyalty. However, some consumers may perceive the discounted products to be lower in quality.

Creating Demand

To sell goods, businesses may need to create demand by using various marketing strategies, such as advertising and sales promotion. **Advertising** is informing consumers about products and encouraging them to buy. Advertisements, or *ads* for short, come in many different forms, but they all have the same purpose—to attract customers. Ads are created to reach a **target audience**, which is a specific group of people who are likely to buy a product.

A **sales promotion** is an incentive offered to customers to increase demand. Examples include coupons, free samples, and customer loyalty programs.

Newspaper and Magazine Advertising

Placing ads in newspapers and magazines is a popular way to reach large numbers of people. The ad may promote a product or a company. Newspaper ads can be used to target people in a specific community. Magazine ads can target those with specific interests, such as sports or food.

Television and Radio Advertising

Television ads are very expensive, but they can reach millions of people. They are written to appeal to a target audience who is likely to be watching a specific program. For example, some groups watch news

branding strategy carrying well-known brand names to attract customers who are loyal to those brands

discount pricing offering the lowest everyday price possible

advertising informing consumers about products and encouraging them to buy

target audience a specific group of people who are likely to buy a product

sales promotion an incentive offered to customers to increase demand

programs. Others are sure to tune in for sporting events. Companies design ads that will appeal to these target audiences. They run the ads on certain shows and at specific times.

Radio stations offer various formats, from news/talk to classical music, to rock and country music. This allows businesses to target their ads to customers with specific interests. Radio ads often involve appeals to emotions. They may use catchy slogans or jingles.

Internet Advertising

More businesses today are using the Internet to promote their products or services. The Internet's vast reach allows businesses to communicate with a large number of people. Many types of advertising can be found on the Internet.

Display advertising uses text, pictures, and animation to grab the user's attention. Such advertisements often invite people to click on a link for more information. Two types of display advertising are banner ads and pop-up ads. *Banner ads* span the top, bottom, or sides of a web page. *Pop-up ads* open new windows and "pop" onto the screen in front of the web page the user is viewing.

Another way that businesses advertise is through *social media marketing*. Many businesses use social media websites, such as Facebook and Twitter, to post frequent updates and provide special offers for their products.

Some sellers send ads in the form of emails to encourage customers to buy. These ads feature pictures and prices of products, special sales events, and discounts. As a customer, you can sign up to receive these emails and are usually able to *opt out*, or unsubscribe, if desired.

Many online retailers customize ads to shoppers who have visited their website. These businesses track a user's visits using *cookies*, which are files created by the website that store information about the web visitor on his or her computer. They enable the website to recognize the shopper in the future. If you have made a previous purchase on the re-tailer's site, it is recorded in the cookie file. Then the next time you visit the site, you may be shown special offers on products tailored to your interests based on previous purchases.

Outdoor Advertising

Some businesses direct their advertising to the masses instead of to a specifically targeted audience. These businesses consider all of the consumers in a general area as potential customers. Billboards and signs may be posted along highways or at store entrances. Local retailers, service businesses, entertainment venues, hotels, and restaurants commonly use outdoor advertising.

Direct Advertising

direct advertising distribution of product information directly to consumers

Direct advertising distributes information about a product directly to consumers. It can include *direct mail*, such as fliers, catalogs, brochures, and circulars sent to target consumers. Another form of direct advertising is *direct sales*, whereby a salesperson goes door to door to show customers a product. One type of direct sales is *party plan marketing*, which is a social event where a host offers products for sale to a group of friends. *Telemarketing* is another type of direct selling in which salespeople call consumers to market a product or service.

Transit Advertising

Transit advertising consists of ads placed on modes of public transportation or in public transportation areas. You may see transit advertising on the sides of buses, trains, and taxis and in train, bus, and subway platforms.

transit advertising ads placed on modes of public transportation or in public transportation areas

Sales Promotions

Most businesses today use some form of sales promotion to entice customers to buy a product. *Coupons* offer instantly redeemable savings on specific products. Some businesses give out free samples of a product to encourage consumers to use it and make additional purchases. Many businesses today have some form of a customer loyalty program. A **customer loyalty program** is designed to encourage repeat business by providing special discounts and other incentives. For example, a *rewards feature* in a customer loyalty program may give customers cash back for repeat purchases. Or it may provide free services, coupons, gift cards, or other forms of payback.

customer loyalty program a program designed to encourage repeat business by providing special discounts and other incentives

CHECKPOINT

How do businesses meet consumer demand?

LO 3-3.2 What Are Buying Strategies?

Sellers have strategies to encourage you to buy. As a consumer, you should have strategies to help you maximize your purchasing power. Some ideas to help you in your role as consumer are given in the following sections.

Before You Shop

Prior to shopping, there are some things you should do to help make the most of your shopping experience.

- *Comparison shop.* **Comparison shopping** involves checking prices, brands, and quality among several sellers to make sure you are getting the best deal. The Internet is a good resource for comparison shopping. By using comparison-shopping sites, you can learn about product prices and features.

comparison shopping checking prices, brands, and quality among several sellers to make sure you are getting the best deal

Looking Ahead

In the near future, you will likely be in the market for a car. Edmunds.com is a website that allows shoppers to quickly compare prices and features of similar vehicles. Access the website and choose a type of vehicle that interests you. Add as many options as you like to each vehicle. Compare the features and prices. What is the invoice price of each vehicle? What is the true market value for each vehicle after options are added? Which vehicle do you think is the best deal? Why?

TIME MANAGEMENT

Why do some people achieve more in a day than others? The answer lies in time management. *Time management* refers to the way that you organize and plan your time for specific activities. Using time-management strategies such as the following can help you be more productive in school, work, and personal activities.

- Be aware of how you are using your time. This is the first step toward managing your activities in a way that makes the best use of your time.
- Identify *peak performance times*, when you are most productive during the day, and *weak performance times*, when you are the least productive. Schedule activities that involve decision making at peak performance times.
- Use a daily or weekly planner to keep track of important dates and times.
- Keep a to-do list; mark off items as they are completed.

- Prioritize your activities so you get the important ones done first.
- Break large projects or tasks into smaller parts, and plan time for completing each part.
- Save some time for doing things you enjoy.
- Do not rush or be pressured for time when making important decisions, such as major purchasing decisions.

Try It Out

Practice your time-management skills by preparing a shopping list for things you would like to buy in the next month. Prioritize the list, putting the items in order of importance. Comparison shop on the Internet. List three locations where you can buy the products on your list, along with the prices at each location. Describe how time management can improve your shopping experiences.

- *Plan your purchases*. Prepare a shopping list of the things you need. Decide ahead of time what you will buy and approximately how much you will spend. Also, plan how you will pay for the items. Planning ahead will help you avoid overspending or buying items that you do not need.
- *Pick the best time to shop*. Shopping can be a fatiguing and stressful activity if you don't shop at a time that works well for you. Do not plan to go shopping when you are experiencing an extreme emotional state. Being hungry, sad, angry, frustrated, or even especially happy can affect your state of mind and your choices.
- *Research businesses*. Use your local Better Business Bureau to be sure you are shopping at a qualified and reputable business. If shopping online, research websites before you place an order.

While You Shop

The following strategies should be used while you shop:

- *Avoid impulse buying*. Take a list with you when you shop, and buy only what is on the list. Avoid products on display that attract your attention but are unnecessary. Do not make last-minute purchases at the checkout line, and do not buy something just because it's on sale.
- *Read labels*. Know ingredients and materials and what they mean. For example, a shirt that is 100 percent cotton will probably shrink.

▶ **FIGURE 3-3.1   Computing Unit prices**

The formula for computing unit prices is:

Price of the item ÷ Number of units per measure

The unit costs of a 15-ounce box of cereal that sells for $1.89 and a 24-ounce box of cereal that sells for $2.59 are computed as follows:

$1.89 ÷ 15 ounces = $0.126 per ounce

$2.59 ÷ 24 ounces = $0.108 per ounce

The 24-ounce container is the better buy, if you will use all 24 ounces.

- *Understand sale terminology.* *Sale* means that goods are offered for sale, but not necessarily at a reduced price. *Clearance* means the business wants to clear out the advertised merchandise, but again, it may not be at a reduced price. *Liquidation* means the business wants to sell everything right away, but not necessarily at reduced prices.
- *Read contracts.* If you are making a purchase that requires a contract, be sure to read and understand it before you sign it.
- *Compute unit prices.* *Unit pricing* is the cost for one unit of an item sold in packages of more than one unit. The lowest unit price for products of comparable quality is the best buy. Figure 3-3.1 shows how to compute unit prices.
- *Compute total cost.* Check the total cost of a product, including supplementary items (such as batteries), shipping and handling charges, finance charges, and other add-ons.

After You Buy

There are also things shoppers must do after they make their purchases.

- *Keep receipts and warranties.* For all major purchases, keep receipts and warranties for possible use later. A *warranty* is a statement guaranteeing the quality and performance of a product or service. Print out and keep warranty statements and sales receipts from online purchases as well.
- *Evaluate your purchase.* Are you satisfied with the product? Is it what you had intended to buy? Are you satisfied with the service you were given? Answering these questions will help you make better decisions in the future.
- *Be loyal.* Shop at businesses that have good reputations and have served you well. Tell others when you have a good experience. Likewise, when you are treated unfairly, share those experiences with others.

≫ CHECKPOINT

Why is comparison shopping important?

3-3 Lesson Assessment

KEY TERMS REVIEW

Match the terms with the definitions. Some terms may not be used.

_____ 1. The distribution of product information directly to consumers

_____ 2. Offering consumers the lowest everyday price possible

_____ 3. A program designed to encourage repeat business by providing special discounts and other incentives

_____ 4. Ads placed on modes of public transportation or in public transportation areas

_____ 5. Informing consumers about products and encouraging them to buy

a.	advertising
b.	branding strategy
c.	comparison shopping
d.	customer loyalty program
e.	direct advertising
f.	discount pricing
g.	sales promotion
h.	target audience
i.	transit advertising

_____ 6. Checking prices, brands, and quality among several sellers to make sure you are getting the best deal

_____ 7. Carrying well-known brand names to attract customers who are loyal to those brands

_____ 8. A specific group of people who are likely to buy a product

CHECK YOUR UNDERSTANDING

9. List three ways that businesses meet customer needs and wants, other than with pricing strategies.

10. Explain the concept of discount pricing as a selling strategy.

11. Explain the concept of a target audience. Provide one example.

12. List three types of advertising that sellers can use to help create demand for a product.

13. List three ways that businesses use the Internet to encourage new sales.

14. Explain how you can use the Internet to enhance your buying skills.

15. List things you can do before you shop to improve your purchasing power.

16. List things you can do while shopping to make better purchase decisions.

17. Discuss things you can do after a purchase to help ensure a better shopping experience now and in the future.

18. How can using effective time-management strategies lead to better buying decisions?

THINK CRITICALLY

19. Companies work hard to earn your business and meet your needs. What is your favorite place to shop? Make a list of how the business meets your needs in the following areas: (a) convenience, (b) customer service, and (c) pricing or branding. Do you think this is part of the business's selling strategy? Explain your answer.

20. Advertising is designed to create demand. How many times have you purchased something because of a TV ad, a newspaper ad, a flier, or some other source? To what needs were the ads appealing? Were you satisfied with your purchase? If you had to do it over again, would you still buy the product or service?

21. There are numerous buying strategies that consumers can use to maximize their purchasing power. Describe what you do before, during, and after you go shopping. For example, do you make a list? Do you stick to the list, or are you easily persuaded by strategic in-store displays and sales promotions? Do you evaluate your purchases? Are there things you would like to change about your personal buying habits? Explain.

EXTEND YOUR LEARNING

22. Goods and services are promoted through advertising. Choose one of the methods of advertising below. Then describe the target audience and how the ads try to reach the target audience.

    a. Watch television for one-half hour. During that period, write down every ad (commercial) you watch. For each ad, describe the group of people you think the ad is targeting. Tell whether the appeal is rational (meets real needs) or emotional (creates a desire for a product). Then tell whether you think the ad is effective and explain why.

    b. Listen to a local radio station for one hour. Write down every commercial you hear. For each ad, describe the people you think are its target audience. Tell whether the appeal is rational or emotional. Then tell whether you think the ad is effective and explain why.

    c. Look through a daily newspaper or magazine. Make a list of the types of advertisements you find. For each type of ad, describe the target audience. Tell whether the appeal is rational or emotional. Then tell whether you think the ad is effective and explain why.

THE ESSENTIAL QUESTION   Refer to The Essential Question on p. 88. Demand is created with various forms of advertising and sales promotion. There are strategies that you can undertake before, during, and after shopping that will help you maximize your purchasing power, such as doing comparison shopping, avoiding impulse buying, and keeping receipts.

THE ESSENTIAL QUESTION   What consumer laws protect you, and how can you protect yourself from consumer fraud?

LEARNING OBJECTIVES

LO 3-4.1   Describe your rights as provided by major consumer protection laws, and list sources of consumer assistance if you have a complaint.

LO 3-4.2   Describe common deceptive practices that defraud consumers.

LO 3-4.3   Discuss your responsibilities as a consumer to protect yourself from consumer fraud.

KEY TERMS

- time-shifting, 97
- space-shifting, 97
- warning label, 99
- deception, 102
- bait and switch, 102
- low-balling, 102
- pyramid scheme, 102
- Ponzi scheme, 103
- pigeon drop, 103
- infomercial, 104

LO 3-4.1 What Are Consumer Rights?

For many years, the consumer's role in the marketplace was viewed as being "buyer beware." Consumers had little protection against unfair practices. However, that position has changed over time. As abuses have become apparent, new rights and protections for consumers have been established.

Laws Defining Consumer Rights

A *bill of rights* is a document containing a formal statement of rights for citizens. The purpose is to protect those rights against infringement from public officials, private citizens, and businesses.

What are the basic provisions of the Consumer Bill of Rights?

Consumer Bill of Rights

One of the most important steps in the direction of consumer protection was the adoption of the *Consumer Bill of Rights* in 1962. It grants consumers the following four basic rights:

1. *The right to safety*: Consumers are protected from unsafe products.
2. *The right to be informed*: Consumers will be given the facts needed to make intelligent and informed product choices.
3. *The right to choose*: Consumers will have access to a variety of quality products and services at competitive prices.
4. *The right to be heard*: Consumers can voice complaints and concerns about a product or service.

Dave Clark Digital Photo/Shutterstock.com

In 1985, the bill was expanded to include four more consumer rights for a total of eight basic rights:

5. *The right to satisfaction of basic needs*: Consumers must have access to basic, essential goods and services, including adequate food, clothing, shelter, health care, and education.
6. *The right to redress*: Consumers must receive fair settlement (such as compensation) for valid claims involving misrepresentation, inferior products, or unsatisfactory services.
7. *The right to consumer education*: Consumers will have access to programs and information that help them make better marketplace decisions.
8. *The right to a healthy environment*: Consumers have the right to live and work in a clean, safe, and healthy environment.

Airline Passenger Rights

In 1999, it became apparent that airline passengers were being treated unfairly. Thus, the *Airline Passenger Bill of Rights Act* was introduced. In 2009 and 2011, the U.S. Department of Transportation (DOT) expanded these rights by adding several more rules. Basic protection for airline passengers now includes the following:

- *Reservations*. Once you have a confirmed reservation, you will be provided a seat on the flight, even if there is no record of your reservation in the airline's computer system.
- *Refunds*. When a ticket is cancelled, you will be issued a refund. If you cancel a ticket for a "nonrefundable fare," you may be able to apply the fare toward a future flight.
- *Delays and cancellations*. Airlines must notify consumers of delays of over 30 minutes as well as cancellations.
- *Bumped flights*. Compensation is required if you are "bumped," either voluntarily or involuntarily, from a flight that is oversold.
- *Extended tarmac delays*. U.S. airlines operating domestic flights cannot permit an aircraft to remain on the tarmac for more than three hours, with exceptions for safety, security, and air traffic control-related reasons.
- *Fee disclosures*. Airlines must disclose all potential fees on their websites, including but not limited to fees for baggage, meals, and canceling or changing reservations.

Consumer Technology Bill of Rights

As a result of technology and its widespread use by consumers, a *Consumer Technology Bill of Rights* was introduced by Congress in 2002. Provisions include the following:

- *Time-shifting*. Consumers have the right to time-shift content that they have legally acquired. Consumers are **time-shifting** when they record video or audio for later viewing or listening. For example, you can record a TV show and watch it later.
- *Space-shifting*. Consumers have the right to use content that they have legally acquired in different places, as long as the use is personal and noncommercial. **Space-shifting** allows media, such as music or movies, stored on one device to be accessed from another place through another device. For example, you can copy the

time-shifting recording video or audio for later viewing or listening

space-shifting storing media, such as music or movies, on one device to be accessed from another place through another device

contents of a CD to a portable music player so that you can listen to it while jogging.

- *Backup copies.* Consumers have the right to make backup copies of purchased CDs, DVDs, and other media in case the original copy is destroyed.
- *Platform of choice.* Consumers have the right to use legally acquired content on whatever device they choose. For example, you can listen to music on your iPod and view DVDs on your HP notebook.
- *Translation.* Consumers have the right to translate legally acquired content into a format that makes it more usable to them. For example, a visually challenged person can modify an electronic book so that it can be read out loud.

Patients' Bill of Rights

Between 1998 and 2001, abuses in managed care and other related medical services led to the following rights:

- *Informed disclosure.* Patients have the right to receive accurate, easily understood information in order to make informed health care decisions.
- *Choice of providers.* Patients have the right to choose their own doctors and other health care providers.
- *Access to emergency services.* Patients have the right to access emergency health care services whenever and wherever the need arises. The health plan insurer must pay for the cost of those services and cannot insist that the patient use a provider on its restricted list.
- *Treatment decisions.* Patients have the right to fully participate in all decisions related to their health care. Patients who are unable to fully participate in these decisions have the right to be represented by parents, guardians, or family members.
- *Respect and nondiscrimination.* Patients have the right to considerate, respectful care from all health care providers.
- *Confidentiality.* Patients have the right to confidentiality regarding their health care information. Patients also have the right to review and copy their own medical records.
- *Complaints and appeals.* Patients have the right to a fair, fast, and objective review of any complaint they have against health care providers.

Consumer Protection Laws

Over the years, Congress has passed many laws to protect consumers from unsafe products and unfair or deceptive business practices. These laws help ensure that consumers get quality goods and services for their money.

Food, Drug, and Cosmetic Act

The *Food, Drug, and Cosmetic Act* of 1938 requires that foods be safe, pure, and wholesome; that drugs and medical devices be safe and effective; and that cosmetics be safe for human use. The law also requires truthful labeling on these products, including the name and address of the manufacturer. In addition, the law mandates that the U.S. Food and Drug Administration (FDA) approves drugs before they can be sold.

Hazardous Substances Act

The *Hazardous Substances Act* of 1960 requires that warning labels appear on all household products that are potentially dangerous to consumers. The purpose of the warning labels is to help consumers safely store and use these products and to provide information about first-aid steps to take if an accident happens. When product defects are unacceptably dangerous, *recalls* are required, meaning the product is returned to the manufacturer for refund or repair.

How can consumers be sure the products they buy are safe?

Kefauver-Harris Drug Amendment

The *Kefauver-Harris Drug Amendment* of 1962 requires drug manufacturers to test drugs for safety and effectiveness before they are sold to consumers. In addition, the amendment requires drug advertising to disclose accurate information about potential side effects of medications. This law also allows the sale of generic drugs. *Generic drugs* are medications with the same composition as the equivalent brand-name drugs, but they are generally less expensive.

Cigarette Labeling and Advertising Act

The *Cigarette Labeling and Advertising Act* of 1965 requires tobacco companies to place a warning label on cigarette packaging regarding the health hazards of smoking. A **warning label** contains information advising consumers of product risks and safety issues.

warning label information on products advising consumers of risks and safety issues

National Traffic and Motor Vehicle Safety Act

The *National Traffic and Motor Vehicle Safety Act* of 1966 established national safety standards for automobiles. The National Highway Traffic Safety Administration enforces provisions of the act. Its responsibilities include increasing public awareness of the need for safety devices, testing for safety, and inspecting vehicles for proper safety equipment.

Care Labeling Rule

The *Care Labeling Rule* of 1971 requires that clothing and fabrics be labeled permanently with laundering and care instructions. *Care labels* give instructions for cleaning, wash and dry temperatures, and other care needed to preserve the product. The labels must stay attached and easy to read for the life of the garment.

Family Educational Rights and Privacy Act

The *Family Educational Rights and Privacy Act (FERPA)* of 1974 is a federal law that protects the privacy of student education records. Information may not be released without the consent of parents or students 18 years of age or older. To protect students from identity theft, Social Security numbers may not be used as student ID numbers.

Yossi Manor/Shutterstock.com

Do you think food labels are helpful? Why or why not?

Nutrition Labeling and Education Act

The *Nutrition Labeling and Education Act* of 1990 requires that all packaged food contain a "Nutrition Facts" label that includes specific information about key vitamins and minerals as well as nutrients (fat, saturated fat, sodium, and cholesterol). The act also developed guidelines regarding the use of nutritional claims. Terms such as "low fat" or "high fiber" can be used only if the foods have met certain criteria by the FDA. The act also requires restaurants to comply with health claims made on signs and menus by making nutritional information available upon request.

Health Insurance Portability and Accountability Act

The *Health Insurance Portability and Accountability Act (HIPAA)* of 1996 protects your health and billing information, including information stored on a computer network, by limiting who can have access to it. Consumers are allowed to have a copy of their health records, have corrections made, know how information is being used, and decide whether to give permission to share the information. The act also states that Social Security numbers cannot be used as a personal identifier for patients.

Sources of Consumer Protection

When you need assistance with a consumer problem, numerous organizations are available to help you. These organizations are found at the federal, state, and local levels and also include private organizations.

Federal Agencies

Many federal government agencies provide information of interest to consumers. Some of these agencies handle consumer complaints, and others direct complaints to agencies or sources that address consumer issues.

- *U.S. Department of Agriculture (USDA)*. The USDA is responsible for developing and executing federal government policy on farming, agriculture, forestry, and food. It works to provide a safe, sufficient, and nutritious food supply for the American people. The USDA Center for Nutrition Policy and Promotion provides dietary and nutrition guidance for consumers.
- *Food and Drug Administration (FDA)*. The FDA enforces laws and regulations preventing distribution of mislabeled foods, drugs, cosmetics, and medical devices. It also requires testing and approval of all new drugs; provides standards and guidelines for poisonous substances; investigates complaints; and conducts research and issues reports, guidelines, and warnings to consumers about unsafe products.
- *Consumer Product Safety Commission (CPSC)*. The CPSC protects consumers from risk of injury or death from potentially hazardous consumer products. It develops and enforces standards for consumer products, bans products that are dangerous, arranges recalls, and researches potential product hazards.

- *Federal Communications Commission (FCC).* The FCC regulates interstate and international communications by radio, television, wire, satellite, and cable. The FCC presides over legal hearings pertaining to matters involving communications.
- *Federal Trade Commission (FTC).* The FTC regulates unfair methods of competition, false or deceptive advertising, deceptive product labeling, and concealment of the true costs of credit. The FTC is also the federal clearinghouse for complaints of identity theft.
- *Federal Aviation Administration (FAA).* The FAA controls air traffic and certifies aircraft, airports, pilots, and other aviation workers. It also writes and enforces air safety regulations.
- *Securities and Exchange Commission (SEC).* The SEC protects investors and oversees the securities (stocks and bonds) markets. It requires companies to disclose certain financial and other information so that investors can make informed decisions about investment options. The SEC also investigates the mishandling of investments by securities professionals.

State and Local Assistance

Most states have a consumer protection agency or a state attorney general's office that handles consumer complaints. Many county and city governments also have consumer protection offices. Consumer leagues and public-interest research groups are also active at the state and local levels. They have websites and publish informational newsletters, pamphlets, and handbooks on current consumer issues.

Private Organizations

There are many private organizations that consumers can access when they need to get information or file complaints.

- *Better Business Bureau (BBB).* The BBB provides free online reports on millions of businesses to help consumers make more informed decisions. Consumers who are dissatisfied with a business transaction can file a complaint with the BBB. The BBB then acts as an intermediary in an attempt to resolve the dispute in a quick and fair manner. Consumers can also view complaints filed against businesses by other consumers.
- *National Consumers League (NCL).* The NCL is the nation's oldest nonprofit consumer organization. It represents consumers on marketplace and workplace issues. It also operates the Fraud.org website, which provides consumers with free information on how to avoid becoming victims of fraud and identity theft.
- *Consumers Union.* Consumers Union is a nonprofit organization best known as the publisher of *Consumer Reports,* a monthly magazine that publishes reviews, comparisons, and ratings of consumer products and services.

Public Officials

National, state, and locally elected officials are also available to you. You can visit them in person, call them, or send an email or a letter. Most public officials have websites where constituents can find contact information. Consumer issues are of interest to them, because these officials represent voters. In some cases, they will investigate and provide direct assistance to consumers. Your voiced concerns may result in new laws and ensure government enforcement of existing ones.

 CHECKPOINT

What consumer protection law has been passed to protect consumers in the area of health care? List two provisions of this law.

LO 3-4.2 How Are Consumers Defrauded?

The marketplace is full of deceptive and misleading information and unfair practices. **Deception** occurs when false or misleading claims are made about the quality, price, or purpose of a particular product. In many cases, little can be done once the consumer has been fooled into making a purchase. To avoid this, it is important to be aware of unfair practices and schemes.

Bait and Switch

deception false or misleading claims made about the quality, price, or purpose of a particular product

Bait and switch is an illegal sales technique in which a business advertises a product with the intent of persuading consumers to buy a more expensive product. The "bait" is the advertised product that draws customers into the store. When they arrive to purchase the product, the salesperson will try to "switch" their interest to a more expensive product, sometimes by telling the customer that the advertised product is sold out.

bait and switch an illegal sales technique in which a business advertises a product with the intent of persuading consumers to buy a more expensive product

Fake Sale

A common consumer fraud is the *fake sale*, which occurs when a business advertises a big sale but keeps the items at regular price. The business may alter the price tags to make them look like there has been a price reduction when there actually is none.

Low-Balling

Repair shops sometimes use a deceptive practice known as low-balling. **Low-balling** is a technique whereby a company advertises a product or service at a low price to lure in customers and then attempts to persuade them that they need additional products or services. For example, a repair shop may offer a discount on brake replacements. But when the mechanic inspects the brakes, he finds several other "necessary" repairs. Customers may wind up paying for a front-end alignment, wheel balancing, or other repairs that are not really as urgent as they are led to believe.

low-balling a technique whereby a company advertises a product or service at a low price to lure in customers and then attempts to persuade them that they need additional products or services

Pyramid Scheme

A **pyramid scheme** is an illegal, multilevel marketing gimmick that promises members (distributors) commissions from their own sales as well as from the sales of other members they recruit. A cash investment is often required to become a distributor. The pyramid consists of managers at the top and many middle and lower distributors who arrange

pyramid scheme an illegal, multilevel marketing gimmick that promises members commissions from their own sales as well as from the sales of other members they recruit

parties where they sell products and recruit new distributors. The managers at the top make big profits by selling the products to the distributors below them in the pyramid—not to the general public. However, most of the lower-level distributors never make a profit or recover their initial investment and are unable to find new members to recruit.

Ponzi Scheme

A **Ponzi scheme** is a fraudulent investment operation in which money collected from new investors is used to pay off earlier investors. Investors give money to an "expert" financial adviser who promises very high returns. For a while, the fraudster maintains the appearance of a legitimate business and pays dividends to the victims. This helps lure in new investors. But actually, the dividends are being paid with money from new investors. The scheme works well as long as new investments are incoming. It falls apart when the "expert" disappears with the money, new investments are slow, investors make withdrawals, or auditors discover problems with the financial records of the investment firm. Although the "expert" often receives a prison term, the investors suffer financial losses because their money usually cannot be recovered.

Ponzi scheme a fraudulent investment operation in which money collected from new investors is used to pay off earlier investors

Pigeon Drop

A scam in which a con artist convinces people to give up their money or personal information in return for a share of a larger sum of money is called a **pigeon drop**. The "pigeon" is the unsuspecting consumer. Con artists often target trusting people who have a source of money, such as senior citizens. In one of the most common pigeon drop scams, a con artist approaches a victim claiming to have found a large sum of money and offering to split it. The con artist sets up a meeting to discuss dividing up the money. In the meantime, the con artist asks the victim to put up some of his or her own money as collateral to prove that he or she is trustworthy. Later, when the victim arrives at the meeting spot, the con artist is nowhere to be found. In another pigeon drop scam that commonly originates online, a con artist convinces victims to use their checking account to assist in the transfer of a large international deposit in return for a portion of the money. The victims give out their checking account information, which is used by the con artist to clean out the account.

pigeon drop a scam in which a con artist convinces people to give up their money or personal information in return for a share of a larger sum of money

Fraudulent Representation

Fraudulent telemarketers or door-to-door solicitors who claim to represent well-known companies or charities are another type of swindle. Consumers may end up buying worthless or unusable products or donating money to a fictitious charity. Before giving money to solicitors, check to verify their identity. Ask them to show official documentation regarding the organization and call to verify that it is real. Investigate charities online through the BBB's Wise Giving Alliance.

Health and Medical Product Fraud

A common type of swindle involves deceptive advertising for expensive "miracle" pills, creams, or other products to enhance the consumer's health and beauty. Deceptive health and medical advertisements carry fake endorsements and pictures of people who have had success using the product. Magazines, newspapers, websites, emails, and flashy tabloids often carry these types of advertisements. Many times, the product proves to be totally ineffective.

Infomercial

infomercial a lengthy paid TV advertisement that includes testimonials and product demonstrations

An **infomercial** is a lengthy paid TV advertisement that includes testimonials and product demonstrations. These advertisements generally last 15 to 30 minutes. Fitness and weight loss, hair growth, cosmetics, and kitchen gadgets are common subjects of infomercials. Some of the product claims are genuine, but many do not deliver on the promises made. Infomercials often contain gimmicks such as an initial shipment for free or at a reduced price. But in accepting the offer, you may have signed up for some other hidden commitment, such as regular monthly shipments.

>> **CHECKPOINT**

How is a Ponzi scheme similar to a pyramid scheme?

LO 3-4.3 How Can Consumers Protect Themselves from Fraud?

Being a responsible consumer means looking out for yourself to avoid making a bad decision. Prevention is your best protection. To protect yourself, be alert to the warning signs of a scam. Educate yourself on products and prices, and seek redress when necessary.

Identify Deceptive Practices

When you hear unrealistic claims, be suspicious. Watch for warning signals in claims or offers made through advertising and by salespeople. Figure 3-4.1 lists common warning signals of possible fraud and deception.

▶ FIGURE 3-4.1 **Warning Signs of Fraud**

Watch out when you hear this:
• You can get something for nothing.
• You can buy a high-quality product for an incredibly low price.
• To receive a prize or "free" product or service, you must supply your credit card or checking account number or pay a high shipping fee.
• You will receive a free gift if you act now.
• You or your home has been specially selected.
• You can attend a demonstration with no obligation to buy.
• If you don't decide right now, you will lose the opportunity.

Shop Online Safely

With online shopping, consumers have the convenience of buying products without leaving their home. Many businesses now have websites. However, Internet shopping has some dangers. Here are some tips to follow when shopping online:

- *Verify website security.* If you're going to shop online, limit yourself to secure websites. The URL of a secure website typically starts with https:// rather than http://. The "s" stands for "secure." Secure websites encrypt data, such as credit card numbers, so that no one else can read them except the sender and receiver. Secure websites may also have a small lock icon in the address bar or somewhere in the window of the browser.
- *Shop at sites you trust.* Research the website before you buy. Try to use sites that you have used before or that are recommended by friends and family.
- *Read the website's privacy policy.* Legitimate online merchants clearly state their privacy policy, explaining how they use the information that you provide and how they protect your privacy. If the policy is not posted, do not trust the site.
- *Use safe payment methods.* The safest way to shop on the Internet is with a credit card or a prepaid gift card on a secure site. If something goes wrong, you can protest the charge through your credit card company. With a prepaid gift card, you do not have to supply personal information.
- *Share only the essentials when you order.* Never provide a Social Security number or other personal information not relevant to the purchase.
- *Know shipping and return policies.* Check the website for cancellation and return policies.
- *Print and keep the confirmation order.* Print at least one copy of what you have ordered as well as the page showing the company name, address, phone number, and legal terms.
- *Use common sense.* If an offer seems too good to be true, it probably is!

Stay Informed

You are responsible for educating yourself about products and services before you buy. To protect yourself, actively seek consumer information in the following ways:

- Use publications such as *Consumer Reports* and consumer review websites to learn about products and services.
- Analyze advertisements before buying to help determine how the product will meet your needs. Be wary of emotional appeals that create a demand for something you don't need.
- Ask questions so that you can fully understand a product and its features. Then follow through to verify the claims made.
- Check consumer protection agency websites to stay informed about the latest consumer scams. Also, report any fraudulent practices that you discover to help keep others informed.

Seek Redress

When you have a complaint or need to solve a problem, you have the right to seek *redress,* or a remedy to the problem. Most businesses will work with you to resolve a problem. Using good communication skills can help you resolve complaints quickly. In addition, follow the steps listed below:

When should you seek legal recourse as a way to resolve a problem?

1. *Take the product back to the store where you bought it.* Calmly explain the problem to the salesperson and provide evidence. If necessary, talk to the manager. If you bought the item online, talk to a customer service representative on the phone. Explain the specifics about the problem, and have copies of relevant information, such as sales receipts and warranties, to support your position.

2. *Stay firm, but not angry.* State that you are dissatisfied and explain why. Ask for the type of redress that you want (refund, replacement, or repair). Be reasonable.

3. *Put your complaint in writing.* If you are not satisfied with the manager's remedy, put your complaint in writing to the store's headquarters or owner. If you still are not satisfied, write to the manufacturer or distributor of the product and state your complaint. Again, be specific about what you want. Be prepared to send copies of evidence that will support your position, including any previous correspondence.

4. *File a complaint with consumer protection agencies.* If you are still dissatisfied with the result, file a complaint with the appropriate consumer protection agency. There may be more than one agency that can assist you. Provide the agency with a full description and copies of your documentation.

5. *As a last resort, seek legal recourse.* Attorneys' fees are expensive, so it is better to try to resolve the issue yourself if possible. Small claims court or other legal remedies may be a less expensive choice. Know what you want and be prepared to negotiate and compromise if the remedy offered is fair.

≫ CHECKPOINT

How can you detect deceptive selling practices?

3-4 Lesson Assessment

KEY TERMS REVIEW

Match the terms with the definitions. Some terms may not be used.

____ 1. False claims about a product

____ 2. Storing media on one device to be accessed from another place through another device

____ 3. A lengthy paid TV ad that includes testimonials and product demonstrations

____ 4. Recording video or audio for later viewing or listening

____ 5. Advertising a product or service at a low price to lure in customers and then persuading them that additional products or services are needed

a. bait and switch

b. deception

c. infomercial

d. low-balling

e. pigeon drop

f. Ponzi scheme

g. pyramid scheme

h. space-shifting

i. time-shifting

j. warning label

____ 6. A fraudulent investment operation in which money collected from new investors is used to pay off earlier investors

____ 7. Advertising a product with the intent of persuading consumers to buy a more expensive product

____ 8. An illegal, multilevel marketing gimmick that promises members commissions from their own sales as well as from the sales of other members they recruit

____ 9. Information on products advising consumers of product risks and safety issues

CHECK YOUR UNDERSTANDING

10. List three important laws that define consumer rights.

11. List five consumer protection laws.

12. How do warning labels protect consumers? Give a specific example.

13. What information must be included on care labels?

14. List three federal agencies that provide consumer protection services.

15. What does the Securities and Exchange Commission (SEC) do to protect consumers?

16. List five methods of defrauding consumers.

17. Explain how infomercials can be misleading for consumers.

18. List four things you can do to protect yourself from fraud.

THINK CRITICALLY

19. If you were writing a new law to protect consumers, what would you include as part of the law?

20. Technology today gives consumers the ability to download songs and movies without paying for them. This deprives musicians and filmmakers of their rightful profit. Sales of CDs and DVDs have dropped dramatically. Do you think there should be some tighter controls on downloading, including laws that provide for criminal penalties? Why or why not?

21. All packaged food must contain a uniform "Nutrition Facts" label that contains specific information about key vitamins, minerals, and nutrients. In addition, restaurants must now make nutritional information available upon request. Why is it important for consumers to have this information?

22. The FDA lifted its advertising ban on pharmaceutical companies and allowed them to market directly to consumers. Since then, targeted ads have appeared on television, and drug sales have soared. Do you think it was a good idea to lift the ban? Why or why not?

EXTEND YOUR LEARNING

23. Copy the ingredients or contents from the labels of the following products: deodorant, breakfast cereal, and bug spray. Do any of the labels carry warnings? What types of precautions are suggested? Why is it important for consumers to be informed of product ingredients or contents?

24. Visit the website for *Consumer Reports* or obtain an issue of the magazine from your library, and answer these questions:
     a. Who publishes this magazine?
     b. Who advertises in the magazine?
     c. How are products tested and compared for safety and/or quality?
     d. Select a tested product. What three key findings about this product would influence your buying decision?

25. Assume you bought a new GPS navigation device at a store last week. It froze up while you were using it, and you were unable to reset it. Because the screen wouldn't turn off, the battery ran down and you replaced it. Now the device won't turn on again. You went back to the store for help, but the manager told you to contact the manufacturer. Because the device was part of a clearance sale, it was sold "as is." Write a letter of complaint. For purposes of this assignment, create information about the manufacturer, the receipt, and the warranty to include in your letter. Specify the redress you are seeking.

THE ESSENTIAL QUESTION   Refer to The Essential Question on p. 96. There are many bills of rights and consumer laws to protect consumers from such things as unsafe products and unfair or deceptive business practices. You can protect yourself by watching for warning signals of fraud; shopping wisely, both in store and online; staying informed; and seeking redress.

Exploring Careers in…
EDUCATION

Do you like to work with people? Are you good at explaining concepts and tasks? If the answer is "yes," a career in education might be right for you. Jobs in education involve teaching children and adults. Some workers in this field, such as a school principal, handle administrative tasks. Others, such as counselors, provide support services related to education. Child care workers provide care for children who have not yet entered school and also work with older children before and after school hours.

Jobs in education are found in public and private schools. Teachers receive the education and training to be able to help others learn. They often teach numerous subjects every day. They put in extra hours meeting with parents and grading homework and exams.

Employment Outlook

- A slower than average rate of employment growth is expected for high school teachers, but an average growth rate is expected for elementary and middle school teachers through 2022.

Job Titles

- Teacher/Instructor
- Principal
- Counselor/Adviser
- Administrator

Needed Education/Skills

- A bachelor's degree in the field you will teach is required.

- A master's degree (or higher) is needed for advancement and tenure positions.
- Excellent communication skills and the ability to work well with others is needed.

What's it like to work in … Education

Rich is a social studies teacher at one of his city's public high schools. He arrives by 7:15 A.M. each morning and prepares for his day in the classroom. His teaching day begins at 8 A.M. with a world history lesson for 24 sophomores. He then teaches two freshmen geography classes and a U.S. history class to 28 juniors before his lunch break. After lunch, he teaches an Advanced Placement (AP) world history class to seniors. This is followed by his planning period, in which he prepares lesson plans and grades papers. In addition, he coaches the swim team for two hours after school every day.

This week, Rich is preparing for parent–teacher conferences. He is expecting parents to have questions and concerns, and he will make suggestions for how they can support their children's efforts.

What About You?

Would you enjoy teaching others a subject that you know well? What subject would you be interested in teaching?

Chapter 3 Assessment

SUMMARY

3-1   Inflation is an increase in the general price levels of goods and services and is measured by the Consumer Price Index (CPI). Inflation reduces purchasing power.

Patterns in changing price levels include disinflation, deflation, reflation, and hyperinflation.

Inflation may also be categorized by its cause: demand-pull inflation and cost-push inflation. There is a direct connection between inflation and employment. Higher inflation usually means more people are employed. Inflation also affects spending, saving, and investing.

3-2   Methods of setting prices in a market economy include cost-recovery pricing, cost-plus pricing, value-based pricing, and market-based pricing.

Rational buying strategies include economizing and optimizing. When used wisely, these strategies help keep prices low. Overspending caused by emotional and impulse buying contributes to inflation.

3-3   Selling strategies used by businesses include making shopping convenient, providing good customer service, and offering products and services to meet consumers' demand. To create demand, businesses use advertising and sales promotions such as customer loyalty programs.

To maximize their purchasing power, consumers should use buying strategies before, during, and after shopping.

3-4   Laws defining consumer rights include the Consumer Bill of Rights, Airline Passenger Bill of Rights, Consumer Technology Bill of Rights, and the Patients' Bill of Rights.

Consumer protection laws are in the area of food, drugs, and cosmetics; hazardous substances; labeling and advertising; traffic and motor vehicle safety; care labeling; nutrition labeling; and privacy.

There are numerous federal agencies that may be contacted for assistance with consumer problems, including the USDA, FDA, CPSC, FCC, FTC, FAA, and SEC. State and local assistance is also available. Private organizations such as the BBB, NCL, and Consumers Union also provide assistance and/or information for consumers.

There are many forms of fraud, including bait and switch, fake sales, low-balling, pyramid schemes, Ponzi schemes, pigeon drops, fraudulent representation, health and medical product frauds, and deceptive infomercials.

Consumers can protect themselves by identifying deceptive practices; shopping smart, both in stores and online; staying informed; and seeking redress.

MAKE ACADEMIC CONNECTIONS

1. **Ethics** When a salesperson works for commissions, he or she may earn no income unless a sale is made. Sometimes, this results in pressuring customers to make purchases they do not really need or want. Some customers are unable to resist this sales strategy. (LO 3-3.1, LO 3-3.2)
   a. Have you ever bought something that you later felt you had been pressured into buying? How satisfied were you with that purchase?
   b. What will you do differently the next time you are faced with this situation?
   c. Ethically speaking, what is wrong with pressuring someone to buy when he or she is not ready or does not really need or want the item?

2. **Social Studies** Prepare a presentation to explain the role of government in consumer protection and its importance. Use visual examples to explain the benefits of governmental consumer protection. (LO 3-4.1)

3. **Communication** Write a paper declaring a bill of rights in an area that concerns you. What rights would you like to have guaranteed to you as a citizen? As you outline your rights, be specific. (LO 3-4.1)

4. **International Studies** Select another country and research its consumer protection laws. How are they different from U.S. laws? (LO 3-4.1)

5. **Research** Perform research to find a recent news story about a business that used deceptive marketing practices, such as bait and switch, fake sales, low-balling, pyramid schemes, Ponzi schemes, pigeon drops, or other gimmicks. Present the deceptive practices and the final outcomes to the class. Create a list of tips on how to avoid becoming a victim of these fraudulent practices and share it with your classmates. (LO 3-4.2)

6. **Economics** Conduct online research about how prices are set in the market economy. Explain the concept of the "invisible hand" of the market and how consumer behavior plays a significant role in what is produced, for whom, and at what price. Prepare a two-page report or a PowerPoint presentation of your findings. (LO 3-2.1)

7. **Communication** When shopping, it is important to be able to communicate your needs to the salesperson or merchant. Think of a product or service you would like to buy. Then write a script of the conversation between you and the salesperson who is trying to sell you the product or service. Be sure you describe the product or service features that will meet your needs. (LO 3-3.1)

8. **Economics** Select a commonly used product, such as gasoline, automobiles, or milk. Track the prices of this product over a 20-year period by creating a line graph. Explain price increases and decreases based on economic conditions, such as inflation and recession. (LO 3-1.1)

Do the Math

1. **Comparing unit prices can help a consumer determine which size or package of a product is the best value. To find the unit price of a product, divide the total price by the number of units.**

   a. Find the unit prices for the following items. (Round to two decimal places.)

   Product A: $3.96 for 24 ounces

   Product B: $3.69 for 12 cookies

   Product C: $25.00 for a case of 36

   Product D: $4.99 for 6 muffins

   Product E: $12.99/for 5 pounds

   b. Determine which of these items has the lowest per-unit cost and, thus, is the best buy. (Round to three decimal places.)

   Product A: $1.99 for a 6-ounce bag or $2.49 for an 8-ounce bag

   Product B: $24.00 for a box of 10 or $36.00 for a box of 15

   Product C: $6.99 for 3 pounds or $8.99 for 5 pounds

2. **A retailer bought a product for $22 and sold it for $36. What is the amount of the markup? What is the percent of markup?**

Take Action

RESEARCH AND REPORT

TEAMWORK

Working with a partner, visit the websites listed below. Then as described, write a short report based on what you learn at each website. Print a copy of each home page, and include it with your report.

a. Visit the Federal Trade Commission's website (www.ftc.gov) or USDA website (www.usda.gov). Select an article that interests you on the site. Prepare a bulleted list of the five most important points in the article.

b. Visit the Better Business Bureau's website (www.bbb.org) and look up the reliability reports on two local businesses. Write a brief summary of the kinds of information that the reports provide about the businesses.

c. Visit the National Consumer League's Fraud.org website (www.fraud.org) and answer the following questions:

   • What services are available to consumers who have complaints?

   • What is the process of filing a complaint?

After completing this project, save your reports and include them in your portfolio.

Business Plans, Inflation, and the Economy

This project is designed to help you begin thinking about your money and the economy. Let's begin with your job. The money you earn affects what you are able to purchase and save. Many people dream of being an entrepreneur or working for themselves. By doing so, you can pursue your interests, make your own decisions, set your own hours, and keep the profits. But there are risks to starting your own business. Just as there is the chance to earn a profit, there is also the possibility of losing money and going out of business. To improve your chances of success, it is important to prepare a business plan that describes your business idea and goals. It should answer questions such as the following: What will the business produce or sell? Who will be operating it? How will it be marketed? How will it be financed? Complete the *Business Plan Worksheet* to help you understand the importance of addressing these issues.

Everyone is a consumer, including employees and business owners. The United States has a market economy. Cost-push inflation, sometimes caused by competition for natural resources, affects prices in a market economy. For example, in 2015, a prolonged drought in California made water a scarce resource that had to be rationed. In some communities, the price of water rose. Rising water prices affected everything, from the agricultural economy, to the price of fresh produce, to the costs associated with doing a carwash for a school fundraiser. The statewide economic cost of the drought for 2015 was estimated to be $2.7 billion. To understand the trade-offs required when scarce resources must be shared by a community, complete the *Cost-Push Inflation Worksheet*.

In addition to a market economy, other economic systems exist throughout the world. In a command economy, the government or central authority controls most of the economic decisions. Consumers have no rights when it comes to deciding what is produced. It is the consumers' responsibility to share resources for the greater benefit of all. In a traditional economy, economic decisions are based on customs and traditions. Members of a traditional economy are responsible for producing the goods needed for survival. Some countries have a mixed economy, which contains elements of more than one type of economic system. To learn more about the various types of economic systems, complete the *Economic Systems Worksheet*.

THINK CRITICALLY

1. How can a business plan help you succeed as an entrepreneur?
2. How might cost-push inflation impact prices consumers must pay?
3. How can various economic systems affect your rights and responsibilities as a consumer?

Decision Making and Planning

Deborah Cheramie/iStockphoto.com

Unit 2 explains how to get started building a plan for financial security with solid financial decisions and planning. Chapter 4 begins with a look at how you can make good financial choices. You'll also learn about the basics of budgeting, such as the importance of preparing a personal budget. The five steps involved in personal financial planning are also discussed.

Chapter 5 discusses banking, including checking and savings accounts and fees you will face. You will learn how to write checks, make online payments, make deposits, and avoid fees. Growing your money through interest earnings is also explained.

In Chapter 6, you will learn how to assess risk and protect your income and property. Risk strategies will be introduced, including reducing, avoiding, transferring, and assuming risk. You will learn about the various types of health and property insurance coverage available to you. Ways to lower your insurance costs while maximizing your benefits are also discussed.

Financial Decisions and Planning

BartekSzewczyk/iStockphoto.com

Good money management begins with taking a careful look at your needs and wants. In this chapter, you will look at where you are now financially and prepare a personal net worth statement. You will study strategies you can use to make better financial choices. You will then explore budgeting and create a simple budget. A five-step financial planning process, which begins with setting your personal and financial goals, is presented. Finally, you will learn about various sources where you can receive good financial advice and ways in which you can protect your financial resources.

Do *This*, **Not** *That*

To make better financial decisions:

- Keep track of the money you receive and spend.
- Prepare a realistic budget and stick to it.
- Avoid expenses that are long-term commitments.
- Create a financial plan that includes goals and timelines.
- Don't fall prey to identity theft scams.

THE ESSENTIAL QUESTION How can you measure whether you are able to meet your financial needs now and in the future?

LEARNING OBJECTIVES

LO 4-1.1 Describe needs and wants, and explain how financial resources help fulfill needs and wants.

LO 4-1.2 Prepare a personal cash flow statement and a personal net worth statement.

LO 4-1.3 Apply a decision-making process to personal financial choices.

KEY TERMS

- needs, 116
- wants, 116
- financial resources, 116
- cash inflows, 117
- cash outflows, 117
- assets, 117
- liabilities, 118
- net worth, 118
- trade-off, 119
- opportunity cost, 119

LO 4-1.1 What Are Needs and Wants?

needs things needed for survival, such as food, water, clothing, shelter, and medical care

wants things people desire for reasons beyond survival and basic comfort

Every person has needs and wants. **Needs** are things you must have for survival, including food, water, clothing, shelter, and medical care. **Wants** refer to things people desire for reasons beyond survival and basic comfort. These items simply allow you to enjoy life more. Examples of wants include new cars, vacations, a large wardrobe, a big-screen TV, and so on. *Luxury items*, which are very costly, often fill emotional wants rather than physical needs.

Resources Limit Choices

financial resources money or other items of value that are used to acquire goods and services

Financial resources include money or other items of value that people can use to acquire goods and services. Although people's financial resources are limited, their wants and needs are unlimited and growing.

What basic needs are represented in this photo? Wants?

Marcio Eugenio/Shutterstock.com

Because most people do not have enough resources to meet all of their needs and wants, they must make choices.

For a person who has few resources, the choices available will also be few. This person may need to spend all of his or her resources to cover basic needs. For a person with more resources, more choices will be available. The amount of money that a person has to spend after needs are met is called *discretionary income*. People who have high discretionary income can consider buying luxury items they may want.

 CHECKPOINT

How are your wants and needs related to your financial resources?

LO 4-1.2 How Are Income and Wealth Measured?

Personal financial statements provide you with a summary of your financial situation. The personal cash flow statement measures your income. Your *wealth*, or items of value minus any debts owed against those items, can be measured using the personal net worth statement. These forms should be prepared on a regular basis to see if you are making progress toward your financial goals.

Personal Cash Flow Statement

The *personal cash flow statement* lists your cash inflows and cash outflows for a period of time. **Cash inflows** include income that you receive from your job, investments, and other sources. You can spend this amount of money without using savings. **Cash outflows** are expenses, or items for which you must spend money. Most people have regular expenses to meet. Some expenses occur on a regular basis, such as rent payments and phone bills. Others happen unexpectedly, such as the cost of replacing a blown tire. It is wise to make saving a planned expense. In order to save, you will need to spend less than you receive in income. Saving increases your wealth.

If your cash inflows exceed your cash outflows, you have a positive cash flow, or *net income*, for the period. If your cash outflows exceed your cash inflows, you have a negative cash flow, or *net loss*, for the period. Comparing monthly cash flow statements over time can help you see whether you are meeting your financial goals. As an example, the personal cash flow statement for Andrea McCall is shown in Figure 4-1.1.

cash inflows income from your job, investments, and other sources

cash outflows expenses, or items for which you must spend money

Personal Net Worth Statement

A *personal net worth statement* shows a person's net worth based on his or her assets and liabilities. **Assets** are money and items of value that you own. For certain assets, such as a car, their value is the price you could get if you sold them. Assets that grow in value are said to *appreciate*. The value of savings bonds, for example, will grow over time. The value of land or a house may also increase over time.

assets money and items of value that you own

ANDREA MCCALL
PERSONAL CASH FLOW STATEMENT
April 1–30, 20--

Cash Inflows		
Work (part-time)	$120.00	
Allowance for household chores	40.00	
Lunch money allowance	60.00	
Savings account interest	2.00	
Total cash inflows		$222.00
Cash Outflows		
Gifts	$ 20.00	
Clothes and shoes	60.00	
Loan payment to parents	20.00	
Lunches	60.00	
Entertainment/miscellaneous	40.00	
Total cash outflows		200.00
Net cash flow		$ 22.00

Other assets, such as cars and electronic items, may *depreciate*, or decrease in value. These items have temporary value that will be used up over time.

liabilities debts that you owe

Debts that you owe are called **liabilities**. The amount owed on a car loan is a liability. The difference between your assets (what you own) and liabilities (what you owe) is called **net worth**. As an example, the personal net worth statement for Jerry Lopez is shown in Figure 4-1.2.

net worth the difference between your assets and liabilities

▶ FIGURE 4-1.2 Personal Net Worth Statement

JERRY LOPEZ
PERSONAL NET WORTH STATEMENT
May 1, 20--

Assets		Liabilities	
Cash and checking account	$ 452.56	Car loan	$1,100.00
Savings account	500.00	Credit card debt	200.98
Savings bonds	300.00	**Total liabilities**	$1,300.98
Baseball card collection	100.00		
Computer, iPod, games	300.00	**Net Worth**	
Car, current value	3,000.00	Assets minus liabilities	3,351.58 ◄
Total assets	$4,652.56	**Total liabilities and**	
		net worth	$4,652.56

Net Worth

⟫⟫ CHECKPOINT

What is the purpose of a personal cash flow statement?

LO 4-1.3 How Can You Make Good Financial Choices?

Buying decisions play an important part in managing your money. Using a step-by-step decision-making process and following financial strategies can help you spend your money wisely and make smart buying decisions.

Decision-Making Process

To help you make good financial decisions, you should use a rational, step-by-step process to define your needs and compare alternatives before making a final decision. When you use a decision-making process, you can use your money in ways that will benefit you most.

Step 1 Define the Problem or Goal

Define the problem you want to solve or a goal you wish to achieve. Then look for ways to resolve it in a manner that fits your financial resources now and in the future. For example, you might need a laptop computer to do online research and to complete homework. Identify all the ways that the laptop can be used and the features it should have to meet your needs.

Step 2 Gather Information

Once you have defined the problem or goal, conduct research to gather information on all possible solutions and their costs. In this example, the solutions could include buying a new laptop, buying a used laptop, or using a computer at the school lab or local library. Each solution has different costs to consider. To purchase a new or used computer with the features you want, you may have to borrow money. To use the computer at the school lab or at a library, you should factor in the time it takes to drive to and from the campus or library and mileage (gas). Also, computer usage may be restricted to certain hours. Keep a record of all the information you gather.

Why should you use a step-by-step decision-making process when making purchase decisions?

Step 3 Compare Choices

To compare your options, list the advantages and disadvantages of each one. You may find that you have to make a **trade-off**, which involves giving up one option in exchange for another that you think is more desirable. The trade-off results in an **opportunity cost**, which is the value of your next best option—what you are giving up. Value can be measured in many ways, such as in dollars, time, convenience, enjoyment, and so forth.

Using a computer at the library would be less costly than buying a laptop. However, if you choose this option, you would have to travel to the library each time you wanted to use the computer and could use it only during the hours the library is open. Thus, the opportunity cost would be the convenience of owning your own laptop. You must decide which you value most—convenience or saving money.

trade-off giving up one option in exchange for another

opportunity cost the value of your next best option—what you are giving up

What is the difference between a trade-off and an opportunity cost?

Step 4   Make a Decision

The decision that you make should be based on careful consideration of the problem and a thorough analysis of the information you collected in your research. The best decision in any situation is the one that best meets your needs, is within your budget, and gives you the most value for your dollar investment.

Step 5   Take Action

After you make a decision, take action to carry out your chosen solution. Because you did a thorough analysis, you can be sure that you have made the best decision you could with the available information.

Step 6   Re-Evaluate Your Choice

After some time has passed, reflect on your decision. Did the option you chose resolve the problem or fill the need for which it was selected? If the answer is "no," or if your needs or goals have changed, follow the process again to make a new decision.

Financial Strategies

Financial choices you make today will affect your finances tomorrow. If you plan ahead, you will be better prepared to use your resources to meet your short-term and long-term needs and wants. Making good financial choices will help prevent worry over financial matters. Follow these strategies to make better financial choices:

- Financial choices should be forward-looking. Ask yourself how a choice will affect your future.
- Consider the *opportunity cost* each time you make a purchase. Doing so will help you decide whether the item or service selected is the best choice.

Building COMMUNICATION SKILLS

READING VOCABULARY

Reading is a basic communication skill. Much of the information you need comes in written form. You read for many reasons, such as to learn new ideas related to school, work, or personal activities. You read directions for completing a task or following a particular route. You also read stories, novels, or poems for pleasure.

Your *vocabulary* is made up of the words you know and understand how to use. Whatever your purpose in reading, improving your vocabulary will help you better understand the material you read. For example, key terms are listed in each chapter of this textbook. Learning these words will help you understand the concepts presented. Use the following strategies to add new words to your vocabulary:

- When you are reading and see a word you do not know, find the meaning in a dictionary at that time, if possible. If you cannot check the dictionary right away, make a note of the word and find it in a dictionary later.
- Try to learn the meaning of a new word from the way it is used in a sentence. Then check a dictionary to see if you are correct.

- Divide a long word into parts. If you know the meaning of one part, you may be able to guess the meaning of the entire word. Again, check a dictionary to see if that meaning is correct.
- If you find a word you do not know when reading a textbook, see if the word is defined in a glossary at the end of the book.
- Practice using new words in conversation or in writing to help you remember their meanings.

Try It Out

Read a newspaper or magazine article about money management. Highlight any words that are new to you. Did you learn their meaning from the article? If not, look up the definition for those words you still do not know. Then read the passage again. Make a list of new terms and their definitions, and then summarize what you learned from reading the article.

- When in doubt about whether to buy a particular item or service, do not make the purchase. If you are not sure of a choice, keep asking questions or doing research until you know enough to make a good decision.
- Do not make snap decisions about financial matters. *Buyer's remorse* occurs when you make a purchase and then later regret it.
- Spend less than your income each month. Set aside money for unexpected expenses.
- Be realistic when deciding which wants you can fill. Learn to enjoy the items you have rather than always wanting more items.
- Read all financial agreements. Ask questions to be sure that you understand what you are agreeing to before signing a document.
- Learn from mistakes that others have made. Listening to the experiences of others can help you avoid the same financial problems.

 **CHECKPOINT**

Why is it important to compare options before buying?

4-1 Lesson Assessment

KEY TERMS REVIEW

Match the terms with the definitions. Some terms may not be used.

_____ 1. Expenses, or items for which you must spend money

_____ 2. Income from your job, investments, and other sources

_____ 3. The act of giving up one option in exchange for another

_____ 4. The value of your next best option

_____ 5. Money or other items of value that are used to acquire goods and services

_____ 6. Money and items of value that you own

_____ 7. Things people desire for reasons beyond survival and basic comfort

_____ 8. The difference between your assets and liabilities

_____ 9. Things needed for survival, such as food, water, clothing, shelter, and medical care

a. assets

b. cash inflows

c. cash outflows

d. financial resources

e. liabilities

f. needs

g. net worth

h. opportunity cost

i. trade-off

j. wants

CHECK YOUR UNDERSTANDING

10. How are wants different from needs? What are some wants that you have?

11. How do financial resources limit a person's spending choices?

12. What is discretionary income? How does it affect your spending?

13. Explain how income is different from wealth.

14. What is the benefit of comparing monthly cash flow and net worth statements over time?

15. How is net cash flow calculated?

16. What are liabilities? Give two examples.

17. How is your net worth calculated?

18. List the six steps for making good financial decisions.

19. Besides the dollar cost, what other costs should you consider when comparing alternative solutions to a problem or goal?

20. List some strategies you can use to make good financial choices.

THINK CRITICALLY

21. Make a list of items that are often considered necessities today but were considered luxuries or were nonexistent in your great-grandparents' time. Explain how these items have increased our standard of living.

22. Financial resources include checking and savings accounts, investments, and other items that can be used to cover your needs and wants. How can you add to and grow your financial resources? Why is it important to plan to do this during your lifetime?

23. What is contained in a personal cash flow statement? What is contained in a personal net worth statement? Why is it important for individuals and families to prepare both of these statements?

24. Some assets appreciate, or increase in value over time, and some assets depreciate, or decrease in value over time. Why do some assets increase while others decrease? Which is the better investment?

25. Think of a recent purchase you have made. What was the trade-off and opportunity cost involved in this purchase? Does every purchase decision have an opportunity cost? Explain your answer.

EXTEND YOUR LEARNING

26. Identifying the income, expenses, assets, and liabilities you have now is a good place to begin planning for your financial future. Create a personal cash flow statement and a personal net worth statement following the steps below. Use spreadsheet software, if available.

    a. Review the personal cash flow statement shown in Figure 4-1.1. Create a similar document using your information.

       - List all of your cash inflows—income you receive from any source during one month.

       - List all of your cash outflows—expenses you pay during the same month.

       - Find the total of your cash inflows and cash outflows. Subtract the two total amounts to find your cash flow. Is it positive or negative?

    b. Review the personal net worth statement shown in Figure 4-1.2. Create a similar document using your information.

       - List all of your assets—money and items of value that you own.

       - List all of your liabilities—money you owe that must be repaid. (*Note:* For each, list the total owed and not the monthly payment.)

       - Find the total of your assets and liabilities. Subtract your liabilities from your assets to find your net worth. Is your net worth positive or negative?

THE ESSENTIAL QUESTION   Refer to The Essential Question on p. 116. You can measure whether you are able to meet your financial needs by preparing a personal cash flow statement and a personal net worth statement.

THE ESSENTIAL QUESTION What is the purpose of budgeting, and how are budgets prepared?

LEARNING OBJECTIVES

LO 4-2.1 Identify the purpose of a personal budget and prepare one.

LO 4-2.2 Describe recordkeeping methods used in the budgeting process.

KEY TERMS

- budget, 124
- fixed expenses, 126
- variable expenses, 126
- charitable giving, 126
- variances, 127
- manual records, 128
- electronic records, 129
- spreadsheet software, 129
- encryption, 130

LO 4-2.1 What Is Budgeting?

budget a spending and saving plan based on expected income and expenses

Budgeting is a critical part of managing your money. A **budget** is a spending and saving plan based on your expected income and expenses. The purpose of a budget is to plan how you will spend and/or save money. A budget is similar to a cash flow statement because both are used to record income (cash inflows) and expenses (cash outflows). However, a cash flow statement differs because it lists *actual* cash inflows and outflows to show how much money you have available on a certain date. A budget lists *estimated* income and expenses to help you create a financial plan. Your goal is to create a financial plan that meets your daily and future spending and saving needs based on your expected income.

Syda Productions/Shutterstock.com

How can budgeting help you plan your spending?

A budget should be designed to help meet financial goals, such as paying for current expenses and saving for the future. To create a budget, begin by looking at the amount you have available to spend or save. Then decide how much of that amount you will save and how much you will spend. You must also choose the items or services for which you plan to spend. Remember that a budget is a plan. Your actual income, saving, and spending may not be exactly as planned. You can compare your actual spending and saving to the budget to see how well you planned. This process will help you create better budgets in the future.

Steps in Preparing a Budget

To prepare a personal budget, there are four simple steps. Figure 4-2.1 shows a sample budget. Look at each part of the budget as you read the steps for preparing a budget in the following sections.

Step 1 Estimate Income

You may have many different sources of *income*. Whether the money is earned or unearned, you should keep track of where it comes from and how often it is received. Because most budgets are prepared once a year, you should calculate income for an entire year. Locate the total estimated yearly income amount, $2,664.00, in the budget in Figure 4-2.1.

You may receive income weekly, monthly, yearly, or on some other schedule. No matter when the income is received, it can be accounted for in terms of a monthly or yearly budget. If you receive income weekly, multiply the weekly amount by 4 to calculate how much that is per month. For example, $10 received per week would be $40 a month. (Rounding is okay as long as your total yearly amount is accurate.) If you receive income once a month, you can multiply it by 12 to get yearly income. When you look at the big picture—how much money comes in and goes out during an entire year—it may change the way you think about money.

Step 2 Plan Savings

Pay yourself first—put money into savings before you consider other expenses. If you plan what you want to spend first, you may have no money left for savings. Enter an amount that you would like to save. After entering expenses, you may need to adjust this amount. You might not be able to save as much as you want and still pay for all expenses. Plan to save some money, however, if at all possible. By saving, you will

▶ FIGURE 4-2.1 **Personal Budget**

ANDREA MCCALL BUDGET FOR 20--			
Income	**Weekly**	**Monthly**	**Yearly**
Work (part-time)	$30.00	$120.00	$1,440.00
Allowance for household chores	10.00	40.00	480.00
Lunch money allowance	15.00	60.00	720.00
Savings account interest	.50	2.00	24.00
Total income	$55.50	$222.00	$2,664.00
Savings			
Deposit to savings account	$ 5.50	$ 22.00	$ 264.00
Expenses			
Gifts	$ 5.00	$ 20.00	$ 240.00
Clothes and shoes	15.00	60.00	720.00
Loan payment to parents	5.00	20.00	240.00
Lunches	15.00	60.00	720.00
Entertainment/miscellaneous	10.00	40.00	480.00
Total expenses	$50.00	$200.00	$2,400.00
Total savings and expenses	$55.50	$222.00	$2,664.00

Aaron Amat/Shutterstock.com

Why should you "pay yourself first" when preparing a budget?

have money to pay for future needs, both expected and unexpected. Locate the yearly savings amount, $264, in the budget in Figure 4-2.1.

Step 3 Estimate Expenses

Expenses are items for which you spend money. Clothes, lunches at school, and bus fares are examples of expenses. You may also make payments on an asset you purchase, such as a car. Other expenses are related to living costs and entertainment. Keeping track of what you spend will help you estimate expenses for the future. If you are trying to control expenses, seeing exactly how much you are currently spending for each expense can be helpful. Locate the expense amounts in the budget in Figure 4-2.1.

There are two types of expenses. Costs that do not change each month are called **fixed expenses**. Examples of fixed expenses are rent, insurance, and car payments. Renters typically have a lease contract stating a monthly rent amount that does not change for the term of the lease. Monthly car payments are usually fixed for the term of the car loan. Fixed expenses remain constant each month and must be paid even when income is less than expected. If income continues to be less than planned, a fixed expense may have to be eliminated. For example, if your income goes down because you lose your job, you may have to sell your car to eliminate the car payment you can no longer afford.

Variable expenses are costs that can go up and down each month. An example of a variable expense is your gas and electric bill. When the weather is cold, the cost of heating your house will go up. Expenses can also vary due to changing prices. For example, as the price of gasoline rises, your transportation expense will also rise. Other examples of variable expenses are costs for food, clothing, and entertainment. If you have less income or higher expenses than expected one month, you may need to decrease your variable expenses. You may choose to spend less on entertainment.

Many people include charitable giving as a part of their monthly expenses. **Charitable giving** is the act of donating money or time to a

fixed expenses costs that do not change each month

variable expenses costs that can go up and down each month

charitable giving the act of donating money or time to a cause in which you believe

FOCUS On...

PHILANTHROPY

Philanthropy is the act of donating money, goods, time, or effort to support a societal cause. *Philanthropists* want to leave the world a better place than they found it. Anyone can be a philanthropist.

After some have accumulated great wealth, they may give large sums of money to others. Philanthropy is the primary source of funding for the fine arts; the performing arts; religious, medical, and humanitarian causes; and private (and some public) schools and universities. Many cultural institutions would not continue to exist without the generosity of private philanthropists.

Many people not possessing great wealth also perform philanthropic acts by donating substantial amounts of their time, effort, and personal resources to charitable causes. When you give your time,

you are giving the most valuable thing you have. You are sharing more than monetary wealth; you are giving of yourself and sharing that which is most precious of all.

Philanthropy is said to be important because it "feeds the soul of the nation." We are all able to enjoy the richness of culture that results when events are sponsored by those who can afford to pay so that those who cannot afford to pay can experience them as well.

Think Critically

1. Conduct online research to locate a charitable organization or foundation. Describe its purpose. How does it add value to society as a whole?
2. If you had the time and/or money, what charitable cause would you support? Why?

---

cause in which you believe. You may donate through your church or a nonprofit organization. For example, you may donate money to the Red Cross to help earthquake victims.

Step 4 Balance the Budget

Find the total of savings and expenses in Figure 4-2.1. This amount should be the same as your total income amount. When these amounts are the same, the budget is in balance. If your savings plus your expenses exceed your income, adjust your budget to make them balance. To do this, you will have to lower your expenses, save a little less, or increase your income.

Preparing a Budget Analysis

You should not expect income, savings, and expenses to be exactly as you planned in a budget. The differences between planned amounts and actual amounts are called **variances**. Looking at the variances in your income and spending amounts can help you plan better when creating budgets in the future.

variances the differences between planned amounts and actual amounts

Budget variances can be favorable or unfavorable. A *favorable variance* occurs when you earn or save more than you estimated or spend less than you planned. An *unfavorable variance* occurs when you earn or save less than you estimated or spend more than you planned.

Figure 4-2.2 shows budget variances—both in dollar amounts and in percentages. To compute the percentages for income and savings amounts, subtract the budgeted amount from the actual amount; then divide the difference by the budgeted amount. To compute the percentages for expense amounts, subtract the actual amount from the budgeted amount; then divide the difference by the budgeted amount.

ANDREA MCCALL **BUDGET VARIANCES FOR AUGUST**				
Income	**Budgeted Amount**	**Actual Amount**	**Dollar Variance**	**Percent Variance**
Work (part-time)	$120.00	$110.00	−$10.00	−8% U
Allowance for household chores	40.00	50.00	10.00	25% F
Lunch money allowance	60.00	60.00	0.00	0%
Savings account interest	2.00	2.00	0.00	0%
Total income	$222.00	$222.00	$ 0.00	0%
Savings				
Deposit to savings account	$ 22.00	$ 22.00	$ 0.00	0%
Expenses				
Gifts	$ 20.00	$ 18.00	$ 2.00	10% F
Clothes and shoes	60.00	70.00	−10.00	−17% U
Loan payment to parents	20.00	22.00	−2.00	−10% U
Lunches	60.00	55.00	5.00	8% F
Entertainment/miscellaneous	40.00	35.00	5.00	13% F
Total expenses	$200.00	$200.00	$ 0.00	0%
Total savings and expenses	$222.00	$222.00	$ 0.00	0%

By looking carefully at variances, you can see where you spent more or less than the estimated amounts. Any variance that is more or less than 10 percent of what you had planned should be looked at carefully. For example, Andrea had planned to spend $60 on clothes and shoes for the month, but she actually spent $70. That is $10 more than budgeted, or a 17 percent difference. Andrea should think about why this happened. She may decide that she needs to revise the budget or change her spending habits. Analyzing variances will help you understand and better estimate your income and expenses.

CHECKPOINT

How does a personal budget differ from a cash flow statement?

LO 4-2.2 What Are Recordkeeping Methods?

Keeping good records will help you prepare a better budget. You can manually keep track of what you are earning, spending, saving, and investing by using pen and paper. Or you may find using an electronic recordkeeping program to be more convenient.

Manual Records

manual records information recorded in hard-copy format using pen and paper

You can keep logs or journals on paper that list types and amounts of income, savings, and expenses. **Manual records** consist of information recorded in *hard-copy* format using pen and paper. You can manually

DEALING WITH CONFLICT

Conflicts are bound to happen sooner or later. People you know will not be able to get along with each other. Maybe you will have a hard time working out a problem with another person. The ability to deal with conflict is an important personal skill—it will help you both in your personal life and in your work life. The next time you must deal with conflict, practice the following skills:

- *Focus on the problem, not the person.* Be objective. Do not let your personal feelings—whether you like or dislike the person—cloud your judgment.
- *Listen actively.* Think about who is speaking and why that person is upset. Repeat a short summary of the problem or complaint to acknowledge that you understand the issue and confirm what you have heard.
- *Do not let your emotions get the best of you.* Remain calm. If the person is upset or angry and not speaking rationally, suggest that you continue your talk later. This will give you and the other person time to think about the issue. Resume talking when you are both calm and can speak in a courteous manner.
- *Stay away from negative talk.* Look for positive ways to address the issue instead of saying things such as "can't," "don't," or "no." Negative words will only make the conflict harder to resolve.
- *Try to negotiate a solution.* Be willing to compromise, when appropriate, to reach a solution that will be acceptable to everyone.

Think Critically

1. Describe a past situation where there was conflict. What did you learn from the experience?
2. What additional conflict resolution skills can you think of to add to the list?

compute your variances and make notations about what to change. You will want to keep these journals over time so you can compare them from year to year. It is important to keep these records in a safe and secure place. This will protect them from fire and other forms of damage and keep them safe from misuse by others.

Electronic Records

Many people prefer to keep **electronic records**, which consist of a *soft-copy* format of your financial information stored on your computer. The advantages of using computerized systems include the ease by which information can be updated, stored, and retrieved and the speed by which new computations and comparisons can be made.

There are several available software packages specially designed for financial planning and recordkeeping. For example, Quicken® is a popular financial management program designed to help you keep track of your income and expenses and create budgets.

You can also use spreadsheet programs, such as Microsoft Excel®, for data entry and budget analysis. **Spreadsheet software** allows you to insert numbers and formulas to compute amounts and then easily change them later as needed. You may need to adjust amounts in a budget several times. This can become quite tedious if done by pen and paper. For example, what if your monthly expenses go up by 8 percent? How will the budget be affected? What if the price of a car you are saving to buy goes up by 10 percent during the time you are saving for it? How much money will you need for the car? Allowing you to answer "what if" questions easily is one

electronic records soft-copy formats of your financial information stored on your computer

spreadsheet software a computer program that allows you to insert numbers and formulas to compute amounts and then easily change them later as needed

of the strengths of a spreadsheet program. When you change a number in Excel that is part of a calculation, all other amounts affected are updated automatically. Because amounts are calculated using formulas, math errors are eliminated (assuming you initially entered the formulas correctly). Excel also allows you to set up worksheets and link them together. A sample budget created in Excel is shown in Figure 4-2.3.

encryption the process of converting data to a coded form

Like manual records, electronic records should be protected from unauthorized uses and users. Passwords and **encryption**, which is the process of converting data to a coded form, will help protect your information. Also, as with any important files you keep electronically, always keep a current backup of your financial records.

▶ FIGURE 4-2.3 **Excel Spreadsheet**

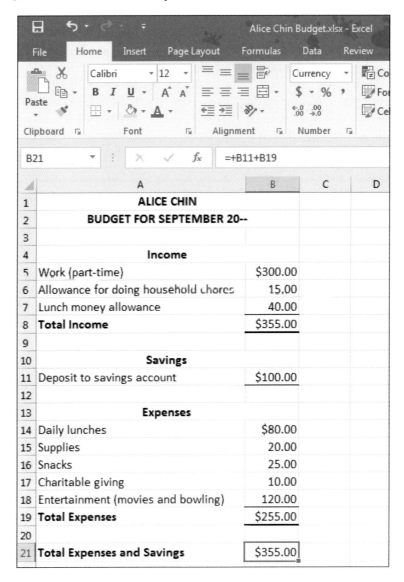

 **CHECKPOINT**

Why is it important to safeguard your financial records?

4-2 Lesson Assessment

KEY TERMS REVIEW

Match the terms with the definitions. Some terms may not be used.

_____ 1. Costs that do not change each month

_____ 2. Soft-copy formats of your financial information stored on your computer

_____ 3. Costs that can go up and down each month

_____ 4. Information recorded in hard-copy format using pen and paper

_____ 5. A spending and saving plan based on expected income and expenses

_____ 6. The differences between planned amounts and actual amounts

_____ 7. A computer program that allows you to insert numbers and formulas to compute amounts and then easily change them later as needed

_____ 8. The process of converting data to a coded form

a. budget

b. charitable giving

c. electronic records

d. encryption

e. fixed expenses

f. manual records

g. spreadsheet software

h. variable expenses

i. variances

CHECK YOUR UNDERSTANDING

9. What is included in a monthly budget?

10. What are the four steps in preparing a budget?

11. How are fixed expenses different from variable expenses?

12. Why is philanthropy important in our society? What can you do to make a difference?

13. Why is it important that a budget be balanced? If your budget does not balance, what can you do to bring it into balance?

14. What is an unfavorable variance?

15. How can budget variances be used to plan better budgets?

16. Why is a good recordkeeping system important?

17. Describe how you can keep financial records manually.

18. What are two ways that you can keep records electronically?

19. How can you use a spreadsheet to help with budgeting?

20. How can you protect your electronic records from unwanted invasions of privacy? How can you protect your manual records?

THINK CRITICALLY

21. Why is it important to prepare a personal budget? It is often said that the mere act of preparing a budget will change one's saving and spending habits. Explain why that would be the case.

22. Why do some expenses go up and down each month? Give examples of items in your family budget that change on a regular basis. What can you do to keep these expenses from rising unexpectedly?

23. Why do some expenses remain the same each month? Give examples of fixed expenses in your family's budget. What can you do to reduce these expenses?

24. Why is it important to budget for charitable giving? How does it affect your budget? Is it a variable or fixed expense?

25. In relation to budgeting, keeping good records is important. How do you plan to keep accurate and complete records of what you are earning, spending, saving, and investing?

EXTEND YOUR LEARNING

26. Review the personal budget shown in Figure 4-2.1. Then create your own personal budget for one month by following the steps described below. You may want to refer back to the personal cash flow statement you created at the end of Lesson 4-1 to see the income (cash inflows) and expenses (cash outflows) you previously identified. Use spreadsheet software to create your budget, if available.

     a. Record your expected income from all sources during the month.

     b. Record an amount you want to save for the month.

     c. Record all of your estimated expenses for the month.

     d. Total the sections of the budget to see if the budget is in balance. If it is not, change the savings or expense amounts to make it balance.

     e. Once the budget has been prepared and balanced, write down what you learned about yourself and your proposed spending and saving habits. How will you change them?

     f. Review your expenses and categorize them as fixed or variable. Do you have more fixed expenses or variable expenses? How do the different types of expenses affect your budget?

     g. Keep good records for a month so you can compare your actual results to your budget. Compute the variance for each income and expense item. Analyze your budget and list ways you might change it.

THE ESSENTIAL QUESTION   Refer to The Essential Question on p. 124. Budgeting helps you plan your spending and savings based on expected income and expenses. Budgets are prepared by using a four-step process either with pen and paper (manually) or electronically with recordkeeping or spreadsheet software.

THE ESSENTIAL QUESTION What is personal financial planning, and how does it help you protect your financial resources?

LEARNING OBJECTIVES

LO 4-3.1 Explain the purpose and steps of financial planning.

LO 4-3.2 List reliable sources of financial advice.

LO 4-3.3 Describe ways you can protect your financial resources.

KEY TERMS

- financial plan, 133
- personal goals, 134
- financial goals, 134
- short-term goals, 134
- intermediate goals, 134
- long-term goals, 134
- timeline, 135
- benchmarks, 135
- financial planner, 136
- phishing, 138
- identity theft, 138

LO 4-3.1 What Is Financial Planning?

Financial planning is a formal process that involves carefully examining your current financial situation and thinking about your future. It requires a long-term commitment. As part of the financial planning process, you will create a financial plan. A **financial plan** is a set of personal and financial goals you want to accomplish, along with steps and a timeline for reaching these goals. Getting a college education, owning a car, and owning a home are examples of personal goals. For each personal goal, you will have a related financial goal. Paying for living expenses, tuition, books, and other related expenses while in college is a financial goal. Saving for a down payment on a car or a house and having a job that provides enough income to make monthly payments are financial goals.

Budgets and financial plans go hand in hand. However, they are not the same. A financial plan is more than a budget. Its purpose is to plan for earning, spending, saving, and investing in a way that will allow you to achieve your goals in the present and the future. By creating a financial plan, you are assuming personal responsibility for your financial health.

Some people create a financial plan by themselves because their finances are not complex enough to require assistance. Other people get advice from experts who can help manage resources and plan for retirement. Whether you do planning by yourself or get help, you will need to complete the five steps of financial planning.

financial plan a set of personal and financial goals, along with steps and a timeline for reaching them

Step 1 Gather Information

The first step in financial planning is to gather information. Everything related to your finances should be considered. The purpose of gathering information is to look at the state of your finances now—your starting point. The following list shows examples of *financial records*, or documents that are used to assess your finances. You may not have all the items listed at this time in your life. However, you can gather or prepare the first three items. Other items may become part of your plan later in life.

- Personal cash flow statement
- Personal net worth statement

- Personal budget
- Checkbook
- Current bank statements
- Investment account statements
- Insurance policies
- Current paycheck stub
- Tax returns
- Will and/or trusts
- Financial contracts for items purchased on credit
- Any other legal documents related to your finances

Step 2 Analyze Information

Take a careful look at the documents and information you have gathered. Find out if any data are missing, and take steps to get the data. Carefully look at each document and make notes about what you see. Review your personal cash flow statement to see what your current sources of income (cash inflows) are. Look at your expenses (cash outflows). Do you have enough income to pay for your expenses and save for the future? If not, try to find ways to increase income and decrease expenses. Review your personal net worth statement. What are your assets? What liabilities do you have? What is your net worth? Review a current monthly or yearly budget. Look at the items for which you spend money. Is there a way you can spend less and save more?

Step 3 Set Goals

personal goals things you want to achieve in your life

financial goals plans for how you will pay for your personal goals

short-term goals things you expect to achieve within one week to one year

intermediate goals things you wish to achieve in the next two to five years

long-term goals things you want to achieve more than five years from now

Two types of goals should be considered when creating a financial plan—personal goals and financial goals. **Personal goals** are the things you want to achieve in your life. Living in your own apartment, owning a car, and taking a two-week vacation are personal goals. Personal goals should be set first because your financial goals will be based on them.

Financial goals describe how you will pay for your personal goals. Financial goals may be short term, intermediate, or long term. **Short-term goals** are what you expect to achieve within one week to one year. A financial plan for the short term tells you on a week-to-week or month-to-month basis what you would like to achieve. Perhaps you would like to save $40 by the end of the month. Perhaps you want to add $200 to your savings account by the end of the year. Using monthly and yearly budgets can help you achieve short-term goals and save for long-term goals.

Intermediate goals are those you wish to achieve in the next two to five years. You may wish to save money for college or for a future purchase or need. You may want to increase your yearly income within three years. These goals take longer to achieve and also require more planning.

Short-term and intermediate-term goals are often stepping-stones to long-term goals. **Long-term goals** typically include what you want to achieve more than five years from now. You may wish to save enough money to buy a car. When you begin working full time, you may want to contribute to a 401(k) to save money for retirement. Achieving long-term goals may require you to save money for a long time. Online financial calculators are available to help you determine the costs of achieving long-term goals. For example, they can calculate how much you should save yearly based on when you want to retire, or how much you should save monthly to pay for college tuition, fees, and expenses.

As part of the goal-setting process, you may experience delayed gratification. Doing without an item you would like to buy now in order to save money to fulfill an intermediate or a long-term goal is an example of *delayed gratification*. For instance, you may have a goal of saving $30 per month to help pay for your college education. This month, you would like to buy a new pair of shoes. However, if you do so, you will not be able to make your savings goal. Doing without the shoes now in order to be able to pay for college later is an example of delayed gratification.

Step 4 Develop a Timeline and Benchmarks

Goals must be measurable. Plan a timeline for putting your goals into action. A **timeline** is a visual display of how long it will take to achieve each phase of your plan. Before creating a timeline, be sure your goals are prioritized based on how soon you need or want to achieve them. For each personal goal, there may be a financial goal you must first achieve. Financial goals can further be divided into parts or steps. For each step, consider how long it will take to complete. Then set a target date for completion.

timeline a visual display of how long it will take to achieve each phase of a plan

In addition to establishing a timeline, goals should include **benchmarks**, which are standards against which progress is measured. Benchmarks may consist of steps or specific actions to take. As you hit each benchmark, you will be another step closer to achieving your overall goal.

benchmarks standards against which progress is measured

The record showing the goals you intend to accomplish with timelines and benchmarks is your financial plan. A sample financial plan for one goal is shown in Figure 4-3.1.

▶ FIGURE 4-3.1 **Financial Plan (One Goal)**

BILL FONG FINANCIAL PLAN Updated April 1, 20--			
Net worth on April 1, 20--: $525.56			
Personal Goal	**Financial Goal**	**Benchmarks**	**Timeline**
Live in my own house in the country.	Buy a house in the country.	1. Save money for a down payment ($12,000)	5 years
		• Set aside $200 per month	Once per month April 8 (next week)
		• Open a separate account for money saved	
		• Talk to a mortgage broker to get prepared	Schedule for April 15
		2. Get a job that provides enough income to make monthly payments	2 years

Step 5 Implement and Evaluate the Plan

Once you have decided on your personal and financial goals, begin working toward achieving them. Check off the items on your timeline as they are completed. Set new benchmarks if you learn about other ways to meet your goals. Most importantly, take a look at your financial plan often. At least once each year, you should evaluate the financial plan and revise it as needed. In doing so, consider the following questions. Some of them may apply now. Others may not apply to you for a few years, or even many years.

- *Is your income and net worth steadily growing over time?* If so, by what amount and percentage?
- *How are your spending habits changing?* What types of things are you buying (needs versus wants), and what are your purchasing plans over time?
- *Who else depends on your income?* Do you have a spouse or children that will be affected by your financial plan? What will they contribute? What needs will they have?
- *What new goals do you need to add and plan for?* Do you need a plan to pay for a college education for your child? Is it time to plan for retirement? As your personal and family goals change, your financial plan should be updated to reflect new goals.

 CHECKPOINT

Why is financial planning important?

LO 4-3.2 Where Can You Get Good Financial Advice?

Financial experts can often be heard on television, radio, and podcasts. A *financial expert* gives advice based on superior knowledge and experience. Many financial experts publish self-help materials in the form of books, videos, and other media. However, there are many other sources of financial advice. Some are better than others, depending on your needs.

Financial Planners

financial planner a professional consultant who provides financial advice

A **financial planner** is a professional consultant who provides financial advice. A CFP (certified financial planner) has completed an education program and has passed CFP Board certification exams. Financial planners (also known as *financial advisers*) help people develop financial plans to meet their financial goals. They review every aspect of their client's financial life, including savings, investments, insurance, and retirement.

The financial planner usually receives a fee for consulting services. Some also receive a commission, or a percentage of the sales, from the investment products (such as stocks, bonds, or life insurance policies) that you purchase. To earn higher commissions, some planners might push the most expensive products instead of the products that best meet the needs of their clients. This is an unethical practice. To avoid this kind of dilemma, hire a financial planner who does not stand to make a profit on the investments you choose.

You will need to share personal information about your income, assets, liabilities, and net worth with your financial planner. You must be able to trust the planner with this sensitive data. The financial planner should follow ethical practices by keeping your information confidential and by not using it for personal benefit. Ask what measures the planner will take to keep your data secure. Also find out if the planner has been in business long, whether any complaints have been filed, and whether he or she has a criminal background.

Newspapers and Magazines

Newspapers have *financial pages* that list securities, such as stocks and bonds, as well as provide other information and advice related to finances. Some newspapers, such as *The Wall Street Journal* and *Barron's*, are entirely devoted to financial news and information.

A number of weekly and monthly magazines publish articles that offer financial advice and smart tips on how to manage your money. Some popular financial magazines include *Business Week*, *Forbes*, *Money*, and *Kiplinger's Personal Finance*.

Why are newspapers and magazines good sources of financial advice?

Seminars and Workshops

Companies that provide financial products such as mutual funds or retirement accounts often provide free seminars and workshops. These events will give you information about how products work. You can also get investment ideas and learn how financial markets work.

Financial Planning Websites

There are many free websites on the Internet to help consumers get started with their financial planning. For example, TeenBusiness is a website dedicated to helping teens learn how to invest and manage their money. The Motley Fool website contains articles on saving and spending, credit and debt, and more. It also contains numerous financial calculators and a community discussion board where you can ask questions and discuss personal finance topics with others. MyMoney .gov is the U.S. government's website dedicated to educating citizens about the basics of personal finance. The site includes advice, financial calculators, and budgeting worksheets. These sites and many others are good resources for young adults starting out on their own.

 **CHECKPOINT**

What should you look for when choosing a financial planner?

Looking Ahead

As a young adult, you should look ahead to determine what steps you need to take to protect you and your finances. The Federal Trade Commission (FTC) provides information to consumers regarding identity theft. Access the FTC's website and click on the Tips & Advice link for consumers. Then answer the following questions: What are some of the warning signs of identity theft? What are some things thieves do with a stolen identity? What are some things you can do to prevent identity theft?

LO 4-3.3 How Can You Protect Financial Resources?

You must protect your financial wealth. There are a number of steps you can take to avoid losing your money.

- Deal only with financial advisers and financial institutions that you know and trust. Before working with a new financial adviser, research his or her background.
- Be aware of the economy and how it affects your personal finances. It is your responsibility to know when to ask questions and make decisions about your investments.
- Keep good records and verify account balances regularly.
- Keep your monthly statements in a safe place, such as a locked drawer, strongbox, or safe.
- Guard your passwords for online banking and investment accounts.
- Store any financial information you keep electronically on a separate storage device, such as a flash drive or CD, rather than on your computer's hard drive.

phishing a common Internet scam that uses email messages to deceive you into disclosing personal information

You should also be aware of phishing scams. **Phishing** is a common Internet scam that uses email messages to deceive you into disclosing personal information. "Phishers" send email messages posing as your bank or other legitimate business. The messages may ask you to verify private information, such as bank account numbers or credit card numbers. Do not respond to such an attempt to get personal information. Banks and legitimate companies don't ask for this information via email. If you give your financial information to these scam artists, you may become a victim of identity theft. **Identity theft** occurs when someone uses your personal information without permission to commit fraud or other crimes. Those who get your personal information may be able to apply for credit in your name or withdraw money from your accounts.

identity theft the use of your personal information by someone else without permission to commit fraud or other crimes

❯❯❯ CHECKPOINT

List two ways you can protect your personal financial information.

KEY TERMS REVIEW

Match the terms with the definitions. Some terms may not be used.

_____ 1. A professional consultant who provides financial advice

_____ 2. Plans for how you will pay for your personal goals

_____ 3. The use of your personal information by someone else without permission to commit fraud or other crimes

_____ 4. A set of personal and financial goals, along with steps and timelines for reaching them

_____ 5. Things you wish to achieve in the next two to five years

_____ 6. Things you want to achieve in your life

_____ 7. A common Internet scam that uses email messages to deceive you into disclosing personal information

_____ 8. Standards against which progress is measured

_____ 9. A visual display of how long it will take to achieve each phase of a plan

a. benchmarks

b. financial goals

c. financial plan

d. financial planner

e. identity theft

f. intermediate goals

g. long-term goals

h. personal goals

i. phishing

j. short-term goals

k. timeline

CHECK YOUR UNDERSTANDING

10. What is the purpose of a financial plan?

11. List the five steps in creating a financial plan.

12. List five types of information or documents that should be gathered as the first step in creating a financial plan.

13. Why are personal goals set before financial goals?

14. What is the difference between short-term, intermediate, and long-term goals?

15. What does delayed gratification mean?

16. Why should goals include benchmarks?

17. How often should you review and update your financial plan?

18. List three sources of good financial advice.

19. Explain the role of personal responsibility and ethics in financial planning.

20. What is phishing? How does it work?

THINK CRITICALLY

21. When preparing a financial plan, is it necessary for you to get advice and help from others, such as a financial planner? Why or why not?

22. Assess your current financial situation. Do you spend all of the money you receive? Are there ways you could adjust your spending so you could save more? Are you satisfied with your current financial position?

23. List a personal goal. Then write a short-term financial goal, an intermediate financial goal, and a long-term financial goal based on your personal goal. Why is it important to set each type of goal?

24. Have you ever experienced delayed gratification? Describe the circumstances and explain whether the decision leading to the delayed gratification was a good one. Did it result in reaching your goal? Why or why not?

25. Why will your financial plan change over time?

EXTEND YOUR LEARNING

26. Prepare a list of three personal goals. For each of these goals, write financial goals, stating the costs and methods to be used to pay the costs. These financial goals should be specific, such as working, saving, borrowing, and so forth. Next to each goal, specify benchmarks (steps that allow you to measure your progress) and timelines (specific dates or timeframes for achieving benchmarks). Then prioritize each of your goals, ranking them one to three.

27. Phishers use many sophisticated means to trick their victims into giving out their personal information. Conduct an online search for articles about recent phishing victims. Select one article and write a summary from the victim's perspective. How was the victim caught off guard? What was the outcome? What advice would the victim give to prevent others from falling prey to similar scams?

28. A long-term financial goal for many people is to save money for retirement. The average American spends 20 years in retirement. How much money do you think you will need in retirement to support yourself? Search online for a retirement planning calculator. How much would you need to start saving today in order to reach that goal?

29. Assume you would like to work as a certified financial planner (CFP) some day. Research the qualifications and skills required. What are the educational requirements? Describe the work environment and characteristics of this occupation. What is the average salary? Compile your research to create a career profile of a CFP.

THE ESSENTIAL QUESTION Refer to The Essential Question on p. 133. Financial planning helps you create a plan for earning, spending, saving, and investing money. By gathering and analyzing your financial information, setting goals, developing a timeline, and implementing the plan (often with the help of a financial adviser), you are taking steps to protect your financial resources.

Exploring Careers in...
MANUFACTURING

Whenever you buy a finished product, someone worked hard to put it together for you. Workers in production plants assemble both finished products and the parts that go into them.

Advances in technology have changed the way in which goods are made. Modern manufacturing systems use robots, computers, motion-control devices, and various sensing technologies. Careful quality control is essential throughout the process.

Manufacturing processes often use teams of workers to produce entire products or components. The teams must all work together, using a wide range of skills and knowledge to perform multiple tasks. Many times, team members rotate through different tasks, rather than specializing in a single task.

Employment Outlook

- A slower than average rate of employment growth is expected.
- Workers with computer skills will have the best job opportunities.

Job Titles

- Assembler
- Fabricator
- Machinist

Needed Education/Skills

- A high school diploma or equivalent is required.
- Experience and additional training is needed for more advanced assembly jobs.
- Dexterity, physical stamina, and excellent technical skills are essential.

What's it like to work in . . . Manufacturing

Elaine works as a team assembler for a local electronics manufacturer. She started as an unskilled worker five years ago, but through training and experience she has advanced to become a team leader.

Elaine arrives for work each morning at the factory at 7 A.M. Her day begins by inspecting all of the tools and work stations. When the other workers on her team arrive by 8 A.M., everything is ready to go. As team leader, Elaine assigns different tasks to workers. If one of the workers is absent, Elaine or one of the other team members will fill in.

This afternoon, Elaine is attending a training session to learn about a new computerized manufacturing system that is being installed to increase workers' output. She will learn how to operate the system and how it will change her team's job duties.

What About You?

Would you like to manufacture high-quality products in an efficient manner? What kind of products would you like to produce? Would you like to be a team leader? Why or why not?

Chapter 4 Assessment

SUMMARY

4-1   Needs are things required for survival, such as food, water, clothing, shelter, and medical care. Wants are the things we desire for reasons beyond survival and basic comfort. Limited financial resources limit our ability to satisfy all needs and wants, which are unlimited and growing.

Income is measured using a personal cash flow statement. A personal net worth statement measures wealth, or net worth, by subtracting liabilities (debts) from assets (items of value that are owned).

The six steps in the decision-making process are (1) define the problem or goal, (2) gather information, (3) compare choices, (4) make a decision, (5) take action, and (6) re-evaluate your choice. Following this six-step process and other financial strategies will help you make better personal financial choices.

4-2   Budgeting is a critical part of making good financial choices. It allows you to analyze what you are spending and saving and make changes as needed.

Budgeting is a four-step process where you estimate income, plan savings, estimate expenses, and balance the budget.

A variance is the difference between a planned amount and the actual amount of an income or expense item in your budget. Analyzing your variances will help you plan spending and saving better in the future.

Manual and computerized recordkeeping methods will help you stay organized and prepare better financial records.

4-3   Financial planning involves examining your current financial situation and thinking about your future. It also involves creating a financial plan that contains goals, benchmarks, and timelines.

Five steps in financial planning are (1) gather information, (2) analyze information, (3) set goals, (4) develop a timeline and benchmarks, and (5) implement and evaluate the plan.

There are many sources of financial advice, including financial planners, financial newspapers and magazines, seminars and workshops, and financial planning websites.

There are a number of ways in which you can protect your financial resources. Phishing is a common Internet scam that uses email messages to get people to disclose their personal information, such as credit card numbers and bank account information. Phishers use this information to commit identity theft.

MAKE ACADEMIC CONNECTIONS

TEAMWORK

1. **Problem Solving** Assume that you belong to a school club that has ten members and two teacher advisers. The club members and advisers are planning to attend a conference in your state capital. Working with a classmate, apply the decision-making process you learned in this chapter to decide how your club should travel to the conference. (LO 4-1.3)

    a. Define the problem or goal. Write a statement that says exactly what you need to decide.

    b. Gather information on all possible solutions for solving the problem or meeting the goal. What methods of transportation might your club use to reach the state capital? (If you live in the state capital, assume you will need to travel 20 miles to the meeting site.) Conduct research as needed to find the cost of each option. Remember to consider the distance both to and from the state capital. Record detailed notes to show how the cost for each item was calculated.

    c. Compare the options you have identified. List the advantages, disadvantages, and opportunity costs of each option.

    d. Make a decision based on your research and evaluation of the information you have gathered. Explain why you chose one option over the others.

    e. Describe how you would take action based on your decision if this were a real situation.

2. **Technology** Use a spreadsheet program to create a budget template that could be used for a monthly and yearly budget. Use the categories shown in Figure 4-2.1. You can add any additional categories that you believe are needed. Insert formulas for calculating totals. (LO 4-2.2)

3. **Economics** Conduct online research for information regarding the budget of the United States, prepared by the President. List the major categories of proposed revenues and expenditures. What are some important provisions of the budget? What is the process for getting the federal budget approved? (LO 4-2.1)

4. **Research** Conduct online research to learn what credentials a good financial planner should have. How can you confirm that the financial planner is legitimate? What kind of background information should you know about your planner? Write a one-page report that provides tips on what to do before hiring a financial planner. (LO 4-3.2)

5. **Communication** Review the financial plan on the next page, and answer the following questions: (LO 4-3.1)

    a. Do you think the personal goals are realistic for a student who is currently a sophomore in high school?

    b. Label each personal goal as short term, intermediate, or long term.

    c. If this student gets a job, how much will she have to earn in take-home pay in order to meet her financial goals?

    d. How can you add to or refine this plan to make it better?

VEERA SEKAR FINANCIAL PLAN Updated April 1, 20--			

Net worth on January 1, 20--: $150

Personal Goals	Financial Goals	Benchmarks	Timeline
1. Get a bachelor's degree in landscape architecture	• Save $2,520 for annual college expenses (books and fees)	• Save $35 per month	• 72 months (begin saving now and continue through college)
	• Get financial aid to cover college tuition	• Apply for financial aid	• January 20-- (next year as junior)
		• Apply for a scholarship	• April 20-- (next year)
2. Own a car	• Save $300 for a car down payment	• Save $25 per month	• 12 months
	• Borrow money from parents	• Get a job so I can repay loan	• Get a summer job and a part-time job by January 1, 20--
3. Take a vacation to Hawaii before starting college	• Save $1,500 for vacation	• Save $50 per month	• 30 months
		• Make reservations early to get the best deal	• January, 20— (in 2 years)
	• Save $300 to buy new clothes for trip	• Save $10 per month	• 30 months

Do the Math

Complete the following problems to build your math skills. You may use spreadsheet software or complete the problems manually.

1. **Michael makes $127 each paycheck and receives four paychecks per month. What is his monthly income? His yearly income?**

2. **Rachelle makes $96 a week and gets paid 52 weeks a year. What is her yearly income? Her average monthly income?**

3. **Maria's budgeted income for July was $539. She earned $522. Compute the variance amount and percent. (Round to the nearest whole percent.) Note if the variance is favorable (F) or unfavorable (U).**

4. **Chin's budgeted entertainment expense was $125. The actual amount he spent was $106. Compute the variance amount and percent. (Round to the nearest whole percent.) Note if the variance is favorable (F) or unfavorable (U).**

Take Action

CREATE A HOUSEHOLD BUDGET

Assume you have graduated from high school and are living on your own. Using Figure 4-2.1 as an example, create a personal budget that will provide for your needs based on the information below. Use spreadsheet software to create the budget, if available.

a. You work 40 hours per week, 4 weeks per month, and earn $8 per hour. Your take-home pay is $224 per week. You also earn $60 per month doing odd jobs, such as mowing grass and babysitting. Enter weekly, monthly, and yearly take-home pay from each source and calculate income totals.

b. Enter an amount you want to save for the month. Use an amount that you think is realistic. You may need to adjust this amount later.

c. List all of your estimated expenses for one month. Assume that health insurance premiums are deducted from your paycheck. Also assume that the taxes withheld from your paycheck are all of the taxes that you must pay. Thus, you do not need to list these items as expenses. A list of typical expenses for a household budget follows. You may add other items that you think would be realistic and leave out items you don't want.

- Rent
- Car payment
- Lunches
- Cell phone
- Utilities
- Entertainment
- Groceries
- Clothing and shoes
- Internet access
- Gasoline
- Satellite or cable TV
- Car license and repairs
- Auto and renters insurance
- Miscellaneous expenses

d. Conduct research to find typical monthly costs for these items in your area. For example, look at advertisements for apartments in a newspaper or online to find rent costs. Ask your parents or other adults how much they usually pay for some of these items. Calculate the total expenses.

e. Calculate the total savings and expenses. Is the budget in balance? If it is not, change the savings or expense amounts (within realistic limits) to make the budget balance. Some ways to balance your budget follow.

- Find an apartment where the utilities are included in the rent.
- Take the bus to work and other places instead of owning a car. You will not have a car payment, gasoline costs, or auto insurance costs. Instead, add the cost of bus fares and occasional taxi fares.
- Consider sharing a two-bedroom apartment with a friend. Your friend would pay half of the rent and utilities.

Save your completed budget in your portfolio.

CHAPTER 5

The Banking System

Daniilantiq/Shutterstock.com

Chapter 5 discusses the banking system in the United States and banking activities for consumers. Many benefits and services are available from financial institutions. Some accounts have fees or restrictions of which consumers should be aware. Banking in this country is centralized through the Federal Reserve System. In this chapter, you will explore how the banking system works and what it means to you as a consumer. You'll also learn about the rights and responsibilities of account holders.

Do *This*, Not *That*

To maximize the use of your money:

- Understand how to use a checking account to make payments and withdrawals.
- Reconcile bank statements to ensure account accuracy.
- Choose a savings option and grow your money through compounding of interest.
- Avoid accounts and services that charge high fees.
- Practice responsible banking by monitoring your accounts.

5-1 Checking Accounts

LEARNING OBJECTIVES

LO 5-1.1   Explain the role of money.

LO 5-1.2   Explain the purpose and use of a checking account.

LO 5-1.3   Prepare checks and deposit slips, and maintain a check register.

LO 5-1.4   Prepare a bank reconciliation and understand account fees and choices.

KEY TERMS

- checking account, 148
- check, 148
- check register, 149
- deposit, 150
- withdrawal, 150
- postdated check, 151
- debit card, 152
- endorsement, 153
- electronic funds transfer, 155
- bank reconciliation, 156

LO 5-1.1 The Role of Money

All economic systems use some form of money or medium of exchange. Money is anything that can be used to settle debt. It should be easily exchangeable and readily accepted in the marketplace. To meet these requirements and be functional, money must be readily divisible, durable, and recognizable as a store of value.

- *Divisibility.* In the United States, money, or *currency*, is divided into denominations for ease in completing transactions. The dollar bill is easily recognizable, and for sums less than a dollar, coins are used. Paper money is also known as *banknotes*, a term more commonly used for currency in other countries. The largest denomination produced for circulation is the $100 bill. When money is counted, it is divided into units. For example, 50 cents is one-half of a dollar. Ten dollars is ten times one dollar. Because money is readily *divisible*, you can buy and sell goods and give and receive the exact "change" for your money.

- *Durability.* Money must be transferred from one person to another. Currency lasts a long time (durability) before it must be reissued. Coins are produced by the U.S. Mint; paper money is produced by the Bureau of Engraving and Printing. As money wears out, new coins and bills replace old ones, which are destroyed.

- *Store of value.* To serve as a medium of exchange, money must have a store of value, or be recognized to represent that value. For example, a $5 bill is readily exchangeable for merchandise of that value. When you accept a $5 bill for something you have sold, you expect to be able to reuse that $5 bill when you wish to do so. Because you have confidence that the paper money can be used again, you will accept it in exchange for goods and services.

To help consumers and businesses manage their money, banks offer many services. The checking account is one of the most commonly used services.

>>> **CHECKPOINT**

What is currency? Describe the purpose of currency and list various types of it.

LO 5-1.2 What Is the Purpose of a Checking Account?

Commercial banks, savings and loans, credit unions, and other financial institutions offer various types of accounts to consumers. Collectively, all these financial institutions will be referred to as *banks*. Checking accounts, savings accounts, certificates of deposit (CDs), and money market accounts are popular account choices. In this lesson, we will focus on checking accounts.

checking account a demand deposit account at a bank on which checks are drawn

A **checking account** is a demand deposit account on which checks are drawn. It provides a safe place to keep money and allows users easy access to the money in the account. It is a *demand deposit account* because the account holder may withdraw money on demand or write checks on the account at any time. Most people have a checking account for the convenience of paying bills by mail. It is not a safe practice to send cash, and it is inconvenient to buy a money order each time.

check a written order to a bank to pay a stated amount to a person or business

A **check** is a written order to a bank to pay a stated amount to the person or business named on the face of the check. Checks are an accepted form of payment for most bills. Checks may also be used to purchase items in stores.

Writing a check for a major purchase is safer than carrying cash. A *canceled check* (one that has been processed) also serves as proof of payment for bills or purchases.

A checking account provides a safe place to keep money. Checking accounts at banks generally are insured by the *Federal Deposit Insurance Corporation (FDIC)* up to the legal limit of $250,000 per depositor per bank. The FDIC is an agency of the federal government. By insuring deposits in banks, the FDIC helps to promote public confidence in the U.S. financial system. Consumers should confirm that a bank's deposits will be insured by the FDIC before opening an account.

Why should you use a checking account rather than cash to pay for purchases and bills?

Jason Stitt/Shutterstock.com

Opening a Checking Account

Often, as little as $50 or $100 (cash or checks) is needed to open a checking account. The account holder will be given some checks when the account is opened. These checks will have blank spaces in which to write information about the account. Personalized checks, which have the account holder's name and other data preprinted on them, will be provided a short time later, usually for a fee. A check register and a checkbook cover are usually included with the checks.

When opening a checking account, the account holder will need to provide personal data. An address, a phone number, a Social Security number, and a photo ID are usually required. In addition, the account holder will sign a *signature card* or form. This paperwork provides an official signature that the bank can compare to the signature written on checks. Some banks are beginning to accept digital signatures using special electronic signature pads. A bank account can be an individual account or a *joint account* that allows two or more persons to write checks on the same account. Each person who is authorized to write checks on the account must have a signature on file with the bank.

Some banks request that the account holder answer a *security question*, such as "What was your first pet's name?" or "What was your mother's maiden name?" The purpose of a security question is to identify the account holder when he or she calls on the phone or accesses an account online.

Keeping a Check Register

Keeping accurate records of checking account transactions is very important. Account holders should verify that the amounts deducted from the account and the amounts added to the account are correct. A **check register** is a tool that can be used to track checking account transactions. It can also provide a record of payments made for bills or purchases. A register can be kept manually or using a computer program such as Excel or Quicken. A manual register is shown in Figure 5-1.1.

check register a tool used to track checking account transactions

▶ FIGURE 5-1.1 **Check Register**

CHECK NO. OR TRANSACTION CODE	DATE	DESCRIPTION OF TRANSACTION	PAYMENT/ DEBIT (–)	FEE (–)	DEPOSIT/ CREDIT (+)	BALANCE $800 00
581	7/1/--	Food Mart Groceries	$ 36 12	20	$	36 32
						763 68
DEP	7/15/--	Deposit Paycheck			220 50	220 50
						984 18
WD	7/16/--	ATM Withdrawal	20 00			20 00
						964 18
582	7/20/--	Bellvue Apts. Rent	600 00	.20		600 20
						363 98
ON	7/22/--	Metro Gas & Electric Online Payment	32 50			32 50
						331 48
SC	7/31/--	Monthly Account Fee July		5.00		5 00
						326 48

deposit money added to a checking or savings account

withdrawal taking money from your account

A **deposit** is money added to a checking or savings account. The money can be in the form of currency, checks, or electronic transfers. When you take money from your account, it is called a **withdrawal**. All deposits, checks, other withdrawals, and fees should be recorded in the check register. The purpose of the transaction can also be recorded. A running balance in the register shows the amount of money in the account.

You should update your check register as often as possible. If you are using a paper check register, try to enter checks, deposits, withdrawals, and other transactions in the register immediately. If you are using an electronic register, you will need a system for entering transactions regularly, such as weekly. By routinely entering all account transactions into the register, you can be sure of how much money is in your account at all times.

In the first column of the register shown in Figure 5-1.1, you would list the check number or a code to identify the transaction. For example, enter a code such as DEP for deposit, WD for withdrawal, ON for online payment, or SC for service charge. The check number *581* is entered on the first line of the register in Figure 5-1.1.

In the Date column, enter the current date. (The characters "--" are used in Figure 5-1.1 to represent the current year.) In the Description of Transaction column, enter the name of the person or business to whom the check is written. You can also enter the purpose for the check. For example, "Groceries" is entered on line 2 of the register in Figure 5-1.1.

In the Payment/Debit column, enter the amount of the check or other withdrawal. If there is a check fee, enter that amount in the Fee column. In the register in Figure 5-1.1, $0.20 is entered as the check fee. When making a deposit, enter the amount in the Deposit/Credit column. Carry the amount of the payment plus any fee or the deposit to the Balance column. Then subtract the payment or add the deposit amount to find the new balance.

CHECKPOINT

What are the benefits of using checks?

LO 5-1.3 How Do You Make Payments and Withdrawals?

An advantage of having a checking account is that the funds are easy to access. The account holder can write a check, use a debit card, withdraw cash at an automated teller machine (ATM), or set up a bill to be paid each month automatically. With an *automatic withdrawal*, money is deducted from your account electronically and transferred to another party on a regular basis. For example, insurance premiums could be deducted from your account and transferred to your insurance company. The main advantage of an automatic withdrawal is that by scheduling bill payments, you do not have to remember to write and mail a check each month (but you do have to remember to record it in your check register).

Writing Checks

A check is a legal document used to transfer money. When you write a check, you are telling the bank to pay money to the person or company named on the check. As the writer of the check, you are called the *drawer*. The bank from which the funds are drawn is called the *drawee*. The person or company named on the check is called the *payee*. The payee can cash the check or deposit it into a bank account.

Figure 5-1.2 shows an example check. Notice that the account holder's name and address are printed on the check. The check number, 581, appears near the top right of the check. Checks should be written in dark ink, such as blue or black. Write legibly. Fill in the spaces, and do not leave space before or after your writing. Follow these steps as you write checks:

1. *Enter the current date.* Checks should not be postdated. A **postdated check** is a check written with a date that will occur in the future. Banks will not hold postdated checks until the future date; they will process them at once without regard to the date.
2. *Enter the name of the payee on the* Pay to the order of *line*. Do not leave this line blank. If you do so and lose the check, anyone can cash the check by simply writing the word *Cash* or his or her own name on the blank line.
3. *Enter the amount of the check in numbers after the dollar sign.* Fill the space, separating dollars and cents clearly.
4. *Write the dollar amount in words.* Do not leave extra space anywhere on the line. Draw a line to the end if the space is not filled. Use the word *and* to separate dollars and cents, such as "Thirty-six and 12/100"——Dollars.
5. *Sign your name.* Write your signature in such a way that it matches how you signed it for the signature card at the bank. Do not leave the signature line blank.
6. *Enter a description.* If desired, describe the purpose of the check on the Memo line. For example, write "groceries," as shown in Figure 5-1.2.

If you make a mistake when writing a check, begin again with a new check. On the check with the error, write VOID in large letters. In the check register, write VOID over the entry in the Description of Transaction column. Draw a line through the check amount and the balance amount. Record the check data again, using the new check number.

Check fraud occurs when someone alters a check by changing its amount to obtain more money from another person's account. *Forgery* is the act of signing another person's name on a check. To help protect yourself, write checks in a proper manner and keep your supply of unused checks in a safe location.

postdated check a check written with a date that will occur in the future

Carley Jackson
Phone: 555-0100
4250 West 18th Avenue
Chicago, IL 60601-2180

581

July 1, 20-- $\frac{2-74}{710}$

PAY TO THE
ORDER OF _Food Mart_ | $36.12

Thirty-six and $^{12}/_{100}$ DOLLARS

For Classroom Use Only

SKY CENTRAL BANK
Chicago, Illinois

MEMO _groceries_ *Carley Jackson*

⑆071000741 ⑈ 08⑈60⑈856⑈

Paying Bills Online

Instead of writing checks, you can pay bills online. It is safer than sending checks through the mail and faster because money leaves your account right away. It's also convenient and saves both postage and the cost of checks.

To pay bills online, you have two choices. First, you can register at the website of the business to which you will be making payments. You will give them your routing number and checking account number. Each month you can authorize a payment, or you can allow the business to take automatic payments (deductions) from your account.

Second, you can pay bills from your own bank. To do this, you must first register at your bank's website. During that process, you establish your personal identification number (PIN) or password to gain entry into your account. Screen prompts will lead you to the bank's online bill payment page, such as the one shown in Figure 5-1.3.

After you set up your list of payees, you can pay bills each month by simply selecting the payee from the list and entering the payment amount. The bank will remove the money from your checking account and send it to the payee's account. Be sure to record these payments in your check register.

Using Debit Cards and ATM Cards

debit card a bank card used to withdraw or deduct money from your checking account

Your bank may issue you a **debit card**, which can be used to withdraw or deduct money from your checking account. It allows you to withdraw cash at an ATM. It also allows you to make purchases by swiping the card through a point-of-sale (POS) terminal at a store's checkout counter. The effect is the same as writing a check, but the money is electronically removed from your account (debited) and transferred to the business's account. You may also be provided with an *ATM card*, which is similar to a debit card, but its use is limited to withdrawals and deposits made at ATM machines. It cannot be used to make purchases.

When using an ATM card or debit card with an ATM or POS terminal, the account holder must also enter a PIN or password. The PIN gives access to the account, so it must be guarded carefully. In some systems, a signature is also required.

Link to Make Payments screen

Down arrow

List of Payees

Click to transmit

Click when you finish paying bills

Date the bill will actually be paid

Enter payment amount

Click to select this payee —————

Symbol for a secure web page

Debit cards do not have all the same protections provided with credit cards. Credit cards allow you to reverse or dispute charges. If a debit card is lost or stolen, funds can be removed from your account. Debit cards should not be used for certain types of purchases, such as online purchases where your account information may be unprotected or purchases requiring deposits for which a hold may be placed on your funds.

Making Deposits

A short time after opening an account, the account holder will usually receive personalized deposit slips, along with checks. Blank deposit slips available at the bank can also be used. Figure 5-1.4 shows a deposit slip for a checking account. Note that the depositor's name and address are printed on the slip. The account number appears at the bottom of the slip.

Deposit slips are commonly used when making a deposit in person at the bank, but they are not needed when making deposits at an ATM. Simply follow the instructions on the ATM screen and get a receipt. Verify that the receipt shows the correct amount of the deposit. Many banks now make it easy to deposit money using a mobile app that allows you to take a picture of the check being deposited; again, no deposit slip is needed. It can take a few days for a deposit to be processed, so the account holder may not have access immediately to the money deposited.

Checks to be deposited must be properly endorsed. An **endorsement** is a signature, with or without instructions, written on the back of a

endorsement a signature, with or without instructions, written on the back of a check

► FIGURE 5-1.4 **Deposit Slip**

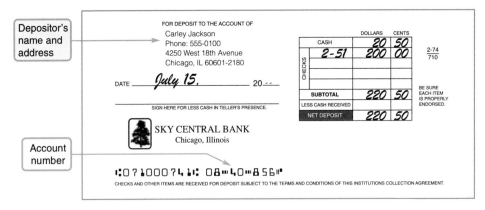

check. It authorizes the bank to cash or deposit the check. If a check is not properly endorsed, it may be returned by the bank to the customer and not deposited. Many checks have an endorsement area printed on the back of the check. If the back of the check is blank, place the check face up, turn the check over while keeping the same edge at the left, and write an endorsement on the left edge of the check.

Some endorsements provide more instructions than others do. Look closely at Figure 5-1.5 as you read about each form of endorsement. With a *blank endorsement*, the signature of the payee is written on the back of the check. The signature must be in ink. This endorsement provides little protection. Anyone who has the check can cash it. This endorsement should be used only when you are at the bank ready to cash or deposit the check.

A *restrictive endorsement* restricts or limits the use of a check. For example, *For deposit only* may be written on the check above the signature of the payee. A *special endorsement* transfers the right to cash the check to someone else. The words *Pay to the order of* and the name of the person or company to whom the check is being transferred are written above the signature of the payee. In some instances, a special endorsement is referred to as an *endorsement in full*.

Third-Party Checks

A special endorsement creates a *third-party check*, which is a check issued by the check writer (drawer) to the payee, who then endorses and

► FIGURE 5-1.5 **Check Endorsements**

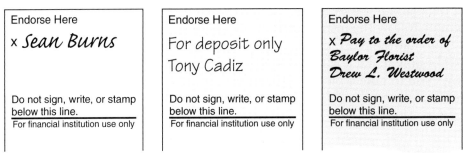

Blank Endorsement   Restrictive Endorsement   Special Endorsement

Building COMMUNICATION SKILLS

READING COMPREHENSION

Good reading skills will help you be more productive at school, at work, and in personal activities. Comprehension is the ability to understand what you have read. Reading for comprehension is also called *study reading*. The goal of this type of reading is to learn and to remember what has been read.

To help improve reading comprehension, read slowly and think about what you are reading. Written material is divided into passages. A passage is a group of paragraphs. Paragraphs are used to introduce and explain ideas. Paragraphs often have a common structure. The first sentence of a paragraph is the topic sentence. It tells you what the paragraph is about. The middle sentences explain the topic. The last sentence of a paragraph sums up or draws a conclusion. To improve understanding as you read, think about the purpose of the paragraph and how it relates to the overall topic of the passage.

Many people take notes of major points in each paragraph. Underlining or highlighting can help identify key points when you are reviewing the material. Comprehension can be improved when you read passages more than once. The first time, look for main ideas and points being made. The second time, focus on vocabulary and details.

Try It Out

Find a newspaper or magazine article about the banking industry. Read the article slowly. For each paragraph, jot down the topic (found in the first sentence). Then read the rest of the paragraph and write a brief phrase about it. Then write a sentence describing what you learned from the article.

---

transfers it to a third party. Many banks will not deposit or cash the check from the third party unless he or she has an account with the bank. If the check is bad, the amount of the check will come out of the third party's account. If a bank refuses to cash a third-party check, you may have to use a check-cashing service. A check-cashing business charges a high fee, often a percentage of the check amount.

Direct Deposits

With a *direct deposit*, wages or benefits are automatically deposited into a bank account electronically. An **electronic funds transfer (EFT)** uses a computer-based system to move money from the drawer's account to the payee's account. EFTs are used for automatic withdrawals and deposits. Many people receive Social Security payments in this manner. Many businesses electronically deposit their employees' net pay. This usually makes it available to employees on the same day it is deposited. The main advantage for account holders is that they have instant access to their money. This method is also safer and more convenient than carrying checks to the bank for deposit.

electronic funds transfer
the use of a computer-based system to move money from the drawer's account to the payee's account

 CHECKPOINT

Why might it be better to use a restrictive endorsement?

LO 5-1.4 How Do You Reconcile a Bank Statement?

Once a month, you will receive a statement from the bank. The *bank statement* may be on paper and arrive by mail, or it may be made available to you electronically. The statement will list checks, other withdrawals, and deposits made to the account. It will show the account's beginning balance and ending balance. Any service charges or other fees that have been debited (charged) to the account and any interest earned will also be listed.

When you get a bank statement, you should compare it to your check register. You will adjust the balance shown in the check register to record interest earned or fees charged. You will adjust the balance shown on the bank statement for checks or other withdrawals and deposits that have not yet been processed by the bank. After adjustments are made, the two balances (check register and bank statement) should be the same. This process is called reconciling a bank statement, or **bank reconciliation**. A form may be provided on the back of the bank statement or on the bank's website for use in reconciling the account. You can also use programs such as Excel to prepare a reconciliation. A sample bank reconciliation is shown in Figure 5-1.6. Follow these steps in bank reconciliation:

bank reconciliation the process of adjusting the check register and bank statement balances so that they agree

1. Enter the date of the reconciliation and the account number on the reconciliation form.
2. Enter the ending balance date and amount from the bank statement on the reconciliation form. The amount probably will not be the same as the balance shown in your check register.
3. Compare your check register with the bank statement. Verify that the amount of each deposit made is shown correctly on the bank statement. Place a check mark in the check mark (✓) column of the register by each deposit that is shown on the bank statement.
4. On the reconciliation form, list the date and amount of any deposits you made that do not appear on the bank statement. These are called *deposits in transit*. Total the deposit amounts. Add the total deposits in transit to the bank statement balance. Place this amount on the Subtotal line.
5. Compare your check register with the bank statement. Verify that the amount of each check you wrote and each ATM or debit card withdrawal you made is shown correctly on the bank statement. Place a check mark in the check mark (✓) column of the register by each check or other withdrawal that is shown on the bank statement.
6. On the reconciliation form, list the check number or code, date, and amount of any checks and other withdrawals you made that do not appear on the bank statement. Checks written that have not yet been processed by the bank are called *outstanding checks*. Total the outstanding amounts. Subtract the total from the Subtotal calculated in Step 4. The amount left is called the adjusted bank balance.
7. Enter the balance date and amount shown in your check register on the reconciliation form.
8. On the reconciliation form, list any fees or charges shown on the bank statement that are not recorded in the register. Total the

RECONCILIATION OF BANK STATEMENT

Date   August 3, 20--

Account No.   942869

Bank Statement Balance on   July 31, 20-- $ 966.68

Add Deposits in Transit and Other Credits

Date	Amount
7/31/20--	220.50

Total Deposits in Transit/Credits   220.50

Subtotal   1,187.18

Deduct Outstanding Checks/Withdrawals

Check No.	Date	Amount
580	7/2/20--	20.00
581	7/29/20--	36.12
ATM	8/1/20--	40.00

Total Outstanding Checks/Withdrawals   96.12

Adjusted Bank Balance $ 1,091.06

Check Register Balance on   August 3, 20-- $ 1,096.06

Deduct Bank Charges

Description	Amount
Service charge, monthly fee	5.00

Total Bank Charges   5.00

Subtotal   1,091.06

Add Interest or Other Credits

Description	Amount

Total Credits   0

Adjusted Check Register Balance $ 1,091.06

amounts. Subtract the total from the check register balance on the form to obtain the Subtotal. Record the fees and charges in your check register, and update the balance.

9. On the reconciliation form, list any interest or other credits (additions) shown on the bank statement that do not appear in the register. Total the interest and other credits. Add this total to the amount calculated in Step 8. Record the interest or other credits in the register and update the balance.

10. Compare the adjusted bank balance and the adjusted check register balance. The two amounts should be the same. If they are not, complete the steps again and check your calculations carefully. If the numbers still are not the same, check your calculations in the check

register. Also, check for *transposition errors*, which occur when numbers are recorded out of order. For example, you may write a check for $62.26 but record the check as $26.62 in your check register. If you find that any kind of mistake has been made, add or subtract the amount of the mistake to correct the check register balance.

With today's modern checking account, you may wish to access the account online and manage it daily, checking items added and deducted.

Truncated Checks

Checks that a bank has processed are called *canceled checks* or *cleared checks*. In the past, banks returned cleared checks to the account holder. Today, to make processing faster and more efficient, many banks exchange check information electronically by producing a digital image of the check. When a paper check is transformed into a digital image, it is said to be *truncated*. Truncated checks are also known as *substitute checks*. Both sides of the check are scanned to produce the digital image. Truncated checks may be viewed (and a copy printed) by accessing your account online. You may also request that a copy be mailed to you, but there is often a charge for this service. You must account for all checks, truncated or otherwise, to be sure they have cleared.

Other Fees and Interest Earnings

Fees and rules for checking accounts vary. Consumers should compare accounts and banks to find the best value for the type of account desired. *Credit unions* are nonprofit financial organizations, and members may be offered free checking accounts with no minimum deposit. Some banks offer free checking accounts to senior citizens and students.

Typical fees include monthly service fees or transaction fees. Monthly service fees range from $5 to $20 a month. Rather than a monthly service fee, some accounts charge a *transaction fee*, such as 20 cents for processing each check. Some accounts may allow ten checks at no charge and then have a set charge for each check after that. One-time fees may be charged for making wire transfers, having insufficient funds to cover a check, or allowing your bank balance to fall below the minimum. Some banks charge a monthly fee for online bill payment privileges. You will see any bank fees on your bank statement. Consider the fees and restrictions for online banking when you choose a bank.

Some checking accounts do not have monthly service or transaction fees. For example, the monthly service fee may be waived if you keep a minimum required balance in your account. Some checking accounts pay interest on the money you keep in the account. You might choose to have an account that pays a lower interest rate on the deposited amount in order to have no monthly fee. When interest is deposited in your account, it must be entered in your check register and added to your balance.

 **CHECKPOINT**

What are some of the checking account fees that banks may charge?

KEY TERMS REVIEW

Match the terms with the definitions. Some terms may not be used.

_____ 1. The process of adjusting checkbook and bank balances so that they agree

_____ 2. A bank card used to withdraw or deduct money from your checking account

_____ 3. A tool used to track checking account transactions

_____ 4. A demand deposit account on which checks are drawn

_____ 5. A check written with a date that will occur in the future

_____ 6. Money added to a checking account

_____ 7. A written order to a bank to pay a stated amount to a person

_____ 8. A signature written on the back of a check

_____ 9. The use of a computer-based system to move funds from the drawer's account to the payee's account

a. bank reconciliation

b. check

c. check register

d. checking account

e. debit card

f. deposit

g. electronic funds transfer

h. endorsement

i. postdated check

j. withdrawal

CHECK YOUR UNDERSTANDING

10. Describe the three characteristics of money that allow it to function as a medium of exchange.

11. What does a bank typically require of a person who wishes to open a checking account?

12. What is the purpose of a signature card?

13. What is the purpose of a check register? What types of data should be in the register?

14. What are the advantages of automatic withdrawal for consumers?

15. What should you do if you make an error while writing a check?

16. What is the difference between a debit card and an ATM card?

17. What is the purpose of a check endorsement? How does a blank endorsement differ from a restrictive endorsement?

18. What is a PIN?

19. What are some advantages of using direct deposit?

20. What is the purpose of completing a bank reconciliation?

THINK CRITICALLY

21. A checking account offers you convenience for bill paying. Many people choose to use cash only. Which do you prefer? Why?

22. Some businesses require payment through automatic withdrawals from your checking account. If other payment methods are used, these businesses may charge you more. Why do you think businesses might prefer automatic withdrawals?

23. Using debit cards is much more convenient than paying cash or writing a check. Many merchants will no longer accept personal checks because there is so much fraud. What is the downside to using your debit card rather than a credit card or cash?

24. Why do you think someone would use a postdated check? What do you think are the dangers of paying a bill with a postdated check?

25. Many banks will not accept third-party checks unless presented by the account holder in person with a photo ID. If the check is bad, the amount of the check comes out of the account holder's account. Why is this a necessary step for banks to take?

26. Many people do not take the time to reconcile their bank accounts. Explain why this isn't a good idea. How does completing a bank reconciliation protect you?

EXTEND YOUR LEARNING

27. You make the transactions listed below during the month of April. Your beginning checking account balance is $218.33. Calculate your new balance at the end of the month, and double-check your work.
    - Check No. 401 on April 1 to Westside Services: $15.00 for haircut
    - Check No. 402 on April 5 to J. Jill. $20.50 for new shirt
    - Cash withdrawal at ATM for $20.00 on April 8
    - Deposit of $25.00 cash on April 10 (gift from uncle)
    - Debit card purchase (DC) of $19.50 on April 11 at Rowe's for food
    - Check No. 403 on April 15 to Bill Baxter: $35.00 for loan payment
    - Cash withdrawal at ATM for $20.00 on April 18
    - Debit card purchase of $9.95 on April 25 at Aston Theater for movie
    - Bank service charge on April 28 for $8.00

THE ESSENTIAL QUESTION   Refer to the essential question on p. 147. The two purposes of a checking account are to provide a safe place to keep money and to allow users easy access to the money in the account to make purchases and pay bills. You should maintain your checking account by recording transactions in a check register and reconciling it with the bank statement each month.

THE ESSENTIAL QUESTION   Why do you need to save money, and how can you do so?

LEARNING OBJECTIVES

LO 5-2.1   Discuss the purpose of savings.

LO 5-2.2   Explain how you can grow your savings with interest.

LO 5-2.3   List and compare savings options and features.

KEY TERMS

- savings account, 161
- liquid, 161
- principal, 162
- simple interest, 162
- compound interest, 163
- annuity, 164
- Rule of 72, 165
- money market account, 166
- certificate of deposit (CD), 167
- U.S. savings bond, 167

LO 5-2.1 What Are the Benefits of Saving?

Saving money is important because it means you are providing for future needs and wants. Saving helps you meet your financial goals. A **savings account** is a demand deposit account designed for the accumulation of money in a safe place for future use. The funds may not be as easily accessible as funds in a checking account. However, the funds are still highly **liquid**, meaning you can generally withdraw your money at any time without penalty. Savings accounts at banks generally are insured by the FDIC up to the legal limit of $250,000 per depositor per bank.

Savings accounts pay interest at a low rate. However, the rate is usually higher than the rate for a checking account. Some banks allow depositors to link their savings and checking accounts. This allows the transfer of money back and forth (by phone or electronically) at the account holder's convenience.

Having a savings account helps you be prepared for emergencies and other unplanned spending. It gives you flexibility so that you can make better buying decisions. For example, if you have savings, you may be able to buy items at sale prices now rather than later. Buying at sale prices now saves money in the long run. Savings accounts also allow you to accumulate money for large purchases, such as a car or a house. Setting aside money today for use later is a first step in becoming financially secure.

Savings accounts can also be used to hold money temporarily while you are preparing to open an investment account. Money that isn't needed until sometime in the future should be invested at a higher rate of return than what savings accounts generally offer.

savings account a demand deposit account designed for the accumulation of money in a safe place for future use

liquid the capability to withdraw money at any time without penalty

❯❯❯ CHECKPOINT

What are the benefits of having a savings account?

FOCUS On...

THE FDIC

The Federal Deposit Insurance Corporation (FDIC) is an independent agency of the U.S. government. The FDIC protects depositors of insured U.S. banks against the loss of deposits if the bank fails. FDIC insurance is backed by the full faith and credit of the U.S. government. Since the FDIC began operation in 1934, no depositor has ever lost a penny of FDIC-insured deposits.

The FDIC covers all types of deposits, including checking accounts, savings accounts, money market deposit accounts, and certificates of deposit (CDs). The FDIC covers accounts at each insured bank, including principal and any accrued interest through the date of the bank's closing, up to the insurance limit. The FDIC does not insure the following:

- Money invested in stocks, bonds, mutual funds, life insurance policies, annuities, or municipal securities, even if purchased at an insured bank
- Valuables stored in the bank's safe deposit boxes
- U.S. treasury bills, bonds, or notes (but these investments are backed by the full faith and credit of the U.S. government)

The standard maximum deposit insurance amount (SMDIA) is $250,000. All accounts at the same bank are added together. For example, if you have $100,000 in savings, $50,000 in checking, and $150,000 in CDs, totaling $300,000, only $250,000 of that amount is insured.

The FDIC insures deposits that a person holds in one insured bank separately from deposits the person holds in another separately chartered and insured bank. For example, if a person has an account at Bank A and an account at Bank B, both accounts are insured separately up to the SMDIA. Funds deposited in other branches of the same insured bank are not separately insured.

Think Critically

1. What is the purpose of FDIC insurance? As a consumer, do you benefit from this insurance?
2. During the Great Depression, many banks failed and people lost their deposits. Do you think such a thing could happen again? Why or why not?

LO 5-2.2 How Can You Grow Your Savings?

Growing your savings is an important part of growing your wealth. One way to do this is by earning interest on your savings. When you earn interest, you are actually getting paid to save money!

Computing Interest

principal sum of money set aside on which interest is paid

simple interest interest computed on principal once in a certain period of time

Money deposited in a savings account will usually earn a set rate of interest. Interest earnings are taxable when they are earned. The sum of money set aside on which interest is paid is called **principal**. Money earned on the principal is called interest. The higher the rate of interest, the more money the account earns.

When interest is computed on the principal once during a certain time period, this is called **simple interest**. The simple interest method assumes that one interest payment will be made at the end of the period. Interest rates are usually given in yearly rates. However, the interest may be paid after a certain number of months. In this case, the months must be converted into a fraction of a year to compute the interest. The formula for calculating simple interest and a sample problem are shown in Figure 5-2.1.

Interest (I)	=	Principal (P) × Rate (R) × Time (T)
	=	$1,000 × 6% Annual Rate × 6 Months
	=	$1,000 × 0.06 × 6/12
	=	$30

Another way of calculating interest is called **compound interest**, which is interest earned on both principal and previously earned interest. Figure 5-2.2 shows how interest compounds. The principal, $100, was put into savings at an annual rate of 6 percent. The interest was then compounded quarterly (four times per year) for three years. An interest rate of 6 percent per year is 1.5 percent quarterly (0.06 ÷ 4 = 0.015).

compound interest interest earned on both principal and previously earned interest

▶ FIGURE 5-2.2 **Compound Interest**

Quarterly Compounding
Annual Interest Rate 6%

Year	Beginning Balance	Rate 6%	Quarter				Ending Balance
			1	2	3	4	
1	$100.00	0.015	$1.50	$1.52	$1.55	$1.57	$106.14
2	$106.14	0.015	$1.59	$1.62	$1.64	$1.66	$112.65
3	$112.65	0.015	$1.69	$1.72	$1.74	$1.77	$119.57

Future Value of Money

The *time value of money* is the concept that a dollar today is worth more than a dollar in the future because the dollar you have today can earn interest. The *future value of money* refers to what it will be worth in the future, after interest has compounded. Future value can be compounded based on a single deposit that is left in an account for a long period of time. It can also be based on a series of deposits that are made over time. To compute future value, you can use future value tables, or you can use a financial (business) calculator that has these tables built into its memory.

When computing future value, you will need to know three things: how much money you can set aside, how long the money will be set aside, and the interest rate it will earn. As each of these rises, the amount by which it will grow also rises. For example, $500 will grow faster than $100. An 8 percent rate of return will grow money faster than 6 percent, and so on.

Saving a Single Sum

Assuming you could set aside $500 and leave it there for ten years at an annual interest rate of 8 percent compounded annually, how much would you have at the end of ten years? To calculate this, you could set up a table, similar to that shown in Figure 5-2.2, or you could use the Future Value (FV) of $1 table, as shown in Figure 5-2.3.

Period	Percent								
	3%	4%	5%	6%	7%	8%	9%	10%	11%
1	1.03000	1.04000	1.05000	1.06000	1.07000	1.08000	1.09000	1.10000	1.11000
2	1.06090	1.08160	1.10250	1.12360	1.14990	1.16640	1.11810	1.21000	1.23210
3	1.09273	1.12486	1.15723	1.19102	1.22504	1.25971	1.29503	1.33100	1.36763
4	1.12551	1.16986	1.21551	1.26248	1.31080	1.36049	1.41158	1.46410	1.51807
5	1.15927	1.21665	1.27628	1.33823	1.40255	1.46933	1.53862	1.61051	1.68506
6	1.19405	1.26532	1.34010	1.41852	1.50073	1.58687	1.66710	1.77156	1.87042
7	1.22987	1.31593	1.40710	1.50363	1.60578	1.71382	1.82804	1.94872	2.07616
8	1.26677	1.36857	1.47746	1.59385	1.71819	1.85093	1.99256	2.14359	2.30454
9	1.30477	1.42331	1.55133	1.68948	1.83846	1.99901	2.17189	2.35795	2.55804
10	1.34392	1.48024	1.62890	1.79085	1.96715	2.15893	2.36736	2.59374	2.83942
11	1.38423	1.53945	1.71034	1.89830	2.10485	2.33164	2.58043	2.85312	3.15176
12	1.42576	1.60103	1.79586	2.01220	2.25219	2.51817	2.81266	3.13843	3.49845
13	1.46853	1.66507	1.88565	2.13203	2.40985	2.71962	3.06581	3.45227	3.88328
14	1.51259	1.73168	1.97993	2.26090	2.57853	2.93719	3.34173	3.79750	4.31044
15	1.55797	1.80094	2.07893	2.39656	2.75903	3.17217	3.64248	4.17725	4.78459
16	1.60471	1.87298	2.18288	2.54035	2.95216	3.42594	3.97031	4.59497	5.31089
17	1.65285	1.94790	2.29202	2.69377	3.15882	3.70002	4.32763	5.05447	5.89509
18	1.70243	2.02582	2.40662	2.54035	3.37993	3.99602	4.71712	5.55992	6.54355
19	1.75351	2.10685	2.52695	3.02560	3.61653	4.31570	5.14166	6.11591	7.26334
20	1.80611	2.19112	2.65330	3.20714	3.86968	4.66096	5.60441	6.72750	8.06231

Using the table, you would go down the Period column to 10 (ten compounding periods). Then you'd go across to the 8% column. The FV factor from the table is 2.15893. If you multiply $500 times 2.15893, you can determine that the future value will be $1,079.47.

Saving on a Regular Basis

annuity a fixed amount set aside on a regular basis over time

Rather than a lump sum, perhaps you could set aside money regularly. When you set aside a fixed amount on a regular basis over time, it is called an **annuity**. Suppose you could set aside $500 per year for ten years at the rate of 8 percent. Instead of the FV of $1 table, you would now use the Future Value (FV) of an Annuity of $1 table, as shown in Figure 5-2.4.

Using the FV of an Annuity of $1 table, go down to period 10 and then across to the 8% column to find an FV factor of 14.48656. Multiply your annual payment of $500 times 14.48656 to determine that you will have $7,243.28 at the end of ten years.

Present Value of Money

In certain cases, you may want to calculate the *present value of money*, which is the amount of money you would need to deposit today in order to accumulate a specific amount in the future. Present value tables are available to help you make this calculation. For example, you may want to save $1,000 for a down payment on a car in four years in a savings account that pays 3 percent interest annually. To determine how much you need to deposit today to reach your savings goal in four years, use

▶ FIGURE 5-2.4 **Future Value of an Annuity of $1**

Period	Percent								
	3%	**4%**	**5%**	**6%**	**7%**	**8%**	**9%**	**10%**	**11%**
1	1.00000	1.00000	1.00000	1.00000	1.00000	1.00000	1.00000	1.00000	1.00000
2	2.03000	2.04000	2.05000	2.06000	2.07000	2.08000	2.09000	2.10000	2.11000
3	3.09090	3.12160	3.15250	3.18360	3.21490	3.24640	3.27810	3.31000	3.34210
4	4.18363	4.24646	4.31013	4.37462	4.43994	4.50611	4.57313	4.64100	4.70973
5	5.30914	5.41632	5.52563	5.63709	5.75074	5.86660	5.98471	6.10510	6.22780
6	6.46841	6.63298	6.80191	6.97532	7.15329	7.33593	7.52334	7.71561	7.91286
7	7.66246	7.89829	8.14201	8.39384	8.65402	8.92280	9.20044	9.48717	9.78327
8	8.89234	9.21427	9.54911	9.89747	10.25980	10.63663	11.02847	11.43589	11.85943
9	10.15911	10.58280	11.02656	11.49132	11.97799	12.48756	13.02104	13.57948	14.16397
10	11.46388	12.00611	12.57789	13.18080	13.81645	14.48656	15.19293	15.93743	16.72201
11	12.80780	13.48635	14.20679	14.97164	15.79360	16.64549	17.56029	18.53117	19.56143
12	14.19203	15.02581	15.91713	16.86994	17.88845	18.97713	20.14072	21.38428	22.71319
13	15.61779	16.62684	17.71298	18.88214	20.14064	21.49530	22.95339	24.52271	26.21164
14	17.08632	18.29191	19.59863	21.10507	22.55049	24.21492	26.01919	27.97498	30.09492
15	18.59891	20.02359	21.57856	23.27597	25.12902	27.15211	29.36092	31.77248	34.40536
16	20.15688	21.82453	23.65749	25.67253	27.88805	30.32428	33.00340	35.94973	39.18995
17	21.76159	23.69751	25.84037	28.21288	30.84022	33.75023	36.97371	40.54470	44.50084
18	23.41444	25.64541	28.13239	30.90565	33.99903	37.45024	41.30134	45.59917	50.39594
19	25.11687	27.67123	30.53900	33.75999	37.37897	41.44626	46.01846	51.15909	56.93949
20	26.87037	29.77808	33.06595	36.78559	40.99549	45.76196	51.16012	57.27500	64.20283

the table in Figure 5-2.5 on page 166. Go down to period 4 and then across to the 3% column to find the PV factor of 0.88849. Then multiply $1,000, the amount you want to have in four years, times 0.88849 to determine the amount you need to deposit today—$888.49.

Rule of 72

A principle called the **Rule of 72** provides a quick formula for computing how long it will take to double money invested at a given interest rate. To apply the Rule of 72, simply divide the annual interest rate into 72. The answer is the number of years it will take at that rate to double the amount invested. For example, if $50 is invested at 6 percent interest, then it will grow to $100 in 12 years (72 ÷ 6 = 12).

Rule of 72 a quick formula for computing how long it will take to double money invested at a given interest rate

 CHECKPOINT

What three things must you know to compute future value?

LO 5-2.3 What Are Your Savings Options?

When choosing savings options and places to save, consider your financial goals. How much money do you want to save and earn in interest for a particular purpose? How much time do you have in which to save?

Period	3%	4%	5%	6%	7%	8%	9%	10%	11%
					Percent				
1	0.97087	0.96154	0.95238	0.94340	0.93458	0.92593	0.91743	0.90909	0.90090
2	0.94260	0.92456	0.90703	0.89000	0.87344	0.85734	0.84168	0.82645	0.81162
3	0.91514	0.88900	0.86384	0.83962	0.81630	0.79383	0.77218	0.75131	0.73119
4	0.88849	0.85480	0.82270	0.79209	0.76290	0.73503	0.70843	0.68301	0.65873
5	0.86261	0.82193	0.78353	0.74726	0.71299	0.68058	0.64993	0.62092	0.59345
6	0.83748	0.79031	0.74622	0.70496	0.66634	0.63017	0.59627	0.56447	0.53464
7	0.81309	0.75992	0.71068	0.66506	0.62275	0.58349	0.54703	0.51316	0.48166
8	0.78941	0.73069	0.67684	0.62741	0.58201	0.54027	0.50187	0.46651	0.43393
9	0.76642	0.70259	0.64461	0.59190	0.54393	0.50025	0.46043	0.42410	0.39092
10	0.74409	0.67556	0.61391	0.55839	0.50835	0.46319	0.42241	0.38554	0.35218
11	0.72242	0.64958	0.58468	0.52679	0.47509	0.42888	0.38753	0.35049	0.31728
12	0.70138	0.62460	0.55684	0.49697	0.44401	0.39711	0.35553	0.31863	0.28584
13	0.68095	0.60057	0.53032	0.46884	0.41496	0.36770	0.32618	0.28966	0.25751
14	0.66112	0.57748	0.50507	0.44230	0.38782	0.34046	0.29925	0.26333	0.23199
15	0.64186	0.55526	0.48102	0.41727	0.36245	0.31524	0.27454	0.23939	0.20900
16	0.62317	0.53391	0.45811	0.39365	0.33873	0.29189	0.25187	0.21763	0.18829
17	0.60502	0.51337	0.43630	0.37136	0.31657	0.27027	0.23107	0.19784	0.16963
18	0.58739	0.49363	0.41552	0.35034	0.29586	0.25025	0.21199	0.17986	0.15282
19	0.57029	0.47464	0.39573	0.33051	0.27651	0.23171	0.19449	0.16351	0.13768
20	0.55368	0.45639	0.37689	0.31180	0.25842	0.21455	0.17843	0.14864	0.12403

What interest rate can you earn on your savings? The amount of time you have to save and the interest you can earn determine how much money you need to save each month or year to meet your goals.

When your savings account has reached a "critical mass," it's time to move it to a permanent investment. In other words, as your savings account continues to grow, it will pass beyond what you might need for emergencies or planned events. When it does, it's time to set it aside for longer periods of time. All these factors should be considered when choosing a savings option.

Methods of Saving

A savings account is one method for saving your money. However, there are many other savings options that you should also consider.

Money Market Accounts

money market account a type of savings account that earns the market rate of interest on the money deposited

A savings option offered by some banks is the **money market account**, which pays the market rate of interest on the money deposited. When interest rates are rising, a money market account will often earn more than a savings account or CD. When rates are falling, however, the interest earned may be less than that paid on a CD. A minimum balance, such as $1,000 or $5,000, is often required to open a money market account. The interest rate also may increase as your balance increases. Restrictions may apply to the account. For example, you are usually limited to a certain number of withdrawals each month. If you make more withdrawals than allowed, you will be charged fees.

Certificates of Deposit

A **certificate of deposit (CD)** is a time deposit (rather than a demand deposit) that pays a fixed rate of interest for a specified length of time. CDs typically pay higher interest rates than a regular savings account. As a time deposit, the funds must be set aside for a fixed period of time. For example, you may put your money into a six-month CD at a guaranteed rate of 3.25 percent. If you leave your money in the CD for the entire six months, you will earn the full 3.25 percent. If you withdraw part or all of it before the six months, you will be penalized. At some banks, you will lose part of your principal, as well as receive no interest on the money deposited. Because a CD pays a higher interest rate than a savings account, it would be a good savings option if you do not need immediate access to the money.

certificate of deposit (CD) a time deposit that pays a fixed rate of interest for a specified length of time

U.S. Savings Bonds

If you are able to commit your money for a longer period of time, you have other choices. One good long-term choice is a savings bond. A **U.S. savings bond** is issued by the federal government and pays a guaranteed minimum rate of interest. These bonds are sold at face value. For example, you would pay $50 for a $50 bond. They must be held for a minimum of one year and can be held for a maximum of 30 years. The bonds are available in any amount from $25 to $10,000.

U.S. savings bond a bond issued by the federal government that pays a guaranteed minimum rate of interest

U.S. savings bonds are considered to be a safe form of saving because they are backed by the U.S. government's full faith and credit. Although you can redeem a savings bond after one year, if it is redeemed in fewer than five years, a three-month interest penalty will be applied.

Looking Ahead

As you begin to work and save money, you'll have many savings options. Before choosing one, it's a good idea to consider the interest you will earn on your savings. Many financial websites include a CD calculator to help you determine how much interest you can earn on a certificate of deposit. By entering principal, time, and interest data into the fields, the calculator will determine the future value for you. Using an online search engine, enter the search terms "CD calculator." Then use the CD calculator to solve the following problem:

You deposit $2,000 in a six-month CD with an interest rate of 1.5 percent compounded monthly. What will your ending balance be? Now suppose you deposit the same $2,000 in a two-year CD with an interest rate of 2 percent compounded monthly. What will your ending balance be?

Why might you consider buying a U.S. savings bond from the TreasuryDirect website?

Savings bonds will continue to earn interest for up to 30 years. When a bond stops earning interest, it should be cashed in or converted to another type of bond. Interest is not taxable until the bond is cashed. If the bond is used for education expenses (for you or your children), the interest may not be subject to federal taxes.

Because it can take several years for a U.S. savings bond to mature, it should be used only as a long-term savings option. U.S. savings bonds can be purchased online only at the U.S. Department of Treasury's Treasury-Direct website. You can also see the current rates being paid on bonds at the site. U.S. savings bonds will be covered more in a later chapter.

Individual Retirement Accounts

Saving for retirement is an important goal for many people. One way to save for retirement is by creating an *individual retirement account (IRA)*. An IRA allows individuals to deposit money into an account during their working years and to delay paying taxes on the money and the interest earned until it is withdrawn after retirement. Because income earned during retirement is often lower than it is during your working years, you will likely be in a lower tax bracket when you withdraw the money, meaning you will pay less tax on it.

IRAs can be set up at a bank or another financial institution. IRAs can also be set up through mutual fund companies, insurance companies, and stockbrokers. Different types of IRAs can be created. The amount of money that can be deposited in the account each year and other rules regarding IRAs are set by the federal government. More information about IRAs can be found in a later chapter.

Places to Save Your Money

Banks and credit unions are the most common places where consumers save their money because accounts are FDIC insured. There are other places to save, however, and some of them are also insured.

Online-Only Banks

Online-only banks often pay higher rates of interest, charge lower fees, and offer lower mortgage and loan rates than traditional banks. One reason is because they don't have the high operating and labor costs that brick-and-mortar banks do. They can pass this savings onto their customers. In addition, online-only banks often have websites that offer more features than found on traditional banks' websites, such as budgeting and financial planning tools.

Online banks are subject to the same laws and regulations as traditional banks, so accounts must be FDIC insured. Before choosing one, research it to learn about the bank's track record. You must have confidence that it is reliable and secure.

Brokerage Firms

In addition to buying and selling stocks and bonds, brokerage or investment firms offer checking and savings account options. They generally pay higher interest rates on savings accounts. However, they may not be insured by the FDIC or any other insurer. If you have a savings account with a brokerage firm, you usually have the flexibility to move money back and forth between savings and an investment option. Brokerage accounts will be covered more in a later chapter.

International Banks

The Internet opens new possibilities for consumers around the world. As an American citizen, you can hold accounts in other countries. Although you may never visit the bank in person, you will receive your statements and account information online. Your money would be insured through the financial network of the bank's home country. In your lifetime, you will see international banking become more commonplace for businesses as well as consumers.

 CHECKPOINT

What should you consider when choosing among savings options?

5-2 Lesson Assessment

KEY TERMS REVIEW

Match the terms with the definitions. Some terms may not be used.

_____ 1. Interest computed on principal once during a certain time

_____ 2. The capability to withdraw money at any time without penalty

_____ 3. A time deposit that pays a fixed rate of interest for a specified length of time

_____ 4. Interest earned on both principal and previously earned interest

_____ 5. A demand deposit account designed for the accumulation of money in a safe place for future use

_____ 6. A bond issued by the federal government

_____ 7. A sum of money set aside on which interest is paid

_____ 8. A fixed amount set aside on a regular basis over time

_____ 9. A quick formula for computing how long it will take to double money invested at a given interest rate

a. annuity

b. certificate of deposit (CD)

c. compound interest

d. liquid

e. money market account

f. principal

g. Rule of 72

h. savings account

i. simple interest

j. U.S. savings bond

CHECK YOUR UNDERSTANDING

10. What is the formula for calculating simple interest?

11. How does compound interest differ from simple interest?

12. What is meant by the future value of money?

13. How is the future value of $1 different from the future value of an annuity of $1?

14. How do a certificate of deposit and a money market account differ from a regular savings account? How are they the same?

15. Why are U.S. savings bonds considered to be a safe form of saving?

16. What is the purpose of an IRA? What types of companies offer IRAs?

17. How do the amount of time you have to save and the interest you can earn relate to achieving financial goals?

18. What is the Rule of 72 that is related to saving?

19. At what point should savings be moved to an investment type of account? Why?

THINK CRITICALLY

20. Why should you put money into savings in addition to having a checking account?

21. Why is it important to be able to set aside money for long periods of time? Why should you, as a young person, start saving early?

22. How can compounding interest help you grow your savings?

23. Why would you choose a CD over a money market account?

24. A regular IRA is tax-deferred. That means you don't pay taxes on the interest earned until you begin withdrawing funds during retirement. Why is it advantageous to defer your income taxes?

EXTEND YOUR LEARNING

TEAMWORK

25. In your local area, there are many banks, credit unions, and other financial institutions that offer savings options such as money market accounts and CDs. With a partner, conduct research using the Internet and the phone book, visiting the Chamber of Commerce, and using other sources as available to locate the following information:

    a. List five banks in your local area. For each one, list the rates on CDs, savings accounts, money market accounts, IRAs, and other types of accounts that may be available.

    b. List five credit unions, savings and loan banks, and other financial institutions in your local area. For each one, list the rates on CDs, savings accounts, money market accounts, IRAs, and other types of accounts that may be available.

    c. List five brokerage firms and other types of businesses that offer savings options in your local area. For each one, list the rates on CDs, savings accounts, money market accounts, IRAs, and other types of accounts that may be available.

    d. List five online-only banks that offer savings options. For each one, list the rates on CDs, savings accounts, money market accounts, IRAs, and other types of accounts that may be available.

    e. Based on the information you have gathered, select the financial institution that best meets your needs in terms of accounts offered. Next to each account, list any costs or disadvantages. Also list any restrictions (such as cosigner and minimum activity).

    f. Prepare a report of your findings and your decision. Include with your report any brochures or other information collected.

THE ESSENTIAL QUESTION Refer to the essential question on p. 161. Saving money will provide you security during your lifetime. Options include savings accounts, money market accounts, certificates of deposit, savings bonds, and IRAs.

LEARNING OBJECTIVES

LO 5-3.1 Describe banking services available to consumers at most banks and credit unions.

LO 5-3.2 Discuss the costs of banking services.

LO 5-3.3 Explain consumer responsibilities for holders of bank accounts.

KEY TERMS

- cashier's check, 172
- certified check, 172
- stop payment, 172
- smart card, 173
- overdraft protection, 173
- Internet banking, 174
- safe deposit box, 174
- bounced check, 175
- inactive account, 176
- floating a check, 177

LO 5-3.1 What Banking Services Are Available to Consumers?

In addition to checking and savings accounts, banks and credit unions offer a number of services for consumers. Some of these are included with your checking account. For example, you may be able to have a "free" checking account if you maintain a minimum balance each month. Other services cost additional money, either on a regular basis, such as monthly or once a year, or as you use them.

Payment Services

cashier's check a check issued against the bank's funds

certified check a personal check that the bank guarantees

A **cashier's check** is a check issued against bank funds. When you buy a cashier's check, the money comes from your account to pay the bank. The money for the payee of the cashier's check comes from the bank's account. A **certified check** is a personal check that the bank guarantees to be good. The bank deducts the amount from your account and holds it in reserve for specific payment of that check. Some people prefer to receive a cashier's check or certified check rather than a personal check because they are more secure.

Some banks issue money orders. A *money order* is a type of check for a specified amount used to pay bills or make payments for which the money is guaranteed. The money order is a safe way to send money through the mail. It does not have your bank's account number or other personal information about you that would be found on a check.

A *traveler's check* is a special form of check that is used instead of cash or personal checks while traveling. When traveler's checks are purchased, money is taken from your bank account to cover them. With the widespread use of ATM machines and credit cards, the need for traveler's checks has diminished.

stop payment an instruction to the bank not to honor a check that has been issued or lost

Another service provided by banks is called stop payment. With a **stop payment**, the bank is instructed not to honor a check you issued or lost. The stop-payment order is generally good for six months. After

that, the check will no longer be honored because checks over six months old are not valid
for cashing or depositing.

Automated Teller Machines (ATMs)

Banks and credit unions provide ATM machines
for their customers. When you use your bank's
ATM machine, you usually are not charged a
fee for the transaction, but you likely will be
charged a fee if you use another bank's ATM.
Your ATM or debit card allows you 24-hour access to your accounts. You can check balances,
withdraw cash, deposit cash and checks, and
transfer money between your accounts.

Bank Cards

Banks and credit unions issue several types of
bank cards. These cards have special features
and are electronically coded, allowing you to
use them for purchases, cash advances, and
deposits. ATM cards and debit cards, discussed
earlier in the chapter, are two types of bank cards.

Why do banks provide ATMs for their customers?

Banks may issue credit cards to their customers who qualify. These
cards often have low, fixed interest rates. Because you are a customer,
you may be offered a higher credit limit.

Similar to debit and ATM cards, banks may issue customers a **smart
card**, or *stored value card*, which contains a computer chip that stores
electronic money. You deposit money to the smart card electronically
when you purchase or renew the card. The card carries an electronic balance. When the money is spent, you can add more money to the card and
continue using it. The advantage of a smart card is that it is not linked to
your checking account, and if it is lost or stolen, the thief cannot access
your bank account. Smart cards often carry the Visa or MasterCard logo,
making them acceptable for most kinds of transactions.

Smart card a card that contains
a computer chip that stores
electronic money

Overdraft Protection

With **overdraft protection**, if you write a check or make a withdrawal
from your account and the account does not have enough money to
cover the transaction, the bank will cover the shortage. This service is
not automatic; you must sign up for it. Still, it is at the discretion of the
bank as to whether it will cover an overdraft. If you have a savings account at the same bank where you have a checking account, the bank
may allow you to use the savings account for overdraft protection. If
you write checks for more money than you have in your checking account, the bank will draw the money from your savings account.

overdraft protection a bank
service that covers a shortage in
your account

Overdraft protection can be a valuable service for consumers. Without it, a check would be returned for *nonsufficient funds (NSF)*. In addition to the original amount of the check, you would have to pay NSF
fees. Although banks may charge a fee for overdraft protection, it is usually less than the costs associated with an NSF check.

Internet Banking

Many banks allow their account holders to access and manage their accounts on the Internet. This is known as **Internet banking**. An access code or PIN number along with a user name is needed. Customers can view their accounts at any time on any day. Internet banking typically allows you to do the following:

- Check account balances
- Check that deposits are posted and checks have cleared
- Monitor activity in your account
- View and print statements
- Transfer money between accounts, such as from checking to savings
- See interest or fees that have been posted
- Pay bills electronically

Internet banking can be as safe as writing paper checks. When deposits and withdrawals are made electronically, nothing can get lost in the mail. Account holders can see exactly how much is in their account at any time.

Safe Deposit Boxes

Many banks and credit unions rent out safe deposit boxes as a service to their customers. A **safe deposit box** is a secure container located in the bank vault. You can use it to store important documents, such as deeds and stock certificates, or valuable jewelry, among other things. The safe deposit box protects items from fire or theft. A safe deposit box usually costs from $50 to $100 a year, depending on the size of the box. Many banks require that the fee for the safe deposit box be electronically debited to your account once a year

To open a safe deposit box, you will need an account at that institution. You will sign a signature card so that the bank can verify who has authority to open the box. You will be given a key for the box, and the bank will also have a key. Both keys must be used to open the box.

Loans

Banks use the money you have on deposit, combined with the deposits of other customers, to make loans. Credit unions also offer loans to their members. Because credit unions are nonprofit organizations, members may get lower interest rates on loans. Some examples of the types of loans provided by banks and credit unions are home mortgage loans, car loans, and personal lines of credit.

Financial Advising

Some banks offer personal financial advising services. They look at your financial situation and recommend financial products, such as mutual funds, that correspond to your goals and resources. Before investing, check options on your own. Be sure the mutual funds and other financial products you purchase have been in existence for a long time and have performed well over time.

Car-Buying Services

Some financial institutions offer *car-buying services*. For a fee, they will find a new or used car of your choice, negotiate the price, and arrange for its delivery. Basically, you are paying the company to negotiate on your behalf. In many cases, the bank or credit union is able to get a better price than you can.

CHECKPOINT

How does a cashier's check differ from a certified check?

LO 5-3.2 What Are the Costs of Banking?

Banks charge their customers fees to help cover their operating costs and to make a profit. Be sure you are aware of what charges can be applied to your account. Fees range from small to large. Before you open any account, you should compare services and fees. In many cases, a credit union will offer you the most services for the least cost.

It pays to ask about *relationship banking*, whereby you work with a bank officer who tries to gain an understanding of your needs and offers services to fulfill those needs. Developing a relationship with your bank allows you to enhance your banking services in a way that could result in lower fees. Your bank may offer suggestions such as carrying higher balances, having multiple accounts, and meeting minimum usage requirements.

What are the benefits of relationship banking?

Monthly Account Fees

Many financial institutions charge a monthly service fee for maintaining a checking account. These fees can average between $5 and $15, or more, a month. Unless you meet a minimum balance requirement or have a special "free" account, you will be charged this fee. Some savings accounts (usually with small balances) also can be charged monthly account fees. Some banks allow you to link all of your accounts together (such as checking and savings accounts) to meet the minimum balance requirement, allowing you to avoid a service fee.

Nonsufficient Fund (NSF) Fees

One particularly high cost of banking is that of covering a bad check. A check that is not honored by a bank and is returned to the payee's bank because of nonsufficient funds is called a **bounced check**. This means the bank returned the check without paying it. When you write a check

bounced check a check that is not honored by a bank and is returned to the payee's bank due to nonsufficient funds

but there isn't enough money to cover it, the check will "bounce" unless you have overdraft protection. The bank will charge you a fee when this happens—often $25 to $30 per check.

When a check bounces, the person or business that deposited it will also be charged a fee. You will be expected to cover that fee as well. A bounced check could cost you $80 or more! If you have overdraft protection, NSF checks will be paid rather than bounced. In this case, you would have to pay the amount of the check plus an overdraft fee. However, the fee would be less than the fees associated with a bounced check.

ATM Fees

Many banks will allow you to use their own ATMs free of charge. If you use an ATM from another bank, however, the other bank will charge you a fee, often $2 or more. Your own bank may charge an additional fee of $2 or more for processing the transaction with the other bank. Several trips to another bank's ATM can be costly. If you have a special account or multiple accounts, you can get some or all of these ATM fees waived.

Special Service Fees

A bank or credit union typically charges a fee for special services, such as a stop payment. There also may be a fee for renting a safe deposit box and obtaining cashier's checks, certified checks, money orders, and traveler's checks.

Inactive Accounts

inactive account a checking or savings account that does not meet minimum usage requirements

Banks and credit unions also charge fees for inactive accounts. An **inactive account** is one that does not meet minimum account usage requirements. If your account does not have transactions (such as deposits, debits, checks, or other uses), the financial institution is not making money from those transactions. Thus, they impose fees to cover their costs of maintaining the account. Inactive account fees typically range from $5 to $15 a month. Clearly, if you have an inactive checking or savings account, the balance can be eaten up because of these charges.

>> **CHECKPOINT**
How can you avoid service fees charged by banks?

LO 5-3.3 What Are Consumer Responsibilities of Banking?

Having a checking and/or savings account is not a right; it is a privilege. Banks, credit unions, and other financial institutions make these accounts available to customers. Using these accounts is a very convenient way to manage money. You have several responsibilities as a consumer.

Maintain Your Balance

Be certain you have money in your account to cover the checks you write. If you do not monitor your account balance carefully, you might write a bad check by mistake. Knowingly writing a bad check is illegal and unethical. Criminal or civil charges can be brought against a person who writes bad checks. Writing bad checks can also affect your credit rating. You may have trouble borrowing money or getting a credit card if you have a poor credit rating.

Writing a check and planning to deposit money later to cover the check before it is processed is known as **floating a check**. You should write a check only when you have enough money in your account to cover it. In today's electronic age, checks are processed very quickly. You should not expect that you will have time to deposit money before a check clears.

What are the risks of floating a check?

floating a check writing a check and planning to make a deposit later to cover it before the check is processed

Monitor Your Account

Reconciling your bank account is one way to be sure that transactions posted to your account are legitimate. You should also be responsible with your checkbook. Keep your blank checks safe. Be careful to whom you give checks. Once someone has your check, he or she can see your name, address, bank routing number, bank account number, and other information that is printed on the check. Thieves can make and use fake checks based on your account information.

If you allow creditors to make automatic withdrawals from your account, monitor these transactions to ensure the correct amount is being withdrawn and only when scheduled.

Know Your Rights

As a consumer, you have rights with respect to banking. The number of laws to protect consumers in credit and financial transactions has been growing since the 1960s. Congress has assigned the Federal Reserve System (the Fed) with the duty of implementing many of these laws. The laws are intended to ensure that consumers receive complete information and fair treatment by banks, lenders, and other financial institutions. Specific duties carried out by the Fed include educating consumers about consumer protection laws, enforcing consumer protection laws, and managing a consumer complaint program.

Consumer Education

According to the Fed, being a well-educated consumer is the best consumer protection in the market. When you know your rights and responsibilities, you can use information provided to shop and compare banking services. The Fed provides consumer information and free educational materials at its website.

NEGOTIATING

Negotiation is the process of reaching an agreement that benefits both parties and enables you to get what is important to you. You may have heard the expression "In life you don't get what you deserve, you get what you negotiate." It's true—people who have good negotiation skills get more of what they want!

The first step in negotiating is to understand your own position. What exactly do you want? In clear, un-emotional words, be able to state your wants or needs. Have solid reasons for your choices.

The second step in negotiating is to understand your opponent's position. What exactly does he or she want? What needs and motives does this person have? When you know his or her needs, you can find ways to meet them while meeting yours too.

Third, create a proposed solution. This usually involves a trade-off—you give up something minor to get something that is important to you. It also means

the other person will give up something to get what he or she wants.

People with good negotiation skills identify what is important to both sides and are willing to compromise in order to reach an agreement. Both sides must feel good about what they are getting and what they are giving up.

Try It Out

Meet with your parents. Decide what you would like to change or have them do for you (such as a raise in your allowance). Then decide what you are willing to do (give up) to get that benefit. Consider their point of view—what is important to them. Are you offering them something of value? Negotiate with your parents and come to an agreement. Did you get at least part of what you wanted?

Consumer Protection Laws

The Fed regularly examines financial institutions to ensure compliance with consumer protection laws and regulations. The condition of banks are evaluated based on several components, including banks' capital, assets, management, earnings, and liquidity.

Consumer Complaint Program

The Fed responds to inquiries and complaints from the public involving consumer protection issues. The Fed maintains information on consumer inquiries and complaints in a database that it regularly reviews to identify trends that should be investigated further or that should be reported to consumers. It aims to uncover unfair or deceptive practices within the banking industry.

It is your responsibility, as a consumer, to file complaints when you believe you have been deceived or defrauded. Only when such violations are reported can appropriate actions be taken to protect you and others from them in the future.

CHECKPOINT

What are the three responsibilities of having a bank account?

KEY TERMS REVIEW

Match the terms with the definitions. Some terms may not be used.

_____ 1. A check that is returned to the payee's bank due to nonsufficient funds

_____ 2. A checking or savings account that does not meet minimum usage requirements

_____ 3. A card that contains a computer chip that stores electronic money

_____ 4. A bank service to temporarily cover a shortage in your account

_____ 5. Writing a check and planning to make a deposit later to cover it before the check is processed

_____ 6. A secure container located in a bank vault

_____ 7. Accessing and managing your account online

_____ 8. An instruction to the bank to not honor a check

_____ 9. A check issued against the bank's funds

a. bounced check

b. cashier's check

c. certified check

d. floating a check

e. inactive account

f. Internet banking

g. overdraft protection

h. safe deposit box

i. smart card

j. stop payment

CHECK YOUR UNDERSTANDING

10. How can you obtain a safe deposit box?

11. What is meant by overdraft protection? How can you prevent the need for it?

12. Why would you ask for a stop payment on a check?

13. What is the purpose of a cashier's check?

14. How is a smart card different from a debit card?

15. What is often the requirement to avoid a monthly service fee on your checking account?

16. What is a "bounced" check? How can you avoid issuing a bad check?

17. What are ATM fees? How can you avoid them?

18. What is an inactive account? Why do banks charge customers who have inactive accounts?

19. How does the Federal Reserve System (the Fed) help protect consumers when dealing with banks?

THINK CRITICALLY

20. Overdraft protection is a service provided by your bank. Consumers must sign up for the service. Why would you want to have this service? What is the downside?

21. Why would you wish to use a cashier's check? Explain why certain transactions (such as purchasing a used car from a private owner) require the use of a cashier's check.

22. People who do not have checking accounts will often use a money order when they need to send money by mail. This is safer than sending cash. Many businesses will not accept cash in the mail. Why is this the case?

23. A safe deposit box is used to store important documents and other valuable items. What items do you or your family have that might be stored in a safe deposit box?

24. Many account holders use the Internet regularly to check their accounts, pay bills, monitor activity, and transfer money between accounts. Why should account holders consider using Internet banking? Is there a downside to this service?

25. Fewer businesses are accepting personal checks as payment for purchases. Discuss possible reasons for this trend. What methods of payment are replacing checks?

EXTEND YOUR LEARNING

ProStockStudio/Shutterstock.com

TEAMWORK

26. For a bank, credit union, and brokerage firm or other type of financial institution, compare the banking services that they offer. Work with a partner to answer the following questions:

    a. List the services that are provided with the financial institution's basic checking and savings accounts. List the fees (if any) that are charged for these basic services.

    b. List the fees for any optional services that are provided, such as overdraft protection/NSF checks, stop payments, cashier's checks, traveler's checks, and online banking.

    c. Is there a debit or ATM card available for the account? Are there restrictions for using the ATM or debit card? Are there fees associated with using the cards? If so, explain.

    d. Is there a charge for an inactive account? What are the minimum usage requirements of the account?

    e. Are other special services provided, such as car-buying or financial advising? Describe these services and any fees for them.

THE ESSENTIAL QUESTION   Refer to the essential question on p. 172. Bank services are likely to include special types of payment, ATMs, bank cards, overdraft protection, Internet banking, safe deposit boxes, loans, and financial advising. Costs include monthly account fees, NSF fees, ATM fees, and other special charges related to cashier's checks, money orders, and stop payments.

Exploring Careers in…
BANKING

The banking industry has many types of jobs that focus on the primary roles of accepting deposits and lending money. Banks (commercial banks, savings and loans, and credit unions) also offer investment and insurance products. In addition to typical banking services, *global banks* lend internationally and trade foreign currencies. *Regional banks* have many branches and ATM locations throughout a multistate area. *Community banks* are based locally and have fewer locations.

Interest on loans is the main source of income for banks. Loans made to businesses and consumers may include student loans, car loans, mortgages, lines of credit, and credit cards.

Employment Outlook

- Employment is expected to grow at an annual rate of 9 percent through 2022.

Job Titles

- Bank teller
- Loan officer
- Branch manager
- New account clerk
- Customer service representative

Needed Education/Skills

- A high school education is required for entry-level positions. A bachelor's degree is required for management positions.
- Good communication and people skills are a must, as most positions require a great deal of customer contact.

What's it like to work in … Banking

Morgan is a supervisor at a branch office for a regional bank. She knows and understands banking because she started as a bank teller several years ago. Morgan oversees her staff of tellers and loan and account specialists.

Morgan works in her office to review the financial data collected from her branch. She must ensure her branch is meeting company goals and operating smoothly and efficiently. Later in the day, she will meet with customers who wish to discuss financial issues regarding their accounts.

Morgan likes working with people and having a variety of tasks every day. She rises to the challenge of working with customers who are sometimes upset with banking fees and regulations. She considers herself a "personal banker" to those she serves. She wants to be sure her customers are getting the best value for their money.

What About You?

Would you enjoy working with the finances of a bank and its customers? Why or why not?

Chapter 5 Assessment

SUMMARY

5-1 All economic systems use some form of money, or medium of exchange. For money to be functional, it must be divisible, durable, and recognizable as a store of value.

A checking account is a demand deposit that provides a safe place to keep money and allows you easy access to the money. A check is a legal document instructing the bank to pay money to the person or company named on the check.

A check register is a record of checks written, deposits made, other withdrawals made, and other charges made to the checking account.

Withdrawals from your checking account can be made by writing a check, making payments online, setting up automatic withdrawals, and using a debit card or an ATM card.

Account holders should reconcile their bank statement by comparing it to their check register.

5-2 A savings account is a demand deposit account designed for the accumulation of money in a safe place for future use.

You can grow your savings by earning interest. Interest is computed using simple and compound interest methods. The future value of money refers to what savings will be worth in the future, after interest has compounded. The present value of money is the amount you would need to deposit today in order to accumulate a specific amount in the future.

In addition to savings accounts, other savings options include money market accounts, certificates of deposit (CDs), savings bonds, and individual retirement accounts (IRAs).

Places to save money include banks, credit unions, online-only banks, brokerage firms, and international banks.

5-3 Banks may offer services such as ATMs, bank cards (including credit, ATM, debit, and smart cards), overdraft protection, Internet banking, safe deposit boxes, loans, and financial advising.

Banks charge fees for their services, including monthly account fees, NSF fees, stop-payment fees, cashier's and traveler's check fees, money order fees, ATM fees, and inactive account fees.

Consumers must maintain minimum balances, reconcile and monitor accounts, and know their rights with respect to banking.

MAKE ACADEMIC CONNECTIONS

1. **Research** Government bonds can be researched and purchased on the TreasuryDirect website (www.treasurydirect.gov). Find information for two types of bonds: I Bonds and EE Bonds. For each type, list the information below. (LO 5-2.3)
   - A brief description of the bond
   - The current interest rate paid on the bond
   - The minimum purchase amount
   - The maximum purchase amount per year
   - The redemption process for the bond

2. **Social Studies** Access the website of the Federal Reserve System (www.federalreserve.gov) and click on the tab for Consumer Information. Search for an article regarding banks or the banking industry. Write a one-page report on what you learn. (LO 5-3.3)

3. **Economics** Create a table listing the various forms of financial exchange, including cash, checks, credit cards, debit cards, smart cards, and electronic funds transfers. Then list the advantages and disadvantages of each form of payment. (LO 5-3.1)

4. **International Studies** Select another country and research its banking systems. Are there international banks that do business in the United States? If so, what accounts or services are available to American businesses and consumers? How are international banks different from U.S. banks? (LO 5-2.3)

5. **Research** Visit a bank website that offers online bill payment. As an alternative, do an online search using the keywords "online banking demo." Write a summary of how the process works. (LO 5-1.3)

6. **History** Today's currency has a long history. Use the Internet to research the roots of U.S. currency. Create a timeline that shows the various types of currency (traditional and nontraditional) that have been used as a medium of exchange throughout history. (LO 5-1.1)

7. **Business Law** Many serious crimes involving checks and checking accounts are committed every day, such as writing bad (NSF) checks and committing check forgery. Research the laws in your state related to these crimes. What are the penalties? How can financial institutions and other businesses help prevent these crimes? What can you do to prevent becoming a victim of such crimes? (LO 5-1.3)

8. **Communication** Assume you are giving a presentation to a group of young students about the benefits of saving. Create an outline of the presentation you will give. For each of the items in your outline, create two to three bullet points that you want to cover in your presentation. Finally, create a handout that you will give to the young students to help reinforce the importance of saving. (LO 5-2.1)

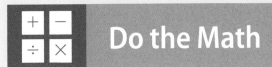

Do the Math

1. **Gloria has an account that draws interest at the rate of 6 percent per year, compounded monthly at 0.5 percent. The amounts listed below were deposited in the account in the current year. What is the balance in the account on December 31 of the current year? (If available, use spreadsheet software to do the computations.)**

   June 1, $50; July 1, $50; August 1, $50; and September 1, $50

2. **Yoshi has an account that draws interest at an annual rate of 5 percent. The interest is compounded quarterly. The amounts listed below were deposited in the account in the current year. What is the balance in the account on December 31 of the current year (after four quarters)? (If available, use spreadsheet software to do the computations.)**

   January 1, $450; April 1, $350; July 1, $200; and October 1, $300

3. **Use the tables in Figures 5-2.3 and 5-2.5 to calculate the future and present value of the amounts below. Round answers to the nearest cent.**

   a. Bill deposits $1,000 and leaves it for 8 years in an account paying 6 percent per year. What is the account's value at the end of 8 years?

   b. Andie wants to save $3,000 in 6 years in an account paying 5 percent per year? How much will she have to deposit today?

Take Action

MANAGE A CHECKING ACCOUNT

In this activity, you will update a check register, complete a deposit slip, write checks, and reconcile a bank statement using the data below and forms supplied by your teacher. Use the current year for dates.

a. Use the following information to complete the check register:
   - Date of the deposit: August 30, 20--
   - Items to be deposited:
     Checks: 456, $108.66
                    589, $50.00
   - Cash received from the deposit: $25.00

b. On August 30, write a check for $15.85 to Quick Pizza for food. Remember to complete the check register before writing the check. Sign your name (first and last) on the check.

c. On August 31, complete the register and write a check for $12.35 to Fresh Cleaners for cleaning services. Sign your name on the check.

d. Reconcile the account; the adjusted balances should be $382.29.

   After you complete this project, save the forms in your portfolio.

Personal Risk Management

6-1 Risk Assessment and Strategies

6-2 Protecting Income

6-3 Protecting Property

In your life, you will face many risks. As you learn about the risks, you can evaluate how serious they are and then decide what to do about them. Avoiding risk, reducing risk, and assuming risk are strategies you can use to help protect yourself. You can transfer risk by buying insurance. Health and life insurance are good ways to protect your income. Homeowners or renters insurance protects against the loss of your home and personal property. Auto insurance protects from losses that might occur to you, your car, and others in a car accident. Planning for risks is a smart way to help guard your financial security, both now and in the future.

Do *This*, Not *That*

When facing risk:

- Realize that not all risks are equal—different strategies are required for different risks.
- Get the right health care coverage to fit your needs.
- Understand how to use insurance to protect your property and income.
- Get auto insurance for your car—it's the law!

LEARNING OBJECTIVES

LO 6-1.1 Explain the concepts of risk.

LO 6-1.2 List the three types of risk that consumers face.

LO 6-1.3 Describe risk assessment and four risk strategies.

KEY TERMS

- risk, 186
- loss, 186
- probability, 186
- risk assessment, 188
- risk reduction, 189
- risk avoidance, 189
- risk transfer, 189
- premium, 190
- risk assumption, 190
- self-insure, 190

LO 6-1.1 What Is Risk?

risk the chance of injury, damage, or economic loss

Risk is the chance of injury, damage, or economic loss. You face risks every day. From the moment you get out of bed, you take chances. You could slip and fall in the bathtub. You could have an accident in the kitchen. You could injure another person or property while driving your car.

There are many types of risk you will face now and in the future. Some risks are avoidable and have a small chance of occurrence. Other risks are unpredictable and unavoidable. Certain risky events may cause serious losses if they happen. A **loss** refers to some type of physical injury, damage to property, or disappearance of property or other assets. The loss might be personal in nature, such as a broken leg or an illness. The loss could be damage or removal of property. For example, you might lose money and other property as a result of theft. Losses could be major and could have a significant effect on your life and future. Losing your job could mean that you cannot make payments on your house or car. Consequently, the lender could seize the property and sell it.

loss a physical injury, damage to property, or disappearance of property or other assets

The likelihood of a risk actually resulting in a loss is called **probability**. Just because you take a risk does not mean you will suffer a loss. And just because you avoid a loss once does not mean you will always do so. You must decide whether the risk and its possible outcome are serious. If the possible loss is serious, you may be able to take steps to lessen the risk or the resulting loss.

probability the likelihood of a risk resulting in a loss

CHECKPOINT

What is a loss?

LO 6-1.2 What Are the Types of Risk?

As a consumer, there are many types of risk that you will face in your lifetime. Three major types of risk that you will face include personal risk, risk of financial loss, and risk of your financial resources. When you understand the risks you are taking, you can take steps to avoid the financial impacts of losses that could occur.

Personal Risk

Taking *personal risk* means you could lose something of personal value. For example, you might break your leg and not be able to participate in an activity that you enjoy. If you do not take your umbrella when the forecast calls for rain, you risk getting wet and cold. This may increase your chances of getting sick. Some personal risks are necessary. If you did not get out of bed in the morning, you could avoid many risks. However, not getting out of bed also means you will accomplish little.

Why is it important to look at losses from a financial standpoint?

Risk of Financial Loss

Some risks will result in financial loss. *Financial loss* refers to a loss in terms of money. The loss can be small or large. Small possible losses should be assessed differently than large possible losses. For example, if you drive without a spare tire, you risk being unable to change a flat tire. Driving without a spare tire could be expensive if you have a flat tire and must pay someone to help you. The money you could lose should be compared to the cost of buying the spare tire.

A large loss might result from driving without auto insurance. If you get into an accident, the damage you could cause to another vehicle or property could cost thousands of dollars. You might have to pay this money out of pocket if you have no insurance. In most states, drivers are required to have insurance. If you drive without insurance, you risk being caught and having to pay a fine and possibly losing your driving privileges.

Risk of Financial Resources

Risk of financial resources is a serious kind of risk. It could jeopardize your future. With this type of risk, more than current income is threatened. You may lose your ability to earn in the future or lose assets you will acquire in the future. For example, you might do something that causes an injury to another person. That person might sue you and win a financial judgment against you in a court of law. This means that the court orders you to pay the person a certain amount of money. Because of the judgment, you could have your wages garnished (withheld) or your assets taken away.

LO 6-1.3 How Can You Manage Risk Using Risk Strategies?

Although it is not possible to avoid all risks at all times, it is possible to understand and manage risk. The first step toward managing risk is assessing your risks. Then you must decide on the best strategy for handling the risks that you have identified.

Risk Assessment

risk assessment the process of identifying risks and deciding how serious they are

Risk assessment is the process of identifying your risks and deciding how serious they are. When you understand your risks and what you could lose, you can make better choices. You may be able to take action to protect yourself from the serious outcomes you could face.

The first step in risk assessment is to identify potential risks. Begin by asking yourself what risks you take on a regular basis, such as the risks that you take by driving a car. Once you have identified your risks, you should assess each one to determine the probability and potential impact on you.

Figure 6-1.1 shows an example of risk assessment. It shows the probability of occurrence for each risk. Then each risk is rated in terms of seriousness. Finally, the chart lists the worst that could happen if each loss occurred.

▶ FIGURE 6-1.1   **Risk Assessment**

Risk	Probability of Occurrence	Seriousness Rating*	Possible Consequences
Losing my job	Medium	10	• Missed payments • Dip into savings • Lower credit rating
Getting in a car accident	Unknown	10	• Personal injury • Lawsuit
Suffering physical injury from snowboarding	Medium	3	• Missed work time • Medical bills
Having bike stolen	Low	2	• New/used bike purchase

*1 is low risk; 5 is medium risk; 10 is high risk.

Building COMMUNICATION SKILLS

READING SPEED

Reading speed affects how much material you can read in a certain amount of time. It also can affect how well you remember or comprehend what you read. To be an effective reader, you must read at a pace that allows you to cover material quickly and still comprehend what you are reading. Use these strategies to help you become a more effective reader:

- Preview the material before reading.
- Read in the order the information is presented.
- Adjust reading speed to suit the material. Technical material or material with a difficult vocabulary may require slower reading. Summaries, review sections, or passages with easy vocabulary allow faster reading.
- Read groups of words at a time.

- Use a pacer to focus your eyes on the page. A *pacer* is a tool such as a pencil or ruler that you move along under the words being read.
- Read in a quiet place where your concentration will not be interrupted.

Try It Out

Using the Internet, locate an article about risk or risk strategies. Read the article following the steps outlined above. Then answer the following questions:

1. What was the main topic of the entire passage?
2. What two or three new things did you learn?
3. What questions do you have after reading the passage? (What additional information would you like to know?)
4. Did you find the passage useful, enlightening, entertaining, or informative? Explain.

Risk Strategies

Based on the nature and seriousness of the risks that you identify in your risk assessment, you should develop a strategy to protect yourself. There are a number of strategies, such as reducing risk, avoiding risk, transferring risk, and assuming risk.

Reducing Risks

Risk reduction involves finding ways to lower your chance of incurring a loss. This can be done by changing your actions or other events. For example, when you go snow skiing, you are taking a risk of personal injury. To reduce that risk, you can take skiing lessons and/or choose the least hazardous slopes. You can reduce your risk of financial loss by having health insurance to pay for any injuries you might suffer.

risk reduction finding ways to lower your chance of incurring a loss

Avoiding Risks

With **risk avoidance**, you stop the behavior or avoid the situation that leads to the risk. For example, instead of snow skiing, you can choose to go ice skating or snowshoeing. This will allow you to avoid the risk of injury from a skiing accident.

Sometimes, however, it is not possible to completely avoid a risk. In such cases, you might use other risk strategies that will lessen the impact of the possible outcomes.

risk avoidance stopping behavior that leads to a risk

Transferring Risks

Risk transfer, also called *risk shifting*, passes risk to another party. An example is when you buy insurance to cover financial losses from damaging events, such as auto accidents, fire, theft, and injury. The price you

risk transfer passing risk to another party

Are you assuming risks? If so, what are the risks, and can they be avoided or transferred?

Bluz60/iStockphoto.com

premium the price you pay for insurance coverage

pay for insurance coverage is called a **premium**. The premium is based on the possible amount of loss to the insurance company. The more risk the insurer takes, the higher the premium. By making insurance premium payments, you shift the risk of financial loss to the insurance company.

Assuming Risks

risk assumption accepting the consequences of risk

Risk assumption involves accepting the consequences of risk. It is also known as *risk retention*. Risks that are not avoided or transferred are retained.

self-insure setting aside money to be used in the event of injury or loss of assets

One method of assuming risk is to **self-insure**, which involves setting aside money to be used in the event of injury or loss of assets. You may decide to risk the chance that something will happen and pay for the costs that arise if it does. By setting aside money, you help cushion the financial burden you could incur due to an injury or a loss.

Many people self-insure as a way to reduce insurance costs. For example, you may choose a health care plan that requires you to pay a higher portion of your medical expenses in exchange for a lower premium. You can use your self-insurance fund to pay for doctor visits or other routine care. However, if you have a serious illness that involves high medical expenses, your insurance policy will pay these bills. This allows you to assume the risk for small or routine expenses and have the insurance company assume the risk for large expenses.

 **CHECKPOINT**

What are the four risk strategies?

KEY TERMS REVIEW

Match the terms with the definitions. Some terms may not be used.

_____ 1. The likelihood of a risk resulting in a loss

_____ 2. Stopping behavior that leads to a risk

_____ 3. Passing risk to another party

_____ 4. The chance of injury, damage, or economic loss

_____ 5. The process of identifying risks and deciding how serious they are

_____ 6. Setting aside money to be used in the event of an injury or loss of assets

_____ 7. Finding ways to lower your chance of incurring a loss

_____ 8. A physical injury, damage to property, or disappearance of property or other assets

_____ 9. The price you pay for insurance coverage

a. loss

b. premium

c. probability

d. risk

e. risk assessment

f. risk assumption

g. risk avoidance

h. risk reduction

i. risk transfer

j. self-insure

CHECK YOUR UNDERSTANDING

10. What kinds of risk do you face each day? What losses would you or your family suffer if one of your risks became a reality?

11. Can you avoid all types of losses? Why or why not?

12. What is meant by personal risk? Provide an example.

13. What is meant by risk of financial loss? Provide an example.

14. What is meant by risk of financial resources? Provide an example.

15. What is the first step toward managing risks? Why is this step important?

16. What is meant by risk avoidance? Provide an example of how you can avoid risk.

17. What is meant by risk transfer? Provide an example of how you can transfer risk.

18. Risks that are not avoided or transferred are retained. What is meant by this statement? Provide an example.

19. What kinds of risk are the best to retain or self-insure?

THINK CRITICALLY

20. Why is it important to consider the risks that you face in life? Everybody faces risk of loss, so why should you be concerned?

21. Why is the risk of financial resources more serious than the risk of financial loss or personal risk? Why is it important to take action to reduce the risk of financial resources?

22. Reducing and avoiding risks usually involve commonsense actions. Give examples of risks that you take and what you can do to reduce and avoid those risks. In reducing and avoiding the risks, do you lessen your quality of life? Explain your answer.

23. Why is it essential to transfer (or shift) certain types of risk? In other words, why don't you just reduce, avoid, and assume these kinds of risks? Give two reasons.

24. Self-insuring can reduce the insurance premiums you must pay, but you take on additional risks of loss. It is a situation that creates trade-offs. In exchange for lower premiums, you will have to pay more out of pocket if a loss occurs. What are the risks versus the benefits of self-insuring? Do you think the benefits outweigh the risks? Why or why not?

EXTEND YOUR LEARNING

25. Everyone faces risks—personal risk, risk of financial loss, and risk of financial resources. Assess some of the risks that you may face. Follow Figure 6-1.1 as an example as you complete the steps below.

   a. Create a chart with the headings shown below. In the Risk column, list four risks that you face.

Risk	Probability of Occurrence	Seriousness Rating	Possible Consequences	Strategies for Managing the Risk

   b. Estimate the likelihood of those events occurring. Add this information to the chart.

   c. Think about the seriousness of each risk, and give it a rating from 1–10, with 10 being the most serious.

   d. List the possible consequences if the risk events should happen.

   e. Consider each possible risk that has a serious consequence. List what you will do to (a) reduce, (b) avoid, (c) transfer, and/or (d) assume the risk.

THE ESSENTIAL QUESTION   Refer to The Essential Question on p. 186. Risk is a part of everyday life. You can manage the three types of consumer risk (personal loss, financial loss, and financial resources loss) by performing a risk assessment and then choosing a strategy to protect yourself.

6-2 Protecting Income

LEARNING OBJECTIVES

LO 6-2.1 Describe group and individual health insurance policies and the types of health insurance coverage and plans.

LO 6-2.2 Explain the need for disability insurance and the types of plans available.

LO 6-2.3 Explain the need for life insurance and the types of coverage available.

KEY TERMS

- health insurance, 193
- fee-for-service plan, 194
- health maintenance organization (HMO), 194
- preferred provider organization (PPO), 194
- stop-loss provision, 196
- disability insurance, 198
- life insurance, 199
- beneficiary, 199
- temporary life insurance, 200
- permanent life insurance, 201

LO 6-2.1 What Is Health Insurance?

Health insurance is a plan for sharing the risk of medical costs resulting from injury or illness. It allows people to pay for high medical expenses. With the passage of the Affordable Care Act (ACA) in 2010, all U.S. citizens must now have health insurance or pay a penalty for failing to do so, unless they qualify for an exemption. Some people have health insurance through a group plan, such as one offered by an employer, whereas others have individual policies.

health insurance a plan for sharing the risk of medical costs resulting from injury or illness

Group Policies

Some people have health insurance through a group plan, such as one offered by an employer. With group insurance, all of those insured have the same coverage and pay a set premium. Because there are more people among which to spread the risk, a group can usually negotiate better coverage and lower premiums than individuals can get on their own. Some employers pay the premiums as a benefit to their employees. In most cases, however, the premium costs are shared between the employer and employee.

Many employers offer health *flexible spending accounts (FSAs)* as part of their benefits package. An FSA allows employees to set aside money to help pay for medical expenses that insurance does not cover. The money set aside is pretax, meaning no federal income taxes have to be paid on it. Deductions are made from the employee's pay to fund the account. The employer may also contribute. However, any unused money that the employee sets aside is forfeited to the employer at the end of the year.

Individual Policies

People can buy individual health insurance policies. Monthly premiums for individual plans are often much higher than those for group plans. One of the purposes of the ACA is to increase the availability and affordability of health insurance. The law set up health insurance exchanges to assist in the purchase of health insurance in each state.

Health insurance exchanges provide standardized health care plans from which uninsured individuals may choose.

Types of Health Care Plans

Health care plans are generally grouped into two types: unmanaged and managed. In addition, government-sponsored health care plans are also available.

Unmanaged Care

An *unmanaged care plan*, or **fee-for-service plan**, allows patients to choose any doctor or other provider for medical services. The insurance policy has a *deductible*, which is the amount of money you must pay each year toward your medical expenses before your insurance company begins to pay for covered medical expenses. For example, if your policy has a $500 deductible, you must pay the first $500 of medical expenses. After that, the insurance company pays a percentage, such as 80 percent, for covered medical services. You must pay the remaining 20 percent.

Deductible amounts vary widely depending on the type of plan. For high-deductible plans, many people choose to open a *health savings account (HSA)* to be used in conjunction with their plan. Money that you deposit in an HSA is used to pay for qualified medical expenses not covered by insurance, including deductibles and co-payments. A *co-payment* is a fixed amount you must pay when you visit a doctor's office or purchase prescription drugs. Contributions to the account are made pretax and are tax-deductible. Money withdrawn from an HSA to pay qualified medical expenses is tax-free. Unlike an FSA, unused money in an HSA isn't forfeited at the end of the year; it continues to grow tax-free. The major advantage of this type of plan is that people manage their own health care dollars.

Managed Care

A *managed care plan* relies on a network of health care providers. Participants in a managed care plan must select doctors, hospitals, and other providers who belong to the network. The insurer exercises significant control over the types of services provided and the maximum benefits allowed for those services. Health maintenance organizations and preferred provider organizations are two common types of managed care plans.

A **health maintenance organization (HMO)** is a group plan that provides prepaid medical care for its members. HMOs usually have their own facilities (clinics and hospitals) and offer a full range of medical services. Patients must choose doctors on the HMO staff, including one doctor to be the primary care physician (PCP). To see a specialist, patients must get a referral from the PCP beforehand. Otherwise, the insurance will not cover the costs. HMOs often do not have deductibles, but patients typically make a co-payment for each office visit. An advantage of belonging to an HMO is the emphasis on preventive care, such as routine physical exams and vaccinations. The goal is to encourage people to get treatment for a minor ailment before it becomes a serious and costly problem.

A **preferred provider organization (PPO)** is a network of independent health care providers (doctors, hospitals, clinics, and labs) that band together to provide health care services for a set fee. Patients can

FOCUS On...

HEALTH CARE REFORM

In 2010, the Affordable Care Act (ACA) was signed into law by President Obama. The ACA is the nation's first comprehensive health care reform law. Included are a number of provisions.

- Individuals cannot be denied coverage for pre-existing conditions, nor can insurance companies charge higher premiums to people who have pre-existing conditions or who become sick.

- Low-income individuals and families are eligible for subsidies (government grants) if they cannot afford insurance.

- Young adults can remain on their parents' health insurance plan until age 26.

- All insurance plans must contain certain minimum coverage standards, called *essential health benefits*, that include things such as emergency care, hospitalization, prescription drugs, and maternity care.

- Annual and lifetime dollar limits on essential health benefits have been eliminated. Previously, many plans required patients to pay the cost of all care exceeding those lifetime benefit limits.

The cost of health care reform will be supported by increases in taxes in several areas. For example, people with "premium" or high-price health policies will be levied a tax. Additional Medicare taxes will be levied against higher-income individuals and against investment income (rather than just earned income).

Critics point out that a major omission from the reform is a control on costs. Due to rising health care costs, employers and employees will be charged higher premiums. Health care costs have risen much faster than inflation and much faster than increases in most other sectors of the economy. Without controls on costs, affordable health care will continue to be out of reach.

Think Critically

1. Do you agree that health care is a right and not a privilege? Why or why not?
2. How can health care costs be better controlled? What changes would you make to the ACA?

---

choose doctors from an approved provider list, but they can also go outside of the plan for care. However, if they choose a provider not on the approved list, they will have to pay a larger percentage of the fee. Patients who stay within the network of providers usually must make a small co-payment per office visit or per prescription. Unlike an HMO, patients are not required to choose a PCP and do not need a referral to see a specialist, but the cost will be higher. Because this type of plan is more flexible than an HMO, it is more expensive.

Government-Sponsored Health Care

Medicare and Medicaid are two forms of insurance established by the federal government to help cover health care costs. Both programs are taxpayer funded, and both have different eligibility requirements and coverage.

Medicare is government-sponsored health insurance for people age 65 or older. Medicare is run by the Social Security Administration (SSA) and funded by employee payroll deductions and matching employer contributions. Retired people pay a monthly premium for Medicare insurance. Medicare will not cover all health care costs for Medicare enrollees. Thus, many enrollees purchase *Medigap* insurance to help pay the additional expenses not covered by Medicare.

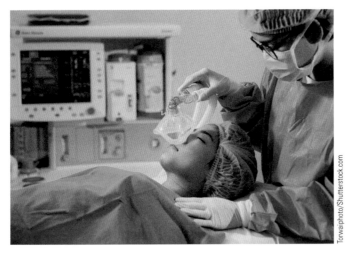

Why are elective surgeries not covered by basic health care?

Medicaid is a form of government-sponsored health insurance for people with low incomes and limited resources. This program helps families who live in poverty and are unable to afford private health insurance or medical care. To be eligible to receive Medicaid, certain income, age, disability, and citizenship requirements must be met.

Types of Coverage

Both group and individual health insurance policies offer similar types of coverage. Typically, health insurance policies cover basic health expenses (medical, hospital, and surgical) and major medical costs. Some policies cover dental and vision needs for a higher premium.

Basic Health Care

Basic health care coverage includes medical, hospital, and surgical costs. It pays for routine physician services, including doctor office visits, annual physical exams, recommended immunizations, X-rays, and laboratory tests. Hospital coverage pays hospital bills for room, board, and medication. Surgical coverage pays for part or all of a surgeon's fees for an operation. Cosmetic and elective surgeries are usually not covered. *Elective surgery* is surgery that you choose to have that is not medically necessary. A facelift to improve appearance and laser eye surgery to improve vision are examples of elective surgery.

Major Medical Costs

Major medical coverage protects against the catastrophic expenses of a serious injury or illness that might cost hundreds of thousands of dollars to treat, such as a bone marrow transplant or kidney transplant. Major medical coverage goes beyond basic health care coverage, and by law, there can no longer be a limit on the amount of lifetime benefits paid for these expenses.

Major medical coverage often has a coinsurance provision that requires the insured to pay a portion (such as 20 percent) of all bills. For a higher premium, a stop-loss provision may be included. A **stop-loss provision** is an insurance clause that sets a maximum that the insured has to pay out of pocket during any calendar year. For example, a $5,000 stop-loss means the insured would have to pay no more than $5,000 for co-payments and deductibles in a year.

Dental and Vision Coverage

Dental insurance covers basic dental services, such as exams, X-rays, cleanings, and fillings. Dental plans often have low deductibles, but they may have an annual dollar limit. Insurers typically pay less for some services, such as crowns, bridges, and braces. Cosmetic dental work, such as teeth whitening, is usually not covered at all.

Vision insurance often pays for an eye exam as well as the costs associated with prescription glasses. Some policies offer limited coverage for prescription sunglasses and contact lenses.

stop-loss provision an insurance clause that sets a maximum that the insured has to pay out of pocket during any calendar year

Supplemental Health Insurance

Standard health insurance policies will not cover all medical events and costs. For this reason, individuals may purchase supplemental insurance. *Supplemental insurance* plans help you pay for services and out-of-pocket expenses that your standard health insurance policy doesn't cover.

Due to high out-of-pocket medical costs, cancer insurance is one type of supplemental health insurance policy that an increasing number of individuals are purchasing. *Cancer insurance* helps to reduce the cost of cancer care. Most plans cover both medical expenses, such as co-payments, medical tests, and extended hospital stays, as well as non-medical expenses, such as home health care, loss of income benefits, and child care expenses. However, to be eligible for cancer insurance, you cannot have a pre-existing cancerous condition. In addition, if you have previously been diagnosed and treated for cancer, you will most likely be ineligible for coverage.

Long-term care insurance is another type of supplemental policy often purchased. *Long-term care insurance* covers the expenses involved in extended care offered in nursing homes, assisted living facilities, or at home by visiting health care professionals. This care generally applies to the elderly, but younger people who suffer debilitating injuries or illnesses may also need this coverage. Although government programs, such as Medicaid, may pay for some long-term care, many people choose to buy long-term care insurance to protect themselves against these costs, which can be extensive and continue to rise.

There are other types of supplemental insurance available. Whether you need supplemental insurance depends on your medical needs and the coverage provided in your standard health insurance policy.

Managing Health Care Costs

The cost of health care is rising rapidly. Patients are paying higher premiums, co-payments, and deductibles. The cost of medicines is also rising. Many people are concerned about finding ways to manage their share of the costs of health care. Following are some suggestions on how you can minimize your health care costs:

- Make sure that medicines and treatments will be covered by insurance before filling prescriptions.
- Use generic drugs when possible.
- Predetermine fees for routine tests and services, and look for less expensive providers. For example, have your cholesterol tested at a local clinic rather than at the doctor's office.
- Choose a high-deductible plan. Although a high-deductible health plan will require you to pay more out of pocket before your insurance coverage begins, your monthly premium will be lower. You can self-insure (or set money aside) to help pay the higher deductible.
- Use an FSA or HSA. These allow you to set aside pretax dollars that you can use toward medical expenses throughout the year.
- Most importantly, stay well. This includes eating a balanced diet, avoiding smoking and excessive drinking, and getting plenty of rest and relaxation.

LO 6-2.2 What Is the Purpose of Disability Insurance?

What is the purpose of disability insurance?

disability insurance insurance that provides income to replace a portion of normal earnings when the insured is unable to work due to a nonwork-related injury or illness

Disability insurance provides income to replace a portion of normal earnings when the insured is unable to work due to a non-work-related injury or illness. (If a person is injured at work or becomes ill because of work conditions, workers' compensation provides coverage.) If a serious accident or illness occurs, recovery can last weeks, months, or even years. During this time, your regular living expenses go on, so disability insurance is an important form of income protection. Generally, there are two types of disability insurance: short term and long term. Most employers offer both short-term and long-term disability group plans, and they may pay for part or all of the plan. Disability insurance can also be purchased as an individual policy through private insurance, but the premium is typically higher.

Short-Term Disability Insurance

Short-term disability insurance covers you if you are temporarily unable to work due to an injury or illness. With short-term disability insurance, you receive a portion of your regular pay (typically 50 to 70 percent) for a short period of time—usually between three to six months. Coverage begins after a waiting period. The waiting period can range from 30 days to 90 days or longer.

Long-Term Disability Insurance

Long-term disability insurance covers you when you are unable to return to work for a long period of time. It usually begins after short-term disability ends and can continue until retirement. Like short-term disability insurance, it typically pays 50 to 70 percent of your regular pay.

Social Security Disability Insurance

If you have Social Security taxes deducted from your paycheck, you are entitled to disability payments from Social Security in the event you become disabled and cannot work. Workers are considered *disabled* if they have a physical or mental condition that prevents them from gainful employment, and the condition is expected to last for at least 12 months or result in death.

Success SKILLS

DEALING WITH HEALTH CARE FRAUD

Health care fraud is the false billing for medical services to insurance companies, government, and individuals. Examples of health care fraud include billing for services not performed; falsifying a diagnosis to justify tests, surgeries, and other unneeded medical treatments; misrepresenting procedures to obtain payment; *upcoding,* or billing for a more costly service than the one provided; *unbundling,* or billing for each stage of the procedure as if it were a separate procedure; billing a patient for more than the co-payment or for services paid by the insurance company; or demanding payment for services which are deemed by the insurance company as excessive charges.

The government has taken powerful steps to fight health care fraud. In a recent year, health care fraud and prevention efforts recovered nearly $3.3 billion. To help avoid and prevent health care fraud, the consumer has responsibilities, including the following:

- Ask questions about services, such as: "Why are they needed?" and "What do they cost?"
- Fill out, sign, and date one claim form at a time.
- Audit bills, verifying that treatments were actually received and questioning any duplications or services not provided.
- Question charges exceeding your co-payment amount.
- Report suspected fraud to insurance companies and government agencies.

Think Critically

1. Why is it important for consumers to take an active role in choosing care and comparing prices for health care services?
2. If you suspect that you have been billed for a service you did not receive or think that there is an error in your bill, what should you do?

To qualify for Social Security disability insurance, you will have to prove the extent of your disability, fill out forms, and have medical exams as required by the Social Security Administration. Benefits are determined in part by your pay and the number of years you have been covered under Social Security.

⟫ CHECKPOINT

How does disability insurance differ from workers' compensation?

LO 6-2.3 Who Needs Life Insurance?

Life insurance pays money to a beneficiary upon the death of the insured person. A **beneficiary** is the person designated to receive the proceeds of the policy. The main purpose of life insurance is to provide protection for those you leave behind who depend on you as a source of income. In addition to providing death benefits, some types of life insurance also build cash value, acting as a form of savings plan. Some reasons why people buy life insurance include the following:

- To provide cash to pay for a funeral
- To pay off a home mortgage and other debts at the time of death

life insurance insurance that pays money to a beneficiary upon the death of the insured person

beneficiary the person designated to receive money from a life insurance policy

How does life insurance provide for its beneficiaries?

- To provide money for a spouse and children to maintain their lifestyle
- To pay for education for children
- To make charitable bequests at death
- To accumulate savings
- To pay inheritance and estate taxes
- To provide cash value that can be borrowed

To buy an individual life insurance policy, you will have to supply a detailed medical history. You also may be required to have a medical exam. Someone with a serious health problem, such as heart disease, may not be able to purchase an individual life insurance policy.

You may also be able to buy life insurance through an employer. *Group life insurance* insures a large number of people under the terms of a single policy. Employers often offer group life insurance as part of their benefits package. Like group health insurance, group life insurance usually provides better coverage and lower premiums than individual policies. Group life insurance also makes it possible for individuals who would not qualify for an individual policy to have life insurance. Another benefit of group life insurance policies is that they are required by law to be portable. *Portable insurance* can be taken with you when you leave your job. In other words, the group policy becomes an individual policy with the same premiums.

Two common types of life insurance are temporary and permanent. Both types have advantages and disadvantages.

Temporary Life Insurance

temporary life insurance
a policy that remains in effect for a specific period of time

Temporary life insurance remains in effect for a specified period of time, such as 20 years. If the insured survives beyond that time, coverage stops with no remaining value. Temporary life insurance is often referred to as *term life insurance*. Term policies are also called "pure" life insurance because they have value only if the insured's death occurs while the policy is in effect. For example, if you have a 20-year term policy, and you die within that period, the policy pays the stated sum, called the *face value*, to the beneficiary. However, if you die after the 20-year term, no benefit will be paid. Parents often buy a term policy to cover the financial needs of their children in case they should die while the children are still young.

There are several different forms of term life insurance. With *decreasing term insurance*, the amount of coverage decreases each year while the premium remains the same. For example, assume a person buys a 20-year decreasing term insurance policy worth $100,000. If the insured dies during the first year of the policy, it pays the full benefit ($100,000). If the insured dies during the second year of the policy, the benefit decreases to $95,000. If the insured dies during the third year of the policy, the benefit decreases to $90,000, and so on. As each year passes, the death benefit decreases by a specified amount. In contrast, *level term insurance* has a death benefit that remains the same from the beginning to the end of the policy, but the premium increases each year.

Renewable term insurance gives the insured the right to renew the policy each year without having to pass a physical exam. The insured can renew the policy until reaching a certain age. The age limit can vary by company and type of policy. At each renewal, the premium increases (because the insured is older and the risk of death increases), but the death benefits remain the same.

Convertible term insurance permits the insured to convert the temporary policy to permanent coverage within a specific time period without providing additional evidence of insurability, such as a medical exam. This type of policy provides the benefit of purchasing less expensive term life insurance now with the option to convert to a permanent policy at a later date, as insurance needs and financial resources change. The premium increases when the policy is converted.

Permanent Life Insurance

Permanent life insurance remains in effect for the insured's lifetime and builds a cash value. *Cash value* is the savings accumulated in a permanent life insurance policy that you would receive if you canceled your policy. To build cash value, a portion of your premiums is deposited into an investment account where it earns interest. When a life insurance policy has a cash value, the insured can borrow against the policy. However, if the amount borrowed is not repaid, the policy will repay it out of the death benefit.

permanent life insurance a policy that remains in effect for the insured's lifetime and builds cash value

There are numerous types of permanent life insurance. Four common types include whole life, limited-pay life, universal life, and variable life.

Whole Life

With a *whole life policy* (also known as *straight life* or *ordinary life*), the insured pays fixed premiums as long as the policy is in effect. The amount of the premium depends on the age of the insured at the time the policy is purchased as well as the amount of the policy and the desired cash value. There is usually an age limit for how long the policy can remain in effect. The policy pays the face value to the beneficiaries upon the death of the insured.

Limited-Pay Life

With a *limited-pay life policy*, the insured pays premiums for a specific number of years or until age 65. At the end of the payment period, the policy is considered "paid up"; the insured pays no more in premiums. However, the policyholder remains insured until his or her death, at which time the policy pays the face value to the beneficiaries.

Universal Life

A *universal life policy* does not have a fixed premium or death benefit. The policyholder can change the amount of the premiums and the death benefit throughout the life of the policy. Thus, the face value of the policy can be lowered or

What are some advantages of permanent life insurance?

raised without rewriting the policy. The advantage of this type of plan is that it allows the policyholder to adjust the death benefit and premiums to fit changing needs. For example, when interest rates are high, the insured can move large sums of money into the policy (by paying higher premiums) and let the earnings grow tax-deferred.

Variable Life

A *variable life policy* combines a death benefit with investment options. As chosen by the policyholder, the insurer invests part of the premium in securities (such as stocks and bonds) within the insurance company's portfolio. Both the death benefit and cash value rise (or fall) with the investment results. Although a minimum death benefit is guaranteed, there is no guaranteed cash value. With some variable life policies, policyholders pay fixed premiums. With others, the premiums can fluctuate because the interest earned on investments may be applied to the premiums, thus reducing the amount the policyholder pays.

 CHECKPOINT

What advantages does group life insurance offer over individual life insurance?

6-2 Lesson Assessment

KEY TERMS REVIEW

Match the terms with the definitions. Some terms may not be used.

_____ 1. A plan for sharing the risk of medical costs resulting from injury or illness

_____ 2. The person designated to receive money from a life insurance policy

_____ 3. Insurance that pays money to the beneficiary upon the death of the insured person

_____ 4. A type of health insurance plan that allows patients to choose any doctor or other provider for medical services

_____ 5. A group plan that provides pre-paid medical care for its members

_____ 6. A policy that remains in effect for the insured's lifetime and builds a cash value

a. beneficiary

b. disability insurance

c. fee-for-service plan

d. health insurance

e. health maintenance organization (HMO)

f. life insurance

g. permanent life insurance

h. preferred provider organization (PPO)

i. stop-loss provision

j. temporary life insurance

_____ 7. A network of independent health care providers that band together to provide health care services for a set fee

_____ 8. An insurance clause that sets a maximum that the insured has to pay out of pocket during any calendar year

_____ 9. Insurance that provides income to replace a portion of normal earnings when the insured is unable to work due to a nonwork-related injury or illness

CHECK YOUR UNDERSTANDING

10. What is the difference between a flexible spending account (FSA) and a health savings account (HSA)?

11. How is a health maintenance organization (HMO) different from a preferred provider organization (PPO)?

12. How is basic health care coverage different from major medical coverage?

13. What are some things you can do to help manage health care costs?

14. How is short-term disability insurance different from long-term disability insurance?

15. List some reasons why people buy life insurance.

16. List the types of temporary life insurance and permanent life insurance.

THINK CRITICALLY

17. Why is it important to find a way to manage the rising costs of health care in this country? (Consider health care spending as a percentage of GDP.)

18. Explain why people who are in good health might prefer to have a high-deductible insurance plan with a health savings account (HSA).

19. Disability insurance is a good way to protect income, yet it is perhaps the most overlooked form of coverage. Why do you think this is so?

20. Life insurance protects others (your family). How much life insurance do you need at this point in your life? How might your insurance needs change over time?

21. Why would you choose temporary life insurance over permanent life insurance? When might you choose permanent insurance instead?

EXTEND YOUR LEARNING

22. You should consider several factors when deciding what type of insurance to buy. Read the following situations, and identify the type of insurance or insurance plan feature you think is right for each one.

    a. You want a life insurance policy that gives you the right to renew the policy on a yearly basis, without having to pass a medical exam. What type of policy should you buy?

    b. You want a health insurance plan that sets a limit on the amount of medical expenses you will have to pay out of pocket in a calendar year. What feature should you request?

    c. You want a health insurance plan that will cover the expenses of at-home professional care in case you need it as you get older. What type of policy should you buy?

    d. You want health insurance that helps you pay for services and out-of-pocket expenses that your standard policy does not cover. What type of insurance should you buy?

    e. You want to choose how part of the premiums you pay for life insurance will be invested. What type of policy should you buy?

    f. You want a life insurance policy that will stay in effect until you die. However, you do not want to pay premiums after you retire. What type of policy should you buy?

THE ESSENTIAL QUESTION   Refer to The Essential Question on p. 193. Health insurance helps you pay for medical costs, which can be expensive. Disability insurance provides you with income to cover daily living expenses in case a serious injury or illness does not allow you to work. Life insurance is needed to protect others who are dependent on you as a source of income.

THE ESSENTIAL QUESTION
What are the various forms of property insurance for home and auto, and what protections do they provide?

LEARNING OBJECTIVES

LO 6-3.1 Explain the need and provisions of homeowners and renters insurance.

LO 6-3.2 Explain the need and types of coverage for auto insurance.

LO 6-3.3 Identify ways to reduce the cost and maximize the benefits of insurance.

KEY TERMS
- homeowners insurance, 205
- liability coverage, 206
- home inventory, 206
- replacement value, 207
- renters insurance, 207
- auto insurance, 208
- collision coverage, 208
- comprehensive coverage, 209
- personal injury protection (PIP), 209
- uninsured/underinsured motorist coverage, 209
- umbrella liability insurance, 212

LO 6-3.1 Why Do You Need Homeowners Insurance?

Regardless of where you live, your property is at risk. *Real property* includes permanent structures, such as buildings and homes. The contents of your home—such as furniture, appliances, and clothing—are called *personal property*. Your property could be destroyed in many ways. Its contents could be lost, damaged, or stolen. **Homeowners insurance** protects property owners from risk of loss to their real and personal property.

homeowners insurance a policy that protects property owners from risk of loss to their real and personal property

Types of Coverage

Homeowners insurance covers property owners' losses from the following three basic types of risk:

1. *Hazards* (fire, water, wind, and smoke that may cause physical damages)
2. *Crimes* (criminal activity such as robbery, burglary, theft, and vandalism)
3. *Liability* (another person's losses due to injuries at your property)

Additional insurance can be purchased to cover natural disasters, such as floods, earthquakes, and hurricanes. If you have particularly valuable possessions, such as expensive jewelry, valuable antiques, or a fine art collection, that are worth beyond what is covered by your basic policy, you can buy extended coverage for the items in the form of an insurance *rider*. To insure valuable items, you likely will need to get an *appraisal*, or an expert's opinion on the market value of the item. An appraisal will give you proof of value in the event the item is damaged, stolen, or destroyed.

Hazards

Fire, water, wind, and smoke can damage or destroy your house. The risk of this type of loss is unpredictable, and the consequences can be serious. For example, if your house is destroyed by a fire and you have no insurance, you would still be legally bound to make your mortgage payment even though you would have no house to live in. Having homeowners insurance provides protection against financial loss from hazards that may cause damage or destruction.

Homeowner's insurance protects not only your home and its contents but also your garage or shed, trees, plants, shrubs, and fences. Some policies also cover the costs of lodging while your house is being repaired or replaced.

Criminal Activity

Theft and vandalism coverage protects your personal belongings if your house is broken into, vandalized, or suffers damage as a result of other criminal acts. After you pay your deductible, you will be reimbursed for the remaining repair expenses and the value of stolen items. Many homeowners insurance policies contain off-premise coverage as well. This protects your possessions if they are with you when you are away.

Why does a property owner need liability coverage?

liability coverage protection against injuries suffered by others while on your property or as a result of your actions

Personal Liability

Liability coverage provides protection if others are injured while on your property or as a result of your actions. For example, if a guest slips and breaks his leg while getting into your swimming pool, you are responsible and must accept personal liability. Liability coverage would pay for the person's medical expenses and any related costs of the injury.

Natural Disasters

Some areas of the country can have hurricanes, floods, or earthquakes. These acts of nature can do a great deal of damage. Coverage for these extreme types of risk is often not included in a basic homeowners insurance policy. For these types of perils, policyholders often use endorsements to add coverage to their homeowners' insurance policy for an additional premium. An *endorsement* is a written amendment to an insurance policy that reflects changes to it. You may also be able to buy insurance from the federal government to cover these risks.

Home Inventory

When items are stolen from your home, destroyed, or damaged, you must file a claim with the insurance company in order to get paid for the items. Could you name all the items in your home if it was destroyed by fire? Do you know the value of all the items? Many people would not be able to give an accurate record of home items from memory. To be prepared in case you need to file a claim, you should create a home inventory. A **home inventory** is a list of all the items of value in your home. Figure 6-3.1 shows part of a home inventory.

home inventory a list of items of value in your home; used for insurance purposes

	A	B	C	D	E
1	HOME INVENTORY				
2	Updated June 1. 20--				
3					
4	Item	Number	Date	Original	Replacement
5	Description	of Items	Purchased	Cost	Value
6	Air cleaner	2	2/12/2015	$110.78	
7	Ionic Pro Model CA-500B				
8	China place setting including dinner	8	5/25/2011	$414.85	
9	plate, salad plate, cup, saucer,				
10	and bread plate. Pattern: Royal				
11	Albert Old Country Roses				
12	Computer monitor, 24-inch flat panel	1	3/18/2014	$149.99	
13	ViewSonic Model VA7000				
14	Sofa, brown leather, 83 inches long	1	4/5/2015	$2,150.48	
15	Brand: Ethan Allen #28945				
16	Television, plasma, 50-inch	1	4/23/2015	$689.56	
17	Sony Model KLV S23A10				
18	Serial # 700 4690				
19					

A home inventory should include a brief description of each item of value (including serial numbers for items such as appliances and computers), the number of items, the purchase date, and the original cost. The inventory should also include a column to list the replacement value of the item. The **replacement value** is the cost of replacing an item regardless of its actual cash (market) value. In other words, it is what you would pay today for an item rather than what you originally paid. It is important to know whether your insurance policy will reimburse you for the actual cash value or replacement value. If you will be paid the replacement value, that amount can be added to the home inventory just before a claim is filed so the price is current.

replacement value the cost of replacing an item regardless of its actual cash (market) value

Once the inventory is complete, a hard copy should be stored in a safe place, such as a fireproof box or safe deposit box. Include documentation that shows proof of ownership and value, such as receipts, pictures, or a videotape of the items. The inventory should be updated regularly. Keeping the inventory in a spreadsheet or database program makes it easy to update.

Renters Insurance

If you rent your residence instead of own it, you don't have to worry about insuring the building; that is the landlord's responsibility. However, your personal belongings are your responsibility to protect. You are also responsible for personal injuries that occur inside your apartment, condo, or rental home. **Renters insurance** protects renters from personal property and liability risks.

renters insurance a policy that protects renters from personal property and liability risks

Personal possessions inside the rental property can be damaged or destroyed by fire, smoke, water, freezing temperatures, or heat. For example, if you rent an apartment and there is a fire in the building, your personal property (couch, chairs, bed, clothing, television, and so on) may suffer damage. Your renters insurance policy will cover the costs of repairing or replacing any damaged or destroyed personal belongings.

Renters insurance even covers your personal belongings when they're not inside your home. For example, if you take your laptop with you on a trip and it is damaged, your renters insurance policy will cover the costs of repairing it.

>>> **CHECKPOINT**

What are some reasons to obtain homeowners or renters insurance?

LO 6-3.2 How Does Insurance Protect Car Owners?

When you drive a car, there are serious risks to people and property. All states have *financial responsibility laws* that require drivers to be prepared to pay for damages caused to others. One way to be prepared is to have auto insurance. **Auto insurance** protects a car owner from losses as a result of accidents and other events. The cost of auto insurance depends on many things, such as the type of car and the age and driving record of the insured.

auto insurance a policy that protects a car owner from losses as a result of accidents and other events

MGkaya/iStockphoto.com

What type of coverage pays for damage to your car if another driver hits you?

Types of Coverage

There are five basic types of auto insurance:

1. Liability
2. Collision
3. Comprehensive
4. Personal injury protection (PIP)
5. Uninsured/underinsured motorist

Full coverage consists of all five basic types of auto insurance purchased together in a single policy. If you have a car loan, you are required to have full coverage.

Liability Coverage

Liability coverage protects the insured against loss as a result of injury to another person or damage to that person's property. It pays nothing toward the insured's own losses. Liability coverage is required by law in most states.

Liability coverage is usually expressed in a series of numbers, such as 100/300/50. The 100 represents how much will be paid for injuries to one person ($100,000). The 300 indicates the total amount that will be paid for all people in an accident ($300,000). The 50 specifies how much property damage will be paid ($50,000). Premiums charged for liability insurance vary according to the amount of coverage.

Collision Coverage

collision coverage a policy that protects against damage to your own vehicle if you hit another car or lose control and roll over

Collision coverage protects against damage to your own vehicle if you hit another car or lose control and roll over. It pays when you are at fault. If you carry only liability insurance, damage to your car will not be covered. If an accident is not your fault, the other driver's insurance will cover the damage.

Collision coverage has a deductible, which typically ranges from as low as $50 to as high as $1,000. The higher the deductible, the lower your insurance premium will be.

Comprehensive Coverage

Protection against damages to your car from causes other than collision or rolling over is provided by **comprehensive coverage**. Examples of other causes of damage include fire, theft, severe weather, falling objects, acts of vandalism, and impacts from hitting an animal, such as a deer. Comprehensive coverage also has a deductible.

comprehensive coverage protection against damages to your car from causes other than collision or rolling over

Personal Injury Protection (PIP)

Personal injury protection (PIP) pays for medical, hospital, and funeral costs of the insured and passengers in the insured's car in the event of an accident, regardless of who is at fault. PIP coverage is mandatory in some states. Discounts for PIP coverage may be available if you have airbags and other safety devices to reduce injuries.

personal injury protection (PIP) coverage for medical, hospital, and funeral costs of the insured and passengers in the event of an accident, regardless of who is at fault

Uninsured/Underinsured Motorist

Uninsured/underinsured motorist coverage provides protection against damages caused by a motorist who is at fault and does not have insurance to pay for your damages. In some cases, the other driver may have insurance but with insufficient coverage to pay for the full extent of your damages. This is known as an *underinsured motorist*. Because of the high number of uninsured drivers on the road, many states require drivers to carry at least uninsured motorist coverage. This insurance also protects you as a pedestrian or bicyclist if you are hit and injured by an uninsured or underinsured motorist.

uninsured/underinsured motorist coverage protection against damages caused by a motorist with no or insufficient insurance

No-Fault Insurance

Some states have passed no-fault insurance laws. With *no-fault insurance*, drivers receive reimbursement for their damages from their own insurer, regardless of who is at fault. The basic idea behind no-fault insurance is to avoid the years of legal battling required to settle a case and determine fault.

Looking Ahead Before you get your first car, you should plan ahead to know how much auto insurance will cost. Every state has laws regarding how much minimum liability coverage for auto insurance is needed. Use the Internet to answer the following questions: What is the minimum amount of liability coverage that is required in your state? Do you think it is wise to purchase only the minimum amount of liability coverage required by law? Explain your answer.

Assigned Risk Pools

Every state has an *assigned risk pool* that consists of drivers with poor driving records who are unable to obtain auto insurance. The state assigns these drivers to different insurers in the state who must provide coverage. Many times, the only coverage offered will be basic liability coverage. In addition, insurance premiums are usually high until the risky driver can reestablish a good driving record.

CHECKPOINT
Which type of auto insurance coverage is required by law in most states?

LO 6-3.3 How Can You Reduce Insurance Costs and Maximize Benefits?

Insurance can be expensive. The costs can be overwhelming if you carry full and maximum coverage for all types of risks to property and income. But there are ways you can reduce costs. This often means raising your overall risk, but in some cases this is necessary so you can manage your budget. You should also carefully review your insurance policy to be sure you are getting the best value for your money.

Reducing Premium Costs

To lower the cost of insurance, you should look for ways to reduce your premiums. You can consider any one or a combination of strategies as described below.

Higher Deductibles

Deductibles are present on many types of coverage. When you raise your deductible from, say, $100 to $500, you will lower your premiums. By assuming more risk yourself, you lower the insurance company's risk.

Discounts

Many insurance companies offer discounts. For example, taking driver's education courses and getting good grades lowers auto insurance rates for teenage drivers. Discounts may also be given if you of are a certain age, if you have a good driving record, or if your vehicle has a high safety rating. Buying more than one type of insurance policy (such as homeowners and auto insurance) from the same company can result in a *multi-line discount*.

Decrease Coverage

In some cases, the cost of insuring against a particular risk may be too great, or the probability that the risk will occur may be too low, to justify paying a higher insurance premium. For example, as your car gets older, it loses value. So instead of full coverage, you may choose to carry only liability coverage and assume the risk of paying for any repairs yourself. By decreasing the amount of coverage and self-insuring, you can lower your premiums. However, if your car is destroyed in an accident that is your fault, you would have to pay to replace it.

Payment Options

If you pay your premiums semiannually or annually, you can usually get lower premiums than if you pay monthly. Some insurance companies will give you lower rates if you pay electronically or if you agree to have your payment automatically deducted from your checking account.

Comparison Shop

Insurance premiums are often set based on geography, customer usage rates, company profitability, types of coverage offered, financial strength ratings, and many other factors. By shopping around and comparing prices, you can save money. There are websites that allow consumers to compare prices of policies from different companies.

You may be able to save money by using an independent agent. An independent insurance agent represents several insurance companies and can do the comparison shopping for you to find the best rates.

Buy Insurance Online

Many insurance companies have websites that allow consumers to buy insurance directly without the use of an insurance agent. Because consumers do not deal with an agent, the cost of these policies may be lower. However, before buying insurance online, conduct research to make sure that the company is reputable.

Piggybacking

Many young drivers get their first insurance as an add-on to their parent's insurance policies. As long as you keep a good driving record, this is most likely your least expensive way to get started. When you go out on your own, you can get a separate policy. Young drivers pay the highest insurance rates because of a higher likelihood of being in an accident. You must build a good driving record to prove you are deserving of lower premiums.

How can you reduce your insurance premiums by buying insurance online?

Maximizing Benefits

Because insurance is costly, it is important to know that you are getting a good value. To make sure you are receiving the best coverage for the premiums you are paying, you should review your coverage and consider purchasing umbrella liability insurance.

Review Coverage

Every year or two, you should review your insurance coverage. For example, as your vehicle gets older and loses value, your premium should be shrinking. You may decide to drop certain types of coverage (such as collision) when your car gets older. For your homeowners insurance, your coverage should increase as your home's replacement value rises.

When reviewing your coverage, check to see if you qualify for any discounts. For example, many insurance companies offer discounts to drivers when they reach a certain age and to homeowners if security features are added to the home. When reviewing coverage, it's also a good time to check prices and comparison shop to be sure your premiums are as low as possible.

Umbrella Liability Insurance

umbrella liability insurance a supplement to your basic auto and homeowners coverage that expands limits and includes additional risks

People who maintain required liability coverage on their vehicle and residence can also purchase an umbrella policy that picks up where the other coverage leaves off. **Umbrella liability insurance** supplements your basic auto and homeowners coverage by expanding limits and including additional risks.

Umbrella liability insurance is designed to protect you from *extraordinary losses*, which are extremely high claims because of unusual circumstances. For example, you may be in an auto accident whereby costs for the other person's injuries are $1 million. If your liability coverage is only for $300,000, you'd be responsible for the remaining $700,000.

Limits for umbrella policies typically begin at $1 million. The cost of umbrella liability insurance is based on the policy limit you choose as well as factors such as your net worth and location. The cost is also influenced by how much of a risk the insurance company thinks you are. This decision is influenced by a number of factors such as your job, driving record, and hobbies. The premium you pay for an umbrella policy is in addition to the premiums for your auto insurance and your homeowners or renters insurance.

〉〉〉 CHECKPOINT

What are some ways that you can reduce the cost of your insurance?

6-3 Lesson Assessment

KEY TERMS REVIEW

Match the terms with the definitions. Some terms may not be used.

_____ 1. Protection against injuries suffered by others while on your property or as a result of your actions

_____ 2. A policy that protects a car owner from losses as a result of accidents

_____ 3. A policy that protects property owners from risk of loss to their real and personal property

_____ 4. Protection against damages to your car from causes other than collision or rolling over

_____ 5. A list of items of value in your home used for insurance purposes

a. auto insurance

b. collision coverage

c. comprehensive coverage

d. home inventory

e. homeowners insurance

f. liability coverage

g. personal injury protection (PIP)

h. renters insurance

i. replacement value

j. umbrella liability insurance

k. uninsured/underinsured motorist coverage

_____ 6. A policy that protects against damage to your own vehicle if you hit another car or lose control and roll over

_____ 7. A policy that protects renters from personal property and liability risks

_____ 8. Protection against damages caused by a motorist with no insurance

_____ 9. Coverage for medical, hospital, and funeral costs of the insured and passengers in the event of an accident

CHECK YOUR UNDERSTANDING

10. What is the difference between real property and personal property?

11. What is the purpose of a home inventory? What details should the inventory include?

12. How is renters insurance different from homeowners insurance?

13. Why do drivers need auto insurance? What are the basic types of auto insurance coverage?

14. If your auto insurance policy has liability coverage of 100/250/100, what does this mean?

15. What is the basic goal behind no-fault insurance?

16. Why should you review your insurance coverage every few years?

17. What is the purpose of having an umbrella liability insurance policy?

THINK CRITICALLY

18. Why do mortgage lenders require borrowers to obtain homeowners insurance as part of the loan contract?

19. Why do standard homeowners insurance policies exclude loss from certain acts of nature, such as floods and earthquakes? How can consumers get protection if they live in an area that is subject to these types of risks?

20. When buying insurance, why is it important to know whether the policy pays replacement value or actual cash value for lost or damaged property?

21. One person's auto insurance is $1,200 per year, and another person's is $800. What factors cause the wide variances in insurance premiums?

22. Liability coverage is required by law in most states. Why is it important for car owners to carry liability coverage? What is the purpose of financial responsibility laws?

EXTEND YOUR LEARNING

TEAMWORK

23. Prices for auto insurance vary depending on the company, the age of the driver, the type of vehicle, and other factors. Descriptions of two drivers follow. Work with a partner to get an annual quote for full-coverage auto insurance for each driver. To find quotes, check online or call a local insurance agent. If you call a local agent, identify yourself as a student, and ask for a typical price for the driver described.

Driver A

Sheila Roberts is 18 years old. She makes good grades in school and has taken a driver's education course. She has had no auto accidents or tickets. The car she will drive is a four-year-old midsize sedan in good working condition. The car is owned by her parents. Sheila wants to be added to her parents' auto policy. She wants two quotes: one for a policy with the lowest deductible and lowest liability coverage available and another for a policy with a higher deductible and higher liability coverage.

Driver B

Joe Chung is 19 years old. His college grades are a C average, and he has not taken a driver's education course. He has had one traffic ticket for speeding. The car that Joe will drive is a two-year-old sports car. He owns the car. Joe wants his own insurance policy (not an add-on to his parents' policy). Because he wants to save money on his premiums, Joe would prefer a higher deductible and the minimum liability coverage.

THE ESSENTIAL QUESTION   Refer to The Essential Question on p. 205. Homeowners insurance protects property owners from risk of loss to their real and personal property. Renters insurance protects renters from personal property and liability risks. Auto insurance protects car owners from losses as a result of accidents and other events. Umbrella liability insurance is available for purchase by property owners, renters, and car owners. It supplements basic auto and property liability coverage by expanding limits and including additional risks.

Exploring Careers in . . .
INSURANCE

When looking to purchase insurance, you may consider contacting an insurance agent. Insurance agents help people select insurance policies that provide the best protection for their property, lives, and health.

Agents spend a lot of time contacting clients to expand their customer base. They also handle policy renewals and process claims when their clients experience a loss. An increasing number offer financial planning services, such as estate planning and retirement planning.

Insurance agents may be captive agents or independent agents. Captive agents work for a single insurance company and sell only policies provided by the company that employs them. Independent agents work for an insurance brokerage and sell the policies of many companies. They match a client with the company that offers a policy with the best rate and coverage.

Employment Outlook

- An average rate of employment growth is expected.
- The Internet has reduced the demand for insurance agents, as many people now do their own research and purchase insurance online.

Job Titles

- Insurance sales agent
- Personal financial adviser
- Insurance underwriter
- Claims adjuster

Needed Education/Skills

- A bachelor's degree in business, finance, or economics is preferred.
- A license is required from the state where the insurance is sold.
- Excellent analytical and communication skills are a must.

What's it like to work in . . . Insurance

Juan works as an independent insurance agent, earning commissions. The amount of his commission depends on the type and amount of insurance sold, and whether the sale is a new policy or renewal.

Today, Juan is meeting with new clients—a young, newly married couple. He will work with them to determine the kinds of risk they may face at this point in their lives, including property, personal, and liability risks. Based on the information he gathers, he will put together an insurance policy that meets their needs. He will then check rates and coverage with several companies to see which one offers the best policy.

What About You?

Are you interested in helping people assess their risks and develop strategies to insure against those risks? What advantages do agents offer that cannot be found online?

Chapter 6 Assessment

SUMMARY

6-1   Risk is the chance of injury, damage, or economic loss. Everyone takes risks that have potential consequences that may be serious.

There are three types of risk: personal risk, risk of financial loss, and risk of financial resources.

Risk can be managed by conducting a risk assessment, which is the process of identifying risks, their probability, their seriousness, and ways to handle them.

Risk strategies include reducing risk, avoiding risk, transferring risk, and assuming risk.

6-2   Health insurance allows people to pay for high medical expenses. Group policies and individual polices are available.

Types of health insurance plans include unmanaged care (fee-for-service), managed (HMOs and PPOs), and government-sponsored plans (Medicare and Medicaid).

Typical health insurance includes basic health care and major medical coverage. Some plans cover dental and vision needs for a higher premium.

Supplemental health insurance plans help pay for services and out-of-pocket expenses that standard health insurance policies do not cover.

Disability insurance provides income when the insured is unable to work due to nonwork-related injury or illness.

Life insurance provides funds to beneficiaries when the insured dies. Temporary life insurance (term life insurance) remains in effect for a specified period of time. Permanent life insurance remains in effect for the insured's lifetime and also builds a cash value.

6-3   Homeowners insurance includes real property and personal property protections. It covers losses from three types of risk: (1) hazards, (2) crimes, and (3) liability. Renters insurance provides similar coverage on the contents of a residence, but not the structure.

Auto insurance protects a car owner from losses as a result of accidents and other events. The five basic types of coverage are (1) liability, (2) collision, (3) comprehensive, (4) personal injury protection (PIP), and (5) uninsured/underinsured motorist.

You can lower premiums by increasing deductibles, looking for discounts, decreasing coverage, choosing cost-effective payment options, comparison shopping, and buying insurance online.

MAKE ACADEMIC CONNECTIONS

TEAMWORK

1. **Research** Financial responsibility laws vary by state. Work with a classmate to learn what the financial responsibility laws of your state require. Using an Internet search engine, enter your state's name and the term *financial responsibility laws*. Read the information you find about the laws for your state. Record the information listed below. (LO 6-3.2)

   • The name and address of the website(s) where you found the information

   • People to whom the financial responsibility laws apply

   • Methods that can be used to meet the requirements of the laws

   • Situations in which individuals may be required to offer proof that they are complying with the laws

   • The minimum amount of each type of insurance that must be carried to satisfy the laws

   • Penalties for breaking the laws

2. **History** Throughout history, natural disasters have created serious economic problems, from repairs and rebuilding to disease and unemployment. Write a two-page report about a natural disaster and its impact on the economy of the area where the event occurred. Examples: the San Francisco Earthquake of 1906, the Thailand (Sumatra) Tsunami of 2004, Hurricane Hugo (Florida), or Hurricane Katrina (Louisiana). (LO 6-3.1)

3. **Government** Research the Affordable Care Act (ACA) that was passed in 2010. Prepare a presentation that explains how the ACA has changed insurance coverage in your family and for the nation. Discuss the benefits as well as the problems and controversies associated with the law. Prepare and use visual aids during your presentation. (LO 6-2.1)

4. **International** Select another country and research its health care laws. Compare the health care and disability coverage options available in the United States and in the other country. Which country's health care laws are more beneficial to patients? Explain why. (LO 6-2.1, LO 6-2.2)

5. **Research** Conduct online research about no-fault insurance laws and how they work. List states that have no-fault insurance provisions. Explain what happens when there is an accident in a state with no-fault insurance laws. (LO 6-3.2)

6. **Communication** Considering the high cost of insurance premiums, what can you (and your family) do to reduce premiums while maintaining the coverage needed for major risks and serious consequences? Prepare a list titled "Insurance Tips" that addresses the following questions: (LO 6-3.3)
   a. How can you reduce premiums by better use of deductibles?
   b. What actions can you take personally to lower premiums?
   c. What other strategies can you use to get the most from the money you spend on insurance?

7. **Ethics** Filing a false insurance claim, whether it is related to health, disability, life, homeowners, or auto insurance, is known as *insurance fraud*. All insurance companies have insurance investigators who are experts at determining whether fraud has occurred. Search the Internet for a recent article about a person or company that committed insurance fraud. Write a brief summary of the article, describing the fraud and the outcome. Share your summary with the class. (LO 6-2.1, 6-2.2, 6-2.3, 6-3.1, 6-3.2)

 Do the Math

1. Takashi Caldwell has health insurance that pays 80 percent of covered charges after a $150 deductible. She received a statement for $350 of covered charges. How much will Takashi have to pay?

2. Ryan Maderas has health insurance that pays 80 percent of covered charges after a $500 deductible. He has a stop-loss provision of $5,000. The insurance company has paid $16,000 (which is 80 percent of the medical expenses after the deductible). Assuming all charges were covered, how much has Ryan paid for medical costs?

3. Mel Adams has homeowners insurance that pays 90 percent of the replacement value of items damaged in a fire. He had a fire in his kitchen, and the electric stove was damaged beyond repair. Mel paid $350 for the stove five years ago. The cash value of the stove before the fire was $100. A new stove with the same features will cost $400. How much will his insurance company pay?

Take Action

PREPARE A HOME INVENTORY

Once you own property, you should take steps to protect it from loss, theft, and damage. Review the example home inventory shown in Figure 6-3.1 and complete the following activities:

a. Create an inventory for the items in one room of your home. You can choose the room where most of your personal items are kept or another room. If possible, use spreadsheet software to create the inventory.

b. If possible, take pictures of or videotape the items in the room to supplement the inventory. Also, include receipts or other verification of the value of the items in your inventory where possible.

c. If your family does not have a complete home inventory, encourage your parents or other adults with whom you live to create one. Prepare a persuasive speech explaining what a home inventory is and why it is important. Also, describe how to make one.

After you complete your home inventory, include a copy of it in your portfolio.

Comparison Shopping, Insurance, and Person-to-Person Payments

Let's discuss buying decisions. Prior to going to the store or going online to make a purchase, you should have an idea of what you need. You should also have an approximate budget in mind before shopping. It is wise to do online research regarding product choices and costs prior to making a purchase. Bear in mind, if an offer seems too good to be true, it may either be a scam or may be an item of inferior quality. Trust your instincts and avoid impulse purchases. Finally, when in doubt, don't make the purchase. Complete the *Before You Buy Worksheet* to practice comparing costs before making a purchase. This worksheet is designed to help you assess before you commit. Assessing before buying is in your best interest.

Comparing costs prior to purchasing helps you use your resources wisely. Another way to manage your resources is to protect your possessions with insurance. In the unfortunate event that some of your insured property is either damaged or stolen, you will need to fill out an insurance claim form. Complete the *Insurance Form Worksheet* to learn the proper way to prepare an insurance claim form.

Payment methods are evolving. With the help of modern technology, consumers can pay one another directly without having to use either cash or checks. Person-to-person (P2P) payments facilitate transactions among service providers (like dog walkers and house painters) and their customers. Complete the *Person-to-Person Payments Worksheet* to understand how to use P2P payment options.

THINK CRITICALLY

1. What difference does it make whether you take the time to do a cost comparison of products before you make a purchase?

2. If the chances of loss or damage to your property are low, why should you spend the money on insurance when you could put the insurance premium money to good use elsewhere?

3. If it has become easier for people to use P2P services to pay one another, why is cash still necessary in our society?

UNIT 3

Managing Credit and Debt

CHAPTER 7 Buying Decisions

CHAPTER 8 Preserving Your Credit

CHAPTER 9 Credit Problems and Laws

Rob Marmion/Shutterstock.com

Unit 3 focuses on financial responsibility and credit. Chapter 7 begins with a discussion on how to be a financially responsible shopper. The rest of the chapter serves as an introduction to credit. You will learn about the various types of credit and the advantages and disadvantages of using credit. You will also learn about the costs of credit and the methods of computing interest on credit.

Chapter 8 begins with a discussion on renting and your responsibilities as a tenant and roommate. It also contains information on long-term debt options and repayment and concludes with a discussion on how to use credit wisely.

Chapter 9 explains common credit problems and how to resolve them. It also provides an overview of bankruptcy, including its purpose and the various types of bankruptcy. Sometimes, bankruptcy may be your best option for relieving debt. You will also discover the many credit laws that have been enacted to help protect consumers.

Buying Decisions

97/iStockphoto.com

Consumers buy products and services every day. Some of those decisions are good; some are not. Chapter 7 is about making good buying choices and using credit wisely. Overuse and misuse of credit can lead to many undesirable outcomes. There are many types of consumer credit. Some types are relatively inexpensive and easy to use. Other types are restrictive, expensive, and can lead to financial disaster. High interest rates, fees, and penalties are often imposed on those who are rated as poor credit risks. Making the right buying decisions and being smart about using credit can maximize your purchasing power.

Do *This*, **Not** *That*

To be financially responsible:

- Live within your means.
- "Pay yourself first," or set aside some money for saving.
- Know how to budget; avoid overspending.
- Pay your bills on time.
- Use credit wisely; don't overextend your credit.

7-1 Designing a Buying Plan

THE ESSENTIAL QUESTION   How can creating a buying plan make you a more responsible shopper?

LEARNING OBJECTIVES

LO 7-1.1   Discuss the consequences of being financially responsible and financially irresponsible.

LO 7-1.2   Design a buying plan and discuss how it is evaluated, financed, and implemented.

KEY TERMS

- systematic decision making, 222
- financial responsibility, 222
- financial irresponsibility, 223
- buying plan, 224
- criteria, 224
- spending limit, 225
- rebate, 226
- extended warranty, 226

LO 7-1.1 How Can You Be a Responsible Shopper?

systematic decision making the process of making choices that reflect goals by considering all of the pros and cons along with the costs

As a consumer, you should shop responsibly to ensure your financial security and freedom. Responsible shopping requires **systematic decision making**, which is the process of making choices that reflect your goals by considering all of the pros and cons along with the costs. Systematic decision making requires you to be financially responsible.

Financial Responsibility

financial responsibility being able to meet your financial goals through planned earning, spending, and saving

Financial responsibility occurs when you plan your earning, spending, and saving so that you meet your financial goals. People who are financially responsible are able to achieve the following goals:

- Live a comfortable lifestyle
- Provide for their own wants and needs
- Enjoy vacations and leisure time
- Save money for known and unknown future events
- Pursue interests, hobbies, and cultural events

The rewards of financial responsibility are satisfaction, independence, and financial freedom. Financially responsible people of all ages understand the deeply rewarding feeling of being able to take care of themselves. In other words, they are not dependent on others, but have learned how to manage their resources so that they are able to pay their own way in life.

Being financially responsible means that you buy goods and services in a responsible manner. You understand the difference between wants and needs. You don't have to borrow money every time something unexpected happens, and if you do have to borrow money, you are able to repay it in a timely manner. You are content and satisfied with the lifestyle that your income is able to provide you. When you are financially

What does it mean to assume responsibility for your own earning, spending, and saving?

<small>RonBailey/iStockphoto.com</small>

responsible, you are able to make payments as agreed and honor your commitments. Your life is structured around sound financial goals that you have set for yourself.

Financial Irresponsibility

Financial irresponsibility is failing to live up to your financial obligations to meet your goals and needs. When people fail to take responsibility, they are unable to sustain their own lifestyle. Financial irresponsibility symptoms include the following:

- Bills are not paid in a timely manner.
- There is inadequate food, clothing, and shelter to live a comfortable lifestyle.
- Money is spent on luxury items while basic needs are not being met.
- A month's worth of paychecks do not last the entire month.
- Borrowed money is not repaid in a timely manner or at all.

When individuals are unable to meet their needs, the costs are high, often unpredictable, and usually overwhelming. Costs of financial irresponsibility include an unhealthy lifestyle and poor health, lack of recreation and fun, and stress. This happens to people in all income groups. Making good choices begins with using systematic decision making, which can be used to set up a buying plan.

financial irresponsibility
failing to live up to your financial obligations to meet your goals and needs

⟫⟫ CHECKPOINT

What are the benefits of being financially responsible?

LO 7-1.2 What Is a Buying Plan?

A **buying plan** is an organized method for making good buying decisions. It will help you stretch your limited resources. It will also help prevent *buyer's remorse*, which is regret over a buying decision you have made. When you make a major purchase or spend a large sum of money, a buying plan can aid in the decision-making process. A buying plan is a more detailed extension of a budget.

Creating a Buying Plan

A buying plan, as shown in Figure 7-1.1, is a five-step process that outlines what it is that you are hoping to achieve. By clearly defining the steps, you will be able to choose wisely.

Step 1 Define Your Spending Goal

Any item you buy should be selected to meet your wants and needs. By evaluating your wants and needs before you shop, you will be better prepared to make good buying decisions. You should also consider how the item relates to meeting the goals you have set in your budget or financial plan. Understand that because your resources will likely be limited, you may have to forego buying other items in order to make your purchase. Thus, you should consider the *opportunity cost*, or the value of what you give up when you make a choice.

Step 2 Choose the Item to Buy

Once you have defined your spending goal, you can then choose the item that will meet your goals. This may include new or used, high-quality, or high-, medium-, or low-cost choices. You may also consider renting the item.

Step 3 Define Criteria

Once you have decided to buy a good or service, you should set criteria for the item. **Criteria** are standards or rules by which something can be judged. For an item you want to purchase, the criteria would be the desired features, functions, and quality of the item. List the criteria that you would consider acceptable before you shop for the item.

▶ FIGURE 7-1.1 **Buying Plan**

Spending Goal	Item	Criteria	Timeline	Spending Limit
1. Define your need, want, or spending goal.	2. List the item(s) that will satisfy your goal.	3. Describe the features or items that represent an ideal choice.	4. Identify when your goal should be met.	5. Set an upper limit on how much you can or are willing to spend.

Step 4 Set a Timeline

For each item you want to buy, decide how soon you want to make the purchase. The *timeline* sets the time frame for making your decision. It may depend on some activity, such as buying a new dress for graduation. It could also depend on the actions of others. For example, you may wait until a store places the item on sale before you make your purchase. Putting a time frame on each planned purchase will help you prioritize. By waiting a day or more, you may decide not to make the purchase.

Step 5 Set a Spending Limit

A **spending limit** is the maximum amount you are willing to pay for an item. Based on the need or want that is being met, how much money are you willing and able to spend? By setting a spending limit, you will not be tempted to spend more than you have planned.

Figure 7-1.2 is an example of a buying plan to buy a washer and dryer.

spending limit the maximum amount you are willing to pay for an item

Implementing a Buying Plan

When you know what type of item or service you need to buy and how much you are willing to spend, you can start to gather specific information. You will want to know what products and services are available, along with their features and prices. You may find that you need to revise your buying plan. For example, you may learn that a product with the specific features you want is not available within your spending limit. When this happens, you must change either the criteria or the spending limit.

Comparison Shopping

Comparison shopping leads to better buying decisions. You can make a better choice when you know all of the options available. Check several sources to find data on prices and features of the product or service. The Internet makes comparison shopping easy. You can browse sites containing product data and prices at your own convenience and without any pressure to buy.

▶ FIGURE 7-1.2 **Buying Plan for a Washer and Dryer**

Spending Goal	Item	Criteria	Timeline	Spending Limit
To wash clothes at home rather than at a laundromat (saving time and money)	Washer and dryer (new or used)	Washer should be heavy-duty, have cycles for different kinds of clothes, and have a bleach dispenser. Dryer should be electric (not gas) and have several heat settings.	1 year or sooner	$850

Building COMMUNICATION SKILLS

INFORMAL SPEAKING

The purpose of *informal speaking* is to share information. Informal speaking often involves getting responses from others. Information is both given and received as other people interact with the speaker. Talking with another person and speaking with several people in a group setting are examples of informal speaking. Follow these guidelines to help you communicate effectively in such situations:

- Express your ideas clearly. Do not assume that others will know as much about the topic as you do.
- Speak clearly. Do not mumble or slur sounds.
- Use standard English. For example, say "give me" instead of "gimme."
- Use proper grammar. For example, say "she does not" (or "doesn't") instead of "she don't."
- Speak at an appropriate volume level. Talk loudly enough to be heard, but not so loudly as to be annoying.

- Use an appropriate tone. *Tone* is a manner of speaking that expresses your attitude or feelings. Make the tone of your voice match the topic being discussed. For example, use a light, friendly tone when talking about plans for an upcoming celebration. Use a more serious tone when discussing problems or important issues.
- Listen to others and give them time to respond.

Try It Out

Gather with a group of your friends. Be prepared to share information with them about a topic that interests you and that you feel might be of interest to them. Follow the procedures outlined above. Then assess how the group reacted. Did anyone ask you questions? Describe their facial expressions (nonverbal feedback). What did you do well (did they understand what you were trying to say)? What would you do differently?

Compare the product or service features to the criteria you have set. Determine which product or service has all the features and the quality you need at the lowest price. Some stores may offer various sales promotions, such as coupons, free product samples, or rebates. A **rebate** is a refund of part of the purchase price of an item. Remember to add taxes, handling charges, and shipping fees when considering the total cost. Some catalog and Internet companies offer free shipping.

rebate a refund of part of the purchase price of an item

Be aware that the lowest price is not always the best price. Compare the warranties and return policies from the various sellers. For expensive items, having a good *warranty* that protects you against product defects can be an important factor. An **extended warranty** is additional coverage that you can buy to pay for repairs or replacements needed beyond the original warranty period. Finally, consider the seller. Do some research to find out if the seller is reputable.

extended warranty additional coverage that you can buy to pay for repairs or replacements needed beyond the original warranty period

Payment Methods

Each purchase involves two choices—what to buy and how you will pay for it. Sometimes your only payment option is cash. At other times, you can choose among payment methods. You may be able to write a check or pay with a debit or credit card. Each payment method offers benefits. Using cash can help prevent overspending. Using a credit card provides protection if you have a problem with the item purchased and want to dispute the charge. For large purchases, such as a car, you may borrow money to pay for the purchase.

Why should you evaluate an item after you make a purchase?

Making the Purchase

Once you have gathered all of your information and decided on the product or service that will best meet your needs, it is time to buy. When making a purchase, check the item carefully to be sure it is in good condition. If the item is in a box, the box should be sealed. It should be clear that the box was not opened and resealed. If the box has been resealed, take the item out and examine it to make sure it is not damaged.

Be sure to keep the receipt. Know the time period within which a product can be exchanged or returned if you find something wrong with it. Sometimes delivery will cost extra. You might be able to save money by picking up a product yourself.

Evaluating the Purchase

Once you buy the product or service and try it out, you should reflect on your purchase. You may find that you feel differently about it after the excitement of buying is gone.

After making a purchase, ask yourself the following questions:

- How satisfied am I with the purchase?
- Did I follow my buying plan?
- Did I get good value for the money I spent?
- Does the product or service meet the want or need for which I purchased it?
- Are there ways I could have done a better job in selecting or buying?
- If I had to do it over again, would I still purchase the item?

Answering these questions will allow you to learn from your buying experience so that you can continue to make good buying decisions. Remember, sometimes the right decision is not buying!

⟩⟩⟩ CHECKPOINT

What are the five steps of creating a buying plan?

7-1 Lesson Assessment

KEY TERMS REVIEW

Match the terms with the definitions. Some terms may not be used.

_____ 1. An organized method for making good buying decisions

_____ 2. The maximum amount you are willing to spend for an item

_____ 3. Being able to meet your financial goals through planned earning, spending, and saving

_____ 4. Standards or rules by which something is judged

_____ 5. The process of making choices that reflect goals by considering all of the pros and cons along with the costs

_____ 6. A refund of part of the purchase price of an item

_____ 7. Failing to live up to your financial obligations to meet your goals and needs

a. buying plan
b. criteria
c. extended warranty
d. financial irresponsibility
e. financial responsibility
f. rebate
g. spending limit
h. systematic decision making

CHECK YOUR UNDERSTANDING

8. How is systematic decision making related to being financially responsible?

9. Describe traits of a person who is financially responsible.

10. When people are living beyond their means, they are said to be financially irresponsible. Explain.

11. Describe the symptoms experienced by someone who is financially irresponsible.

12. What are the advantages of using a buying plan?

13. Why is it important to set a spending limit before you go shopping for an item?

14. How does a rebate affect the price of an item you are purchasing?

15. Under what circumstances would you buy an extended warranty?

16. What payment methods are available when making a purchase?

17. Why is it important to keep your receipt after making a purchase?

18. What questions should you ask yourself when evaluating a purchase?

THINK CRITICALLY

19. Why is it important for you to be financially responsible at this point in your life? How do you plan to be financially responsible throughout your life? (Give examples of what you will do.)

20. What are the costs of financial irresponsibility? Why do people who do not take financial responsibility seriously incur these costs?

21. Why is the opportunity cost an important factor in a buying plan?

22. Why is it important to set a timeline when planning a purchase? Is it ever a good idea to wait overnight before making a commitment to make a large purchase?

23. Why might you choose to use a credit card for a purchase rather than paying cash? Why might you choose to use cash?

24. Would you choose a product that came with a warranty over a similar product that had no warranty? Why or why not? What is the value of an extended warranty when purchasing an appliance or computer?

EXTEND YOUR LEARNING

25. In this activity, you will make a buying plan. Begin by creating a table with five columns and four rows with the headings shown below. Follow Figure 7-1.2 as an example.

Spending Goal	Item	Criteria	Timeline	Spending Limit

a. Identify three needs or wants for which you would like to purchase products or services. List them in the Spending Goal column.

b. Identify products or services that would fill each need or want. List them in the Item column.

c. Identify the criteria (features) that are important for each product or service. List them in the Criteria column.

d. Set a time frame in which you want to make each purchase. List the time frames in the Timeline column.

e. Determine the maximum price you are willing and able to pay for each purchase. List the prices in the Spending Limit column.

THE ESSENTIAL QUESTION   Refer to The Essential Question on p. 222.
By creating a buying plan, you make better and wiser buying decisions. You make purchases in a more responsible manner.

THE ESSENTIAL QUESTION   What should you consider when getting started with credit?

LEARNING OBJECTIVES

LO 7-2.1 Compare the types of credit.

LO 7-2.2 List and explain the advantages and disadvantages of credit.

KEY TERMS

- credit, 230
- debt, 230
- credit card, 230
- store account, 230
- revolving credit, 231
- charge card, 231
- consumer loan, 231
- installment credit, 231
- collateral, 232
- line of credit, 232
- service credit, 232

LO 7-2.1 What Types of Credit Can Consumers Get?

credit the ability to borrow money and pay it back later

debt money that must be repaid

Credit is the ability to borrow money and pay it back later. It is the most commonly used method of payment in the United States today. The purpose of credit is to allow buyers to purchase items and pay for them in the future. The person who borrows money is called a *debtor*, and the money that must be repaid is called **debt**. A *creditor* is a person or business that loans money to others. Creditors charge money for this service in the form of interest and fees.

A good way to get started with credit is to open a savings or checking account and get an ATM card and a debit card. Once you prove that you can manage those accounts and have a steady source of income, you will have a much better chance of qualifying for credit.

When you apply for most forms of credit, you will need to fill out a credit application. The application will ask for your name, address, and Social Security number. You will also be asked questions such as where you work, how much you make, and how long you have worked there. The creditor must determine that you are creditworthy.

There are different types of credit available. They are designed to meet different consumer needs.

Credit Cards

credit card a plastic card linked to a credit account that can be used to make purchases

A **credit card** is a plastic card linked to a credit account that can be used to make purchases. Credit cards are available from banks and other companies, and are usually issued through a provider such as Visa, MasterCard, or Discover. With a credit card, you can buy products or get cash at ATMs around the world.

store account a credit account that allows you to charge items or services only at that store or with that merchant

Department stores, gas companies, and other retail merchants may also offer their own credit cards. A **store account** allows you to charge items or services only at that store or with that merchant. Store credit customers may receive discounts, advance notice of sales, and other privileges not offered to cash customers or to customers using other credit cards.

Bank and store credit cards are a type of revolving credit. With **revolving credit**, the account holder can charge to the account repeatedly, up to a maximum limit. The account holder makes payments, usually each month. The entire debt or part of the debt can be paid each month. The account can have an ongoing balance, but a minimum monthly payment is usually required. Interest is charged on outstanding balances. Interest on credit cards can be quite high. Credit cards also may charge an annual fee.

revolving credit an account on which the account holder can charge repeatedly up to a maximum limit

Charge Cards

A **charge card** is a form of credit card for which the cardholder must pay the balance in full by the due date. A 25-day billing period is common. Because charge card balances must be paid in full each month, there are no interest charges. Thus, charge cards often require a large annual fee, but they usually have high or no credit limits. If the bill is not paid on time, late fees and other penalties may apply. Charge cards are widely accepted nationwide and internationally. Examples of charge cards include American Express and Diners Club.

charge card a form of credit card for which the cardholder must pay the balance in full by the due date

Consumer Loans

Banks and credit unions loan money to consumers. Consumer finance companies and sales finance companies also make consumer loans. A **consumer loan** is a direct loan of cash made to a consumer at a fixed interest rate for a set period of time. It does not allow continuous borrowing or varying payment amounts. For example, a consumer might borrow $1,000 at 8 percent interest for one year. The consumer (debtor) is required to make regular payments, which include interest, for a set period of time to repay the loan.

consumer loan a direct loan of cash made to a consumer at a fixed interest rate for a set period of time

Would you prefer to have a credit card or charge card? Why?

The terms of some loans may allow the consumer to use the money borrowed as desired. Other loans may specify how the money is to be used. For example, the loan may be for home repairs or for the purchase of a car.

Installment credit is a type of consumer loan used to finance the purchase of a single high-priced item through a series of equal payments made over a set period of time. Consumers often use installment credit

Installment credit Credit used to finance the purchase of a single high-priced item through a series of equal payments made over a set period of time.

> FIGURE 7-2.1 **Installment Payment Plan**

Amount borrowed	$1,200.00
Annual rate of interest	16%
Number of monthly payments	36
Amount of monthly payment (including both principal and interest)	$42.19
Total amount to be repaid (36 payments of $42.19)	$1,518.84
Total interest paid for the loan	$318.84

to pay for very expensive items, such as cars, major appliances, or real estate. For example, a customer might buy a refrigerator for $1,200 and agree to pay 16 percent yearly interest on a three-year payment plan. Figure 7-2.1 shows the payments for this loan.

In some cases, the lender may require the borrower to offer security for the loan. Property that can be used as security for a loan is called **collateral**. Land, a house, a car, or the product purchased with the loan are examples of items that can be used as collateral. If the borrower does not repay the loan, the lender may take possession of the collateral and sell it to get the money owed.

collateral property that can be used as security for a loan

If the borrower does not have collateral to offer as security, the lender may require that the loan have a cosigner. A *cosigner* is a person who signs a loan agreement with the borrower and agrees to repay the loan if the borrower does not make the payments. The cosigner must have a good credit record.

Lines of Credit

line of credit a preapproved loan amount that a debtor can borrow as needed with no collateral

A **line of credit** is a preapproved loan amount that a debtor can borrow as needed with no collateral. It is available through banks, credit card companies, and other lenders. With a line of credit, the maximum amount that can be borrowed is set so you will know how much you have available to finance a purchase. It allows you the flexibility of knowing that you have credit on hand in case you need it. No interest is charged on the unused portion of the line of credit.

Service Credit

service credit the ability to receive services and pay for them later

Almost everyone uses some type of service credit. **Service credit** is the ability to receive services and pay for them later. Your telephone and utility services are provided a month in advance; then you are billed. Service credit is also extended by doctors, dentists, lawyers, dry cleaners, and others. These businesses provide services in advance that you pay for later.

CHECKPOINT

How is a store account different from a bank credit card?

FOCUS On...

WHAT'S IN A CREDIT REPORT?

A *credit report* is a statement of your credit history issued by a credit bureau. It is a complete record of your borrowing and repayment performance. This record provides a basis of your creditworthiness and helps creditors determine your ability to pay new debt. Based on your credit report, you can be granted or denied new credit. You also can be re-evaluated for a credit limit increase (or decrease).

Every person who uses credit has a credit report on file at a credit bureau. A *credit bureau* is a business that gathers, stores, and sells credit information to business members. Maintaining these files is big business. About once a month, business members transmit data about your credit borrowing and payments to one of the three national credit bureaus—TransUnion, Experian, and Equifax.

The credit bureaus enter the data into your credit file and store it under your Social Security number. Local and regional credit bureaus have access to the big three national credit bureaus, making everyone's information widely available.

Reports from different credit bureaus may be arranged differently, but they typically contain the following sections.

- *Summary of information*: A summary of positive items, such as credit card accounts in good standing, and negative items, such as accounts that are past due. (Negative information stays on your credit report for seven years, excluding bankruptcy which stays on for ten years.)
- *Public record information*: Information found in public records, such as lawsuits, judgments, bankruptcy filings, marriage, divorce, and property purchase and sale.

- *Credit information*: A list of credit accounts that have been reported to the credit bureau along with each account's balance and the current payment status.
- *Account detail*: The monthly balances and credit limits for each account.
- *Requests for credit history*: A list of every business that has sought information from your credit file as well as requests that you have made to inspect your credit records.
- *Personal information*: Information that you have given when you have applied for credit.

Credit reports sometimes contain errors. That is why you should review your credit report at least once a year. You can challenge information that you believe is incorrect. The error must be corrected if you can prove it is wrong. You must write a letter explaining the error as well as provide evidence. Even if the credit bureau decides the information in your credit file is correct, it must keep your letter of explanation and issue it along with the credit report.

Authorized users of your credit report include more than potential creditors. Employers, banks, insurance companies, landlords, and others may access your credit report to help them decide whether to do business with you. A credit report provides evidence of your financial responsibility–or lack of it!

Think Critically

1. Do you believe that credit bureaus have too much power because they can gather information about you, sell it, and use it without your knowledge or consent? Why or why not?
2. What can you do to protect your credit report from containing information that could be harmful to you?

LO 7-2.2 What Are the Advantages and Disadvantages of Credit?

People use credit for a variety of reasons. Credit provides many benefits when used wisely; however, many people get into trouble each year by not using credit carefully. Like most things in life, there are advantages and disadvantages to using credit. When making a purchase, be sure the advantages of using credit outweigh the disadvantages.

Advantages of Credit

Credit is important because it offers many advantages.

- *Increased purchasing power.* Credit can greatly expand your purchasing power and raise your standard of living. For example, most people are not able to purchase expensive items, such as a car or house, simply by saving money and paying cash. Credit allows you to purchase these items and pay for them over time. As a result, you can enjoy these items now instead of later. In addition to things you want, credit also allows you to purchase things in life that you need. For example, the cost of education continues to rise, and most Americans will need to obtain a loan to pay for college.

- *Security.* Using a credit card is safer than carrying a large amount of cash with you. If you lose cash, there is no way to replace it. If you lose a credit card, you can simply call the company and report your lost or stolen card. The company will freeze your account, and you will not be held responsible for charges you did not make.

- *Convenience.* Credit is convenient. Most businesses now accept credit cards. Many accounts on which you make regular payments can be set up to be billed automatically to a credit card each month. Consumers can also use credit cards to get a *cash advance*, which is money borrowed against the credit card. This is convenient for consumers traveling far from home.

- *Leverage.* Consumers have more leverage when using credit instead of cash or other methods of purchase. With credit, you can withhold payment for disputed items while the dispute is being investigated. With a debit card, check, or cash, money has already been paid for the purchase, which can make it more difficult to settle a dispute and get a refund.

- *Benefits.* Credit customers often get special benefits. Department store credit cardholders, for example, receive advance notices of sales and special offers not available to the general public. Also, credit cards may have incentive programs for their customers. For example, some credit cards have a *rewards program* in which you earn points, cash back, airline miles, or other special awards that you can redeem at a later date.

Disadvantages of Credit

Although credit has several benefits, it also has disadvantages.

- *Finance charge.* An item purchased on credit and paid for over time costs more because of the finance charge. For example, a finance charge of 18 percent a year is 1½ percent per month. On a $1,000 balance, the finance charge would be $15 per month. The larger your balance and the longer you take to pay it off, the greater the finance charge. You will learn more about the finance charge later in the chapter.

- *Reduction of future buying power.* When you use credit, you tie up future income by committing to make payments. Part of everything you earn in the future will go toward what you bought in the past. This can result in funds being unavailable when you need to purchase other products.

EVALUATE YOUR CREDIT SCORE

Credit bureaus use a point system to compute credit scores for consumers. In a *point system*, the credit bureau assigns points based on various factors. When your points are added up, they result in a credit score. Your *credit score* tells potential creditors the likelihood that you will repay debt as agreed. The most common credit score used by creditors is the FICO score, which ranks individuals on a scale from 300 to 850. The higher your score, the greater the chance you will be a good credit risk.

FICO scores are calculated based on five factors:

- Payment history (35 percent)
- Amounts owed (30 percent)
- Length of credit history (15 percent)
- New credit from recently opened accounts (10 percent)
- Types of credit used (10 percent)

As you can see, payment history carries the most weight. This refers to how well you pay your debts as agreed. Any liens, collections, or past-due accounts will greatly affect your score in a negative way. The amount you owe in proportion to your credit limits is another important factor. For example, if your credit limit is $1,000 and your balance is $750, you are using 75 percent of your available credit. This would adversely affect your score. You should try to keep your credit usage at 50 percent or less of credit available.

An excellent FICO score is in the 740 to 850 range. Those with this score will get the best loan terms. A very good score is in the 670 to 739 range. This is often the minimum range to get a mortgage loan. Average to below average scores range from 580 to 669. Those with average scores will likely pay higher interest rates. Below 580 often means lack of credit or poor credit. A poor FICO score will make it difficult to get loans and credit. It should be noted that these range values change from time to time.

To improve your FICO score, you should pay your debts promptly—on or before the due date. Pay more than the minimum amount required. Reduce your outstanding credit (amounts owed) compared to total credit available. Keep a good mix of credit types, such as credit accounts, credit cards, installment loans, and mortgages. Too much revolving credit will count against you. And finally, check your credit report on a regular basis to make sure that it contains correct information.

Think Critically

1. Why should you be concerned about your FICO score even if you aren't planning to apply for credit any time soon?
2. What can you do to improve your FICO score?

- *Overspending.* Buying on credit can lead to overspending. Because no cash leaves your bank account, you may not realize how much you are really spending. Using credit too much can result in debts so high that you can never pay them off. Failure to fulfill financial agreements will result in a poor credit record.

- *Identity theft.* Having a credit card means that you run the risk that your account information could be stolen, allowing someone else to make purchases on your credit card without your knowledge. Credit card fraud is discussed further in Chapter 9.

>>> CHECKPOINT

What are some of the advantages and disadvantages of credit?

KEY TERMS REVIEW

Match the terms with the definitions. Some terms may not be used.

____ 1. The ability to borrow money and pay it back later

____ 2. Property that can be used as security for a loan

____ 3. A credit account that allows you to charge items or services only at that store or with that merchant

____ 4. The ability to receive services and pay for them later

____ 5. An account on which the account holder can charge repeatedly up to a maximum limit

____ 6. A form of credit card in which the cardholder must pay the balance in full by the due date

____ 7. A plastic card linked to a credit account that can be used for making purchases

a. charge card
b. collateral
c. consumer loan
d. credit
e. credit card
f. debt
g. installment credit
h. line of credit
i. revolving credit
j. service credit
k. store account

____ 8. A direct loan of cash made to a consumer at a fixed interest rate for a set period of time

____ 9. Credit used to finance the purchase of a single high-priced item through a series of equal payments made over a set period of time

CHECK YOUR UNDERSTANDING

10. What are the purposes of credit? Why is it important?

11. List several types of consumer credit.

12. How are credit cards different from charge cards?

13. What information is contained in a credit report?

14. Give two examples of collateral that might be used to secure a loan.

15. What is the responsibility of a cosigner on a loan?

16. How is a credit score computed?

17. Does credit provide consumers with more or less leverage than cash? Why?

18. How is a line of credit different from other types of loans?

19. How does credit reduce a consumer's future buying power?

THINK CRITICALLY

20. Think of the items you own. For each item, identify whether it was purchased with cash or credit. If it was purchased on credit, give a brief explanation as to what type of credit was used and why.

21. As long as you maintain a good credit record, you will receive many credit offers. The better your credit rating, the better the interest rate you are offered on new accounts. Why is this true?

22. Why is it important for you to be financially responsible in the payment of your credit obligations? What will happen if you aren't responsible?

23. Why should your credit score be important to you? Suppose you purchase everything with cash and do not use credit. What will happen to your credit score? Why should you be concerned?

24. Assume an interest rate of 20 percent and a minimum payment of $30 on a credit card balance of $1,000. Using a financial calculator or an online calculator, compare the total cost of reducing the balance to zero by making minimum payments versus making above-minimum payments of $100 a month. Why is it important to pay off credit card debt quickly?

EXTEND YOUR LEARNING

25. To get a credit card, consumers typically must fill out a credit application. Complete the credit application provided by your teacher using the following information:

    - Use your name and address. For a home phone, use *606-555-1234*. For a business phone, use *606-555-0132*. Enter a fictitious address.

    - For the date of birth, use *August 1, 1994*.

    - For a Social Security number, use *000-11-0000*.

    - For an email address, enter *myname@provider.com*.

    - For the other items in the Personal Data, enter fictitious data.

    - For the Employment section, enter fictitious data.

    - In the Other Credit Accounts section, write *Sears store account* in the Type or Name box. Enter *34289-10* for the account number. Enter *$240* for the current balance.

    - In the Bank Accounts section, place a check mark to indicate that you have a checking account. Write the name of a local bank and use the name of your city. For the account number, write *45892-4509*.

    - Sign your name and enter the current date at the bottom of the form.

THE ESSENTIAL QUESTION Refer to The Essential Question on p. 230. When getting started with credit, you should consider the various types of credit that are available and the advantages and disadvantages of using credit.

THE ESSENTIAL QUESTION   What are the different types of interest, and what methods are used to compute credit card interest?

LEARNING OBJECTIVES

LO 7-3.1   Explain the various costs of credit.

LO 7-3.2   Discuss methods used for calculating interest.

KEY TERMS

- finance charge, 238
- minimum payment, 238
- fixed interest rate, 239
- variable interest rate, 240
- balance transfer, 240
- cash advance, 240
- penalty, 240
- grace period, 241
- billing cycle, 241

LO 7-3.1 What Are the Costs of Credit?

finance charge the total dollar amount of all interest and fees you pay for the use of credit

Credit usually involves interest and other fees. The total dollar amount of all interest and fees you pay for the use of credit is called the **finance charge**. The finance charge is the price that you pay for the privilege of using someone else's money to buy goods and services now. It increases the cost of the items you purchase on credit.

When credit is extended, there often is a credit agreement that acts as a contract. The credit agreement outlines the interest rate, various fees, and other terms and conditions associated with the use of credit. Before opening a credit account, be sure you understand all of the credit policies that will affect your overall cost of credit.

Why is it important to know the finance charge on a loan?

Real Deal Photo/Shutterstock.com

Minimum Payment

minimum payment the amount you are required to pay each month on a credit account

The **minimum payment** is how much you are required to pay each month on a credit account. Minimum payments typically range from 2 to 5 percent of the balance owed. Thus, if you owe $1,000, your monthly payment would be $20 to $50. This payment includes both principal and interest. The minimum payment due and the payment due date must be disclosed on your monthly credit card statement. Figure 7.3-1 shows a portion of a credit card statement.

The minimum payment can be changed at any time. However, current credit card legislation prevents creditors from *more than* doubling the minimum payment. For example, a credit card company can raise minimum payments from 2 percent to 4 percent, but not to 5 percent.

▶ FIGURE 7-3.1 Credit Card Statement (partial)

Summary of Transactions

Previous Balance	Payments and Credits	Cash Advances	Purchases and Adjustments	Finance Charges	New Balance Total
$2,102.42	$2,144.81	$0.00	$1,259.61	$0.00	$1,217.22

Finance Charge Schedule

Category	Corresponding Annual Rate	Balance Subject to Finance Charge
Cash Advances		
A. Balance Transfers, Checks	15.97%	$0.00
B. ATM, Bank	15.97%	$0.00
C. Purchases	15.97%	$0.00

Total Minimum Payment Due

Due Date	Past Due Amount	Current Payment	Minimum Payment Due
8/25/—	$0.00	$15.00	$15.00

Interest Rate

When you carry an ongoing balance on your credit card, you will have to pay interest on your account. The interest rate affects your monthly payment and how fast you can pay off your balance. Interest charges can be avoided by paying your balance in full each month.

A credit card interest rate is expressed as an annual percentage rate (APR), which must be shown on the credit card statement. The APR is the best indicator of what credit costs. The higher the APR, the more you will pay. To calculate the rate each month, divide the APR by 12. For example, if the APR is 18 percent, the monthly interest rate on carrying a balance is 1½ percent. Sometimes a credit card company offers a low introductory rate for a specific period of time as a way to get you to open a new account or switch cards. After the introductory period, the interest rate increases.

A credit card's APR may be a fixed or variable rate. A **fixed interest rate** is set and does not change from month to month. The Credit

fixed interest rate an interest rate that is set and does not change from month to month

 **Looking Ahead**

Before getting a credit card, it pays to compare. CreditCards.com is a credit card comparison and information website. Its mission is to provide consumers with the largest variety of credit cards online.

Visit the CreditCards.com website and answer the following questions: What are the different categories of credit cards offered to consumers? Why do you think banks and issuers offer so many different types of credit cards? Which credit card designed for students would you choose? Why?

CARD Act of 2009 states that fixed rates cannot be raised for at least one year, though there are certain exemptions. After that time, the rate can be raised, but only with an advance notice of 45 days. If you accept the increased rate, it applies only to new charges—not existing balances. If you do not accept the new rate, your account will be closed, and you will have to pay off your existing balance at the old rate.

A **variable interest rate** goes up and down with inflation and other economic conditions. Variable interest rates are often tied to the prime rate. The *prime rate* is the interest rate that banks offer to their most creditworthy business customers. Today, most credit card companies use variable rates.

Fees

Credit card issuers make money by charging fees. These fees are one of the biggest costs of using credit. Before selecting a credit card, be aware of the following fees that you could be charged.

- *Annual Fees.* Many credit card issuers charge an annual fee. The fee can range from $40 to up to $100 or more, and you must pay it whether or not you use the card. The annual fee might be a one-time charge on your credit card, or it might be divided and charged to your account monthly.
- *Transaction Fees.* Credit card companies offer many services. You may be allowed to pay your bill by phone. You may do a **balance transfer** by moving a balance from one credit card account to another. In many cases, you will be charged a transaction fee for using such services.
- *Cash Advance Fees.* Some cards will give you a **cash advance**, which is money borrowed against your credit card account. You can use an ATM or go to a bank to withdraw cash up to your cash advance limit. Cash advances may also be in the form of *access checks*, which are checks issued by the credit card company that can be used for purchases. There is often a fee for this service in addition to interest charges, which are often higher than the interest charges on regular credit card purchases.
- *Penalty Fees.* If you exceed your credit limit, make a late payment, fail to make a minimum payment, or try to make a payment with a check that bounces, you can be charged a penalty. A **penalty** is a fee charged for violating a term of the credit agreement. Under the Credit CARD Act of 2009, penalty fees were capped to prevent excessive charges being passed on to cardholders. Most customers will be charged $25 for one late payment—$35 if payments are late more than once within six billing cycles. Also, penalty fees are not permitted to be higher than the minimum payment due.

variable interest rate an interest rate that goes up and down with inflation and other economic conditions

balance transfer moving a balance from one credit card account to another

cash advance money borrowed against your credit card account

penalty a fee charged for violating a term of the credit agreement

>> **CHECKPOINT**

What are some of the fees associated with using credit?

LO 7-3.2 How Is Interest Computed on Credit?

The cost of using revolving credit, such as a credit card, varies based on the method the creditor uses to compute the interest (finance charge) on the unpaid balance. Most credit cards have a **grace period**, which is the amount of time you have to pay your current credit card balance in full to avoid paying interest. The grace period is the time between your billing cycle end date and your credit card bill due date. The **billing cycle** is the period of time between billings, during which purchases, payments, fees, and interest charges are posted to your account. Creditors may calculate the interest using one of three basic methods, each resulting in different interest charges.

Adjusted Balance Method

When creditors use the *adjusted balance method*, the interest is calculated based on the amount owed after you have paid your bill each month. The charges made during the billing cycle are added to the balance at the beginning of the period. The payment received is subtracted from this amount to find the adjusted balance. The interest is calculated using the formula Principal (P) × Rate (R) × Time (T). In this case, the adjusted balance is the principal. The interest amount is added to the adjusted balance to find the new balance (amount owed), as shown in Figure 7-3.2. (A 30-day billing cycle and a 360-day year are used for computing interest.)

Previous Balance Method

When creditors use the *previous balance method*, interest is calculated based on the outstanding balance at the end of the previous billing cycle. Charges and payments in the current billing cycle are not included. The new balance is the previous balance plus interest and charges and minus any payments made, as shown in Figure 7-3.3.

Average Daily Balance Method

Most creditors use the average daily balance method for computing interest. With the *average daily balance method*, an adjusted balance is

▶ FIGURE 7-3.2 **Adjusted Balance Method**

Previous Balance		$500.00
Charges:	$30.00	
	50.00	
	80.00	
Total Charges		160.00
Payment		−100.00
Adjusted Balance		$560.00
Interest for 1 Month (18% Yearly): $560 × 18% × 30/360		8.40
New Balance (Amount Owed)		$568.40

▶ FIGURE 7-3.3 Previous Balance Method

Previous Balance	$500.00
Interest for 1 Month (18% Yearly): $500 × 18% × 30/360	7.50
Charges: $30.00	
50.00	
80.00	
Total Charges	160.00
Payment	−100.00
New Balance (Amount Owed)	$567.50

computed for each day of the month. The adjusted balance is the balance from the previous day plus charges and minus payments received on that day. The adjusted balances for all days are added and then divided by the number of days in the billing cycle. This amount is the average daily balance, on which interest is calculated. The interest is added to the balance on the last day of the billing cycle to find the new balance, as shown in Figure 7-3.4.

▶ FIGURE 7-3.4 Average Daily Balance Method

Previous Balance $500.00

Daily Balances:

	Previous Balance	Charges	Payments	Adjusted Balance
Day 1	$500.00	$0.00	$0.00	$500.00
Day 2	$500.00	$0.00	$0.00	$500.00
Day 3	$500.00	$30.00	$0.00	$530.00
Day 4	$530.00	$50.00	$0.00	$580.00
Day 5	$580.00	$80.00	$0.00	$660.00
.				
.				
.				
Day 25	$660.00	$0.00	$100.00	$560.00
Day 26	$560.00	$0.00	$0.00	$560.00
Day 27	$560.00	$0.00	$0.00	$560.00
Day 28	$560.00	$0.00	$0.00	$560.00
Day 29	$560.00	$0.00	$0.00	$560.00
Day 30	$560.00	$0.00	$0.00	$560.00

Average Daily Balance	$563.67
Interest for 1 Month (18% Yearly): $563.67 × 18% × 30/360	8.46
New Balance (Amount Owed): $560.00 (Day 30 balance) + $8.46 =	$568.46

▶▶ CHECKPOINT

Which method of computing is used by most creditors?

7-3 Lesson Assessment

KEY TERMS REVIEW

Match the terms with the definitions. Some terms may not be used.

_____ 1. The total dollar amount of all interest and fees you pay for the use of credit

_____ 2. The period of time between credit card billings

_____ 3. An interest rate that goes up and down with inflation and other economic conditions

_____ 4. The amount of time you have to pay your credit card balance in full to avoid paying interest

_____ 5. An interest rate that is set and does not change from month to month

_____ 6. The amount you are required to pay each month on a credit account

_____ 7. Moving a balance from one credit card account to another

_____ 8. A fee charged for violating a term of the credit agreement

a. balance transfer
b. billing cycle
c. cash advance
d. finance charge
e. fixed interest rate
f. grace period
g. minimum payment
h. penalty
i. variable interest rate

CHECK YOUR UNDERSTANDING

9. What is the finance charge?
10. List some costs associated with using credit.
11. What does the minimum payment amount on a credit card statement indicate?
12. What is a credit card's annual percentage rate (APR)?
13. Why do credit card companies offer low introductory rates?
14. Explain the difference between credit card accounts that have fixed interest rates and those that have variable interest rates.
15. What is a cash advance?
16. When might a credit cardholder incur a penalty fee?
17. Describe how interest may be computed on credit cards using three common methods.
18. Why is it important for consumers to know the grace period and billing cycle of their credit cards?

THINK CRITICALLY

19. Credit card companies can raise the required minimum payment at their discretion. How can this adversely affect a credit cardholder?

20. Credit card statements must indicate how long it will take you to pay off your current balance, making only minimum payments, and provide the total interest you will be charged. How is this information useful to you?

21. The Credit CARD Act of 2009 required that creditors not raise the interest rate on existing balances when raising fixed rates. How does this work to your advantage?

22. Whenever you exceed your credit limit, make late payments, fail to make a minimum payment, or try to make a payment with a check that bounces, you can be charged a penalty. When this happens, it is also reported to the credit bureau. Why would this adversely affect your credit score?

EXTEND YOUR LEARNING

23. Credit card companies have different rates, fees, penalties, and other terms. Study the two examples of credit card terms that follow. Evaluate these two credit card offers. Which one would you choose? Why?

    Credit Card A: This card has a special introductory APR of 0 percent for the first 18 months and for any balance transfers made within the first 60 days. After that, a fixed interest rate of 12.99 percent applies. There is an annual fee of $50, and a transaction fee of 3 percent on all purchases made outside of the United States. This card also has a rewards feature that gives you back 1 percent in cash each year.

    Credit Card B: This card has a special introductory APR of 0 percent for the first 12 months and for any balance transfers made within the first 30 days. After that, a variable rate of 10.99 to 20.99 percent applies. This card has no rewards feature, no annual fee, no transaction fees, and no penalty fees for making late payments for the first 12 months.

24. Bankrate offers useful information about credit cards and interest rates. Visit Bankrate's website and answer the following questions:
    a. What is the current average fixed rate?
    b. What is the current average variable rate? Has this rate risen or fallen over the past three months?
    c. What three credit card types have the lowest average interest rates? What are the pros and cons of each of these credit card types?

THE ESSENTIAL QUESTION Refer to The Essential Question on p. 238. A fixed interest rate remains constant, whereas a variable rate changes with inflation and other economic conditions. The three methods of computing credit card interest are the adjusted balance method, previous balance method, and average daily balance method, each resulting in different interest charges.

Exploring Careers in...
CREDIT

When you apply for credit, your application is handled by credit clerks who gather data from your credit history to evaluate the risk and potential rewards of granting you credit. A lender's credit policies will determine which applications are granted or denied.

Many factors can be considered when deciding whether to grant credit to an applicant. Most credit clerks will check the individual's credit score and credit report to see what kind of customer he or she is likely to be. In many cases, credit clerks will also call credit departments of businesses to get information about applicants' credit standing. Employment status and financial history are also considered. Many times, credit clerks will contact references and/or previous employers listed on the individual's application for verification.

Employment Outlook

- A slower than average rate of employment growth is expected.
- Openings will arise as a result of closer attention to credit policies by lenders.

Job Titles

- Credit authorizer
- Credit checker
- Credit clerk
- Credit analyzer

Needed Education/Skills

- A high school diploma is required, although some college courses in accounting and other business-related courses are often preferred.

- Most credit clerks learn their duties through on-the-job training.
- Trustworthiness, strong math skills, and good judgment are essential.

What's it like to work in . . . Credit

Ian is a credit clerk at the local credit union. He receives between 30 and 50 applications a day from credit union members who want car loans, mortgages, lines of credit, and personal loans.

As part of the approval process, Ian checks the applicant's credit score online and also prints out a copy of the applicant's credit report to review. He also considers the applicant's history with the credit union, account balances, and employment status.

At the end of each workday, Ian meets with his supervisor to go over the approved applications. He will also be prepared to discuss why some credit applications were rejected.

What About You?

Would you like to analyze credit data? Would you like to help people get financing for important purchases? Does a job in credit appeal to you? Why or why not?

Chapter 7 Assessment

SUMMARY

7-1 Being a responsible shopper requires financial responsibility, which involves planning your earning, spending, and saving to meet financial goals. Financial irresponsibility will result in the inability to sustain your lifestyle.

Designing a buying plan involves defining your spending goal, choosing the item to buy, defining criteria, setting a timeline, and setting a spending limit.

Implementing a buying plan involves comparison shopping, choosing among payment methods, making the purchase, and evaluating the purchase so you can make better choices in the future.

7-2 Credit is the ability to borrow money with the agreement to pay it back later, usually with interest.

Types of credit available to consumers include revolving credit (credit cards and store accounts), charge cards, consumer loans (installment credit), lines of credit, and service credit.

Advantages of credit are increased purchasing power, security, convenience, leverage, and special benefits such as rewards. Disadvantages of credit are the finance charge on items purchased, the decreased ability to spend in the future, the tendency to overspend, and the risk of identity theft.

7-3 Interest and fees you pay for the use of credit are called finance charges.

The minimum payment is how much you are required to pay each month on a credit account.

Interest rates may be fixed or variable. A fixed rate of interest is set and does not change from month to month. A variable rate of interest goes up and down with inflation and other economic conditions.

Common fees charged by credit card issuers include annual fees, transaction fees, cash advance fees, and penalty fees if you exceed your credit limit, make a late payment, fail to make a minimum payment, or try to make a payment with a check that bounces.

Creditors calculate interest by using the adjusted balance method, previous balance method, or average daily balance method. The interest charge varies depending on the method used.

MAKE ACADEMIC CONNECTIONS

TEAMWORK

1. **Research** Comparison shopping leads to better buying decisions. Assume you are ready to buy a car. Work with two classmates to complete this activity. (LO 7-1.2)
   a. Make a list of criteria that the car should have.
   b. Each team member should search the Internet, look at sales brochures, or use other sources to find the following information about two cars from two different sources:
      - Car name or brand
      - Car make or model number
      - Criteria on your list that the car meets
      - Price of the car
      - Other costs that will apply, such as taxes or added options (for example, a sunroof or a GPS navigation system)
      - Car rebates or other special offers
      - Car warranty
   c. As a group, compare the information from the two sources. Consider car prices and other charges. Discuss whether each car meets the criteria you listed. Compare warranties and special offers.
   d. As a group, decide which car you would buy. Explain why.

2. **History** Research credit in the United States, starting with the 1950s, when most households had a single income and credit cards were rare. Write a report, dividing your work into decades and commenting on how and why credit has changed, including the costs of credit. (LO 7-2.1, LO 7-3.1)

3. **Economics** Conduct online research on the Credit CARD Act of 2009. Select five regulations set forth by the act. Prepare PowerPoint slides or other visual aids that describe each regulation. (LO 7-3.1)

4. **Ethics** Credit scores, such as FICO, are a major factor in whether a lender will grant you credit. Sometimes, your credit score might be the only consideration, regardless of your circumstances. Do you think this is fair? Why or why not? What other factors do you think should be taken into consideration? (LO 7-2.2)

Do the Math

1. Assume you have a credit card balance of $1,000. Your interest rate on the credit card is 18 percent, and your minimum monthly payments are $50. At this rate, how long will it take to pay off your credit card? What would your payment need to be to pay it off in three years? How long would it take to pay off your debt if your interest rate is 14 percent and your minimum monthly payments are $50? Use a financial calculator or an online calculator to do your computations.

ProStockStudio/Shutterstock.com

2. **The table below shows the activity on your credit card for the past month. Compute the new balance using the (a) adjusted balance method, (b) previous balance method, and (c) average daily balance method. Use spreadsheet software, if available, to complete the problems below, or do them manually. Round to the nearest cent.**

Credit Card Activity		
Previous Balance		$800.00
Charges:	September 5	$35.78
	September 18	$124.87
	September 21	$528.00
Payments	September 22	$750.00
Annual Interest Rate	14%	

Take Action

EVALUATE CREDIT CARD OFFERS

Credit card offers can vary considerably. Shopping for a credit card involves making decisions similar to those involved in making purchases. You should follow the same steps as in a buying plan. First, think about why you want or need a credit card. Next, consider how you will use it. Set criteria that you want the credit card agreement to meet. Then, do comparison shopping to find the card that most closely matches the criteria you have set.

Assume that you are ready to apply for a credit card. You will use the card to make shopping more convenient. You plan to pay the entire balance each billing period to avoid paying interest charges. The card should have a low annual fee ($50 or less) or no annual fee, a reasonable APR, a low introductory rate, and a rewards program that interests you.

a. Use the Internet to perform searches using terms such as *low credit rates*, *credit card offers*, or *credit card application*.

b. Visit several websites that provide information about credit card offers. Read the information about fees and interest rates. Find a card that meets your criteria.

c. Choose a card. List its features and describe its rewards program. Explain why you selected this card over other cards you considered.

Save the list of credit card features and your reasons for selecting the credit card in your portfolio.

Preserving Your Credit

antoniodiaz/Shutterstock.com

Individual responsibilities change as you venture out on your own and live as an independent adult. Although debt is often necessary to have the basic comforts of life, a responsible person will pay off those debts in a timely manner. Renting and purchasing decisions must be entered into carefully. In this chapter, you will learn about planning and decision making as you move into new living arrangements independent of your parents. You'll also discover how to manage credit in ways that minimize your costs and risks while maximizing the value you receive.

Do *This*, Not *That*

To effectively manage debt:

- Know your rights and responsibilities before signing a contract.
- Understand financing options when taking on debt.
- Monitor your credit on a regular basis.
- Pay more than the minimum payment on any existing debt.
- Do not take on new debt unless it is necessary.

8-1 Identifying Financial Issues

THE ESSENTIAL QUESTION What factors should you consider before renting a place and living with a roommate?

LEARNING OBJECTIVES

LO 8-1.1 Discuss living arrangements and financial issues with other members of your household.

LO 8-1.2 Describe contractual rights and responsibilities for landlords and tenants.

KEY TERMS

- roommate, 250
- shared responsibility, 250
- living habits, 250
- security deposit, 251
- logistics, 251
- contract, 252
- consideration, 252
- lease, 252
- rental agreement, 252
- eviction, 255
- property manager, 255

LO 8-1.1 What Are Shared Responsibilities?

roommate a person with whom you share living space, living expenses, and other responsibilities

shared responsibility two or more people who each agree to bear a portion of an obligation

After you leave your parents' home and go to college or move into your own residence, you will likely share physical space and financial resources with one or more other persons. A **roommate** is a person with whom you share living space, living expenses, and other responsibilities. **Shared responsibility** occurs when two or more people each agree to bear a portion of an obligation. For example, if you share an apartment with a roommate, both of you will share the responsibility of paying the rent on time. You must take your responsibilities seriously because any missteps can lead to financial and credit problems.

Living Arrangements

living habits your daily routine, or the way you choose to live your life

Choosing a roommate is an important decision. When doing so, you should consider your living habits. **Living habits** describe your daily routine, or the way you choose to live your life. It's important that your living habits are compatible with those of your roommate. Otherwise, you are likely to have immediate and serious difficulties living together. Questions to ask before entering into a living arrangement may include the following:

- Do you smoke or drink? How do you feel about those who do?
- Do you like a clean living area at all times, or are you more easy-going and casual about your environment?
- How should the division of household chores be handled?
- What is your social life like? Do you intend to have frequent visitors?
- Do you have steady employment or another source of income to ensure that you can pay your share of the expenses?
- What are your leisure activities? What activities will you share with (or impose on) your roommate?
- What type of transportation do you have? Will you need to share transportation? If so, what are the costs, and how will you divide them?
- What are some of your future goals? Do you want to continue your education, work full time, or travel?

By discussing these issues, you will know, understand, and appreciate each other's needs, values, and differences. You will have an idea of what it will be like to live together and what each person can expect from the other(s). Reaching an understanding ahead of time will help reduce conflict later.

Financial Issues

When living with a roommate, there are numerous expenses to consider, such as those listed below.

- *Moving costs.* Moving costs include the time and money spent in packing, loading, transporting, unloading, and unpacking. This may involve paying for a professional mover to do these things for you or renting a truck or trailer and using your own labor.
- *Deposit and fees.* Your landlord will require a security deposit before you can move in. A **security deposit** is a refundable amount paid to cover possible damages to property caused by a tenant. There may also be nonrefundable fees, such as for cleaning and changing the locks. Utility companies may also charge a security deposit to turn on services.
- *Installation charges.* When you move into a new residence, you will pay installation charges, such as for telephone, cable TV, and Internet services.
- *Living expenses.* After moving in, certain expenses will occur regularly, including rent, utilities, cable TV, Internet, groceries, transportation costs (gasoline, bus fares, etc.), and household supplies.

security deposit a refundable amount paid to cover damages to property caused by a tenant

You will need to decide if one person is solely responsible for an expense or whether it will be divided among roommates. Each roommate is responsible for meeting the obligations to which he or she agrees. If part or all of the rent, utilities, or other joint costs are not paid on time, then all tenants are in jeopardy. Thus, it is important to work out the logistics of how your expenses will be paid. **Logistics** is the act of making a plan and carrying it out to ensure that an event takes place. A good plan is to create a group budget. *Group budgeting* allows for the careful allocation of expenses so that each person pays his or her share. The budget should be prepared and put into writing. Figure 8-1.1 is an example of a group budget.

logistics the act of making a plan and carrying it out to ensure that an event takes place

To pay expenses, each person could have a separate bank account for individual expenses, and the group could have a joint account to pay shared expenses. Each person could make a deposit into the joint account by a certain date each month. Then roommates could take turns writing checks to pay for rent, utilities, and other expenses incurred throughout the month.

Why is it important to create a group budget with your roommates?

FIGURE 8-1.1 Group Budget

Expense	Monthly Cost	Robert's Share	Bill's Share	Juan's Share
Rent	$900	$300	$300	$300
Utilities (average)	150	50	50	50
Cable/TV/Internet	105	35	35	35
Gas/insurance/repairs	120	40	40	40
Groceries	600	200	200	200
Household supplies	90	30	30	30
Totals	$1,965	$655	$655	$655

⟫⟫⟫ CHECKPOINT

What are the financial issues that should be agreed upon before moving in with a roommate?

LO 8-1.2 What Are Contractual Rights and Duties?

During your lifetime, you will enter into many agreements with other individuals and businesses. A **contract** is a legally binding agreement that specifies the rights and duties of each party to the agreement. To be legally binding, a contract requires **consideration**, which is something of value exchanged for something else of value. For example, you may agree to pay money for a couch that the furniture store agrees to deliver to your residence.

Many contracts are oral agreements, where you promise to do or give something in exchange for something provided to you. Because oral contracts may be more difficult to enforce, many businesses as well as consumers prefer to put their agreements in writing.

As a tenant renting property from a landlord, you (and your roommates) will be entering into a contract. There are two types of rental contracts: leases and rental agreements. A **lease** is a written agreement that allows a tenant to use property for a set period of time at a set rent payment. A lease typically runs for six months, a year, or longer. A **rental agreement** is a written contract that allows you to leave any time as long as you give the required notice. A rental agreement is also called a *month-to-month agreement* because the agreement does not bind you to pay rent for a period of time longer than a month, as a lease does. Both a lease and a rental agreement include provisions for security deposits, termination of contract, rent payments, tenant and landlord responsibilities, and various other matters. Figure 8-1.2 is an example of a lease agreement.

contract a legally binding agreement that specifies the rights and duties of each party to the agreement

consideration something of value exchanged for something else of value

lease a written agreement that allows a tenant to use property for a set period of time at a set rent payment

rental agreement a written contract that allows you to leave any time as long as you give the required notice

RESIDENTIAL LEASE AGREEMENT
AND SECURITY DEPOSIT RECEIPT

THIS INDENTURE, made this <u>29th</u> day of <u>October</u> , 20 <u>--</u> , between

<u>Brendan Martin</u> , hereinafter designated the Lessor

or Landlord, and <u>Teresa Thomas</u> , hereinafter designated the Lessee,

WITNESSETH: That the said Lessor/Landlord does by these presents lease and demise the residence

situated at <u>614 Dundas Street</u> in <u>Cincinnati</u> City,

<u>Hamilton</u> County, <u>Ohio</u> State,

of which the real estate is described as follows:

614 Dundas Street, Cincinnati, Ohio,

upon the following terms and conditions:

1. **Term:** The premises are leased for a term of <u>one (1)</u> years, commencing the <u>1st</u> day of <u>November</u> , 20 <u>--</u> , and terminating the <u>31st</u> day of <u>October</u> , 20 <u>--</u> .

2. **Rent:** The Lessee shall pay rent in the amount of $ <u>900.00</u> per month for the above premises on the <u>1st</u> day of each month in advance to Landlord.

3. **Utilities:** Lessee shall pay for service and utilities supplied to the premises, except <u>None</u> which will be furnished by Landlord.

4. **Sublet:** The Lessee agrees not to sublet said premises nor assign this agreement nor any part thereof without the prior written consent of Landlord.

5. **Inspection of Premises:** Lessee agrees that he has made inspection of the premises and accepts the condition of the premises in its present state, and that there are no repairs, changes, or modifications to said premises to be made by the Landlord other than as listed herein.

6. **Lessee Agrees:**
(1) To keep said premises in a clean and sanitary condition;
(2) To properly dispose of rubbish, garbage, and waste in a clean and sanitary manner at reasonable and regular intervals and to assume all costs of extermination and fumigation for infestation caused by Lessee;
(3) To properly use and operate all electrical, gas, heating, plumbing facilities, fixtures, and appliances;
(4) To not intentionally or negligently destroy, deface, damage, impair, or remove any part of the premises, their appurtenances, facilities, equipment, furniture, furnishings, and appliances, nor to permit any member of his family, invitee, licensee, or other person acting under his control to do so;
(5) Not to permit a nuisance or common waste.

7. **Maintenance of Premises:** Lessee agrees to mow and water the grass and lawn, and keep the grass, lawn, flowers, and shrubbery thereon in good order and condition, and to keep the sidewalk surrounding said premises free and clear of all obstructions; to replace in a neat and workmanlike manner all glass and doors broken during occupancy thereof; to use due precaution against freezing of water or waste pipes and stoppage of same in and about said premises and that in case water or waste pipes are frozen or become clogged by reason of neglect of Lessee, the Lessee shall repair the same at his own expense as well as all damage caused thereby.

8. **Alterations:** Lessee agrees not to make alterations or do or cause to be done any painting or wallpapering to said premises without the prior written consent of Landlord.

9. **Use of Premises:** Lessee shall not use said premises for any purpose other than that of a residence and shall not use said premises or any part thereof for any illegal purpose. Lessee agrees to conform to municipal, county and state codes, statutes, ordinances, and regulations concerning the use and occupation of said premises.

10. **Pets and Animals:** Lessee shall not maintain any pets or animals upon the premises without the prior written consent of Landlord.

11. **Access:** Landlord shall have the right to place and maintain "for rent" signs in a conspicuous place on said premises for thirty days prior to the vacation of said premises. Landlord reserves the right of access to the premises for the purpose of:
(a) Inspection;
(b) Repairs, alterations, or improvements;
(c) To supply services; or
(d) To exhibit or display the premises to prospective or actual purchasers, mortgagees, tenants, workmen, or contractors. Access shall be at reasonable times except in case of emergency or abandonment.

12. **Surrender of Premises:** In the event of default in payment of any installation of rent or at the expiration of said term of this lease, Lessee will quit and surrender the said premises to Landlord.

13. **Security Deposit:** The Lessee has deposited the sum of $ <u>900.00</u> , receipt of which is hereby acknowledged, which sum shall be deposited by Landlord in a trust account with <u>Citizens</u> bank; savings and loan association, or licensed escrow, <u>Cincinnati</u> branch, whose address is <u>201 Main Street, Cincinnati, Ohio</u>
All or a portion of such deposit may be retained by Landlord and a refund of any portion of such deposit is conditioned as follows:
(1) Lessee shall fully perform obligations hereunder and those pursuant to Chapter 207, Laws of 1973, 1st Ex Session or as may be subsequently amended.
(2) Lessee shall occupy said premises for <u>one (1)</u> months or longer from date hereof.
(3) Lessee shall clean and restore said residence and return the same to Landlord in its initial condition, except for reasonable wear and tear, upon the termination of this tenancy and vacation of apartment.
(4) Lessee shall have remedied or repaired any damage to apartment premises.
(5) Lessee shall surrender to Landlord the keys to premises.
Any refund from security deposit, as by itemized statement shown to be due to Lessee, shall be returned to Lessee within fourteen (14) days after termination of this tenancy and vacation of the premises.

IN WITNESS WHEREOF, the Lessee has hereunto set his hand and seal the day and year first above written.

/s/ *Brendan Martin*   /s/ *Teresa Thomas*
LANDLORD   LESSEE
610 Dundas Street
Cincinnati, Ohio
ADDRESS
(Acknowledgment)

READING A LEASE AGREEMENT

A *lease* is a property rental agreement that specifies the rights and duties of the landlord and tenant. A lease gives both the landlord (the *lessor*) and the tenant (the *lessee*) the security of knowing the property is committed for a fixed period of time. But the lease can also be a trap if you don't understand its provisions before you sign.

For example, many lessors offer "specials" to those who sign leases for a year or longer. These specials may include reduced monthly rent, reduced deposits and fees, and other concessions. But in most cases, if you need to terminate the lease before the agreed-upon time, there can be enormous consequences. In a typical "special" lease offer, the lessor may state that regular monthly rent is $800. If the lessee signs a one-year lease, the rent will be reduced to $750 and the move-in fee will be reduced from $300 to $200. The savings are significant. However, the lease also states that if the lessee terminates the agreement prior to one year, he or she must repay the entire rent reduction and the balance of the reduced fee.

Suppose you are the lessee and you must move out early, at the beginning of the eighth month. If your lease agreement prohibits *subleasing*, which allows you to find another tenant to take over the rest of your lease,

you would have to pay back seven months' worth of reduced rent ($50 × 7) plus the additional $100 move-in fee, for a total of $450. In addition, you are still obligated to pay the remaining five months' rent (at the regular rate of $800) until the lessor can find another tenant to take your place. Although the lessor has to make every "reasonable" effort to re-rent your place, he or she has no incentive to try to lease yours first if there are other units available. As you can see, this type of "deal" can be very expensive and harmful to your budget.

Before you sign a lease agreement, be sure to read it carefully and understand your commitments. You may be able to negotiate better terms at the beginning— before you sign the contract.

Think Critically

1. Check online for listings of rental housing in your area. Do you see any lease specials? Describe them.
2. Do you know someone who is leasing property? Ask to see the person's lease agreement. Or find a sample lease agreement online. What potentially expensive provisions does it contain?

Tenant Rights and Responsibilities

Tenants have the right to possess and enjoy the rented property. They can come and go as they please, have guests, and use the property as a residence. They also have the right to use common areas, such as hallways, lawns, swimming pools, meeting rooms, and other amenities provided on the property.

Tenants also have numerous responsibilities—both to the landlord and to other tenants. Tenants have the obligation to do the following:

- Read, understand, and abide by the terms of the rental contract.
- Use the rental unit only for the purpose for which it is intended. For example, if the tenant plans to rent a place to use for a business, this must be discussed with the landlord before the lease or rental agreement is signed.
- Take proper care of the property, including recreational facilities and laundry facilities.
- Report any needed repairs in a timely manner, and give the landlord access to the unit to make repairs or perform maintenance.

- Respect the rights of other tenants. For example, some agreements require that noise levels be restricted between the hours of 10 P.M. and 8 A.M.
- Pay the rent on or before the due date. Failure to make a rent payment on time could result in late fees or possibly eviction. **Eviction** is the legal process of removing a tenant from rental property. When this happens, tenants will also be held liable for any property damage and other charges that result from not meeting their contractual duties. If the eviction goes to court and the judge rules in favor of the landlord, it will be reported to credit bureaus. This will reflect poorly on the tenant's credit score, making it difficult for the tenant to rent property in the future.
- Give at least 30 days' written notice of intent to move.

eviction the legal process of removing a tenant from rental property

Landlord Rights and Responsibilities

Landlords have the right to receive their monthly payments for rent in a timely manner. They also have the right to inspect the property, with proper notice, to make sure it is receiving proper care, and not abuse, from the tenant. They can retain security deposits for damages caused by the tenant.

Landlords have many responsibilities. They must provide a convenient way for tenants to pay rent. They must make sure the buildings and grounds are clean, sanitary, and safe. Landlords are also required by law to provide a dwelling that is habitable (livable) at all times. A dwelling is considered habitable if the following conditions are met:

- The exterior (including roof, walls, doors, and windows) is weatherproof and waterproof.
- Floors, walls, ceilings, stairs, and railings are in good repair.
- Elevators, halls, stairwells, and exits meet fire and safety regulations. Smoke detectors are required in each unit in most states.
- Adequate locks are provided for all outside doors, and working latches are provided for all windows.
- Plumbing facilities comply with local and state sanitation laws and are in good working condition.
- Water supply provided is safe and adequate.
- Lighting, wiring, heating, air-conditioning, and appliances are in good condition and comply with local and state building and safety codes.

In many cases, the owner of an apartment complex will hire either an on-site manager or a property manager to carry out various duties. An *on-site manager* lives at the property and provides or arranges for repair and maintenance work, collects the rent, and supervises the safety of all common areas. A **property manager**, or *off-site manager*, does not live on-site, but is hired to take care of the rental property. The property manager is responsible for collecting rent, hiring people to make repairs and maintain the property, managing the budget, and providing an accounting to the owner. Property managers charge a fee for the service of assuming these responsibilities for the owner.

property manager an off-site manager hired to take care of rental property

>>> CHECKPOINT

What are a tenant's responsibilities when renting property?

KEY TERMS REVIEW

Match the terms with the definitions. Some terms may not be used.

_____ 1. The act of making a plan and carrying it out to ensure that an event takes place

_____ 2. A legally binding agreement that specifies the rights and duties of each party to the agreement

_____ 3. Something of value exchanged for something else of value

_____ 4. Occurs when two or more people each agree to bear a portion of an obligation

_____ 5. The process of legally removing a tenant from rental property

_____ 6. Your daily routine, or the way you choose to live your life

_____ 7. A written agreement that allows a tenant to use property for a set period of time at a set rent payment

_____ 8. A person with whom you share living space, living expenses, and other responsibilities

_____ 9. A refundable amount paid to cover possible damages to property caused by a tenant

a. consideration

b. contract

c. eviction

d. lease

e. living habits

f. logistics

g. property manager

h. rental agreement

i. roommate

j. security deposit

k. shared responsibility

CHECK YOUR UNDERSTANDING

10. What living habits and areas of compatibility should be discussed before moving in with a roommate?

11. Provide three examples of living expenses that are commonly divided among roommates.

12. What is the purpose of a group budget?

13. Explain logistics as it relates to payment of monthly rent and other living expenses by roommates.

14. What is the difference between a lease and a rental agreement?

15. List several provisions that would appear in a lease or rental agreement.

16. List three rights of tenants.

17. What are the possible consequences of an eviction?

18. What are three characteristics of a habitable dwelling?

19. How is an on-site manager different from a property manager?

THINK CRITICALLY

20. Why should you discuss shared responsibilities with potential roommates before moving in together?

21. Why is it important to consider living habits before entering into living arrangements with other people? Does this also apply to families or only to unrelated persons? Explain your answer.

22. Why is it important to discuss attitudes about money and spending with others before moving in together?

23. Why do people enter into written agreements? Isn't it just as good to have an oral agreement? Why or why not?

24. Why do tenants need to be aware of their rights and responsibilities? What might happen if a tenant does not understand his or her obligations to other tenants?

25. Why are landlords responsible for providing a safe and habitable residence for their tenants?

EXTEND YOUR LEARNING

26. Assume you have agreed to rent a three-bedroom apartment with two other roommates. You are Roommate #1. The costs of moving in and renting are listed below:

Cost of rental truck	$ 60
Cost of security deposit	300
Pet deposit for Roommate #2	200
Monthly rent	900
Average monthly utilities	99
Household supplies	60
Household groceries	300
Special diet needs for Roommate #3	100

a. Using Figure 8-1.1 as an example, prepare a group budget. Because Roommate #3 has special diet needs, she won't share the costs of household groceries.

b. Assume Roommate #3 moves out. Revise the group budget. Assume you could move to a two-bedroom apartment on the same premises for rent of $650 per month. There are no moving costs, but the security deposit remains at $300 (and you must return Roommate #3's share of the deposit from the first apartment).

THE ESSENTIAL QUESTION   Refer to The Essential Question on p. 250. When renting a place to live with a roommate, you must consider living habits, financial issues, the type of rental contract desired, and the obligations and responsibilities of both the tenant and the landlord.

8-2 Long-Term Debt Repayment

THE ESSENTIAL QUESTION What long-term debts will you face, and what is the best way to repay them?

LEARNING OBJECTIVES

LO 8-2.1 Discuss long-term debt options for the purchase of high-priced items.

LO 8-2-2 Explain the purpose of a debt repayment plan.

KEY TERMS

- down payment, 258
- trade-in, 258
- preapproved loan, 259
- refinancing, 259
- mortgage, 260
- rent-to-own agreement, 262
- debt repayment plan, 262
- balloon payment, 264
- prepayment penalty, 264

LO 8-2.1 What Are Long-Term Debt Options?

Many high-priced items that have an extended life can be financed with long-term debt. *Long-term debt* is a loan that is payable over a period longer than a year. Examples include car loans and mortgages. Most forms of long-term debt involve making monthly payments. *Amortization* is the process of dividing up your debt obligation, plus interest, into equal monthly payments over a set period of time.

Buying a Car

Although some people opt to pay cash, the majority of car buyers finance their cars by getting a loan. Typically, a *car loan* is set up as an installment loan with monthly payments. With an *installment loan*, you will make regular payments for a set period of time. The period of time and the amount of your monthly payment will be based on the loan amount and interest rate charged.

A car loan typically requires the buyer to make a down payment. A **down payment** is a cash deposit toward the purchase price that is paid up front. It reduces the amount of the loan. If you have an existing car, you may use it as a **trade-in** by applying its value to the down payment. Other car-buying costs include the title fee, the annual registration fee, and sales taxes.

Based on your monthly income and living expenses, you can determine how much money you can afford to pay each month for the car payment. You should also factor in the costs of insurance, gasoline, maintenance, and repairs. Keep in mind that the car will *depreciate*, or go down in value, over time. The down payment and loan structure should be such that the loan principal is paid down faster than the car depreciates. You do not want to have an *upside-down* loan, which means you owe more on the car than it is worth.

down payment a cash deposit toward the purchase price that is paid up front

trade-in something of value applied toward the down payment of a new purchase

Financing Options

Before buying a car, you should consider getting preapproved at a bank or credit union. With a **preapproved loan**, a maximum loan amount is established and approved in advance. Knowing you have been pre-approved for a loan and knowing your loan limit allows you to focus on negotiating the best deal for the car. Most financial institutions offer car loan terms of 36, 48, 60, or 72 months. Although longer terms mean lower payments, they result in more total interest being paid and a greater chance of having an upside-down loan.

In addition to banks and credit unions, most car dealerships also offer financing through auto manufacturers. On particular models and at particular times of the year, they may offer you better terms than those available from other sources. For example, you may be able to get a 0 percent loan. Use caution with this type of financing. Don't allow a special promotional loan rate to influence you to buy a more expensive car.

There are many online tools available to help you calculate an auto loan payment schedule. By entering information such as the price of the car, the loan term, and the interest rate, you can calculate your monthly payments, including the total interest you will pay over the life of the loan.

preapproved loan a loan for which a maximum amount is established and approved in advance

How can you get a loan to buy a car?

Leasing

Rather than purchasing a new car, you might consider leasing. A *car lease* allows you to use the car for a set period of time and make monthly lease payments. You do not own the car; rather, you are simply renting its use. Leasing can be an attractive option because a monthly lease payment is typically less than a monthly car loan payment. This is because the lease payments are designed to cover only the value of the car you use up during the lease period. You may need a down payment, and you will probably be limited in the number of miles you can drive the car annually. If you exceed this limit, you may have to pay a penalty. At the end of the lease period, you may have the option to buy the car for its expected value at the end of the agreement. As with any rental agreement, you will be responsible for routine maintenance. But if something major happens, such as engine failure, the leasing company usually pays for it (because it is the legal owner).

Debt Repayment

As you make your monthly car payments (which include both principal and interest), the balance of your loan goes down. The loan is set up so that more interest than principal is paid off in the first payments. As the interest is paid down, you will begin paying off more of the principal. If you can pay off the debt early, you may be able to save interest costs.

During the term of the loan, you may find that you can refinance it at a lower rate of interest. **Refinancing** involves paying off an existing

refinancing paying off an existing loan with a new loan that usually has better terms

loan with a new loan that usually has better terms, such as a lower interest rate. For example, at the time you buy a car, the best interest rate may be 8 percent. But within a couple of years, your credit rating may improve and/or the interest rates for car loans may drop. In such cases, it may be worth it to refinance your loan. By moving to a loan with a 5 percent rate, for example, you could save hundreds of dollars in interest costs.

Buying a House

At some point, you are likely to find that owning a house is better than paying rent. There are significant reasons for owning rather than renting. In most cases, with a house, you will own something that is going up in value, or *appreciating*. As your house is appreciating, you are also paying down your debt obligation. Thus, you are building equity in your property and gaining wealth. *Equity* is the difference in the property's value and what you owe on it. As a renter, you do not build equity in the property.

Owning property also gives you tax advantages. On your federal tax return, you can deduct the interest you pay on your house loan. You can also deduct the property taxes you pay. These deductions will lower your total tax liability. As a renter, you do not get these tax deductions.

In addition, most people believe that owning their own house gives them security, independence, and privacy. They can do what they want with the house, and they are able to come and go as they please without worrying about rules in the rental agreement. In some cases, however, there are neighborhood restrictions and homeowners' association rules to follow.

Financing Options

When buying a house, you will most likely be required to make a down payment. If you qualify, lenders will provide a loan for the balance of the price. A loan used to purchase real estate is called a **mortgage**. To qualify for a mortgage, you must complete an extensive loan application. The lender will check your credit history, employment history, and references. The lender will also look at the type and amount of your current debts, the amount and source of your income, and your creditworthiness. Based on this information, the lender will judge if you can handle the monthly mortgage payments, which as a general rule, should not exceed 25 to 35 percent of your take-home (net) pay. Payments on a mortgage are made over an extended period, such as 15 or 30 years. Monthly loan payments include principal and interest.

There are several types of loans available. Banks and mortgage lenders may offer a *conventional loan*, where you make a large down payment (often between 10 and 30 percent of the purchase price) and pay the balance in equal monthly payments for up to 30 years (360 payments). An *FHA loan* is a government-sponsored loan that allows for a smaller down payment but requires you to pay a monthly mortgage insurance premium as well as the principal and interest. The FHA (Federal Housing Administration) insures your loan, making

mortgage a loan used to purchase real estate

Building COMMUNICATION SKILLS

FORMAL SPEAKING

The purpose of a formal speech is to convey information, entertain, or persuade. When preparing a speech, begin with a clear statement of the goals you want to accomplish. These goals will guide you as you prepare the content of the speech.

Use an outline to develop the content. The outline should have three main parts: the introduction, the body, and the conclusion. The introduction briefly explains your topic. The body gives the details or substance of the speech. The conclusion is a summary or request for action.

As you develop the content, consider the audience who will hear the speech. Why will these people be listening? What do they have in common (age, place of work or residence, hobbies, other interests)? How much do they already know about the topic? Answering these questions will help you create content that will accomplish your goals.

Many formal speeches are presented using visual aids, such as electronic slides. Projection equipment and software such as Microsoft PowerPoint® are often used. The slides help illustrate points and add interest to the speech. Slides should list only the main points being covered. If more detailed information must be shared, use a handout for that material.

A time limit is often set for formal speeches. Practice delivering the speech so you can stay within the required time limit. As you deliver the speech, be aware of your body language. Engage your audience by making eye contact with people. Also, use an appropriate tone, rate, and volume. Speaking with confidence and enthusiasm will keep your audience interested. Pause briefly after important points to allow listeners to think about them.

Effective formal speaking often takes lots of practice and refining of skills over time. After you make a speech, evaluate yourself. Think about what you did well and what you could do better the next time. You may also want to ask the audience to evaluate the speech.

Try It Out

Create a classroom presentation on topics related to car loans or mortgages. Prepare an outline, develop the content, and use PowerPoint slides to guide you through the presentation. Practice your speech so that it will be limited to ten minutes. Evaluate your presentation in terms of your audience's reaction, and make suggestions for improvement.

---

it less risky for banks to lend the money. FHA programs are available to first-time homebuyers, low-income buyers, and others who qualify.

There are a few types of government-backed loans that may not require a down payment. VA loans, which are backed by the U.S. Department of Veterans Affairs (VA), are available for military veterans. Also available is the U.S. Department of Agriculture's (USDA) Rural Development loan. To qualify, houses must be located in an eligible rural area as defined by the USDA, and borrowers must meet certain income and credit score requirements.

Several mortgage loan calculators are available online. Based on the loan amount, interest rate, and number of payments, you can calculate what your monthly payment (for principal and interest) will be over the life of your loan.

In addition to the mortgage, there are several other costs associated with buying a home, including title insurance, filing fees, and closing costs. *Closing costs* are the expenses incurred in transferring ownership from buyer to seller in a real estate transaction. Closing costs include charges for the appraisal fee, credit report fee, loan assumption fee, and recording fee. You will also have to pay property taxes and homeowners insurance each year.

Debt Repayment

Mortgages are usually structured in one of two ways: fixed-rate mortgages and adjustable-rate mortgages. With a *fixed-rate mortgage*, the interest rate stays the same for the full term of the loan. Thus, your amortized monthly house payment will not change. With an *adjustable-rate mortgage (ARM)*, the interest rate changes in response to the movement of interest rates in the economy. Thus, your monthly payment is likely to change often. For most people, a fixed monthly payment is the better option. If interest rates drop, you can refinance the loan to get a better rate and save interest costs.

Renting to Own

rent-to-own agreement a contract in which a portion of the renter's monthly payment is applied toward the purchase price of the rented item

If you do not have enough money for a down payment or do not qualify for a mortgage, you may want to look for a seller who will offer a rent-to-own agreement. Under a **rent-to-own agreement**, a portion of the renter's monthly payment is applied toward the purchase price of the rented item. The price is locked in. If the renter elects to buy the house at the end of the lease agreement, he or she has already made a portion or all of the down payment. When people don't have enough money to make a down payment, the rent-to-own option can be a good way of getting the house they want now while at the same time applying money toward its purchase. The purchase option is also known as a *right of first refusal*. In other words, the owner of the property must first give the renter the right to buy the property before it is put on the open market for sale. However, if you decide not to buy the house, no part of your rent payments is returned to you.

XuRa/Shutterstock.com

Why would you use a rent-to-own agreement to buy a house?

 CHECKPOINT

What are the costs of buying a car?

LO 8-2.2 What Is a Debt Repayment Plan?

debt repayment plan a strategy for paying off debt in a way that reduces the total interest paid

A **debt repayment plan** is a strategy for paying off debt in a way that reduces the total interest paid. By making the required monthly payments, your debt will be paid off in a fixed number of years. But if you can pay a little extra with each monthly payment, you will bring down your debt much faster and save money on interest costs.

To create a debt repayment plan, prioritize your debts based on the interest rates. You should focus first on paying off the debt with the highest interest rate, because it will provide you the greatest savings with early payoff. Once it is paid off, you can turn your attention to the account with the next highest interest rate and pay a little extra on it each month. Then once that debt is paid off, focus on the debt with the next highest interest rate, and so on. Continue this pattern until all debts are paid off.

Figure 8-2.1 shows how adding just $30 more to a monthly payment will reduce the number of payments and total interest charges. The result is that you will pay off the loan six months early and save $180 in interest charges.

Student Loan Debt

Many who attend college can do so only with the aid of student loans. This form of debt is known as a *deferred-payment loan*, because you are able to postpone making payments on it until you have completed your education.

Student loans are available from the federal government through its FAFSA (Free Application for Federal Student Aid) website or from private lenders, such as banks. Interest rates are generally low. You must reapply for student loans annually, and the terms of these loans, including the interest rate, may change each year. The FAFSA program will *consolidate*, or combine, all of your student loans into one monthly loan payment when you complete your education. The interest rate on the consolidated loan will be fixed, and your payment will be much lower than the combined payments of the separate loans.

Under special circumstances, the federal government may forgive part, or all, of your federal student loans. *Loan forgiveness* is a program by the federal government to encourage young people to consider "giving back" to society by performing public service. To qualify, you must meet certain requirements and either work full time in a public service job or teach in an elementary or secondary school that serves low-income communities.

Mortgage Debt

When incurring mortgage debt, you may have a choice of debt instruments. For example, rather than a 30-year mortgage on a house, you might want to choose a 15-year mortgage. With a 15-year mortgage, you can generally get a lower interest rate (because the term of the loan

▶ FIGURE 8-2.1 **Paying Off Debt Early**

Making Required Payments		Making Larger-than-Required Payments	
Amount borrowed	$5,000	Amount borrowed	$5,000
Interest rate	18%	Interest rate	18%
Number of payments	36	Number of payments	30
Monthly payment	$180	Monthly payment	$210
Total interest paid	$1,480	Total interest paid	$1,300

is shorter), but your fixed monthly payment will be considerably higher. Or, you could choose the 30-year mortgage and make additional payments toward the principal when possible to reduce the interest charges and the duration of the loan.

balloon payment a large lump-sum payment that must be paid at a set time

Some mortgages will have a balloon payment. A **balloon payment** is a large lump-sum payment that must be paid at a set time. The balloon payment is typically the last loan payment. For example, a mortgage may have equal monthly payments of $800 for ten years and a final balloon payment of $5,000. Having this type of loan might be beneficial to some buyers. When interest rates are high, a buyer can get a lower rate, and thus a lower monthly payment, by agreeing to the balloon payment. If the buyer does not want to make the large balloon payment, he or she may refinance the loan before the payment is due. At that time, the buyer may qualify for a fixed-rate mortgage with a more favorable interest rate.

Prepayment Penalty

prepayment penalty a fee charged if you repay a loan before the agreed-upon time

Some types of loans may have penalties for early repayment. A **prepayment penalty** is a fee charged if you repay a loan before the agreed-upon time. For example, suppose you borrow money and agree to repay the loan over a 15-year period. A short time later, you decide to pay off the entire loan balance. The loan agreement may specify a 30- to 90-day interest penalty. The lender has certain costs related to setting up the loan. These costs are spread over the life of the loan. If the loan is repaid early, the lender charges a penalty fee to cover these costs. An example of a 60-day interest penalty on a $10,000 loan that is paid off after one year is shown in Figure 8-2.2.

Repaying a debt early still may be a wise choice, even with a prepayment penalty. If the penalty amount is less than the interest you would owe if you paid on the original schedule, paying off the debt would be to your advantage. Paying debt off early helps your credit score and frees up cash to be used for other purposes (such as savings).

Often, the prepayment penalty is lowered or eliminated after the first few years of the loan. If you want to pay it off early, you may choose to wait until the prepayment penalty period has expired. It's always a good idea to be sure you understand any prepayment penalties before you sign a loan agreement.

▶ FIGURE 8-2.2 **Prepayment Penalty**

Terms: $10,000, 5-year loan at 8% with a 60-day interest penalty for early repayment after 1 year	
Initial balance	$10,000.00
Monthly payment	202.76
Current loan balance	8,305.60
60-day interest penalty ($8,305.60 × 8% × 60/360)	110.74
Balance to be paid at early repayment	8,416.44

CHECKPOINT

What is the purpose of a debt repayment plan?

KEY TERMS REVIEW

Match the terms with the definitions. Some terms may not be used.

_____ 1. Something of value applied toward the down payment of a new purchase

_____ 2. A strategy for paying off debt in a way that reduces the total interest paid

_____ 3. A fee charged if you repay a loan before the agreed-upon time

_____ 4. A loan for which a maximum amount is established and approved in advance

_____ 5. A contract in which a portion of the renter's monthly payment is applied toward the purchase price of the rented item

_____ 6. A cash deposit toward the purchase price that is paid up front

_____ 7. A loan used to purchase real estate

_____ 8. Paying off an existing loan with a new loan that usually has better terms

a. balloon payment

b. debt repayment plan

c. down payment

d. mortgage

e. preapproved loan

f. prepayment penalty

g. refinancing

h. rent-to-own agreement

i. trade-in

CHECK YOUR UNDERSTANDING

9. What is meant by amortization?

10. Why is it a good idea to get preapproved for a loan before shopping to buy a car?

11. How can refinancing a loan save you money?

12. What are the advantages of leasing rather than buying a car?

13. What are the advantages of buying a house rather than renting?

14. What information does a lender need to obtain in a loan application for a mortgage?

15. What costs are involved in buying a home?

16. How is an FHA loan different from a conventional loan?

17. How is a fixed-rate mortgage different from an adjustable-rate mortgage (ARM)?

18. When is it beneficial to have a loan with a balloon payment?

19. What is a deferred-payment loan and for what purposes is such a loan granted?

20. What is the purpose of a prepayment penalty?

THINK CRITICALLY

21. Why should you make a substantial down payment when buying a car?

22. If you don't have cash to use as a down payment, you could use your existing car as a trade-in. Explain how this can save you money.

23. Under what circumstances would you want to consider refinancing a debt?

24. Why is it best to have a large down payment (20 percent or more) when you are buying a house and financing the purchase with a 30-year mortgage?

25. Why should you pay more than the required amount of a monthly payment as part of your debt repayment plan?

26. If you acquire several student loans through your college years, why is it to your advantage to consolidate those loans upon graduation?

27. What should you consider when thinking about the early payoff of a loan with a prepayment penalty?

EXTEND YOUR LEARNING

28. Search for mortgage (home loan) and auto loan calculators on the Internet. Use them to determine the monthly payments and total interest for the life of the loans in each of the following scenarios:

    a. Joe Chin bought a house for $180,000. He made a 20 percent down payment. Joe secured a loan for the balance of the purchase price at 6.5 percent interest for 30 years.

    b. Louisa Perez bought a house for $300,000. She made a 10 percent down payment. Louisa secured a loan for the balance of the purchase price at 5.95 percent interest for 30 years.

    c. Mary Roberts bought a house for $255,000. She made a 5 percent down payment. Mary secured a loan for the balance of the purchase price at 6.75 percent interest for 15 years.

    d. Nathan Reynolds bought a car for $15,000. He made a down payment of $3,000. Nathan secured a loan for the balance of the purchase price at 8 percent interest for four years.

    e. Troy Parker also bought a car for $15,000 and made a $3,000 down payment. He secured a loan for the balance of the purchase price at 4 percent interest for four years.

THE ESSENTIAL QUESTION   Refer to The Essential Question on p. 258. Long-term debts may include buying a car or house or getting a student loan. The most efficient way to pay off long-term debts is to devise a debt repayment plan. A debt repayment plan will reduce the total interest paid.

THE ESSENTIAL QUESTION What are some ways that you can practice good credit management?

LEARNING OBJECTIVES

LO 8-3.1 List ways that you can effectively manage your use of credit.

LO 8-3.2 Explain how to avoid credit costs and risky loan practices.

KEY TERMS

- credit management, 267
- 20/10 Rule, 268
- unused credit, 270
- predatory lending, 270
- loan shark, 270
- easy access credit, 270
- title loan, 270
- equity stripping, 271
- payday loan, 272
- advance-fee loan, 272

LO 8-3.1 How Can You Manage Credit Use?

When you begin using credit, plan to use it wisely. Go slowly; do not use too much credit at first. It is very important to establish credit when you do not need it so that it will be available to you when you do. Build a solid credit history by paying all credit bills on time. Later, when you want to use credit, you will be considered a low (good) risk. You may also be able to borrow at lower interest rates than someone who is considered a high (bad) risk.

Exercising good **credit management** involves establishing and following an individual plan for using credit wisely. It requires you to recognize your limits and plan your use of credit. There are a number of ways to practice good credit management, including adjusting your spending and use of credit based on the current state of the economy, carefully examining credit offers, and effectively managing and periodically assessing your debt load.

credit management establishing and following an individual plan for using credit wisely

Consider the Economy

When the economy is doing well, consumers may feel optimistic about the future. This optimism often leads to increased buying. During good economic times, interest rates are usually rising. Thus, rather than buying on credit, this would be a good time to save money and earn interest on those savings.

The opposite is true when the economy is slowing down. People may feel pessimistic, and this can lead to decreased buying. Because people are buying less, prices may be dropping. This may be a good time to buy because you can get better values. If you do not spend all of your money (and credit) during the good economic times, you will have money available to spend when prices are more favorable.

Study Credit Offers

You most likely will receive credit offers soon after you begin working. These offers are mailed, emailed, or found in advertisements. If you

Why is it important to read the fine print of a credit offer before you accept it?

want to take advantage of one of these offers, carefully examine each one and compare the *disclosure terms,* which typically include the following:

- APR
- Grace period for payments
- Minimum finance charge on unpaid balances
- Finance charge calculation method
- Fees (annual fee, transaction fees, cash advance fees, and penalty fees)

Be sure to read all of the fine print in any credit offer before accepting it. What may appear to be a great deal can be a very expensive lesson that hurts your credit rating. Keep an eye out for credit terms described in the fine print, such as the following:

- *Low introductory rate.* Interest rates may be as low as 0 percent for the first year. However, the fine print may tell you that if you are late by even one day in making a payment, the rate will rise to 25 to 30 percent or more. The fine print may also state that the introductory rate may be subject to change without notice.
- *Fixed APR.* The offer may say the interest rate is fixed, but the fine print may say the rate is subject to change and can be "adjusted" (raised) at the option of the creditor.
- *Closure or inactivity fees.* These fees may be assessed if you close your account, do not use it for a certain period of time, or fail to reach a set annual spending limit.

Manage and Assess Your Debt Load

A *debt load* is the amount of outstanding debt at a particular time. Whether your debt load is acceptable to you will depend on your ability to make regular payments, your ability to pay off the debt quickly if necessary, and your level of comfort with the amount of debt you owe.

A common suggestion for effectively managing your debt load is to use the 20/10 Rule. The **20/10 Rule** is a plan to limit the use of credit to no more than 20 percent of your *yearly* take-home pay, with payments of no more than 10 percent of *monthly* take-home pay. Mortgages and monthly payment commitments for housing are not included in the 20/10 rule limits.

Debt represents future earnings already spent. Unfortunately, many people never assess how much future income they have already committed to debt and whether the types and sources of credit they use are the most advantageous to them. You can avoid this trap by periodically making a careful assessment of your debt load throughout your life and taking corrective action if necessary.

20/10 Rule a plan to limit the use of credit to no more than 20 percent of your yearly take-home pay, with payments of no more than 10 percent of monthly take-home pay

LO 8-3.2 How Can You Reduce and Avoid Credit Costs?

Credit can be costly if the appropriate precautions aren't taken. You need to look for ways to reduce costs and to avoid fraudulent credit practices.

Avoid Unnecessary Credit Costs

If you use credit wisely, costs can be kept to a minimum. Here are several ways that you can reduce your costs:

- *Pay cash for small purchases.* You shouldn't charge small purchases unless you plan to pay them off at the end of the month to avoid finance charges.
- *Keep the number of credit accounts you have to a minimum.* Most credit counselors recommend having no more than two or three credit cards. The more cards you have, the greater the temptation to buy without thinking and to overextend yourself.
- *Comparison shop when getting a loan or credit card.* When looking to apply for a credit card, compare the costs of credit from at least three different sources. When planning a large purchase, such as a car, get preapproved for a loan. That way you will know the dollar amount you can spend and the interest rate you can get, which you can compare to other offers.
- *Examine your monthly credit card statement for accuracy.* When you receive a credit card statement, check it closely to ensure that the charges listed are correct, payments are recorded, credits for returned items are posted, fees and penalties applied are permitted, and the interest amount and new balance are correct.

Looking Ahead

What if credit cards of the future were 100 percent secure? As a way to combat fraud, credit card companies in the United States are phasing out magnetic stripe credit cards and upgrading to cards embedded with anti-theft chip technology. This technology is known as EMV (named after its developers—Europay, MasterCard, and Visa). Many foreign countries, such as Europe and Asia, have been using EMV credit cards for years. Using the Internet, conduct research to answer the following questions: How do EMV cards work? Why has the United States been so slow to use EMV technology? What are the advantages and disadvantages of EMV cards? Do you think these cards will be a solution to credit card fraud?

- *Always pay your bills on time or early.* If possible, schedule your payments through your checking account online using *automatic withdrawals*. This ensures that your payment is processed on time and helps you avoid penalty fees or increased interest rates due to late or missed payments.
- *Pay off your balances as quickly as you can.* Credit card companies charge interest on outstanding balances. If you have the financial means to do so, pay the full amount owed on your credit card each month. This way you can avoid paying interest charges.
- *Do not increase spending when your income increases.* Instead of spending the income, use it to pay off credit card debt or put it in your savings.
- *Accept only the amount of credit you need.* Although having credit available when you need it can be comforting, unused credit can count against you. **Unused credit** is the remaining credit available to you on current accounts; it is your credit limit minus your current balance. For example, if your credit limit is $2,000 and you owe $800, your unused credit is $1,200. Other creditors may be reluctant to lend you money because you could at any time access the other $1,200, thereby increasing your debt and reducing your ability to repay their loan.
- *Take advantage of credit incentive programs.* With a *rewards program* or *rebate program*, you can get back a portion of what you spent in credit purchases for the year or earn points that you can redeem at a later date. However, be aware that credit cards that offer credit incentive programs can have high annual fees and interest rates.

Avoid Risky Loan Practices

Some lenders take advantage of people by engaging in **predatory lending**, or unfair, deceptive, and fraudulent loan practices. Some loan practices are illegal. Because they have poor credit ratings or have not used credit wisely in the past, some people may not qualify for conventional loans from banks, credit unions, and other traditional lenders. When borrowers are desperate, they may seek risky loans through nontraditional lenders that often charge very high interest rates. In states where there are no *usury laws* that limit interest rates, illegal loan practices can flourish.

A **loan shark** is a person who offers illegal loans at very high interest rates and often uses intimidation, such as threats of violence, to enforce repayment. Because of the high interest rates, loans offered by predatory lenders and loan sharks are almost impossible to repay, leaving the borrowers in worse financial shape than before the loan was taken out.

Another example of a risky loan practice is **easy access credit**, which can be obtained quickly and easily but often comes with high or hidden costs. Examples include title loans, payday loans, and others.

Title Loans

A **title loan** is a type of short-term, secured loan with a high interest rate that uses the title on your vehicle as collateral. With a title loan, the lender places a *lien* (a financial claim against property) on the

unused credit the remaining credit available to you on current accounts

predatory lending unfair, deceptive, and fraudulent loan practices

loan shark a person who offers illegal loans at very high interest rates and often uses intimidation to enforce repayment

easy access credit type of credit that can be obtained quickly and easily but that often comes with high or hidden costs

title loan a short-term loan with a high interest rate that uses the title on your vehicle as collateral

STRESS MANAGEMENT

Stress is a state of mental or physical tension. Many types of changes in life can cause stress. The change can be good, such as getting a new job, or it can be bad, such as being ill. Stress is not always harmful. Sometimes stress can cause a person to take actions or learn new ways to handle a situation that can be helpful. In other instances, stress can cause problems. Emotional upset, trouble sleeping or concentrating, and even disease can be caused by too much stress.

Everyone experiences stress in daily life. Because too much stress can be harmful, you need to learn to manage factors that cause stress and take steps that will help you cope with stress. The key to stress management is finding things that will work for you. Follow these guidelines to help you control and cope with stress:

- *Identify situations that cause negative stress in your life.* Take whatever steps you reasonably can to avoid or change these situations. For example, if you are unable to pay your credit card bills, determine what you need to do to improve your situation.
- *Accept things you can't change.* Many sources of stress are unavoidable and beyond our control, such as the death of a loved one or an economic recession.

Rather than stressing out over these types of events, focus on the things you can control.

- *Seek counseling to help you deal with serious stressful events.* For example, if you are having credit problems, credit counselors are available to help you find ways to manage your money.
- *Make time for fun and relaxation.* Set aside time to relax or do something you enjoy such as a hobby or other leisure activity. Constantly focusing on your problems will only lead to more stress.
- *Reach out to family and friends.* Talking with and getting a family member's or friend's advice can help relieve stress.
- *Get enough rest and sleep, eat a healthy diet, and stay physically active.* A healthy lifestyle will help you become more physically fit and better able to cope with stress.

Think Critically

1. Using the Internet, locate and read three articles on managing stress. Describe what you learned from the articles. What are some additional tips for managing stress?
2. What have you learned about stress that you can apply to your life?

---

borrower's car title in exchange for a loan amount between 25 and 50 percent of the car's value. When the loan is repaid, the lien is removed and the car title is returned to its owner. If the borrower defaults on his or her payments, then the lender can repossess the vehicle and sell it to repay the borrower's outstanding debt.

Title loans are a very expensive form of credit. They have a much higher interest rate than most forms of credit, sometimes well over 100 percent, and are only for a short period of time, such as 15 to 30 days. This makes it very difficult for borrowers to pay off the loan on time.

Equity Stripping

Equity stripping is the unethical practice of extending a loan to a distressed homeowner who cannot afford the loan payments, resulting in the lender taking possession of the home. A lender points out that the homeowner has equity (value) in the home and can use the home as collateral for the loan. The lender may even encourage the borrower to overstate her or his income to get the loan. Although the borrower

equity stripping the unethical practice of extending a loan to a distressed homeowner who cannot afford the loan payments, resulting in the lender taking possession of the home

may not have enough income to make the loan payments, the lender approves the loan. If the borrower starts missing payments, the lender will foreclose and take the home.

Payday Loans

payday loan a cash advance from your next paycheck

A **payday loan** is a cash advance from your next paycheck. A borrower writes a check to the lender for the amount he or she wants to borrow, plus a fee for borrowing the money. The lender gives the borrower the amount of the check (less the fee) and agrees to hold the check until the borrower's next payday. On that day, the lender deposits the check to receive repayment for the loan. With other payday loans, the borrower gives the lender his or her checking account information so that the lender can access the account for payment on the due date. A payday loan is simple and fast, but the interest and fees paid are usually substantial. Figure 8-3.1 shows how to calculate the APR on a payday loan.

Advance-Fee Loans

advance-fee loan a type of loan that includes a large fee up front

With an **advance-fee loan**, a lender guarantees a loan if the borrower pays a large fee up front. The fee may range from $100 to several hundred dollars. These loans may be scams. Legitimate lenders never "guarantee" a loan or credit card before you apply, especially if you have bad credit. You may be asked to call a fee-based "900" number to learn more about the loans. It is illegal for companies doing business by phone in the United States to promise you a loan or credit card and ask you to pay for it before they deliver.

Rent-to-Own Agreements

Although rent-to-own agreements can be legitimate, such as those used for houses, some of them can be risky. When used to buy personal property, such as furniture or electronics, the total price you will have paid for the item is often much higher than if you had purchased the item outright. For example, suppose you rent-to-own a television that sells for $220. You make weekly payments of $10. After making 78 weekly payments, you own the television. You have paid a total of $780 for an item that sells for $220. This amount compares to paying a loan interest rate of approximately 210 percent!

▶ FIGURE 8-3.1 Payday Loan

The formula for computing the annual percentage rate of a payday loan is:

Loan fee ÷ Loan amount × Number of days in the year ÷ Loan term in days

If you borrow $350 for two weeks (14 days) and pay a loan fee of $50, the annual percentage rate would be calculated as follows:

$50 ÷ $350 × 360 ÷ 14 = 3.67, or 367% APR

 **CHECKPOINT**

What makes a loan risky?

KEY TERMS REVIEW

Match the terms with the definitions. Some terms may not be used.

_____ 1. The unethical practice of extending a loan to a distressed homeowner who cannot afford the loan payments, resulting in the lender taking possession of the home

_____ 2. A person who offers illegal loans at very high interest rates and often uses intimidation to enforce repayment

_____ 3. A plan to limit the use of credit to no more than 20 percent of your yearly take-home pay, with payments of no more than 10 percent of monthly take-home pay

_____ 4. Unfair, deceptive, and fraudulent loan practices

_____ 5. The remaining credit available to you on current accounts

_____ 6. Following an individual plan for using credit wisely

_____ 7. A type of loan that includes a large fee up front

_____ 8. A short-term loan with a high interest rate that uses the title on your vehicle as collateral

_____ 9. Type of credit that can be obtained quickly and easily but often comes with high and hidden costs

a. 20/10 Rule

b. advance-fee loan

c. credit management

d. easy access credit

e. equity stripping

f. loan shark

g. payday loan

h. predatory lending

i. title loan

j. unused credit

CHECK YOUR UNDERSTANDING

10. What does exercising good credit management involve?

11. Why should you consider the economy when planning credit purchases?

12. List three things you should look for in the fine print of a credit offer.

13. What is meant by *debt load*, and why should it be monitored?

14. Does the 20/10 Rule apply to all types of credit? Explain your answer.

15. List three ways you can reduce and avoid costs of credit.

16. How can you use comparison shopping when choosing a credit card?

17. Explain why it is important to have unused credit.

18. What is the advantage of using automatic withdrawals to pay your credit card bill each month?

19. Provide two examples of types of predatory lending.

THINK CRITICALLY

20. Why do interest rates rise during good economic times? What is your best strategy to maximize the benefits of credit while minimizing interest paid on credit?

21. You receive an offer in the mail for a credit card that has a 0 percent interest rate for the first six months. You are thinking about signing up for the card. What are the dangers of taking a credit card that offers a low introductory rate such as this?

22. Why should you keep the number of credit cards you use to a minimum?

23. When is it advisable to use credit during poor economic times? When is this not a good practice?

24. Why should you comparison shop when seeking to get a loan for a new car purchase?

25. To avoid the practice of equity stripping, what advice would you give to a low-income homeowner who needs to borrow money?

26. If you get a payday loan of $500 for two weeks (14 days) for a fee of $100, what is the APR? (*Hint*: Use 360 as the number of days in a year.)

27. Do you feel that the advantages of using credit outweigh the disadvantages? Why or why not?

EXTEND YOUR LEARNING

28. Find three advertisements of offers for loans or credit cards by using the Internet, newspapers, or magazines, or by visiting your local bank or credit union. The loans may be car loans, mortgage loans, or student loans. Find the information below for each loan or credit card offer. Compile this information in a table.

   * Type of loan or credit card

   * Interest rate charged and whether it is fixed or variable (adjustable)

   * Length of the loan in months or years

   * Disclosure terms (APR, grace period, minimum finance charge, finance charge calculation method, and fees)

   Evaluate each offer. Do you think the lender or credit card company is reputable? Are any of the terms questionable? Which loan or credit card offer has the most favorable terms for the borrower?

THE ESSENTIAL QUESTION   Refer to The Essential Question on p. 267. Practice good credit management by adjusting your spending and use of credit based on the current state of the economy, carefully examining credit offers, effectively managing and periodically assessing your debt load, avoiding and reducing unnecessary credit costs, and being aware of risky loan practices.

Exploring Careers in...
CRIMINAL INVESTIGATION

Criminal investigators, or detectives, are law enforcement officers who gather facts and collect evidence for criminal cases. Detectives work at the local, state, and federal level.

Criminal investigators have a variety of job duties. They conduct interviews with suspects and witnesses, examine records, and observe the activities of suspects. They also have the power to obtain warrants and arrest suspects. They must also write reports and keep detailed records. They are oftentimes called upon to testify in court.

Detectives usually specialize in investigating one type of crime, such as fraud or homicide. They are typically assigned cases on a rotating basis and work on them until an arrest is made and trial is completed or until the case is dropped.

Employment Outlook

- A slower than average rate of employment growth is expected.

Job Titles

- Detective
- Criminal investigator
- Law enforcement officer
- Agent
- Special agent

Needed Education/Skills

- A high school diploma is required, although college coursework or a college degree is sometimes required.
- Most detectives must graduate from their agency's training academy before completing a period of on-the-job training.

- Detectives normally begin their career as police officers.
- Good judgment, excellent communication skills, and physical stamina are essential.

What's it like to work in ... Criminal Investigation

Raji is a detective with the city police department. He was promoted to the detective position two years ago, after spending the previous eight years as a police officer.

Raji investigates crimes involving fraud that occur within the city limits. He spends most of his time assessing and collecting evidence, talking with witnesses and suspects, and preparing reports for the district attorney, who will decide if there is sufficient evidence to charge a suspect. Although Raji works in an office, he spends much of his time out in the field.

Today, Raji is interviewing the victim of a fraudulent scam. He will be doing computer searches as well to try to match evidence and data to previous fraudulent crimes committed in the area.

What About You?

Would you find satisfaction in protecting the people of your community? Would a career in criminal investigation appeal to you? What types of crime would you like to investigate?

Chapter 8 Assessment

SUMMARY

8-1 Before entering into a shared living arrangement, you should learn each other's living habits and establish a group budget.

A contract is a legally binding agreement that specifies the rights and duties of each party to the agreement. A lease is a contract between a landlord and a tenant.

Tenant responsibilities include paying rent on time, obeying the rules, and taking reasonable care of the property. Landlords are responsible for providing a safe, sanitary, and habitable place for tenants to live.

8-2 Long-term debt is used to finance large purchases, such as a car or house. Most financing options require a cash down payment and monthly payments spread over several years.

Before buying a car, you should get a preapproved loan. Preapproval allows you to find out how much money you will be qualified to borrow.

Financing options for cars include a loan from your bank or credit union, as well as manufacturer financing. Leasing a car is another option.

Financing a home requires a mortgage. Financing options for a mortgage include conventional loans requiring higher down payments or FHA loans requiring smaller down payments and mortgage insurance. Mortgage loans may have a fixed or adjustable interest rate.

A debt repayment plan is a strategy for paying off debt in a way that reduces the total interest paid.

Student loans defer payment until you have completed your education. Upon graduation, the loans may be consolidated into one loan with one lower monthly payment.

Some loans may include a balloon payment and prepayment penalties.

8-3 Good credit management involves using credit based on the current state of the economy, carefully examining credit offers, and effectively managing and periodically assessing your debt load.

To reduce and avoid credit costs, keep credit accounts to a minimum; comparison shop; examine your monthly statement for accuracy; always pay bills on time; pay off balances as quickly as you can; accept only the amount of credit you need; take advantage of credit incentive programs; and avoid risky lending practices, such as title loans, equity stripping, payday loans, advance-fee loans, and rent-to-own agreements.

MAKE ACADEMIC CONNECTIONS

1. **Ethics** Using the Internet, research the usury laws in effect in your state. What is the maximum interest rate that lenders may charge? Which state(s) has the highest usury interest rate? Which state(s) has the lowest? Should more be done to restrict interest rates? (LO 8-3.2)

2. **Research** Using the community resources in your area, find out the installation fees and security deposits required for the following services: (a) electricity, (b) cable or satellite TV, and (c) water. Are any of these fees and deposits refundable? If so, under what conditions? (LO 8-1.1)

3. **Economics** Home values change over time. Prepare a two-page report or give a presentation on how housing prices have changed in your local area over the past ten years. Provide reasons for the changes. Cite two or three sources for the information in your report. (LO 8-2.1)

4. **Communication** Make a list of the types of long-term debt that you think you will incur over the next ten years. Then describe your financing options and debt repayment plans for your debts. (LO 8-2.1, LO 8-2.2)

 Do the Math

1. Determine the required amounts in each of the following scenarios:

Loan amount (principal)	$250,000
Appraisal fee	$500
Lender's inspection fee	$250
Credit report fee	$50
Loan origination fee	1% of loan amount
Notary public fee	$60
Document recording fees	$75
Title search	$250
Survey fee	$250
Flood certification	$30
Buyer's attorney fees	$750

a. The following charges are part of the closing costs for a mortgage loan. What is the total amount of the closing costs?

b. Albert Morrison took out a loan for $90,000 at 10 percent interest for 15 years. His monthly payments are $967.14. He has made payments for 2 years (24 payments) and now wants to repay the loan early. The current principal balance owed is $84,257.19. The loan agreement specifies a $468 prepayment penalty. Will Albert save money by repaying the loan (current balance plus penalty) at this time? If so, how much will he save?

c. Sue Thomson bought a house for $178,750. She is getting a mortgage for $145,000. If a mortgage is for more than 80 percent of the value of the home, Sue's lender requires that the borrower purchase mortgage insurance. Will Sue have to purchase the insurance?

2. **Different forms of credit have different costs. You have decided you need a laptop computer and printer. The purchase price for both is $1,200. Compare the following options: (a) paying for the equipment using a credit card, (b) renting them to own, or (c) leasing them. After evaluating the details that follow, indicate which option you would choose and why.**

a. You can buy the computer and printer with your credit card and pay for them over the course of one year. The interest rate is 18.99 percent. For the first 11 months, you will pay $110 each month. In the last month, you will pay the remainder of the outstanding balance. (For the purposes of this problem, assume there will be no other charges or fees on the credit card bill.) The credit card company uses the adjusted balance method to compute interest (see Chapter 7). What is the total amount (purchase price plus interest) you will pay?

b. You can rent and buy the computer and printer from a rent-to-own company. You will pay fixed monthly rental payments of $200. What is the total you will pay for the equipment using this option?

c. You can lease the computer and printer for one year. You will be required to make monthly payments of $125. What is the total amount that you will pay for one year's use if you choose this option?

Take Action

GROUP PRESENTATION

TEAMWORK

Work with two or three classmates to complete this activity. Develop a presentation based on a topic related to using credit, such as one of the following:

- The housing market in your local area or state
- The employment market in your local area or state
- The new and used car markets in your local area or state
- Interest rates in the economy
- Comparison of interest rates and other credit terms for different lenders in your area

a. Conduct research on the topic. Use local newspapers, magazines, and the Internet.

b. Create an outline of the main points to include in your presentation. Then write down the details you want to cover. Include how the information you found could or should affect use of credit by consumers in your area.

c. Prepare a slideshow, transparencies, handouts, or other visual aids that you can use during your speech.

d. Assign roles for the presentation. Practice as a group.

Review the *Building Communications Skills: Formal Speaking* feature in this chapter to help you prepare and deliver the presentation to your class. Save your presentation materials in your portfolio.

Credit Problems and Laws

Gpointstudio/iStockphoto.com

In this chapter, you will learn how to resolve problems with credit and protect yourself from unethical and illegal practices. Avoiding credit problems is not always possible. Sometimes you must resolve disputes and take positive steps to protect your creditworthiness. In extreme situations, the solution may be to file for bankruptcy. There are many laws and agencies that help protect consumer interests in the areas of credit reporting, billing, collections, and the granting or denial of credit.

Do *This*, Not *That*

To avoid problems with credit:

- Recognize the warning signs that your debt load is too high.
- Safeguard your personal information against identity theft.
- Get credit counseling to help create a budget.
- Use federal and state agencies for assistance in resolving complaints.
- Know and use the laws that support consumer rights.

THE ESSENTIAL QUESTION What issues can result from credit use, and what actions can you take to resolve them?

LEARNING OBJECTIVES

LO 9-1.1 Recognize how to avoid collection, garnishment, and foreclosure procedures.

LO 9-1.2 Explain how to dispute errors on billing statements and the methods that can be used to resolve disputes.

LO 9-1.3 Explain how to avoid credit scams and fraud.

KEY TERMS

- loan modification, 281
- credit delinquency, 281
- repossession, 281
- foreclosure, 281
- garnishment, 282
- disputing a charge, 282
- documentation, 283
- dispute letter, 283
- alternative dispute resolution (ADR), 284
- credit card fraud, 286
- identity theft, 287
- credit repair, 288

LO 9-1.1 What Problems Can Arise from Debt?

Every year, millions of consumers get into financial trouble because they have too much debt. Often this happens because of a job loss, illness, or other event that disrupts income and the ability to pay existing credit obligations.

There are many warning signs that debt has become a problem:

- Your credit card balances are at or near your credit limit.
- You are able to make only minimum payments on your balances.
- You often make late payments.
- You may skip some payments in order to make other payments.
- You often pay one credit card by shifting the balance to another credit card.
- Credit card companies are reducing your credit limit.
- Your credit score is falling because you have too much credit.
- You are receiving phone calls from debt collectors.
- You are unable to save or invest any money because of debt obligations.
- You worry about how you will be able to pay your bills.

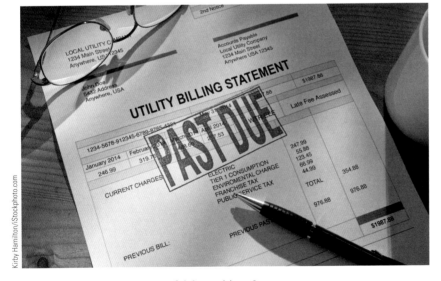

What might be some causes of debt problems?

Kirby Hamilton/iStockphoto.com

If you experience debt problems, there are certain actions you can take to help resolve them. These actions may help you preserve your credit rating:

- *Call each creditor.* As soon as you have problems paying bills, call each of your creditors and discuss your situation with them.
- *Negotiate lower payments or other ways to meet your obligations.* Most creditors want to work with you to find a solution. For example, you may be granted a temporary loan modification. A **loan modification** is a new loan arrangement that allows you to make reduced payments, usually on a temporary basis. Lenders will often lower or postpone payments, reduce interest, or make other special arrangements so you can avoid penalties.
- *Follow up.* Confirm any agreement reached with a written letter or email stating your understanding of the agreement.
- *Meet your new agreement duties.* Make payments according to the new arrangement.
- *Keep your creditors informed of your situation.* If you need more help, ask early. Ignoring a bad situation will only make it worse.

If debt continues to build and no action is taken to resolve the problem, you may experience several negative consequences.

loan modification a new loan arrangement that allows you to make reduced payments, usually on a temporary basis

Credit Delinquency

A credit contract requires that you make payments on time. When you do not make payments on time, your account is in delinquency. **Credit delinquency** is the failure to pay your debts as required by agreement or by law. When you are delinquent, your credit rating and credit score will drop dramatically. You will find it difficult to get credit when you need it.

credit delinquency failure to pay debts as required by agreement or by law

Repossession and Foreclosure

A loan that has *collateral* pledged for repayment is a *secured loan.* If the borrower does not make payments as agreed upon, the property used as collateral can be taken away to pay the debt. **Repossession** is the act of taking an asset used as collateral, such as a car, and selling it to pay the debt. Having an item repossessed hurts the borrower's credit rating.

If a homeowner fails to make house payments, he or she may face foreclosure. **Foreclosure** is the legal process of taking possession of a house (property) when the borrower does not make mortgage payments

repossession the act of taking an asset used as collateral and selling it to pay the debt

foreclosure the legal process of taking possession of the house (property) when the borrower does not make mortgage payments as agreed

Looking Ahead

If you face credit problems in the future, you may have some of your assets repossessed. Vehicles are among the most frequently repossessed assets. Visit the website of the Federal Trade Commission (FTC) and read about vehicle repossession. Then answer the following questions: When does a creditor or lender have permission to seize your vehicle? What happens to the personal belongings left inside a repossessed vehicle? How can a borrower get the repossessed vehicle back?

as agreed. The creditor may be able to force a sale of the property. Money from the sale is used to pay the debt. In addition to losing the house and being evicted, the debtor may lose the money he or she has paid so far as mortgage payments. The debtor also may have to pay foreclosure costs, which can include attorneys' fees, court costs, interest charges, and other expenses of collection. Foreclosure will negatively affect a debtor's credit rating.

Collection Agencies

If payments on your credit account are overdue, your account may be turned over to a collection agency. Collection agencies legally have the right to represent the creditor to collect the amount due. If there is a dispute with your account, collection cannot begin until the dispute is resolved. If you do not pay your debt, the collection agency may file a lawsuit on behalf of the creditor to get a judgment against you. A *judgment* is a ruling of a court of law. If there is a judgment against you, the collection agency can attempt to collect on the judgment in several ways. It may take your assets to repay the debt, levy (freeze) your bank account, or garnish your wages to pay the debt you owe. **Garnishment** is a legal process that allows part of an employee's paycheck to be withheld for payment of a debt. The money is paid directly from the employer to the creditor.

garnishment a legal process that allows part of an employee's paycheck to be withheld for payment of a debt

With a collection proceeding, you will have to pay interest, collection fees, and certain other costs of the collection agency. This is in addition to the debt amount owed. Collection costs can sometimes exceed the debt amount.

CHECKPOINT

Why should you avoid delinquencies, repossessions, and foreclosures?

LO 9-1.2 How Can You Resolve Credit Errors?

When buying goods and services, there may be times when you think that you have been cheated or that an error has been made. You may be due some type of adjustment to your account. To get redress (a remedy), you must take action.

Disputing Charges

disputing a charge the process of informing a credit company of an error on your bill

When you receive a credit account statement, examine it closely. If you find a charge on the statement that you did not make or that is for the incorrect amount, take action right away to dispute the charge. **Disputing a charge** is the process of informing a credit company of an error on your bill. It generally means that you are asking the credit issuer to reverse the charge on your account.

To dispute a charge, you must follow procedures outlined by your credit issuer. The process usually begins with a telephone call to discuss the problem. Provide any information and **documentation**, or records, such as receipts, that support your claim. Whenever you talk to a person about a dispute, write down the date, the person's name and title, the phone number, and the details discussed. Follow up your phone call with a written letter explaining what happened.

documentation records that support your claim

Figure 9-1.1 shows a **dispute letter**, which is a letter written to inform a credit company of an incorrect charge on your account. The letter should begin with your return address and the date. Read the credit account information to find the proper address to which you should send a dispute letter. Often, the address is not the same one you use for payments, and the letter should not be mailed with a payment. Include your credit account number in a subject line. State the problem with the account clearly. Give the details needed to make the problem easy to understand. State any earlier steps you have taken related to the problem, such as any phone calls you have made. Indicate that you are enclosing a copy of the statement that contains the error. Continue to communicate with the credit company until the dispute is resolved.

dispute letter a letter written to inform a credit company of an incorrect charge on your account

▶ FIGURE 9-1.1 **Dispute Letter**

4550 Bay View Road
Hamburg, NY 14075-4450
April 7, 20—

Credit Company
P.O. Box 87483
Wilmington, DE 19850-7483

Dear Sir or Madam

DISPUTE ON ACCOUNT 2444 2344 2317 3243

Please register this dispute of a charge on my recent credit card statement, which is dated April 2, 20—. The incorrect charge is circled on the enclosed copy of the statement.

I called to report this error today and talked to Melanie Smith in your Customer Service Department. The charge is for $46.42 for the purchase of gasoline in Houston, Texas, on March 20, 20—. I did not make this purchase. I have never been to Texas. I have not loaned my credit card to another person or given permission to anyone to use my account. I have had my card with me at all times, and it is not lost or stolen.

Please remove this incorrect charge from my credit account. If you have any questions about this dispute, please call me at 716-555-0134.

Sincerely,

Joy B. Adams

Joy B. Adams

Enclosure: Credit Statement

Methods for Settling Credit Disputes

A consumer may have trouble settling a dispute with a creditor. Rather than give up, the consumer can seek alternative dispute resolution. If that method does not settle the dispute, the consumer might file a lawsuit.

Alternative Dispute Resolution

alternative dispute resolution (ADR) a method of settling a dispute using a neutral third party

Alternative dispute resolution (ADR) is a method of settling a dispute using a neutral third party. ADR is much less expensive than going to court. It is usually much faster also. Typical ADR processes include negotiation, mediation, and arbitration.

Whenever there is a dispute, negotiation is usually the first step in trying to resolve it. *Negotiation* is a process in which a neutral third person, a negotiator, assists two parties in reaching a compromise that is acceptable to both sides. During negotiation, both parties express their point of view and how they want to see the issue resolved. The negotiator guides the discussion and helps the parties reach a compromise. The compromise usually involves both sides giving and getting something in return.

When the parties cannot negotiate a settlement, the next level of ADR is called mediation. *Mediation* is a non-binding dispute resolution method in which an independent third person, a mediator, helps the parties to reach a voluntary settlement. The mediator usually works with both sides separately. However, if the parties seem able to do so, the mediator may allow them to speak to each other. The mediator listens and helps both sides sort out the issue. The mediator proposes a solution and, if the parties agree, prepares a settlement document for the parties to sign.

Arbitration, the highest level of ADR, involves an independent third person, an arbitrator, who is a legal authority appointed to help resolve a dispute. Arbitrators have subject matter expertise, which means they have a legal or professional background related to the issue involved. Arbitration may be voluntary or binding. With *voluntary arbitration*, the arbitrator listens to both sides and makes a recommendation but cannot impose it. Both parties are free to accept or reject it. With *binding arbitration*, the arbitrator makes a decision that is binding on both parties. The parties must agree before arbitration begins that they will accept the decision as final.

Marcin Balcerzak/Shutterstock.com

What are the benefits of alternative dispute resolution?

Filing a Lawsuit

When attempts to resolve a dispute have failed, a consumer may decide to take the matter to court. The amount of the dispute will determine which type of court hears your case.

SUCCESS SKILLS

DEALING WITH DIFFICULT PEOPLE

At some point in your life, you will most likely find yourself in a situation in which someone is causing conflict or problems. This may occur at school, at work, or at home.

Dealing with people in difficult situations starts with focusing on the person causing the conflict. First, consider who the person is. If the person creating the problem is someone you do not have to see or deal with beyond the current situation, the best option may be simply to ignore the person's negative comments or bad behavior. However, if the person is someone you see on a regular basis, such as a classmate, coworker, or neighbor, you may have no choice but to deal with the person. Although it may not be comfortable, bringing the situation to the forefront and dealing with it is often the best way to resolve it. Use the following techniques to address the situation:

- Deal with the issues head-on. This is a good way to keep the problem from getting worse.
- Meet the person in a private setting to discuss the issues.
- Stop and think before you say anything. Don't let your emotions get the best of you.

- Ask the person to explain his or her position or situation.
- Listen to what the person is saying, and repeat the concerns.
- Ask for suggestions about how the problem could be resolved.
- Talk to others affected by the behavior. Find out what changes they would like to see.

There may be times where you cannot resolve a problem alone. In this case, you may have to use alternative dispute resolution (ADR) techniques. Unfortunately, difficult situations and people can sometimes lead to lawsuits. In all cases, it's important to know your options for resolving conflict.

Think Critically

Describe a situation where you had to deal with a difficult person. How did you handle it? Did you and the other person feel that it was resolved fairly? What could you have done differently? What will you do the next time a similar situation arises? What did you learn from the experience?

A *small claims court* is a court of limited jurisdiction that resolves cases involving small amounts (usually less than $5,000). Attorneys are typically not allowed in small claims court. Also, there is no jury; a judge decides the matter. Small claims courts are easy to use. The *plaintiff* files a document called a *complaint*, which outlines the issues of the case. The complaint is served on the *defendant*. If the defendant disagrees with the complaint, the court sets a hearing date. At the hearing, the plaintiff presents his or her side of the case, and the defendant does the same. After hearing the arguments from both sides, the judge proclaims a judgment. This process usually takes from a few weeks to a few months.

For larger dollar amounts, regular trial courts settle disputes. Attorneys represent each side. The first step is hiring an attorney to represent you. The attorney will try to negotiate a settlement for you. If that fails, a lawsuit is filed. When a case goes to trial, the judge or jury will make a decision (called the *verdict*). If you win the lawsuit, you get a judgment against the defendant. This process often takes many months. It may also cost hundreds or thousands of dollars in attorneys' fees.

>>> **CHECKPOINT**

What should you do if you find an error on your credit card statement?

LO 9-1.3 How Can You Protect Yourself Against Credit Fraud and Scams?

Every year, millions of American consumers lose money to credit fraud and scams. They can drain your finances and hurt your credit. There are warning signs to look for and actions you can take to avoid becoming a victim.

Credit Card Fraud

You may have improper charges made to your credit accounts. When someone intentionally uses your credit account to steal money or goods, this is a crime called **credit card fraud**.

credit card fraud intentionally using someone's credit account to steal money or goods

Thieves steal credit card information in numerous ways. The most common way is by using a lost or stolen credit card. Thieves also use skimming devices to steal credit card information. When the credit card is run through a skimmer, the device stores the credit card information. Skimming often occurs at retail stores, restaurants, and gas stations, where cardholders let their cards out of their sight. Credit card information can also be stolen from your mail or discarded trash as thieves sort through it to get copies of credit card statements.

The Internet has opened a whole new avenue for thieves to steal credit card information. The most common way is by hacking unsecure websites and stealing the financial data stored on those sites. Thieves also use phishing scams (discussed in Chapter 4) and *spam*, or junk email, to trick consumers into supplying their credit card information.

If you are a victim of credit card fraud, notify the creditor as soon as possible. Take steps such as the following to help prevent credit card fraud:

- Carry only the cards you need.
- Keep a list of your credit card numbers, their expiration dates, and the phone number and address of each card issuer in a safe place.
- Notify creditors immediately if your card is lost or stolen.
- Verify purchases and account balances when you receive a statement.
- Tear up old receipts and statements containing your account numbers when you no longer need them.
- Do not lend your credit card to others.
- Destroy expired cards by cutting them up.
- Do not give out any credit card information over the phone or online to people or businesses you don't know. Be sure businesses are reputable.
- When shopping online, verify website security. A secure website's URL starts with https:// rather than http://. Secure websites also have a small lock icon in the address bar or somewhere in the window of the browser.

- Don't store your credit card information on the merchant's website. Although this makes shopping faster and easier, your credit card information could be at risk if the company experiences a data breach.
- Monitor your credit activity. You may be able to monitor your credit activity yourself online, or you may consider enrolling in a *credit protection service*, which is a plan that provides credit monitoring for a fee. The service will notify you of any changes to your credit file and send you an alert if any change or suspicious activity occurs.
- Check your credit report regularly. Consumers have the right to one free copy of their credit reports from each the three major credit bureaus annually.

Identity Theft

According to the U.S. government, identity theft is one of the fastest-growing crimes in the United States. **Identity theft** occurs when someone uses your personal information without your permission to commit fraud or other crimes. A thief may use your Social Security number, bank account numbers, and credit card numbers to make purchases, take out loans, and apply for new credit accounts. He or she may even take a job and file tax returns using your name and personal data.

Only certain businesses have the right to your Social Security number, including motor vehicle departments, tax departments, and businesses that report income, such as banks and employers. If you are asked for your Social Security number by any other person or business, ask why it is needed and what law requires you to give your number.

Identity theft using someone's personal information without his or her permission to commit fraud or other crimes

Why do consumers need to guard against identity theft?

If you find you are a victim of identity theft or credit card fraud, take the following steps quickly:

1. *Close or freeze your credit account(s).* Call the fraud department of your credit issuer and explain that someone has stolen your identity. Ask to have your account closed or frozen. Change your log-in, password, and personal identification number (PIN).
2. *Have a fraud alert placed on your credit reports.* Contact the credit bureaus about a fraud alert. This can help stop someone from opening a credit account in your name.

3. *File a complaint with the Federal Trade Commission (FTC).* Its complaint form is available online. Based on the information you provide, the FTC will create an Identity Theft Affidavit. Print a copy of the affidavit and keep it for your records.
4. *File a report with your local police.* Call the police department and ask to fill out a police report for identity theft. Obtain a copy of the report. Your police report, along with your Identity Theft Affidavit, will entitle you to certain protections, such as ensuring that debts will not reappear on your credit report.
5. *Contact other government agencies.* The agencies that issued your identification documents, such as a driver's license, need to be informed so you can get a replacement document. Ask the agency to place an alert in your file so that another person cannot get an identification document in your name. You should also file a report with the Social Security Administration to have an alert placed in your file.

Credit Repair Scams

credit repair a scam in which a company claims to be able to "fix" your poor credit record and give you a clean credit history—for a price

Credit repair scams take advantage of consumers who want to improve their credit rating. With **credit repair**, a company claims to be able to "fix" your poor credit record and give you a clean credit history—for a price. However, the services these companies offer are nothing more than what you can do for yourself—for free. Many of the claims these companies make are false. Regardless of what they say, these companies cannot remove accurate information regarding overdue or unpaid bills from your credit report. They cannot change your credit score. Any advice they give is already available to you free of charge from various government and nonprofit agencies.

Beware of credit repair offers that do the following:

- *Require you to pay a fee before the company performs any service.* It is illegal for credit repair companies to charge you before they have performed any services.
- *Fail to explain your legal rights.* Credit repair companies are required by law to explain your legal rights in a written contract. The contract must also detail the services they will perform and the total cost.
- *Suggest that you create a "new credit identity."* Companies that promise you a "new credit identity" often will provide you with a nine-digit number, called a credit profile number (CPN) that looks like a Social Security number, or they may direct you to apply for an employer identification number (EIN) from the IRS. However, it is illegal to use these numbers to apply for new credit or to default on previous loans.
- *Recommend that you not contact the creditors yourself.* Actually, the opposite is true. You should contact creditors yourself when you are having debt problems to try to work out a new payment arrangement.

>>> **CHECKPOINT**
Why is credit repair considered a scam?

9-1 Lesson Assessment

KEY TERMS REVIEW

Match the terms with the definitions. Some terms may not be used.

_____ 1. Failure to pay debts as required by agreement or by law

_____ 2. Records that support your claim

_____ 3. A new loan arrangement that allows you to make reduced payments, usually on a temporary basis

_____ 4. A letter written to inform a credit company of an incorrect charge on your account

_____ 5. A legal process that allows part of an employee's paycheck to be withheld for payment of a debt

_____ 6. The process of informing a credit company of an error on your bill

_____ 7. The act of taking an asset used as collateral and selling it to pay the debt

_____ 8. A method of settling a dispute using a neutral third party

a. alternative dispute resolution (ADR)

b. credit card fraud

c. credit delinquency

d. credit repair

e. dispute letter

f. disputing a charge

g. documentation

h. foreclosure

i. garnishment

j. identity theft

k. loan modification

l. repossession

_____ 9. The legal process of taking possession of a house (property) when a borrower does not make mortgage payments as agreed

CHECK YOUR UNDERSTANDING

10. What are three warning signs that indicate debt has become a problem?

11. What should you do if you cannot meet your debt obligations?

12. What is a collection agency? Why might your credit account be turned over to a collection agency?

13. If one of your creditors obtains a legal garnishment order against you, what is likely to occur?

14. Explain how to dispute an error on your credit statement.

15. What should be included in the body of a dispute letter?

16. What are three ADR processes?

17. Explain the process of filing a lawsuit in small claims court.

18. What are some ways that you can protect yourself from credit card fraud when shopping online?

THINK CRITICALLY

19. Why should you try to work out alternate arrangements with creditors? If you can't pay, why not just stop making payments?

20. Why is it a bad idea to have a credit delinquency and to allow it to reach the point of being turned over to a collection agency?

21. Why should the tone of a dispute letter be firm, but not angry?

22. Why is it important to keep good records, especially sales receipts, when you purchase products and services on credit?

23. Explain how each of the three ADR processes (negotiation, mediation, and arbitration) work.

24. Why is filing a lawsuit your last step in settling a dispute with a creditor?

25. Do you think the costs associated with credit repair services are justified? Explain your answers.

26. Why is identity theft one of the fastest-growing crimes in the United States? Explain how thieves are able to get consumers' credit card information in order to commit fraud.

EXTEND YOUR LEARNING

27. Write a few sentences for each situation below, explaining what you would do to resolve it. Be sure to include any outside source of information or support you would seek.

    a. You tried to use your credit card, and it was rejected. When you called your credit card company, you were told that your balance is over the limit. You have not used your card recently, and based on your latest statement information, there should be well over $1,000 worth of credit available on it. What should you do?

    b. A representative from your bank called and told you about a special offer. You will receive a free safe deposit box and a $50 gift if you open a money market account. You verified your personal information with the caller. After the call, you phoned the bank to ask a question about the deal, but you found that no one at your bank knew anything about such an offer. What should you do?

    c. You took your car to have the brakes replaced. When the mechanic did the job, he also found that your muffler needed replacing. You authorized him to do the work and paid the bill with your credit card. After you got home, you noticed another bill showing that your spouse had the muffler replaced two weeks earlier. What should you do?

THE ESSENTIAL QUESTION   Refer to The Essential Question on p. 280. Credit use can result in too much debt, which can lead to credit delinquency, garnishment, repossession, or foreclosure. Credit use also opens up risks such as credit card fraud and identity theft. To resolve credit problems, you may need to take part in alternative dispute resolution or even a lawsuit.

THE ESSENTIAL QUESTION   Why might you consider bankruptcy, and what other debt relief options do you have?

LEARNING OBJECTIVES

LO 9-2.1 Explain the reasons for and purposes of bankruptcy, and list and describe types of bankruptcy.

LO 9-2.2 List strategies for avoiding bankruptcy.

KEY TERMS

- bankruptcy, 291
- bankruptcy fraud, 291
- Chapter 7 bankruptcy, 292
- discharge, 292
- exemption, 292
- Chapter 13 bankruptcy, 293
- Chapter 11 bankruptcy, 294
- credit counseling, 294
- debt settlement program, 295
- debt consolidation, 295
- equity loan, 295

LO 9-2.1 What Is Bankruptcy?

Credit that is used wisely can be a valuable tool in reaching financial goals. When credit is not used wisely, however, the consumer may build debt to the point that it can never be repaid. **Bankruptcy** is a legal procedure to relieve a person of excessive debt. Bankruptcy is granted by a federal court.

Bankruptcy petitions may be voluntary or involuntary. In a *voluntary bankruptcy*, the debtor files a petition with the court asking to be declared bankrupt. Creditors can also petition the court to force a debtor into bankruptcy. This situation is called *involuntary bankruptcy*.

Generally, bankruptcy should be a last resort. However, there are cases where people may be forced to declare bankruptcy or where bankruptcy is the only practical choice. Some common reasons why people seek bankruptcy include the following:

- Excessive medical bills (even with insurance coverage)
- Small business failure
- Poor financial planning (overspending, unwise use of credit)
- Losing employment and being overextended
- Having no savings or emergency fund to access when unexpected events (losses) occur

Bankruptcy Laws

There are two purposes of bankruptcy law. One purpose is to protect debtors and give them a "fresh start." A fresh start is needed when bills are so high that they could never be repaid. Bankruptcy laws are in place to help people in hopeless situations get back on their feet. The second purpose is to ensure fair treatment for creditors.

Bankruptcy fraud is the abuse of bankruptcy laws in a way that favors the debtor and defrauds creditors. People who do not reveal or who try to hide assets from the bankruptcy court are committing bankruptcy fraud. For example, it is illegal to transfer money or other assets

bankruptcy a legal procedure to relieve a person of excessive debt

bankruptcy fraud the abuse of bankruptcy laws in a way that favors the debtor and defrauds creditors

to someone else so that the assets cannot be located. Assets must be disclosed so that creditors can receive a fair share of the debt repaid. Creating debts with the intent of denying creditors payment for goods and services is also illegal and unethical.

If the court suspects that a person is committing bankruptcy fraud, it may dismiss the bankruptcy case and prosecute for fraud. Bankruptcy fraud is a serious federal crime that can carry large fines and prison time.

Types of Bankruptcy

There are three common types of bankruptcy: Chapter 7, Chapter 13, and Chapter 11. Chapter 7 bankruptcy and Chapter 13 bankruptcy are for individuals; Chapter 11 bankruptcy is for business owners. Depending on the type of bankruptcy granted, all debt may be erased, or a plan may be adopted to pay back some of the debt over a set period of time. With all three forms of bankruptcy, the debtor has an *automatic stay*, which provides immediate protection from any further action by creditors, including collection of debts.

Chapter 7 Bankruptcy

Chapter 7 bankruptcy the forfeiture of an individual's assets in exchange for the discharge of debts

discharge a court order that pardons the debtor from having to pay debts

exemption property that a debtor in bankruptcy does not have to forfeit to pay off creditors

Also known as *straight bankruptcy* or *liquidation bankruptcy*, **Chapter 7 bankruptcy** involves the forfeiture of an individual's assets in exchange for the discharge of debts. A **discharge** is a court order that pardons the debtor from having to pay debts. The debtor's assets are sold (liquidated), and the money is used to repay as much of the debt as possible. Then all remaining debts (with a few exceptions) are discharged.

Most debts can be discharged. This includes credit card balances, bank loans, medical bills, and court judgments. There are some types of debt, however, that are not discharged by bankruptcy, such as income tax debt, student loans, government fines for criminal charges, child support, and alimony.

While Chapter 7 bankruptcy requires debtors to give up most of their assets to erase their debts, debtors may keep certain amounts and types of property based on certain exemptions. An **exemption** is property that a debtor in bankruptcy does not have to forfeit to pay off creditors. Exemptions typically include assets considered necessary for survival. Federal bankruptcy exemptions include a limited amount of equity in a residence, interest in a vehicle, personal property and furnishings, clothing, some jewelry, and tools of a trade, including books and equipment. The amounts for these exemptions are adjusted by the federal government every three years. In addition to federal bankruptcy exemptions, some states have their own unique set of bankruptcy exemptions.

auremar/Shutterstock.com

Why does bankruptcy law allow exemptions for certain property, such as tools of trade?

Building COMMUNICATION SKILLS

PERSUASIVE SPEAKING

When the focus of public speaking is to convince people to take action or to support an idea or position, it is called *persuasive speaking*. For example, people who run for public office engage in persuasive speaking.

To be effective, persuasive speeches should be relevant, interesting, and decisive. The speaker must be believable and capture the listeners' attention as information and logical conclusions are presented. Persuasive speaking is challenging because you may have people in the audience who are biased against your ideas or position, and you must change their minds in order to gain their support.

When writing a persuasive speech, open with remarks that will get the attention of the audience. Clearly state the position or action you want the listeners to support. The main body of your speech should provide the audience with several convincing reasons to support your viewpoint. Provide supporting data or quotes from credible sources that will strengthen your position. You may also want to address the counterargument or any opposing views. This gives you the chance to address any possible negative reactions, objections, or questions the audience may have. Conclude your speech with a call to action.

The next time you hear a campaign speech, listen carefully to what is being said. Also listen to the techniques used in presenting the speech. How did the person get your attention? What problems were discussed? What solutions were proposed? Was the speaker believable? Apply the techniques that you think were effective to your next speech.

Try It Out

Prepare a 10- to 15-minute persuasive speech about a credit practice that you believe is unfair and needs to be changed. List at least one important point you wish to make. It should convince people to do or not to do something. Conduct research, prepare an outline, and practice your speech. After giving your speech to the class, evaluate your effectiveness. How did the audience react to your speech?

Bankruptcy laws passed in 2005 have made it more difficult for a person to file for Chapter 7 bankruptcy. To qualify for Chapter 7, the debtor has to get credit counseling six months before filing and satisfy a *means test*. This test requires the debtor to confirm that his or her income does not exceed a certain amount. It prevents people with high incomes from filing for Chapter 7. The amount varies by state. In addition, the debtor also has to complete a debtor education course before debts can be discharged.

Chapter 13 Bankruptcy

Also known as *individual debt adjustment* or *reorganization bankruptcy*, **Chapter 13 bankruptcy** involves a repayment plan for some of an individual's debt. Rather than liquidate assets, Chapter 13 bankruptcy allows debtors to follow a court-approved plan to pay back as much debt as they can over a three- to five-year period. After that time, the remaining balances on debts are discharged if all the payments were made as specified in the plan.

Chapter 13 bankruptcy is designed for debtors who have a good source of steady income. It is used mostly by homeowners and working people. In addition, debtors who do not qualify for Chapter 7 bankruptcy may file for Chapter 13 bankruptcy.

Chapter 13 bankruptcy a repayment plan for some of an individual's debt

Chapter 13 bankruptcy forces creditors to stop interest and late penalties. While a Chapter 13 plan is in effect, creditors cannot start or continue collection efforts. They must accept what the bankruptcy court decides will be their settlement. In some cases, creditors who have made *unsecured loans* (loans without collateral) receive no more than 10 to 30 percent of the amount owed to them.

Chapter 11 Bankruptcy

Chapter 11 bankruptcy is a reorganization form of bankruptcy for businesses that allows them to retain possession of their assets and continue operating under court supervision as they repay their restructured debts. The purpose of Chapter 11 bankruptcy is to make sure that the business can remain viable after the bankruptcy proceeding.

Chapter 11 bankruptcy is most often associated with large corporations. However, it can be used by small businesses. In rare cases, individuals can file Chapter 11 bankruptcy. For example, wealthy individuals who have a number of investment properties may have debts that are too high to qualify for Chapter 13 but do qualify for Chapter 11.

Chapter 11 bankruptcy a reorganization form of bankruptcy for businesses that allows them to retain possession of their assets and continue operating under court supervision as they repay their restructured debts

CHECKPOINT

When might bankruptcy be your best option?

LO 9-2.2 How Can Bankruptcy Be Avoided?

Consumers should try to avoid bankruptcy if possible. Bankruptcy damages a person's credit rating. It stays on the credit record for up to ten years. It prevents the consumer from getting low interest rates on credit accounts or loans. Bankruptcy can make it difficult to obtain credit, buy a home, or even get a job. Thus, it pays to try to find other ways to solve debt problems. Be sure to research any organizations you might use to verify they are reputable.

Credit Counseling

credit counseling a service to help consumers manage credit and avoid bankruptcy

Credit counseling is a service to help consumers manage credit and avoid bankruptcy. Credit counseling is typically free and is available through nonprofit and government-sponsored organizations and other groups. Credit counselors are certified and trained in consumer credit, money and debt management, and budgeting. They discuss your entire financial situation with you, including your income, expenses, debt, and goals, and help you develop a personalized budget plan.

When your financial situation is serious and needs immediate action, your credit counselor may suggest you enroll in a debt management plan. With a *debt management plan*, you make a single monthly payment to a credit counseling organization that distributes the funds to creditors based on a payment schedule. The organization uses your money to pay your unsecured debts (such as credit cards) according to the payment plan that the counselor develops with you and your creditors. Typically, the counselors are able to negotiate with the creditors to get lower interest rates and to waive fees. While the debt management plan is in effect, you must agree not to use credit.

Debt Settlement

In a **debt settlement program**, a company negotiates with your creditors on your behalf to reduce the amount of debt you owe. This type of program is not the same as credit counseling or a debt management plan in that it is typically offered by a for-profit company, meaning the services are not free. The company usually requires you to make monthly payments into an account administered by a third party. When enough money has accumulated, the company then pays off the negotiated amount of debt to the creditors in one lump sum.

How can credit counseling help you avoid bankruptcy?

debt settlement program a type of debt relief service in which a company negotiates with your creditors on your behalf to reduce the amount of debt you owe

There are many risks associated with a debt settlement program. First, many of these companies charge high fees for their services. Also, they may make promises or guarantees they cannot keep (such as reducing your debts by 50 percent or more). In addition, your creditors have no obligation to agree to negotiate a settlement of the amount you owe. Therefore, there is a possibility that the company will not be able to settle some of your debts, even if you pay the required monthly payments to the company.

Debt Consolidation

Debt consolidation is the process of getting one loan with a single monthly payment to pay off all of your debts. The single payment is usually much less than the total of the minimum payments on a number of loans or debts.

debt consolidation the process of getting one loan with a single monthly payment to pay off all of your debts

Consolidation loans are available through banks and other financial institutions. There are finance companies that specialize in consolidation loans to pay off credit card debt. Many debt consolidation loans require collateral to secure the loan. If you have equity in your home, your debt consolidation might take the form of an equity loan. An **equity loan** is a second mortgage or debt secured with the equity in your home. For example, if your house is valued at $150,000 and your mortgage is $120,000, then you have equity of $30,000. This amount could be borrowed to pay off high-interest credit cards and accounts. The interest rate is generally much lower, making the payments more affordable. You should know, however, that failure to pay the second mortgage can result in losing your home to foreclosure.

equity loan a second mortgage or debt secured with the equity in your home

⟩⟩ CHECKPOINT

Why is it best to avoid filing for bankruptcy?

KEY TERMS REVIEW

Match the terms with the definitions. Some terms may not be used.

_____ 1. The abuse of bankruptcy laws in a way that favors the debtor and defrauds creditors

_____ 2. The process of getting one loan with a single monthly payment to pay off all of your debts

_____ 3. Property that a debtor in bankruptcy does not have to forfeit to pay off creditors

_____ 4. A legal procedure to relieve a person of excessive debt

_____ 5. A court order that pardons the debtor from having to pay debts

_____ 6. A repayment plan for some of an individual's debt

_____ 7. A service to help consumers manage credit and avoid bankruptcy

_____ 8. A second mortgage or debt secured with the equity in your home

_____ 9. The forfeiture of an individual's assets in exchange for the discharge of debts

a. bankruptcy

b. bankruptcy fraud

c. Chapter 7 bankruptcy

d. Chapter 11 bankruptcy

e. Chapter 13 bankruptcy

f. credit counseling

g. debt consolidation

h. debt settlement program

i. discharge

j. equity loan

k. exemption

CHECK YOUR UNDERSTANDING

10. Provide three common reasons why people seek bankruptcy.

11. How is voluntary bankruptcy different from involuntary bankruptcy?

12. What are the two purposes of bankruptcy law?

13. What is meant by bankruptcy fraud? Give two examples of bankruptcy fraud.

14. When filing for bankruptcy, what does it mean to receive an automatic stay?

15. What is a means test? Explain how it applies to bankruptcy.

16. How is Chapter 11 bankruptcy different from Chapter 13 bankruptcy?

17. How is a debt settlement program different from a debt management plan?

18. What can happen if you are unable to pay back an equity loan?

THINK CRITICALLY

19. Why should some people consider bankruptcy rather than trying to pay off their debts? Give examples.

20. Why would a business or other lender want to force another person (debtor) into involuntary bankruptcy? What is the purpose of involuntary bankruptcy?

21. What is the major advantage of Chapter 7 bankruptcy? What is the major disadvantage?

22. Why do bankruptcy laws require credit counseling before a person can declare bankruptcy?

23. Why would you choose Chapter 13 over Chapter 7 bankruptcy?

24. Why would businesses (large and small) choose Chapter 11 bankruptcy?

25. Explain why enrolling in a debt management plan may be the best option for many consumers who wish to avoid bankruptcy. What do they gain?

EXTEND YOUR LEARNING

26. When consumers have serious problems making payments and managing their debt, they may seek advice. Some credit counseling agencies offer free advice; others charge a fee. In some cases, bankruptcy may be the only course available. Consumers may seek legal advice in filing for bankruptcy. Some bankruptcy lawyers will give an initial consultation that is free. During this free session, the client explains her or his situation, and the attorney evaluates the options.

    a. Visit the U.S. Trustee Program website (www.justice.gov/ust) to find a list of approved credit counseling agencies. You can also search the Web using the term *approved credit counseling agencies*. List the names and addresses of three credit counseling agencies that are approved for residents of your state.

    b. List three services provided by the credit counseling agencies.

    c. Conduct an online search using the term *bankruptcy attorney*. Provide the names of three bankruptcy attorneys in your local area.

    d. Review each of the attorney's websites, and answer the following questions: What types of claims do these attorneys make about bankruptcy? What kinds of fees do they charge? Is there a free initial consultation? What other kinds of information do the websites provide about bankruptcy?

THE ESSENTIAL QUESTION   Refer to The Essential Question on p. 291. You may consider bankruptcy when bills are so high they cannot be repaid. Other than declaring bankruptcy, you can receive credit counseling, enroll in a debt settlement program, or get a debt consolidation loan to help pay off debt.

9-3 Consumer Protection

THE ESSENTIAL QUESTION What protections are available to consumers who are having credit problems?

LEARNING OBJECTIVES

LO 9-3.1 Describe the purpose of consumer advocacy groups and government consumer protection agencies.

LO 9-3.2 List and explain consumer protection laws that are related to credit.

KEY TERMS

- consumer advocacy, 300
- Fair Credit Reporting Act, 301
- Truth in Lending Act, 302
- Fair Credit Billing Act, 302
- Fair Debt Collection Practices Act, 302
- Equal Credit Opportunity Act, 303
- Credit Card Accountability Responsibility and Disclosure Act, 303

LO 9-3.1 What Help Is Available to Consumers?

When you need help with a consumer problem, numerous organizations are available to assist you. These organizations are found at the federal, state, and local levels and also include consumer advocacy groups.

Federal Agencies

There are many federal agencies that protect and help consumers. Some of these agencies handle consumer complaints, and others direct complaints to agencies or sources that address consumer issues. All of these agencies maintain websites that offer an abundance of helpful information to consumers.

The U.S. government's official website (www.usa.gov) offers consumers a wealth of information. Hundreds of topics can be researched, including identity theft, fraud, scams, recalls, credit reports, and debt abuse. In addition, the website publishes the annual *Consumer Action Handbook*, which is a free resource that contains general information about your consumer rights. It also provides helpful consumer tips about shopping for goods and services, understanding credit, and filing complaints about a purchase. It includes a consumer assistance directory with contact information for consumer protection offices in government agencies. The *Consumer Action Handbook* can be downloaded and printed free of charge.

Federal Trade Commission

The Federal Trade Commission (FTC) regulates unfair methods of competition, false or deceptive advertising, deceptive product labeling, and the concealment of the true costs of credit. The FTC is also the federal clearinghouse for complaints of identity theft. The FTC's Bureau of Consumer Protection enforces federal consumer protection laws,

What kinds of information are available online to assist you with consumer-related problems?

helping to enhance consumer confidence. The Bureau also oversees the U.S. National Do Not Call Registry. More information about the FTC can be found at www.ftc.gov.

Consumer Financial Protection Bureau

The Consumer Financial Protection Bureau (CFPB) is an independent bureau within the Federal Reserve System that provides consumers with information to help them make good financial decisions. It is designed to assist and protect consumers from abusive practices in the financial services industry, including institutions that provide mortgages, credit cards, and other types of loans. At the website of the bureau (www.consumerfinance.gov), you can file complaints if you have issues with financial products or services; get questions answered; and access information to make comparisons among credit products and providers.

Federal Bureau of Investigation

The Federal Bureau of Investigation (FBI), which is part of the U.S. Department of Justice, is the nation's federal law enforcement organization. As part of its job duties, the FBI investigates various types of fraud (Internet fraud, bankruptcy fraud, mortgage fraud), identity theft, and other crimes. You can learn about current scams and get tips on how to avoid them on its website (www.fbi.gov).

State and Local Assistance

Most states have a consumer protection agency, or the state attorney general may handle consumer complaints. Many county and city governments also have consumer protection offices. Consumer leagues and public-interest research groups are also active at the state and local levels, with newsletters, pamphlets, handbooks, and websites on current consumer issues. City and county government offices and local offices of consumer groups can be found on the Internet and in the telephone book.

FOCUS On...

TELEMARKETING FRAUD

Although many legitimate companies solicit or contact consumers by telephone, there are also many con artists who use the telephone to commit telemarketing fraud. Most of the time, they are taking advantage of people's insecurity or willingness to believe that it's their lucky day, which is rarely the case.

Older people are often targeted. This is because they are at home, are more likely to have savings, and are often lonely and willing to talk to people. Some people find it difficult to hang up on others or to say "no," even when they really don't want the product or service.

To help protect yourself from telemarketing fraud, it's important to recognize the danger signs. These include the following:

- *Requests for personal information.* A fraudulent telemarketer may ask for personal information, such as a bank account number, credit card number, or Social Security number, for "identification" or "verification" that you won a prize. Never give this type of information to unsolicited callers.
- *Pressure to act immediately.* Many fraudulent telemarketers use a high-pressure sales approach, urging you to "act now" because the offer won't be available later.
- *Use of scare tactics.* Some telemarketers use scare tactics, such as impersonating bankers or government officials, to frighten people into sending money or providing financial information.

- *Demands to send money by a wire transfer or overnight delivery.* This is often used by fraudulent telemarketers to get your money before you change your mind.
- *Offers for something too good to be true.* Many fraudulent telemarketers make promises to do something, such as recover money or repair credit, in exchange for an upfront fee.
- *Refusal to send written information.* The caller may tell you that printed material is not available yet.

Consumers have rights when it comes to telemarketing. You can register your home phone and mobile phone numbers on the National Do Not Call Registry website (www.donotcall.gov) to stop most of these calls. You can report telemarketers who continue to call and violate your rights at the donotcall.gov website and at the National Consumers League's Fraud.org website (www.fraud.org).

If you do buy something from a telemarketer, always use a credit card. This way, you can dispute the charge if it turns out to be fraudulent.

Think Critically

1. Why are some consumers easy targets for telemarketing fraud?
2. Do you have a plan for dealing with callers who interrupt your time at home and try to sell you something you do not want? Explain.

Consumer Advocacy Groups

consumer advocacy the process of helping consumers resolve problems

The process of helping consumers resolve problems is called **consumer advocacy**. Consumer advocacy groups are mostly nonprofit organizations that promote consumer rights. They often provide information about laws related to consumer rights. Many of the groups actively work to get laws passed that will be beneficial to consumers. Some consumer advocacy groups focus on a single area, such as food safety. Other groups address a wide range of issues. Several of these groups deal with consumer issues related to using credit. Figure 9-3.1 provides a list of several nonprofit consumer advocacy groups.

The websites for these organizations provide valuable information for consumers. Some websites allow users to post complaints about company practices or fraud and read complaints posted by other consumers.

300   CHAPTER 9   Credit Problems and Laws

Better Business Bureau	Promotes responsible business practices in the marketplace to build trust between buyers and sellers
Consumer Action	Promotes consumer rights, publishes educational materials, and advocates for consumers in the media and before lawmakers
Consumer Federation of America	Works to advance pro-consumer policies on a variety of issues before state and federal legislatures, regulatory agencies, and the courts
Consumers Union	Provides advice about products and services in its publication *Consumer Reports*
National Consumers League	Operates Fraud.org (formerly the National Fraud Information Center) and addresses a wide range of issues in the marketplace
Public Citizen	Addresses issues such as the consumers' right to seek redress; clean and safe energy sources; and strong health, safety, and environmental laws

CHECKPOINT

What are three federal agencies that provide protection to consumers?

LO 9-3.2 What Consumer Credit Rights Are Protected by Law?

The federal government has passed a number of laws that protect consumers from unfair credit practices. These laws also outline consumer responsibilities. Each law is intended to remove some of the problems and confusion surrounding the use of credit.

Check Your Credit Report

The **Fair Credit Reporting Act** regulates the collection, dissemination, and use of consumer credit information. This act gives you the right to know what is in your credit report and entitles you to a free copy every 12 months from each of the three major credit bureaus (Equifax, Experian, and TransUnion). Annual Credit Report.com, which was created by the three major credit bureaus, is a centralized service for requesting your free annual credit reports. The act also gives you the right to know who has received your credit report in the last year (or two years for employment purposes). A credit bureau may not provide your credit report to an employer unless you give that employer written permission to make the request.

Fair Credit Reporting Act a law that regulates the collection, dissemination, and use of consumer credit information

You may see your credit report at no charge within 60 days of a credit denial. In addition, the act gives you the right to dispute inaccurate or incomplete information in your report. The credit bureau must correct or delete any inaccurate or incomplete information in your report within 30 days. If potentially damaging information in the file is correct, you can write a statement giving your side of the story to be added to the file, which must be made available to those who see your credit report.

Know the Cost of Credit

Truth in Lending Act a law that requires lenders to fully inform consumers about the cost of credit in a loan or credit agreement

The Consumer Credit Protection Act, better known as the **Truth in Lending Act**, requires lenders to fully inform consumers about the cost of credit in a loan or credit agreement. Before the agreement is signed, the following information must be given in writing:

- Description of the item being purchased
- Cash price of the item being purchased
- Down payment or trade-in price
- Amount financed
- Any service fees or other costs being added to the price
- Finance charge
- Annual percentage rate (APR)
- Deferred-payment price
- Amounts and dates of payments
- Method of computing finance charge in case of early payoff

The Truth in Lending Act requires that consumers be given a grace period of three days to change their minds about a credit agreement. The act also limits a person's liability to $50 after a credit card is reported lost or stolen. There is no liability when a card is reported lost prior to its illegal use.

Resolve Billing Errors

Fair Credit Billing Act a law that sets requirements for resolving billing disputes

The **Fair Credit Billing Act** sets requirements for resolving billing disputes. This law helps consumers resolve errors on their accounts in a timely manner. The law applies only to open-end credit, such as store or credit card accounts; it does not apply to installment loans.

You have 60 days from the day a bill is received to file a dispute. The creditor must acknowledge the complaint within 30 days. Then the creditor must either correct the error or show why the bill is correct within 90 days. You are not liable for the amount in dispute while the error is being investigated. However, you must still make payments on all other amounts.

All credit card companies must have billing error policies. They must tell their customers how to report errors. Figure 9-3.2 shows an error-correction policy for a credit card company.

Protect Against Debt Collection Practices

Fair Debt Collection Practices Act a law that protects consumers from abusive collection practices by creditors and collection agencies

The **Fair Debt Collection Practices Act** protects consumers from abusive collection practices by creditors and collection agencies. For example, threats, obscenities, and false and misleading statements to intimidate the consumer into paying are not allowed. It also restricts the time and frequency of collection practices, such as telephone calls, and restricts contacts at places of employment. Also, debt collectors are required to verify

In Case of Errors or Inquires About Your Bill

The Fair Credit Billing Act requires prompt resolution of errors. To preserve your rights, follow these steps:

1. Do not write on the bill. On a separate piece of paper, write a description as listed below. A telephone call will not preserve your rights.
   a. Your name and account number
   b. Description of the error and your explanation of why you believe there is an error (send copies of any receipts or supporting evidence you may have; do not send originals)
   c. The dollar amount of the suspected error
   d. Other information that might be helpful in resolving the disputed amount
2. Mail your letter as soon as possible. It must reach us within 60 days after you receive your bill.
3. We will acknowledge your letter within 30 days. Within 90 days of receiving your letter, we will correct the error or explain why we believe the bill is correct.
4. You will receive no collection letters or collection action regarding the amount in dispute, nor will it be reported to any credit bureau or collection agency.
5. You are still responsible for all other items on the bill and for the balance less the disputed amount.
6. You will not be charged a finance charge against the disputed amount unless it is determined that there is not an error in the bill. In this event, you will be given the normal 25 days to pay your bill from the date the bill is determined to be correct.

the accuracy of the bill and give the consumer the opportunity to dispute it. Any disputed amounts must be resolved before they can be collected.

Obtain Freedom from Discrimination

The **Equal Credit Opportunity Act** protects consumers from discrimination in the granting or denying of credit. *Discrimination* is the act of treating people differently based on prejudice rather than individual merit. The act makes it illegal to discriminate on the basis of the following factors:

- Gender
- Race
- Color
- Age
- Marital status
- Religion
- National origin

> **Equal Credit Opportunity Act** a law that protects consumers from discrimination in the granting or denying of credit

In addition, the act states that if you are denied credit, the denial must be in writing and list a specific reason for the denial. The law benefits consumers because factors other than the consumer's creditworthiness cannot be used when evaluating whether to grant credit.

Know Credit Card Practices

The **Credit Card Accountability Responsibility and Disclosure Act** (also known as the Credit CARD Act) is a comprehensive reform to credit card law to establish fair practices related to credit. It is designed to limit abusive practices by credit card companies and provide more protection to consumers.

> **Credit Card Accountability Responsibility and Disclosure Act** a comprehensive reform to credit card law to establish fair practices related to credit

Why do you think the Credit CARD Act has special credit provisions for those under the age of 21?

The act contains a number of provisions:

- Credit card issuers must give a 45-day written notice of any interest rate increase.
- Credit card issuers can no longer charge you a late fee greater than your minimum payment.
- Monthly credit card statements must include information on how long it will take you to pay off your balance if you make only minimum payments.
- Credit card issuers are required to mail your statement at least 21 days before your payment is due, and your monthly due date must be the same date each month.
- Double-cycle billing, or the practice of applying a finance charge on both the current balance and the previous month's balance, is prohibited.

Young consumers receive additional protection under the act. Credit card issuers must now verify proof of income or otherwise require a co-signer before issuing a credit card to someone under the age of 21. Also, credit card issuers cannot raise the credit limit for cardholders under the age of 21 who have a cosigner, unless the cosigner has given written permission to do so.

 CHECKPOINT

What are three federal laws that help protect consumers from unfair credit practices?

9-3 Lesson Assessment

KEY TERMS REVIEW

Match the terms with the definitions. Some terms may not be used.

_____ 1. A comprehensive reform to credit card law to establish fair practices related to credit

_____ 2. A law that protects consumers from discrimination in the granting or denying of credit

_____ 3. A law that regulates the collection, dissemination, and use of consumer credit information

_____ 4. A law that protects consumers from abusive practices by creditors and collection agencies

a. consumer advocacy

b. Credit Card Accountability Responsibility and Disclosure Act

c. Equal Credit Opportunity Act

d. Fair Credit Billing Act

e. Fair Credit Reporting Act

f. Fair Debt Collection Practices Act

g. Truth in Lending Act

_____ 5. A law that requires lenders to fully inform consumers about the cost of credit in a loan or credit agreement

_____ 6. A law that sets requirements for resolving billing disputes

CHECK YOUR UNDERSTANDING

7. What information is contained in the *Consumer Action Handbook*?

8. What duties does the FTC have regarding consumer protection?

9. Provide three examples of consumer advocacy groups.

10. How often can you see your credit report free of charge? What website can you use to get a free credit report?

11. List the basic provisions of the Truth in Lending Act.

12. Explain the procedures for resolving billing errors under the Fair Credit Billing Act.

13. List debt collection activities that were made illegal under the Fair Debt Collection Practices Act.

14. List the items that cannot be used as a basis for determining whether credit should be granted or denied.

15. Give three provisions of the Credit Card Act of 2009.

THINK CRITICALLY

16. How have consumers benefited from the creation of the Consumer Financial Protection Bureau (CFPB)?

17. How does a consumer advocacy group help consumers? What issues do you think are important for advocacy groups to understand and work on today?

18. Why is it important for consumers to report fraud to consumer advocacy groups and government assistance sources? In most cases, you don't get your money back, so why bother to report it?

19. Which of the provisions of the Credit CARD Act do you think is most important? Explain why.

20. Do you think it is fair that young consumers must now either have a job or have a cosigner to get credit? Explain your answer.

EXTEND YOUR LEARNING

TEAMWORK

ProStockStudio/Shutterstock.com

21. Working in a small group, select a consumer advocacy group from Figure 9-3.1 or another group approved by your teacher. Search the Internet or other sources to find information about this group. Write a summary of the information you find. Include the points listed below and other information you think would be helpful for consumers to know about the group. Give a short presentation or prepare a brochure about this group and include the following information:
    - The group's name
    - When the group was founded
    - The main activities or mission of the group
    - Services offered to consumers by the group
    - Publications or websites published by the group
    - How the group is organized (nonprofit or government-sponsored)

22. Visit the FTC's website and answer the following questions:
    a. What services are available to consumers?
    b. What is the process of filing a complaint?
    c. What are three types of scams discussed on the website? Provide a short description of a type of scam for each category.

THE ESSENTIAL QUESTION   Refer to The Essential Question on p. 298. You can protect yourself by seeking help from consumer protection agencies at the federal, state, and local levels, as well as from consumer advocacy groups. You can also protect yourself by knowing the various consumer protection laws and rights.

Exploring Careers in . . .
ARCHITECTURE

Architects are responsible for the design of various structures, from houses and office buildings to shopping malls and recreational facilities. They are concerned with creating structures that are visually appealing as well as safe, functional, sustainable, and durable.

Architects spend most of their time in an office. They meet with clients to discuss the objectives, requirements, and budget of a project; prepare construction plans and drawings; and also consult with other architects and engineers. They also visit building sites to ensure that contractors are following the design, keeping to the schedule, using the specified materials, and meeting work-quality standards.

Employment Outlook

- A faster than average rate of employment growth is expected.

Job Titles

- Architect
- Architectural engineer
- Architectural designer
- Commercial designer

Needed Education/Skills

- A five-year professional degree from a school accredited by the National Architectural Accrediting Board (NAAB) is required in most states.
- A passing grade on the Architect Registration Exam is required.
- Graduates must complete at least a three-year paid internship at an architectural firm before they can take the exam.
- Strong analytical, technical, and visualization skills are needed.

What's it like to work in . . . Architecture

Bill works for a local architectural firm. He was hired full-time last year after passing the Architect Registration Exam and spending the previous four years as a paid intern.

Most of Bill's time is spent in his office, which is equipped with computer-aided design and drafting (CADD) and building information modeling (BIM) technology for creating designs and drawings. He also spends time visiting worksites.

This morning, Bill is meeting with clients who are considering hiring the firm to design a new downtown office complex. Later in the day, Bill is driving to a construction site to review the progress of a shopping center that his firm was contracted to design.

What About You?

Are you highly skilled in computer technology? Do you have strong creativity and technical skills? Would a job in architecture appeal to you? If so, what types of structures would you like to design?

SUMMARY

9-1 Credit delinquencies can result in your assets being repossessed or foreclosed or your account being turned over to a collection agency.

To dispute a charge on a credit card statement, you should call and write a letter to the credit card company. If that doesn't work, alternative dispute resolution (ADR) and lawsuits are methods you can use to resolve credit disputes.

Identity theft occurs when someone uses your personal information without your permission to commit fraud or other crimes. Credit card fraud is a common form of identity theft.

9-2 Bankruptcy laws are designed to help people get a "fresh start" and to provide fair treatment to creditors competing for the debtor's assets.

In Chapter 7 bankruptcy, the debtor gives up property in exchange for having debts discharged. In Chapter 13 bankruptcy, debtors follow a court-approved plan to pay back as much debt as possible over a three- to five-year period. Chapter 11 bankruptcy is a reorganization form of bankruptcy for businesses that allows them to retain possession of assets and continue operating under court supervision as they repay their restructured debt.

Credit counseling, debt settlement programs, and debt consolidation are ways of avoiding bankruptcy.

9-3 Organizations at the federal, state, and local levels and consumer advocacy groups provide information, help, and protection for consumers.

The Fair Credit Reporting Act gives you the right to view your credit report and dispute inaccurate or incomplete information.

The Truth in Lending Act requires lenders to fully inform consumers about the cost of credit in a loan or credit agreement.

The Fair Credit Billing Act sets conditions for resolving billing disputes.

The Fair Debt Collection Practices Act protects consumers from abusive collection practices by creditors and collection agencies.

The Equal Credit Opportunity Act protects consumers from discrimination in the granting or denying of credit.

The Credit Card Accountability Responsibility and Disclosure Act (Credit CARD Act) is a comprehensive reform to credit card law to establish fair practices related to credit.

MAKE ACADEMIC CONNECTIONS

TEAMWORK

1. **Research** Work with two classmates to find out where or how you could file complaints in the situations described below. Review the information presented in this chapter and search the Internet if needed. (LO 9-3.1)
   a. You were the victim of a telemarketing scam. The caller offered to send you money if you provided your Social Security number and bank account number.
   b. You bought items from a business on the Internet. The company did not send the merchandise that was ordered.
   c. An investment scheme promised you a 50 percent return on your money in less than a year. You invested $1,000, and you have not heard from the company since.

2. **Business Law** Due to Marcia's overspending on extravagant items, she has credit card bills and loans that she cannot repay. She decides to file for Chapter 7 bankruptcy to relieve her of all of her debt. Her father recently died and left her a large inheritance including a large sum of money, his house, and many antiques. She plans to transfer all of these assets, along with other items she wants to keep, to another relative until her bankruptcy is final and then reclaim them afterward. Her overdue accounts were turned over to a collection agency. The collection agent has been calling Marcia three times a day, often during work and late in the evening. The agent has threatened to visit her at work if she doesn't pay her bills. What legal issues are evident in this situation? (LO 9-2.1, LO 9-3.2)

3. **Economics** The number of home foreclosures rises during poor economic times. Research the impact of foreclosures on communities and our economy. Prepare a one-page report. (LO 9-1.1)

4. **History** Look up the Bankruptcy Act of 1898 online. Write a two-page report covering the following: (a) events that led to the passage of the act, (b) how long the law was in effect, and (c) how it was different from subsequent bankruptcy laws. (LO 9-2.1)

5. **International Studies** Conduct online research and prepare a presentation about bankruptcy laws in another country. Compare them to the U.S. bankruptcy laws. Which do you think are more beneficial for consumers? Why? (LO 9-2.1)

6. **Research** Use the Internet to find articles about recent fraudulent credit scams aimed at unsuspecting consumers and businesses. Prepare a PowerPoint presentation or a role-play that describes one of the scams. Conclude the presentation or role-play with a list of tips on how to avoid the scam. (LO 9-1.3)

7. **Technology** Some people blame technology for the increase in identity theft because of the easy access to personal information provided by the Internet. Explore how technology is being used as a way to protect consumers from identity theft. Present your findings to the class in a five-minute presentation. (LO 9-1.3)

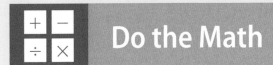

Do the Math

1. Rey Mercado has a house valued at $250,000. His mortgage is for $180,000. How much money can he borrow if the bank will lend 80 percent of the equity in the home?

2. Your credit card was stolen. You reported the theft within 24 hours. Before the theft was reported, the thief charged $2,450 at a jewelry store and $1,245 at an electronics store. How much of the fraudulent charges will you have to pay?

3. Jacki Marshall owes a balance of $5,000 on one credit card that charges 19 percent interest. She can pay off the balance in two years with monthly payments of $252.04. She has another credit card with a balance of $7,500 that charges 20 percent interest. She can pay off the balance in two years with monthly payments of $381.72. Jacki owns a home valued at $150,000. She can get a home equity loan for $12,500 at 8 percent interest. Jacki can repay the loan in two years with monthly payments of $565.34. How much money will Jacki save if she takes out a home equity loan to pay off the credit card balances?

Take Action

WRITE A LETTER DISPUTING A CHARGE

Upon checking your credit card statement, you see that you were charged $85 for the purchase of a pair of shoes at the Fancy Foot Shoe Outlet on May 8, 20—. You have a receipt that shows a $58 purchase at the Fancy Foot Shoe Outlet on that date. Using Figure 9-1.1 as a reference, write a dispute letter to the credit card company using the following guidelines:

a. Use your return address. Use May 12, 20—, as the letter date.

b. Use the following letter address and an appropriate salutation.

Credit Company

P.O. Box 87483

Wilmington, DE 19850-7483

c. Use a subject line that indicates you have a dispute on Account 2444 2344 2317 1111.

d. State that you are registering a dispute. Explain the problem, and ask for a credit of the extra amount charged on your statement. Indicate that you are enclosing a copy of the statement and a copy of your receipt.

e. Use an appropriate letter closing and your full name. Add an enclosure notation at the end of the letter.

After you finish writing the letter, proofread it carefully and correct any errors. Include a copy of the dispute letter in your portfolio.

Customer Loyalty Programs, Guarding Your Credit, and Debt Load

Shopping is big business in America. Retailers and restaurants work hard to earn your loyalty. They often provide incentives to get you into their store initially and to keep you returning. Incentives can be in several forms, including coupons, sales promotions, and loyalty programs. Loyalty programs provide incentives in the form of rewards for making frequent purchases. The loyalty programs encourage consumers to spend money at stores, and in turn, the stores are able to collect consumer behavior data from the purchases. The data is used by retailers to create highly targeted incentive programs. However, consumers need to beware of personalized offers they receive from retailers because they can blur the line between wants and needs. Consumers may end up spending more than they intended on items they don't really need. Getting a discount on excess spending doesn't provide any real benefit to a monthly budget. To understand the motivation of retailers and restaurants, complete the *Customer Loyalty Programs Worksheet*.

To protect your credit, you should understand how to guard yourself from credit card fraud and other forms of identity theft. You must take control over your own credit history, credit report, and credit score monitoring. The website of the Federal Reserve System answers questions consumers have about credit. Visit the site at www.federalreserve.gov and click on the "Consumer Information" link. Review the Fed's advice about guarding your credit and understanding your credit report and credit score. Being educated is an important step you can take to protect your credit now and in the future. Complete the *Guard Your Credit Worksheet* to help you identify the latest tips for safeguarding and managing credit.

Understanding your debt load will help you plan for your future. *Debt* represents future earnings already spent. Many people do not consider how much of their future income they have committed to past or current expenses. For example, most people need student loans to complete their post-secondary education plans. But the debt incurred through student loans can affect future spending. Your *debt load* is the amount of outstanding debt at any given point in time. Complete the *Debt Load Worksheet* to help you understand your feelings and expectations about debt. Planning finances to minimize or eliminate debt is an important personal financial strategy.

THINK CRITICALLY

1. What benefit do retailers and restaurants receive from customer loyalty programs?

2. What steps should you take to guard your credit for current and future uses?

3. Why is it important to try to minimize your debt?

UNIT 4

Saving and Investing

CHAPTER 10 Basics of Saving and Investing

CHAPTER 11 Saving and Investing Options

CHAPTER 12 Buying and Selling Investments

Unit 4 explains how to save and invest for the long term to achieve future financial security. Chapter 10 covers the basics of saving and investing, including reasons why you should set aside money for the future and how to meet your goals for retirement. It also discusses risk related to investing, as well as strategies for lowering risk and maximizing return.

Chapter 11 discusses the various low-risk, medium-risk, and high-risk savings and investing options. Remember, the more risk you are willing to take, the higher the return you can expect.

Chapter 12 focuses on buying and selling securities (stocks and bonds). It stresses the importance of doing research before you invest. You may need to seek competent and professional advice in order to make the best investment decisions. The chapter concludes with a discussion of the regulatory agencies and other sources of protection available to you as an individual investor.

Basics of Saving and Investing

Rido/Shutterstock.com

Saving and investing can help you accomplish short-term, intermediate, and long-term goals. Although some aspects of saving and investing overlap, there is a difference between the two. Savings can provide for your short-term needs and goals. Once you start setting aside money on a permanent basis, you will be in a position to make investments and grow your wealth. Through sustained saving and investing, you will be able to achieve your personal financial goals. Your plan should be based on solid principles of investing. Consider the risk involved and the amount you can expect to earn.

Do *This*, Not *That*

To maximize your savings and investing potential:

- Pay yourself first.
- Do not invest before considering the risks.
- Consult with a financial professional.
- Diversify your investments to offset losses.
- Track and monitor your savings and investments.

LEARNING OBJECTIVES

LO 10-1.1 Explain how saving and investing are related and how saving leads to investing and wealth.

LO 10-1.2 Describe how saving and investing help you achieve personal goals.

LO 10-1.3 Explain how investing prepares you for retirement and beyond.

KEY TERMS

- savings, 314
- investing, 314
- emergency fund, 314
- contingencies, 314
- liquidity, 315
- wealth, 315
- financial security, 316
- retirement, 318
- estate, 318
- foundation, 319

LO 10-1.1 How Are Saving and Investing Related?

savings money set aside for the future

Money set aside for the future is called **savings**. Another definition of savings is *deferred spending*. In other words, money not spent today allows for needs to be met in the future. Saving money is important because it means you are planning for future needs and wants.

When you are saving money, the emphasis is on *safety of principal*, which involves protecting the balance in your account. A savings account, a certificate of deposit, and a money market account, which are FDIC-insured, are all good, safe ways to save.

investing a strategy to earn more on your money than the rate of inflation

When savings accumulate above what you might need for short-term goals and emergencies, you have money that can be used for investing. **Investing** is a strategy to earn more on your money than the rate of inflation. Thus, the purpose of investing is to make your money grow. Investing is sometimes explained as using money to make more money. For example, you may use money to buy real estate, such as a house. You might also buy shares of stock in a corporation. Your hope is that the house and stocks will increase in value over the years that you own them. That way, you will have more money when you sell the investments than when you bought them. Saving and investing are related, because it is the setting aside of money (savings) that provides the funds that can be used for investing.

Savings Provide Security

emergency fund money set aside for unplanned expenses

When you set aside money, you have a reserve or emergency fund that you can count on. An **emergency fund** is an amount of money set aside for unplanned expenses. An emergency fund gives you a sense of security—knowing you can take care of contingencies should they arise.

contingencies unplanned or possible events

Contingencies are unplanned or possible events. For example, suppose you are driving home from work and a tire blows out. You need money to pay for a new tire, towing, or other related expenses. An emergency fund will provide for contingencies such as this. Experts recommend that you set aside three to six months' net pay in this fund.

Liquidity is a measure of how quickly an asset can be turned into cash. For example, a regular savings account is very liquid because you can withdraw your money at any time without penalty. Within your plan for financial security, it is important to have some liquid assets that are available to cover unexpected needs.

liquidity a measure of how quickly an asset can be turned into cash

wealth the accumulation of assets over your lifetime

Investments Provide Wealth

As investments continue growing, they lead to **wealth**, which is the accumulation of assets over your lifetime. Financial success grows from the assets that you build up over time.

There are a number of different investment choices. Even money left in a regular savings account or money market account for a long period can be considered a type of investment. However, the interest rate and the money earned on such accounts are typically low compared to other types of investment choices.

Most investments that are considered long-term, strategic choices are designed to stay ahead of inflation. When your investments are growing at a rate faster than the rate of inflation, you are accumulating wealth. When inflation is growing faster than your investments, your wealth is actually shrinking. It is important to make good investment choices that will lead to increased value over the long run.

With any investments, you have the potential for great gain. However, you do not know how much you will earn on the money you invest. You may even lose the money you invest. For example, with some investments, such as stocks, you may have temporary setbacks due to market conditions that are beyond your control. However, your gains from investments will typically exceed your losses over the 30- or 40-year period you will be investing money.

How can investments help you increase your wealth?

CHECKPOINT

How does saving lead to investing?

LO 10-1.2 How Can You Benefit from Saving and Investing?

Both saving and investing offer many benefits. Saving money is a *pay-yourself-first strategy* that helps you meet personal goals. It also reduces your dependence on using credit. Investing is a proven way to strengthen your financial position over time.

Meet Personal Goals

Short-term goals involve things you want to get done within the next few days, weeks, months, or year. For example, you may wish to attend a special event, such as a concert. Another short-term goal may involve planning for a vacation. Having a savings plan will enable you to cover costs such as hotel reservations and airline tickets.

Intermediate goals are those you want to accomplish in the next two to five years. Intermediate goals require more planning than short-term goals and often require more savings as well. An example of an intermediate goal for some people may be to get married. Weddings not only take a while to plan (sometimes up to a year or longer), but they can also be expensive. You will need money to pay for the ceremony, flowers, attire, photographer, reception, and so forth. Savings can help cover these expenses. Other examples of intermediate goals may include owning a car and going to college. Accomplishing these goals will require a financial plan that includes saving for down payments and earning income sufficient to make the monthly payments.

Saving and investing are also required in order to meet long-term goals. *Long-term goals* include those that you wish to accomplish more than five years from now. For example, many people want to own a home. You may need to save money for a few years in order to afford the down payment. People who plan to have children in the future also need to plan for the expenses involved in raising children. Housing, food, clothing, medical care, and child care are examples of expenses that parents must meet for at least 18 years. Planning for retirement is another long-term goal. All people need to think about investing for retirement to help pay for their living expenses when they are no longer working.

Build Financial Security

financial security the ability to meet current and future needs while living comfortably

Financial security should be one of your goals throughout life. **Financial security** is the ability to meet current and future needs while living comfortably. It means having enough resources so that you can have food, proper clothing, a safe and comfortable place to live, medical care, and other items that you need.

For most people, financial security is built on saving and investing over time. When you first begin working and living on your own, you may need to spend most of your earnings to cover current expenses. You can save and invest more as your career and income progress. As you save and invest, you can start to build the resources that will provide for your future security.

 **Looking Ahead**

Weddings can be a huge expense. A large wedding can cost $25,000 or more. This does not include the cost of a honeymoon. How much would your "dream wedding" cost? Make a guess. Then go online to find prices for typical wedding expenses. There are many online wedding calculators that can help you estimate these costs. Based on your research, what will your wedding cost you? How close was your guess? How much would you have to save each month to pay for your dream wedding, presuming that you have five years to save for it?

▶ FIGURE 10-1.1 **Personal and Financial Goals**

Personal Goal	Financial Goal	Benchmarks	Timeline
Short-Term Goals			
Camping trip next summer	Buy camping gear; buy supplies; pay for transportation	Save $50/month	6 months
Attend concert	Pay for ticket, hotel, food, and transportation	Save $75/month	4 months
Intermediate Goals			
Share wedding expenses	Pay half of expenses for reception hall, flowers, caterer, and photographer	Save $100/month	2 years
Own a car	Put a down payment on a new car	Save $100/month; invest at a safe rate	5 years
Long-Term Goals			
Own a house	Buy a house to meet family needs; need $50,000 down payment	Invest $500/month at growth rate to beat inflation	8 years
Add a swimming pool	Construct inground pool at new home	Invest $150/month at high rate of return	10 years

Being financially secure enables you to meet your personal goals. Once your basic needs are met, you can begin thinking about your short-term, intermediate, and long-term goals. By creating a financial plan that lists goals, benchmarks, and timelines (such as the one you learned about in Chapter 4), you can determine how you will save or invest to meet your goals. A sample financial plan is shown in Figure 10-1.1.

CHECKPOINT

What are the benefits of investing?

LO 10-1.3 How Does Investing Prepare You for Retirement and Beyond?

Most people need to plan for the time when they can stop working and start enjoying more leisure time. They will want to be able to live comfortably without worrying about how their bills will be paid. Many people also wish to plan their estates to make sure their finances are in order at the time of their death.

Retirement Planning

retirement a period of time, usually in later years, when you are not working and need to meet expenses through other income sources

Retirement is the period of time, usually in later years, when you are not working and need to meet expenses through other income sources. Sources of retirement income include personal retirement plans, such as individual retirement accounts (IRAs); employer-sponsored retirement plans, such as 401(k) plans; Social Security benefits; and savings and investments. Some costs, such as those related to working and a mortgage, are eliminated during retirement. Other costs, such as groceries and utilities, tend to stay the same or rise slightly. Some costs, such as medical care and prescriptions, tend to increase significantly.

Planning for retirement involves thinking about what you would like to do and how you would like to live after you are no longer working, and the amount of monthly income you will need to support this lifestyle. Retirement plans should also include how to pay for long-term medical care if it is needed.

You should begin planning for retirement even as you begin your first career. The sooner you begin investing, the longer your money will have to grow for your retirement. Figure 10-1.2 compares amounts invested at the same rate for varying amounts of time.

Estate Planning

estate all that a person owns (assets), minus debts owed, at the time of that person's death

An **estate** is all that a person owns (assets), minus debts owed, at the time of that person's death. Assets can include bank accounts, investments, property, and other items of value. Money that is not used for living expenses, travel, and leisure activities will add to one's estate. Life insurance proceeds are also part of the estate. When people die, their assets pass to other people. *Estate planning* is the process of preparing a plan for transferring property during one's lifetime and at one's death. The goal of estate planning is to make known how you want your possessions distributed and to provide for a smooth transfer of your possessions to your loved ones upon your death.

▶ FIGURE 10-1.2 **Investment Growth Over Time**

Amount Invested	Interest Rate	Investment Term	Maturity Value
$10,000 investment	6%	20 years	$32,071
$10,000 investment	6%	30 years	$57,435
$1,000 investment	8%	30 years	$10,063
$1,000 investment	8%	40 years	$21,725
$1,000 per year investment	5%	20 years	$33,066
$1,000 per year investment	5%	30 years	$66,439
$1,000 per year investment	5%	40 years	$120,800
$100 per month investment	7%	25 years	$81,007
$100 per month investment	7%	30 years	$121,997
$100 per month investment	7%	40 years	$262,481

HAVING A WILL AND HEALTH CARE DIRECTIVE

Estate planning often involves preparing a will. A *will* is a document that passes title of property after a person dies. For property held in joint names, you do not need a will. But if you have property in your name only, then a will lets you decide where the property goes at your death. If you die without a will, you are said to be *intestate*. In that event, your property will be distributed according to the laws of the state in which you live. Most states require that you reach the age of majority (18 in most states) in order to make a valid will.

In your will, you will name *heirs*, or people who will inherit your money and property. You will also name an *executor*, or person who will be in charge of carrying out your wishes when you die. When you die, your estate must go through probate. *Probate* is the legal process of proving that a deceased person's will is valid and then administering and distributing that person's estate upon death.

A *simple will* is a short document that lists the people whom you want to be your heirs and what you want each to receive. You can prepare a simple will yourself or with the help of an attorney. There are inexpensive "will kits" and will-writing software that are available for purchase online and at office supplies stores. A simple will can cost from a few hundred dollars to a thousand dollars or more.

A *holographic will* is written in a person's own handwriting. In some states, a holographic will is legally valid if it is entirely written in your handwriting, is dated and signed, and clearly expresses your intent to make it your will.

A *trust will* is a long and complicated document whereby you set up trusts as a way to leave your assets to your beneficiaries. Trusts are generally preferred when children are young and a legal guardian needs to be appointed to care for them and their inheritance. Trust wills typically cost several thousand dollars and must be prepared by attorneys and tax advisers.

In addition to a will, many people also design and sign a *health care directive*. Also called a *living will*, this document describes your wishes at the end of your life. It specifies the type of effort you would want taken in the event you will not recover from an injury or illness. It should also state your preferences in the event some of your organs can be recovered and used to help others. It's important to appoint someone to make these decisions for you. If there is no such document or person appointed, health care workers will preserve life and will not terminate life support, even if you cannot recover.

Think Critically

1. If you were to write a simple will, whom would you list as your heirs?
2. What type of health care directive would you prefer to have? Are you, or would you like to be, an organ donor?
3. What may happen if a person dies intestate and there are many potential heirs for his or her estate?

In addition to leaving possessions to loved ones, many people designate a portion of their estate for philanthropic causes. They make allowances for donations to their favorite charity, university, and/or church. They may request that money go toward the establishment of a foundation. A **foundation** is a fund or an organization established and maintained for the purpose of supporting an institution or a cause. Foundations usually seek to help others, achieve a social objective, and/or enrich the community. They support specific activities, such as education, research, veterans' benefits, or cultural literacy.

foundation a fund or an organization established and maintained for the purpose of supporting an institution or a cause

▶▶▶ CHECKPOINT

How do living expenses tend to change for retirees?

10-1 Lesson Assessment

KEY TERMS REVIEW

Match the terms with the definitions. Some terms may not be used.

_____ 1. A measure of how quickly an asset can be turned into cash

_____ 2. A fund or an organization established and maintained for the purpose of supporting an institution or a cause

_____ 3. The accumulation of assets over your lifetime

_____ 4. Unplanned or possible events

_____ 5. Money set aside for the future

_____ 6. A period of time, usually in later years, when you are not working but are able to meet expenses through other income sources

_____ 7. A strategy to earn more on your money than the rate of inflation

_____ 8. The ability to meet current and future needs while living comfortably

_____ 9. Money set aside for unplanned expenses

a. contingencies

b. emergency fund

c. estate

d. financial security

e. foundation

f. investing

g. liquidity

h. retirement

i. savings

j. wealth

CHECK YOUR UNDERSTANDING

10. How is investing money different from saving money?

11. Why are savings accounts often safer than other investments?

12. What is the purpose of an emergency fund?

13. List two short-term goals that could be reasons for saving.

14. List two intermediate goals that most people need savings and investments to achieve.

15. Give two examples of long-term goals that can be met with money from investments.

16. What should be included in a financial plan? Why is it important to create one?

17. When should you begin retirement planning?

18. What is meant by estate planning?

19. What is the purpose of a foundation?

20. What is the purpose of a will?

THINK CRITICALLY

21. Why is it important to keep your savings safe (take almost no risk) as you begin saving and investing?

22. Why is it important for people to have enough liquidity? In other words, why shouldn't you put all of your savings into a long-term investment?

23. Why is it important for investments to provide a greater return than the rate of inflation?

24. Why is it important to pay yourself first? Give two reasons.

25. How is planning for short-term goals different from planning for intermediate and long-term goals?

26. Why should you be concerned about retirement planning throughout your life?

27. How can you ensure that your property will be distributed as you intended upon your death?

28. What factors should you consider when planning your estate? Why should you consider charitable donations and possibly setting up a foundation as you plan your estate?

29. If you were to receive an inheritance from someone's estate, what would you do with the money? How might you invest?

EXTEND YOUR LEARNING

30. People have many purposes for saving and investing. These purposes can be defined in terms of goals, including short-term, intermediate, and long-term goals.

    a. Create a table with four columns, similar to the one shown in Figure 10-1.1. The column headings should be as follows:

       Personal Goal   Financial Goal   Benchmarks   Timeline

    b. List at least one short-term, one intermediate, and two long-term personal goals in the table.

    c. List a financial goal for each personal goal. Include benchmarks (steps to take that allow you to measure your progress) and a timeline for each goal.

    d. Enter the total amount of money you think you will need to meet each goal.

    e. Write a paragraph about your financial plan, explaining what might happen to change your goals over time.

THE ESSENTIAL QUESTION   Refer to The Essential Question on p. 314. Saving and investing provides wealth and security, allows you to meet personal goals, and provides financial security after you retire.

LEARNING OBJECTIVES

LO 10-2.1 Discuss the concept of risk versus return.

LO 10-2.2 List and explain the types of risk that are faced by individual investors.

LO 10-2.3 Describe the tax advantages available with certain types of investments.

KEY TERMS

- return on investment (ROI), 323
- investment risk, 324
- inflation risk, 324
- bond, 324
- industry risk, 324
- political risk, 325
- market risk, 325
- nonmarket risk, 325
- stock, 325
- company risk, 325
- tax deferral, 326
- tax-exempt, 326

LO 10-2.1 How Is Risk Related to Return?

When selecting an investment, you must weigh the risk involved against the possible return expected. The higher the risk you are willing to take, the greater your possible return will be. If you are not willing to take much risk, then you cannot expect high returns. *Risk-free investments* are those guaranteed by the government, such as U.S. government savings bonds and Treasury securities. Savings accounts, money market accounts, and CDs that are insured by the FDIC are also risk-free. As a result, the guaranteed rate of interest is low compared to rates for other investments.

The ideal investment would have all of the following features:

- The principal is safe (no risk).
- The rate of return (earnings) is high.
- The investment is *liquid* (you can get your money quickly without a penalty).
- You can invest quickly and easily.
- The costs of investing are low, both in terms of the amount invested as well as investment fees.
- The earnings and long-term gains are tax-free or tax-deferred.

How much risk are you willing to take with your savings?

RapidEye/iStockphoto.com

Unfortunately, there are no investments that meet all of these criteria. Therefore, you must decide how much risk you are willing to take and what rates of return will meet your goals.

Growth of Principal

When money is deposited into a savings account, the *principal*, or base amount on which interest is computed, should get larger over time. The principal grows when you deposit more money into the account. The principal also grows through the compounding of interest (as described in Chapter 5). Interest is calculated and added to the initial principal amount, which becomes the new principal amount. Interest is later calculated based on the new principal amount. This cycle continues, with the interest added to the previous principal amount each time it is calculated. As the principal increases over time, the value of the investment grows.

Return on Investment

When you put money into an investment, you expect its value to grow over time. The amount that the savings or investment grows is called the *return*. **Return on investment (ROI)** is a performance measure used to evaluate the efficiency of an investment. ROI calculates the amount of return on an investment in relation to the investment's cost. It is calculated by dividing the amount you gained (either in interest or in increased value) by the amount you invested, and the result is expressed as a percentage. The gain could also include other amounts you received, such as dividends. A *dividend* is a portion of a corporation's profits distributed to stockholders.

return on investment (ROI) a performance measure used to evaluate the efficiency of an investment

Figure 10-2.1 shows the calculation of ROI for two different investment choices. By comparing the ROI for different investment choices, you can see which has the best return.

 CHECKPOINT

What are risk-free investments?

▶ FIGURE 10-2.1 **Return on Investment (ROI)**

Example 1:	Bought an investment for $500; received dividends of $18 for the year.
	Gain: $18
	ROI: $18 ÷ $500 = 3.6% (annual ROI)
Example 2:	Bought an investment for $500 on March 1; sold it on October 1 for $525.
	Gain: $25
	ROI: $25 ÷ $500 = 5%
	Note: The 5% was calculated after only 7 months. The annual ROI would be higher. Calculate the annual ROI as follows:
	0.05 ÷ 7 months × 12 months = 8.6% (annual ROI)

Building COMMUNICATION SKILLS

GOOD NEWS MESSAGES

A *good news message* is one that the reader will find favorable or be happy to receive. Good news messages are often written to inform people that their requests have been granted. Other examples of good news messages include thank-you letters and congratulatory messages.

When writing a message that is good news, use a direct approach. The answer or main point of the message should be placed early in the message. For example, the opening of a good news letter might be "Congratulations, Mr. Mendez. You have been selected to receive a $5,000 scholarship." Details should be presented in later paragraphs. The message should close by reiterating the main point. The closing may also include a forward-looking statement, such as "We look forward to serving your needs in the future."

A good news message should be clear, leaving no doubt about the answer or point to be shared. The letter should be complete, giving all the details needed. The letter should also be concise. It should use enough words to sound friendly and courteous, but not be too wordy.

Try It Out

You work at a bank. The bank is making special offers to its best customers. Customers who qualify can receive higher interest rates on savings and have free access to various bank services. Using the guidelines discussed above, write a letter to a customer to give her the "good news."

LO 10-2.2 What Types of Risk Do Investors Face?

investment risk the potential for change in the value of an investment

Few investments go up in value all of the time. In fact, some investments decrease in value over time. **Investment risk** is the potential for change in the value of an investment. You are looking for investment choices that, on average, go up more than they go down. The goal is to have investments that are worth more at the end of the year than they were worth at the beginning of the year. There are several kinds of investment risk.

Inflation Risk

inflation risk the chance that the rate of inflation will rise faster than your investment rate of return

When prices are rising rapidly in the economy, your investment may lose value. **Inflation risk** is the chance that the rate of inflation will rise faster than your investment rate of return. When this occurs, your investment loses value.

bond a debt instrument that is issued by a corporation or government

For example, assume you bought a bond. A **bond** is a debt instrument that is issued by a corporation or government. Basically, the bond issuer is borrowing from an investor. The issuer must pay the bondholder the principal (the original amount of the loan) plus interest when the bond matures. Suppose the bond has a fixed interest rate of 5 percent. If inflation is lower than 5 percent, your investment is holding its value. If inflation rises to 7 or 8 percent, however, your investment is losing value. You will not be able to purchase as many goods or services with the dollars earned on your investment.

Industry Risk

industry risk the chance that factors affecting an industry as a whole will affect the value of an investment

Industry risk is the chance that factors affecting an industry as a whole will affect the value of an investment. For example, suppose you invest in a company that is in the oil industry. If oil prices and profits rise, then your investment is likely to gain in value. If alternate energy sources are found, however, then investments in the oil industry could lose value. People might start buying other types of fuel, and the price of oil could drop. Industry risk occurs in all types of businesses.

Political Risk

Political risk is the chance that actions taken by the government will affect the value of your investment. For example, an increase or a decrease in taxes or the passing of a new law can have an effect on the value of investments. The stock market sometimes reacts positively when a new president is elected in the United States. Political events, such as wars, in this country and in other countries can significantly affect the stock markets.

political risk the chance that actions taken by the government will affect the value of an investment

Market and Nonmarket Risk

Market risk is the chance that changes in the business cycle—periods of economic growth or decline—will affect the value of an investment. When the economy is doing well, the financial markets usually follow and vice versa.

market risk the chance that changes in the business cycle will affect the value of an investment

Nonmarket risk is the chance that events unrelated to market trends will affect the value of an investment. Nonmarket risk is entirely unpredictable and uncontrollable. For example, terrorist acts and natural disasters, such as earthquakes and hurricanes, affect investments in the short term.

nonmarket risk the chance that events unrelated to market trends will affect the value of an investment

Company Risk

Many people invest by buying **stock,** which is an ownership interest in a publicly held company. **Company risk** is the chance that activities or events that affect a company will change the value of an investment in that company.

stock ownership interest in a publicly held company

company risk the chance that activities or events that affect a company will change the value of an investment in that company

Stock in a company can go up or down in value due to a number of reasons. Poor management or unexpected events, such as product recalls or employee strikes, may negatively affect a company's performance, which in turn can negatively affect stock prices. During hard economic times when companies are unable to pay dividends to their stockholders, stock prices tend to fall. During periods when the company does well and pays good dividends, stock prices tend to rise.

Investment Risk Versus Gambling

It should be noted that a *game of chance*, or gambling, is hardly ever a good investment for building wealth. When you are betting, your chances of winning are much less than 50 percent. Even if you do win at times, your overall losses will far exceed your overall gains. A good rule of thumb is "When you can't afford to lose, then you can't afford to play." Games of chance should be considered entertainment only—not ways to make money. Traditional investments such as stocks, on the other hand, are proven ways to earn income.

CHECKPOINT

Name various types of investment risk.

LO 10-2.3 What Are Tax Advantages of Investing?

Investors may realize some important tax advantages for setting aside money over the long term. They include tax deferral and tax exemption.

Tax Deferral

tax deferral a postponement of taxes to be paid

When you set aside money for retirement using certain investment options, such as an IRA or a 401(k) plan, the money may be tax-deferred. **Tax deferral** is a postponement of taxes to be paid. There are no taxes on investment gains until the money is withdrawn from the account. Also, you may not have to pay taxes on the amounts you contribute to the account until later. And when you withdraw the money upon retirement, you will likely be in a lower tax bracket because your income is lower, meaning you will pay less tax.

Tax Exemption

tax-exempt an investment that is not subject to taxation

When an investment is **tax-exempt**, it is not subject to taxation. For example, interest earned on U.S. Treasury securities and Series EE and Series I savings bonds is exempt from state and local income taxes. Interest earned on municipal bonds issued by state and local governments may be free from all income taxes.

People with higher incomes may choose tax-exempt investments because their tax rates are high. Suppose a person is in a 35 percent tax bracket. If $1,000 is earned on an investment, $350 is paid in tax. If this person invests in a tax-exempt bond and earns $1,000 in interest, there is no tax. Interest rates paid on tax-free investments are often lower than market rates, but the tax-free investment may be the better choice, as shown in Figure 10-2.2.

> ## ≫ CHECKPOINT
> **What are two tax advantages that investing offers?**

 FIGURE 10-2.2 Investment Comparison Based on Tax Rates

INVESTMENT COMPARISON	
Taxable	**Tax-Free**
Corporate bond at 7% interest	Government bond at 5% interest
The investor pays federal tax at a rate of 35%. The investor keeps 65% (100% − 35%) of the interest earned. The rest (35%) is paid in tax.	The investor keeps all the interest earned at 5%.
0.07 × 0.65 = 0.0455 = 4.55% earnings after taxes	

KEY TERMS REVIEW

Match the terms with the definitions. Some terms may not be used.

_____ 1. The chance that changes in the business cycle will affect the value of an investment

_____ 2. The potential for change in the value of your investment

_____ 3. A postponement of taxes to be paid

_____ 4. A performance measure used to evaluate the efficiency of an investment

_____ 5. The chance that factors affecting an industry as a whole will affect the value of an investment

_____ 6. Ownership interest in a publicly held company

_____ 7. A debt instrument issued by a corporation or government

a. bond

b. company risk

c. industry risk

d. inflation risk

e. investment risk

f. market risk

g. nonmarket risk

h. political risk

i. return on investment (ROI)

j. stock

k. tax deferral

l. tax-exempt

_____ 8. An investment that is not subject to taxation

_____ 9. The chance that the rate of inflation will rise faster than your investment rate of return

CHECK YOUR UNDERSTANDING

10. Explain how risk and return are related to each other.

11. Describe the ideal investment.

12. How does compounding of interest lead to the growth of principal?

13. How is return on investment (ROI) calculated?

14. Explain how a bond is both a debt instrument and an investment.

15. What might occur at a company that would cause the company's stock to go up or down?

16. Why are games of chance not a good investment?

17. How are tax-deferred investments different from tax-exempt investments?

18. Under what circumstances can an investment with 5 percent interest bring you higher returns than an investment with 7 percent interest?

THINK CRITICALLY

19. Why is the return on investment (ROI) an important tool for evaluating your investments?

20. Explain how a fixed-rate investment can lose value when the rate of inflation is higher than the fixed rate.

21. Why are political risk and nonmarket risk difficult to measure and predict?

22. There is an E. coli breakout on a cruise ship which leads to the cancellation of reservations on other cruise ships. What kind of risk is this to the owners of cruise ships? Why does this happen?

23. Why is it important for some investors to choose tax-deferred or tax-exempt investments?

EXTEND YOUR LEARNING

24. The criteria for an ideal investment are as follows:

    - The principal is safe.
    - The rate of return is high.
    - The investment is liquid.
    - You can invest quickly and easily.
    - The costs of investing are low, both in terms of the amount invested as well as investment fees.
    - The earnings and long-term gains are tax-free or tax-deferred.

    For each situation below, explain which two criteria you think would be the most important for choosing a savings plan or an investment.

    a. Joshua plans to create an emergency fund to pay for unexpected expenses.

    b. Maria wants to see her money grow over several years. She has a separate fund for emergencies that is in a liquid, no-risk account.

    c. Chin wants to save money for retirement. He has a separate fund for emergencies that is in a liquid, no-risk account. He has other investments to help achieve other long-term goals.

25. You are in the 28 percent tax bracket and are considering investing $10,000. Option A pays 8 percent interest and is taxable. Option B pays 6 percent interest and is tax-free. If you earn interest of $750 on Option A and $600 on Option B, how much must be paid in taxes for each option? How much will you keep after taxes? Assuming the risk for both investments is the same, which is the better investment choice?

THE ESSENTIAL QUESTION   Refer to The Essential Question on p. 322. When making investment choices, the investor should weigh the risk involved against the possible return expected. The buyer should also consider tax advantages that certain types of investments offer.

10-3 | Strategies for Saving and Investing

LEARNING OBJECTIVES

LO 10-3.1 Explain the concept of systematic saving and investing.

LO 10-3.2 Describe how you can lower investment risk through diversifying and building an investment portfolio.

LO 10-3.3 Explain how you can maximize investment return by understanding the financial marketplace and the economy.

KEY TERMS

- systematic saving, 329
- systematic investing, 329
- investment tracking, 330
- market timing, 330
- dollar-cost averaging, 331
- diversification, 331
- portfolio, 331
- financial market, 333
- bull market, 334
- bear market, 334

LO 10-3.1 What Are Systematic Saving and Investing Strategies?

Systematic means regular, orderly, or done according to a plan. **Systematic saving** is a strategy that involves regularly setting aside cash that can be used to achieve goals. The amount should be the most you can comfortably afford to save each pay period. Some people find it convenient to have a set amount withheld automatically each month from their paychecks. Others make a monthly payment to a savings plan, just like paying a bill. Some people set aside a bonus or a portion of a raise they receive at work. After money is set aside in savings, it should remain there until used to meet a planned goal. Once you have excess savings beyond what you need for emergencies, daily expenses, and short-term goals, you can begin investing.

Systematic investing is a strategy that involves a planned approach to making investments on a regular basis. When you first start investing, you may wish to buy safe and liquid investments. In later years, you may want to take more risk so your principal can grow faster over time. Systematic saving and investing are important for building financial security in the long term.

systematic saving a strategy that involves regularly setting aside cash that can be used to achieve goals

systematic investing a strategy that involves a planned approach to making investments on a regular basis

Long-Term Focus

A systematic saving and investing plan is designed for growth in the long run, not for short-term results. Investors may need to hold investments for 20 or more years to get the returns they want. In any given year, investments may actually lose money. Over time, however, gains exceed losses on sound investments. For example, suppose your investments in the stock market have grown at an annual rate of more than 7 percent over any 20-year period of time. This does not mean that, in any given year, your investments earned 7 percent. In fact, in some years, the return may have been very low. In other years, the return may have been more than 10 percent. Investors must plan to hold investments for the long term to achieve substantial growth over time. As a young person, you should set saving and investing goals that focus on the future.

Investment Tracking

investment tracking a technique for making investment choices by following the prices of stocks and other investments over time

Investment tracking is a technique for making investment choices by following the prices of stocks and other investments over time. Stock prices may be tracked on Internet sites and are also shown in many newspapers. You might want to track a stock that interests you for several weeks to see how much the price changes. By tracking stocks and other investment choices over time, you can decide whether you are satisfied with the performance. Then when you are convinced it is a good match with your investment goals, you can buy the stock.

Those who track investments tend to keep data in the form of charts and graphs. These tools allow you to visualize how an investment does over time. They reveal *trends*, or general ups and downs, that can be compared with the performance of other investments under the same conditions. The chart in Figure 10-3.1 shows changes in the price of a stock over a period of 12 years. In general, the trend is upward, although there are times when the price falls and recovers.

Market Timing

market timing buying and selling stocks based on what the market is expected to do

Those who have a good understanding of the economy and general conditions in the financial markets are able to make good investment choices. **Market timing** involves buying and selling stocks based on what the market is expected to do. Stockbrokers, analysts, and others who make their living buying and selling investments get a good "feel" for when the time is right to buy, hold, or sell. They are able to advise their clients based on experience, trend lines, and analyses. Based on this data, they can match investor goals with investment opportunities.

▶ FIGURE 10-3.1 Stock Trend Line

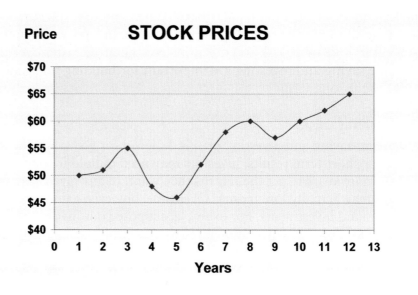

It should be noted that market timing can be risky and difficult. This is because not all economic and world events are predictable. However, over time and with experience, many investors develop a certain sense of market timing.

Dollar-Cost Averaging

Another strategy for buying stocks or other investments is dollar-cost averaging. With **dollar-cost averaging**, a person invests the same amount of money on a regular basis, such as monthly, regardless of market conditions. The amount is invested regardless of whether stock prices are high or low. Sometimes the investor pays a higher stock price and gets fewer shares. Sometimes the stock price is low, and more shares are purchased. Overall, the dollar cost per share may be less than the average price. Using this strategy, investors do not have to study the stock market to try to determine the best time to buy stocks.

dollar-cost averaging investing the same amount of money on a regular basis regardless of market conditions

 CHECKPOINT

What is meant by systematic saving and investing?

LO 10-3.2 How Can You Reduce Investment Risk?

Individual investors should look for ways they can reduce their overall risks of investing. Diversifying investments and building an investment portfolio can help lessen the risks.

diversification holding a variety of investments for the purpose of reducing overall risk

Diversify

Diversification involves holding a variety of investments for the purpose of reducing overall risk. When one type of investment goes down in value, there may be others that go up. Thus, the losses in one area are offset by the gains in others. It is important for investors to choose more than one type of investment. This is to avoid "having all your eggs in one basket." If a company fails, the investor could lose everything if he or she has only that one investment.

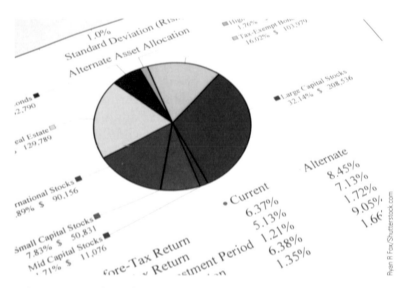

Why is it wise to diversify your investments?

Build a Portfolio

Once you are able to make investments on a regular basis, you can begin to build a portfolio. A **portfolio** is a collection of investments. In order to lower risk over time, the portfolio should be diversified.

portfolio a collection of investments

DOLLAR-COST AVERAGING

The dollar-cost averaging strategy involves the systematic purchase of an equal dollar amount of the same stock at regular intervals. The result is usually a lower average cost per share. For example, an investor purchased $100 worth of stock at various prices every quarter for one year, as shown below. Over that time, the average price of the stock was $8. However, by investing at regular intervals, the investor's average cost per share was lower ($7.41).

Quarterly Investment		Share Price ($)		Number of Shares
$100	÷	$10	=	10
$100	÷	7	=	14.29
$100	÷	5	=	20
$100	÷	10	=	10
$400		$32		54
Total invested				Total number of shares

Average share price = $8 ($32 ÷ 4)

Average cost per share = $7.41 (total invested ÷ number of shares: $400 ÷ 54)

Ending value = $540 (last share price × number of shares: $10 × 54)

Try It Out

You purchased $200 worth of stock every quarter for one year and paid the following share prices: Quarter 1 – $5; Quarter 2 – $10; Quarter 3 – $8; Quarter 4 – $4. Calculate these values: (a) average share price; (b) average cost per share; (c) ending value. Did you benefit from dollar-cost averaging?

You should start building your portfolio with a strong foundation of safe investments. For example, insured savings accounts and CDs are safe investments. When you feel secure enough to take more risk and you have additional money to invest, you should add some relatively safe, low-risk investments. These might include U.S. savings bonds and conservative mutual funds. A *mutual fund* is a professionally managed collection of stocks, bonds, and other investments. Mutual funds have specific objectives, such as growth (high earnings) or balance (good earnings with acceptable risk). Mutual funds allow investors to have diversified holdings within one investment.

A portfolio can also include some higher-risk choices that have the potential for high returns. Growth stocks and real estate are examples. Some people also include *speculative* investments, which have high earnings potential but carry a high risk. With speculative investments, you can make—or lose—a great deal of money in a short period of time. For this reason, some people include only a few or no speculative investments in their portfolios.

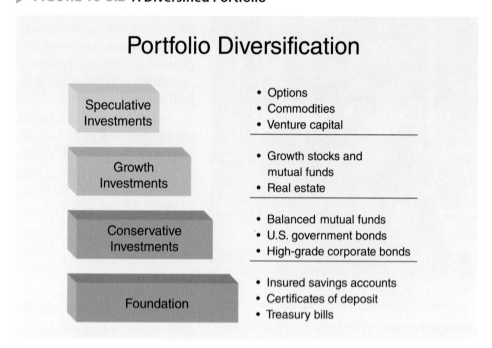

Portfolio Diversification

Speculative Investments
- Options
- Commodities
- Venture capital

Growth Investments
- Growth stocks and mutual funds
- Real estate

Conservative Investments
- Balanced mutual funds
- U.S. government bonds
- High-grade corporate bonds

Foundation
- Insured savings accounts
- Certificates of deposit
- Treasury bills

Over time, the portfolio should gain in value at a rate greater than the rate of inflation. The investor must decide how much of each type of investment to include. Investment choices will vary based on the person's age, income, family situation, goals, and attitude toward risk.

A sample portfolio is shown in Figure 10-3.2. You will learn more about the various types of investments listed in this figure in Chapter 11.

≫ CHECKPOINT
What is a portfolio?

LO 10-3.3 How Can You Maximize Investment Return?

Investors should consider economic conditions when forming an investment strategy. Understanding the economy and how it affects the **financial market**, or any place where investments are bought and sold, will help you make better investment choices.

There will always be periods of growth and decline in the economy that cause market prices to rise and fall. Whether the economy is experiencing growth or decline will affect your decisions about when to invest, what investments to buy, and how much to invest.

financial market any place where investments are bought and sold

Bull Market

During periods of economic growth, the unemployment rate is low, profits are good, and people are optimistic. Under these economic conditions, the market for many investments is growing. Consumer

bull market a prolonged period of rising stock prices and general feeling of investor optimism

Why is profit taking common during a bull market?

confidence in the country's economy can drive up stock prices. A prolonged period of rising stock prices and general feeling of investor optimism is referred to as a **bull market**.

Investors who think that the market will continue in a growth trend may choose this time to buy stock. They think the stock will grow in value. Other investors choose to sell their investments during a bull market. They want to sell at the current high prices before the market begins a downward trend. This practice is referred to as *profit taking*. This selling activity may cause prices to drop for a while. However, the drop in prices does not mean that the bull market has ended. As long as the general trend of upward prices continues, it is still considered a bull market.

There is no set time span for how long a bull market lasts. In the past, some have lasted several months, whereas others have lasted several years.

Bear Market

bear market a period of steadily decreasing stock prices and investor pessimism

When the economy experiences a general slowdown, the market for investments is declining. Stock prices usually fall—some sharply—and continue falling, often 20 percent or more, as people take their money out of the markets. This period of steadily decreasing stock prices and investor pessimism is referred to as a **bear market**.

During a bear market, many people are fearful of losing their money and sell their investments. However, this can be a good time to buy stocks that are sound investments, because prices are lower. This increases the chance of making a profit when the stock is sold at some future date. At times in a bear market, there may be a lot of buying activity. This may cause a temporary rise in stock prices but does not end the bear market. As long as the general trend is toward declining stock prices, it is still considered a bear market.

Bear markets are usually short and savage. The average bull market often lasts three to five times as long as a bear market.

⟫ CHECKPOINT
How is a bull market different from a bear market?

10-3 Lesson Assessment

KEY TERMS REVIEW

Match the terms with the definitions. Some terms may not be used.

_____ 1. A technique for making investment choices by following the prices of stocks over time

_____ 2. Holding a variety of investments for the purpose of reducing overall risk

_____ 3. Buying and selling stocks based on what the market is expected to do

_____ 4. A strategy that involves regularly setting aside cash that can be used to achieve goals

_____ 5. A prolonged period of rising stock prices and general feeling of investor optimism

_____ 6. A strategy that involves a planned approach to making investments on a regular basis

_____ 7. A collection of investments

_____ 8. Any place where investments are bought and sold

_____ 9. Investing the same amount of money on a regular basis regardless of market conditions

a. bear market

b. bull market

c. diversification

d. dollar-cost averaging

e. financial market

f. investment tracking

g. market timing

h. portfolio

i. systematic investing

j. systematic saving

CHECK YOUR UNDERSTANDING

10. Explain how to save and invest using a systematic strategy.

11. Describe the investment tracking process.

12. What is the advantage of using dollar-cost averaging as an investment strategy?

13. How does diversification lower investment risks?

14. List three types of investments that would be considered low risk.

15. What are some factors that will affect the types of investments that a person may need in an investment portfolio?

16. When the economy is growing and stock prices are rising, why might an investor sell stocks?

17. When the economy is slowing down and stock prices are falling, why might an investor buy stocks?

THINK CRITICALLY

18. Why does systematic investing begin with systematic saving?

19. Why is systematic investing a long-term plan?

20. Why would you use a chart or graph to display the history of a stock's price over time?

21. Why would an investor choose dollar-cost averaging over market timing or investment tracking?

22. Why should a portfolio include a solid foundation of safe investments?

23. Why would an investor choose to invest in speculative stocks or investments? Why should this type of investment be used sparingly?

24. How does the economy affect investment (buy and sell) decisions?

25. Why do people buy in bull markets and sell in bear markets? Is there a flaw to this strategy? Explain.

EXTEND YOUR LEARNING

26. A good investment portfolio is diversified. It should include low-risk, safe options as well as higher-risk options. It should also include various types of investments, as shown in Figure 10-3.2. Conduct research to find an example of each type of saving or investment option listed below. Then create a table and provide a short description of each one, including the expected annual rate of return (interest earned). Based on your research, select one option from each category to create your diversified portfolio.

Foundation
- Savings account
- Treasury bill

Conservative Investments
- Mutual fund
- U.S. government bond

Growth Investments
- Stock
- Real Estate

Speculative Investments
- Commodities
- Venture capital

THE ESSENTIAL QUESTION Refer to The Essential Question on p. 329. With systematic saving and investment strategies, you will set aside money regularly and have a planned approach for making investments. This will help you build a diversified portfolio and understand how to react to changes in the economy.

Exploring Careers in...
MARKETING

Marketing managers are in charge of planning, directing, and coordinating the marketing activities for a business. They estimate the demand for products that an organization and its competitors offer. They identify potential markets for the organization's products and monitor trends that indicate the need for any new product. Marketing managers often work with sales, public relations, and product development departments.

Marketing managers must understand perceptions as well as wants and needs of consumers. They must develop pricing and promotional strategies that keep companies profitable while also ensuring that customers' needs are being met.

Employment Outlook

- An average rate of employment growth is expected.
- Marketing managers are highly desirable by organizations; thus, the competition for these positions is strong.

Job Titles

- Marketing manager
- Marketing research manager
- Marketing director
- Marketing coordinator

Needed Education/Skills

- A bachelor's degree in a field related to marketing is usually required. Coursework in advertising, management, communications, and finance is recommended.
- Previous work experience in marketing is preferred.

- Computer skills are essential, along with creativity and excellent communication and analytical skills.

What's it like to work in . . . Marketing

Anne works as a marketing manager for a cosmetics company. She is the head of the organization's marketing department and manages a team of marketing specialists.

Today, Anne and her team are meeting with the product development department to discuss the marketing campaign for a new cosmetic line targeting teenagers. She has researched the product line and has developed a promotional strategy to reach the target audience.

Anne loves her job because it is different every day. She is able to use her creativity and imagination. Her ideas have resulted in successful marketing campaigns and awards for her team.

What About You?

Do you enjoy analyzing trends and data? Do you like conducting research? Would you like working with teams in a very competitive and creative environment? Would a career as a marketing manager appeal to you? Why or why not?

Chapter 10 Assessment

SUMMARY

10-1 Saving and investing are related because excess money set aside in savings provides the funds that can be used for investing.

Saving and investing provide the funds needed to meet short-term, intermediate, and long-term goals.

Saving and investing provide the means for meeting expenses and enjoying leisure activities during your retirement years. Estate planning will help protect your savings and investments after your death.

10-2 Risk and return are related. Risk-free investments are guaranteed but have low return. High-risk investments offer higher returns.

Return on investment (ROI) is a performance measure used to evaluate the efficiency of an investment. The ROI allows you to compare different investment choices.

All investors face investment risks, including inflation risk, industry risk, political risk, market and nonmarket risk, and company risk.

Saving and investing can provide tax advantages when gains are tax-deferred or tax-exempt.

10-3 Systematic saving is a strategy that involves regularly setting aside cash that can be used to achieve goals. Systematic investing is a strategy that involves a planned approach to making investments on a regular basis.

A systematic saving and investing plan is designed for growth in the long run, not for short-term results.

Investment tracking and market timing are techniques for buying and selling investments, but neither can guarantee results.

Using dollar-cost averaging, a person invests the same amount of money on a regular basis regardless of market conditions or prices.

Investors can reduce their risk through diversification, which involves owning a variety of investments, and by building a portfolio, or collection of investments.

To maximize investment return, investors can sell stocks during a bull market (period when the economy is growing and stock prices are increasing) and buy stocks during a bear market (period when the economy is declining and stock prices are decreasing).

MAKE ACADEMIC CONNECTIONS

TEAMWORK

1. **Research** Work with two classmates to prepare an oral report. Search the Internet to find stories, biographies, or other data about three successful and wealthy entrepreneurs or businesspersons of your choice. (LO 10-1.1, LO 10-1.3)

   a. How did they get started building wealth? Describe their early years, successes, failures, business ventures, and so forth.

   b. Do they participate in or sponsor any foundations or other organizations that benefit others? If so, describe them and their purpose.

   c. Have they published books, articles, media programs, or other items to tell others how to succeed? If so, describe them.

   d. Evaluate each person based on his or her contributions to society, ethics displayed, and methods of accumulating wealth.

2. **Technology** Search the Internet for a savings calculator. Plug in different numbers and note the results. For example, enter a savings amount compounded annually, then quarterly, and then monthly. Note the differences that occur because of the different compounding methods. Then try different savings amounts using the same compounding method. How does saving just a little more each month affect your total savings in, say, ten years? Then try different interest rates with the same savings amounts and compounding method. Summarize your conclusions. (LO 10-2.1)

3. **Research** If you inherit money, you may have to pay a state or federal inheritance or estate tax. What tax rates apply in your state and at the federal level? How do these two taxes differ? (LO 10-1.3)

4. **Economics** Explain the concept of a business cycle. If the economy is growing, how would that affect your investment choices? If the economy is slowing, how would that affect your choices? Consult *The Economist* magazine and find an article about the business cycle. Where are we at this point in time (recession, recovery, peak, or trough)? Explain what present economic conditions mean in terms of investing. (LO 10-2.2, LO 10-3.3)

5. **Social Studies** Access the Internet to learn about foundations that solicit donations from individuals. Select one and create a promotional brochure, including the history of the foundation, what kind of activities it engages in (how it uses the money collected), and how it benefits society. (LO 10-1.3)

6. **History** Conduct research about the history of the New York Stock Exchange (NYSE) in New York City. How long has it existed? What is its purpose? What goes on there? Prepare a written report, including a timeline of important events throughout the history of the stock exchange. (LO 10-3.3)

7. **Communication** You and your friend are thinking about investing in some stock together. You are trying to convince your friend that dollar-cost averaging will be your best choice as a long-term investment strategy. Write a paragraph that provides support for your position. (LO 10-3.1)

1. John bought stock for $350. A year later, he sold it for $385. What is his gain in dollars? What is his return on investment? (Round to the nearest whole percent.)

2. Samantha sold her collection of model cars for $600. She had purchased them for $520 a year earlier. What is her gain in dollars? What is her return on investment? (Round to the nearest whole percent.)

3. Pedro bought 25 shares of a stock for $150 a share. He received dividends of $3 per share each year for 5 years. After 5 years, Pedro sold the stock for $155 a share. What is his gain in dollars? What is his return on investment? (Round to the nearest whole percent.)

Take Action

TRACK STOCK PRICES

Tracking a stock's price for several weeks or months before buying the stock is a common investment strategy. Stock prices are available online and in the financial pages of newspapers. Typically, the user must enter or find a symbol (a series of letters) that represents the company. For example, the symbol for Apple Inc. is AAPL. If you do not know the symbol for the company, you can find it online by entering *stock symbol lookup* in a search engine.

Depending on the Internet site or newspaper, various information is provided about the stock. The opening price of the stock, the closing price (also called Last Trade), and any change in the stock price are usually shown, as in the example here.

a. Select a large corporation with which you are familiar.

b. Access the Internet and find a site that gives stock quotes. You can find websites by entering the keywords *stock quotes* in a search engine. Search to find the stock symbol for the company if you do not know it.

c. Find the Close (Last Trade) price for the stock for the current date. Record the date and the price. Continue to track and record the Close (Last Trade) price of the stock every one to three days for the following two or three weeks as your teacher directs.

Apple Inc. (AAPL)	
Date	9/1/—
Close (Last Trade)	107.72
Change	⇓ 5.04
Previous Close	112.76
Open	110.18

d. Using Figure 10-3.1 as an example, create a line chart to show the changes in the stock price. Use *Days* or *Weeks* instead of *Years* for your chart.

Include your investment tracking information and line chart in your portfolio.

Saving and Investing Options

Annabaek/iStockphoto.com

As an investor, you can choose among savings and investing options that have low, medium, or high risk. No single investment is likely to meet all of your needs. You will learn to consider risk, liquidity, and rate of return as you choose investments. You will have different investment goals at different times during your life. Making good choices involves an understanding of your financial goals, the risk you are willing and able to assume, and how each potential choice will act and react with market and economic conditions.

Do *This*, **Not** *That*

To make good saving and investment choices:

- Determine the amount of risk you are willing to take.
- Know the various saving and investing options and their risk levels.
- Start with low-risk investments and work your way up to medium- and high-risk investments.
- Avoid speculative investments unless you can afford potentially large losses.

11-1 Low-Risk Choices

THE ESSENTIAL QUESTION Why should all investors choose some liquid, low-risk investments?

LEARNING OBJECTIVES

LO 11-1.1 List low-risk savings options, and discuss their features.

LO 11-1.2 List low-risk investing options, and discuss their advantages and disadvantages.

KEY TERMS

- illiquid, 342
- maturity date, 343
- early withdrawal penalty, 344
- premium bond, 345
- discount bond, 345
- coupon rate, 346
- callable bond, 346
- convertible bond, 347
- zero-coupon bond, 347
- bond rating, 347
- annuity, 349

LO 11-1.1 What Are Low-Risk Savings Options?

Savings is money set aside to meet future needs. Having savings allows you to meet your short-term and long-term needs, both expected and unexpected. There are a number of different savings options available. Most are generally considered low risk; thus, they pay a lower rate of return. Many savings options are liquid, meaning they can be converted to cash easily. Others are **illiquid**, which means they are not convertible to cash quickly or without a penalty. Investors may choose these options because they typically pay higher returns than those that are liquid. Many investors seek to balance their investments. They want to have some options that provide higher returns and some that are liquid that can be converted to cash quickly.

illiquid not convertible to cash quickly or without a penalty

Savings Accounts

A savings account in a bank, credit union, or other insured financial institution is a good option to choose for meeting short-term needs. Savings accounts usually do not have withdrawal penalties. Some or all of the money can be withdrawn at any time. Thus, savings accounts are liquid. However, the account may have some restrictions. For example, the depositor may be able to write only a limited number of checks per month on the account and/or must maintain a minimum balance to avoid fees. A savings account typically pays a low interest rate. The rate is usually higher, though, than for a checking account. A savings account should be considered a safe place to put money.

Money Market Accounts

A *money market account* is another low-risk, liquid savings option. Brokerage firms as well as banks and other financial institutions offer money market accounts.

342   CHAPTER 11   Saving and Investing Options

How can a savings account help meet short-term needs?

There are two different kinds of money market accounts: money market deposit accounts and money market funds. A *money market deposit account* is similar to a savings account, but it offers a higher rate of interest in exchange for larger-than-normal deposits. This type of account pays the market rate of interest. In other words, the rate of interest earned on the account changes with general market conditions. Banks often pay a higher interest rate as your account balance increases. These accounts are insured by the FDIC.

A *money market fund* is a type of mutual fund that invests in low-risk securities (such as U.S. Treasury bills). Money market funds are not FDIC insured, but they are generally considered safe because they invest in short-term government securities. Therefore, the chance of losing your principal (amount deposited) is very low. On average, money market funds will pay a higher interest rate than money market deposit accounts.

With money market accounts, you usually are limited to a certain number of withdrawals each month and must maintain a minimum balance. Because money market accounts offer a more competitive rate, they are a better cushion against inflation than a savings account.

Certificates of Deposit

A *certificate of deposit (CD)* is money set aside for a specific length of time at a fixed interest rate—for example, six months at 6 percent interest. Most CDs have terms of a few months to five years. A CD typically pays a higher interest rate than a money market account or savings account. But a typical CD is not a liquid investment. You must pay a heavy penalty if you withdraw the money before the stated time. CDs purchased at banks and credit unions are safe because they are insured by the FDIC. Thus, a CD is a low-risk, illiquid investment. The biggest risk you face with a CD is *inflation risk* because the fixed rate of return may be lower than the cost of living, or the general level of prices. This causes your money to lose value.

Withdrawal Penalties

A CD has a set **maturity date**, which is the date on which an investment becomes due for payment. You may redeem it for cash, renew it for the same time period, or purchase a new certificate for a different time period. Typically, within a stated number of days after the maturity date, your certificate will renew automatically if you do not redeem it.

maturity date the date on which an investment becomes due for payment

Certificate of Deposit
Amount deposited: $5,000.00
Interest rate: 5% yearly
Term: 5 years

Penalty for Early Withdrawal
If the money is withdrawn before 5 years, the penalty imposed will equal 365 days' interest, whether earned or not.

Sample Scenario
The money is withdrawn after 180 days.

$5,000.00 × 0.05 × 180/365 = $123.29 interest earned
$5,000.00 × 0.05 × 365/365 = $250.00 penalty

$5,000.00	amount deposited
+ 123.29	interest earned
$5,123.29	
− 250.00	early withdrawal penalty
$4,873.29	amount received at early withdrawal

early withdrawal penalty a fee imposed to discourage depositors from withdrawing the money before the stated time period

If you take out any part of your money early, you will pay an **early withdrawal penalty**, which is a fee imposed to discourage depositors from withdrawing the money before the stated time period. This penalty could be anywhere from 90 days' interest to the loss of part of your principal, depending on the terms of your CD. Figure 11-1.1 shows an example of the penalty terms for a CD.

Jumbo CDs

CDs pay higher interest when money is set aside for a long period of time. They also pay higher interest for large amounts. A *jumbo CD* is for a large sum of money, usually $100,000 or more. CDs that pay higher rates of interest often have higher withdrawal penalties. You can earn good interest on this type of CD if you are able to leave your money on deposit for the full term. However, the risk on a jumbo CD is greater than that of a traditional CD. Because the FDIC insures up to $250,000 of your money in a single account, any amount invested in a jumbo CD that exceeds that amount is at risk. For example, if you invest $250,000 in jumbo CD that earns 6 percent interest for one year, the $15,000 in interest you earned would not be insured by the FDIC.

Life Insurance Savings Plans

When you buy permanent life insurance, the policy has a savings feature that gains in cash value. *Cash value* is the amount of savings accumulated in a permanent life insurance policy that you will receive if you cancel your policy. To build cash value, a portion of your premiums is deposited into an investment account where it earns interest. The interest rate varies with short-term rates in the economy. However, policies may contain a "surrender charge," which is a penalty that you must pay if you cancel the policy and withdraw its cash value.

Many life insurance policies allow you to borrow money against the policy's cash value. However, if this loan is not repaid, the life insurance death benefit is reduced by the amount of the loan.

Life insurance savings are illiquid. Some people think these plans are a good choice because the built-in savings feature "forces them to save." But, these investments are only as safe as the company from which you buy. Life insurance savings plans are not insured.

Brokerage Accounts

You can open an account at an investment company. This account may pay interest like a savings account, or it may be used to buy and sell investments. Money is taken from the account to buy them. When they are sold, money is put back into the account. Interest earnings are low but may be higher than for checking or savings accounts in banks. Brokerage accounts usually are not insured. However, they are considered low risk when placed with a reputable investment company. A brokerage account is liquid and works a lot like a checking account. There may be restrictions such as a limit to the number of checks you can write in a month or year.

 CHECKPOINT

Give three examples of low-risk savings options.

LO 11-1.2 What Are Low-Risk Investing Options?

Investments vary in term, risk, rate of return, and relative liquidity. For your initial investments, you will likely want to consider fairly safe investments, even though their returns will be relatively low. Even as you grow as a sophisticated investor, however, you should continue to include some low-risk investments as part of your portfolio.

Bonds

A *bond* is basically a loan that a buyer makes to a bond issuer. Thus, it is a form of holding debt as an investment. Bonds are generally a safe investment because they have a fixed interest rate.

Some bonds are sold at face value. The *face value* is the amount the bondholder will be repaid on the *maturity date*. Investors earn a return on bonds through interest that accumulates each day they own the bond. Investors can also earn a return if they sell the bond before maturity for a price higher than they paid for it. A bond that sells for more than its face value is called a **premium bond**. However, bonds can also decrease in value, especially if current interest rates are higher than the bond's fixed interest rate. A bond that sells for less than its face value is a **discount bond**. For example, if a bond pays a fixed interest rate of 6 percent, and current interest rates are higher than 6 percent and rising, the bond may have to be sold at an amount lower than face value to attract buyers.

premium bond a bond that sells for more than its face value

discount bond a bond that sells for less than its face value

Bonds may be issued by corporations, state and local governments, and the federal government. There are three basic types of bonds: corporate, municipal, and U.S. Treasury.

Corporate Bonds

Corporate bonds are issued by corporations to raise money. Bonds are a form of borrowing for the company. The money is used for various purposes, such as building new factories or buying equipment.

Corporate bonds pay a **coupon rate**, which is the fixed rate of interest that is paid semiannually for the life of a bond. The rate is set at the time the bond is issued and typically does not change. The interest is subject to income tax.

Corporate bonds are typically offered for sale in multiples of $1,000 or $5,000. All corporate bonds are issued with a stated face value and have a maturity date. Bond maturities typically range from 1 to 30 years. At maturity, the bond can be redeemed for face value.

Corporate bonds can be purchased at a discount. Figure 11-1.2 illustrates how you can make money buying a corporate bond at a discount. When you redeem the bond, you must pay taxes on the interest as well as on any gains you make. In Figure 11-1.2, you would pay taxes on the $400 interest earned and on the $200 gain you realized from the discount.

There are many types of corporate bonds, including those listed below.

- *Callable bonds.* A bond may be issued with a call provision. A **callable bond** has a clause that allows the issuer to repay the bond before the maturity date. The amount paid to the bondholder is typically higher than the face value. For example, a ten-year, $1,000 bond issued in 2016 with a maturity date of 2026 may be

coupon rate the fixed rate of interest that is paid semiannually for the life of a corporate bond

callable bond a bond with a clause that allows the issuer to repay the bond before the maturity date

▶ FIGURE 11-1.2 **Return on a Corporate Bond**

Corporate Bond
Face value: $5,000 Discount rate: 4% Coupon rate: 4% yearly (paid semiannually) Term: 2 years
Purchase price: $5,000 × 0.04 = $200 discount amount $5,000 − $200 = $4,800 discounted purchase price
Semiannual interest: $5,000 × 0.04 = $200 interest per year ($100 semiannual payment) $200 × 2 years = $400 total interest received
Return on investment: At the end of the second year, the bond is redeemed for $5,000 (face value).
$ 5,400 total amount received ($5,000 face value + $400 interest) −4,800 amount invested $ 600 total profit in dollars
$600 ÷ $4,800 = 0.125 = 12.5% total return on investment

callable in 2021. If interest rates fall, the corporation may choose to call the bonds and pay $1,020 to the bondholder. The corporation can then reissue the bonds at a lower interest rate.

- *Convertible bonds.* A **convertible bond** is one that can be exchanged for shares of common stock at the option of the bondholder. If you see that the company is doing especially well and/or you are willing to take more risk, you can exchange your bond for an equivalent number of shares of stock. For example, assume you purchase a $1,000 bond that is convertible to 50 shares of the company's common stock. You should convert the bond to stock whenever the price of the stock reaches $20 ($1,000 ÷ 50), or higher. Convertible bonds are attractive to investors because it gives them flexibility.

  convertible bond a bond that can be exchanged for shares of common stock at the option of the bondholder

- *Zero-coupon bonds.* A **zero-coupon bond** is a type of corporate bond that is sold at a deep discount, does not provide interest payments, and is redeemable for its face value at maturity. They may be sold at as much as 50 to 75 percent below face value. For example, you might buy a zero-coupon bond for $9,500. In ten years, at the maturity date, you might redeem the bond for $19,000. You can also make money by selling the bond before maturity at a higher price than what you paid for it.

  zero-coupon bond a type of corporate bond that is sold at a deep discount, does not provide interest payments, and is redeemable for its face value at maturity

The risk involved in investing in a corporate bond varies. The level of risk depends on the issuing company's ability to make interest payments and repay the bond. To help investors evaluate the risk level of corporate bonds, independent rating services, such as Standard & Poor's and Moody's, rate bonds according to their safety. A **bond rating** tells the investor the risk category that has been assigned to a bond. The rating is based on the creditworthiness of the issuing corporation.

bond rating tells the investor the risk category that has been assigned to a bond

An *investment-grade bond* is considered a high-quality, low-risk bond. It has a rating of Aaa, Aa, A, or Baa by Moody's and AAA, AA, A, or BBB by Standard & Poor's. The higher the rating, the lower the interest rate you will earn. *Speculative-grade bonds* have low ratings. These bonds are sometimes called *junk bonds* or high-yield bonds. They are considered medium to high risk. However, they are attractive to some investors because they pay higher interest rates than investment-grade bonds.

Municipal Bonds

Municipal bonds are issued by states, counties, cities, and towns. They are used to pay for projects such as roads or public buildings. The minimum investment in a municipal bond is usually $5,000. The interest is exempt from federal taxes (and often state and local taxes as well). Municipal bonds generally pay a lower interest rate than corporate bonds. However, because of the tax advantage, a municipal bond is sometimes a better deal than a corporate bond that pays a higher interest rate.

U.S. Government Savings Bonds

When you buy a savings bond, you are lending money to the U.S. government. *Savings bonds* help pay for the U.S. government's borrowing needs. They are considered one of the safest investments because they are backed by the full faith and credit of the U.S. government.

Building COMMUNICATION SKILLS

BAD NEWS MESSAGES

A *bad news message* is one that the reader will not find favorable or will not be happy to receive. Examples of bad news messages include rejection letters (in response to job applications, scholarships, etc.) and negative announcements (such as a change in company policy that affects employees).

When writing a message that is bad news, use an indirect approach. With an indirect approach, the writer attempts to break the news gently and keep the reader's goodwill. A bad news message should use a friendly tone.

Begin the letter with a buffer statement. A *buffer statement* is a positive or neutral statement that cushions, or buffers, the bad news that will follow. This statement also lets the reader know what the letter is about without revealing the bad news. An example of a buffer statement would be "Thank you for the order you placed for the new Sony HD widescreen notebook computer."

Next, give an explanation or details about the issue at hand. Include any positive news about the issue. For example, "This particular model has had the highest sales of all our notebooks since it was introduced earlier this month."

In the next paragraph, state the denial or other bad news. Make the explanation clear. Give details as needed and facts or logical reasoning to support the unfavorable news. For example, "Unfortunately, the popularity of this particular model has led to a temporary backorder situation, and the shipment of your order will be delayed."

Close the letter on a positive note. Bad news can often be cushioned by talking about what can be done rather than just stating what cannot be done. The purpose of the closing is to maintain goodwill. For example, "We anticipate your order will ship out next week. Thank you for your business, and please accept the enclosed $10-off coupon that you can use on your next purchase with us."

Try It Out

You are a financial adviser. Using the guidelines above, write a letter to a client explaining that he has incurred a loss on the sale of a corporate bond because the issuing corporation is financially unstable. Convince the client that it is best to take the loss and focus on better investment options.

U.S. government savings bonds are available in two forms: Series EE and Series I. They are available in any amount from $25 to $10,000, and you can buy up to $10,000 worth of bonds in a year. Both Series EE and Series I savings bonds are sold at face value. For example, you would pay $100 for a $100 bond. They must be held for a minimum of one year and can be held for a maximum of 30 years. Interest is added to the bond monthly and paid when the bond is redeemed. However, if the bonds are redeemed within five years, you must pay a three-month interest penalty. The two forms of bonds differ in how they earn their interest. Series EE savings bonds earn a fixed rate of interest. Series I savings bonds earn a fixed rate of interest in combination with a semiannual adjustment for inflation. The interest that both Series EE and Series I savings bonds earn is subject to federal income tax, but not state or local income tax. Thus, these bonds make a good tax shelter. A *tax shelter* is an investment that allows you to legally avoid or reduce income taxes.

Series EE and Series I savings bonds are no longer sold at banks, credit unions, or other financial institutions. They can be bought online only at the U.S. Department of Treasury's TreasuryDirect website (www.treasurydirect.gov). Paper certificates are no longer issued.

U.S. Government Treasury Securities

U.S. Treasury securities are considered safe investments because they are backed by the U.S. government. They are subject to federal income tax but are exempt from state and local income taxes. There is no minimum term of ownership for U.S. Treasury securities. They can be purchased at a bank, through a broker, or online at the TreasuryDirect website.

There are four types of U.S. Treasury securities:

- *Treasury bills.* These bills, called T-bills, are available for a minimum purchase of $100. They are issued for terms of 4, 13, 26, and 52 weeks. T-bills are typically sold at a discount rather than face value. For example, you might pay $990 for a $1,000 bill. When the bill matures, you would be paid $1,000. The difference between the purchase price and face value constitutes the earnings on the bill.
- *Treasury notes.* These notes, called T-notes, are available for a minimum purchase of $100. They are issued for terms of 2, 3, 5, 7, and 10 years. They earn a fixed rate of interest, set at the time the note is issued, every six months until maturity.
- *Treasury bonds.* These bonds, called T-bonds, are issued for a minimum of $100 with a 30-year maturity. They pay interest every six months until they mature. Interest rates are generally higher than rates for either T-bills or T-notes because of the longer maturity.
- *Treasury Inflation-Protected Securities (TIPS).* These securities are issued for a minimum purchase of $100. They are issued in terms of 5, 10, and 30 years. The face value of a TIPS increases with inflation (and decreases with deflation), as measured by the Consumer Price Index (CPI). When a TIPS matures, you are paid the adjusted face value or the original face value, whichever is greater. Interest is paid semiannually, at a fixed rate, on the adjusted face value. Thus, interest payments rise with inflation and fall with deflation.

Annuities

An **annuity** is a contract in which you make a lump-sum payment or series of payments that earn interest and, in return, receive regular disbursements, often after retirement. Annuities are typically purchased from a life insurance company. Generally, you will receive income monthly, with disbursements continuing for as long as you live or for a specified number of years. Taxes are deferred on the interest until you begin receiving your disbursements. The payments from an annuity are normally used as a supplement to retirement income. Annuities are not insured. They are fairly safe, but only as safe as the company with which you invest.

annuity a contract in which you make a lump-sum payment or series of payments that earn interest and, in return, receive regular disbursements, often after retirement

 CHECKPOINT

List three types of U.S. government savings bonds and/or securities.

KEY TERMS REVIEW

Match the terms with the definitions. Some terms may not be used.

_____ 1. A contract in which you make a lump-sum payment or series of payments that earn interest in return for regular disbursements, often after retirement

_____ 2. A bond that the issuer has the right to pay off before the maturity date

_____ 3. A bond that sells for more than its face value

_____ 4. A fee imposed to discourage depositors from withdrawing the money before the stated time period

_____ 5. The fixed rate of interest that is paid semiannually for the life of a corporate bond

_____ 6. Not convertible to cash quickly or without a penalty

_____ 7. A bond that can be exchanged for shares of common stock at the option of the bondholder

_____ 8. A bond that sells for less than its face value

_____ 9. A type of corporate bond that is sold at a deep discount, does not provide interest payments, and is redeemable for the face value at maturity

_____ 10. The risk category assigned to a bond

a. annuity

b. bond rating

c. callable bond

d. convertible bond

e. coupon rate

f. discount bond

g. early withdrawal penalty

h. illiquid

i. maturity date

j. premium bond

k. zero-coupon bond

CHECK YOUR UNDERSTANDING

11. Why is a savings account considered a low-risk savings option?

12. How are money market deposit accounts different from money market funds?

13. Why is a certificate of deposit (CD) more illiquid than a savings account?

14. Explain the purpose of early withdrawal penalties for CDs.

15. How do investors earn a return on bonds?

16. How are Series EE savings bonds different from Series I savings bonds?

17. How are T-bonds different from T-bills and T-notes?

18. Explain how an annuity can help provide financial security during retirement.

19. How can an investment be considered low risk if it is not insured?

THINK CRITICALLY

20. Why is it important to make some low-risk investments that are illiquid?

21. Why would an investor choose to take an early withdrawal penalty?

22. Why would you select a money market account over a savings account?

23. Why might an individual choose to put his or her money in a life insurance policy? How does this savings option potentially carry more risk than other low-risk options?

24. When a bond sells at a discount, do you pay more or less than the face value of the bond? Why might a bond issuer sell the bond at a discount?

25. Series EE savings bonds carry a fixed rate of interest, whereas Series I savings bonds have a variable rate component. Which is better? Why?

26. Why might investors choose corporate bonds over U.S. government savings bonds or Treasury securities?

27. Why might investors choose U.S. government savings bonds or Treasury securities over corporate bonds?

EXTEND YOUR LEARNING

28. In the two cases below, consider the risk and liquidity of savings and investing options. Give advice to each of the investors.

    a. Lee is working full time. He started his first job six months ago. After paying bills, he has $300 a month remaining. Rather than spend this money, he has decided to set it aside for the future. He has signed an annuity contract whereby he will pay $300 a month for the next 20 years. Then he will start receiving payments from the annuity, or he can leave the money there to gain more earnings until he retires. He has no savings account or other investments at this point. Has Lee made a good investment choice? Are there other options that might be better for him to consider for his portfolio at this time?

    b. Juanita is working part time while she goes to college. Because she has a scholarship, she is able to save $50 a month. Juanita has decided to deposit the $50 she saves each month in her savings account. Although the account pays little in interest, she is able to avoid a monthly service fee of $8 because she has enough money to meet minimum deposit requirements. What do you think of Juanita's decision? Are there other good options that she might consider for saving or investing her money?

THE ESSENTIAL QUESTION   Refer to The Essential Question on p. 342.
Savings options that are liquid allow you to meet short-term needs and emergencies. Low-risk investment options provide safety and offer protection when the financial market turns volatile.

THE ESSENTIAL QUESTION What are some good medium-risk investment choices, and why are they important to your investment strategy?

LEARNING OBJECTIVES

LO 11-2.1 List and describe medium-risk investment options.

LO 11-2.2 List and discuss retirement accounts and options available to individual investors.

LO 11-2.3 List and describe retirement accounts available through employers.

KEY TERMS

- mutual fund, 352
- asset allocation, 353
- common stock, 354
- preferred stock, 354
- traditional IRA, 356
- Roth IRA, 357
- Keogh plan, 357
- 401(k) plan, 359
- 403(b) plan, 360
- rollover, 360

LO 11-2.1 What Are Medium-Risk Investment Options?

To earn a higher return, investors must be willing to take some risk. Medium-risk investments will increase your return without raising the risk beyond reason. With many medium-risk choices, the investor can choose how much risk he or she is willing to take. When first making medium-risk investments, investors may be wise to use the services of financial experts.

mutual fund a professionally managed group of investments bought using a pool of money from many investors

Why is it a good idea to begin investing with a mutual fund?

Don Farrall/Getty Images

Mutual Funds

A **mutual fund** is a professionally managed group of investments bought using a pool of money from many investors. Mutual funds are operated by professional fund managers who use the pooled money to buy stocks, bonds, and other securities based on market research they have conducted. Mutual funds are often thought of as a good way to get started with medium-risk investments. It is a relatively inexpensive way for investors who do not have the time or expertise to manage their own portfolio.

Each fund is focused on a specific investment strategy or objective. An investor buys shares in the fund with the strategy that best matches the investor's goals and risk comfort level. Figure 11-2.1 describes various types of mutual funds by their objectives.

Mutual Fund Type	Description
Balanced funds	Invest in a diversified portfolio that includes some low-risk, some medium-risk, and some high-risk stocks. These funds strive for balance between growth and income. The objective is to reduce overall risk while maximizing return.
Bond funds	Invest primarily in bonds. If the bonds are tax-free, this advantage is passed along to investors.
Global funds	Invest in international companies, new industries in foreign countries, and companies in the world marketplace.
Growth funds	Invest in companies that are expected to grow over the long run. Gains will be made when the companies reach their potential. They are often considered to be high-risk investments in the short run.
Income funds	Invest in bonds and stocks that produce steady and reliable dividend and interest payments that are passed along to investors.
Index funds	Invest in securities to match a market index with the goal of having returns similar to those of that index.
Money market funds	Invest in short-term securities that go up or down with current interest rates and the economy.
New venture funds	Invest in new and emerging businesses and industries. These are considered high-risk (but also high-return) choices.
Precious metal funds	Invest in companies that are associated with precious metals, such as gold, silver, and platinum.
Stock funds	Invest primarily in stocks. They could be categorized into types of stocks—blue chips, technology, medical, etc.

With mutual funds, the investor can exercise **asset allocation**, which involves choosing a combination of funds within a single mutual fund company. The investor can pick investments that have a variety of risks. An example of asset allocation is shown in Figure 11-2.2.

asset allocation choosing a combination of funds within a single mutual fund company

Stocks

When you buy stock in a corporation, you become a stockholder. A *stockholder* owns shares of the company. Stockholders receive income in two ways. One way is by receiving *dividends*, or money paid to stockholders from the corporation's profits. Stock that pays annual dividends is attractive to an investor who needs the income (such as for retirement).

The other way to get income from stock is by selling it at a price that is higher than the price you paid for it. This increase in value is referred to as *capital gain*. Buying stocks and holding them for growth

ASSET ALLOCATION		
Percent of Holdings	Type of Fund	Reason for Choice
20%	Bond fund	For stability and to offset risk of other funds
20%	Growth fund	To invest in high-risk choices that could grow greatly over time
20%	Global fund	To benefit from world economic growth
20%	Money market fund	To provide liquidity and short-term gains
15%	Income fund	To receive income in the form of dividends
5%	New venture fund	To invest in emerging, young businesses that could become highly profitable and provide a high return

is a long-term strategy. You are betting that the value of the stock will go up over time. As a young, beginner investor, stocks should be considered a long-term investment.

Stocks generally carry more risk than investment choices with a fixed interest rate because a stockholder's earnings can go up or down, depending on the company's performance. Stocks in well-established companies are reasonably safe, whereas stocks in less-stable companies can be quite risky. However, a diversified portfolio of stocks of various risk levels can achieve a medium overall risk.

Stocks and other securities are purchased through a stockbroker. Stockbrokers will be discussed in Chapter 12.

Types of Stock

common stock a type of stock that pays a variable dividend and gives owners (stockholders) voting rights

Many companies issue two types of stock: common stock and preferred stock. **Common stock** pays a variable dividend and gives owners (stockholders) voting rights. However, dividends are not guaranteed. If the company does well, the stockholder shares in the profit in the form of dividends. Common stockholders can vote on issues such as who the company directors will be or whether to issue additional stock.

preferred stock a type of stock that guarantees a fixed dividend but does not provide voting rights

Preferred stock guarantees a fixed dividend but does not provide voting rights. Preferred stockholders are paid a set dividend regardless of how the company is doing. Because there is less risk, preferred stock generally costs more than common stock. If the company goes bankrupt, preferred stockholders would be paid before common stockholders.

Investors often classify stocks (common and preferred) into different categories. Each category has a different level of risk. Which category is best for you will depend on how much risk you are willing to assume. Many investors choose to buy stocks in several categories to diversify their risk. Some of the categories of stock include the following:

- *Income stocks.* Stocks in corporations that have a consistent history of paying high dividends to stockholders are income stocks. Investors choose income stocks to get current income in the form of dividends.

TRACKING INVESTMENTS

People who buy investments should check the progress of their investments. A good way to do this is to set up a spreadsheet that shows purchase price, monthly or yearly change in value, percentage change in value, and ending value. This allows you to track each investment over time. It also allows you to compare investments. Most importantly, it helps you to decide when it is time to change your investment strategy. If one type of investment is going steadily down in value over time, or not increasing as fast as others, it may be time to make a change.

You can also track your investments using various online tracking tools, such as Google Finance. Its "Portfolios" feature allows you to create a portfolio that resides on the Google site. The portfolio tracker keeps tabs on the performance of your various stock and mutual fund holdings. As you make transactions, you enter the changes into your portfolio, and Google Finance registers the appropriate adjustments. The portfolio tracker also provides a customized listing of current news stories related to the companies in which you have invested. The Google Finance portfolio charting tool generates a performance chart that allows you to review the performance of the investments in your portfolio. You can set the chart to review performance of your investments for up to the past ten years.

Try It Out

Choose five different investments from a local newspaper or online, such as three stocks, a mutual fund, and a CD. Assume you will invest a total of $15,000 ($3,000 in each). Set up a spreadsheet to keep track of the progress of the investments for a month. At the end of the month, compare the current values of each investment to the initial price or cost. Evaluate your choices—which one was the best? The worst?

- *Growth stocks.* Stocks in corporations that reinvest their profits into the business so that it can grow are growth stocks. These corporations may pay little or no dividends. Instead of current income, investors buy growth stocks for future capital gains. If the stock is worth more in the future, the investor can sell it to make a profit.
- *Blue chip stocks.* Stocks of large, well-established corporations with a solid record of profitability are blue chip stocks. Investors choose them for their safe and stable, but moderate, returns.
- *Defensive stocks.* Stocks that remain stable and pay dividends during an economic decline are defensive stocks. These companies are not affected as much by the ups and downs of the economy because demand for their products remains fairly consistent.

Personal Residence

Most financial experts believe that buying your own home is the best investment you will ever make. They also agree that home ownership is not always liquid. You must be willing to wait to sell when the market is on the upswing. Because the costs of buying are so high, it usually takes several years to make a profit. However, over the long run, the value of a home often grows faster than the rate of inflation, thus making home ownership a fairly safe investment.

Owning your own house is a good tax shelter. If you sell your house and the home was your primary residence (you lived in the house for at least two years out of the five years prior to its sale), you do not have to pay taxes if the gains from the sale are below $250,000 ($500,000 for married couples filing joint income taxes). Any gain beyond the $250,000 may be subject to *capital gains tax*, depending on your tax bracket. In addition, certain costs associated with home ownership may be treated as tax deductions or credits.

While investing in your own home carries little risk, investment in other types of real estate can be very risky. Investing in real estate not used as a primary residence is covered in greater depth later in the chapter.

≫ CHECKPOINT

Why is preferred stock less risky than common stock?

LO 11-2.2 What Are Individual Retirement Account Options?

A retirement account is a good way to meet long-term needs and financial goals. You can open a retirement account as an individual. You deposit funds in an account to be withdrawn at retirement. You must manage the account by choosing the types of investments in the account. Earnings on the investments remain in the account, allowing them to compound and grow faster. These investments are considered to be medium-risk. Individual retirement accounts offer either a tax-deferred or tax-free way of saving for retirement, making them excellent tax shelters.

Individual Retirement Accounts

An *individual retirement account (IRA)* is a retirement savings plan that allows individuals to set aside a specified amount of money each year. IRAs are set up at banks and other financial companies, but they are managed by the investor.

The amount that can be set aside in an IRA is limited and changes periodically. In 2015, the maximum contribution limit was $5,500 (or $6,500 if you are age 50 or older). Those who do participate in a retirement plan at work can also contribute to an IRA; however, the maximum they can contribute depends on their income.

You can begin withdrawing money from an IRA at age 59½. If money is withdrawn before age 59½, a 10 percent early withdrawal penalty will be assessed. In addition, the money withdrawn is subject to federal and state income taxes in the year of withdrawal.

Traditional IRA

traditional IRA an individual retirement account in which contributions are tax-deductible and grow tax-deferred.

A **traditional IRA** is an individual retirement account in which contributions are tax-deductible and grow tax-deferred. The money you contribute to a traditional IRA (up to the maximum contribution limit) may qualify for a tax deduction. Thus, you will not have to pay taxes on

Why should young people consider a Roth IRA?

contributions to the account or the account's earnings until the money is withdrawn during retirement. At that time, your income will likely be lower than it was while you were working. As a result, you will be in a lower tax bracket and will pay less tax. Although you don't have to start making withdrawals when you turn 59½, you must begin to do so by age 70½. Otherwise, a penalty will be assessed.

Roth IRA

A **Roth IRA** is an individual retirement account in which contributions are taxed, but earnings are not. Contributions are not tax-deductible. With a Roth IRA, you pay tax on your income before you put it into the account. You do not receive a tax deduction for contributions. After a five-year holding period, and at age 59½, you can begin making tax-free withdrawals. This is the opposite of a traditional IRA, for which you pay tax on the earnings as well as the contributions when you withdraw the money during retirement. Unlike a traditional IRA, you are not required to make withdrawals by age 70½.

Roth IRA an individual retirement account in which contributions are taxed, but earnings are not

Keogh Plans

A **Keogh plan** is a tax-deferred retirement plan for self-employed individuals. It is also available to their employees. However, employees do not contribute to the plan. All contributions come from the business owner, and the contribution rate set by the business owner must be applied uniformly to all employees.

Keogh plans can be structured in various ways. A self-employed person may set an annual goal for funding the plan. In 2015, Keogh contributions were limited to $210,000 or 100 percent of self-employment income (whichever is less). This type of plan may allow high-earning self-employed individuals to save more for retirement than they would with other plans. A Keogh plan may also be set up as a profit-sharing plan. In 2015, contributions to Keogh plans that are based on profit-sharing are restricted to $53,000 or 25 percent of earned income (whichever is less). *Earned income* is your net income

Keogh plan a tax-deferred retirement plan for self-employed individuals

after subtracting business expenses, including any contributions to the plan for employees.

The contributions made by a self-employed individual are tax-deductible. Earnings on Keogh plans are also tax-deferred. Withdrawals cannot be made before age 59½ without a penalty being assessed and must begin by age 70½.

Simplified Employee Pension Plans

A *simplified employee pension (SEP) plan* (often called a *SEP-IRA*) is a tax-deferred retirement plan for small business owners and their employees. Many self-employed individuals also use SEPs because they are easier to set up than Keogh plans. With a SEP plan, all contributions come from the employer; employees cannot contribute. Employers can make an annual tax-deductible contribution of up to 25 percent of the employee's salary or $53,000 (in 2015), whichever is less. These contributions go into a traditional IRA that each employee sets up at a financial institution. Withdrawals cannot be made before age 59½ without penalty and must begin by age 70½.

> ## CHECKPOINT
>
> **Why might someone want to open an individual retirement account?**

LO 11-2.3 What Retirement Plans Are Available through Employers?

An employer-sponsored retirement plan is another way to help meet long-term needs and financial goals. Many employers provide some type of retirement plan for their employees. With an *employer-sponsored retirement plan*, the employee and possibly the employer contribute money to the employee's retirement savings. Employer-sponsored retirement plans may be part of an employee's benefits package.

Employer-sponsored retirement plans provide significant tax advantages for employees because the money is tax-deferred. It is not taxed until the employee actually receives it (at retirement).

Defined-Benefit Plans

Some larger employers provide defined-benefit plans for their employees. A *defined-benefit plan* is an

Why is an employer-sponsored retirement plan an important part of a benefits package?

Johnny Grieg/iStockphoto.com

Planning for your retirement is important. However, knowing where to start is often the hardest part. Conduct online research and analysis about retirement planning and the tools available to help you meet your retirement needs. After doing so, answer the following questions: How can you get started with a retirement plan? Why should you begin saving early? What online tools can help you create and manage your retirement plan? What are the benefits of a 401(k) plan? Why should you participate in an employer-matching program?

employer-sponsored retirement plan whereby retired workers receive a set monthly amount for life, beginning at retirement, based on their wages earned and number of years of service. A pension plan is an example of a defined-benefit plan. Employees typically do not contribute to the plan; instead, the employer makes the entire contribution. Defined-benefit plans are tax-deferred. Employees pay taxes on the money when received after retirement.

Typically, employees must work for the company for a certain number of years to become *vested*, or entitled to the full amount in the plan. Once vested, the employee cannot lose the money in the account if he or she leaves the job.

Pension plans are offered by fewer companies now than in the past. These plans are disappearing because employers must make pension payments even when the investments in the plan do poorly or lose value because of poor economic conditions.

Defined-Contribution Plans

A *defined-contribution plan* is an employer-sponsored retirement plan whereby employees receive a periodic or lump-sum payment based on their account balance and the performance of the investments in their account. Employees are not promised a specific amount of benefits at retirement. Employees pay a set amount or percentage of their salary into a retirement account each month, which is then invested. Contributions are not taxed until they are withdrawn at retirement. The employer may choose to make contributions to the plan. The plan specifies the amount the employer will contribute, if anything. When employees retire, they are paid a benefit based on contributions made to their account and investment gains or losses.

Defined-contribution plans are more common than defined-benefit plans at most companies today. Two types of defined-contribution plans are 401(k) and 403(b) plans.

401(k) Plans

A **401(k) plan** is a tax-deferred retirement plan for employees offered by businesses that operate for a profit. Under a 401(k) plan, employees choose the percentage of salary they want to contribute to their account. The employer deducts this amount from their paychecks and puts it into the employees' individual accounts. Taxes are deferred until the money

401(k) plan a tax-deferred retirement plan for employees offered by businesses that operate for a profit

is withdrawn at retirement. An investment company manages the accounts and invests the money. Usually, employees may select the types of investments they want from among several options offered by the plan.

Employers may "match" employee contributions by some percentage. For example, for every $1 of salary that employees contribute to their account, the employer may add 10 cents (a 10 percent match). The employer's contribution is pure profit to the employee. In the preceding example, the 10 percent match is the same as making an immediate 10 percent return on your money. Any time you are able to get a *money match*, you should set aside as much money as you possibly can. This will maximize your return and lead to accumulation of wealth.

Employees cannot withdraw funds from their 401(k) plan without penalty before age 59½, except in the event of death, disability, or financial hardship. They must also begin making withdrawals by age 70½, or pay a penalty.

403(b) Plans

403(b) plan a tax-deferred retirement plan for employees of schools, government units, and nonprofit organizations

A **403(b) plan** is a tax-deferred retirement plan for employees of schools, government units, and nonprofit organizations. Teachers, nurses, doctors, and ministers are examples of people who qualify for 403(b) plans.

Although the rules may vary slightly, the 403(b) plan operates like a 401(k) plan. Employees contribute a percentage of their salary toward this tax-deferred account. Employers may make matching contributions. Employees are allowed to choose investments for the money deposited. Earnings and contributions are not taxed until the money is withdrawn. Money cannot be withdrawn without penalty before age 59½, and withdrawals must begin before age 70½.

Portability

rollover the process of moving a retirement account balance to another qualified account without incurring a tax penalty

Most employee-sponsored retirement accounts are *portable*—you can take the account with you when you leave a job. A **rollover** is the process of moving a retirement account balance to another qualified account without incurring a tax penalty. For example, you may be working for a company that has a 401(k) or a 403(b) retirement account. If you leave your job, you can take the money you contributed with you. If the account is vested, you can also take with you the money your employer contributed. You can roll over your 401(k) to an individual IRA account or to an account provided by a new employer. By doing this, you can continue to defer taxes on the money and its earnings until you retire and withdraw the cash. If you take a cash payout instead of doing a rollover, you will have to pay tax on the full amount that year plus a 10 percent penalty if you are under age 59½.

▶▶ CHECKPOINT

How is a 401(k) plan different from a 403(b) plan?

KEY TERMS REVIEW

Match the terms with the definitions. Some terms may not be used.

_____ 1. A tax-deferred retirement plan for employees offered by businesses that operate for a profit

_____ 2. An individual retirement account in which contributions are taxed, but earnings are not

_____ 3. The process of moving a retirement account balance to another qualified account without incurring a tax penalty

_____ 4. A professionally managed group of investments bought using a pool of money from many investors

_____ 5. A type of stock that guarantees a fixed dividend but does not provide voting rights

_____ 6. An individual retirement account in which contributions are tax-deductible and grow tax-deferred

_____ 7. Choosing a combination of funds within a single mutual fund company

_____ 8. A type of stock that pays a variable dividend and gives owners (stockholders) voting rights

_____ 9. A tax-deferred retirement plan for self-employed individuals

a. 401(k) plan

b. 403(b) plan

c. asset allocation

d. common stock

e. Keogh plan

f. mutual fund

g. preferred stock

h. rollover

i. Roth IRA

j. traditional IRA

CHECK YOUR UNDERSTANDING

10. What is the purpose of asset allocation?

11. Which type of mutual fund has a better potential for high returns: a bond fund or a stock fund? Which of these two funds has a higher risk?

12. Describe two ways to receive income from stocks.

13. How can retirement plans help you meet long-term goals and financial plans?

14. List three types of retirement accounts that can be opened by an individual.

15. How are traditional IRAs and Roth IRAs similar? How are they different?

16. What does it mean to be vested, and how does that affect portability?

17. What is the difference between a defined-benefit plan and a defined-contribution plan?

THINK CRITICALLY

18. Why is owning your own home a good investment for most people? Explain the concept of tax shelter as it relates to this investment.

19. If available, why should you start setting money aside in an employer-sponsored retirement plan as soon as you begin working?

EXTEND YOUR LEARNING

20. Three types of mutual funds are described below.

    Balanced Fund: This fund seeks current income, long-term growth of capital and income, and preservation of capital. This is a low-risk fund.

    Index Fund: This fund seeks above-average returns by investing primarily in stocks. The fund's risk profile is similar to that of the Standard & Poor's 500 Index. This is a medium-risk fund.

    Growth Fund: This fund seeks long-term gains by investing at least 80 percent of its assets in stocks of companies with above-average earnings growth. This is a high-risk fund.

    Returns for each fund over eight years are shown in the following table:

Year	Balanced Fund	Growth Fund	Index Fund
2008	14.01%	6.53%	28.84%
2009	3.89%	58.17%	12.37%
2010	−1.83%	−13.52%	−7.75%
2011	−5.23%	−33.59%	−10.87%
2012	−18.91%	−24.88%	−22.85%
2013	18.21%	34.83%	23.67%
2014	6.78%	4.94%	8.78%
2015	6.84%	11.82%	7.60%

   a. Using spreadsheet software, create a line graph or bar graph to compare the returns data for the three funds. As an alternative, you can create a chart manually using graph paper.

   b. Use *RETURNS COMPARISON* for the title of the graph. Include a legend to identify the line or bar for each fund.

   c. Which fund had the highest return in any one year? Which fund had the lowest return in any one year? Which fund had the smallest amount of change over the years? Which two funds had similar returns? Which fund would you choose and why?

THE ESSENTIAL QUESTION   Refer to The Essential Question on p. 352. Good medium-risk investment options include mutual funds, stocks, your personal residence, and retirement accounts. Medium-risk investments will increase your return without raising the risk beyond reason.

11-3 High-Risk Choices

THE ESSENTIAL QUESTION   What makes investing in collectibles, precious metals, gems, business ventures, and real estate so risky?

LEARNING OBJECTIVES

LO 11-3.1 Discuss high-risk investment choices, including futures contracts, options, collectibles, precious metals, and gems.

LO 11-3.2 Describe how you can invest in business ventures, including starting or buying a business.

LO 11-3.3 Explain real estate investing, both direct and indirect.

KEY TERMS

- futures contract, 363
- commodity, 363
- option, 363
- collectibles, 364
- precious metals, 364
- gems, 364
- franchise, 366
- direct investing, 367
- indirect investing, 369

LO 11-3.1 What Are High-Risk Investment Options?

High-risk investment options involve considerable uncertainty. If you are willing to take the risks involved with these choices, you stand to make high returns over time. However, you also risk big losses if your investments perform poorly.

Futures and Options

A **futures contract** is an obligation to buy or sell stock or a specific commodity for a set price on a set date in the future. A **commodity** is an item that has the same value across the market with little or no difference in quality among producers. Examples include farm products (such as wheat, soybeans, and cattle) and metals (such as gold and silver).

Buying and selling a futures contract does not transfer ownership. It spells out the terms under which the commodity will be bought or sold at a later date. Futures contracts are often used by sellers and buyers as a way to *hedge*, or reduce the likelihood of losing money in the future. For example, a farmer could sell a futures contract to deliver 5,000 bushels of wheat one year from today. In this case, the farmer knows in advance what he will be paid for the wheat. If prices of wheat fall during the year, the farmer can make money because he or she is being paid a set price; if prices rise, however, the farmer will lose money.

An **option** is the right, but not the obligation, to buy or sell stock or a specific commodity for a set price within a set time period. A *call option* is the right to buy shares of stock or a commodity at a set price by a certain expiration date. A *put option* is the right to sell stock or a commodity at a fixed price until the expiration date. An investor who thinks the price of a stock or commodity will increase during a short period of time may decide to purchase a call option. On the other hand, an investor who feels that the price of a stock or commodity will decrease

futures contract an obligation to buy or sell stock or a specific commodity for a set price on a set date in the future

commodity an item that has the same value across the market with little or no difference in quality among producers

option the right, but not the obligation, to buy or sell stock or a commodity for a set price within a set time period

during a short period of time may purchase a put option to safeguard the investment. Options are very risky and not for the inexperienced investor.

Because you have no control over what happens to the price of commodities, investing in them through futures and options is very risky. Investors who have an in-depth knowledge of how the market for a particular product fluctuates may be able to do well trading commodities.

Why are collectibles considered a risky investment?

Collectibles

collectibles physical assets that appreciate in value over time because they are rare or desired by many

Collectibles are physical assets that appreciate in value over time because they are rare or desired by many. Collectibles include such things as antiques, baseball cards, coins, stamps, and fine art. Some of these items do go up in value, but others do not. And if you need to sell your collectible, you may not be able to find a buyer who is willing to pay what you believe your investment is worth.

Buying collectibles is a very risky investment choice. When collecting, have a clear goal in mind. Decide whether you are collecting items as an investment or whether you are simply buying items for your own enjoyment. If you are buying items as an investment, conduct market research to learn which items may increase in value. Also, learn how to distinguish between an authentic item and a replica. Being able to prove authenticity is very important.

Precious Metals

precious metals rare metals that have known value around the world

Precious metals are rare metals that have known value around the world. Gold, silver, and platinum are examples of precious metals. They are usually rare, natural substances that have high economic value. However, the prices of precious metals can swing widely over time. These price swings make precious metal investments risky.

You can buy gold, silver, and platinum as coins, medallions, jewelry, and bullion. Storage can be difficult due to bulk and weight. Instead of physically taking possession, you may wish to have ownership in the form of a certificate that indicates your ownership status and the storage location. You can also buy metals indirectly by investing in the stocks of companies that mine, store, or own them. Other metals in which you can invest include aluminum, tin, copper, lead, nickel, and zinc. Prices for precious metals can be found in the financial pages of newspapers and online at various financial websites.

Gems

gems natural, precious stones such as diamonds, rubies, sapphires, and emeralds

Gems are natural, precious stones such as diamonds, rubies, sapphires, and emeralds. Prices are usually high and subject to change. Gems have their highest value in jewelry. However, buying jewelry at retail prices

FOCUS On...

DAY TRADERS

Day traders are individuals who attempt to make money by buying and selling stocks and bonds over short periods of time. These investments are not held for long-term growth. They are held just long enough for the day trader to try to make a profit. When the day trader sees a stock's price rising, the stock is sold for a quick profit. When the day trader sees prices dropping for stocks that are good values, the trader buys. If the prices rise again, the trader sells the stock to make a profit. However, if the prices do not rise again, the trader takes a loss.

Day traders must be aware of general market conditions. They also must be familiar with companies, products, and industries in which they trade. By carefully watching the market and keeping track of trends, day traders can make considerable profits over time. However, day trading can be very risky. Day traders often suffer severe financial losses, especially in their first months of trading, and many never graduate to profit-making status at all. In addition, because they trade so often, day traders must pay high trading commissions, fees, and expenses. These costs require them to earn large profits just to break even.

Think Critically

1. When stock prices rise, day traders make profits by selling stock. This activity causes the market to drop in value. Some people find this practice annoying at best and unethical at worst. How might it affect your overall portfolio?
2. Day traders must pay ordinary tax rates on their gains because they hold their stock for less than a year. Some have proposed those rates should be higher than regular tax rates. Why do you think this is so?

often involves very high markups, from 50 to 500 percent or more. Prices must increase substantially in the world market before you can recover the cost and make a profit from reselling your jewelry. Owning gems is risky because the market for them is small and unpredictable. There may be no ready market (willing buyer) when you want to sell. Fraud is also a common risk that investors will face when purchasing gems. Unless you are working with a professional appraiser, judging whether a stone is real can be very difficult.

 CHECKPOINT

What is the difference between a futures contract and an option?

LO 11-3.2 How Do You Invest in Business Ownership?

There are several ways that entrepreneurs can get involved in business ownership. If you own a business by yourself, it is known as a *sole proprietorship*. If you form a business with one or more other persons, it is called a *partnership*. These forms of small business ownership allow you to work for yourself. They are also considered risky because you will be responsible for any losses or for sharing any losses. In many cases, proprietors and partners commit their personal assets, cash, and lines of credit to get and keep the business going.

Starting a Business

If you decide to go into business for yourself, you'll need a solid plan. More than half of all small businesses fail each year, often because of poor planning and inadequate funding. Starting a business is a very risky investment. If the business succeeds, however, it can be a profitable investment. As you learned in Chapter 2, you'll need a business plan. A business plan includes a statement of the company mission, the financing needs, the marketing plan, the management plan, and the operating plan for the company. The business plan attempts to show how the business will make a profit. It is used by potential lenders to evaluate your chances for success and to show you are worthy of funding.

New businesses are started every year, some in garages or spare rooms. As they grow, they expand until they need a larger site, investors, and employees. The goal may be to go public through an *initial public offering (IPO)* so you can sell stock in the company to the general public. At this point, the business takes on a life of its own, and the founder becomes a stockholder of a corporation.

Buying a Business

Rather than starting your own business, you may wish to purchase an existing business. You can purchase the business's assets, including inventory, store location, fixtures, and other items of value. An existing business often has an established customer base and a track record of success. However, your initial costs will be higher because you'll have to buy the business for its market value. Also, you will have to make sure beforehand that the business is a sound investment. Many businesses are for sale because they are not making a profit or they have other serious problems, such as a poor reputation with customers or poor location.

franchise a contract that gives you the right to sell a company's products and services

Some small business owners may choose to buy a franchise. A **franchise** is a contract that gives you the right to sell a company's products and services. These businesses are less risky because most franchises are well known and have established products or services and customer bases. Franchising opportunities exist in virtually every field, from hotels to restaurants, to hair salons.

Why is investing in a franchise like Dunkin' Donuts less risky than starting your own business?

Forming Business Ventures

A *business venture* is a new business or business idea that is backed by investors who expect a return on their investment. Investors may join together to develop a new product idea or business strategy.

They may patent a new product and bring it to market themselves, or they may sell it to another business to be developed further and marketed. Setting up a business venture for investment purposes can be risky, but it also provides investment opportunities that otherwise would not be affordable.

Some affluent individuals use their own money to help small businesses get started. These *angel investors* (also known as *venture capitalists*) offer cash as well as their business experience and expertise. In exchange, they often require some control of the business as well as a large ownership interest, such as 50 percent or more. When profits are made, they will be repaid for their loan.

Some people who decide to make a cash investment in a business venture while letting others operate the business are treated as *silent partners*. Silent partners share the profits as a return on the investment but are not liable for the business losses or liabilities.

CHECKPOINT

What is included in a business plan?

LO 11-3.3 How Do You Invest in Real Estate?

When you invest in real estate, you are buying land and any buildings on it. The rewards can be great when one of these investments gains substantial value over time. However, real estate is an illiquid investment because a property can take months or even years to sell. Also, some real estate investments are speculative and can result in a substantial loss. You can invest in real estate directly or indirectly.

Direct Investing

With **direct investing**, the investor holds legal title to the property and has control over management decisions. Types of real estate that you can buy directly include vacant land or lots and rental properties.

direct investing the investor holds legal title to a property and has control over management decisions

Vacant Land or Lots

The purchase of *vacant land*, or unimproved property, is often classified as speculative investing. The investor is buying now with the hope that the property will increase substantially in value in the long run. For example, a vacant lot today may be in a sparsely populated area. But 20 or 30 years from now, it may be the prime location for a new shopping mall or housing subdivision. Because it is speculative in nature, most lenders will not provide financing (loans) for the purchase of vacant land.

Some people also buy vacant land to meet long-term goals, such as building a house. Many people expect that for retirement, they can develop the property or use it for recreation purposes.

Rental Property

Individuals can buy real estate beyond a family home. If you buy a house, duplex, apartment complex, vacation property, or other type of property and rent it to tenants, you will receive rental income. Buying rental real estate has risks and responsibilities.

Although the tenant (renter) must take reasonable care of the property, the owner is responsible for repairs and maintenance. This may mean fixing or replacing the roof, painting, and other upkeep. In addition to these expenses, other costs of ownership include mortgage payments, property taxes, and property insurance. When the *rental income* exceeds your costs of ownership, you have a *positive cash flow*. When rental income does not exceed all of these costs, the result is a *negative cash flow*. Without enough cash to pay the costs, the owner must get cash from other sources. This situation is often referred to as "feeding the investment" because the investment (in this case, rental property) is unable to generate enough revenue to pay its own costs.

Rental property has many tax advantages. As the owner, you can deduct all the expenses of ownership, including property taxes. You can also deduct for *depreciation*, which is the decline in the value of the property due to normal wear and tear. Depreciation is really a "write-off" for tax purposes because your property will likely increase, not decrease, in overall value. Some day the mortgage on the rental property will be paid off, and the rent collected will be profit for the investor.

You should consider the risks of owning a rental property. For example, tenants may damage the property or fail to pay the rent. In addition, vacancies can decrease rental income, cutting into your profits. Under poor economic conditions, the property may lose value, resulting in a loss when the property is sold.

Would you consider buying rental property as an investment? Why or why not?

Indirect Investing

With **indirect investing**, investors have a third person do the actual buying and selling of property. A *trustee* is an individual or institution that manages assets for someone else. The trustee holds the title to the property. Real estate investment trusts and real estate syndicates are examples of indirect investments using a third-party trustee.

indirect investing investors have a third person do the actual buying and selling of property

Real Estate Investment Trusts

A *real estate investment trust (REIT)* is a corporation that pools the money of many individuals to invest in real estate projects. REITs are also known as real estate stocks. A REIT may own and operate income-producing property, such as an apartment building that rents to families or a factory building that rents to a business. A REIT may lend money to real estate developers. It may also invest in securities backed by real estate mortgages (investments in debt).

A REIT is similar to a mutual fund in that it allows you to invest in the portfolios of large-scale properties through the purchase of shares of stock. You can buy and sell REIT shares at will, making them highly liquid. Many REITs are publicly traded on stock markets. Because of the nature of real estate, REITs fluctuate with market conditions. When the real estate investments do well, dividends (profits) are distributed to the shareholders. They often outperform many other investments over the long run.

Real Estate Syndicates

A *real estate syndicate* is a group of investors who pool their money to purchase, operate, and then resell a single high-priced property. This is a temporary association of individuals whose purpose is to raise a large amount of capital to purchase property that they could not obtain on their own.

The organizer of the syndicate is called the *general partner*. The people who contribute the capital are called *limited partners*. In a real estate syndicate, the general partner forms a partnership and assumes unlimited liability for all of the debts of the partnership. By assuming unlimited liability, the general partner's responsibility extends beyond the initial investment to his or her personal assets if the investment incurs debt. The general partner then sells participation units to the limited partners. Limited partners have no management responsibility, and their liability is limited to the amount of their investment. After expenses related to the property and operations are paid, any remaining cash is distributed to the partners, often on a quarterly basis, until the property is resold.

 CHECKPOINT

List two examples of real estate investing (direct or indirect).

KEY TERMS REVIEW

Match the terms with the definitions. Some terms may not be used.

_____ 1. An obligation to buy or sell stock or a specific commodity for a set price on a set date in the future

_____ 2. Physical assets that appreciate in value over time because they are rare or desired by many

_____ 3. The investor holds title to the property and has control over management decisions

_____ 4. The right, but not the obligation, to buy or sell stock or a commodity for a set price within a set time period

_____ 5. A contract that gives you the right to sell a company's products or services

_____ 6. Natural, precious stones such as diamonds, rubies, sapphires, and emeralds

_____ 7. An item that has the same value across the market with little or no difference in quality among producers

_____ 8. Investors use a third person to do the actual buying and selling of property

a. collectibles

b. commodity

c. direct investing

d. franchise

e. futures contract

f. gems

g. indirect investing

h. option

i. precious metals

CHECK YOUR UNDERSTANDING

9. Give three examples of commodities.

10. Why are futures contracts often used as a "hedge" against losing money in the future?

11. What is the difference between a put option and a call option?

12. Why is it important to study the business plan when considering a business venture investment?

13. How can a venture capitalist help you start a business?

14. What risks are associated with owning rental property?

15. What are two ways in which an investor can make money on rental property?

16. How does a real estate investment trust (REIT) work? Why is it safer than a direct investment in rental property?

THINK CRITICALLY

17. Name some collectibles you have seen, collected, or read about that have increased substantially in value over the years. What would you like to collect?

18. Why are precious metals and gems considered risky investments? Why would investors be willing to take the risk?

19. If you want to invest in some form of business ownership, what can you do to reduce your risk?

20. Why is real estate considered an illiquid investment? Why might this be a factor for some investors?

21. Why is the purchase of vacant land speculative, or highly risky?

22. When investing in rental property, why is the need for a positive cash flow so important?

23. If investing in rental property is risky, why do many people do it?

EXTEND YOUR LEARNING

24. The Internet has provided a new way for buyers and sellers of collectibles to find each other. Search the Internet for websites dealing with a collectible that interests you. How is this item bought and sold online? Is there an association or club for your collectible? If so, how does the site help collectors?

25. Suppose your investment portfolio is well balanced, with short-term investments, stocks, bonds, and mutual funds. You own your own home. Recently, you unexpectedly received a large sum of money. You want to take some risk and invest the money in hopes of making a high return.

    a. You are considering the high-risk investment options listed below. Which option would you choose?

    - Buy futures contracts for a commodity
    - Buy a painting by a well-known, popular artist
    - Purchase a one-carat diamond ring in a platinum setting
    - Invest in a small business venture
    - Buy a vacant lot in an area of town that is undeveloped
    - Buy a condominium to rent

    b. Give an advantage and a disadvantage of your choice.

THE ESSENTIAL QUESTION   Refer to The Essential Question on p. 363. There may be no ready market (willing buyer) for collectibles, precious metals, and gems when you want (need) to sell. Startup businesses are risky because the money you invest is lost if the company fails. There is a chance that real estate may not increase in value over the long run, and because it is illiquid, it can take a long time to sell.

Exploring Careers in...
COMPUTER PROGRAMMING

Computer programmers write software programs. They turn the program designs created by software developers into instructions that a computer can follow. The instructions are written in a language known as *code*. Most programmers specialize in writing programs in a particular type of computer language, such as Java and C++.

Programmers must test the program at various stages. If a program does not work correctly, they check the code for mistakes and correct them. This process is known as *debugging*. They must also maintain the program and make any updates when needed. Changes in hardware, operating systems, and equipment often require revisions to the programs in order for them to operate properly.

Employment Outlook

- An average rate of employment growth is expected.

Job Titles

- Computer programmer
- Programmer
- Program analyst
- Software developer

Needed Education/Skills

- A bachelor's degree in computer science or a related field is desired, although some employers will hire programmers with an associate's degree.
- Continuing education to keep up with changing technology is recommended.
- Being highly detail oriented and possessing strong analytical and troubleshooting skills are necessary.

What's it like to work in ... Computer Programming

Jayce works as a computer programmer for a large marketing firm. She works alone at the computer for many hours a day but meets with other team members to communicate problems and proposed solutions.

Today, Jayce is meeting with the company's software developers, who are presenting her with a program design for a new marketing research software. Jayce's job will be to create the software program by using the Java programming language. She must have the program up and running within three months.

As Jayce writes the program, she will test it at various stages to make sure it is working correctly. If it isn't, she must figure out where the error is in the code and fix it so the program will function to meet the needs of the marketing department.

What About You?

Do you enjoy working with computers? Do you have an aptitude for writing detailed instructions that are logical and systematic? Do you enjoy problem solving? Would a job as a computer programmer appeal to you? Why or why not?

Chapter 11 Assessment

SUMMARY

11-1 Low-risk saving options include savings accounts, money market accounts, CDs, life insurance savings plans, and brokerage accounts. Because these options are low risk, they pay a lower rate of return. Savings accounts and money market accounts have a high degree of liquidity. CDs and life insurance savings plans are illiquid; early withdrawal penalties apply to money withdrawn before a set period of time.

Low-risk investment options include corporate bonds, municipal bonds, U.S. government savings bonds, U.S. government Treasury securities, and annuities purchased from a life insurance company. Corporate bonds are rated based on their safety. Municipal bonds, U.S. government savings bonds, and Treasury securities offer tax advantages.

11-2 Mutual funds use money pooled from many investors to buy stocks, bonds, and other securities that fit the fund's specific investment objective. An investor buys shares in the fund that best matches the investor's goals and risk comfort level.

Stockholders earn income through dividends and capital gains.

Preferred stock is less risky than common stock. Categories of stock include income stocks, growth stocks, blue chip stocks, and defensive stocks.

Buying a home has risks, but it provides tax advantages and can provide a good return when home values rise faster than inflation.

Individual retirement account options include traditional IRAs, Roth IRAs, Keogh plans, and simplified employee pension (SEP) plans.

Employer-sponsored retirement accounts include defined-benefit plans, such as pension plans, and defined-contribution plans, such as 401(k) and 403(b) plans.

11-3 High-risk investment choices include futures contracts, options, collectibles, precious metals, and gems.

Starting or buying a business or forming a business venture with other investors are ways to invest in business ownership.

If you invest in real estate directly, you own legal title to the property and have control over management decisions. Examples of direct investing include purchasing vacant land and rental property.

If you invest in real estate indirectly, a trustee holds legal title on behalf of the investor group. Examples of indirect investing include real estate investment groups (REITs) and real estate syndicates.

MAKE ACADEMIC CONNECTIONS

TEAMWORK

1. **Research** Work with a classmate to complete this activity. (LO 11-1.1, LO 11-1.2, LO 11-2.1, LO 11-2.2, LO 11-2.3, LO 11-3.1, LO 11-3.2, LO 11-3.3)

    a. Complete the following grid of investments based on risk, return, and liquidity. In each square of the grid, write one or more investments that fit the criteria. For example, in the first square, write the name of a savings or investing option that is liquid and has low risk. Write *None* in a square if no investment meets both the criteria.

	Low Risk	Medium Risk	High Risk
Liquid			
Low Return			
Medium Return			
High Return			

    b. Pick one type of investment from each column (one with low risk, one with medium risk, and one with high risk) that you would consider having in your portfolio. Give an advantage and a disadvantage of each one.

2. **Ethics** Many companies have stopped offering pension plans. Some companies that still provide the plans have not funded them at the needed level. Other companies have changed the rules that govern their pension plans to reduce benefits. A company might also declare bankruptcy. These actions often leave employees without some of their promised retirement benefits. The Pension Benefit Guaranty Corporation (PBGC) is a federal corporation created by the Employee Retirement Income Security Act of 1974. Its mission is to protect retirement incomes of millions of U.S. workers with pension plans. When a pension plan fails, workers may receive some benefits from the PBGC. Although the employer's actions may not be illegal, some people think it is unethical to deny retired workers the benefits they were promised. What effect has this type of activity had on U.S. workers and their families? What message does this convey about the importance of retirement planning? (LO 11-2.3)

3. **Economics** When you buy U.S. savings bonds, notes, and bills, you are lending money to the U.S. government. As such, it is part of the national debt. Conduct online research on the national debt and prepare a two-page report on how much it is, what types of debt are involved, and what it means to you as a current or future taxpayer. (LO 11-1.2)

4. **History** Gold is a commodity. Most of the U.S. gold supply is stored at Fort Knox. What is meant by the "gold standard"? Does the United States have a gold standard today? How much gold does the United States currently have? Conduct online research and prepare a brief history of the importance of gold to the U.S. economy. (LO 11-3.1)

Do the Math

1. You have a CD for $1,000. The interest rate is 5 percent annually, and the term is 5 years. The CD has an early withdrawal penalty. If the money is withdrawn before 36 months, interest is paid for the time the money is in the account, but a 6-month interest penalty is deducted. If you withdraw the money after 12 months, what penalty will you pay? How much money will you get?

2. You purchased a house for $125,000. You spent $15,000 for repairs, remodeling, property taxes, and other expenses. You sold the house one year later for $160,000. How much profit did you make on the house? What is your return on investment?

3. You purchased 100 shares of stock at $125 per share. One year later, the price of the stock has risen to $150 per share. What is the percentage increase in the stock price?

Take Action

RESEARCH MUTUAL FUNDS

Investing in mutual funds is a good way to have a diversified portfolio and balance risk.

a. Use the Internet to find sites about mutual funds. Use a search engine and enter the search terms *mutual funds, mutual fund list,* or *types of mutual funds.*

b. Review two or three websites that describe mutual funds. Choose one fund. For that fund, record the following information:
   - Fund name
   - Fund trading symbol
   - Strategy or objective of the fund (such as balance or growth)
   - Holdings (list of investments the fund contains)
   - Performance in recent years (percent of return each year)

c. Find the selling price of a share in the mutual fund. (You may have to visit a different website that provides market quotes to find the price.) The price will likely be labeled NAV (for net asset value). The NAV is the price of one share in the fund at the close of trading on a particular day.

d. What do you think is the risk level of this mutual fund—low, medium, or high? Prepare a report describing your findings and making a recommendation for the purchase/rejection of this mutual fund.

Include the information you collected about mutual funds in your portfolio.

Buying and Selling Investments

Justin Lane/Epa/Landov

Chapter 12 covers the basics of buying and selling investments. Much information about investing is available. Some information is free; some is costly. You can hire a full-service broker, or you can take a more active role in building and maintaining your investment portfolio. Either way, there are effective strategies for purchasing that will save you both time and money. You will also learn about regulatory agencies and financial reform legislation that are designed to inform and protect you, the investor, when you buy and sell securities.

Do *This*, Not *That*

When choosing a broker or financial planner:

- Choose someone with whom you are comfortable.
- Ask how your confidential and personal data will be protected.
- Consider fees charged.
- Ask about his or her investing philosophy.
- Use the Financial Industry Regulatory Authority's online "BrokerCheck" tool to verify the person's credentials.

12-1 Researching Investments and Markets

LEARNING OBJECTIVES

LO 12-1.1 Describe the types of financial information found in magazines, newspapers, newsletters, and other public sources.

LO 12-1.2 Discuss the kinds of advice and assistance that are available from financial experts.

LO 12-1.3 Explain how financial markets are designed for securities transactions.

KEY TERMS

- annual report, 378
- prospectus, 378
- full-service broker, 380
- discount broker, 380
- primary market, 382
- secondary market, 382
- securities exchange, 382
- auction market, 382
- over-the-counter (OTC) market, 383
- stock dividend, 383
- stock split, 384

LO 12-1.1 What Are Sources of Investing Information?

Investors need to know about the economy and current market trends. They also need to learn about specific companies or funds in which they may want to invest. Keeping informed about current market conditions helps investors make better choices. There are several sources that provide investing information.

Magazines

A number of weekly and monthly magazines specialize in business and financial information. These magazines contain news, articles, market analysis, and expert opinions on various topics related to investing and the economy. Some of the more popular business and financial magazines include *Business Week*, *Forbes*, *Investor's Business Daily*, *Money*, and *Kiplinger's Personal Finance*. All of these publications also offer financial news and data at their websites.

You can also find good information in news magazines such as *Time*, *Newsweek*, and *U.S. News & World Report*. These magazines contain articles related to world events that affect the economy and investments. Many news magazines also have regular features that include financial advice.

Newspapers

One of the best sources for current information is the financial pages of newspapers. The financial pages list price quotes for securities. *Securities* include stocks, bonds, mutual funds, and other investments. The financial pages also include other information related to investing, such as news articles and commentary. Reading the financial pages daily will help you keep track of the financial market and obtain information to make better investment choices.

The Wall Street Journal is a daily newspaper that provides detailed coverage of the business and financial world. *Barron's* is a weekly newspaper that also provides charts of trends, financial news, and technical analysis of financial data. Both of these publications offer online subscriptions as well as access to free articles and data at their websites.

Investor Services and Newsletters

Companies called investor services provide extensive data to clients. Major services include Standard & Poor's Financial Services, Moody's Investors Service, and Value Line. Their publications can be found in public libraries and brokerage firms, as well as online. They contain precise current and historical financial data.

Many investors subscribe to weekly or monthly *investment newsletters*. These newsletters provide the latest financial data and information as well as advice and commentary. Subscription costs for newsletters vary.

Company Reports

annual report a company's report to shareholders about the financial position of the company

The Securities and Exchange Commission (SEC) requires all corporations that sell stock to the public to prepare a yearly annual report. An **annual report** is a company's report to shareholders about the financial position of the company. It provides a summary of a corporation's profits or losses for the year and its prospects for the future. It also provides information about the company stock and dividends. Investors can use the information from annual reports in conjunction with current stock prices to evaluate the corporation as an investment prospect or to compare one company to another. Figure 12-1.1 describes a few key figures that investors can use to make these comparisons.

You can find annual reports online at the SEC's website. Corporations often publish their financial performance data in the "Investors" section of their websites.

The Prospectus

prospectus a legal document issued by an investment company that provides details about the securities it offers for sale

The SEC also requires that all mutual fund companies provide potential buyers with a prospectus. A **prospectus** is a legal document issued by an investment company that provides details about the securities it offers for sale. A fund prospectus contains a summary of the fund's portfolio of investments, its objectives, and financial statements showing past performance.

You can find company prospectuses at EDGAR, a database maintained by the SEC. You may also find a company's prospectus at its corporate website.

Investment Clubs

Joining an investment club is a good way to get investing information. An *investment club* is a group of friends, relatives, or acquaintances who share an interest in studying companies for the purpose of making investments. They meet on a regular basis. Members of an investment club share responsibility for researching and presenting possible purchases. Each investment club member usually contributes an amount, such as $25–$50, that is deposited in a joint account. The money is then used to purchase and hold investments in the club's partnership based on the research conducted and recommendations made by the members.

Figure	Description
Current stock price	The amount investors are willing to pay for a share of ownership in the company.
Number of employees	Increases or decreases in the number of employees can reflect growth or downsizing.
Market cap (capitalization)	The total value of a company in the stock market (total shares outstanding times price per share). This figure, along with revenue, indicates the size of a company.
Revenue	The amount of money received from business activities. This may be mostly from sales of products and/or services to customers.
Net income or profit	The amount of money earned after deducting all the business's expenses. To investors, this number is more important than revenue.
Profit margin	Profit shown as a percentage. It is the net income divided by revenue for the same period.
P/E ratio	The price-earnings ratio compares the selling price of a company's common stock to the annual profits (earnings) per share. Fast-growing or high-risk companies may have higher P/E ratios than slow-growing or low-risk companies. This ratio is an important measure of a stock's value.
Current ratio	A measure of a company's ability to pay its current debts from current assets. It indicates a company's liquidity and financial strength. The current ratio is calculated by dividing the total current assets by the total current liabilities.

Investment clubs may have stated goals and buy investments, ranging from low risk to high risk, to help reach those goals. The level of risk taken is often related to the club's knowledge and experience.

The Internet

One of the best ways to find investing information is to use the Internet. As previously mentioned, print publications and companies have websites that provide valuable investing information. Search engines such as Google, Yahoo!, or Bing™ allow users to search for data on almost any investment topic. You can use search engines to find data on specific companies, stocks, bonds, mutual funds, the financial market, and the economy. There are a number of free educational sites for investors. Some websites maintain and compile financial information to help investors analyze and understand the market. Figure 12-1.2 lists some Internet sites that investors might find helpful.

 CHECKPOINT

What types of financial information can be found in print sources?

Site Name	Information/Features Provided
Bloomberg www.bloomberg.com	News articles; market data for stocks, bonds, currency, mutual funds, commodities, and other securities; investment tools; online tutorials for investing; and other features.
CNNMoney.com money.cnn.com	Current financial news and information to help investors make better decisions.
Kiplinger www.kiplinger.com	Tools to help beginners get started. Investors can use this site to track investments in both stocks and mutual funds.
Morningstar www.morningstar.com	Articles related to investments and stocks in the news, research reports, newsletters, and portfolio tracking and other tools.
Reuters www.reuters.com	Business and investing articles, stock quotes, bond and currency news, and investment tracking tools.

LO 12-1.2 What Professional Advice Is Available?

Choosing which stock, bond, mutual fund, or other investment to buy is an important decision. With so much data available in online and print sources, investors may feel overwhelmed. They may not understand all the data or know how to compare companies or funds. Thus, many investors opt to seek advice from experts when deciding how to invest.

Stockbrokers

A *stockbroker* is a licensed professional who buys and sells securities on behalf of others. The broker will make commissions on the items that the investor buys. Stocks, bonds, and mutual funds are examples of securities traded through stockbrokers.

There are two general categories of stockbrokers: full-service and discount. A **full-service broker** is a qualified stockbroker who provides advice about what securities to buy and sell. A full-service broker will consider his or her client's investment goals and risk tolerance levels. The information provided, along with the broker's knowledge about the market and securities, will be used to select stocks or other investments to help the client reach his or her goals. The broker will recommend the best timing for stock trades and will carry out the transactions. The broker will charge a commission and/or fee for services. The client will receive regular reports of activity and account balances. Merrill Lynch, Morgan Stanley, and Edward Jones are examples of full-service brokerage firms.

A **discount broker** is a qualified stockbroker who buys and sells securities at a reduced commission but provides limited services to clients. A discount broker has the same qualifications as a full-service broker. However, discount brokers provide little or no investment advice to clients, nor do they help manage assets. Because of the limited

full-service broker a qualified stockbroker who provides advice about what securities to buy and sell

discount broker a qualified stockbroker who buys and sells securities at a reduced commission but provides limited services to clients

FULL-SERVICE OR DISCOUNT BROKERS?

There is a healthy competition between full-service brokers and other types of brokers. A smaller fee for services is one reason people choose discount or online brokers. There are other factors to consider as well. One factor is the amount of information available and how much it costs. If you have to pay extra to get the information you need to make good choices, then discount brokers may not save you money in the long run.

Another factor to think about is the amount of help you will need to make wise investment choices. If you do not have the time or expertise to study the market, you may find that your investment choices are not very profitable. You may be better off paying higher fees for sound investment advice from a full-service broker.

Investors should also look at how easy it is to buy and sell. Investors must compare services in terms of the type of trading they want to do. For example, do you want to trade online or by phone? Where is the nearest brokerage office? How often do investors receive statements? What is the charge for services such as research? What are the fees that will be charged for opening an account? Are there minimum deposits? Consider all these factors carefully to help decide which type of broker is right for you.

Think Critically

1. For your initial step into investing, would you use a full-service broker or a discount broker? Why?
2. When you become a seasoned investor, after many years of successful investing, which would you be more likely to use—a full-service broker or a discount broker? Why?

amount of services offered, the fees or commissions charged by a discount broker are much lower than those charged by a full-service broker. Charles Schwab, E*TRADE, and TD Ameritrade are examples of discount brokerage companies.

Because of the increasing popularity of inexpensive trading, many full-service brokers offer discount trading at their website. Investors can perform many activities online, such as place buy and sell orders, transfer money among investment accounts, and track the progress of their investments.

Financial Planners

A *financial planner* is an adviser who helps people make investment decisions to meet stated goals. *Certified financial planners (CFPs)* have completed education requirements and have passed CFP Board certification exams. CFPs are required to have a minimum of three years experience in the financial planning field. Financial planners work for investment and brokerage firms and at financial institutions. Typically, investors are asked to provide confidential information about assets, liabilities, net worth, and income. They also list their goals, such as saving for retirement or paying for a child's college education. The planner considers this information and suggests options that will help meet the investor's goals. The adviser usually receives a fee for consulting services.

In addition to providing advice, some financial planners sell financial products, such as stocks, bonds, and life insurance policies. They receive a commission on the products they sell. Generally, you will get better advice when the adviser does not stand to make a profit on the investments you choose to buy.

Financial Institutions

Some banks, credit unions, and other financial institutions provide their customers with financial advice. Personal bankers at these companies are licensed to sell securities that are endorsed by the company. These *licensed personal bankers* make a commission on products they sell. Some banks offer their own brand of securities. Investors can choose the bank's investment account, which is similar to owning shares of a mutual fund.

> ## »» CHECKPOINT
> How does a discount broker differ from a full-service broker?

LO 12-1.3 How Are Financial Markets Structured?

primary market the financial market in which new issues of securities are sold

When securities (stocks and bonds) are bought or sold on the financial market, they are said to be traded. Securities can be traded in the primary market or secondary market. The **primary market** is the financial market in which new issues of securities are sold. Securities are purchased directly from the issuing company. New security issues are often in the form of initial public offerings. An *initial public offering (IPO)* is a company's first sale of its stock to the public. IPOs are often made by small or young companies seeking to expand their business. They can do this with the money raised by selling stock. Small investors often are not able to purchase securities in the primary market.

secondary market the financial market in which previously issued securities are bought and sold

The **secondary market** is the financial market in which previously issued securities are bought and sold. The buyer is trading with an investor who already owns the stock. After stock is sold in the primary market, it can be resold many times in the secondary market.

Investors can use the services of a broker to trade securities. Securities may be listed on securities exchanges or in the over-the-counter market. Investors can also trade securities directly.

Securities Exchanges

securities exchange a marketplace where brokers buy and sell securities for their clients

A **securities exchange** is a marketplace where brokers buy and sell securities for their clients. Securities listed on the exchange have been accepted for trading at that exchange. The largest organized exchange in the United States is the New York Stock Exchange (NYSE). To have stock listed with the NYSE, a company must meet minimum requirements pertaining to income and revenue, market value, and the number of public shares of stock. Brokers must be members of the NYSE to do business on the NYSE trading floor.

auction market a market in which buyers enter competitive bids and sellers enter competitive offers at the same time

The NYSE is a form of auction market. In an **auction market**, buyers enter competitive bids and sellers enter competitive offers at the same time. Stock is sold to the highest bidder (buyer) and bought from the lowest offeror (seller).

NASDAQ is another popular securities exchange. It is a *dealer market*, rather than an auction market, because dealers (or stock traders) work directly with other dealers to buy and sell NASDAQ securities without the use of brokers. NASDAQ is a completely computerized network and does not have a physical location (trading floor).

Over-the-Counter Market

When securities are bought and sold through brokers but not through a stock exchange, the transaction is over the counter. The **over-the-counter (OTC) market** is a network of brokers who buy and sell securities of corporations that are not listed on a securities exchange. A stock might be traded in the OTC market because the company is small and unable to meet exchange listing requirements. However, some large, well-known companies are also traded over the counter. Trades are completed by telephone or computer networks.

over-the-counter (OTC) market a network of brokers who buy and sell securities that are not listed on a securities exchange

Direct Investing

Direct investing involves buying securities directly from a corporation. You do not use a broker. There are many forms of direct investing. Buying U.S. government savings bonds is a form of direct investing that carries low risk. Many companies have direct investing plans that allow individual investors to purchase stock.

Direct investing offers many advantages. By buying directly, you avoid brokerage and other purchasing fees. You may also be able to obtain shares at prices lower than on open exchanges. Another advantage is that you are aware of the investments you have at all times. When you buy direct, you make the decisions about the items to buy and sell and the timing of the trades. People who participate in direct investing can use a spreadsheet to keep track of their investments, as shown in Figure 12-1.3.

Why do some investors choose direct investing instead of using brokers?

Reinvesting

When investors forego a cash dividend to receive more shares of stock in a company, this is a form of *reinvesting*. By acquiring more shares of stock, stockholders have the opportunity to grow their wealth. Many corporations issue a stock dividend instead of a cash dividend. A **stock dividend** is a dividend paid in the form of new shares of stock. For example, with a 10 percent stock dividend, you would receive 10 new shares of stock for every 100 shares of stock you currently own. The price per share does not change. Having more shares of stock grows wealth. In the future, you will receive more dividends and have more shares of stock to sell.

stock dividend a dividend paid in the form of new shares of stock

	A	B	C	D	E	F	G
1	STOCK RECORD						
2	Stock A:						
3	Purchase Date	No. of Shares	Price Paid per Share	Sold Date	No. of Shares	Price Rec'd per Share	ROI
4	12/2/20--	500	$55.25				
5	3/30/20--	100	$58.45	12/28/20--	100	$68.00	21.9%
6							
7	Date		Closing Price			Average Price Paid:	$55.78
8	1/30/20--		$55.00				
9	2/1/20--		$57.25				
10	3/1/20--		$58.95				
11	4/1/20--		$52.50				
12	5/1/20--		$53.78				
13	6/1/20--		$57.50				
14	7/1/20--		$59.32				
15	8/1/20--		$59.25				
16	9/1/20--		$60.35				
17	10/1/20--		$65.50				
18	11/1/20--		$70.65				
19	12/1/20--		$68.50				
20							
21	Average Price:		$59.88				
22	Highest Price:		$70.65				
23	Lowest Price:		$52.50				
24							

stock split the issuance of more stock to current shareholders in some proportion to the stock they already own

Reinvesting may also take the form of a stock split. A **stock split** occurs when a company issues more stock to current shareholders in some proportion to the stock they already own. A two-for-one split means that for every share you own, you get an additional share of stock. For example, assume you own 100 shares of stock at $50 par value per share. (*Par value* is the stated value of the stock at the time it is issued.) After a 2:1 split, you would own 200 shares at $25 par value per share. In other words, the number of shares increases by the same multiple that par value decreases. Although your total stock value is still $5,000, now you have more shares. Because the selling price of the stock is lower, it encourages investors to buy more. As investors buy more stock, the share price often rises, along with the total value of your stock.

Stock dividends and stock splits involve no brokerage fees or costs to investors, and they are not taxable income. Many corporations choose these forms of rewarding investors (rather than paying cash dividends) to preserve their cash and use it for growth purposes.

 CHECKPOINT

How is the primary market different from the secondary market?

12-1 Lesson Assessment

KEY TERMS REVIEW

Match the terms with the definitions. Some terms may not be used.

_____ 1. A qualified stockbroker who provides advice about what securities to buy and sell

_____ 2. A qualified stockbroker who buys and sells securities at a reduced commission but provides limited services to clients

_____ 3. A marketplace where brokers buy and sell securities for their clients

_____ 4. The financial market in which previously issued securities are bought and sold

_____ 5. A dividend paid in the form of new shares of stock

_____ 6. The financial market in which new issues of securities are sold

a. annual report

b. auction market

c. discount broker

d. full-service broker

e. over-the-counter (OTC) market

f. primary market

g. prospectus

h. secondary market

i. securities exchange

j. stock dividend

k. stock split

_____ 7. A network of brokers who buy and sell securities that are not listed on a securities exchange

_____ 8. A company's report to shareholders about the financial position of the company

_____ 9. The issuance of more stock to current shareholders in some proportion to the stock they already own

CHECK YOUR UNDERSTANDING

10. List three magazines and/or newspapers that give information and advice about spending and investing.

11. Describe the type of information available in a company annual report.

12. What information is contained in a prospectus?

13. What must a financial planner do to become certified?

14. What is an initial public offering (IPO)? What is its purpose?

15. How many times may a stock be sold in the primary market? In the secondary market?

16. What is the difference between an auction market and a dealer market? Provide an example of each.

17. What is meant by reinvesting?

18. How are stock dividends different from stock splits?

THINK CRITICALLY

19. Why might an investor want to subscribe to an investment newsletter?

20. Why would you use the Internet to find information on investing? What kinds of information might you research online?

21. Why would someone buy stock on a securities exchange rather than in the over-the-counter (OTC) market?

22. Why would you invest directly with a company? Why would you reinvest?

23. Why would a company choose to reward investors with a stock dividend rather than a cash dividend?

24. How do investors benefit from stock splits?

EXTEND YOUR LEARNING

25. Choose three corporations to research online. Create a table that compares the three companies, using the format shown below. Enter the names of the companies in the top row and then complete the rest of the table. After doing so, answer the questions below.

Company name			
Industry or primary business			
Current stock price			
Revenue			
Net income			
Profit margin			
P/E ratio			
Current ratio			

a. Which company had the highest revenue?

b. Which company had the highest net income?

c. Which company had the highest P/E ratio?

d. Did each company have a current ratio of 1 or above? If not, which ones did not?

e. Would you consider one or more of these companies a good investment? Why or why not?

THE ESSENTIAL QUESTION   Refer to The Essential Question on p. 377. Sources of investing information include magazines, newspapers, investor services and newsletters, annual reports, prospectuses, investment clubs, websites, stockbrokers, financial planners, and financial institutions.

LEARNING OBJECTIVES

LO 12-2.1 Explain how to set up a brokerage account and begin the process of buying and selling.

LO 12-2.2 Describe techniques to use when buying and selling securities.

KEY TERMS

- market order, 388
- limit order, 388
- stop order, 388
- discretionary order, 388
- selling short, 389
- buying on margin, 390
- buy and hold, 390
- stock turning, 391
- round lot, 391
- odd lot, 391

LO 12-2.1 How Are Stocks Bought and Sold?

The purchase and sale of securities in the financial markets is a simple process. It involves setting up an investment account, requesting a transaction, and having the broker take action.

Set Up an Account

To get started buying and selling securities, begin by choosing your venue. Set up an account at a full-service broker, a discount broker, or at your bank or other financial institution. This will allow for the transfer of money that goes along with the buying and selling of securities.

Setting up an account is as simple as opening a new savings or checking account. You must provide identification information such as your Social Security number. Most brokerage accounts require a minimum deposit or a regular monthly deposit amount.

The account will house your transactions, and you will receive monthly or quarterly statements. You will be in charge of managing your account. Most accounts can be accessed online with a unique username and password, allowing you to monitor your account's activity. If you would like to make changes in your asset allocations or types of investments, you will need to follow specific procedures for requesting those changes.

Place Transactions

Once you have decided to buy or sell a stock, there are four types of transactions, called *orders*, that you can request.

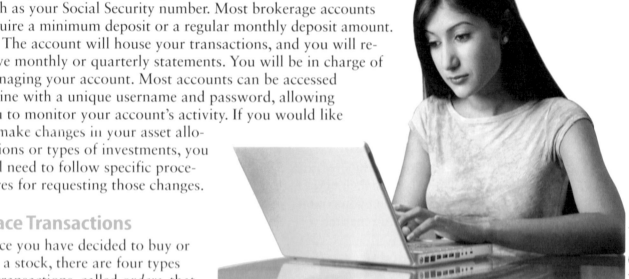

How can you set up a brokerage account?

Market Order

A **market order** is a request to buy (or sell) a stock at the current market price. In an auction market, the broker will try to get you the best price. However, there is no guarantee of what you will pay (or receive). Stock is auctioned to the highest bidder, so you may or may not get the price you hoped. For example, you may have $1,000 in your brokerage account and make a request to buy as many shares of XYZ stock as can be purchased for that amount. At the end of the day, you may have purchased 20 shares at the current market price of $50 per share.

Limit Order

limit order a request to buy (or sell) a stock at a specific price

A **limit order** is a request to buy (or sell) a stock at a specific price. When you are buying, a limit order guarantees that you will not pay more than a set dollar amount. When you are selling, the order guarantees that you will not get less than a specific dollar amount. For example, you may tell your broker to buy stock when it drops to $40 per share. If the price does not go that low, the purchase will not be made. The broker will wait until the price hits $40 and then buy the shares of stock.

Stop Order

stop order a request to sell a stock when it reaches a certain price

A **stop order** is a request to sell a stock when it reaches a certain price. This type of order protects you from a sudden drop in price. It also allows you to capture profits when a higher price is reached. For example, you may own 100 shares of ABC stock. You purchased them for $25 a share, and currently the price is $27 (down from a high of $33). You ask your broker to sell your shares if and when they reach $25 a share. Thus, if the market price drops to $25, your broker will sell your stock at the best possible price (market price), which may be lower than the price specified in the stop order. The selling price is not guaranteed.

Discretionary Order

discretionary order an order to buy (or sell) a stock that allows the broker to get the best possible price

A **discretionary order** is an order to buy (or sell) a stock that allows the broker to get the best possible price. The broker also determines the best time to make the transaction. Discretionary orders give the broker the power to use her or his experience and judgment to make good decisions. For example, you may place $1,000 into your account and ask your broker to buy shares of JKL stock as soon as they reach their best price. Your broker would research that stock and see what is likely to be the best price and the best time to purchase it.

Take Action

Following the investor's decision to move forward with a transaction, the broker then takes action. Figure 12-2.1 illustrates the steps that take place when you contact your broker to complete a purchase of stock in an auction market.

 CHECKPOINT

What are the four types of stock market transactions that can be placed?

To buy stock traded on the New York Stock Exchange, an investor would take the steps described below.

1. The investor contacts the broker and asks him or her to buy shares of stock.

2. The broker relays the order electronically to a clerk at the stock exchange.

3. The clerk gives the message to a floor broker.

4. The floor broker goes to the trading post at which this stock is traded.

5. The floor broker negotiates a buy from the floor broker for the stock being sold.

6. After the trade is made, the floor broker relays a message to the clerk and to the consolidated ticker tape (a digital display that shows securities transactions).

7. The sale appears on the ticker tape.

8. A confirmation is sent to the investor's broker.

9. The broker notifies the investor that the transaction is complete.

10. The investor's account reflects money exchanged for stock at the price and quantity agreed upon.

LO 12-2.2 When Should You Buy or Sell?

When you buy securities, you are committing to a long-term investment. Unlike your 401(k), annuity, or mutual fund, which are managed by professionals, personal investing requires you to make your own choices. As an investor, you will need to develop a strategy for buying and selling stocks.

Using Cash

By setting aside cash for investing, you will be ready to buy and sell stock or other securities when you feel it is a good time to do so. In Chapter 10, you learned about *market timing* and *investment tracking* strategies to help you decide when it is time to buy or sell. You can use your brokerage account to make stock trades when the time is right.

Using Credit

If you do not have enough cash to make the type of purchase you want, there are still ways you can *leverage* it. In other words, you can borrow money to complete the trade.

Selling Short

Selling short involves selling stock that has been borrowed from a broker and replacing it at a later date. You are hoping to buy back the stock at a lower price than you sold it for, thus making a profit. Selling short is highly risky. You are betting that stock prices will drop. If prices for the stock rise, you will lose money because you must replace the borrowed stock with stock purchased at a higher price.

selling short selling stock that has been borrowed from a broker and replacing it at a later date

buying on margin borrowing money from your broker to buy stock

Buying on Margin

Buying on margin involves borrowing money from your broker to buy stock. You must open a margin account and sign a contract with a broker called a *margin agreement*. To establish a margin account, you must deposit a minimum amount of cash or *eligible securities* (securities that your broker considers valuable collateral). Once the account is open, you can borrow up to 50 percent of the purchase price of a stock. For example, if you have $2,000 in your margin account and want to buy 100 shares of stock at $20 per share, you could use $1,000 from your margin account and borrow $1,000, with interest, from your broker. You are using a leverage strategy by borrowing money to buy stock. Because you can buy more stocks with less of your own money, you increase your chances of making a profit.

When buying on margin, you are betting that the stock will increase in value. Unfortunately, if the value of the stock does not increase, you will have to make up the difference. When the market value of a margined stock decreases by a certain percentage, you will receive a *margin call* from the broker. This means you must pledge additional cash or securities as collateral for the loan or sell the stock to avoid defaulting on the loan. Buying on margin is a risky strategy. Figure 12-2.2 illustrates the process of buying on margin.

Buying Patterns

When buying stocks and other investments, there are several buying patterns to consider. Each of these has its advantages and its disadvantages.

Buy and Hold

buy and hold a plan to purchase and keep stock for the long term

Buy and hold is a plan to purchase and keep stock for the long-term. Buy-and-hold investors make money in three ways.

1. They will receive cash dividends over the years.
2. If the price of the stock goes up, they will have long-term capital gains when the stock is sold.
3. Stock dividends or stock splits may occur, giving investors additional shares of stock.

▶ FIGURE 12-2.2 **Buying on Margin Example**

1. Marco invests $5,000 and borrows $5,000 at an annual interest rate of 5 percent from a brokerage firm. He buys 500 shares at $20 per share ($10,000 purchase price). He uses the stock as collateral for the loan (as required by the Fed).

2. Six months later, the stock has increased in value to $30 per share. Marco sells the stock for $15,000 (500 × $30 = $15,000). He pays the broker commissions and fees of $150.

3. From his net proceeds of $14,850 ($15,000 – $150), Marco repays the $5,000 loan plus $125 interest ($14,850 – $5,125 = $9,725). When he subtracts the $5,000 originally invested, Marco has made $4,725 profit.

Note: There is no guarantee that the stock price will rise. If the stock price drops, Marco has to pay interest on the loan and wait to sell the stock. If he sells when the price has dropped, he will lose money (principal).

Stock Turning

Some investors and experts believe that you should be moving your stock investments regularly. **Stock turning** is a strategy of making regular and systematic changes in stock ownership based on trends in the economy. With stock turning, you change your stock ownership on a regular basis, such as monthly or quarterly, or more often if it is warranted. Based on observations of how stocks are doing, you sell one and replace it with another. For example, if energy stocks are falling but precious metals are rising, you would sell one and buy the other. Understanding the economy and its signals can help you do this. You will not always earn profits, but with careful timing, you may be able to gain more than you lose. The hope is that when you see a particular stock dropping, you can sell it before it hits bottom. And when you see a particular stock rising rapidly, you can buy it before it hits the top.

stock turning a strategy of making regular and systematic changes in stock ownership based on trends in the economy

Watch and Wait

The watch-and-wait investor will make a selection of securities and prepare a *comparative analysis* periodically, usually every two or three years. This strategy involves comparing how investments have done since the last analysis. It may also compare current choices to other possible choices in the financial market. When the analysis is complete, the investor decides what to do. Some securities will be kept, some will be sold, and new securities will be added.

Managing Costs

As you buy and sell your securities and other investments, you will want to manage your costs. There are techniques you can use to minimize your expenses. For example, when you use direct investing, you are able to save all fees of buying and selling. By using a reinvestment strategy that includes stock dividends and stock splits, you can avoid transaction fees and other costs.

Type of Transaction

Stockbrokers make money when stocks are bought and sold for clients. Some brokerage firms have minimum commission fees. Additional fees may be charged based on the number of shares and on the value of the stock being traded. On the trading floor of a stock exchange, stocks are traded in round lots or odd lots. A **round lot** is exactly 100 shares or multiples of 100 shares of stock. An **odd lot** is fewer than 100 shares of stock. Brokerage firms usually charge higher per-share fees for trading in odd lots. Thus, you can manage your costs of buying and selling by purchasing in round lots.

round lot exactly 100 shares or multiples of 100 shares of stock

odd lot fewer than 100 shares of stock

Using Discount Brokers

Using discount brokers rather than full-service brokers can save you money. Discount brokers usually charge a flat fee per transaction. However, for odd lots or small amounts, they often charge higher fees. For example, when the trade amount is less than $1,000, the transaction fee may be higher.

READING THE STOCK LISTINGS

To make wise investments in the stock market, it is a good idea to track the progress of your investments by reading the stock listings. Whether you choose to follow your stocks in a financial newspaper or online, you should see a listing similar to the one below.

- *Column 1.* This column lists stocks alphabetically by name. You will notice that stock names are abbreviated. This abbreviated name is called the stock's *ticker symbol*.
- *Columns 2, 3, and 4.* These columns show the highest, lowest, and closing price for the stock on the previous day. The closing price is the final price at the end of the trading for the day.
- *Column 5.* This column, called net change, compares the closing price today with the closing price of the day before. A minus means the price has gone down. A plus means the price has risen.
- *Columns 6 and 7.* These columns show the highest and lowest price the stock sold for during the year.
- *Column 8.* This column shows the cash dividend per share for the year, listed in dollars and cents. For the ExeB stock, 2.50 means that if you owned 100 shares

of this company, you would have received a dividend of $250 for the year.

- *Column 9.* Yld % stands for *percent yield*, or the percentage of the current price the dividends represent. Divide the amount of annual dividends (Column 8) by the closing price (Column 4).
- *Column 10.* The P/E ratio (price/earnings ratio) is the price of a share of stock divided by the corporation's earnings per share over the last 12 months. A low P/E ratio may indicate a solid investment, whereas a high P/E ratio may indicate higher risk.
- *Column 11.* This column shows sales in hundreds of shares (round lots) from the previous day. Multiply the number by 100 to get the number of shares.

Try It Out

Using the stock listings in a newspaper or online, find and record the information described above for two stocks. Which stock paid higher dividends? Which stock had the smaller net change? Which stock had the lower P/E ratio? How can you use this information to make investment decisions?

Stock	High	Low	Close	Net Change	52 wks High	Low	Div	Yld%	P/E Ratio	Sales 100s
1	2	3	4	5	6	7	8	9	10	11
Enger	46.38	45.50	46.00	–.50	58.75	44.00	2.20	4.8	12	109
ExeB	46.00	43.00	44.00	+1.00	57.00	32.00	2.50	5.7	11	48

Timing and Combining

Investors can also save money by making their trades all at once rather than at different times. By timing purchases (and sales) so that they are bundled, you can save on total transaction fees. When buying and selling, investors should check with their brokers or bank financial advisers about ways to save fees and maximize returns.

CHECKPOINT

How can you control your investment costs?

KEY TERMS REVIEW

Match the terms with the definitions. Some terms may not be used.

_____ 1. Exactly 100 shares or multiples of 100 shares of stock

_____ 2. A plan to purchase and keep stock for the long term

_____ 3. An order to buy (or sell) a stock that allows the broker to get the best possible price

_____ 4. A strategy of making regular and systematic changes in stock ownership based on trends in the economy

_____ 5. A request to buy (or sell) a stock at the current market price

_____ 6. Borrowing money from your broker to buy stock

_____ 7. Selling stock that has been borrowed from a broker and replacing it at a later date

_____ 8. A request to buy (or sell) a stock at a specific price

_____ 9. Fewer than 100 shares of stock

a. buy and hold

b. buying on margin

c. discretionary order

d. limit order

e. market order

f. odd lot

g. round lot

h. selling short

i. stock turning

j. stop order

CHECK YOUR UNDERSTANDING

10. List the steps in a stock buying transaction on a stock exchange.

11. What are two leverage strategies that you can use to buy and sell stocks?

12. Why is selling short risky?

13. How can you buy stocks on margin?

14. What are three ways to gain wealth by using a buy-and-hold strategy?

15. What is the purpose of stock turning?

16. How does the watch-and-wait strategy work?

17. Is it to your advantage to purchase stock in round lots or odd lots? Why?

18. What is an advantage of using a discount broker rather than a full-service broker?

19. How can you reduce the costs of stock purchases and sales by bundling trades?

THINK CRITICALLY

20. Why would an investor choose to place a limit order or a stop order?

21. Why do some investors leverage stock purchases by selling short and buying on margin rather than pay cash for stocks?

22. Which of the three buying patterns would you choose? Why?

EXTEND YOUR LEARNING

23. When using the watch-and-wait buying strategy, investors must track their stock's performance. Create a spreadsheet like the one in Figure 12-1.3 to track the following:

    a. Assume you purchased 400 shares of Stock A at $65.30 per share on December 2 last year. Record the following closing prices for the stock over the next year.

Date	Closing Price	Date	Closing Price
1/1/20–	$65.50	7/1/20–	$71.86
2/1/20–	$68.25	8/1/20–	$80.92
3/1/20–	$67.30	9/1/20–	$83.91
4/1/20–	$70.52	10/1/20–	$85.45
5/1/20–	$72.80	11/1/20–	$88.50
6/1/20–	$70.45	12/1/20–	$85.00

    b. Enter formulas to find the average price, highest price, and lowest price of the stock for the prices recorded.

    c. On March 30, you bought another 100 shares of Stock A at $69.00 per share. And on December 28, you sold 100 shares of stock at $86.00 per share. Enter these data in the spreadsheet.

    d. Enter a formula to find the average price paid per share for the stocks you have purchased, including your initial purchase. (Multiply the price by the number of shares for each purchase. Add the two amounts. Divide by the total number of shares purchased.)

    e. Enter a formula to find the return on investment (ROI) for the 100 shares you sold. Use the average price paid per share for the stocks you purchased (see part d) in the ROI formula. (*Reminder*: ROI = Total Amount Received – Total Amount Paid ÷ Total Amount Paid)

    f. Create a line chart to show the closing price for Stock A for each of the 12 prices recorded. Use *STOCK A PRICES* for the chart title.

THE ESSENTIAL QUESTION   Refer to The Essential Question on p. 387. Buying and selling securities involves three steps: (1) set up an investment account, (2) request a transaction, and (3) have the broker take action.

THE ESSENTIAL QUESTION   How do regulatory agencies and laws protect investors?

LEARNING OBJECTIVES

LO 12-3.1 Describe agencies that regulate and supervise the securities and financial industry.

LO 12-3.2 Explain how financial reform laws enhance consumer protections in the financial markets.

KEY TERMS

- oversight, 395
- National Credit Union Administration (NCUA), 396
- Financial Industry Regulatory Authority (FINRA), 396
- Pension Benefit Guaranty Corporation (PBGC), 397
- Commodity Futures Trading Commission (CFTC), 397
- Office of the Comptroller of the Currency (OCC), 397
- Securities and Exchange Commission (SEC), 397
- Sarbanes-Oxley (SOX), 399
- Wall Street Reform Act, 399

LO 12-3.1 What Regulatory Agencies Help Consumers?

Banks, brokerage companies, and other financial businesses are limited and controlled by a number of agencies created by the U.S. Congress. These agencies make or enforce rules and regulations. Most of these agencies provide **oversight**, or supervision of activities to ensure that investors' rights are protected.

oversight supervision of activities to ensure that investors' rights are protected

Federal Deposit Insurance Corporation

The *Federal Deposit Insurance Corporation* (FDIC) is an independent agency created by Congress in 1933 in response to the bank failures in the 1920s and 1930s. People and businesses that had made deposits in these banks lost their money. The purpose of the FDIC is to promote public confidence in the banking system. It insures depositor accounts up to $250,000. The FDIC also supervises banks and other financial institutions to maintain a stable and sound banking system. It monitors practices at banks, including advising and investment activities, to ensure that lawful and ethical practices are being used. All federally chartered banks must participate in the FDIC program.

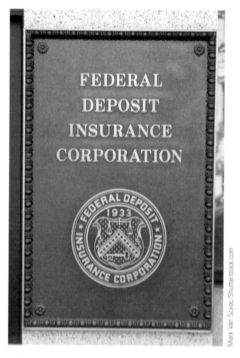

What is the FDIC's role in the economy?

The FDIC also provides consumer resources. At the FDIC website, you can find information about savings and investing resources and banking and money topics. There is also a wealth of information about consumer protection financial education and literacy.

National Credit Union Administration

National Credit Union Administration (NCUA) an independent federal agency that charters and supervises credit unions

The **National Credit Union Administration (NCUA)** is an independent federal agency that charters and supervises credit unions. Savings deposits in member credit unions are insured through the National Credit Union Share Insurance Fund (NCUSIF) for up to $250,000.

The NCUA operates the MyCreditUnion.gov website, a source of financial information and personal finance tips designed to help individuals make good financial decisions. The site also contains various tools, such as a savings and retirement calculator and the NCUA Share Insurance Estimator, which can be used to compute the amount of NCUSIF coverage available for different accounts.

Financial Industry Regulatory Authority

Financial Industry Regulatory Authority (FINRA) a private, nonprofit organization that regulates firms selling securities in the United States

The **Financial Industry Regulatory Authority (FINRA)** is a private, nonprofit organization that regulates firms selling securities in the United States. FINRA's mission is to protect investors by making sure the U.S. securities industry operates fairly and honestly. FINRA monitors trading on the NASDAQ stock market and other selected markets. It registers member firms, writes rules to govern their behavior, and enforces these rules. Firms that break the rules may be charged high fines to discourage illegal and unethical practices.

FINRA also tests and licenses stockbrokers. Investors can find information about licensed brokers on the FINRA website. FINRA also provides materials on its website to educate the public about investing. You can find information about different types of investments, tips on how to choose an investment professional, and current news about investment scams.

Looking Ahead

As you begin to earn money, you'll most likely open a checking and/or savings account at a bank or credit union. To ensure your deposits are safe, you should choose an FDIC-insured or NCUA-insured institution. Both agencies are designed to promote public confidence in the banking system and to protect deposits. Access the FDIC's website (www.fdic.gov) and the NCUA's website (www.ncua.gov) to answer the following questions: Why were these agencies created? How are they funded? What does FDIC and NCUA insurance cover? What does it not cover? How many bank or credit union failures has the FDIC or NCUA reported over the past year (or most recent year recorded on its website)?

Pension Benefit Guaranty Corporation

The **Pension Benefit Guaranty Corporation (PBGC)** is a federal corporation whose primary purpose is to protect the retirement incomes of workers with defined-benefit pension plans. The corporation was established by the Employee Retirement Income Security Act (ERISA) of 1974.

Although the PBGC is a federal agency, it is not funded with tax dollars. Instead, the PBGC is funded by insurance payments from companies that offer pension plans to their workers and recoveries in bankruptcy from former plan sponsors. It also earns money from investments.

When a PBGC-covered pension plan ends or fails for some reason, the PBGC pays some benefits to the retired workers. However, retirees may not get all the benefits promised by the company. For example, health care benefits may not be covered. The maximum benefit is set by law and varies according to the year in which your plan ended and your age at the date you begin receiving benefits. Maximum monthly guaranteed benefit tables are provided on the PBGC website. You can also find information on the following topics at the website:

- How to find out if your pension plan is insured by PBGC
- How a pension plan can end
- What benefits likely will be provided to workers in the plan
- What survivor benefits are available
- How to start collecting pension benefits

Pension Benefit Guaranty Corporation (PBGC) a federal corporation whose primary purpose is to protect the retirement incomes of workers with defined-benefit pension plans

Commodity Futures Trading Commission

The **Commodity Futures Trading Commission (CFTC)** is a government agency that regulates futures and options markets in the United States. When the CFTC was first created, most futures trading took place in the agricultural sector. Over the years, futures trading has become varied and complex. Through effective oversight and regulation, the CFTC seeks to protect investors against manipulation, abusive trade practices, and fraud.

Commodity Futures Trading Commission (CFTC) a government agency that regulates futures and options markets in the United States

Office of the Comptroller of the Currency

The **Office of the Comptroller of the Currency (OCC)** is a government agency that charters, regulates, and supervises all national banks. The OCC was established in 1863 as a bureau of the U.S. Treasury. Its mission is to ensure that national banks operate in a safe and sound manner, provide fair and equal access to financial services, treat customers fairly, and comply with applicable laws and regulations. It also issues rules, legal interpretations, and decisions about banking, lending practices, bank investments, community development, and other aspects of bank operations.

Office of the Comptroller of the Currency (OCC) a government agency that charters, regulates, and supervises all national banks

Securities and Exchange Commission

The **Securities and Exchange Commission (SEC)** is the primary overseer and regulator of the U.S. securities markets. It oversees securities exchanges, brokers and dealers, investment advisers, and mutual funds. The SEC works with other federal and state agencies and with private organizations, such as FINRA.

Securities and Exchange Commission (SEC) the primary overseer and regulator of the U.S. securities market

The SEC tries to maintain fair and orderly markets and promote business growth. It also enforces securities laws. Typical law violations include insider trading, accounting fraud, and the issuance of false information about companies or securities. The primary goal of the SEC is to protect investors. The SEC requires public companies to provide meaningful and accurate data to the public, including financial reports. Having this data helps investors make informed investment decisions.

Department of the Treasury

The *U.S. Department of the Treasury* is the primary federal agency responsible for the economic security of the United States. It has a wide range of duties related to financial issues, including the following:

- Producing all currency and coinage of the United States
- Paying all bills of the United States
- Supervising national banks
- Managing the federal finances
- Managing the U.S. national debt
- Enforcing federal finance and tax laws
- Prosecuting tax evaders, counterfeiters, and forgers

Information about many saving and investing topics is available online at the Department's website (www.treasury.gov). The Department of the Treasury is a member agency of the U.S. Financial Literacy and Education Commission. The commission has a website called MyMoney.gov, which is dedicated to teaching the basics of financial education. The site provides consumers with information about topics such as saving and investing, borrowing, retirement planning, and owning a business. Tools such as a financial savings calculator and budgeting worksheets are also available at the website.

Internal Revenue Service

The *Internal Revenue Service (IRS)* is a bureau of the U.S. Department of the Treasury. Its role is to help taxpayers understand and meet their tax responsibilities. It also seeks to ensure that those who owe taxes pay them. Both interest (from bonds) and cash dividends (from stocks) are forms of taxable income and must be reported on tax returns.

Taxpayers must ensure that all investing activity is properly reported to the IRS. Investors who sell stocks, bonds, options, or other securities must file Form 8949 and Schedule D of Form 1040 to report capital gains and losses.

What is the primary role of the IRS?

The Federal Reserve System

The *Federal Reserve System* (the Fed) is the central bank of the United States. Its purpose is to provide the nation with a safe and flexible financial system. Its activities are in four general areas as follows:

- Setting monetary policy
- Providing financial services to the U.S. government, financial institutions, and the public
- Supervising and regulating the banking system
- Keeping the country's financial systems and markets stable

 CHECKPOINT

List four regulatory agencies that help consumers.

LO 12-3.2 What Are Financial Reform Laws?

Financial reform laws are designed to protect consumers as they participate in the financial markets. Regulatory reform has been deemed necessary because of large-scale fraud that has taken place in the financial markets. Such fraud can lead to economic consequences, including recession, business failures, job loss, devaluation of stocks, and severe financial distress.

Sarbanes-Oxley

The Public Company Accounting Reform and Investor Protection Act of 2002, more commonly known as **Sarbanes-Oxley (SOX)**, set new and stronger standards for public companies and accounting firms regarding the reporting of financial results of business operations. The law was created in response to financial scandals at large companies. These scandals involved fraud or misconduct by company officers that resulted in losses for investors and company employees. SOX requires improved financial reporting, audits, and accounting services for public companies. It also established the Public Company Accounting Oversight Board, an agency that oversees and regulates accounting firms in their roles as auditors of public companies.

Sarbanes-Oxley (SOX) a law that set new and stronger standards for public companies and accounting firms regarding the reporting of financial results of operations

Dodd–Frank Wall Street Reform

Officially known as the *Dodd–Frank Wall Street Reform and Consumer Protection Act of 2010*, simplified as the **Wall Street Reform Act**, this law's numerous provisions are intended to decrease various risks in the U.S. financial system and enhance investor and consumer protections throughout the system. The act is designed to create and maintain a stable financial system. It was passed in 2010 as a response to the financial crisis of 2007–2009. The imposed requirements will affect more than the financial markets of Wall Street. Businesses across all financial services, not just banking, will feel the impact. It is the most extensive overhaul of laws governing our nation's lending institutions since the 1930s. The law will also affect consumers in many ways.

Wall Street Reform Act a law that seeks to decrease various risks in the U.S. financial system and enhance investor and consumer protections throughout the system

Building COMMUNICATION SKILLS

A New Consumer Agency

The act established the Consumer Financial Protection Bureau (CFPB) to prevent predatory lending and to make it easier for consumers to understand the terms of a loan. The CFPB seeks to protect consumers' financial security by regulating credit and debit cards, payday and consumer loans, credit reporting, debt collection, and financial advisory services.

Credit Scores

All consumers can get one free credit report a year from the credit bureaus. This provision of the act also permits the consumer to get an actual credit score along with that free credit report. Consumers also have the right to a copy of their credit score if they are turned down for a loan, or if they are offered a rate other than the rate that the lender gives its best customers.

Interchange Fees

The act cracks down on debit card "swipe fees" that retailers pay to banks when their customers buy products and services using debit cards. The Fed now caps those fees, making them more reasonable and proportional to the amount of the purchase.

Liar Loans

Lenders are now required to document a borrower's income before originating a mortgage loan and must verify the borrower's ability to repay the loan. Part of the problem that caused the housing collapse in 2008–2010 was the number of mortgages made to consumers who could not afford to make the payments. They did not have to "qualify" for those mortgages; the loans were granted on stated (undocumented) income rather than verified income.

How did liar loans contribute to the 2008–2010 housing collapse?

Credit Rating Monitoring

The act established the Office of Credit Ratings to regulate credit rating agencies in the financial market industry. The office has the responsibility of ensuring that credit rating agencies, such as Moody's and Standard & Poor's, provide meaningful and reliable credit ratings of entities they evaluate. The agencies were criticized for misleading investors and helping to create the financial crisis of 2007–2009 by overrating the value of investments.

New Oversight Power

The act created a new ten-member Financial Stability Oversight Council (FSOC), headed by the Treasury Secretary, to monitor large financial firms whose failure could cause a widespread economic collapse. It also provides for orderly liquidations or restructurings if these firms become too weak and prevents taxpayer money from being used to bail out such firms. The FSOC also has the authority to break up large banks that may pose a *systemic risk* (risk of collapse of the entire financial system) because of their size.

Increased Insurance Supervision

The act created a new Federal Insurance Office (FIO), which identifies large insurance companies that pose a systemic risk. The FIO's authority extends to all types of insurance other than health insurance. It gathers information about the insurance industry and ensures that affordable non-health insurance is available to minorities and other underserved communities.

 **CHECKPOINT**

What is the purpose of Sarbanes-Oxley?

KEY TERMS REVIEW

Match the terms with the definitions. Some terms may not be used.

_____ 1. A government agency that charters, regulates, and supervises all national banks

_____ 2. An independent federal agency that charters and supervises credit unions

_____ 3. A federal corporation whose primary purpose is to protect the retirement incomes of workers with defined-benefit pension plans

_____ 4. Supervision of activities to ensure that investors' rights are protected

_____ 5. A government agency that regulates futures and options markets in the United States

_____ 6. The primary overseer and regulator of the U.S. securities market

_____ 7. A private, nonprofit organization that regulates firms selling securities in the United States

_____ 8. A law that sets new and stronger standards for public companies and accounting firms regarding the reporting of financial results of business operations

a. Commodity Futures Trading Commission (CFTC)

b. Financial Industry Regulatory Authority (FINRA)

c. National Credit Union Administration (NCUA)

d. Office of the Comptroller of the Currency (OCC)

e. oversight

f. Pension Benefit Guaranty Corporation (PBGC)

g. Sarbanes-Oxley (SOX)

h. Securities and Exchange Commission (SEC)

i. Wall Street Reform Act

CHECK YOUR UNDERSTANDING

9. What is meant by government oversight of the securities industry?

10. What is the mission of the Financial Industry Regulatory Authority (FINRA)?

11. What is the purpose of the Pension Benefit Guaranty Corporation (PBGC)?

12. List three duties of the U.S. Department of the Treasury.

13. What services does the Internal Revenue Service (IRS) offer consumers? What do investors need to do to be in compliance with IRS rules?

14. What prompted passage of the Wall Street Reform Act? How does this law help consumers?

THINK CRITICALLY

15. Why did Congress create the FDIC in 1933? Is it still needed today?

16. How would investors be affected if public corporations did not have to report financial data as required by the SEC?

17. Why are financial reform laws dealing with the stock market needed?

EXTEND YOUR LEARNING

18. Investors who sell stocks and bonds will need to complete tax Form 8949 and Schedule D of Form 1040 to report their capital gains and losses. Visit the IRS's website (www.irs.gov) and print out these two forms. Write your name and use *000-22-1111* as the Social Security number on each of the forms.

    a. Part I of Form 8949 is used to report the sale of assets held for one year or less. Check box (A) and enter the following data in columns (a)–(e).

Description of Property	Date Acquired	Date Sold	Proceeds	Cost or Other Basis
Stock A, 100 shares	4/1/2015	9/30/2015	$1,050	$900
Stock B, 300 shares	3/20/2015	11/3/2015	$3,000	$2,500

   Skip columns (f) and (g). Calculate the amount of gain or loss for each stock (Proceeds – Cost). Enter the amount in column (h). Then enter the totals for columns (d), (e), and (h) on line 2.

    b. Transfer the totals to line 1b of Schedule D. Leave lines 4–6 blank. Find the total of Part I and enter the amount on line 7.

    c. Part II of Form 8949 is used to report activity for assets held more than one year. Check box (D) and enter the following data in columns (a)–(e):

Description of Property	Date Acquired	Date Sold	Proceeds	Cost or Other Basis
Stock C, 200 shares	5/15/2012	8/30/2015	$3,000	$2,400
Stock D, 100 shares	6/20/2014	7/31/2015	$900	$1,000

   Skip columns (f) and (g). Calculate the amount of gain or loss for each stock (Proceeds – Cost). Enter the amount in column (h). Enter the totals for columns (d), (e), and (h) on line 2. Enter any amount that is a loss in parentheses.

    d. Transfer the totals to line 8b of Schedule D. Leave lines 11–14 blank. Find the total of Part II and enter the amount on line 15.

    e. Complete Part III of Schedule D.

THE ESSENTIAL QUESTION   Refer to The Essential Question on p. 395.
Financial reform laws protect consumers as they participate in the financial markets. Agencies provide oversight to ensure that investors' rights are protected.

Exploring Careers in...
AGRICULTURE

Much of the food bought for consumption in homes is grown or raised on farms and ranches. Farmers, ranchers, and other agricultural workers bring vegetables, fruit, meat, eggs, and milk to your supermarket.

Most of the work done on farms and ranches is hard physical labor. Agricultural workers feed and care for livestock, operate heavy machinery, and participate in outdoor work. Farmers typically work long hours. Those who plant crops often work from sunrise to sunset during planting and harvesting season. Those who raise livestock must tend to and care for their animals every day, year-round.

Although farming can be profitable, there is a lot of risk and uncertainty involved. Production and income are strongly influenced by factors that are uncontrollable, such as weather conditions and fluctuations in market prices.

Employment Outlook
- A slower than average rate of employment growth is expected through 2022.

Job Titles
- Rancher
- Farmer
- Agricultural worker
- Farm manager
- Agricultural manager

Needed Education/Skills
- Self-employment skills and experience in agriculture, mechanics, and equipment operation are important.

- Physical ability to operate heavy machinery and tend to crops and animals is essential.
- Physical stamina to work long hours outdoors is required.

What's it like to work in ... Agriculture

Jeremy works at a dairy farm where he handles 300 cows every day, year-round. Jeremy makes sure they are properly cared for, including feeding and milking them twice a day. He enjoys working with the animals and taking care of them to ensure they are healthy.

The barn contains modern equipment used for milking. Jeremy is responsible for making sure all equipment is working properly, that sanitary requirements are being met, and that the milk meets standards for sales and shipment. Today, Jeremy is supervising the installation of a new device that will streamline the milking process and provide a better filter for the milk as it passes into the holding tanks.

What About You?

Do you like working outdoors? Do you enjoy working with and caring for plants and animals? Would a job in agriculture appeal to you? Why or why not?

SUMMARY

12-1 Sources of financial information for investors include magazines, newspapers, investment newsletters, company reports, prospectuses, investment clubs, and the Internet.

Professionals such as stockbrokers, financial planners, and licensed personal bankers can help investors choose securities to buy or sell.

Securities can be traded in the primary or secondary market. In the primary market, investors buy securities directly from the issuing company. In the secondary market, investors buy securities from previous owners.

A securities exchange is a place where brokers or dealers buy and sell stock. The over-the-counter (OTC) market is a network of brokers who buy and sell securities of corporations that are not listed on a securities exchange.

Direct investing involves buying securities directly from a corporation.

Reinvesting occurs when investors forego a cash dividend to receive more shares of stock in a company. Reinvesting may occur in the form of a stock dividend or a stock split.

12-2 You begin investing by setting up a brokerage account. Four different types of stock market orders can be placed when trading on a securities exchange: market orders, limit orders, stop orders, and discretionary orders. Brokers will place orders on your behalf.

Selling short and buying on margin are leverage strategies for buying and selling securities. Both techniques are risky.

Investor buying patterns include buy and hold, stock turning, and watch and wait. Market timing is a factor with each.

Investors can minimize costs by using direct investing, reinvesting, purchasing in round lots, using discount brokers, and bundling purchases.

12-3 Many regulatory agencies oversee and control the financial markets. They seek to protect consumers by providing stable markets and enforcing fair trading practices.

The Sarbanes-Oxley Act of 2002 helps protect consumers by setting forth new and stronger financial reporting standards for U.S. public companies and for accounting firms.

The Wall Street Reform Act of 2010 was designed to decrease various risks in the U.S. financial system and enhance investor and consumer protections throughout the system.

MAKE ACADEMIC CONNECTIONS

1. **History** Select a regulatory agency that provides information, assistance, and protections for consumers and/or investors. Research the history of the agency—when it was formed, what its original mission was, and what it does today. Visit its website and gather information about the state of the country and the economy at the time the agency was formed. Give a presentation of your findings. State whether you believe the agency is meeting its mission and whether the agency is still needed today. (LO 12-3.1)

2. **Communication** You are on the board of directors for a new corporation. Instead of paying cash dividends to the stockholders this year, you think it would be in the corporation's and stockholders' best interest to pay stock dividends. Write a persuasive letter to the other board members asking them to take this action. (LO 12-1.3)

3. **Ethics** Brokers earn fees for buying and selling securities for clients. The more trades they make, the more money they earn. When a broker is constantly buying and selling stocks for a client, the client may or may not be making profits. Trading securities primarily to make money from sales commissions is called *churning*. Churning is illegal under rules of the SEC. Churning can be hard to prove. Investors sign a waiver that states that brokers are not responsible for losses in stock trades. How will you know if churning is occurring? What should you do if you think you have been a victim of churning? What advice would you give others to avoid becoming a victim of churning? (LO 12-2.1, 12-2.2)

4. **Economics** In the decade following the stock market crash of 1929, many new federal laws were passed, and many new federal agencies were created. Research that ten-year period of time and write a paper explaining what was occurring in the economy that called for new regulations, laws, and agencies. Is it possible for such an economic event to happen today? (LO 12-3.1, 12-3.2)

5. **Consumer Economics** Visit the MyMoney.gov website, which was developed by the federal government to educate citizens on financial management. View several of the resources and tools available. Prepare a presentation describing two of the resources and/or tools. Explain how they could be useful for consumers who need some help managing their finances. (LO 12-1.1)

6. **Ethics** In 2001, Enron Corporation was involved in a massive stock fraud scheme. Enron's stock plummeted, and it filed bankruptcy. Stockholders lost their entire investment. Prepare a history of the Enron scandal. What ethics issues were involved? Discuss reforms that were put in place as a result of the Enron stock scandal. How do the reforms enhance corporate responsibility and protect you as an investor? (LO 12-3.2)

7. **Careers** Assume you would like to work as a broker some day. Research the qualifications and skills required. What are the educational requirements? Describe the work environment and characteristics of this occupation. What is the average salary? Compile your research into a "career profile" of a broker. (LO 12-1.2)

Do the Math

1. You plan to buy 35 shares of stock for $22.18 per share. If you use a full-service broker, you must pay a 2 percent commission on the purchase price. You must also pay $10.00 because it is an odd-lot sale and $15.00 because it is a small purchase. Investment advice is included at no extra cost. What is the total amount you must pay? If you use a discount broker, you will pay a fee of $34.95 for the odd-lot purchase. You have already paid $100.00 for an investment newsletter to help you decide which stock to buy. Which broker would you use and why?

2. You want to leverage your investment by selling short. You borrow 100 shares of stock in XYZ Corporation from your broker on January 2. You immediately sell all 100 shares at $60 a share. On April 1, you instruct your broker to purchase 100 shares of XYZ stock at $53 a share, which you return to your broker. What is your return on investment?

Take Action

RESEARCH AN INVESTMENT CHOICE

Before buying stock in a company, investors should learn about the company, its history, and its outlook for the future. Work with a classmate to complete the following steps:

a. Choose a company that interests you to research.

b. Do research to learn all you can about the company. Look for information in magazine and newspaper articles and on the Internet. If possible, get a copy of the company's annual report. Keep a record of the source information for all the articles you read, whether in print or online.

c. Write a report or give an oral report to present what you have learned about the company. Include several of the following points and others that you think would help an investor decide whether to buy stock in the company.

TEAMWORK

- Company name and trading symbol
- Industry to which the company belongs
- Major products or services the company sells
- Number of employees
- Brief history of the company
- Newsworthy topics, such as plans for expansion or new products

- Current stock price
- High and low stock prices over the last year
- Revenue and income for last year
- P/E ratio and current ratio
- Dividends paid
- Stock splits
- Risk level for the company stock

Include the information you have collected about the company in your portfolio.

Saving and Investing

Getting started saving will help you meet your goals for financial security in the future. Money set aside today can be used for investing tomorrow. For your own personal savings plan, you should set aside a predetermined amount each month. This should be an amount that you know you can afford. This is beyond your personal emergency needs. It is money you will be setting aside permanently. Complete the *Savings Plan Worksheet* to help you get started. It will show you how setting aside even a small amount of money each month can help you save to make a purchase many years in the future. This worksheet will also show how the effects of compounding interest will help your savings grow.

After you have provided for savings, you can begin investing. Sometimes that's right away; other times, you may want to wait until you feel more financially secure. But you should know that all types of investing involve some degree of risk. When choosing investments, you should be comfortable with the risk you are taking. The more risk you are willing and able to endure, the larger the potential returns. If you choose low-risk investments, your money is likely to be safe, but you will see lower returns. Medium-risk investments will increase your return without raising the risk too much. High-risk options offer the possibility of a high rate of return, but you also risk big losses if the investments perform poorly. You need to balance out a desire to grow your investments with the peace of mind that can come from knowing that your investments are secure. Complete the *Risk Assessment Worksheet* to help you identify your personal risk preferences.

When making investments, consumers frequently use the services of a financial adviser. However, not all financial advisers are equal. Many financial advisers adhere to high ethical standards and comply with the laws and regulations that govern the financial planning industry. Unfortunately, there are some advisers who do not adhere to legal and ethical requirements. Therefore, it is important to thoroughly research a financial adviser before doing business with him or her. Complete the *Financial Adviser Research Worksheet* to learn some tips regarding the best way to research financial advisers.

THINK CRITICALLY

1. Why is it important to start saving systematically? How can setting aside even a small amount of savings each month help you achieve future financial goals?

2. Do you think you would prefer low-risk, medium-risk, or high-risk investments? Why is it important for you to know and understand your investment risk tolerance level?

3. Why were agencies formed to regulate and monitor the behavior of financial advisers?

GLOSSARY

20/10 Rule a plan to limit the use of credit to no more than 20 percent of your yearly take home pay, with payments of no more than 10 percent of monthly take-home pay

401(k) plan a tax-deferred retirement plan for employees offered by businesses that operate for a profit

403(b) plan a tax-deferred retirement plan for employees of schools, government units, and nonprofit organizations

A

advance-fee loan a type of loan that includes a large fee up front

advertising informing consumers about products and encouraging them to buy

alternative dispute resolution (ADR) a method of settling a dispute using a neutral third party

annual report a company's report to shareholders about the financial position of the company

annuity (1) a contract in which you make a lump-sum payment or series of payments that earn interest and, in return, receive regular disbursements, often after retirement; (2) a fixed amount set aside on a regular basis over time

asset allocation choosing a combination of funds within a single mutual fund company

assets money and items of value that you own

auction market a market in which buyers enter competitive bids and sellers enter competitive offers at the same time

auto insurance a policy that protects a car owner from losses as a result of accidents and other events

B

bait and switch an illegal sales technique in which a business advertises a product with the intent of persuading consumers to buy a more expensive product

balance transfer moving a balance from one credit card account to another

balloon payment a large lump-sum payment that must be paid at a set time

bank reconciliation the process of adjusting the check register and bank statement balances so that they agree

bankruptcy a legal procedure to relieve a person of excessive debt

bankruptcy fraud the abuse of bankruptcy laws in a way that favors the debtor and defrauds creditors

bear market a period of steadily decreasing stock prices and investor pessimism

benchmarks standards against which progress is measured

beneficiary the person designated to receive money from a life insurance policy

benefits forms of compensation in addition to salary or wages

billing cycle the period of time between credit card billings

bond a debt instrument that is issued by a corporation or government

bond rating tells the investor the risk category that has been assigned to a bond

bounced check a check that is not honored by a bank and is returned to the payee's bank due to nonsufficient funds

branding strategy carrying well-known brand names to attract customers who are loyal to those brands

budget a spending and saving plan based on expected income and expenses

bull market a prolonged period of rising stock prices and general feeling of investor optimism

business cycle the alternating periods of growth and decline in the economy

buy and hold a plan to purchase and keep stock for the long term

buying on margin borrowing money from your broker to buy stock

buying plan an organized method for making good buying decisions

C

callable bond a bond with a clause that allows the issuer to repay the bond before the maturity date

cash advance money borrowed against your credit card account

cash inflows income from your job, investments, and other sources

cash outflows expenses, or items for which you must spend money

cashier's check a check issued against the bank's funds

certificate of deposit (CD) a time deposit that pays a fixed rate of interest for a specified length of time

certified check a personal check that the bank guarantees

Chapter 7 bankruptcy the forfeiture of an individual's assets in exchange for the discharge of debts

Chapter 11 bankruptcy a reorganization form of bankruptcy for businesses that allows them to retain possession of their assets and continue operating under court supervision as they repay their restructured debts

Chapter 13 bankruptcy a repayment plan for some of an individual's debt

charge card a form of credit card for which the cardholder must pay the balance in full by the due date

charitable giving the act of donating money or time to a cause in which you believe

check a written order to a bank to pay a stated amount to a person or business

check register a tool used to track checking account transactions

checking account a demand deposit account at a bank on which checks are drawn

collateral property that can be used as security for a loan

collectibles physical assets that appreciate in value over time because they are rare or desired by many

collision coverage a policy that protects against damage to your own vehicle if you hit another car or lose control and roll over

commission a set fee or percentage of a sale paid to an employee instead of or in addition to salary or wages

commodity an item that has the same value across the market with little or no difference in quality among producers

Commodity Futures Trading Commission (CFTC) a government agency that regulates futures and options markets in the United States

common stock a type of stock that pays a variable dividend and gives owners (stockholders) voting rights

company risk the chance that activities or events that affect a company will change the value of an investment in that company

comparison shopping checking prices, brands, and quality among several sellers to make sure you are getting the best deal

compound interest interest earned on both principal and previously earned interest

comprehensive coverage protection against damages to your car from causes other than collision or rolling over

consideration something of value exchanged for something else of value

consumer advocacy the process of helping consumers resolve problems

consumer loan a direct loan of cash made to a consumer at a fixed interest rate for a set period of time

contact a person you know

contingencies unplanned or possible events

contract a legally binding agreement that specifies the rights and duties of each party to the agreement

convertible bond a bond that can be exchanged for shares of common stock at the option of the bondholder

cost-plus pricing setting a price based on production cost plus a markup

cost-push inflation rising prices as a result of rising production costs

cost-recovery pricing setting an introductory price high to recover the research and development (R&D) costs

coupon rate the fixed rate of interest that is paid semiannually for the life of a corporate bond

cover letter a letter that accompanies a resume, introducing the applicant to a prospective employer

credit the ability to borrow money and pay it back later

credit card a plastic card linked to a credit account that can be used to make purchases

Credit Card Accountability Responsibility and Disclosure Act a comprehensive reform to credit card law to establish fair practices related to credit

credit card fraud intentionally using someone's credit account to steal money or goods

credit counseling a service to help consumers manage credit and avoid bankruptcy

credit delinquency failure to pay debts as required by agreement or by law

credit management establishing and following an individual plan for using credit wisely

credit repair a scam in which a company claims to be able to "fix" your poor credit record and give you a clean credit history—for a price

criteria standards or rules by which something is judged

customer loyalty program a program designed to encourage repeat business by providing special discounts and other incentives

D

debit card a bank card used to withdraw or deduct money from your checking account

debt money that must be repaid

debt consolidation the process of getting one loan with a single monthly payment to pay off all of your debts

debt repayment plan a strategy for paying off debt in a way that reduces the total interest paid

debt settlement program a type of debt relief service in which a company negotiates with your creditors on your behalf to reduce the amount of debt you owe

deception false or misleading claims made about the quality, price, or purpose of a particular product

deflation a decrease in the general level of prices for goods and services

demand the willingness and ability of consumers to buy goods and services

demand-pull inflation higher prices as a result of consumers wanting to buy more goods and services than producers supply

dependent a person who depends on you for more than half of his or her support

deposit money added to a checking or savings account

direct advertising distribution of product information directly to consumers

direct investing the investor holds legal title to a property and has control over management decisions

disability insurance insurance that provides income to replace a portion of normal earnings when the insured is unable to work due to a nonwork-related injury or illness

discharge a court order that pardons the debtor from having to pay debts

discount bond a bond that sells for less than its face value

discount broker a qualified stockbroker who buys and sells securities at a reduced commission but provides limited services to clients

discount pricing offering the lowest everyday price possible

discretionary order an order to buy (or sell) a stock that allows the broker to get the best possible price

disinflation rising prices with the rate of increase slowing down

disposable income money available to spend or save after taxes have been paid

dispute letter a letter written to inform a credit company of an incorrect charge on your account

disputing a charge the process of informing a credit company of an error on your bill

diversification holding a variety of investments for the purpose of reducing overall risk

dividends a portion of a corporation's profits distributed to stockholders

documentation records that support your claim

dollar-cost averaging investing the same amount of money on a regular basis regardless of market conditions

down payment a cash deposit toward the purchase price that is paid up front

E

early withdrawal penalty a fee imposed to discourage depositors from withdrawing the money before the stated time period

easy access credit type of credit that can be obtained quickly and easily but that often comes with high or hidden costs

economizing saving as much as possible and spending money only when necessary

economy all of the activities related to making and distributing goods and services in a geographic area or country

electronic funds transfer the use of a computer-based system to move money from the drawer's account to the payee's account

electronic records soft-copy formats of your financial information stored on your computer

emergency fund money set aside for unplanned expenses

emotional buying the process of purchasing products based on desire rather than logic

encryption the process of converting data to a coded form

endorsement a signature, with or without instructions, written on the back of a check

entrepreneur a person who takes the risks of being selfemployed and owning a business

Equal Credit Opportunity Act a law that protects consumers from discrimination in the granting or denying of credit

equity loan a second mortgage or debt secured with the equity in your home

equity stripping the unethical practice of extending a loan to a distressed homeowner who cannot afford the loan payments, resulting in the lender taking possession of the home

estate all that a person owns (assets), minus debts owed, at the time of that person's death

ethics a set of moral values that people consider acceptable; the study of what is right versus

eviction the legal process of removing a tenant from rental property

excise tax a tax charged on the purchase of specific goods and services

exemption (1) a person claimed as a dependent on a tax return; (2) property that a debtor in bankruptcy does not have to forfeit to pay off creditors

extended warranty additional coverage that you can buy to pay for repairs or replacements needed beyond the original warranty period

F

Fair Credit Billing Act a law that sets requirements for resolving billing disputes

Fair Credit Reporting Act a law that regulates the collection, dissemination, and use of consumer credit information

Fair Debt Collection Practices Act a law that protects consumers from abusive collection practices by creditors and collection agencies

fee-for-service plan a type of health insurance plan that allows patients to choose any doctor or other provider for medical services

finance charge the total dollar amount of all interest and fees you pay for the use of credit

financial aid money received from an outside source to help pay for education

financial goals plans for how you will pay for your personal goals

Financial Industry Regulatory Authority (FINRA) a private, nonprofit organization that regulates firms selling securities in the United States

financial irresponsibility failing to live up to your financial obligations to meet your goals and needs

financial market any place where investments are bought and sold

financial plan a set of personal and financial goals, along with steps and a timeline for reaching them

financial planner a professional consultant who provides financial advice

financial resources money or other items of value that are used to acquire goods and services

financial responsibility being able to meet your financial goals through planned earning, spending, and saving

financial security the ability to meet current and future needs while living comfortably

fixed expenses costs that do not change each month

fixed interest rate an interest rate that is set and does not change from month to month

floating a check writing a check and planning to make a deposit later to cover it before the check is processed

follow-up contact with a prospective employer after the interview but before hiring

foreclosure the legal process of taking possession of the house (property) when the borrower does not make mortgage payments as agreed

Form 1040EZ the short tax return form designed for single and joint filers with no dependents or itemized deductions

Form W-2 a form used to report taxable income that a worker received during the calendar year

foundation a fund or an organization established and maintained for the purpose of supporting an institution or a cause

franchise a contract that gives you the right to sell a company's products and services

full-service broker a qualified stockbroker who provides advice about what securities to buy and sell

futures contract an obligation to buy or sell stock or a specific commodity for a set price on a set date in the future

G

garnishment a legal process that allows part of an employee's paycheck to be withheld for payment of a debt

gems natural, precious stones such as diamonds, rubies, sapphires, and emeralds

goal a desired outcome, based on one's values, for which a plan of action is developed carried out

grace period the amount of time you have to pay your current credit card balance in full to avoid paying interest

grant money given to pay for educational expenses that does not have to be repaid

gross domestic product (GDP) the value of all goods and services produced in a country in a given time period

gross pay total salary or wages earned during a pay period

H

hard skills measurable physical and mental abilities that allow you to complete a job

health insurance a plan for sharing the risk of medical costs resulting from injury or illness

health maintenance organization (HMO) a group plan that provides prepaid medical care for its members

home inventory a list of items of value in your home; used for insurance purposes

homeowners insurance a policy that protects property owners from risk of loss to their real and personal property

hyperinflation rapidly rising prices that are out of control

I

identity theft the use of your personal information by someone else without permission to commit fraud or other crimes

illiquid not convertible to cash quickly or without a penalty

impulse buying purchasing something on the spur of the moment without thinking it through or any planning

inactive account a checking or savings account that does not meet minimum usage requirements

in-cash payments money in the form of a check, a debit card, or other direct payment given to a person needing assistance

indirect investing investors have a third person do the actual buying and selling of property

industry risk the chance that factors affecting an industry as a whole will affect the value of an investment

inflation an increase in the general level of prices for goods and services

inflation risk the chance that the rate of inflation will rise faster than your investment rate of return

infomercial a lengthy paid TV advertisement that includes testimonials and product demonstrations

in-kind payments payments made indirectly on a person's behalf or paid in a form other than money

Installment credit Credit used to finance the purchase of a single high-priced item through a series of equal payments made over a set period of time.

interest money earned on savings accounts and other funds

intermediate goals things you wish to achieve in the next two to five years

Internet banking accessing and managing your account online

investing a strategy to earn more on your money than the rate of inflation

investment risk the potential for change in the value of an investment

investment tracking a technique for making investment choices by following the prices of stocks and other investments over time

J

job application a form that asks basic questions about the applicant's background, such as work history, education, skills, and references

job description describes what a job would be like, including the tasks performed and skills needed

job interview a face-to-face meeting with a potential employer to discuss a job opening

job market the job openings that are available when you are ready to go to work

job shadowing spending time observing a worker in a type of job that interests you

K

Keogh plan a tax-deferred retirement plan for self-employed individuals

L

lease a written agreement that allows a tenant to use property for a set period of time at a set rent payment

liabilities debts that you owe

liability coverage protection against injuries suffered by others while on your property or as a result of your actions

life insurance insurance that pays money to a beneficiary upon the death of the insured person

limit order a request to buy (or sell) a stock at a specific price

line of credit a preapproved loan amount that a debtor can borrow as needed with no collateral

liquid the capability to withdraw money at any time without penalty

liquidity a measure of how quickly an asset can be turned into cash

living habits your daily routine, or the way you choose to live your life

loan modification a new loan arrangement that allows you to make reduced payments, usually on a temporary basis

loan shark a person who offers illegal loans at very high interest rates and often uses intimidation to enforce repayment

logistics the act of making a plan and carrying it out to ensure that an event takes place

long-term goals things you want to achieve more than five years from now

loss a physical injury, damage to property, or disappearance of property or other assets

low-balling a technique whereby a company advertises a product or service at a low price to lure in customers and then attempts to persuade them that they need additional products or services

M

manual records information recorded in hard-copy format using pen and paper

market economy an economy based on the laws of supply and demand

market order a request to buy (or sell) a stock at the current market price

market risk the chance that changes in the business cycle will affect the value of an investment

market timing buying and selling stocks based on what the market is expected to do

market-based pricing setting a price to be competitive with prices of similar products currently being sold

markup the percentage amount added to production cost to obtain the price of an item

maturity date the date on which an investment becomes due for payment

Medicare tax a tax that pays for medical care for retired persons age 65 and older who receive Social Security benefits

minimum payment the amount you are required to pay each month on a credit account

minimum wage the lowest pay rate allowed by law for each regular hour of work

money market account a type of savings account that earns the market rate of interest on the money deposited

mortgage a loan used to purchase real estate

mutual fund a professionally managed group of investments bought using a pool of money from many investors

N

National Credit Union Administration (NCUA) an independent federal agency that charters and supervises credit unions

needs things needed for survival, such as food, water, clothing, shelter, and medical care

net pay the amount of your paycheck after deductions

net worth the difference between your assets and liabilities

nonmarket risk the chance that events unrelated to market trends will affect the value of an investment

normal profit a profit that allows a business to survive and grow

O

odd lot fewer than 100 shares of stock

Office of the Comptroller of the Currency (OCC) a government agency that charters, regulates, and supervises all national banks

on-the-job training learning as you do the work

opportunity cost the value of your next best option—what you are giving up

optimizing getting the highest value for the money spent

option the right, but not the obligation, to buy or sell stock or a commodity for a set price within a set time period

overdraft protection a bank service that covers a shortage in your account

oversight supervision of activities to ensure that investors' rights are protected

over-the-counter (OTC) market a network of brokers who buy and sell securities that are not listed on a securities exchange

overtime pay pay received for hours worked in addition to regular hours

P

payday loan a cash advance from your next paycheck

penalty a fee charged for violating a term of the credit agreement

Pension Benefit Guaranty Corporation (PBGC) a federal corporation whose primary purpose is to protect the retirement incomes of workers with defined-benefit pension plans

permanent life insurance a policy that remains in effect for the insured's lifetime and builds cash value

personal goals things you want to achieve in your life

personal injury protection (PIP) coverage for medical, hospital, and funeral costs of the insured and passengers in the event of an accident, regardless of who is at fault

personal leave paid time away from work for personal reasons

phishing a common Internet scam that uses email messages o deceive you into disclosing personal information

pigeon drop a scam in which a con artist convinces people to give up their money or personal information in return for a share of a larger sum of money

political risk the chance that actions taken by the government will affect the value of an investment

Ponzi scheme a fraudulent investment operation in which money collected from new investors is used to pay off earlier Investors

portfolio a collection of investments

postdated check a check written with a date that will occur in the future

preapproved loan a loan for which a maximum amount is established and approved in advance

precious metals rare metals that have known value around the world

predatory lending unfair, deceptive, and fraudulent loan practices

preferred provider organization (PPO) a network of independent health care providers that band together to provide health care services for a set fee

preferred stock a type of stock that guarantees a fixed dividend but does not provide voting rights

premium the price you pay for insurance coverage

premium bond a bond that sells for more than its face value

prepayment penalty a fee charged if you repay a loan before the agreed-upon time

primary market the financial market in which new issues of securities are sold

principal sum of money set aside on which interest is paid

probability the likelihood of a risk resulting in a loss

productivity a measure of the efficiency with which goods and services are made (comparison of total output to total input)

profit sharing a benefit that allows employees to share a portion of the business's profits

property manager an off-site manager hired to take care of rental property

property tax a wealth tax based on the assessed value of owned real estate

prospectus a legal document issued by an investment company that provides details about the securities it offers for sale

public goods government provided goods and services paid for by taxes

pyramid scheme an illegal, multilevel marketing gimmick that promises members commissions from their own sales as well as from the sales of other members they recruit

R

rational buying the process of selecting goods and services based on need, want, and logical choices

rebate a refund of part of the purchase price of an item

refinancing paying off an existing loan with a new loan that usually has better terms

reflation high prices followed by lower prices and then high prices again

rental agreement a written contract that allows you to leave any time as long as you give the required notice

renters insurance a policy that protects renters from personal property and liability risks

rent-to-own agreement a contract in which a portion of the renter's monthly payment is applied toward the purchase price of the rented item

replacement value the cost of replacing an item regardless of its actual cash (market) value

repossession the act of taking an asset used as collateral and selling it to pay the debt

resume a summary of your work experience, education, skills, interests, and other qualifications (your skill set) that qualify you for a job opening

retirement a period of time, usually in later years, when you are not working and need to meet expenses through other income sources

retirement plan an account into which employees voluntarily contribute a portion of their earnings for their retirement; employers may match these contributions

return on investment (ROI) a performance measure used to evaluate the efficiency of an investment

revolving credit an account on which the account holder can charge repeatedly up to a maximum limit

risk the chance of injury, damage, or economic loss

risk assessment the process of identifying risks and deciding how serious they are

risk assumption accepting the consequences of risk

risk avoidance stopping behavior that leads to a risk

risk reduction finding ways to lower your chance of incurring a loss

risk transfer passing risk to another party

rollover the process of moving a retirement account balance to another qualified account without incurring a tax penalty

roommate a person with whom you share living space, living expenses, and other responsibilities

Roth IRA an individual retirement account in which contributions are taxed, but earnings are not

round lot exactly 100 shares or multiples of 100 shares of stock

Rule of 72 a quick formula for computing how long it will take to double money invested at a given interest rate

S

safe deposit box a secure container located in a bank vault

sales promotion an incentive offered to customers to increase demand

sales tax a tax levied as a percentage of the purchase price of goods and services sold to consumers

Sarbanes-Oxley (SOX) a law that set new and stronger standards for public companies and accounting firms regarding the reporting of financial results of operations

savings money set aside for the future

savings account a demand deposit account designed for the accumulation of money in a safe place for future use

scholarship a cash allowance awarded to a student to help pay for education

secondary market the financial market in which previously issued securities are bought and sold

Securities and Exchange Commission (SEC) the primary overseer and regulator of the U.S. securities market

securities exchange a marketplace where brokers buy and sell securities for their clients

security deposit a refundable amount paid to cover damages to property caused by a tenant

self-insure setting aside money to be used in the event of injury or loss of assets

self-training learning new skills from reading and practicing on your own

selling short selling stock that has been borrowed from a broker and replacing it at a later date

service credit the ability to receive services and pay for them later

shared responsibility two or more people who each agree to bear a portion of an obligation

short-term goals things you expect to achieve within one week to one year

sick leave paid time away from work due to illness

simple interest interest computed on principal once in a certain period of time

skill set the unique skills and abilities that you bring to the job market

Smart card a card that contains a computer chip that stores electronic money

social network a group of friends and acquaintances who keep in contact and share information

Social Security tax a withholding tax that pays for Old-Age, Survivors, and Disability Insurance (OASDI) benefits

soft skills nontechnical skills needed by most workers for success on the job

space-shifting storing media, such as music or movies, on one device to be accessed from another place through another device

spending limit the maximum amount you are willing to pay for an item

spreadsheet software a computer program that allows you to insert numbers and formulas to compute amounts and then easily change them later as needed

stock ownership interest in a publicly held company

stock dividend a dividend paid in the form of new shares of stock

stock split the issuance of more stock to current shareholders in some proportion to the stock they already own

stock turning a strategy of making regular and systematic changes in stock ownership based on trends in the economy

stop-loss provision an insurance clause that sets a maximum that the insured has to pay out of pocket during any calendar year

stop order a request to sell a stock when it reaches a certain price

stop payment an instruction to the bank not to honor a check that has been issued or lost

store account a credit account that allows you to charge items or services only at that store or with that merchant

subsidized student loan a loan on which the student pays no interest until he or she has graduated or is no longer in school

supply the quantity of goods and services that producers are willing and able to provide

systematic decision making the process of making choices that reflect goals by considering all of the pros and cons along with the costs

systematic investing a strategy that involves a planned approach to making investments on a regular basis

systematic saving a strategy that involves regularly setting aside cash that can be used to achieve goals

T

target audience a specific group of people who are likely to buy a product

tax deferral a postponement of taxes to be paid

tax-exempt an investment that is not subject to taxation

temp agency an employment agency that provides part-time and full-time jobs on a temporary basis

temporary life insurance a policy that remains in effect for a specific period of time

time value of money a concept that says a dollar you receive in the future will be worth less than a dollar you receive in the present (today)

timeline a visual display of how long it will take to achieve each phase of a plan

time-shifting recording video or audio for later viewing or listening

title loan a short-term loan with a high interest rate that uses the title on your vehicle as collateral

trade-in something of value applied toward the down payment of a new purchase

trade-off giving up one option in exchange for another

traditional IRA an individual retirement account in which contributions are tax-deductible and grow tax-deferred.

transfer payments money and benefits received from local, state, or federal governments

transit advertising ads placed on modes of public transportation or in public transportation areas

Truth in Lending Act a law that requires lenders to fully inform consumers about the cost of credit in a loan or credit agreement

tuition the expense paid by students for the instruction at a school

U

U.S. savings bond a bond issued by the federal government that pays a guaranteed minimum rate of interest

umbrella liability insurance a supplement to your basic auto and homeowners coverage that expands limits and includes additional risks

unearned income money received from sources other than working

uninsured/underinsured motorist coverage protection against damages caused by a motorist with no or insufficient insurance

unsubsidized student loan a loan that starts charging interest from the time the loan is made

unused credit the remaining credit available to you on current accounts

use tax a tax charged on the use, storage, or consumption of a good that was purchased in one state but used in another state

V

value a principle that reflects the worth you place on an idea or action

value-based pricing setting a price based on how much consumers are willing to pay

variable expenses costs that can go up and down each month

variable interest rate an interest rate that goes up and down with inflation and other economic conditions

variances the differences between planned amounts and actual amounts

W

Wall Street Reform Act a law that seeks to decrease various risks in the U.S. financial system and enhance investor and consumer protections throughout the system

wants things people desire for reasons beyond survival and basic comfort

warning label information on products advising consumers of risks and safety issues

wealth the accumulation of assets over your lifetime

withdrawal taking money from your account

Workers' compensation an insurance plan that pays medical and disability benefits to employees injured on the job

Z

zero-coupon bond a type of corporate bond that is sold at a deep discount, does not provide interest payments, and is redeemable for its face value at maturity

INDEX

Investment portfolio, 332–334
Investment risk, 325
    vs. gambling, 326
    reduction, 332–334
    return and, 324
Investment tracking, 331
Investments. *See also* Savings; specific types of
        investment
    agencies regulating, 396–402
    in business ownership, 366–368
    cash for, 390
    collectibles as, 365
    direct, 368–369, 384
    diversification for, 332
    economy and, 334
    gems as, 365–366
    high-risk options for, 364–366
    ideal, features of, 323
    illiquid, 343
    indirect, 370
    for intermediate goals, 317
    long-term focus of, 330–331
    for long-term goals, 317, 330–331
    medium-risk options for, 353–357
    precious metals as, 365
    principles of, 323–324
    purpose of, 315–327
    real estate as, 368–370
    return on, 324
    risk options for, 346–350
    risks of, 325
    for short-term goals, 317
    sources of information on, 378–381
    strategies for, 330–332
    systematic, 330
    tax advantages of, 327
    wealth and, 316
Investor newsletters, 379
Investor's Business Daily, 378
Involuntary bankruptcy, 292
IPO. *See* Initial public offering (IPO)
IRA. *See* Individual retirement accounts (IRA)
IRS. *See* Internal Revenue Service (IRS)

J

Job application, 24
Job description, defined, 5
Job fairs, 22
Job interview, 28
Job market, defined, 3
Job openings
    cooperative work experience in, 23
    employment agencies for, 22–23

    job fairs, 22
    job scouts, 22
    placement centers for, 24
    social networking sites, 20–21
    state employment offices for, 23
    temp agencies for, 23
    websites for, 21–22
Job shadowing, 23
Job title, 5
Joint account, 149
Journalism careers, 35
Judgment, 283
    financial, 187
Junk bonds, 348

K

Kefauver-Harris Drug Amendment of 1962, 99
Keogh plan, 358–359
Kiplinger's Personal Finance, 378

L

Land, investments in, 368
Landlords
    rights and responsibilities, 256
Lawsuits
    filing, 285–286
Lease, 253, 254, 255, 260
Leisure time, 318
Lessee, 255. *See also* Tenants
Lessor, 255. *See also* Landlords
Level term insurance, 201
Liability, 118
    coverage, 206, 208
    personal, 206
Liar loans, 401
Life insurance
    explanation of, 44, 199–200
    group, 200
    permanent, 201–202
    savings plans, 345–346
    term, 200–201
Lifelong learning, 6
Limit order, 389
Limited-pay life insurance, 202
Line of credit, 233
Liquid, 161, 323
Liquidation, meaning of, 93
Liquidity, 316
Listening. *See also* Communication skills
    comprehensive, 52
    creative, 84
    critical, 84

N

NASDAQ stock market, 383
National Consumers League (NCL), 101
National Credit Union Administration
(NCUA), 397
National Credit Union Share Insurance Fund
(NCUSIF), 397
National Traffic and Motor Vehicle Safety Act of
1966, 99
Natural disasters, 206
government transfer payments for, 49–51
Needs, 116
Negotiation, 178, 285
Net income, 117
Net loss, 117
Net pay, defined, 58
Net worth, 118
Newspapers, 137
advertising in, 89
investment information in, 378–379
Newsweek, 378
New York Stock Exchange (NYSE), 383
No-fault insurance laws, 209
Nonmarket risk, 326
Nonsufficient funds (NSF), 173, 175–176
Nonverbal communication, 3
Normal profit, defined, 82
Nutrition Labeling and Education Act
of 1990, 100

O

*Occupational Outlook Handbook
(OOH)*, 4, 5
Odd lot, 392
Office of the Comptroller of the Currency
(OCC), 398
Off-site manager, 256
Online brokers, 382
Online-only banks, 169. *See also* Banks
Online shopping, 105
On-site manager, 256
On-the-job training, defined, 7
Opportunity cost, 119, *225*
Optimizing, defined, 85
Outdoor advertising, 90
Outstanding checks, 156
Overdraft protection, 173
Oversight, 396
Over-the-counter (OTC) market, 384
Overtime pay, defined, 40

P

PAs. *See* Physician assistants
Paid holidays, 43
Par value, 385
Partial scholarship, 16
Partnership, 366
Party plan marketing, 90
Patients' Bill of Rights, 98
Pay bills online, 152
Pay to the order of, 154
Pay without work, 43–44
Paycheck deductions, 58–62
Payday loans, 273
Payee, 151
Payments
methods for, 227
services, 172–173
transfer, 49–51
Pay-yourself-first strategy, 316
Penalties
explanation of, 241
Penalty fees, 269
Pension Benefit Guaranty Corporation
(PBGC), 398
Pension plans, 45, 360
Perks, defined, 46
Permanent life insurance, 201–202
limited-pay, 202
universal, 202
variable, 202
whole life, 201
Personal cash flow
statement, 117
Personal goals, 134
Personal identification number (PIN), 152
Personal injury protection (PIP), 209
Personal leave, defined, 43
Personal liability, 206
Personal net worth statement, 117–118
Personal property, 205
Personal residence, 356–357
Personal risk, 187
Persuasive message, 401
Persuasive speaking, 294
Philanthropists, 127
Philanthropy, 127
Phisher, 138
Phishing, 138, 287
Physician assistants (PAs), 6
Pigeon drop, 103
Piggybacking, 211
Plaintiff, 286

Securities, 378
  buying and selling, 388–393
  government bonds and, 350
  primary market for, 383
  secondary market for, 383
Securities and Exchange Commission (SEC), 101,
    398–399
Securities exchange, 383
Security deposit, 252
Security question, 149
Self-employment, 31–32
  advantages of, 31
  disadvantages of, 31
Self-insure, 190
Self-training, defined, 7
Selling short, 390
Selling strategies, 88–91
Seminars, 137
Service credit, 233
Shared responsibility, 251–253
  explanation of, 251
Shopping
  comparison, 91, 211, 226–227,
      270
  online, 105
Short-term disability insurance, 198
Short-term goals, 134, 317
Sick leave, defined, 43
Signature card, 149
Silent partners, 368
Simple interest method, 162
Simple will, 320
Simplified employee pension (SEP) accounts, 359
Skill set, defined, 3
Skimming, 287
Small claims court, 286
Smart card, 173
Social media marketing, 90
Social network, 20
Social Security Administration (SSA), 195
Social Security benefits, 51
Social security disability insurance, 198
Social security tax, 59–60
  defined, 59
Soft-copy format, recordkeeping and, 129
Soft skills, defined, 3
Sole proprietorship, 366
Space-shifting, right for, 97–98
Spam, 287
Speaking. *See also* Communication skills
  informal, 227
  persuasive, 294
Special endorsement, 154
Special service fees, 176

Speculative-grade bonds, 348
Speculative investments, 333
Spending limit, 226
Spreadsheet software, 129
Standard maximum deposit insurance amount
    (SMDIA), 162
Standard & Poor's Corporation, 348
Standard & Poor's Financial Services, 379
State and local assistance, for consumer protection,
    101
Stock dividends, 49, 384
  defined, 49
stock options, 46
Stockbrokers, 381–382
Stockholders, 49, 354
Stock split, 385
Stock turning, 392
Stocks, 354–356
  buying and selling, 388–393
  buyout timing, 393
  common, 355
  cost management of, 392–393
  explanation of, 326
  preferred, 355
  transactions for, 388–389
  types of, 355–356
Stop-loss provision, 196
Stop order, 389
Stop payment, 172
Store account, 231
Store location, convenient for sales promotion, 88
Stored value card, 173
Stress management, 272
Student loans
  debt, 264
Study reading, 155
Subsidized student loan, 16
Substitute checks, 158
Supplemental health insurance, 197
Supply, defined, 11
Systematic decision making, 223
  financial responsibility and, 223
Systematic investing, 330
Systematic saving, 330
Systems analyst, 5

T

Take-home pay, 58
Target audience, 89
  defined, 89
Tax collection, career in, 69
Tax deferral, 327
Tax-deferred retirement plans, 45